RESEARCH HANDBOOKS IN EUROPEAN LAW

This important series presents a comprehensive analysis of the latest thinking, research and practice across the field of European Law. Organised by theme, the series provides detailed coverage of major topics whilst also creating a focus on emerging areas deserving special attention. Each volume is edited by leading experts and includes specially-commissioned chapters from distinguished academics as well as perspectives from practice, providing a rigorous and structured analysis of the area in question. With an international outlook, focus on current issues, and a substantive analysis of the law, these *Handbooks* are intended to contribute to current debate as well as providing authoritative and informative coverage.

Forming a definitive reference work, each *Handbook* will be essential reading for both scholars in European law as well as for practitioners and policymakers who wish to engage with the latest thinking and ongoing debates in the field.

Titles in this series include:

Research Handbook on European State Aid Law
Edited by Erika Szyszczak

Research Handbook on EU Internet Law
Edited by Andrej Savin and Jan Trzaskowski

Research Handbook on EU Private International Law
Edited by Peter Stone and Youseph Farah

Research Handbook on European Social Security Law
Edited by Frans Pennings and Gijsbert Vonk

Research Handbook on EU Agriculture Law
Edited by Joseph A. McMahon and Michael Cardwell

Research Handbook on EU Criminal Law
Edited by Valsamis Mitsilegas, Maria Bergström and Theodore Konstadinides

Research Handbook on EU Public Procurement Law
Edited by Christopher Bovis

Research Handbook on EU Public Procurement Law

Edited by

Christopher Bovis

University of Hull, UK

RESEARCH HANDBOOKS IN EUROPEAN LAW

Edward Elgar PUBLISHING

Cheltenham, UK • Northampton, MA, USA

Published by
Edward Elgar Publishing Limited
The Lypiatts
15 Lansdown Road
Cheltenham
Glos GL50 2JA
UK

Edward Elgar Publishing, Inc.
William Pratt House
9 Dewey Court
Northampton
Massachusetts 01060
USA

A catalogue record for this book
is available from the British Library

Library of Congress Control Number: 2016931738

This book is available electronically in the **Elgar**online
Law subject collection
DOI 10.4337/9781781953266

MIX
Paper from responsible sources
FSC® C013056

ISBN 978 1 78195 325 9 (cased)
ISBN 978 1 78195 326 6 (eBook)

Typeset by Columns Design XML Ltd, Reading
Printed and bound in Great Britain by TJ International Ltd, Padstow

Contents

Contributors

Marta Andrecka
Assistant Professor, Centre for Enterprise Liability, Faculty of Law, Copenhagen University, Denmark

Rick Canavan
Senior Lecturer, Nottingham Trent University, United Kingdom

Roberto Caranta
Professor of Law, University of Turin, Italy

Charles Clarke
Associate, Gibson Dunn, Brussels, Belgium

Dacian C. Dragos
Center for Good Governance Studies, Babes Bolyai University, Cluj Napoca, Romania

Steven van Garsse
Professor of Adminsitrative Law, University of Antwerp, Professor of Law, University of Hasselt and Head of Flemish PPP Knowledge Centre (Vlaams Kenniscentrum), Belgium

Mihalis Kekelekis
Senior Officer at the Competition and State Aid Directorate of the EFTA Surveillance Authority

Emanuela Matei
Counsel, Mircea and Partners, Bucharest

Kine Neslein
Senior Associate at Wikborg Rein Advokatfirma in Oslo, Norway

Erik Olsson
Partner Advokatfirman Kahn Pedersen, Stochmolm, Sweden

Spyros Panagopoulos
Senior Legal Counsel, European Central Bank, Frankfurt, Germany

Oana S. Pantilimon Voda
Senior Legal Adviser at Corvers Legal and Commercial Affairs

Kristian Pedersen
Partner, Advokatfirman Kahn Pedersen, Stochholm, Sweden

Albert Sanchez Graells
Senior Lecturer in Law, University of Bristol, United Kingdom

Sarah Schoenmaekers
Assistant Professor – Advocaat (Belgium), Faculty of Law, Department of International and European Law, University of Maastricht, Belgium

Tünde Tátrai
Assistant Professor, Corvinus University of Budapest, Hungary

Martin Trybus
Professor of European Law and Policy, Director, Institute of European Law, Birmingham Law School, University of Birmingham, United Kingdom

Editor

Christopher Bovis
Professor of European and International Business Law, University of Hull, United Kingdom

Preface

The regulation of public procurement in the European Union has multiple dimensions. As a discipline of European law, it is directly relevant to the fundamental principles of the internal market. Public procurement regulation is a necessary component of the principles of free movement of goods and services, the right of establishment and the prohibition of discrimination of nationality grounds. It is also a policy instrument. The identification of public procurement as a major non-tariff barrier has revealed the economic importance of its regulation.[1] Procurement by Member States is often susceptible to a policy that favours indigenous undertakings and national champions at the expense of more efficient competitors. The policy dimension of public procurement regulation aims at market integration across the EU. Through the principles of transparency, non-discrimination and objectivity in the award of public contracts, it is envisaged that the regulatory system will bring about competitiveness in the relevant product and geographical markets, will increase import penetration of products and services destined for the public sector, will enhance the tradability of public contracts across the common market, will result in significant price convergence and finally it will be the catalyst for the needed rationalization and industrial restructuring of the European industrial base.

The regulation of public procurement has been a priority for the European Union since the 1986 Single European Act, a legislative framework which paved the way for the conclusion of the Maastricht Treaty on European Union. The White Paper for the Completion of the Internal Market[2] and the Single European Act represented the conceptual foundation of the regulation of public markets of the Member States. The identification of public procurement as a significant non-tariff barrier has offered ample evidence on the economic importance of its regulation.[3] Savings and price convergence appeared as the main arguments for liberalizing the trade patterns of the demand (the public and utilities sectors) and supply (the industry) sides of the public procurement equation.[4] The regulation of public procurement exposes an economic and a legal approach to the integration of public markets in the European Union. On the one hand, the economic approach to the regulation of public procurement aims at creating an

---

1 See Commission of the European Communities, *The Cost of Non-Europe, Basic Findings, Vol.5, Part.A; The Cost of Non-Europe in Public Sector Procurement* (Luxembourg: Official Publications of the European Communities 1988). Also the Cechinni Report *1992 The European Challenge* (Aldershot, Wildwood House 1988).

2 See European Commission, *White Paper for the Completion of the Internal Market* (COM) 85 310 fin. (1985).

3 See Commission of the European Communities, *The Cost of Non-Europe*, *op.cit.* Also the Cechinni Report *op.cit.*

4 The European Commission claimed that the regulation of public procurement could bring substantial savings of €20 billion or 0.5% of GDP to the European public sector. See European Communities, *The Cost of Non-Europe*, *op.cit.*

integral public market across the European Union. Through the principles of transparency, non-discrimination and objectivity in the award of public contracts, it is envisaged that the public procurement regulatory system will bring about competitiveness in the relevant product and geographical markets, will increase import penetration of products and services destined for the public sector, will enhance the tradability of public contracts across the common market, will result in significant price convergence and finally it will be the catalyst for the needed rationalisation and industrial restructuring of the European industrial base.[5] A combination of legal and economic objectives project upon public procurement regulation principles of public sector management such as transparency, accountability, fiscal prudency and competition and make public procurement regulation a necessary ingredient for the EU integration process. The commonly accepted assumption is that public procurement is not subject to the same commercial pressure or organisational incentives for sound management as private sector procurement which is underpinned by the foundations of strong competition. This has prompted the imposition, not only by the EU but by many international jurisdictions, of legal and regulatory disciplines to encourage the better use of public financial resources, to introduce greater efficiency and to reduce the risk of favouritism or corruption in public purchasing. EU public procurement rules exist in order to introduce a regulatory discipline in the relevant markets. Legislation, policy guidelines and jurisprudence have all played their role in determining the need for integrated public markets in the European Union, where sufficient levels of competition influence the most optimal patterns in resource allocation for supplying the public sector as well as the public utilities with goods, works and services.

The degree and level of importance of public procurement in the European Union and the constant evolution of its regulation which reveals indissoluble links with European law prompted the review of the substantive public procurement Directives.[6] The financial stakes for public procurement regulation in the EU and the Member States are high. Currently, the total public expenditure directed by the Member States in procuring goods, works and services accounts for over €2 trillion. Public procurement in the Member States is a highly fragmented and complex process, notably in relation to the extent of centralization or decentralization which varies amongst Member States as a function of the organization of their public administration. There is a large and heterogeneous range of over 250,000 contracting authorities across the EU which annually undertake in excess of 2 million procedures for the award of public contracts.[7] The vision and aspirations of European Institutions towards a Single Market Act[8] have

---

[5] See Commission of the European Communities, *Statistical Performance for keeping watch over public procurement*, 1992. Also the *The Cost of Non-Europe*, *op.cit.*

[6] See *Green Paper on the modernisation of EU public procurement policy: Towards a more efficient European Procurement Market* COM (2011) 15/47.

[7] An approximate 20% of total public expenditure on goods, works and services is covered by the EU public procurement directives. The estimated value for these contracts is €420 billion in 2009–10. Three-quarters of the value of procurement advertised in accordance with EU rules is for construction work and services. Supplies make up only a quarter of all procurement.

[8] See European Commission, Communication to the European Parliament, the Council, the Economic and Social Committee and the Committee of the Regions, *Towards a Single Market Act* COM(2010) 608 final.

identified public procurement reforms as the most essential components of competitiveness and growth[9] and as indispensable instruments of delivering public services.[10]

Public procurement regulation is an essential component of the single market[11] because public procurement has been identified as a considerable non-tariff barrier and a hindrance to a genuinely competitive single market. Economic justifications for its regulation are based on the assumption that by introducing competitiveness into the relevant markets of the Member States, their liberalization and integration will follow. This result, in theory, would increase import penetration of products and services destined for the public sector, would enhance the tradability of public contracts across the common market and would bring about significant savings and price convergence. However, Member States retain substantial discretion for the regulation of public procurement outside the scope of the EU Directives.[12] Several Member States regulate public procurement below EU thresholds within the same act as the contracts covered by the EU Directives and also require the use of open, fair and competitive procedures, which have similar features to those laid down in the Directives. There are areas where national rules and procedures are often similar for contracts above and below the EU thresholds, such as rules for qualitative selection, evaluation of tenders, award criteria, abnormally low tenders, technical specifications, framework agreements and electronic procurement. Other Member States provide a lighter regime for contracts below the EU thresholds, which may take the form of administrative guidance rather than formal legislation and offer shorter time limits for submission of applications and tenders and less demanding rules for publication and for selection of tenders.

The legal approach to the regulation of public procurement reflects on a modality which facilitates the functions of the common market. In parallel with the economic arguments, legal arguments have emerged supporting the regulation of public procurement as a necessary ingredient of the fundamental principles of the Treaties, such as the free movement of goods and services, the right of establishment and the prohibition of discrimination of nationality grounds.[13] The legal significance of the regulation of public procurement has been well documented through the Court's jurisprudence. The liberalization of public procurement indicates the need to eliminate preferential and

---

[9] See European Commission, Communication, Europe 2020, *A strategy for smart, sustainable and inclusive growth*, 3 March 2010, COM (2010) 2020 final.

[10] See European Commission, *Guide to the application of the European Union rules on state aid, public procurement and the internal market to services of general economic interest, and in particular to social services of general interest*, 7 December 2010, SEC(2010) 1545 final. See European Commission, *Buying Social: A Guide to Taking Account of Social Considerations in Public Procurement*, SEC(2010) 1258, final.

[11] See European Commission, *Towards a Single Market Act, op.cit.*

[12] Large amounts of public expenditure on goods and services to provide health, education and social services (over 6% of GDP) are spent in ways which are not covered by the EU public procurement Directives. Also, public contracts below the EU thresholds fall outside the scope of the EU public procurement Directives but they are of significant importance. Below-threshold procurement was estimated at around €250 billion in 2008 or around 2% of EU GDP.

[13] See C. Bovis, 'Recent Case Law relating to Public Procurement: A Beacon for the Integration of Public Markets' (2002) 39 *Common Market Law Review* 1025–56.

discriminatory purchasing patterns by the public sector and create seamless intra-community trade patterns between the public and private sectors. Procurement by Member States and their contracting authorities is often susceptible to a rationale and a policy that tend to favour indigenous undertakings and national champions[14] at the expense of more efficient competitors (domestic or Community-wide). As the relevant markets (product and geographical) have been sheltered from competition, distorted patterns emerge in the trade of goods, works and services destined for the public sector. These trade patterns represent a serious impediment in the functioning of the common market and inhibit the fulfilment of the principles enshrined in the Treaties.[15]

The European Court of Justice has viewed the public procurement legal framework through two approaches: a positive one, revealing the flexibility of the regulatory regime and at the same time a restrictive one reflecting on the interpretation of the regime. The Court's approaches provide intellectual assistance to the efforts of European institutions in order to strengthen the three principles (non-discrimination, objectivity and transparency) underlying the regulation of public procurement.[16] The positive approach of the Court comprises its attempts to eliminate discrimination and non-tariff barriers in the fields of technical standards (product specification and standardization) and the selection procedures (quantitative and qualitative suitability criteria). The Court's judicial positivism through the observance of non-discrimination and objectivity principles epitomizes the integral role of public procurement in the attainment of the fundamental principles of the Treaty, specifically the right of establishment and the freedom to provide services. On the other hand, the Court's restrictive approach serves the principle of objectivity, with particular reference to the use of the award procedures for public contracts.

The above pattern also reflects on a strategic goal of the European judiciary: to vest the public procurement regime wherever possible with direct effect. Arming the public procurement rules with direct effect will enhance access to justice at national level, improve compliance, increase the quality of the regulatory regime and finally streamline the public procurement process across the common market by introducing an element of uniformity. By conferring direct effect upon the public procurement directives and inviting national courts to play a prominent role in future public

---

[14] The term *implies* a firm with more than a third of its turnover made in its own country and which has enjoyed formal or informal government protection. The term has been defined by Abravanel and Ernst, 'Alliance and acquisition strategies for European national champions' (1992) 2 *The McKinsey Quarterly* 45–62.

[15] See Communication from the European Commission to the Council, the European Parliament, the Economic and Social Committee, and the Committee of the Regions, 'Working together to maintain momentum' 2001 Review of the Internal Market Strategy, Brussels, 11 April 2001, COM(2001)198 final. Also European Commission, Commission Communication, Public procurement in the European Union, Brussels, 11 March 1998, COM (98) 143.

[16] See the recital of Directive 89/440, [1989] OJ L210/1 amending the original works Directive 71/305 concerning co-ordination of procedures for the award of public works contracts, stating that '... it is necessary to improve and extend the safeguards in the directives that are designed to introduce transparency into the procedures and practices for the award of such contracts, in order to be able to monitor compliance with the prohibition of restrictions more closely and at the same time to reduce disparities in the competitive conditions faced by nationals of different Member States'.

procurement litigation, the Court has hinted towards its preference for a decentralized enforcement of the public procurement regime. However, the most important lesson law and policy makers have learnt from the Court's approaches to public procurement is the potential of its regulation with regard to policy formulation at both national and European levels.

In its jurisprudence, the Court has reflected on the relative importance of public procurement to the fundamental freedoms of the common market, namely the right of establishment and the freedom to provide services. The approach taken by the Court has revealed a positive yet restrictive interpretation of the Directives. By conferring direct effect upon their provisions where appropriate and inviting national courts to play a prominent role in future public procurement litigation, the Court has hinted towards its preference for a decentralized enforcement of the Directives. The Court's jurisprudence has also played an important function in delineating key concepts within the public procurement legal framework, such as contracting authorities and award criteria. This has exposed a significant characteristic of the EU Public Procurement Law: flexibility. The Court developed a *ratione*, which recognizes discretion in the hands of contracting authorities, discretion which is integral to the legal framework, compatible to the attainment of the fundamental freedoms of the common market and complementary with other policies.

The Court gradually abandoned the formality test in determining the relationship between an entity and the state and instead adopted the functionality and dependency tests to define contracting authorities. In addition, dualism and the dual capacity of contracting authorities are irrelevant to the applicability of public procurement Directives. The Court inferred that commerciality and competitiveness might render the public procurement rules inapplicable. The Court accepted, in principle, the complementarity of relevant policies of the European integration process, such as social policy and the protection of the environment, by conferring discretion to contracting authorities to award public contracts by reference to employee protection as well as socio-economic and environmental considerations.

The influence of neo-liberal economic theory on public procurement regulation has taken the relevant *acquis* through the paces of liberalization within the European Union and with reference to the World Trade Organization. Anti-trust and its remedies have played a seemingly important role in determining the necessary competitive conditions for the supply side to service the public sector. However, we have seen the emergence of a *sui generis* market place where the mere existence and functioning of anti-trust is not sufficient to achieve the envisaged objectives. Public markets require a positive regulatory approach in order to enhance market access. Whereas anti-trust and the neo-liberal approach to economic integration depend heavily on price competition, public procurement regulation requires a system which primarily safeguards market access. Such regulatory system could be described as public competition law. The above represents the first departure from the *stricto sensu* neo-liberal perspective of public procurement. A policy orientation has emerged mainly through the jurisprudential approach of the regime and the willingness of the Court to expand on the element of flexibility that is inherent in the public procurement Directives.

The neo-liberal versus the ordo approach reflects the frequently rehearsed debate about the origins of anti-trust law and policy *per se*. The European integration has benefited from a system where the neo-liberal approach has contributed to the functioning of an environment of workable competition. However, consistently the rigidity of the neo-liberal influence has been diluted with policy considerations, often attributed to national policy requirements. The reflection of the above picture is presented in public procurement regulation, although there are certain differences: the Court has allowed for a flexible policy-oriented application of public procurement, where in anti-trust the Commission has eroded the strict neo-liberal approach of competition rules with the plethora of policy considerations. Nevertheless, the similarity of balancing an economic exercise with policy choice is remarkable.

Subsequent generations of legal instruments which regulate public procurement in the EU have intended to simplify and modernize a regulatory regime which aims at establishing gradually a public market in the European Union. This regulatory regime seeks to accomplish unobstructed access to public markets through transparency of public expenditure relating to procurement, improved market information, elimination of technical standards capable of discriminating against potential contractors and uniform application of objective criteria of participation in tendering and award procedures. The public procurement regulatory regime has three principal objectives: simplification, modernization and flexibility.

The objective of simplification has materialised through the codification of supranational administrative law in the form of an EU Directive which covers all public sector procurement. The objective of modernization is met by introducing a number of regulatory innovative concepts. The ability of bodies governed by public law to tender for public contracts alongside private undertakings is a significant development. The use of framework procurement could assist in bringing the public sector closer to a seamless supply chain management. The introduction of electronic procurement and the use of information technology in public purchasing could process the logistics of public sector purchasing faster and more efficiently. The introduction of the competitive dialogue envisages facilitating the award of complex projects such as public-private partnerships and trans-European networks.

The objective of flexibility is demonstrable through the relaxation of the competitive tendering regime, and the disengagement of the public procurement rules in industries that operate under competitive conditions in the utilities sectors indicates the links between procurement regulation and anti-trust. The non-applicability of the regime to telecommunications entities is an important development indicative of the future legal and regulatory blueprints.

The regulation of public procurement reflects on two opposite dynamics: one of a community-wide orientation and one of national priorities. The influence of neo-liberal economic theory on public procurement regulation has taken the relevant regime through the paces of the liberalization. However, the emergence of a *sui generis* market place where the mere existence and functioning of anti-trust is not sufficient to achieve the envisaged objectives is evident. Public markets require a positive regulatory approach in order to enhance market access. Whereas anti-trust and the neo-liberal approach to economic integration depend heavily on price competition, public procurement regulation requires a system which primarily safeguards market access. Such regulatory system could be described as public competition law. The above scenario represents a departure from the *stricto sensu* neo-liberal perspective of public procurement. A policy orientation has emerged mainly through the jurisprudential approach of the regime and the willingness of the Court to expand on the element of flexibility that is inherent in the public procurement Directives. The Court has allowed for a flexible policy-oriented application of public procurement, where in anti-trust the Commission has eroded the strict neo-liberal approach of controlling market power with the plethora of policy considerations.

Public procurement is a powerful exercise. It carries the aptitude of acquisition; it epitomizes economic freedom; it depicts the nexus of trade relations amongst economic operators; it represents the necessary process to deliver public services; it demonstrates strategic policy options. Public procurement as a discipline expands from a simple topic of the common market, to a multi-faceted tool of European regulation and governance covering policy choices and revealing an interesting interface between centralised and national governance systems. This is where the legal effects of public procurement regulations are felt most. Litigation and jurisprudential inferences will be extremely important in understanding the thrust of the new regime. The role of the Court has been instrumental in shaping many of the newly introduced concepts and in the future will be invaluable in interpreting the new regime and pronounce on the compatibility of national provisions with *acquis communautaire*.

The strategic importance of public procurement for the European integration process has been recognised by the 2011 Single Market Act[17] which has prompted a series of reforms to the EU Public Procurement *acquis*.[18] These reforms aim at linking public procurement directly with the European 2020 Strategy which focuses on growth and competitiveness. The importance of a liberalized and integrated public procurement regime as an essential component of the Single Market has been clearly established.[19] The conceptual origins of public procurement regulation in the European Union can be traced in policy instruments which identified purchasing practices of Member States as considerable non-tariff barriers and as hindering factors for the functioning of a genuinely competitive internal market.[20] Economic justifications for regulating public procurement have pointed towards introducing competitiveness into the relevant markets in order to increase cross-border trade of products and services destined for the public sector and to achieve price transparency and price convergence across the European Union, thus achieving significant savings.[21] The need for competitiveness and transparency in public procurement markets is also considered as a safeguard to

---

17 See European Commission, Communication, Europe 2020, *A strategy for smart, sustainable and inclusive growth*, 3 March 2010, COM (2010) 2020 final.

18 See Green Paper on the modernization of EU public procurement policy: *Towards a more efficient European Procurement Market*, COM(2011)15/47.

19 See European Commission, *Towards a Single Market Act op.cit.*

20 See European Commission, *White Paper for the Completion of the Internal Market*, COM (85) 310 fin, 1985; also Green Paper on Public Procurement in the European Union: *Exploring the way forward*, European Commission 1996; also European Commission, Communication on Public Procurement in the European Union, COM (98) 143.

21 See Commission of the European Communities, *The Cost of Non-Europe*, *op.cit.* Also the Cechinni Report *op.cit.*

fundamental Treaty principles,[22] such as the free movement of goods and services, the right of establishment and the prohibition of discrimination on grounds of nationality.[23]

The current public procurement *acquis*[24] has prescribed a different regulatory treatment to public sector procurement and utilities procurement. First, a more relaxed regime for utilities procurement, irrespective of their public or privatized ownership has been justified and accepted as a result of the positive effects of liberalization of network industries which has stimulated sectoral competitiveness.[25] Secondly, a codified set of rules, covering supplies, works and services procurement in a single legal instrument[26] for the public sector aims at producing legal efficiency, simplification and compliance in order to achieve the opening up of the relatively closed and segmented public sector procurement markets. A decentralized dimension of the public procurement rules has been introduced by the procurement Remedies Directives,[27] which nevertheless, suffered from serious deficiencies, as they did not provide for effective review procedures between the stages of contract award and contract conclusion. Thus, the Remedies Directives have been inadvertently promoting direct awards and the so-called 'race to sign' the relevant contract to ensure immunity from any redress, based on the *pacta servanta sunt* principle. In addition, during both pre-contractual and post-contractual stages there were no effective deterrents for breach of either procedural or substantive public procurement rules. These deficiencies were pointed at by the Court in numerous instances, which resulted in the amending Remedies Directive[28] introducing new themes such as a clear divide between pre-contractual and post-contractual stages, a balance between effective review of public contracts and need of efficient public procurement, a strict standstill requirement for contract conclusion, including direct awards by contracting authorities and extensive communication and monitoring requirements.

The European Institutions through the enactment of the 2011 Single Market Act[29] have identified public procurement reforms as essential components of competitiveness

---

22 See Cases C-223/99, *Agora Srl v Ente Autonomo Fiera Internazionale di Milano* and C-260/99, *Excelsior Snc di Pedrotti Runa & C v Ente Autonomo Fiera Internazionale di Milano* [2001] ECR 3605; C-360/96, *Gemeente Arnhem Gemeente Rheden v BFI Holding BV* [1998] ECR 6821; C-44/96, *Mannesmann Anlangenbau Austria AG et al v Strohal Rotationsdurck GesmbH* [1998] ECR 73.

23 See D. Drijber and H. Stergiou, 'Public Procurement Law and Internal Market Law' (2009) 46 *Common Market Law Review* 805–46.

24 See Directive 2004/18, [2004] OJ L134 on the coordination of procedures for the award of public works contracts, public supply contracts and public service contracts and Directive 2004/17, [2004] OJ L134 coordinating the procurement procedures of entities operating in the water, energy, transport and postal services sectors.

25 See C. Bovis, 'Developing Public Procurement Regulation: jurisprudence and its influence on law making' (2006) 43 *Common Market Law Review* 461–95.

26 See Directive 2004/18, *op.cit.*

27 See the Public Sector Remedies Directive 89/665 [1989] OJ L395/33, and the Utilities Remedies Directive 92/13, [1992] OJ L76/14.

28 See Directive 2007/66, [2007] OJ L335/31.

29 See European Commission, *Towards a Single Market Act*, *op.cit.*

and growth[30] and as indispensable instruments of delivering public services.[31] The results of previous public procurement reforms have been registered in a positive manner. The public sector Directive represents a notable example of codification of supranational administrative law. The main influence for the codification of the public sector Directive can be traced in important judicial developments, in particular case-law on the definition of contracting authorities, the use of award procedures and award criteria, and the possibility for contracting authorities to use environmental and social considerations as criteria for the award of public contracts. The modernization objective of the reforms focusing on the ability of private undertakings, which pursue activities of general interests of non-commercial or industrial character to tender for public contracts alongside bodies governed by public law, is a significant development influenced by the Court's rulings. The flexibility objective of the public procurement regulatory regime reflects on the relaxation of the competitive tendering regime and the disengagement of the public procurement rules in industries that operate under competitive conditions in the utilities sectors indicate the links between procurement regulation and anti-trust. The non-applicability of the regime to telecommunications entities is an important development indicative of the future legal and regulatory blueprints.

The Court of Justice of the European Union has inferred where further reforms are needed. The substantive public procurement rules and mainly the public sector Directive suffer from legal porosity as a result of exhaustive harmonisation. Exhaustive harmonisation represents a *de lege lata* approach to public procurement regulation on the part of the European legislature. Such approach has developed certain deficiencies. The effectiveness of the procurement rules is compromised and the Court has applied, through a rule of reason approach, a hybrid transplant of EU legal principles to the public procurement Directives in order to control their porosity. However, this treatment is temporary and not conducive to legal certainty and legitimate expectation.

The reforms of the public procurement regime have been focused mainly upon the way service concessions and contracts awarded by a contracting authority to another contracting authority on the basis of exclusive rights are regulated, in the light of the interface of the public procurement *acquis* with the Services Directive.[32] On the other hand, public-public partnerships and in-house contractual relations between contracting authorities or undertakings upon which the former exercise control similar to that exercised over their own departments and the controlled entities are operationally dependent on them link conceptually very well with public contracts awarded by utilities to their affiliated undertakings and public service contracts relating to services of general economic interest and contracts having the character of a revenue-producing

---

[30] See European Commission, *A strategy for smart, sustainable and inclusive growth, op.cit.*

[31] See European Commission, *Guide to the application of the European Union rules on state aid, public procurement and the internal market to services of general economic interest, and in particular to social services of general interest, op.cit.* See European Commission, *Buying Social, op.cit.*

[32] See Directive 2006/123/EC of the European Parliament and of the Council of 12 December 2006 on services in the internal market [2006] OJ L376/36).

monopoly, and as such reflect on the positive dimension of inherent flexibility in the public procurement Directives.

Public contracts which fall below the stipulated value thresholds (sub-dimensional contracts) represent the most difficult category for reform. On the one hand, they encapsulate a significant amount of Member States' public expenditure which escapes the clutches of the public procurement *acquis*. On the other hand, the Court is keen to subject these contracts to some form of competition and has supplemented the public procurement Directives with EU law principles which ensure a parallel process of procurement with dimensional public contracts. This development has created uncertainty in the market place and resulted in a dysfunctional application of procurement rules to those contracts. The administrative and procedural burdens on the part of contracting authorities often surpass any potential efficiency benefits resulting from competitively tendering sub-dimensional contracts. In addition, adequately sufficient safeguards against intentional division of dimensional contracts into lots in order to avoid the applicability of the public procurement Directives exist in the current *acquis*.

The Single Market Act relies on a simplified public procurement regime in the EU, which will result from procedural efficiencies and from streamlining the application of the substantive rules. Public procurement regulation will play a pivotal role for the delivery of the European 2020 Growth Strategy.

This research handbook aims to provide the reader with a comprehensive analysis of the law, jurisprudence and regulation of public procurement in the European Union. It is structured into five thematic parts, consisting of 19 substantive chapters.

In the Introduction, public procurement as a discipline within the European economic and legal integration is considered.

Part 1 comprises six chapters which offer the reader a trajectory of the development, evolution and application of the public procurement *acquis*.

Chapter 1 entitled 'The principles of public procurement regulation' presents a thematic overview of the reformed public procurement regime by revealing the new concepts in public procurement regulation relevant to the public sector and also relevant to the procurement of utilities. It also exposes the new dynamics with regard to the new public procurement regime on concessions. Chapter 2 entitled 'Public procurement and contracting authorities' examines case-law relating to the notion of of contracting authorities and also provides for a codified approach of the concept of contracting authorities under the Court's jurisprudence, their relation with private sector undertakings, the conditions for pursuing services of general interest as part of public procurement contracts, especially the criteria for defining bodies governed by public law and the tests used by the Court to define the existence of state control over an entity which is construed as contracting authority. Chapter 3 entitled 'Public contracts in public procurement regulation' examines the concept of public contracts in public procurement. The Court has dealt with the notion of public contracts in cases regarding public service concessions, vertical procurement and subcontracting, procurement and state aid, procurement and services of general interest, needs in general interest and ccontracts financing public services. Chapter 4 entitled 'Public procurement and frameworks' has the purpose to offer an exposition of the nature and purpose of the framework agreement at large and to then focus in on the framework agreement as it is defined and conceived for the purposes of European public procurement regime. The chapter will consider the concept, definition and forms of framework agreement and how frameworks may be operated, established and breaches of them remedied. Finally, this chapter will turn to examine, whether, notwithstanding their wide usage, frameworks are in fact capable in principle and in fact of delivering the efficiencies and cost benefits that they appear to herald while maintaining fairness and transparency. Chapter 5 entitled 'Public procurement and award criteria' investigates the Court's case-law in relation to award criteria and presents a comprehensive analysis of the two criteria laid down in the public procurement Directives. It provides for the conditions under which contracting authorities award public contracts. The Court has many opportunities to pronounce on the features of the award criteria, namely the lowest price or the most economically advantageous offer. The chapter explores the Court's views in relation to the following topics: the meaning of abnormally low offers, the compatibility of mathematical matrixes, the evaluation of the lowest offer, the factors included in the most economically advantageous offer and policy considerations, such as employment, protection of the environment as part of the award criteria. Chapter 6 entitled 'Sub-dimensional public procurement in the European Union' focuses on contracts that fall outside the ambit of the Public Sector Directive – the sub-dimensional public procurement. The analysis applies also to contracts above and below the thresholds set out for Annex XVI services (non-priority services), the latter being only in part subjected to EU law rules anyway.

Part 2 comprises of four chapters which offer the reader a comprehensive approach of strategic procurement.

Chapter 7 entitled 'Innovative and sustainable procurement: framework, constraints and policies' examines cases where no solutions yet exist on the market; innovative procurement enables public purchasers to get technologically innovative solutions developed according to their specific needs. By steering product development upstream in the product development process, public purchasers are better positioned to improve the quality, effectiveness and efficiency of their public services, while the private business sector operates within an increasingly competitive environment. Such an approach contributes to achieving better value for money as well as wider economic, environmental and societal benefits in terms of generating new ideas, translating them into innovative products and services and thus promoting sustainable growth. Chapter 8 entitled 'Innovative public-private partnerships' attempts to identify and analyze what are the available ways in which to procure innovative Public-Private Partnerships under the Public Sector Directive. Chapter 9 entitled 'Strategic EU public procurement and small and medium size enterprises' examines the understanding of SMEs' involvement in public procurement in the EU. The study provides an overview of EU public procurement policy with regard to the facilitation of a wider SMEs' involvement and a description and analysis of the barriers SMEs face in entering the public procurement market and the available countermeasures. Chapter 10 entitled 'Public procurement and services of general economic interest' investigates the role of public procurement in the financing of SGEIs by focusing on the link between the application of the State aid rules and the public procurement framework.

Part 3 comprises of three chapters which offer the reader a comprehensive analysis of the justiciability of public procurement.

Chapter 11 entitled 'Judicial activism and public procurement' offers a critical assessment of the impact of the Court's jurisprudence upon public procurement regulation. The chapter establishes that judicial activism represents the most influential factor in the evolution of the public procurement *acquis* and serves as the prelude to legislative and policy reforms to continuous modality changes in delivering public services. Chapter 12 entitled 'The Remedies Directive in public procurement' deals with legal remedies available to individuals at national level and access to justice in public procurement disputes. The objective of this chapter is to assess the progress made by Member States to decentralize enforcement of public procurement rules by creating the appropriate legal frameworks that encourage aggrieved contractors to seek justice. Chapter 13 entitled 'The role of the European Court of Justice in public procurement' examines the role of the Court in public procurement law by exploring some areas where the Court's jurisprudence has been of particular importance for the development of public procurement law, namely concessions, the exemptions for in-house cooperation, environmental considerations, selection processes and the effectiveness of remedies.

Part 4 comprises of three chapters which offer the reader an evaluation of the relationship between public procurement and competition.

Chapter 14 entitled 'Public procurement and competition: some challenges arising from recent developments in EU public procurement law' explores the recent OECD push for more competition in public procurement and its role as an influential factor in the 2014 reform of EU public procurement rules. Afterwards, it critically assesses three of the main challenges to keeping public procurement precompetitive: (i) the difficult balance in terms of procurement transparency created by the clash between competition and corruption concerns; (ii) the magnification of the undesired (potential) anti-competitive effects of public procurement that centralized procurement may generate, as well as its increasing use as an improper tool of market regulation; and (iii) the possible competitive distortions and the potential advantages resulting from the generalization of eProcurement. Chapter 15 entitled 'Public procurement and State aid' presents an overview of both the public procurements and State aid rules and discusses their interplay in the light of the modernization of EU public procurement which presents certain opportunities to increase convergence between the application of the EU public procurement and State aid rules. Chapter 16 entitled 'EU public procurement and probity' deals with the connection between public procurement and corruption; it examines the legal background – including the previous Public Procurement Directives and the current new Directives – to the prevention of corruption and fraud in procurement procedures and concludes that the use of traditional instruments may be inadequate in the struggle for ethical public procurement. Prevention and access to relevant, procurement-related information on the part of the legislator are as much part of the subject matter as the independent audit activity of the contracting authorities and the focus on the real meaning and content of probity.

Part 5 comprises of three chapters which offer the reader an evaluation of the relationship between public procurement and public services.

Chapter 17 entitled 'The new EU defence procurement regime' comprehensively covers the procurement of armaments and other security sensitive goods and services. The objective of the chapter is to explain the use of Article 346 TFEU and other security exemptions in defence and security procurement inside the EU internal market. Chapter 18 entitled 'Public service partnerships' evaluates the relationship between public procurement and public private partnerships. It appraises recent legal, policy and judicial developments that have emerged as a result of the involvement of the private sector in the delivery of public services and in particular their financing. The concept of public-private partnerships is gaining momentum across the common market and policy makers are keen to see the relevant model as a credible and effective delivery mechanism. Chapter 19 entitled 'Concessions and public procurement' covers the evolution of the phenomenon of concession and public private partnerships, provides for a comprehensive analysis of the structure of such arrangements and a detailed analysis of legal developments in the fields of concession contracts at Community level and demonstrates that the procurement of public-private partnerships must adhere to the newly adopted concessions Directive which has enshrined principles of transparency, objectivity and non-discrimination that underpin the public procurement regime.

Acknowledgments

It would have been very difficult to complete this project without the involvement of a number of people to whom here I record my indebtedness. First, I express my gratitude to the contributors of the *Research Handbook on EU Public Procurement*.

It is also with deep appreciation that I thank Domenica Melfi and Lorenzo Jovannoti. Finally, I am eternally indebted to Joliet Lamar.

Christopher Bovis
October 2015

Introduction

The intellectual paternity of public procurement regulation can be traced in a neo-liberal economic approach to market integration.[1] Public procurement in the European Union has been significantly influenced by the internal market project. The White Paper for the Completion of the Internal Market[2] and the Single European Act provide for the conceptual foundations of the regulation of public markets of the Member States. The identification of public procurement as a major non-tariff barrier has revealed the economic importance of its regulation.[3] Savings and price convergence appeared as the main arguments for liberalizing the trade patterns of the demand (the public and utilities sectors) and supply (the industry) side of the public procurement equation.[4] The economic approach to the regulation of public procurement aims at the integration of public markets across the EU. Through the principles of transparency, non-discrimination and objectivity in the award of public contracts, it is envisaged that the regulatory system will bring about competitiveness in the relevant product and geographical markets, will increase import penetration of products and services destined for the public sector, will enhance the tradability of public contracts across the common market, will result in significant price convergence and finally it will be the catalyst for the needed rationalization and industrial restructuring of the European industrial base.[5]

In parallel with the economic arguments, legal arguments have emerged supporting the regulation of public procurement as a necessary ingredient of the fundamental principles of the European Treaties, such as the free movement of goods and services, the right of establishment and the prohibition of discrimination on nationality grounds.[6] The legal significance of the regulation of public procurement in the common market

[1] See Bovis, 'Public Procurement and the Internal Market of the 21st Century: Economic Exercise versus Policy Choice', Chapter 17 in O'Keeffe and Tridimas (eds), *EU Law for the 21st Century: Rethinking the New Legal Order*, Oxford: Hart Publishing 2005.

[2] See European Commission, *White Paper for the Completion of the Internal Market*, (COM) 85 310 fin., 1985.

[3] See Commission of the European Communities, *The Cost of Non-Europe, Basic Findings, Vol.5, Part.A; The Cost of Non-Europe in Public Sector Procurement*, Official Publications of the European Communities, Luxembourg, 1988. Also the Cechinni Report *1992 The European Challenge*, Aldershot: Wildwood House, 1988.

[4] The European Commission has claimed that the regulation of public procurement could bring substantial savings of ECU 20 bn or 0.5% of GDP to the (European) public sector. See European Communities, *The Cost of Non-Europe, op.cit.*

[5] See Commission of the European Communities, Statistical Performance for keeping watch over public procurement, 1992. Also *The Cost of Non-Europe, Basic Findings, Vol.5, Part.A; The Cost of Non-Europe in Public Sector Procurement, op.cit.*

[6] See Bovis, 'Recent Case Law Relating to Public Procurement: A Beacon for the Integration of Public Markets' (2002) 39(5) *Common Market Law Review* 1025–56.

has been well documented. It reflects the wish of European institutions to eliminate preferential and discriminatory purchasing patterns by the public sector and create seamless intra-community trade patterns between the public and private sectors. Procurement by member states and their contracting authorities is often susceptible to a rationale and policy that tends to favour indigenous undertakings and *national champions*[7] at the expense of more efficient domestic or Community-wide competitors. As the relevant product and geographical markets have been sheltered from competition, distorted patterns emerge in the trade of goods, works and services destined for the public sector. These trade patterns represent a serious impediment in the functioning of the common market and inhibit the fulfillment of the principles enshrined in the Treaties.[8]

The European Court of Justice has been instrumental in interpreting the public procurement legal framework. The Court has provided intellectual assistance to the efforts of European institutions in order to strengthen the three principles (non-discrimination, objectivity and transparency) underlying the regulation of public procurement,[9] to eliminate discrimination and non-tariff barriers in the fields of technical standards (product specification and standardization) and the selection procedures (quantitative and qualitative suitability criteria). The jurisprudence of the Court also reflects on a strategic goal of the European judiciary: to vest the regime wherever possible with direct effect. Arming the public procurement rules with direct effect will enhance access to justice at national level, improve compliance, increase the quality of the regulatory regime and finally streamline the public procurement process across the common market by introducing an element of uniformity. By conferring direct effect upon the public procurement directives and inviting national courts to play a prominent role in future public procurement litigation, the Court has hinted towards its preference for a decentralised enforcement of the public procurement regime. However, the most important lesson law and policy maker have learnt from the Court's jurisprudence reflects on a *rule of reason approach* which propels public procurement regulation as an instrument of policy making at national and European levels.

---

7 The term implies a firm with more than a third of its turnover made in its own country and has enjoyed formal or informal government protection. The term has been defined by Abravanel, and Ernst (1992), 'Alliance and Acquisition Strategies for European National Champions' (1992) 2 *The McKinsey Quarterly* 45–62.

8 See Nicolaides (ed.), *Industrial Policy in the European Community: A Necessary Response to Economic Integration,* Dordrecht: Martinus Nijhoff, 1993.

9 See the recital of Directive 89/440, [1989] OJ L210/1 amending the original works Directive 71/305 concerning co-ordination of procedures for the award of public works contracts, stating that '... it is necessary to improve and extend the safeguards in the directives that are designed to introduce transparency into the procedures and practices for the award of such contracts, in order to be able to monitor compliance with the prohibition of restrictions more closely and at the same time to reduce disparities in the competitive conditions faced by nationals of different Member States'.

1. A THEMATIC OVERVIEW OF PUBLIC PROCUREMENT REGULATION

European Directives which govern the award of public contracts in the supplies, works and services sectors, as well as in the public utilities[10] have been adopted by the European Union after a considerable amount of debate and consultation.[11] The new Directives reflect on the 1996 European Commission's Green Paper on Public Procurement[12] and the following 1998 Commission's Communication.[13] The Directives have been seen as an integral part of the Commission's 2000 Work Programme, which pledges to modernize the relevant legislation for the completion of the internal market and at the same time implement the Lisbon European Council's call for economic reform within the internal market.

The Directives are based upon two premises: *simplification* and *modernization*. Drawing on the wealth of experience from the application and implementation of previous legal regimes and the Court's jurisprudential inferences to public procurement regulation, the new Directives are set to achieve the challenging objective to fully integrate public sector purchasing in the common market and abolish any remaining non-tariff barriers.

Although the same fundamental principles underpin procurement liberalization in both the government and utilities sectors, the new regime maps a clear-cut *dichotomy* between the public sector and the utilities. Their separate regulation reveals the diametrically opposed nature of the contracting authorities/entities under these sectors and reflects on the process of transformation that utilities have been undergoing over

---

[10] See Directive 2004/18 on the coordination of procedures for the award of public works contracts, public supply contracts and public service contracts [2004] OJ L134 and Directive 2004/17 coordinating the procurement procedures of entities operating in the water, energy, transport and postal services sectors [2004] OJ L134. The new Directives amend the existing regime which is applicable until 31 January 2016 and includes the following instruments: the Public Supplies Directive 93/36/EC, [1993] OJ L199, as amended by Directive 97/52/EC [1997] OJ L328 and Directive 2001/78/EC [2001] OJ L285; the Public Works Directive 93/37/EC [1993] OJ L199, amended by Directive 97/52/EC [1997] OJ L328 and Directive 2001/78/EC [2001] OJ L285; The Utilities Directives 93/38/EC [1993] OJ L199, amended by Directive 98/4/EC [1998] OJ L101; the Public Services Directive 92/50/EEC [1992] OJ L209, amended by Directive 97/52/EC [1997] OJ L328 and Directive 2001/78/EC [2001] OJ L285; the Remedies Utilities Directive 92/13/EEC [1992] OJ L076; the Public Remedies Directive 89/665/EEC [1989] OJ L395.

[11] See the proposal from the European Commission [2001] OJ C29E/11 and [2002] OJ C203E/210; the opinion of the Economic and Social Committee [2001] OJ C193/7; the opinion of the Committee of the Regions [2001] OJ C144/23; the opinion of the European Parliament of 17 January 2002 [2002] OJ C271E/176), Council Common Position of 20 March 2003 [2003] OJ C147/1) and Position of the European Parliament of 2 July 2003. See also the Legislative Resolution of the European Parliament of 29 January 2004 and Decision of the Council of 2 February 2004.

[12] See the Green Paper on Public Procurement in the European Union: Exploring the way forward, European Commission 1996.

[13] See European Commission, Communication on Public Procurement in the European Union, COM(98) 143.

the past decade. Their change in ownership from public to private has stimulated commercialism and competitiveness and provided for the justification of a more relaxed regime and the acceptance that utilities, in some form or another represent *sui generis* contracting authorities which do not need a rigorous and detailed regulation of their procurement.

The dichotomy in regulation which the new public procurement regime has established to separate public sector procurement from utilities procurement exposes an insight into current market conditions and political priorities across the European Union, as well as an indication that the main emphasis should be placed on attempts to open up the public sector.

The merger of the rules governing supplies, works and services procurement into a single legal instrument represents a successful attempt on the part of the European Union to codify supranational administrative provisions which have the aim to harmonize domestic legal regimes, public or private, which co-ordinate the award of public contracts. The codification, apart from the obvious benefits of legal certainty and legitimate expectation, has two important implications: legal efficiency and compliance discipline. As far as legal efficiency is concerned, the new codified Directive will speed up and streamline its implementation process by Member States, especially the new arrivals from the 2004 Accession Treaty, and provide for a one-stop shop reference point in national legal orders, augmented by the Court's vesting of direct effectiveness upon the Directive's predecessors in numerous occasions. On the other hand, codification will enhance compliance, as it will remove any remaining uncertainties over the applicability of the previously fragmented regime and afford contracting authorities a disciplined method in dispersing their procurement functions. The main influence of the codified public sector procurement Directive can be traced in important recent case-law developments[14] from the European Court of Justice, in particular case-law on the definition of contracting authorities, the use of award procedures and award criteria, and the possibility for contracting authorities to use environmental and social considerations as criteria for the award of public contracts.[15]

As far as utilities procurement is concerned, the two main reasons for the introduction of a distinctive legal regime which aims at coordinating procedures for the award of contracts in the utilities sectors revolve around the relations of the state with such entities. First, the numerous ways in which national authorities can influence the

---

[14] For a comprehensive analysis of the public procurement case law, see Bovis, 'Recent Case Law Relating to Public Procurement: A Beacon for the Integration of Public Markets', (2002) 39(5) *Common Market Law Review* 1025–56.

[15] See Communication from the European Commission to the Council, the European Parliament, the Economic and Social Committee, and the Committee of the Regions, 'Working together to maintain momentum' 2001 Review of the Internal Market Strategy, Brussels, 11 April 2001, COM(2001)198 final. Also, European Commission, Commission Communication, Public procurement in the European Union, Brussels, 11 March 1998, COM (98) 143. See Commission Interpretative Communication on the Community law applicable to public procurement and the possibilities for integrating social considerations into public procurement, COM (2001) 566, 15 October 2001. Also, Commission Interpretative Communication on the Community law applicable to public procurement and the possibilities for integrating environmental considerations into public procurement, COM(2001) 274, 4 July 2001.

purchasing behaviour of these entities, such as participation in their capital and representation in their administrative, managerial or supervisory bodies. Secondly, the closed nature of the markets in which utilities operate, as a result of special or exclusive rights granted by the Member States, necessitates the operation of a procurement regulatory regime which ensures on the one hand compliance with the fundamental principles of the EU Treaties and on the other hand compatibility with anti-trust and sector specific regulation in the utilities sectors.

2. THE CONCEPTS IN PUBLIC SECTOR PROCUREMENT

The codified public sector Directive has introduced a series of new concepts which are the product of jurisprudential inferences and policy refining of the previous legal regimes. They intend to modernize public purchasing and align the procurement of government and its agencies with that of utilities which operate in a more commercially oriented environment.

2.1 Eligibility of Bodies Governed by Public Law to Tender

The new public sector Directive clearly accepts that entities which are covered by its rules can participate in the award of public contracts, alongside private sector undertakings. Member States should ensure that the participation of a body governed by public law as a tenderer in a procedure for the award of a public contract does not cause any distortion of competition in relation to private tenderers. The eligibility of bodies governed by public law to participate in tendering procedures has been influenced by case-law.[16] There is a protection mechanism built in Article 55(e) of the public sector Directive, which specifies that in case of abnormally low tenders, the contracting authority may reject those tenders, if it establishes that the tenderer is the recipient of state aid which may have been granted illegally. The onus to prove the legitimacy of the state aid rests with the tenderer.

It should be mentioned that the existing Directives provide for an automatic disqualification of an 'obviously abnormally low offer'. The term has not been interpreted in detail by the Court and serves rather as an indication of a 'bottom limit'.[17] The Court, however, pronounced on the direct effect of the relevant provision requiring contracting authorities to examine the details of the tender before deciding the award of the contract and to seek from the tenderer an explanation for the price submitted.

---

[16] See Case C-94/99, *ARGE Gewässerschutzt v Bundesministerium für Land-und Forstwirtschaft,* para 30, judgment of 7 December 2000, where the Court ruled that directly or indirectly subsidized tenders by the state or other contracting authorities or even by the contracting authority itself can be legitimately part of the evaluation process.

[17] Case 76/81, *SA Transporoute et Travaux v Minister of Public Works* [1982] ECR 457.

The debate over the terminology of 'obviously abnormally low' tenders surfaced when the Court held[18] that rejection of a contract based on mathematical criteria without giving the tenderer an opportunity to furnish information is inconsistent with spirit of the public procurement Directives. The Court, following previous case-law,[19] ruled that the contracting authorities must give an opportunity to tenderers to furnish explanations regarding the genuine nature of their tenders, when those tenders appear to be abnormally low. However, the Court did not analyze the meaning of 'obviously'. It seems, in the author's view, that the term 'obviously' indicates the existence of precise and concrete evidence as to the abnormality of the low tender. On the other hand, the wording 'abnormally' implies a quantitative criterion left to the discretion of the contracting authority. Nonetheless, if the tender is just 'abnormally' low, it could be argued that it is within the discretion of the contracting authority to investigate the genuine offer of a tender. *Impresa Lombardini*[20] followed *Transporoute* and maintained the unlawfulness of mathematical criteria used as an exclusion of a tender which appears abnormally low. Yet, it held that such criteria may be lawful if used for determining the abnormality of a low tender, provided an *inter partes* procedure between the contracting authority and the tenderer that submitted the alleged abnormal low offer presents the opportunity to clarify the genuine nature of that offer. Contracting authorities must take into account all reasonable explanations furnished and avoid limiting the grounds on which justification of the genuine nature of a tender should be made. In *ARGE*,[21] the rejection of a tender based on the abnormally low pricing attached to it got a different twist in its interpretation. Although the Court ruled that directly or indirectly subsidized tenders by the state or other contracting authorities or even by the contracting authority itself can legitimately be part of the evaluation process, it did not elaborate on the possibility of rejection of an offer, which is appreciably lower than those of unsubsidized tenderers by reference to the abnormally low disqualification ground.[22]

---

18 See Case 103/88, *Fratelli Costanzo S.p.A. v Comune di Milano*, [1989] ECR 1839; Case 296/89, *Impresa Dona Alfonso di Dona Alfonso & Figli s.n.c. v Consorzio per lo Sviluppo Industriale del Comune di Monfalcone*, judgment of 18 June 1991.

19 See Case 76/81 *Transporoute*, [1982] ECR 417, *op.cit.*

20 See Cases C-285/99 & 286/99, *Impresa Lombardini SpA v ANAS*, judgment of 27 November 2001.

21 See Case C-94/99, *ARGE Gewässerschutzt v Bundesministerium für Land-und Forstwirtschaft*, para 30, judgment of 7 December 2000.

22 In *ARGE* the Court adopted a literal interpretation of the Directives and concluded that if the legislature wanted to preclude subsidized entities from participating in tendering procedures for public contracts, it should have said so explicitly in the relevant Directives. See paras 26 *et seq* of the Court's judgment. Although the case has relevance in the fields of selection and qualification procedures and award criteria, the Court made no references to previous case-law regarding state aids in public procurement, presumably because the *Dupont de Nemours* precedent is still highly relevant.

2.2 Joint and Centralized Procurement

The public sector Directive aims at introducing a regime where procurement can benefit from scale economies and streamlining planning, operation and delivery. In the light of the diversity of public procurement contracts in Member States, contracting authorities have been given the freedom to make provision for contracts for the design and execution of work to be awarded jointly. The decision to award contracts jointly must be determined by qualitative and economic criteria, which may be defined by national law. According to Article 1(10) of the public sector Directive, a central purchasing body is a contracting authority which: (i) acquires supplies and/or services intended for contracting authorities, or (ii) awards public contracts or concludes framework agreements for works, supplies or services intended for contracting authorities.

2.3 Official List of Contractors

The public sector Directive provides for a central system of certification of private and public organizations for the purposes of providing evidence of financial and economic standing as well as levels of technical capacity in public procurement selection and qualification procedures. Such systems must be mutually recognized by all Member States and registration of entities in official lists of contractors, suppliers or service providers is influenced by the Court's case-law,[23] where an economic operator belonging to a group claims the economic, financial or technical capabilities of other companies in the same group in support of its application for registration. Member States may determine the level of requirements to be met for such registrations and the period of their validity, in particular requirements for joint and several liability where an operator relies on the financial standing of another company in the same group.

2.4 The Competitive Dialogue

The competitive dialogue is the most publicized change brought about by the new public procurement regime. Its inception is attributed to three reasons: (i) the inability of open or restricted procedures to facilitate the award of complex public contracts, including concessions and public-private partnerships; (ii) the exceptional nature of negotiated procedures without prior advertisement;[24] and (iii) the restrictive

---

[23] See Case C-76/81, *SA Transporoute et Travaux v Minister of Public Works* [1982] ECR 457; Case C-27/86, *Constructions et Enterprises Industrielles S.A (CEI) v Association Intercommunale pour les Autoroutes des Ardennes*; Case C-28/86, *Ing.A. Bellini & Co. S.p.A. v Regie de Betiments*; Case C-29/86, *Ing.A. Bellini & Co. S.p.A. v Belgian State* [1987] ECR 3347; Case C-389/92, *Ballast Nedam Groep NV v Belgische Staat* [1994] 2 CMLR 836; Case C-5/97, *Ballast Nedam Groep NV v Belgische Staat,* judgment of 18 December 1997; Case C-176/98, *Holst Italia v Comune di Cagliari,* judgment of 2 December 1999.

[24] Negotiated procedures without prior advertisement are exceptionally allowed 'when for technical or artistic reasons or reasons connected with the protection of exclusive rights the services could only be procured by a particular provider ... and ... in cases of extreme urgency brought about by events unforeseeable by the contracting authority'. In Cases C-199/85,

interpretation[25] of the grounds for using negotiated procedures with prior advertisement.

Article 29 of the public sector Directive establishes the competitive dialogue as an award procedure, alongside open, restricted and negotiated procedures. The competitive dialogue must be used exceptionally in cases of particularly complex contracts, where the use of the open or restricted procedures will not allow the award of the contract, and the use of negotiated procedures cannot be justified. A public contract is considered to be particularly complex where the contracting authorities are not able to define in an objective manner the technical specifications which are required to pursue the project, or they are not able to specify the legal or financial make-up of a project.

The procedure is very complex, as it has three main phases and many options within these phases. First, the advertisement phase according to Article 29(2) obliges contracting authorities to publish a contract notice or a descriptive document outlining their needs and basic specifications of the project. After that phase and before launching a competitive dialogue for the award of a contract, contracting authorities may, using a technical dialogue, seek or accept advice which may be used in the preparation of the specifications, provided that such advice does not have the effect of precluding competition.

Secondly, a selection phase reduces the candidates to be invited to the competitive dialogue according to the relevant provisions of Articles 44 to 52 of the public sector Directive.[26] The minimum number of candidates should be three but it could be lower if there is sufficient evidence of competitiveness in the process or the limited number of initial respondents to the contract notice precludes the invitation of at least three candidates.

Thirdly, the competitive dialogue is opened by the commencement of the award phase in accordance with Article 29(3). Contracting authorities must open a dialogue

---

Commission v Italy [1987] ECR 1039 and C-3/88, *Commission v Italy* [1989] ECR 4035, the Court rejected the existence of exclusive rights and regarded the abuse of this provision as contrary to the right of establishment and freedom to provide services which are based on the principle of equal treatment and prohibit not only overt discrimination on grounds of nationality, but also all covert forms of discrimination, which, by the application of other criteria of differentiation, lead to the same result. Interestingly, in Case 199/85, *Commission v Italy, op.cit*, the Court elucidated that exclusive rights might include contractual arrangements such as know-how and intellectual property rights. For urgency reasons brought by unforeseen events to contracting authorities the Court established two tests: (i) the need of a justification test based on the proportionality principle, and (ii) the existence of a causal link between the alleged urgency and the unforeseen events (see C-199/85, *Commission v Italy, op.cit*; C-3/88, *Commission v Italy, op.cit*; Case C-24/91, *Commission v Spain* [1994] 2 CMLR 621; Case C-107/92, *Commission v Italy*, judgment of 2 August 1993; Case C-57/94, *Commission v Italy*, judgment of 18 May 1995; Case C-296/92, *Commission v Italy*, judgment of 12 January 1994).

[25] The grounds for using this procedure are confined to: (i) the nature of the works or services or risks attached thereto do not permit overall pricing and (ii) the nature of the services is such that specifications cannot be established with sufficient precision. See Article 7(2)(c) of the Works Directive and Articles 11(2)(b) and 11(2)(c) of the Services Directive.

[26] Articles 44 to 46 of the Public Sector Directive 2004/18 govern the conduct of the procedure for verification of the suitability and choice of participants and award of contracts, criteria for qualitative selection, and suitability to pursue a professional activity.

with the candidates selected, the aim of which is to identify the means best suited to satisfying their needs. They may discuss all aspects of the contract with the chosen candidates, ensuring equality of treatment among all tenderers. In particular, they must not provide information in a discriminatory manner which may give some tenderers an advantage over others. Contracting authorities may not reveal to the other participants' solutions proposed or other confidential information communicated by a candidate participating in the dialogue without prior agreement granted from that candidate.

Contracting authorities may provide for the competitive dialogue to take place in successive stages in order to reduce the number of solutions to be discussed with the candidates in accordance with Article 29(4). They may continue the dialogue until they can identify the solution or solutions which are capable of meeting their needs. Having declared that the dialogue is concluded and having informed the participants, contracting authorities must ask them to submit their final tenders on the basis of the solution or solutions presented and specified during the dialogue.

After this phase is over (closure of the competitive dialogue), there are four stages until the contract award. First, contracting authorities must ask all remaining candidates to submit their final tenders (Article 44(4)). Secondly, these tenders need to be finalized prior to their evaluation (Article 29(6)). Thirdly, the selection of the winning tenderer must take place in accordance with the criteria stipulated in the contract notice (Article 29(7)) and fourthly the winning tenderer must provide further clarification and his commitment to undertake the project (Article 29(7)).

The tenders must contain all the elements required and considered necessary for the performance of the project. They may be clarified, specified and fine-tuned at the request of the contracting authority. However, any additional information must not involve any changes to the basic features of the tender or the call for tender, nor allow for variations which are likely to distort competition or have a discriminatory effect. In the author's view, there is a great deal of uncertainty over the meaning of clarification, additional provision of tender specification and the extent of fine-tuning, to the degree of compromising the competitiveness and integrity of the procedure.

Contracting authorities must assess the tenders received on the basis of the award criteria laid down in the contract notice or the descriptive document and must choose the most economically advantageous tender in accordance with Article 53. At the request of the contracting authority, the tenderer identified as having submitted the most economically advantageous tender may be asked to clarify aspects of the tender or confirm commitments contained in the tender provided this does not have the effect of modifying substantial aspects of the tender or of the call for tender and does not risk distorting competition or discriminating against other candidates.

Overall, the competitive dialogue has addressed many of the features that are important during the award of complex projects and are currently being addressed by negotiated procedures with prior advertisement. In comparison with these procedures, the competitive dialogue allows also for a limited number of participants (three in number), introduces a staged approach to tendering and permits elimination of participants during its internal phases. However it allows significant scope for post-tender negotiations, but it restricts the award of a contract to complete offers.

2.5 Framework Procurement

The existing utilities Directives have introduced framework agreements as a selection and tendering procedure which is influenced to a large extent by the benefits of chain supply management and partnering schemes operating in the private sector. The new utilities Directive has maintained the framework agreements regime in virtually unaltered format as laid down in Article 17(3). Within the provisions of the new utilities Directive, when an entity established a framework agreement under the relevant procedures which are common to other public contracts covered therein, subsequent individual contracts concluded under the framework agreement may be awarded without having recourse to a call for competition. Individual contracts which have been awarded under a framework agreement could be subject to the reopening of tendering procedures, provided the contracting entity does not invite new tenderers to participate. The Directive specifically stipulates that misuse of framework agreements may distort competition and trigger the application of the relevant rules, particularly with reference to concerted practices which lead to collusive tendering.

The new public sector Directive has for the first time introduced framework procurement to the public sector contracting authorities. According to Article 1(5) of the public sector Directive, a framework agreement is an agreement between one or more contracting authorities and one or more economic operators, the purpose of which is to establish the terms and conditions of public contracts to be awarded during a given period, in particular with regard to price and, where appropriate, the quantity of supplies, works or services envisaged.

Contracting authorities may establish framework agreements in accordance with the provisions of the public sector Directive relating to advertising, time limits and conditions for the submission of tenders. The parties to the framework agreement must be chosen by applying the award criteria set in accordance with Article 53. Article 53 refers to the award criteria being the most economically advantageous offer or the lowest price. When the award is made to the tender most economically advantageous from the point of view of the contracting authority, various criteria linked to the subject-matter of the public contract in question, for example, quality, price, technical merit, aesthetic and functional characteristics, environmental characteristics, running costs, cost-effectiveness, after-sales service and technical assistance, delivery date and delivery period or period of completion. When the award criterion refers to the lowest price only, no other factors should play a part. Contracting authorities may subsequently enter into contracts based on such framework agreements during their term of validity either by applying the terms set forth in the framework agreement or, if terms and conditions for the conclusion of contracts have not been fixed in advance, by reopening competition between the parties to the framework agreement. The reopening of competition should comply with certain rules[27] the aim of which is to guarantee the

[27] According to Article 32(4) of the Public Sector Directive 2004/18, the conditions for reopening competition within a framework agreement include: (a) for every contract to be awarded, contracting authorities must consult in writing the economic operators capable of performing the contract; (b) contracting authorities must fix a time limit which is sufficiently long to allow tenders for each specific contract to be submitted, taking into account factors such

required flexibility and to guarantee respect for the general principles, in particular the principle of equal treatment.

Contracts based on a framework agreement must be awarded in accordance with the procedures of Article 32, which must be applied only between the contracting authorities and the economic operators originally party to the framework agreement. The duration of a framework agreement may not exceed four years, unless exceptional cases justify its extension. Framework agreements can be established between contracting authorities and a single economic operator according to Article 32(3) in exceptional circumstances which must be justified by the nature of the framework agreement, or with several economic operators according to Article 32(4). The latter must be at least three in number, provided that there are a sufficient number of economic operators to satisfy the selection criteria or there are a sufficient number of admissible tenders which meet the award criteria. Contracting authorities are under an obligation not to use framework agreements improperly or in such a way as to prevent, restrict or distort competition.

2.6 Electronic Procurement

The rapid expansion of electronic purchasing systems in private sector procurement and the continuous development of electronic purchasing techniques have made an impact with the public sector Directive. Electronic procurement can contribute in increasing competition and streamlining public purchasing, particularly in cases where repetitive purchasing allows efficiencies to be achieved both in time and in financial terms.

2.6.1 Dynamic purchasing systems

Article 1(6) of the public sector Directive provides for the establishment of dynamic purchasing systems. A dynamic purchasing system is an electronic process which allows contracting authorities to utilize techniques available to the private sector in order to procure supplies or services of repetitive nature. Any economic operator which submits an indicative tender in accordance with the specification and meets the selection criteria should be allowed to join such a system. This purchasing technique allows contracting authorities, through the establishment of a pre-selected list of tenderers, to have a particularly broad range of tenders as a result of the electronic facilities available, and to ensure, in principle, optimum use of public funds through broad competition.

The use of dynamic purchasing systems is described in Article 33 of the public sector Directive. In order to set up a dynamic purchasing system, contracting authorities must follow the open procedure in all its phases up to the award of the contracts. All the tenderers satisfying the selection criteria and having submitted an indicative tender which complies with the technical specification must be admitted to

---

as the complexity of the subject-matter of the contract and the time needed to send in tenders; (c) tenders must be submitted in writing, and their content must remain confidential until the stipulated time limit for reply has expired; (d) contracting authorities must award each contract to the tenderer who has submitted the best tender on the basis of the award criteria set out in the specifications of the framework agreement.

the system; indicative tenders may be improved at any time provided that they continue to comply with the overall specifications.

With a view to setting up the system and proceeding to the award of contracts under that system, contracting authorities must use solely electronic means in accordance with Article 42(2) to (5). For these purposes contracting authorities must:

(a) publish a contract notice making it clear that a dynamic purchasing system is involved;
(b) indicate in the specification, amongst other matters, the nature of the purchases envisaged under that system, as well as all the necessary information concerning the purchasing system, the electronic equipment used and the technical connection arrangements and specifications;
(c) offer by electronic means, on publication of the notice and up to the expiry of the system, unrestricted, direct and full access to the specification and to any additional documents and must indicate in the notice the internet address at which such documents may be consulted.

Contracting authorities must give every economic operator participating in the dynamic purchasing system the possibility of submitting an indicative tender throughout the entire period of such system. Each specific contract must be the subject of an invitation to tender. Before issuing the invitation to tender, contracting authorities must publish a simplified contract notice inviting all interested economic operators to submit an indicative tender within a time limit of at least 15 days. The duration of a dynamic purchasing system may not exceed four years, except in duly justified exceptional cases. Contracting authorities are under an obligation not to levy any charges attributed to the operation of dynamic purchasing systems to the interested economic operators admitted to such systems

2.6.2 Electronic auctions

According to Article 1.7 of the public sector Directive an electronic auction is a repetitive process involving an electronic device for the presentation of new prices which are revised downwards, or new values concerning certain elements of tenders. The presentation of such financial information occurs after an initial full evaluation of the tenders, enabling them to be ranked using automatic evaluation methods.

Article 54 of the public sector Directive stipulates the parameters for the use of electronic auctions. In open, restricted or negotiated procedures, contracting authorities may decide that the award of a public contract must be preceded by an electronic auction when the contract specifications can be established with precision. In the same circumstances, an electronic auction may be held on the reopening of competition among the parties to a framework agreement as provided for in the second indent of the second subparagraph of Article 32(4) and on the opening for competition of contracts to be awarded under the dynamic purchasing system referred to in Article 33. The electronic auction must be based: (i) either solely on prices when the contract is awarded to the lowest price, or (ii) on prices and/or on the new values of the features of the tenders indicated in the specification when the contract is awarded to the most economically advantageous tender.

Contracting authorities who decide to hold an electronic auction must indicate their intention in the contract notice. The contract specifications must include, *inter alia*, the following details:

(a) the features, the values for which will be the subject of electronic auction, provided that such features are quantifiable and can be expressed in figures or percentages;
(b) any limits on the values which may be submitted, as they result from the specifications relating to the subject of the contract;
(c) the information which will be made available to tenderers in the course of the electronic auction and, where appropriate, when it will be made available to them;
(d) the relevant information concerning the electronic auction process;
(e) the conditions under which the tenderers will be able to bid and, in particular, the minimum differences which will, where appropriate, be required when bidding;
(f) the relevant information concerning the electronic equipment used and the arrangements and technical specifications for connection.

When the contract is to be awarded on the basis of the most economically advantageous tender, the invitation must provide the full evaluation framework in accordance with the respective weighting of the award criteria. The invitation must also state the mathematical formula to be used in the electronic auction to determine automatic re-rankings on the basis of the new prices or new values submitted. That formula must incorporate the weighting of all the criteria fixed to determine the most economically advantageous tender. Where variants are authorized, a separate formula must be provided for each variant. After closing an electronic auction contracting authorities must award the contract in accordance with Article 53 on the basis of the results of the electronic auction. Contracting authorities may not have improper recourse to electronic auctions nor may they use them in such a way as to prevent, restrict or distort competition or to change the subject-matter of the contract, as specified in the contract notice and defined in the specifications.

2.7 The Award Criteria and the Introduction of Policies in Public Procurement

2.7.1 Contractual performance and public procurement

Conditions relating to the performance of public contracts are compatible with the public sector Directive provided that they are not directly or indirectly discriminatory and are indicated in the contract notice or in the contract documents. They may, in particular, be intended to favour on-site vocational training, the employment of people experiencing particular difficulty in achieving integration, the fight against unemployment or the protection of the environment.

The new public sector Directives and the new utilities Directives remain silent over the possibility of expressly authorizing social or environmental consideration as part of the award criteria of public contracts. Although the draft Directives, at the insistence of the European Parliament, contained specific provisions relevant to workforce matters as part of the award criteria, such provisions were omitted from the final text. The Commission has adopted a myopic view that considerations related to contractual performance cannot be used as criterion for the award of the contract. The Court had the opportunity to correct the Commission's interpretation and point to the right direction of its judgments,[28] where a condition relating to the employment of long-term unemployed persons or the protection of the environment can legitimately constitute a criterion for the award of the contract. However, the new public procurement regime has failed to adopt previous jurisprudential inferences and clarify the position of contacting authorities over the legitimacy of pursuing socio-economic and environmental policies through public procurement.[29]

Examples of conditions relevant to contractual performance in public contracts may include requirements to recruit long-term job-seekers or to implement training measures for the unemployed or young persons, to comply in substance with the provisions of the International Labour Organization (ILO) Conventions, assuming that such provisions have not been implemented in national law, and to recruit more handicapped persons than are required under national legislation.

However, according to Article 19 of the public sector Directive, a specific category of public sector contracts are regarded as reserved contracts. This is the only concession the Commission afforded Member States in relation to the socio-economic dimension of the award criteria of public contracts. Member States may reserve the right to participate in public contract award procedures to sheltered workshops or provide for such contracts to be performed in the context of sheltered employment programmes where most of the employees concerned are handicapped persons who, by reason of the nature or the seriousness of their disabilities, cannot carry on occupations under normal conditions. The contract notice must make reference to this provision.

In addition, the laws, regulations and collective agreements, at both national and Community level, which are in force in the areas of employment conditions and safety at work apply during performance of a public contract, providing that such rules, and their application, comply with Community law. In cross-border situations, where workers from one Member State provide services in another Member State for the purpose of performing a public contract, Directive 96/71/EC concerning the posting of workers in the framework of the provision of services[30] lays down the minimum conditions which must be observed by the host country in respect of such posted workers. If national law contains provisions to this effect, non-compliance with those obligations may be considered to be grave misconduct or an offence concerning the professional conduct of the economic operator concerned, liable to lead to the exclusion of that economic operator from the procedure for the award of a public contract.

---

[28] See Case 31/87, *Gebroeders Beentjes v The Netherlands* [1989] ECR 4365 at para 14; Case C-225/98, *Commission v French Republic (Nord-Pas-de-Calais)* [2000] ECR I-7445), at para 52; Case C-513/99, *Concordia Bus Finlandia v Helsingin Kaupunki et HKL-Bussiliikenne* [2002] ECR I-7213, at para 31.

[29] For a detailed analysis of the ordo-liberal versus the neo-liberal approach in public procurement regulation, see Bovis, 'Public Procurement and the Internal Market of the 21st Century: Economic Exercise versus Policy Choice', Chapter 17 in *EU Law for the 21st Century: Rethinking the New Legal Order*, footnote 9, *op.cit.*

[30] See [1997] OJ L18/1.

2.7.2 The most economically advantageous offer

The most economically advantageous offer as an award criterion has provided the Court with the opportunity to balance the economic considerations of public procurement with policy choices. Although in numerous instances the Court has maintained the importance of the economic approach[31] to the regulation of public sector contracts, it has also recognized the relative discretion of contracting authorities to utilize non-economic considerations as award criteria.

The meaning of the most economically advantageous offer[32] includes a combination of factors chosen by the contracting authority, including price, delivery or completion date, running costs, cost-effectiveness, profitability, technical merit, product or work quality, aesthetic and functional characteristics, after-sales service and technical assistance, commitments with regard to spare parts and components and maintenance costs, security of supplies. The above list is not exhaustive and the factors listed therein serve as a guideline for contracting authorities in the weighted evaluation process of the contract award. The Court reiterated the flexible and wide interpretation of the relevant award criterion[33] and had no difficulty in declaring that contracting authorities may use the most economically advantageous offer as award criterion by choosing the factors which they want to apply in evaluating tenders,[34] provided these factors are mentioned in hierarchical order or descending sequence in the invitation to tender or the contract documents,[35] so that tenderers and interested parties can clearly ascertain the relative weight of factors other than price for the evaluation process. However, factors which have no strict relevance in determining the most economically advantageous offer by reference to objective criteria do involve an element of arbitrary choice and therefore should be considered as incompatible with the Directives.[36]

A question was put before the Court in *Concordia*[37] intended to assess the integral function of the factors that comprise the most economically advantageous offer for contracting authorities. The question was as to whether, under the most economically advantageous offer, each individual award factor has to provide an economic advantage which directly benefits the contracting authority, or whether it is sufficient that each

---

31 See Case C-380/98, *The Queen and H.M. Treasury, ex parte University of Cambridge* [2000] ECR I-8035 at para 17; Case C-44/96, C-44/96, *Mannesmann Anlangenbau Austria AG et al v Strohal Rotationsdurck GesmbH,* [1998] ECR I-73 at para 33; Case C-360/96, *Gemeente Arnhem Gemeente Rheden v BFI Holding BV*, [1998] ECR I-6821 at paras 42 and 43; Case C-237/99, *Commission v France*, judgment of 1 February 2001 (OPAC), at paras 41 and 42.

32 See Article 26 of Directive 93/36, Article 30 of Directive 93/37, Article 34 of Directive 93/38 and Article 36 of Directive 92/50.

33 Case 31/87, *Gebroeders Beentjes v The Netherlands*, [1989] ECR 4365.

34 Case C-324/93, *R. v The Secretary of State for the Home Department, ex parte Evans Medical Ltd and Macfarlane Smith Ltd*, judgment of 28 March 1995, where the national court asked whether factors concerning continuity and reliability as well as security of supplies fall under the framework of the most economically advantageous offer, when the latter is being evaluated.

35 See para 22 of *Beentjes*.

36 See para 37 of *Beentjes*.

37 See Case C-513/99, *Concordia Bus Finlandia v Helsingin Kaupunki et HKL-Bussiliikenne,* [2002] ECR I-7213. The case concerns, *inter alia*, the permissibility of environmental considerations as part of the award criteria.

individual factor has to be measurable in economic terms, without the requirement that it directly provides an economic advantage for the contracting authority in the given contract.

Although there is wide discretion conferred on contracting authorities in compiling the relevant factors, subject to the requirements of relevance to the contract in question and their publicity, their relative importance, in economic terms, remains somehow unknown. In other words, the discretion conferred to contracting authorities would permit a wide range of factors to feature as part of award criteria in public contracts, without the need to demonstrate a direct economic advantage to a contracting authority which is attributable to each of these factors. On the contrary, if each individual factor has to establish a measurable (in quantifiable terms) economic advantage to the contracting authority, which is directly attributed to its inclusion as part of the award criterion, the discretion of contracting authorities is curtailed, since they would be required to undertake and publicise in the tender or contract documents a clear cost-benefit analysis of the relevant factors that comprise in their view the most economically advantageous offer.

2.7.2.1 Social considerations In *Beentjes*,[38] the Court ruled that social policy considerations and in particular measures aiming at the combating of long term unemployment could only be part of the award criteria of public contracts, especially in cases where the most economically advantageous offer is selected. The Court accepted that the latter award criterion contains features that are not exhaustively defined in the Directives, therefore there is discretion conferred on contracting authorities to specify what would be the most economically advantageous offer for them. However, contracting authorities cannot refer to such measures as a selection criterion and disqualify candidates who could not meet the relevant requirements. The selection of tenderers is a process, which is based on an exhaustive list of technical and financial requirements expressly stipulated in the relevant Directives and the insertion of contract compliance as a selection and qualification requirement would be considered *ultra vires*. The Court held that a contractual condition relating to the employment of long term unemployed persons is compatible with the public procurement Directives, if it has no direct or indirect discriminatory effect on tenders from other Member States. Furthermore, such a contractual condition must be mentioned in the tender notice.[39] Rejection of a contract on the grounds of a contractor's inability to employ long-term unemployed persons has no relation to the checking of the contractors' suitability on the basis of their economic and financial standing and their technical knowledge and ability. The Court maintained that measures relating to employment could be utilised as a feature of the award criteria only when they are part of a contractual obligation of the public contract in question and on condition that they do not run contrary to the fundamental principles of the Treaty. The significance of that qualification has revealed the Court's potential stance over the issue of contract compliance in public procurement.

In the recent case *Nord-pas-de-Calais*, the Court considered whether a condition linked to a local project to combat unemployment could be considered as an award

---

[38] See Case 31/87, *Gebroeders Beentjes B.V v The Netherlands, op.cit.*

[39] See Case 28/86 *Bellini* [1987] ECR 3347.

criterion of the relevant contract. The Court held that the most economically advantageous offer does not preclude all possibility for the contracting authorities to use as a criterion a condition linked to the campaign against unemployment provided that that condition is consistent with all the fundamental principles of Community law, in particular the principle of non-discrimination deriving from the provisions of the Treaty on the right of establishment and the freedom to provide services.[40] Furthermore, even if such a criterion is not in itself incompatible with Directive 93/37, it must be applied in conformity with all the procedural rules laid down in that directive, in particular the rules on advertising.[41] The Court therefore accepted the employment considerations as an award criterion, part of the most economically advantageous offer, provided it is consistent with the fundamental principles of Community law, in particular the principle of non-discrimination and it is advertised in the contract notice.

The Court's rulings in *Beentjes* and *Nord-pas-de-Calais* have opened an interesting chapter in public procurement jurisprudence. *Beentjes* started a debate on the integral dimensions of contract compliance and differentiated between the *positive* and *negative* approaches. A positive approach within contract compliance encompasses all measures and policies imposed by contracting authorities on tenderers as suitability criteria for their selection in public procurement contracts. Such positive action measures and policies intend to complement the actual objectives of public procurement, which are confined in economic and financial parameters and are based on a transparent and predictable legal background. Although the complementarity of contract compliance with the actual aims and objectives of the public procurement regime was acknowledged, the Court has been reluctant in accepting such a flexible interpretation of the Directives and based on the literal interpretation of the relevant provisions disallowed positive actions of a social policy dimension as part of the selection criteria for tendering procedures in public procurement. However, it should be mentioned that contract compliance could incorporate not only unemployment considerations, but also promote equality of opportunities and eliminate sex or race discrimination in the relevant market.[42] Indeed, the Directives on public procurement stipulate that the

---

40 See *Beentjes*, para 29.

41 See, to that effect, para 31, where the Court stipulated that an award criterion linked to the campaign against unemployment must be expressly mentioned in the contract notice so that contractors may become aware of its existence.

42 There are a number of legal instruments relevant to social policy at Community level that may apply to public procurement. They include, in particular, Directives on safety and health at work (for example, Council Directive 89/391 on the introduction of measures to encourage improvements in the safety and health of workers at work, and Directive 92/57 on the implementation of minimum safety and health requirements at temporary or mobile construction sites), working conditions and the application of employment law (for example, Directive 96/71/EC of the European Parliament and of the Council concerning the posting of workers in the framework of the provision of services [1997] OJ L18/1, and Directive 2001/23 on the safeguarding of employees' rights in the event of transfers of undertakings, businesses or parts of undertakings or businesses [2001] OJ L82/16, codifying Directive 77/187/EEC), Directive 2000/43/EC implementing the principle of equal treatment between persons irrespective of racial or ethnic origin [2000] OJ L180/22; and Directive 2000/78/EC establishing a general framework for equal treatment in employment and occupation ([2000] OJ L303/16).

contracting authority may require tenderers to observe national provisions of employment legislation when they submit their offers. The ability to observe and conform to national employment laws in a Member State may constitute a ground of disqualification and exclusion of the defaulting firm from public procurement contracts. In fact, under such interpretation, contract compliance may be a factor of selection criteria specified in the Directives, as it contains a *negative approach* to legislation and measures relating to social policy.[43]

2.7.2.2 Environmental considerations In *Concordia*,[44] the Court was asked, *inter alia*, whether environmental considerations such as low emissions and noise levels of vehicles could be included amongst the factors of the most economically advantageous criterion, in order to promote certain types of vehicles that meet or exceed certain emission and noise levels. The Advocate-General in his opinion[45] followed the *Beentjes* principle, establishing that contracting authorities are free to determine the factors under which the most economically advantageous offer is to be assessed and that environmental considerations could be part of the award criteria, provided they do not discriminate against alternative offers, and that they have been clearly publicized in the tender or contract documents. However, the inclusion of such factors in the award criteria should not prevent alternative offers that satisfy the contract specifications being taken into consideration by contracting authorities.[46] Criteria relating to the environment, in order to be permissible as additional criteria under the most economically advantageous offer must satisfy a number of conditions, namely they must be objective, universally applicable, strictly relevant to the contract in question, and clearly contribute an economic advantage to the contracting authority.[47]

Under Article 6 of the EU Treaty, environmental protection requirements are to be integrated into the definition and implementation of the Community policies and activities referred to in Article 3 of the EU Treaty, in particular with a view to promoting sustainable development. The public sector Directive clarifies how contracting authorities may contribute to the protection of the environment and the promotion of sustainable development, whilst ensuring fairness and competition in the award of public contracts. Article 50 of the public sector Directive deals with environmental

[43] It should be mentioned that adherence to health and safety laws have been considered by a British court as part of the technical requirements specified in the Works Directive for the process of selection of tenderers; see *General Building and Maintenance v Greenwich Borough Council*, [1993] IRLR 535. Along these lines, see the Commission's Interpretative Communication on the Community law applicable to public procurement and the possibilities for integrating social considerations into public procurement, COM (2001) 566, 15 October 2001.

[44] See Case C-513/99, *Concordia Bus Finlandia v Helsingin Kaupunki et HKL-Bussiliikenne* [2002] ECR I-7213.

[45] See the opinion of Advocate General Mischo delivered on 13 December 2001.

[46] Clearly the Advocate General wanted to exclude any possibility of environmental considerations being part of selection criteria or disguised as technical specifications, capable of discriminating against tenderers that could not meet them. See the debate in this article on selection and qualification and technical standards, pp. 2–5.

[47] See the analysis of the Advocate General Mischo in his opinion of *Concordia*, paras 77 to 123.

management standards. It provides that contracting authorities may require the production of certificates drawn up by independent bodies attesting the compliance of the economic operator with certain environmental management standards, they must refer to the Community Eco-Management and Audit Scheme (EMAS) or to environmental management standards based on the relevant European or international standards certified by bodies conforming to Community law or the relevant European or international standards concerning certification. Contracting authorities must recognize equivalent certificates from bodies established in other Member States. They must also accept other evidence of equivalent environmental management measures from economic operators.

In appropriate cases, in which the nature of the works and/or services justifies applying environmental management measures or schemes during the performance of a public contract, the application of such measures or schemes may be required. Environmental management schemes, whether or not they are registered under Community instruments such as Regulation (EC) No 761/2001 (EMAS),[48] can demonstrate that the economic operator has the technical capability to perform the contract. Moreover, a description of the measures implemented by the economic operator to ensure the same level of environmental protection should be accepted as an alternative to environmental management registration schemes as a form of evidence.

2.8 Small and Medium Enterprises and Subcontracting

In order to encourage the involvement of small and medium-sized undertakings in the public contracts procurement market, it is advisable to include provisions on subcontracting. According to Article 25 of the public sector Directive the contracting authority, in the contract documents, may ask or may be required by a Member State to ask the tenderer to indicate in his tender any share of the contract he may intend to subcontract to third parties and any proposed subcontractors. This indication must be without prejudice to the question of the principal economic operator's liability. The theme of public procurement and subcontracting originates in the original Works Directives where contracting authorities are allowed to specify to concessionaires a minimum percentage of the works to be subcontracted. Along these lines, Article 60 of the public sector Directive provides that the contracting authority may either: (a) require the concessionaire to award contracts representing a minimum of 30 per cent of the total value of the work for which the concession contract is to be awarded, to third parties, at the same time providing the option for candidates to increase this percentage, this minimum percentage being specified in the concession contract, or (b) request the candidates for concession contracts to specify in their tenders the percentage, if any, of the total value of the work for which the concession contract is to be awarded which they intend to assign to third parties.

---

[48] See Regulation (EC) No 761/2001 of the European Parliament and of the Council of 19 March 2001 allowing a voluntary participation by organizations in a Community eco-management and audit scheme (EMAS) [2001] OJ L114/1.

2.9 Procurement and Culture

The award of public contracts for certain audiovisual services in the field of broadcasting should allow aspects of cultural or social significance to be taken into account which render application of procurement rules inappropriate. For these reasons, an exception must therefore be made for public service contracts for the purchase, development, production or co-production of off-the-shelf programmes and other preparatory services, such as those relating to scripts or artistic performances necessary for the production of the programme and contracts concerning broadcasting times. However, this exclusion should not apply to the supply of technical equipment necessary for the production, co-production and broadcasting of such programmes. A broadcast should be defined as transmission and distribution using any form of electronic network.

2.10 Procurement and Probity

The award of public contracts to economic operators who have participated in a criminal organization or who have been found guilty of corruption or of fraud to the detriment of the financial interests of the European Communities or of money laundering should be avoided. Where appropriate, the contracting authorities should ask candidates or tenderers to supply relevant documents and, where they have doubts concerning the personal situation of a candidate or tenderer, they may seek the cooperation of the competent authorities of the Member State concerned. The exclusion of such economic operators should take place as soon as the contracting authority has knowledge of a judgment concerning such offences rendered in accordance with national law that has the force of *res judicata*. If national law contains provisions to this effect, non-compliance with environmental legislation or legislation on unlawful agreements in public contracts which has been the subject of a final judgment or a decision having equivalent effect may be considered an offence concerning the professional conduct of the economic operator concerned or grave misconduct. Non-observance of national provisions implementing Council Directives 2000/78/EC[49] and 76/207/EC[50] concerning equal treatment of workers, which has been the subject of a final judgment or a decision having equivalent effect may be considered an offence concerning the professional conduct of the economic operator concerned or grave misconduct.

Article 45 of the public sector Directive deals with the personal situation of the candidate or tenderer. It provides that any candidate or tenderer who has been the subject of a conviction by final judgment of which the contracting authority is aware

---

[49] See Council Directive 2000/78/EC of 27 November 2000 establishing a general framework for equal treatment in employment and occupation [2000] OJ L303/16).

[50] See Council Directive 76/207/EEC of 9 February 1976 on the implementation of the principle of equal treatment for men and women as regards access to employment, vocational training and promotion, and working conditions [1976] OJ L39/40. amended by Directive 2002/73/EC of the European Parliament and of the Council [2002] OJ L269/15.

for one or more of the reasons listed below must be excluded from participation in a public contract:

(a) participation in a criminal organization, as defined in Article 2(1) of Council Joint Action 98/733/JHA;[51]
(b) corruption, as defined in Article 3 of the Council Act of 26 May 1997[52] and Article 3(1) of Council Joint Action 98/742/JHA[53] respectively;
(c) fraud within the meaning of Article 1 of the Convention relating to the protection of the financial interests of the European Communities;[54]
(d) money laundering, as defined in Article 1 of Council Directive 91/308 on prevention of the use of the financial system for the purpose of money laundering.[55]

3. THE CONCEPTS IN UTILITIES PROCUREMENT

3.1 Remit and Extent of Coverage

As a result of the liberalization process in public utilities across the European Union and the introduction of sector-specific regulation covering the operational interface of such entities, the regulation of their purchasing practices no longer requires the rigidity and disciplined structure of that of public sector authorities. Under the remit of flexibility envisaged by the new regime, utilities procurement has undergone a dramatic restructuring with effects varying from the relaxation of the competitive tendering regime to the total disengagement of the public procurement rules in industries that operate under competitive conditions, especially in the telecommunications and water sectors. The new utilities procurement Directive does not regard telecommunication utilities as contracting entities, since the sector has been subjected to competitive forces adequate enough to ensure its commercial character operation.

The exiting utilities Directive 98/38/EC covers, at present, certain contracts awarded by contracting entities operating in the telecommunications sector. One of the consequences of telecommunications regulation has been the introduction of effective competition, both *de jure* and *de facto*, in this sector. The Commission, being aware of this development, has published a list of telecommunications services[56] which may already be excluded from the scope of the existing utilities Directive by virtue of Article 8 of the existing utilities Directive.

---

[51] See [1998] OJ L351/1.
[52] See [1997] OJ C195/1.
[53] See [1998] OJ L358/2.
[54] See [1995] OJ C316/48.
[55] See [1991] OJ L166/77 as amended by Directive 2001/97/EC of the European Parliament and of the Council of 4 December 2001 [2001] OJ L344/76.
[56] See [1994] OJ L336/1.

There are three milestones in EU telecommunications regulation. First, the actions which followed the 1987 Green Paper[57] opened the door for partial sector liberalization and set in motion the process of an integrated telecommunications market. Although the corporate structure of operators was left untouched and voice telephony and television broadcasting were excluded, some fundamental principles were established and created the necessary conditions for subsequent regulatory reforms. In particular, the liberalization of terminal equipment,[58] the community-wide interoperability,[59] the separation of regulatory and operational functions of public telecommunications operators,[60] the application of competition law to public telecommunications operators and private sector providers[61] and the installation of an Open Network Provision (OPN) to determine the level of competitiveness between public monopolies and private telecommunications providers.[62] The period that followed the 1992 Review[63] and the 1994 Green Paper[64] resulted, gradually, in a full liberalization of alternative infrastructures,[65] cable television networks and mobile networks. Voice telephony regulation and the liberalization of the relevant market were envisaged as the subsequent phase.

Secondly, the fully liberalized period, a period, which included the introduction of a competition regime in the telecommunications sector with the so-called full competition Directive (Directive 96/19EC).[66] This period witnessed significant regulatory adjustments in the field of OPN, such as interconnectivity and licensing provisions and

---

[57] See European Commission, Towards a Dynamic Economy – Green Paper on the Development of the Common Market for Telecommunications Services and Equipment, COM (87) 290.

[58] Directive 88/301EEC on liberalizing terminal equipment in telecommunications is the first instrument that followed the 1987 Green Paper. The Directive required the abolition of exclusive rights for import, marketing, connection, bringing into service or maintenance of telecommunications terminal equipment.

[59] See Directive 91/263EEC replacing Directive 86/361EEC on the initial stage of the mutual recognition of type approval for telecommunications terminal equipment. The Directive has been consolidated by Directive 98/13EC on telecommunications terminal equipment and satellite earth station equipment, including mutual recognition of its conformity. The system has been replaced with a mutual recognition framework by virtue of Directive 99/5EC on radio equipment and telecommunications terminal and mutual recognition of their conformity.

[60] See Directive 90/388EC (the Services Directive) as subsequently amended. The original Directive did not apply to television or radio broadcasting, telex mobile telephony paging, satellite services and voice telephony.

[61] See the Commission's Guidelines on the application of EC Competition Rules in the telecommunications sector [1991] OJ C233/2.

[62] See Directive 90/387EEC on the OPN Framework and Directive 92/44EEC on the ONP Leased Lines.

[63] See European Commission, Review of the Situation in the telecommunications services sector, 1992, SEC (92) 1048 fin.

[64] See European Commission, Part I – Principles and Timetable, 1994, COM (94) 440 fin and Part II – A common approach to the provision of infrastructures for telecommunications in the European Union, 1995, COM (94) 682 fin.

[65] Telecommunications infrastructure owned by parties different than local telecommunications operators.

[66] See Directive 96/19EC [1996] OJ L74 amending Directive 90/388EEC with regard to the implementation of full competition in telecommunications markets.

voice telephony and universal service liberalization.[67] In addition, common frameworks for interconnection of networks and licensing and authorization were provided by Directive 97/33EC[68] (the so-called Interconnection Directive) and by Directive 97/13EC[69] (the so-called Licensing Directive) respectively. The advent of competitiveness in the relevant markets introduced the notion of significant market power (SMP) in telecommunications markets,[70] a development which will provide a regulatory yardstick for future generations of legal and policy instruments.

Thirdly, the current phase of telecommunications regulation embraces the notion of convergence and the creation of a common regulatory framework for telecommunications, media and information technologies.[71] The most significant legislative measure has been the adoption of the Competition Directive 2002/76EC[72] on competition in the markets for electronic communications networks and services. The Directive consolidates all previous instruments and its main purpose is to reaffirm the obligation of Member States to abolish exclusive and special rights in the field of telecommunications. Furthermore, four additional Directives consolidate the telecommunications regime: the Framework Directive 2002/21EC[73] on a common regulatory framework for electronic communications networks and services; the Authorization Directive 2002/20EC;[74] the Universal Service Directive 2002/22EC[75] on universal service and users' rights relating to electronic communications networks and services; and the Access Directive 2002/19EC[76] on access to interconnection of electronic communications networks and associated facilities.

The regulatory process of telecommunications in the European Union is centred on the national regulatory authorities (NRAs), which will provide the necessary interface

---

67 The envisaged regulatory adjustments were enacted by virtue of Directive 97/51EC [1997] OJ L295/23 and Directive 98/10EC on the application of OPN to voice telephony and universal service for telecommunications in a competitive environment.

68 See Directive 97/33EC [1997] OJ L199/32.

69 See Directive 97/13EC [1997] OJ L117/15.

70 See Article 4(3) of the Interconnection Directive 97/33EC regarding universal service and operability through the applications of OPN.

71 See European Commission, Green Paper on the convergence of telecommunications, media and information technologies, COM (97) 623.

72 See Directive 2002/76EC [2002] OJ L249/21, which consolidates the Services Directive 90/388EEC as amended by the Satellite Directive 94/46EC, the Cable Directive 95/51EC, the Mobile Directive 96/2EC, the full Competition Directive 96/19EC and the Cable Ownership Directive 1999/64 amending the Services Directive in relation to the requirement that telecommunications networks and cable TV networks owned by a single operator are separate legal entities.

73 See Directive 2002/21EC [2002] OJ L108/33, which effectively replaces the OPN Framework Directive 90/387EEC, as amended by 97/51EC, and repeals Directives 90/387EEC, 92/44, the Interconnection Directive 97/33EC, the Licensing Directive 97/13EC, the Voice Telephony Directive 98/10EC and the Telecommunications Data Protection Directive 97/66EC.

74 See Directive 2002/20EC, which effectively repeals all existing licensing and authorization instruments.

75 See Directive 2002/22EC [2002] OJ L108/51 which replaces the relevant provisions of the Interconnection Directive 97/33EC and the Voice Telephony Directive 98/61EC.

76 See Directive 2002/19 [2002] OJ 2002 L108/7, which replaces the relevant provisions of the Interconnection Directive 97/33EC and OPN Leased Lined Directive 92/44EC.

for implementing Community principles in line with national legal frameworks and market conditions. As a consequence of the above progress in the telecommunications sector and its relevant markets, the Commission considers that it is no longer necessary to regulate purchases by entities operating in this sector.

On the other hand, Directive 93/38/EC excludes from its scope purchases of voice telephony, telex, mobile telephone, paging and satellite services. Those exclusions were introduced to take account of the fact that the services in question could frequently be provided only by one service provider in a given geographical area because of the absence of effective competition and the existence of special or exclusive rights. The introduction of effective competition in the telecommunications sector removes the justification for these exclusions. The Commission has therefore included the procurement of such telecommunications services within the remit of the new utilities Directive.

Conversely, the postal sector which was previously excluded from procurement regulation is now covered (only from 1 January 2009) in order to allow sufficient time for transitional measures in the postal services sector of Member States. Taking into account the further opening up of Community postal services to competition and the fact that such services are provided through a network by contracting authorities, public undertakings and other undertakings, contracts awarded by contracting entities providing postal services should be subject to the rules of this Directive, create a framework for sound commercial practice and allow greater flexibility than is offered by the new utilities Directive 2004/18/EC. For a definition of the activities in question, it is necessary to take into account the definitions of Directive 97/67/EC on common rules for the development of the internal market of Community postal services and the improvement of quality of service.[77]

The new concepts of Directive 2004/17 embrace the links of the state with utilities through special or exclusive rights and the notion of affiliated undertakings as a potential subject of utilities procurement coverage. Finally, the new regime introduces grounds for exemption for entities operating in competitive markets.

3.2 Special or Exclusive Rights in the Utilities

The remit and thrust of public procurement legislation has traditionally relied on the connection between contracting authorities and the state. However, that connection may be weak in covering entities which operate in the utilities sector and have been privatised. The *Foster* principle[78] established that state accountability could not embrace privatised enterprises.[79] The enactment of the Utilities Directives[80] brought under the procurement framework entities operating in the water, energy, transport and

[77] See [1998] OJ L15/14. Directive as last amended by Regulation (EC) No 1882/2003 [2003] OJ L284/1).

[78] See Case 188/89, *Foster v British Gas* [1990] ECR I-1313, in which the European Court of Justice ruled that a Directive capable of having direct effect could be invoked against a body which is subject to the *control* of the State and has been delegated special powers.

[79] This was the view of Advocate General Lenz in Case 247/89, *Commission v Portugal* [1991] ECR I-3659.

[80] EC Directive 90/531, as amended by EC Directive 93/38 [1993] OJ L199.

telecommunications sectors. A wide range of these entities are covered by the term *bodies governed by public law*, which is used by the existing utilities Directives for the contracting entities operating in the relevant sectors.[81] Interestingly, another category of contracting authorities under the existing utilities Directives includes *public undertakings*.[82] The term indicates any undertaking over which the state may exercise direct or indirect dominant influence by means of ownership, or by means of financial participation, or by means of laws and regulations, which govern the public undertaking's operation. Dominant influence can be exercised in the form of a majority holding of the undertaking's subscribed capital, in the form of majority controlling of the undertaking's issued shares, or, finally in the form of the right to appoint the majority of the undertaking's management board. Public undertakings may cover utilities operators, which have been granted exclusive rights of exploitation of a service. Irrespective of their ownership, they are subject to the utilities Directive in as much as the *exclusivity* of their operation precludes other entities from entering the relevant market under substantially the same competitive conditions.

Entities in the utilities sector enjoying special or exclusive rights conferred on them by Member States have been covered by the utilities procurement regime. The intention of the legislature was to eliminate government interference over the purchasing behavior of the recipients of such rights arising from the pressure exercised by the respective governments as a condition of granting the special or exclusive rights and the inability of the recipient entity to resist such pressure as a result of the non-competitive environment of its operation. Traditionally, special or exclusive rights were demonstrable when the right to expropriate property or the right to place utility networks on, under or over highways were conferred upon the recipient. Also, a connection with an entity enjoying special or exclusive rights brought any supplier of a utility network within the remit of utilities procurement.

For the purposes of the new utilities Directive and in accordance with Article 2(3), 'special or exclusive rights' means rights granted by a competent authority of a Member State by way of any legislative, regulatory or administrative provision the effect of which is to limit the exercise of activities defined in Articles 3 to 7 to one or more entities, and which substantially affects the ability of other entities to carry out such activity.[83]

The new utilities Directive provides for a more restrictive definition of the notion of special or exclusive rights than its predecessor. The consequence of the definition is depicted in three ways: first, the availability of a procedure for the expropriation or use of property and the ability of an entity to place network equipment on, under or over a public highway for the purpose of constructing networks or port or airport facilities, do not automatically constitute exclusive or special rights within the meaning of the Directive; secondly a special or exclusive right does not exist merely due to the fact that an entity supplies drinking water, electricity, gas or heat to a network which is

---

81 See Article 1(1) of Directive 93/38.

82 See Article 1(2) of Directive 93/38.

83 The activities covering special or exclusive rights embrace the following utilities sectors: gas, heat and electricity, water, postal services, transport services, exploration for, or extraction of, oil, gas, coal or other solid fuels, as well as ports and airports.

itself operated by an entity enjoying special or exclusive rights granted by a competent authority of a Member State; and thirdly, rights granted by Member State through acts of concession, to a limited number of undertakings on the basis of objective, proportionate and non-discriminatory criteria that allow any interested party fulfilling those criteria to enjoy those rights are not considered special or exclusive rights.

The practical implication of the definition of special or exclusive rights under the new utilities Directive is the non-applicability of the regime to the entities that do not meet the conditions but are still covered under the existing regime.

The influence of the Court's jurisprudence in the restrictive application of special or exclusive rights is evident. The Court's approach in the *British Telecommunications*[84] case does not allow the application of the sector-specific definition of leased (licensed) lines in the telecommunications sector to the respective utilities procurement definition of special or exclusive right. In that case the Court ruled that special or exclusive rights under the Leased Lines Directive[85] did not exist as a result of the licenses conferred by Member States to entities.

The situation could be more complicated as entities compete for such special or exclusive rights such as concessions or public-private partnerships on the basis of objective, proportionate and non-discriminatory criteria which can restrict market access to other undertakings and by definition limit the number of interested parties. The analogous application of the *British Telecommunications* judgment is dubious, as the Court remained silent over such a scenario. The Commission however has indicated[86] that where Member States do not enjoy discretion in the conferral of special or exclusive rights, by definition they cannot detrimentally influence the procurement behavior of the recipient of such rights and as a consequence the utilities procurement regime need not apply.

3.3 Affiliated Undertakings

Article 13 of the existing Utilities Directive provides for the exclusion of certain contracts between contracting authorities and affiliated undertakings. The term affiliated undertaking, for the purposes of Article 1(3) of the Utilities Directive, is one the annual accounts of which are consolidated with those of the contracting entity in accordance with the requirements of the Seventh Company Law Directive.[87] These are service contracts which are awarded to a service-provider which is affiliated to the contracting entity and service contracts which are awarded to a service-provider which is affiliated to a contracting entity participating in a joint venture formed for the purpose of carrying out an activity covered by the Directive.

---

[84] See Case C-302/94, *R v Secretary of State for Trade and Industry ex parte British Telecommunications plc* [1996] ECR I-6417.

[85] See EC Directive 92/44 [1992] OJ L165/27.

[86] See European Commission, Explanatory Memorandum of the Proposal for the directive co-coordinating the procurement procedures of entities operating in the water, energy and transport sectors, COM (2000) 276 fin.

[87] See Council Directive 83/349 [1983] OJ L193/1).

The explanatory memorandum of the Utilities Directive[88] stated that this provision relates to three types of service provision within groups. These categories, which may or may not be distinct, are: the provision of common services such as accounting, recruitment and management; the provision of specialized services embodying the know how of the group; the provision of a specialized service to a joint venture. The exclusion from the provisions of the Directive is subject, however, to two conditions: the service-provider must be an undertaking affiliated to the contracting authority and, at least 80 per cent of its average turnover arising within the European Community for the preceding three years, derives from the provision of the same or similar services to undertakings with which it is affiliated. The Commission is empowered to monitor the application of this Article and require the notification of the names of the undertakings concerned and the nature and value of the service contracts involved.

Interestingly, the new utilities regime also excludes from its remit contracts awarded to affiliated undertakings. Article 23 of the new utilities Directive excludes contracts awarded by a contracting entity to an affiliated undertaking, or by a joint venture, formed exclusively by a number of contracting entities for the purpose of carrying out activities which are covered by the utilities Directive to an undertaking which is affiliated with one of these contracting entities.

Under the new utilities procurement regime, the term affiliated undertaking means any undertaking the annual accounts of which are consolidated with those of the contracting entity in accordance with the requirements of the Seventh Council Directive 83/349 on consolidated accounts.[89] In cases of entities which are not subject to that Directive, affiliated undertaking means any undertaking over which the contracting entity may exercise, directly or indirectly, a dominant influence within the meaning of Article 2(1)(b), or any undertaking over which the contracting entity may exercise a dominant influence by virtue of ownership, financial participation or the rules which govern it.

3.4 Competitive Markets in Utilities

Privatized utilities could, in principle, be excluded from the procurement rules when a genuinely competitive regime[90] within the relevant market structure would rule out purchasing patterns based on non-economic considerations. The new utilities Directive should not apply to markets where the participants pursue an activity which is directly exposed to competition on markets to which access is not limited within the relevant Member State. The new utilities Directive has therefore introduced a procedure, applicable to all sectors covered by its provisions that will enable the effects of current or future opening up to competition to be taken into account. Such a procedure should

---

88 See COM (91) 347-SYN 36 1.

89 See [1983] OJ L193/1, as last amended by Directive 2001/65/EC [2001] OJ L283/28).

90 The determination of a genuinely competitive regime is left to the utilities operators themselves. See Case C 392/93, *The Queen and H.M. Treasury, ex parte British Telecommunications PLC* [1993] OJ C287/6. This is perhaps a first step towards self-regulation which could lead to the disengagement of the relevant contracting authorities from the public procurement regime.

provide legal certainty for the entities concerned, as well as an appropriate decision-making process, ensuring, within short time limits, uniform application of standards that result in the disengagement of the relevant procurement rules.

Direct exposure to competition should be assessed on the basis of objective criteria, taking account of the specific characteristics of the sector concerned. The implementation and application of appropriate Community legislation liberalizing a utility sector will be considered to provide sufficient grounds for determining if there is free access to the market in question. Such appropriate legislation should be identified in an annex which will be provided by the Commission. The Commission will, in particular, take into account the possible adoption of measures entailing a genuine opening up to competition of sectors other than those for which legislation is already mentioned in Annex XI, such as that of railway transport services. Where free access to a given market does not result from the implementation of appropriate Community legislation, it should be demonstrated that such access is uninhibited *de jure* and *de facto*.

Article 30 of the new utilities Directive provides for the procedure for establishing whether a given activity of a utility entity is directly exposed to competition. The question of whether an activity is directly exposed to competition shall be decided on the basis of criteria that are in conformity with the Treaty provisions on competition, such as the characteristics of the goods or services concerned, the existence of alternative goods or services, the prices and the actual or potential presence of more than one supplier of the goods or services in question. When a Member State considers that access to the relevant market activity is free, it must notify the Commission and provide all relevant facts, and in particular of any law, regulation, administrative provision or agreements, where appropriate together with the position adopted by an independent national authority that is competent in relation to the regulation of the activity concerned. The Commission can issue a Decision which verifies that the relevant activity is provided in a competitive environment. Such verification is also presumed if the Commission has not adopted a Decision concerning the inapplicability of the utilities Directive within a certain period.[91]

The disengagement of the utilities procurement regime as a result of the operation of the relevant entities in competitive markets by virtue of Article 30 of the new utilities Directive does not apply to the WTO Government Procurement Agreement. This represents a legal *lacuna* as the procedural flexibility envisaged in the European procurement regulatory regime does not cover entities covered under the GPA. Rectification of the problem would require amendment to the GPA with the conferral of concessions and reciprocal access rights to the GPA signatories.

[91] According to Article 68(2), for the adoption of a Decision the Commission shall be allowed a period of three months commencing on the first working day following the date on which it receives the notification or the request. However, this period may be extended once by a maximum of three months in duly justified cases, in particular if the information contained in the notification or the request or in the documents annexed thereto is incomplete.

4. THE REFORM OF THE PUBLIC PROCUREMENT DIRECTIVES

European institutions have introduced three new legal instruments which amend the public procurement Directives. In particular, Directive 2014/24/EU will replace Public Sector Directive 2004/18; Directive 2014/25/EU will amend the Utilities Directive 2004/17; and a new Directive 2014/23/EU on concessions to regulate the award of concessions.

Concessions regulation represents the most significant development of the reform agenda of the EU in public procurement regulation. The main principles envisaged in the proposed Concessions Directive are: legal certainty and better access to the concession markets. The current public procurement regime only partially applies to works concessions; service concessions are exempt. The Commission believes that the lack of a consistent framework for concessions across the EU means that concessions are often awarded without any transparent or competitive process and that, as a result, contracting authorities are often failing to achieve best value, and some economic operators, in particular SMEs, are denied access to the market.

Concessions are usually long term, complex arrangements where the concessionaire assumes responsibilities and risks traditionally borne by the contracting authorities and normally falling within their remit. Contracting authorities and entities should be allowed considerable flexibility to define and organise the procedure leading to the choice of concessionaire. The duration of a concession should be limited in order to avoid market foreclosure and restriction of competition.

The rules of the legislative framework applicable to the award of concessions are clear and simple. Member States or public authorities should remain free to define and specify the characteristics of the services to be provided, including any conditions regarding the quality or price of the services. They should duly reflect the specificity of concessions as compared to public contracts and should not create an excessive amount of bureaucracy.

The scope of the concessions Directive indicates that it fully applies only to concessions with a cross-border interest with a value of at least €5 million. Service concessions of a value between €2.5 million and €5 million and concessions for social and other specific services are only subject to limited obligations under the Draft Directive, including the obligation to publish a concession award notice.

The concessions Directive does not apply to concessions awarded between contracting authorities or to concessions awarded by contracting authorities to affiliated undertakings or joint ventures. The Draft Directive also sets out various other specific exemptions such as concessions contracts for the provision or exploitation of electronic communications, as well as water and waste sectors.

The concessions Directive will not apply retrospectively. However, contracting authorities should be mindful that an extension of the duration of an existing concession may qualify as a new concession and would therefore have to comply with the rules of the concessions Directive.

If an existing concession were to be substantially modified during its term it will be considered to be a new concession and the Directive will apply. Under the Directive, providing the overall nature of the contract is not altered, a modification of a value of less than 5 per cent of the initial contract value shall not be considered to be substantial. Modifications of the concession resulting in a minor change of the contract below the threshold should always be possible without the need to carry out a new concession procedure (Article 42). A new concession procedure is required in case of material changes to the initial concession, in particular to the scope and content of the mutual rights and obligations of the parties, including the distribution of intellectual property rights. Such changes demonstrate the parties' intention to renegotiate essential terms or conditions of that concession.

Non-economic services of general interest should not fall within the scope of the Concession Directive. It is appropriate to exclude from the full application of this Directive only those services which have a limited cross-border dimension, such as certain social, health, or educational services (Articles 8, 10, 11, 12, 14, 15 and 21). These services are provided within a particular context that varies widely amongst Member States, due to different cultural traditions. In the case of mixed contracts, the applicable rules should be determined in accordance with the main subject of the contract where the different parts which constitute the contract are objectively not separable.

In the concession award procedures, contracting authorities or contracting entities should be allowed to use award criteria or concession performance conditions relating to the works, or services to be provided under the concession contract in any respect and at any stage of their life cycles from extraction of raw materials for the product to the stage of disposal of the product, including factors involved in the specific process of production, provision or commercialisation of those works or services or a specific process during a later stage of their life cycle, even where such factors do not form part of their material substance and so on. Contracting authorities and entities should further be given the possibility to exclude economic operators which have proven unreliable, for instance because of serious or repeated violations of environmental or social obligations, including rules on accessibility for disabled persons or other forms of grave professional misconduct, such as violations of competition rules or of intellectual property rights.

The concessions Directive outlines rules for the publication and award of concession contracts and sets time limits for various stages of the procurement process. Contracting authorities wishing to award a concession will be required to publish a concession notice (using a standard form and containing prescribed information). Potential tenderers must be given at least 52 days from the date on which the concession notice was sent to apply, although this time limit may be reduced by five days if tenderers are able to apply electronically. Within 48 days of awarding a concession, a contracting authority must send a concession award notice giving the results of the concession award procedure.

The concessions Directive also introduces a standstill period for concession awards to be appealed by extending the scope of the Remedies Directive so that it applies to all concession contracts above the relevant threshold. Not later than 48 days after the award of a concession, the contracting authorities and contracting entities shall send a concession award notice on the results of the concession award procedure. In view of the detrimental effects on competition, awarding concessions without prior publication should only be permitted in very exceptional circumstances.

The concessions Directive does not outline any specific procurement procedure for the award of concessions and, in order to promote flexibility, instead sets out procedural guarantees of transparency, consistency and objective criteria which contracting authorities must fulfil when awarding a concession. In order to comply with these requirements, the contracting authority must give a description of the concession, the technical specifications, the award criteria and the minimum requirements to be met in the contract notice, the invitation to submit tenders or the concession documents. The award criteria must relate to the economic, financial and technical capacity of the party and be listed in descending order of importance. The contracting authority should also establish in advance and communicate to all participants the rules on the organisation of the concession award procedure, including the rules on communication, the stages of the procedure and timing. Throughout the procurement process, a contracting authority must ensure that the parties are treated fairly and equally. Contracting authorities should take care to ensure that the information provided to tenderers throughout the tender process does not give some tenderers an advantage over others, and retain records relevant to the procedure.

Before awarding the concession a contracting authority needs to ensure that the tender complies with the requirements, conditions and criteria set out in the concession notice, the invitation to tender and the concession documents, and that the tenderer is not excluded from participating in the award. Assuming that the tenderer is compliant, the contracting authority must, as soon as possible, then inform each tenderer of decisions reached concerning the award of a concession. Upon request from the party concerned, the contracting authority must, as quickly as possible (and within 15 days from receipt of a written request) inform any unsuccessful candidates of the reasons for the rejection of their application.

The concessions Directive limits the duration of concession contracts to 'the time estimated to be necessary for the party contracting with the contracting authority to recoup the investments made in operating the works or service together with a reasonable return on the invested capital'.

The Commission may, every three years, request that Member States transmit a monitoring report covering an overview of the most frequent causes of incorrect application of the rules for the award of concessions contracts, including possible structural or recurring problems in the application of the rules and possible cases of fraud and other illegal behaviour. All Decisions adopted prior to the entry into force of the new concesision Directive adopted on the basis of Article 30 of Directive 2004/17/EC will apply.

PART 1

A THEMATIC APPROACH TO PUBLIC PROCUREMENT REGULATION

1. The principles of public procurement regulation

Christopher Bovis

THE PRINCIPLE OF TRANSPARENCY

One of the most important principles of the Public Procurement Directives is the principle of transparency. The principle of transparency serves two main objectives: the first is to introduce a system of openness in public purchasing of the Member States, so a greater degree of accountability should be established and potential direct discrimination on grounds of nationality should be eliminated. The second objective aims at ensuring that transparency in public procurement represents a substantial basis for a system of best practice for both parts of the equation, but in particular relevant to the supply side, to the extent that the latter has a more *proactive* role in determining the needs of the demand side. Transparency in public procurement is achieved through community-wide publicity and advertisement of public procurement contracts over certain thresholds by means of publication of three types of notices in the Official Journal of the European Communities: Periodic Indicative Notices (PIN); Invitations to tender; and Contract Award Notices (CAN).

THE EFFECTS OF THE PRINCIPLE OF TRANSPARENCY

The principle of transparency, which serves as the ignition of public procurement regulation, has imprinted some significant effects in the regime, namely the effect of price competitiveness, the effect of flexibility and the effect of verification in the delivery of public services.

The Effect of Price Competitiveness

Transparency, as a principle in public purchasing, has an obvious trade effect, that of price competitiveness. If more interested suppliers are aware of a contracting authority's determination to procure, an element of competition automatically occurs; this sort of competitive pattern would probably be reflected in the prices received by the contracting authority, when it evaluates the offers. The fact that more suppliers are aware of a forthcoming public contract and the fact that interested suppliers are aware that their rivals are informed about it, indicates two distinctive parameters which are relevant to savings and value for money. The first parameter focuses on value for money for the demand side of the equation of public purchasing and reveals the possibility for contracting authorities to compare prices (and quality). The second parameter has an effect on the supply side of the equation (the suppliers) which amongst other things can no longer rely on the lack of price comparisons when serving the public sector. Openness in public procurement, by definition, results in price competition and the benefits for contracting authorities appear achievable.

However, transparency and openness in public purchasing pose a question over long-term savings and value for money considerations. Price competition, as a result of the awareness of forthcoming public contracts, represents a rather static effect in the value for money process. The fact that more and more interested suppliers are aware and do submit tenders, in the long run, appears rather as a burden. If transparency and the resulting price competitiveness are based on a *win-to-win* process, the potential benefits for contracting authorities could easily be counterbalanced by the administrative costs in tender evaluation and replies to unsuccessful tenders. Furthermore, the risk management factor is much higher in a win-to-win purchasing scenario. Price competitiveness represents also some threats for contracting authorities, to the extent that quality of deliverables as well as the delivery process itself could be jeopardised, if contracting authorities deal with different and unknown contractors. It could thus be argued here that price competitiveness, as a trade effect potentially beneficial for the demand side of the public purchasing equation, has a static character. It seems that it does not take into account medium or long-term purchasing patterns, as well as counter effects of competition. Two elements deserve further analysis here:

The first raises questions over the aggregate loss of the economy through transparent competitive purchasing patterns. For example, if a large number of interested suppliers submit their offer to a particular contracting authority, two types of costs should be examined. First, the cost which is attributed to the response and tendering stage of the procurement process: human and capital resources are directed by the suppliers towards the preparation of documents and the submission of the offers. If one of these suppliers wins the contract, those remaining will have suffered an unrecoverable loss. If that aggregate loss exceeds the benefit/saving accomplished by the contracting authority by following transparent and competitive purchasing patterns, value for money has not been achieved. Secondly, along the same lines, the evaluation and selection process during tendering represents a considerable administrative cost to the contracting authorities. If the principle of transparency complements the principle of equal treatment, contracting authorities should give the same attention to all interested suppliers that have submitted a response. Downsizing the list through evaluation and assessment based on stipulated criteria is by no means an inexpensive exercise. Human and capital resources have to be directed by contracting authorities towards meeting that cost. If the latter exceeds the potential savings achieved through the competitive tendering route, then value for money is unaccomplished.

The second element that deserves attention relates to the definition of price competitiveness in public purchasing as well as its interrelation with anti-trust law and policy. A question which arises in price competitive tendering patterns is *what would be the lowest offer contracting authorities can accept.* If the maximisation of savings is the only achievable objective in the public procurement process, the transparent/competitive pattern cannot guarantee and evaluate safeguards in relation to under-priced offers. If the supply side responds to the perpetuated competitive purchasing pattern by lowering prices, contracting authorities could face a dilemma: where to stop. It should be mentioned here that the European rules provide for an automatic disqualification of an 'abnormally low offer'. The term has not been interpreted in detail by the judiciary at European and domestic levels and serves rather as a 'lower bottom limit'.[1] Also, when an offer appears low, contracting authorities may request clarifications from the tenderer in question. Contracting authorities face a dilemma in evaluating and assessing low offers other than abnormal ones. It is difficult for them to identify dumping or predatory pricing disguised behind a low offer for a public contract. In addition, even if there is an indication of anti-competitive price fixing, the European public procurement rules do not provide for any disqualification procedure. The suspension of the award procedures (or even the suspension of the conclusion of the contract itself) would be unlikely without a thorough and exhaustive investigation by the competent anti-trust authorities.

The *De Minimis* Principle

The public procurement Directives are applicable only if certain value thresholds are met. The application of the Directives is subject to monetary considerations in relation to the value of the relevant contracts. There is a clear-cut distinction of coverage of the public procurement rules upon contracts representing transactions between the public sector and the industry of a certain economic substance and volume. Contracts below the required thresholds are not subject to the rigorous regime envisaged by the Directives. However, contracting authorities are under the explicit obligation to avoid discrimination on nationality grounds and apply all the provisions related to the fundamental principles of the Treaties of Rome and Maastricht. The thresholds laid down are as follows.

One could question the reason behind the separation of public procurement regulation into dimensional and sub-dimensional nature as a result of the relevant thresholds. Interestingly enough, it was thought that contracts above the thresholds laid down by the Directives could embrace the majority of the public procurement requirements in the Member States, thus eliminating the danger of discriminatory public purchasing for those contracts left outside the ambit of the Directives. However, a careful monitoring of procurement systems in the Member States has revealed that sub-dimensional procurement appears at least three times the size of dimensional public purchasing,[2] a fact that renders the application of the Directives only partly responsible for the integration of public markets in the European Community.

The Dimensionality of Public Procurement

The dimensional nature of public procurement by virtue of the monetary applicability of the relevant rules introduces *a de minimis criterion*, where certain thresholds in relation to the value of the contracts are utilised for the applicability of the Directives. The dimensional public procurement should, in principle, encompass the majority of

[1] See Case 76/81, *SA Transporoute et Travaux v Minister of Public Works* [1982] ECR 457; Case 104/75, *SA SHV Belgium v La Maison Ideale et Societe Nationale du Longement*, before the Belgian Conseil d'Etat, judgment of 24 June 1986 of the Belgian Conseil d'Etat.

[2] See, European Commission, *The Use of Negotiated Procedures as a Non-Tariff Barrier in Public Procurement*, Brussels, CC 9364, 1995.

procurement requirements of Member States and their contracting authorities. However, the legislation on public procurement has had little effect on the principle of transparency, as empirical investigation of the patterns of contracting authorities of Member States concerning their publication record in relation to their contracts reveals a rather gloomy picture. The volume of public purchasing which is advertised and tendered according to the requirements of the relevant Directives in comparison with the total volume of public procurement of the Member States appears disproportionate and beyond expectation, bearing in mind the vital importance that has been given to the principle of transparency for the opening-up of the public markets in the European Union. The percentages of public contracts advertised in the Official Journal by Member States reveal the relatively low impact of the public procurement legislation on the principle and objectives of transparency in European public markets. Clarification of the above impact of the law upon the transparency patterns which contracting authorities have established should be sought by exploring three scenarios.

The first scenario is based on the distinction between dimensional and sub-dimensional public procurement in the Member States. The European Directives allow the division of public contracts into lots without any justification from contracting authorities. This in most cases may result in intentional contravention of the Directives, as sub-dimensional (below certain thresholds) public contracts escape their applicability. As sub-dimensional public procurement escapes from the mandatory publication requirement, contracting authorities tend to divide contracts into separate lots. It should be mentioned that the Directives stipulate the prohibition of intentional division of contracts into lots with a view to avoiding the relevant thresholds, but the provision presents practical difficulties in its observance and enforcement. Until the time of writing, there is no case or complaint before national courts or before the European Court of Justice relating to the intentional division of contracts into lots with lower thresholds in order to avoid the application of the Directives. The relevant thresholds which require the mandatory publication requirement clearly result in a segmentation of the public markets in quantitative terms by creating a *dimensional forum* which is subject to the rigorous legal regime. A *de minimis* rule applies to contracts below the thresholds, which exempts them from the provisions of the Directives. The sub-dimensional public procurement is only subject to the principle of non-discrimination at European level, whereas at domestic level, national tendering rules regulate the award of these contracts.

The second scenario is based on the excessive utilisation of award procedures without prior publication. Indeed, the Directives allow, under certain circumstances the award of contracts through direct negotiations with a contractor. Although the European Court of Justice condemned the above practice in a number of cases before it, the actual utilisation of negotiated procedures without prior publication is widespread. Finally, the third scenario implies the blunt violation of Community law by Member States by avoiding the publication of tender notices in the Official Journal of the European Communities.

Bearing in mind the relative absence of complaints and subsequent litigation concerning non-advertisement of public contracts before national courts or the European Court of Justice, the third scenario reflects to a large extent the underlying reason for the lack of transparency in public procurement. In fact, intentional division of contracts into lots with a view to avoiding the Directives and excessive and unjustified recourse to award procedures without prior publication amounts to a blunt violation of Member States' obligations arising from the relevant Directives and also from primary Treaty provisions.

The Flexibility Effect

Transparency in public procurement is linked with the *flexibility* inherent in the regulatory regime, which is demonstrated through certain doctrines established by the ECJ. These include the doctrines of *functionality* and *dependency* in order to define the notion of contracting authorities, as well as the doctrines of *dualism, commercialism* and *competitiveness* in order to determine the remit and thrust of public procurement rules.

The doctrine of functionality

Functionality depicts a flexible and pragmatic approach in the applicability of the procurement Directives. Entities and bodies which have been set up by the state to carry out tasks entrusted to them by legislation, but are not formally part of the state's administrative structure, could not fall under the remit of the term 'contracting authorities', since they are not formally part of the state; neither are all criteria for the definition of bodies governed by public law present.[3] The functional dimension of contracting authorities has earmarked the departure from the formality test, which has rigidly positioned an entity under state control on *stricto sensu* traditional public law grounds.[4] Functionality, as an ingredient of assessing the relationship between an entity and the state demonstrates, in addition to the elements of management or financial control, the importance of constituent factors such as the intention and purpose of establishment of the entity in question.[5] The doctrine of functionality supports the principle of transparency, as its application enhances the span and remit of the public procurement regulation.

---

[3] This is particularly the case of non-governmental organisations (NGOs) which operate under the auspices of the central or local government and are responsible for public interest functions. See Article 9 of the Public Sector Directive. In particular, bodies governed by public law (i) must be established for the specific purpose of meeting needs in the general public interest not having an industrial or commercial character; (ii) they must have legal personality; and (iii) they must be financed, for the most part, by either the state, or regional or local authorities, or other bodies governed by public law; or subject to management supervision by these bodies, or having an administrative or supervisory board, more than half of whose members are appointed by the state, regional or local authorities or by other bodies governed by public law.

[4] The formality test and the relation between the state and entities under its control was established in Cases C-249/81, *Commission v Ireland* [1982] ECR 4005; C-36/74 *Walrave and Koch v Association Union Cycliste International et al.* [1974] ECR 1423.

[5] See Case 31/87, *Gebroeders Beentjes B.V. v State of Netherlands* [1988] ECR I-4635; Cases C-353/96, *Commission v Ireland* and C-306/97, *Connemara Machine Turf Co Ltd v Coillte Teoranta*, judgment of 17 December 1998; Case C-323/96, *Commission v Kingdom of Belgium*, judgment of 17 September 1998.

The doctrine of dependency

The assessment of the third criterion of bodies governed by public law, namely that they 'must be financed, for the most part, by either the state, or regional or local authorities, or other bodies governed by public law; or must be subject to management supervision by these bodies, or must have an administrative or supervisory board, more than half of whose members are appointed by the state, regional or local authorities or by other bodies governed by public law', assumes that there is a close dependency of these bodies on the State, in terms of corporate governance, management supervision and financing.[6] These dependency features are alternative, thus even the existence of one feature satisfies the entire third criterion and renders the public procurement rules applicable.

Management supervision by the state or other contracting authorities entails not only administrative verification of legality or appropriate use of funds or exceptional control measures, but the conferring of significant influence over management policy, such as the narrowly circumscribed remit of activities, the supervision of compliance, as well as the overall administrative supervision.[7] Dependency, in terms of overall control of an entity by the state or another contracting authority presupposes a control similar to that which the state of another contracting authority exercises over its own departments. However, the 'similarity' of control denotes lack of independence with regard to decision-making, thus a contract between a contracting authority and an entity, where the former exercises a control similar to that which it exercises over its own departments and at the same time that entity carries out the essential part of its activities with the contracting authority, is not a public contract, irrespective of that entity being a contracting authority or not.[8] The similarity of control as a reflection of dependency reveals another facet of the thrust of contracting authorities: the non-applicability of the public procurement rules for in-house relationships.

The receipt of public funds from the state or a contracting authority is an indication that an entity could be a body governed by public law. However, this indication is not an absolute one.[9] Only specific payments made to an entity by the state or other public authorities have the effect of creating or reinforcing a specific relationship of subordination and dependency. The funding of an entity within a framework of general considerations indicates that the entity has close dependency links with the state or other contracting authorities.

If there is a specific consideration for the state to finance an entity, such as a contractual nexus, the dependency ties are not sufficiently close to allow the entity

---

[6] This type of dependency resembles the Court's definition in its ruling on state controlled enterprises in Case 152/84 *Marshall v Southampton and South West Hampshire Area Health Authority* [1986] ECR 723.

[7] See Case C-237/99, *Commission v France*, judgment of 1 February 2001.

[8] See Case C-107/98, *Teckal Slr v Comune di Viano,* judgment of 18 November 1999.

[9] See Case C-380/98, *The Queen and H.M. Treasury, ex parte University of Cambridge*, judgment of 3 October 2000. The Court stipulated that the proportion of public finances received by an entity, as one of the alternative features of the third criterion of the term bodies governed by public law must exceed 50% to enable it meeting that criterion. For assessment purposes of this feature, there must be an annual evaluation of the (financial) status of an entity for the purposes of being regarded as a contracting authority.

financed by the state meeting the third criterion of the term 'bodies governed by public law'. Such relationship is analogous to the dependency that exists in normal commercial relations formed by reciprocal contracts, which have been negotiated freely between the parties. The existence of a contract between the parties, apart from the specific considerations for funding, indicates strongly evidence of supply substitutability, in the sense that the entity receiving the funding faces competition in the relevant markets.

The doctrine of dependency brings entities which are dependent on public authorities within the remit of public procurement regulation, but exonerates in-house relationships.

The doctrine of dualism

The dual capacity of an entity as a public service provider and a commercial undertaking respectively, and the weighting of the relevant activity in relation to the proportion of its output, should be the decisive factor in determining whether an entity is a body governed by public law. This argument appeared for the first time when it was suggested[10] that only if the activities in pursuit of the 'public services obligations' of an entity supersede its commercial thrust, could the latter be considered as a body covered by public law and a contracting authority.

In practice, the suggestion implied a selective application of the public procurement Directives in the event of dual capacity entities. This is not entirely unjustified as, on a number of occasions,[11] the public procurement Directives themselves utilize thresholds or proportions considerations in order to include or exclude certain contracts from their ambit. However, the ECJ ruled out a selective application of the Directives in the case of dual capacity contracting authorities based on the principle of legal certainty. It substantiated its position on the fact that only the purpose for which an entity is established is relevant in order to classify it as body governed by public law and not the division between public and private activities. Thus, the pursuit of commercial activities by contracting authorities is incorporated with their public interest orientation aims and objectives, without taking into account their proportion and weighting in relation to the total activities dispersed, and contracts awarded in pursuit of commercial purposes fall under the remit of the public procurement Directives. The ECJ recognized the fact that by extending the application of public procurement rules to activities of a purely industrial or commercial character, an onerous constraint would probably be imposed upon the relevant contracting authorities, which may also seem unjustified on the

---

[10] See Case C-44/96, *Mannesmann Anlangenbau Austria. v Strohal Rotationsdurck GesmbH, op.cit.* For a comprehensive analysis of the case, see the annotation by Bovis in (1999) 36 *Common Market Law Review* 205–25.

[11] For example, the relevant provisions stipulating the thresholds for the applicability of the Public Procurement Directives (Article 3(1) of Directive 93/37; Article 5(1) of Directive 93/36; Article 14 of Directive 93/38; Article 7(1) of Directive 92/50); the provisions relating to the so-called 'mixed contracts' (Article 6(5) of Directive 93/37), where the proportion of the value of the works or the supplies element in a public contract determines the applicability of the relevant Directive; and finally the relevant provisions which embrace the award of works contracts subsidised *directly* by more than 50% by the state within the scope of the Directive (Article 2(1)(2) of Directive 93/37)).

grounds that public procurement law, in principle, does not apply to private bodies which carry out identical activities.[12] The above situation represents a considerable disadvantage in delineating the distinction between private and public sector activities and their regulation, to the extent that the only determining factor appears to be the nature of the organization in question. The Court suggested that that disadvantage could be avoided by selecting the appropriate legal instrument or framework for the objectives envisaged or pursued by public authorities.

The doctrine of dualism specifically implies that contracting authorities may pursue a dual range of activities; to procure goods, works and services destined for the public, as well as participate in commercial activities. They can pursue other activities in addition to those which meet needs of general interest not having an industrial and commercial character. The proportion between activities pursued by an entity, which on the one hand aim to meet needs of general interest not having an industrial or commercial character, and commercial activities on the other is irrelevant for the characterization of that entity as a body governed by public law. What is relevant is the intention of establishment of the entity in question, which reflects on the 'specificity' requirement. Also, specificity does not mean exclusivity of purpose. Specificity indicates the intention of establishment to meet general needs. Along these lines, ownership or financing of an entity by a contracting authority does not guarantee the condition of establishment of that entity to meet needs of general interest not having industrial and commercial character.

There is considerable risk of circumventing the public procurement Directives, if contracting authorities award their public contracts via private undertakings under their control, which cannot be covered by the framework of the Directives. Under the domestic laws of the Member States, there is little to prevent contracting authorities from acquiring private undertakings in an attempt to participate in market activities. In fact, in many jurisdictions the socio-economic climate is very much in favour towards public-private sector partnerships, in the form of joint-ventures or in the form of private financing of public projects. The default position is the connection between the nature of a project and the aims and objectives of the undertaking, which awards it. If the realization of a project does not contribute to the aims and objectives of an undertaking, then it is assumed that the project in question is awarded 'on behalf' of another undertaking, and if the latter beneficiary is a contracting authority under the framework of public procurement law, then the relevant Directives should apply. The ECJ applied the *Strohal* lines to *Teckal*,[13] where the exercise of a similar control over the management of an entity by a contracting authority prevents the applicability of the Directives.

The dual capacity of contracting authorities is irrelevant to the applicability of public procurement rules. If an entity is a contracting authority, it must apply public procurement rules irrespective of the pursuit of general interest needs or the pursuit of commercial activities. Also, if a contracting authority assigns the rights and obligations of a public contract to an entity which is not a contracting authority, that entity must

[12] See C. Bovis, *The Liberalisation of Public Procurement in the European Union and its Effects on the Common Market*, Aldershot: Ashgate, 1998, Chapter 1, p. 16 *et seq.*

[13] Case C-107/98, *Teckal Slr v Comune di Viano*, *op.cit.*

follow public procurement rules. The contrary would be acceptable if the contract fell within the remit of the entity, which is not a contracting authority, and the contract was entered into on its behalf by a contracting authority.

Dualism's irrelevance for the applicability of public procurement represents a safeguard for the *acquis communautaire*. Dualism could be viewed as recognition of contractualised governance, where the demarcation between public and private activities of the public sector has become difficult to define, as well as a counterbalance of commerciality. If commercialism might shield the activities of a contracting authority from the application of public procurement rules, dualism provides for the necessary inferences to subject dual capacity entities to the public procurement *acquis*.

The doctrines of commercialism and competitiveness

Commercialism and its relationship with needs in the general interest represents the most important link between profit-making and public interest, as features which underpin the activities of bodies governed by public law. The criterion of 'specific establishment of an entity to meet needs in the general interest having non-commercial or industrial character' has attracted the attention of the ECJ,[14] where analogy was drawn from public undertakings jurisprudence, as well as case-law relating to public order to define the term *needs in the general interest.*[15] The concept was approached through a direct link with that of 'general economic interest', as defined in Article 90(2) EC.[16] The concept 'general interest' denotes the requirements of a community (local or national) in its entirety, which should not overlap with the specific or exclusive interest of a clearly determined person or group of persons[17]. However, the problematic requirement of the *specificity* of the establishment of the body in question was approached by reference to the reasons and the objectives behind its establishment. Specificity of the purpose of an establishment does not mean exclusivity, in the sense that other types of activities can be carried out without escaping classification as a body governed by public law.[18]

On the other hand, the requirement of non-commercial or industrial character of needs in the general interest has raised some difficulties. The Court had recourse to case law and legal precedents relating to public undertakings, where the nature of

---

[14] See Cases C-223/99, *Agora Srl v Ente Autonomo Fiera Internazionale di Milano* and C-260/99 *Excelsior Snc di Pedrotti runa & C v Ente Autonomo Fiera Internazionale di Milano,* judgment of 10 May 2001; C-360/96, *Gemeente Arnhem Gemeente Rheden v BFI Holding BV,* judgment of 10 November 1998; C-44/96, *Mannesmann Anlangenbau Austria AG et al. v Strohal Rotationsdurck GesmbH,* judgment of 15 January 1998.

[15] See the Opinion of Advocate-General Léger, point 65 of the Strohal case.

[16] See Case C-179/90, *Merci Convenzionali Porto di Gevova,* [1991] ECR I-5889; General economic interest as a concept represents 'activities of direct benefit to the public'; point 27 of the Opinion of Advocate-General van Gerven.

[17] See Valadou, *La notion de pouvoir adjudicateur en matière de marchés de travaux,* Semaine Juridique, 1991, Ed. E, No.3. p. 33.

[18] See Case C-44/96, *Mannesmann Anlangenbau Austria, op.cit.*

industrial and commercial activities of private or public undertakings was defined.[19] The industrial or commercial character of an organization depends much upon a number of criteria that reveal the thrust behind the organization's participation in the relevant market. The state and its organs may act either by exercising public powers or by carrying on economic activities of an industrial or commercial nature by offering goods and services on the market. The key issue is the organization's intention to achieve profitability and pursue its objectives through a spectrum of commercially motivated decisions. The distinction between the range of activities which relate to public authority and those which, although carried out by public persons, fall within the private domain is drawn most clearly from case-law and judicial precedents of the Court concerning the applicability of competition rules of the Treaty to the given activities.[20]

The ECJ in *BFI*[21] had the opportunity to clarify the element of non-commercial or industrial character. It considered that the relationship of the first criterion of bodies governed by public law is an integral one. The non-commercial or industrial character is a criterion intended to clarify the term 'needs in the general interest'. In fact, it is regarded as a category of needs of general interest. The Court recognised that there might be needs of general interest which have an industrial and commercial character, and it is possible that private undertakings can meet needs of general interest which do not have industrial and commercial character. The acid test for needs in the general interest not having an industrial or commercial character is that the state or other contracting authorities choose themselves to meet these needs or to have a decisive influence over their provision.

In the *Agora* case[22] the Court indicated that if an activity which meets general needs is pursued in a competitive environment, there is a strong indication that the entity which pursues it is not a body governed by public law. The reason can be found in the relationship between competitiveness and commerciality. Market forces reveal the commercial or industrial character of an activity, irrespective of the latter meeting the needs of general interest or not. However, market competitiveness as well as profitability cannot be absolute determining factors for the commerciality or the industrial nature of an activity, as they are not sufficient to exclude the possibility that a body governed by public law may choose to be guided by considerations other than economic ones. The absence of competition is not a condition necessarily to be taken into account in order to define a body governed by public law, although the existence of significant competition in the market place may be indicative of the absence of a need in the general interest, which does not carry commercial or industrial elements. The Court reached this conclusion by analysing the nature of the bodies governed by public law contained in Annex 1 of the Works Directive 93/37 and verifying that the intention of

---

[19] For example see Case 118/85 *Commission v Italy* [1987] ECR 2599 at para 7, where the Court had the opportunity to elaborate on the distinction of activities pursued by public authorities.

[20] See Case C-364/92, *SAT Fluggesellschafeten* [1994] ECR I-43; also Case C-343/95, *Diego Cali et Figli* [1997] ECR I-1547.

[21] See Case C-360/96, *Gemeente Arnhem Gemeente Rheden v BFI Holding BV, op.cit.*

[22] see Case C-223/99, *Agora Srl v Ente Autonomo Fiera Internazionale di Milano, op.cit.*

the state to establish such bodies has been to retain decisive influence over the provision of the needs in question.

Certain activities, which by their nature fall within the fundamental tasks of the public authorities, cannot be subject to a requirement of profitability and therefore are not meant to generate profits. It is possible, therefore, that the reason for drawing a distinction between bodies whose activity is subject to the public procurement legislation and other bodies, could be attributed to the fact that the criterion of 'needs in the general interest not having an industrial or commercial character' indicates the lack of competitive forces in the relevant marketplace. The concept of the state encapsulates an entrepreneurial dimension to the extent that it exercises *dominium.* Although the state as entrepreneur enters into transactions with a view to providing goods, services and works for the public, this type of activities does not resemble the characteristics of entrepreneurship, in as much as the aim of the state's activities is not the maximisation of profits but the observance of public interest. The relevant markets into which the state enters can be described as public markets. Public markets are the *fora* where *public interest* substitutes *profit maximisation.*[23]

Competitive Markets in Utilities

Privatized utilities could, in principle, be excluded from the procurement rules when a genuinely competitive regime[24] within the relevant market structure would rule out purchasing patterns based on non-economic considerations. The new utilities Directive should not apply to markets where the participants pursue an activity which is directly exposed to competition on markets to which access is not limited within the relevant Member State. The new utilities Directive has therefore introduced a procedure, applicable to all sectors covered by its provisions, that will enable the effects of current or future opening up to competition to be taken into account. Such a procedure should provide legal certainty for the entities concerned, as well as an appropriate decision making process, ensuring, within short time limits, uniform application of standards that result in the disengagement of the relevant procurement rules.

Direct exposure to competition should be assessed on the basis of objective criteria, taking account of the specific characteristics of the sector concerned. The implementation and application of appropriate Community legislation liberalizing a utility sector will be considered to provide sufficient grounds for determining if there is free access to the market in question. Such appropriate legislation should be identified in an annex which will be provided by the Commission. The Commission will, in particular, take into account the possible adoption of measures entailing a genuine opening up to competition of sectors other than those for which legislation is already mentioned in

---

[23] Flamme et Flamme, *Enfin l'Europe des Marchés Publics,* Actualité Juridique – Droit Administratif, 20 November 1989, p. 653, argue along the same lines.

[24] The determination of a genuinely competitive regime is left to the utilities operators themselves. See Case C 392/93, *The Queen and H.M. Treasury, ex parte British Telecommunications PLC* [1993] OJ C287/6. This is perhaps a first step towards self-regulation which could lead to the disengagement of the relevant contracting authorities from the public procurement regime.

Annex XI, such as that of railway transport services. Where free access to a given market does not result from the implementation of appropriate Community legislation, it should be demonstrated that such access is uninhibited *de jure* and *de facto*.[25]

THE PRINCIPLE OF ACCOUNTABILITY

The effects of the principle of accountability on public procurement regulation have been felt through four main effects; the objectivity of the regime, the probity of procurement practices, the regime's contract compliance and finally the regime's judicial redress.

The Effect of Objectivity

Standardization and the doctrine of equivalence

National technical standards, industrial product and service specifications and their harmonization have been considered priority areas for the common market. The ECJ has proactively approached the discriminatory use of specification requirements and standards.[26] It established the 'equivalent standard' doctrine, where contracting authorities are prohibited from introducing technical specifications or trade marks which mention products of a certain make or source, or a particular process which favours or eliminates certain undertakings, unless these specifications are justified by the subject and nature of the contract and on condition that they are only permitted if they are accompanied by the words 'or equivalent'. The rules on technical standards and specifications have been brought in line with the new policy which is based on the mutual recognition of national requirements, where the objectives of national legislation are essentially equivalent, and on the process of legislative harmonization of technical standards through non-governmental standardization organizations (CEPT, CEN, CENELEC).[27]

---

[25] According to Article 68(2), for the adoption of a Decision the Commission shall be allowed a period of three months commencing on the first working day following the date on which it receives the notification or the request. However, this period may be extended once by a maximum of three months in duly justified cases, in particular if the information contained in the notification or the request or in the documents annexed thereto is incomplete. The disengagement of the utilities procurement regime as a result of the operation of the relevant entities in competitive markets by virtue of Article 30 of the new utilities Directive does not apply to the WTO Government Procurement Agreement. This represents a legal *lacuna* as the procedural flexibility envisaged in the European procurement regulatory regime does not cover entities covered under the GPA. Rectification of the problem would require amendment to the GPA with the conferral of concessions and reciprocal access rights to the GPA signatories.

[26] See Case C-45/87, *Commission v Ireland*, [1988] ECR 4929; also Case C-359/93, *Commission v The Netherlands*, judgment of 24 January 1995.

[27] See Article 7 of Directive 88/295. See the White Paper on Completing the Internal Market, paras 61–79; also Council Resolution of 7 May 1985 [1985] OJ C136, on a new approach in the field of technical harmonization and standards.

Standardization and specification can act as a non-tariff barrier in public procurement contracts in two ways: first, contracting authorities may use apparently different systems of standards and specifications as an excuse for disqualification of tenderers. It should be maintained here that the description of the intended supplies, works or services to be procured is made by reference to the Common Product Classification, the NACE (General Industrial Classification of Economic Activities within the European Communities) and the Common Procurement Vocabulary (CPV); however, this type of description is of generic nature and does not cover industrial specifications and standardization requirements. Secondly, standardization and specification requirements can be restrictively defined in order to exclude products or services of a particular origin, or narrow the field of competition amongst tenderers. National standards are not only the subject of domestic legislation, which, of course, need to be harmonized and mutually recognized across the common market. One of the most significant aspects of standardization and specification appears to be the operation of voluntary standards, which are mainly specified at industry level. The above category presents difficulties in the attempts to harmonize, as any approximation and mutual recognition of standards relies on the willingness of the industry in question. Voluntary standards and specifications are used quite often in the utilities sector, where the relevant procurement requirements are complex and cannot be specified solely by reference to 'statutory' standards, thus leaving a considerable margin of discretion in the hands of the contracting authorities, which may abuse it during the selection and qualification stages of the procurement process.

Selection and qualification

During the selection and qualification process of tenderers, contracting authorities vet all candidates according to objectively defined criteria which aim at eliminating arbitrariness and discrimination. The selection criteria are determined through two major categories of qualification requirements: (i) legal, and (ii) technical/economic. Contracting authorities must strictly follow the homogeneously specified selection criteria for enterprises participating in the award procedures of public procurement contracts in an attempt to abolish potential grounds for discrimination on grounds of nationality and exclude technical specifications which are capable of favouring national undertakings.

The relevant provisions of the procurement Directives relating to the criteria of a tenderer's good standing and qualification are directly effective.[28] These criteria comprise of grounds for exclusion from participation in the award of public contracts, such as bankruptcy, professional misconduct, failure to fulfil social security obligations and obligations relating to taxes. They also refer to the technical ability and knowledge of the contractor, where proof of them may be furnished by educational or professional qualifications, previous experience in performing public contracts and statements on the contractor's expertise.

In principle, there are automatic grounds for exclusion, when a contractor, supplier or service provider: (i) is bankrupt or is being wound up; (ii) is the subject of proceedings

---

[28] See Case C-76/81, *SA Transporoute et Travaux v Minister of Public Works*, [1982] ECR 457.

for a declaration of bankruptcy or for an order for compulsory winding up; (iii) has been convicted for an offence concerning his professional conduct; (iv) has been guilty of grave professional misconduct; (v) has not fulfilled obligations relating to social security contributions; and (vi) has not fulfilled obligations relating to the payment of taxes.

However, for the purposes of assessing the financial and economic standing of contractors, an exception to the exhaustive list covering the contractors' eligibility and technical capacity is provided for, where, in particular, contracting entities may request references other than those expressly mentioned therein. Evidence of financial and economic standing may be provided by means of references including: (i) appropriate statements from bankers; (ii) the presentation of the firm's balance sheets or extracts from the balance sheets where these are published under company law provisions; and (iii) a statement of the firm's annual turnover and the turnover on construction works for the three previous financial years. The non-exhaustive character of the list of references in relation to the contractors' economic and financial standing was recognized by the ECJ,[29] where the value of the works which may be carried out at one time may constitute a proof of the contractors' economic and financial standing. The contracting authorities are allowed to fix such a limit, as the provisions of the public procurement Directives do not aim at delimiting the powers of Member States, but at determining the references or evidence which may be furnished in order to establish the contractors' financial and economic standing. The Court in another case referred to by a Dutch court[30] maintained that the examination of a contractor's suitability based on its good standing and qualifications and its financial and economic standing may take place simultaneously with the award procedures of a contract.[31] However, the two procedures (the suitability evaluation and bid evaluation) are totally distinct processes which shall not be confused.[32]

Award criteria

Throughout the evolution of the public procurement *acquis*, the procedural phase in the procurement process culminated in the application of objectively determined criteria which demonstrate the logic behind the behaviour of contracting authorities. There are two criteria on which the contracting authorities must base the award of public contracts:[33] (a) the most economically advantageous tender, or (b) the lowest price.

The most economically advantageous tender When the award is made to the tender most economically advantageous from the point of view of the contracting authority, various criteria linked to the subject-matter of the public contract in question, for

---

[29] See Cases C-27/86, 28/86, 29/86, *Constructions et Enterprises Industrielles S.A (CEI) v Association Intercommunale pour les Autoroutes des Ardennes*; Case 28/86, *Ing.A. Bellini & Co. S.p.A. v. Regie de Betiments*; Case 29/86, *Ing.A. Bellini & Co. S.p.A. v Belgian State* [1987] ECR 3347.

[30] See Case C-31/87, *Gebroeders Beentjes B.V. v State of Netherlands* [1988] ECR 4635.

[31] See Case C-28/86, *Bellini* [1987] ECR 3347, *op.cit.*

[32] See Case C-71/92, *Commission v Spain*, judgment of 30 June 1993.

[33] Article 53 of the Public Sector Directive.

example, quality, price, technical merit, aesthetic and functional characteristics, environmental characteristics, running costs, cost-effectiveness, after-sales service and technical assistance, delivery date and delivery period or period of completion, can be taken into consideration. The above listed criteria which constitute the parameters of the most economically advantageous offer are not exhaustive.[34]

The Court reiterated the wide interpretation of the relevant award criterion[35] and had no difficulty in declaring that contracting authorities may use the most economically advantageous offer as an award criterion by choosing the factors which they want to apply in evaluating tenders,[36] provided these factors are mentioned, in hierarchical order or descending sequence in the invitation to tender or the contract documents,[37] so that tenderers and interested parties can clearly ascertain the relative weight of factors other than price for the evaluation process. However, factors which have no strict relevance in determining the most economically advantageous offer by reference to objective criteria do involve an element of arbitrary choice and therefore should be considered as incompatible with the Directives.[38]

Criteria related to the subject matter of the contract A question arose as to whether and under what conditions a contracting authority can apply, in its assessment of the most economically advantageous tender for a contract for the supply of electricity, a criterion requiring that the electricity supplied be produced from renewable energy sources.[39] In principle, that question referred to the possibility of a contracting authority laying down criteria that pursue advantages which cannot be objectively assigned a direct economic value, such as advantages related to the protection of the environment. The Court held that that each of the award criteria used by the contracting authority to identify the most economically advantageous tender must not necessarily be of a purely economic nature.[40] The Court therefore accepted that where the contracting authority decides to award a contract to the tenderer who submits the most economically advantageous tender it may take into consideration ecological criteria, provided that they are linked to the subject-matter of the contract, do not confer an unrestricted freedom of choice on the authority, are expressly mentioned in the contract documents or the tender notice, and comply with all the fundamental principles of Community law, in particular the principle of non-discrimination.[41]

---

34 Article 53(1)(a) of the Public Sector Directive.

35 Case 31/87, *Gebroeders Beentjes v The Netherlands*, *op.cit*, para 19.

36 Case C-324/93, *R. v The Secretary of State for the Home Department, ex.parte Evans Medical Ltd and Macfarlane Smith Ltd*, judgment of 28 March 1995, where the national court asked whether factors concerning continuity and reliability as well as security of supplies fall under the framework of the most economically advantageous offer, when the latter is being evaluated.

37 See para 22 of *Beentjes*.

38 See para 37 of *Beentjes*.

39 See Case C-448/01, *EVN AG, Wienstrom GmbH and Republik Österreich*, judgment of 4 December 2003.

40 See Case C-513/99 *Concordia Bus Finland* [2002] ECR I-7123, para 55.

41 See *Concordia Bus Finland*, para 69.

The lowest price When the lowest price has been selected as the award criterion, contracting authorities must not refer to any other qualitative consideration when deliberating the award of a contract. The lowest price is a sole quantitative benchmark that intends to differentiate the offers made by tenderers.[42] However, contracting authorities can reject a tender, if they regard the price attached to it as abnormally low.

Abnormally low tenders In cases where tenders appear to be abnormally low in relation to the goods, works or services, the contracting authority must request in writing details of the constituent elements of the tender which it considers relevant before it rejects those tenders.[43] The clarification details[44] may relate in particular to:

(a) the economics of the construction method, the manufacturing process or the services provided;
(b) the technical solutions chosen and/or any exceptionally favourable conditions available to the tenderer for the execution of the work, for the supply of the goods or services;
(c) the originality of the work, supplies or services proposed by the tenderer;
(d) compliance with the provisions relating to employment protection and working conditions in force at the place where the work, service or supply is to be performed;
(e) the possibility of the tenderer obtaining state aid.

Where a contracting authority establishes that a tender is abnormally low because the tenderer has obtained state aid, the tender can be rejected on that ground alone only after consultation with the tenderer where the latter is unable to prove, within a sufficient time limit fixed by the contracting authority, that the aid in question was granted legally.[45] Where the contracting authority rejects a tender in these circumstances, it must inform the Commission of their decision.

The debate over the terminology of 'obviously abnormally low' tenders surfaced when the Court held[46] that rejection of a contract based on mathematical criteria without giving the tenderer an opportunity to furnish information is inconsistent with spirit of the public procurement Directives. The Court, following previous case-law,[47] ruled that the contracting authorities must give an opportunity to tenderers to furnish explanations regarding the genuine nature of their tenders, when those tenders appear to be abnormally low. Unfortunately, the Court did not proceed to an analysis of the wording 'obviously'. It rather seems that the term 'obviously' indicates the existence of precise and concrete evidence as to the abnormality of the low tender. On the other hand, the wording 'abnormally' implies a quantitative criterion left to the discretion of

---

42 See Article 53(1)(b) of the Public Sector Directive.

43 Article 55 of the Public Sector Directive.

44 Article 55(1) of the Public Sector Directive.

45 Article 55(3) of the Public Sector Directive.

46 See Case C-103/88, *Fratelli Costanzo S.p.A. v Comune di Milano* [1989] ECR 1839; Case 296/89, *Impresa Dona Alfonso di Dona Alfonso & Figli s.n.c. v Consorzio per lo Sviluppo Industriale del Comune di Monfalcone*, judgment of 18 June 1991.

47 See Case C-76/81 *Transporoute,* [1982] ECR 417, *op.cit.*

the contracting authority. However, if the tender is just 'abnormally' low, it could be argued that it is within the discretion of the contracting authority to investigate the genuine offer of a tender. *Impresa Lombardini*,[48] followed the precedent established by *Transporoute* and maintained the unlawfulness of mathematical criteria used as an exclusion of a tender which appears abnormally low. Nevertheless, it held that such criteria may be lawful if used for determining the abnormality of a low tender, provided an *inter partes* procedure between the contracting authority and the tenderer that submitted the alleged abnormal low offer presents the opportunity to clarify the genuine nature of that offer. Contracting authorities must take into account all reasonable explanations furnished and avoid limiting the grounds on which justification of the genuine nature of a tender should be made. Both the wording and the aim of the public procurement Directives direct contracting authorities to seek explanation and reject unrealistic offers, informing the Advisory Committee.[49] In *ARGE*,[50] the rejection of a tender based on the abnormally low pricing attached to it got a different twist in its interpretation. Although the Court ruled that directly or indirectly subsidized tenders by the state or other contracting authorities or even by the contracting authority itself can be legitimately part of the evaluation process, it did not elaborate on the possibility of rejection of an offer, which is appreciably lower than those of unsubsidized tenderers by reference to the 'abnormally low' disqualification ground.[51]

The Effect of Probity in Public Sector Integration

The award of public contracts to economic operators who have participated in a criminal organization or who have been found guilty of corruption or of fraud to the detriment of the financial interests of the European Communities or of money laundering should be avoided. Where appropriate, the contracting authorities should ask candidates or tenderers to supply relevant documents and, where they have doubts concerning the personal situation of a candidate or tenderer, they may seek the cooperation of the competent authorities of the Member State concerned. The exclusion of such economic operators should take place as soon as the contracting authority has knowledge of a judgment concerning such offences rendered in accordance with national law that has the force of *res judicata*. If national law contains provisions to

---

48 See Cases C-285/99 & 286/99, *Impresa Lombardini SpA v ANAS*, judgment of 27 November 2001.

49 The Advisory Committee for Public Procurement was set up by Decision 77/63 [1977] OJ L13/15, and is composed of representatives of the Member States belonging to the authorities of those States and has as its task to supervise the proper application of Public Procurement Directives by Member States.

50 See Case C-94/99, *ARGE Gewässerschutzt, op.cit.*

51 In *ARGE* the Court adopted a literal interpretation of the Directives and concluded that if the legislature wanted to preclude subsidized entities from participating in tendering procedures for public contracts, it should have said so explicitly in the relevant Directives. See paras 26 *et seq.* of the Court's judgment. Although the case has relevance in the fields of selection and qualification procedures and award criteria, the Court made no references to previous case-law regarding state aids in public procurement, presumably because the *Dupont de Nemours* precedent is still highly relevant.

this effect, non-compliance with environmental legislation or legislation on unlawful agreements in public contracts which has been the subject of a final judgment or a decision having equivalent effect may be considered an offence concerning the professional conduct of the economic operator concerned or grave misconduct. Non-observance of national provisions implementing the Council Directives 2000/78/EC[52] and 76/207/EC[53] concerning equal treatment of workers, which has been the subject of a final judgment or a decision having equivalent effect may be considered an offence concerning the professional conduct of the economic operator concerned or grave misconduct.

Article 45 of the public sector Directive deals with the personal situation of the candidate or tenderer. It provides that any candidate or tenderer who has been the subject of a conviction by final judgment of which the contracting authority is aware for one or more of the reasons listed below must be excluded from participation in a public contract:

(a) participation in a criminal organization, as defined in Article 2(1) of Council Joint Action 98/733/JHA;[54]
(b) corruption, as defined in Article 3 of the Council Act of 26 May 1997[55] and Article 3(1) of Council Joint Action 98/742/JHA[56] respectively;
(c) fraud within the meaning of Article 1 of the Convention relating to the protection of the financial interests of the European Communities;[57]
(d) money laundering, as defined in Article 1 of Council Directive 91/308 on prevention of the use of the financial system for the purpose of money laundering.[58]

The Effect of Contract Compliance and the Rule of Reason

The most economically advantageous offer as an award criterion has provided the Court with the opportunity to balance the economic considerations of public procurement with policy choices. Although in numerous instances the Court has maintained the importance of the economic approach[59] to the regulation of public sector contracts, it

---

[52] See Council Directive 2000/78/EC of 27 November 2000 establishing a general framework for equal treatment in employment and occupation [2000] OJ L303/16).

[53] See Council Directive 76/207/EEC of 9 February 1976 on the implementation of the principle of equal treatment for men and women as regards access to employment, vocational training and promotion, and working conditions [1976] OJ L39/40, amended by Directive 2002/73/EC of the European Parliament and of the Council [2002] OJ L269/15).

[54] See [1998] OJ L351/1.

[55] See [1997] OJ C195/1.

[56] See [1998] OJ L358/2.

[57] See [1995] OJ C316/48.

[58] See [1991] OJ L166/77, as amended by Directive 2001/97/EC of the European Parliament and of the Council of 4 December 2001 [2001] OJ L344/76).

[59] See Case C-380/98, *The Queen and H.M. Treasury, ex parte University of Cambridge* [2000] ECR I-8035 at para 17; Cases C-44/96, C-44/96, *Mannesmann Anlangenbau Austria AG et al. v Strohal Rotationsdurck GesmbH* [1998] ECR 73, para 33; Case C-360/96, *Gemeente*

has also recognised the relative discretion of contracting authorities to utilize non-economic considerations as award criteria.

The term *contract compliance*[60] could be best defined as the range of secondary policies relevant to public procurement, which aim at combating discrimination on grounds of sex, race, religion or disability.[61] When utilized in public contracts, contract compliance is a system whereby, unless the supply side (the industry) complies with certain conditions relating to social policy measures, contracting authorities can lawfully exclude tenderers from selection, qualification and award procedures. The concept is well known and practiced in North American jurisdictions and in particular in the United States,[62] as it has been in operation for some time in an attempt to reduce racial and ethnic minority inequalities in the market and to achieve equilibrium in the workforce market.

Apparently, the potential of public purchasing as a tool capable of promoting social policies has been met with considerable scepticism. Policies relevant to affirmative action or positive discrimination have caused a great deal of controversy, as they practically accomplish very little in rectifying labour market equilibria. In addition to the practicality and effectiveness of such policies, serious reservations have been expressed with regard to their constitutionality,[63] since they could limit, actually and potentially, the principles of economic freedom and freedom of transactions.[64]

Contract compliance legislation and policy is familiar to most European Member States, although the enactment of public procurement Directives has changed the situation dramatically.[65] The position of European Institutions on contract compliance

---

Arnhem Gemeente Rheden v BFI Holding BV, [1998] ECR 6821, paras 42 and 43; C-237/99, *Commission v France* [2001] ECR 934, at paras 41 and 42.

60 See Bovis, 'The Compatibility of Compulsory Tendering with Transfer of Undertakings: the case of Contract Compliance and the Acquired Rights Directive', Chapter 21 in Collins, Davies and Rideout (eds), *Legal Regulation of the Employment Relations*, London: Kluwer, 2000.

61 See ILEA Contract Compliance Equal Opportunities Unit, *Contract Compliance: a brief history*, London, 1990.

62 For a detailed analysis see P.E. Morris, 'Legal Regulation of Contract Compliance: an Anglo-American Comparison' (1990) 19 *Anglo-American Law Review* 87.

63 In particular in the US, see Case 93-1841 *Adarand Constructors v Pena*, 1995 Annual Volume of US Supreme Court. The United States Supreme Court questioned the constitutionality in the application of contract compliance as a potential violation of the equal protection component of the Fifth Amendment's Due Process Clause and ordered the Court of Appeal to re-consider the employment of socio-economic policy objectives in the award of federal public procurement contracts.

64 For an overview of the Social Policy in North American systems, see Cnossen and Bovis, 'The Framework of Social Policy in Federal States: An Analysis of the Law and Policy on Industrial Relations in USA and Canada', (1996) 12 *International Journal of Comparative Labour Law and Industrial Relations.*

65 For example, in the United Kingdom, every initiative relating to contract compliance has been outlawed by virtue of the Local Government Act 1988. Contract compliance from a public law perspective has been examined by T. Daintith, in 'Regulation by Contract: the new prerogative' (1979) 32 CLP 41. For a comprehensive analysis of the issue of contract compliance in relation to public contracts across the European Community, see McCrudden, *Contract Compliance and Equal Opportunities*, Oxford: Oxford University Press 1997.

has been addressed in three instances before the European Court of Justice.[66] The Court maintained that contract compliance with reference to domestic or local employment cannot be used as a selection criterion in tendering procedures for the award of public contracts. The selection of tenderers is a process which is based on an exhaustive list of technical and financial requirements expressly stipulated in the relevant Directives and the insertion of contract compliance as a selection and qualification requirement would be considered *ultra vires*. The Court ruled that social policy considerations can only be part of award criteria in public procurement, and especially in cases where the most economically advantageous offer is selected, provided that they do not run contrary to the basic principles of the Treaty and that that have been mentioned in the tender notice.

The Court's approach has also opened an interesting debate on the integral dimensions of contract compliance and the differentiation between the *positive* and *negative* approaches. The concept of positive approach within contract compliance encompasses all measures and policies imposed by contracting authorities on tenderers as suitability criteria for their selection in public procurement contracts. Such positive action measures and policies intend to complement the actual objectives of public procurement which are confined in economic and financial parameters and are based on a transparent and predictable legal background. Although the complementarity of contract compliance with the actual aims and objectives of the public procurement regime was acknowledged, the Court (and the European Commission) were reluctant in accepting such an over-flexible interpretation of the Directives and based on the literal interpretation of the relevant provisions disallowed positive actions of a social policy dimension as part of the selection criteria for tendering procedures in public procurement.

However, contract compliance can incorporate not only unemployment considerations, but also promote equality of opportunities and eliminate sex or race discrimination in the relevant market.[67] Indeed, the Directives on public procurement stipulate that the contracting authority may require tenderers to observe national provisions of employment legislation when they submit their offers. The ability to observe and conform to national employment laws in a Member State may constitute a ground of

[66] See Case 31/87, *Gebroeders Beenjes B.V v The Netherlands* [1989] ECR 4365. Also see Case C-360/89, *Commission v Italy* [1992] ECR 3401.

[67] There are a number of legal instruments relevant to social policy at Community level, that may apply to public procurement. They include, in particular, Directives on safety and health at work (for example, Council Directive 89/391 on the introduction of measures to encourage improvements in the safety and health of workers at work, and Directive 92/57 on the implementation of minimum safety and health requirements at temporary or mobile construction sites), working conditions and the application of employment law (for example, Directive 96/71/EC of the European Parliament and of the Council concerning the posting of workers in the framework of the provision of services [1997] OJ L18/1, and Directive 2001/23 on the safeguarding of employees' rights in the event of transfers of undertakings, businesses or parts of undertakings or businesses [2001] OJ L82/16, codifying Directive 77/187/EEC), Directive 2000/43/EC implementing the principle of equal treatment between persons irrespective of racial or ethnic origin [2000] OJ L180/22 and Directive 2000/78/EC establishing a general framework for equal treatment in employment and occupation [2000] OJ L303/16).

disqualification and exclusion of the defaulting firm from public procurement contracts.[68] In fact, under such interpretation, contract compliance may be a factor of selection criteria specified in the directives, as it contains a *negative approach* to legislation and measures relating to social policy.

There are arguments both in favour of and against incorporating social policy considerations in public procurement.[69] The most important argument in favour focuses on the ability of public procurement to promote parts of the Member States' social policy, with particular reference to long-term unemployment, equal distribution of income, social exclusion and the protection of minorities. Under such a positively oriented approach, public purchasing could be regarded as an instrument of policy in the hands of national administrations with a view to rectifying social equilibria. Contract compliance in public procurement could also cancel the stipulated aims and objectives of the liberalisation of the public sector. The regulation of public markets focuses on economic considerations and competition. Adherence to social policy factors could derail the whole process, as the public sector will pay more for its procurement by extra or hidden costs for the implementation of contract compliance in purchasing policies.[70]

A rule of reason in public procurement

In European Union law, the rule of reason serves as an expansion of the determined exemptions from a prohibition principle.[71] The rule of reason is a juridical development where the Court interprets the margins of discretion allotted to an executive authority (Member States and/or the Commission), as well as the grounds, the limits and the levels of deviation from a prohibition's exemptions. For public procurement, a rule of reason has emerged through the application of the most economically advantageous offer criterion. The Court, through a steady accumulation of case-law adopted a bi-focal stance: positive yet restrictive. Where the rules allow for discretion, the Court did not claw back any margin of appreciation from Member States and their contracting authorities; in fact, in many instances, it gradually expanded the grounds of flexibility in the award procedures.

The meaning of the most economically advantageous offer includes a series of factors chosen by the contracting authority, including price, delivery or completion date, running costs, cost-effectiveness, profitability, technical merit, product or work

---

[68] It should be mentioned that adherence to health and safety laws have been considered by a British court as part of the technical requirements specified in the Works Directive for the process of selection of tenderers; see *General Building and Maintenance v Greenwich Borough Council* [1993] IRLR 535. Along these lines, see the Commission's Interpretative Communication on the Community law applicable to public procurement and the possibilities for integrating social considerations into public procurement, COM (2001) 566, 15 October 2001.

[69] See Kruger, Nielsen and Brunn, *European Public Contracts in a Labour Law Perspective*, Copenhagen: DJOF Publishing, 1997.

[70] See Bovis, 'Social Policy Considerations and the European Public Procurement Regime' (1998) 3 *International Journal of Comparative Labour Law and Industrial Relations*.

[71] See the application of the rule of reason to the principle of free movement of goods and also the competition law principle prohibiting cartels and collusive behavior.

quality, aesthetic and functional characteristics, after-sales service and technical assistance, commitment with regard to spare parts and components and maintenance costs, security of supplies. The above list is not exhaustive and the factors listed therein serve as a guideline for contracting authorities in the weighted evaluation process of the contract award.

The Court reiterated the flexible and wide interpretation of the relevant award criterion[72] and had no difficulty in declaring that contracting authorities may use the most economically advantageous offer as award criterion by choosing the factors which they want to apply in evaluating tenders,[73] provided these factors are mentioned in hierarchical order or descending sequence in the invitation to tender or the contract documents,[74] so that tenderers and interested parties can clearly ascertain the relative weight of factors other than price for the evaluation process. However, factors which have no strict relevance in determining the most economically advantageous offer by reference to objective criteria do involve an element of arbitrary choice and therefore should be considered as incompatible with the public procurement Directives.[75]

A debate has arisen whether, under the most economically advantageous offer, each individual award factor has to provide an economic advantage which directly benefits the contracting authority, or, alternatively, it is sufficient that each individual factor has to be measurable in economic terms, without the requirement that it directly provides an economic advantage for the contracting authority in the given contract.

This debate intends to shed light on the integral function of the factors that comprise the most economically advantageous offer for contracting authorities. Although there is wide discretion conferred to them in compiling the relevant factors, subject to the requirements of relevance to the contract in question and their publicity, their relative importance, in economic terms, remains somehow unknown. If the second alternative were accepted, the discretion conferred on contracting authorities would permit a wide range of factors to feature as part of award criteria in public contracts, without the need to demonstrate a direct economic advantage to a contracting authority which is attributable to each of these factors. On the contrary, if each individual factor has to establish a measurable (in quantifiable terms) economic advantage to the contracting authority, which is directly attributed to its inclusion as part of the award criterion, the discretion of contracting authorities is curtailed, since they would be required to undertake and publicize in the tender or contract documents a clear cost-benefit analysis of the relevant factors that comprise in their view the most economically advantageous offer.

There are two instances where the rule of reason as applied in public procurement brought the relevant regime in line with European policy. The first is the case of transfer of undertakings, where the Court expanded the remit of the Acquired Rights

---

[72] See Case 31/87, *Gebroeders Beentjes v The Netherlands*, *op.cit*, para 19.

[73] See Case C-324/93, *R. v The Secretary of State for the Home Department, ex.parte Evans Medical Ltd and Macfarlane Smith Ltd* [1995] ECR 563, where the national court asked whether factors concerning continuity and reliability as well as security of supplies fall under the framework of the most economically advantageous offer, when the latter is being evaluated.

[74] See para 22 of *Beentjes*.

[75] See para 37 of *Beentjes*.

Directive to the public procurement contractual relations.[76] The second instance is the permissibility of environmental factors[77] as part of the award criteria for public contract and the explicit recognition of the environmental policy of the European Union as being complimentary to all legal and policy activities of the common market.

The latter development reveals also the importance of public procurement in relation to harmonization and even standardization of national policies. Public procurement in such cases serves as a conveyer belt for transferring homogenous legal or policy standards across the common market. The protection of the environment as an award criterion in public contracts is a classic example of the potential of public procurement regulation as an instrument of public policy. There will be instances in the future where positive integration will be required by European Institutions and Member States equally in areas such as social security, business ethics and anti-corruption policies. Harmonization of laws and policies within the common market has traditionally sought a common denominator amongst divergences and differences of national administrations. Under an ordo-liberal approach, the rule of reason seems an essential tool to convey effectively rights and obligations of Community law.

There is no attempt yet to instil a type of European public policy across the common market. Not only have the legal and political differences of Member States dictated that such an approach would face considerable resistance, the very need for a common denominator of public policy in the European Union has been questionable. However, if the European Union is to become a serious competitor to major trading forces in the world, perhaps the introduction of such a common denominator is something that requires further consideration. Productivity rises, competitiveness, industrial restructuring exercises, privatization, employment relations, taxation, and corporate governance are mere examples of the features which the European Union and its Member States will be facing in a post-enlargement era. Public procurement could play a role in carrying over the European legal and policy standards into national systems.

Judicial Redress and its Impact on Accountability

The inadequacy of existing remedies at national level to ensure compliance and enforcement of the public procurement *acquis* was highlighted by their inability to correct infringements and ensure a correct application of the substantive public

---

[76] See Directive 77/62 [1977] OJ C61/26, as amended by Directive 98/50 [1998] OJ L132 and consolidated by Directive 2001/23 [2001] OJ L82/16. For a comprehensive analysis of the implications of transfer of undertakings in public procurement see Case C 29/91, *Dr Sophie Redmond Stichting v Bartol* [1992] ECR 3189; Case C 382/92, *Commission v United Kingdom* [1994] ECR 2435; Case 24/85, *Spijkers v Gebroders Benedik Abbatoir CV* [1986] ECR 1123; Case C 209/91, *Rask v ISS Kantinservice* [1993] ECR 5735; Case C 392/92, *Schmidt v Spar und Leihkasse der fruherer Amter Bordersholm, Kiel und Cronshagen* [1994] ECR 1320; Case C 392/92, *Schmidt v Spar und Leihkasse der fruherer Amter Bordersholm, Kiel und Cronshagen* [1994] ECR 1320; Case C 48/94, *Rygaard v Stro Molle Akustik* [1995] ECR 2745; Case C-324/86, *Tellerup* [1998] ECR 739.

[77] See Case C-513/99, *Concordia Bus Finlandia Oy Ab v Helsingin Kaupunki et HKL-Bussiliikenne* [2002] ECR 7213.

procurement rules. The enactment of the Remedies Directives[78] has brought a decentralized dimension into the application of public procurement rules. The liberalization of public procurement to community-wide competition demands a substantial increase of the efficiency levels regarding the availability of redress measures introduced within national legal systems which provide interested parties, at least, the same treatment in public procurement litigation, as in other forms of litigation. The remedies Directives have revealed three fundamental doctrines in public procurement regulation; the doctrine of procedural autonomy, the doctrine of effectiveness and the doctrine of procedural equality.

The doctrine of procedural autonomy

Member States have wide discretion to establish the procedural framework for review procedures and the logistics for its operation. The existence of national legislation which provides that any application for review of decisions of contracting authorities must be commenced within a specific time-limit and that any irregularity in the award procedure relied upon in support of such application must be raised within the same period is compatible with public procurement *acquis*,[79] provided that, in pursuit of fundamental principle of legal certainty, such specific time limits are reasonable.[80]

The doctrine of effectiveness

Member States are required to provide for a review procedure so that an applicant may set aside a decision of a contracting authority to award a public contract to a third party, prior to the conclusion of the contract.[81] That right of review for tenderers must be independent of the possibility for them to bring an action for damages once the contract has been concluded.[82] A national legal system that makes impossible to contest the award decision because of the award decision and the conclusion of the contract occurring at the same time deprives interested parties of any possible review in order to have an unlawful award decision set aside or to prevent the contract from being concluded. Complete legal protection requires that a reasonable period must elapse between the decision which awards a public contract and the conclusion of the contract itself, as well as a duty on the part of contracting authorities to inform all interested parties of an awarding decision.

---

[78] See the public sector Remedies Directive 89/665 [1989] OJ L395/33, and the utilities Directive 92/13 [1992] OJ L76/14.

[79] See Case C-470/99, *Universale-Bau AG, Bietergemeinschaft* [2002] ECR I-11617.

[80] See Case C-261/95, *Palmisani* [1997] ECR I-4025, para 28, and Case C-78/98 *Preston and Others* [2000] ECR I-3201, para 33.

[81] See Case C-212/02, *Commission v Austria*, judgment of 24 June 2004, unpublished.

[82] See Case C-81/98 *Alcatel Austria and Others* [1999] ECR I-7671, para 43.

The doctrine of procedural equality

Time limits and periods to contest the legality of act or decisions of contracting authorities[83] remain within the discretion of Member States, subject to the requirement that the relevant national rules are not less favourable than those governing similar domestic actions.[84]

[83] See Case C-92/00, *Hospital Ingenieure Krankenhaustechnik Planungs- GmbH (HI) and Stadt Wien,* [2002] ECR I-5553.

[84] See Case C-390/98 *Banks v Coal Authority and Secretary of State for Trade and Industry* [2001] ECR I-6117, para 121; Case C-453/99 *Courage and Crehan* [2001] ECR I-6297, para 29.

2. Public procurement and contracting authorities

Charles Clarke

UNDERLYING PRINCIPLE OF PUBLIC PROCUREMENT

The term 'contracting authority' is a decisive element of the public procurement legal framework, as it determines the applicability of the relevant rules,[1] encompassing the State, regional or local authorities, bodies governed by public law and associations formed by one or several of such authorities or one or several of such bodies governed by public law.[2] Importantly, a far-reaching and transparent definition of the term *contracting authorities* is a crucial component in providing a clear understanding of the Public Procurement Directives' remit. The structure of the Directives is such, to embrace the *purchasing behaviour* of all entities, which have a close association or connection with the State.[3] These entities, although not officially part of the state, disperse public funds in pursuit or on behalf of the public interest. State (executive and judiciary),[4] regional and local authorities are normally easy to recognise; however, it is sometimes difficult to determine whether the role of other bodies or associations means that they fall within the legal framework of a 'contracting authority'. This chapter seeks to identify the legal remit of the term, 'contracting authority' within the Public Procurement arena; through determining the European Courts' interpretation of the types of authorities which are caught by the Public Procurement Directives.

Public procurement law regulates the purchasing by public sector bodies and certain utility sector bodies of contracts for goods, works or services;[5] regulation of such activities is coordinated by the current EU Directive 2004/18/EC.[6] The current Utilities Directive[7] has encapsulated entities operating in the water, energy, transport and telecommunications sectors, forcing them within the remit and structure of public procurement law where there is a positive link between the state and the contracting

---

[1] See C. Bovis, '*EU Public Procurement Law*', European Law Studies Series, Cheltenham, UK and Northampton, MA, USA: Edward Elgar, 2008, at p. 192.

[2] See Article 1(9) of Directive 2004/18/EC (OJ L 94, 28.3.2014, pp. 65–242).

[3] See Case 24/91, *Commission v Kingdom of Spain* [1994] ECR I-1989; and Case 247/89, *Commission v Portugal* [1991] ECR I-3659.

[4] See Case C-323/96, *Commission v Kingdom of Belgium* [1998] ECR I-5063, para 1; Case 14/83, *Von Colson* [1984] ECR 1891.

[5] See S. Arrowsmith (ed.), 'EU Public Procurement Law: an Introduction' (2011), available 25 January 2016 at http://www.nottingham.ac.uk/pprg/documentsarchive/asialinkmaterials/eupublicprocurementlawintroduction.pdf; and S.E. Kalsmose-Hjelmborg, P. Jakobsen and S.T. Poulsen, *Public Procurement Law: The EU Directive on Public Contracts*, Copenhagen: Djøf Pub., 2006, at pp. 8–90.

[6] See Directive 2004/18/EC, *op. cit.*

[7] See Directive 2004/17/EC (OJ L 134, 30.4.2004, pp. 1–113).

authority. The Utilities Directive also covers *public undertakings*.[8] The term 'public undertakings' covers entities over which the State exerts *direct* or *indirect* authority through ownership, financial participation, or by means of laws and regulations, which administer the public undertaking's daily operation. Under the Utilities Directive, 'public undertakings' cover utilities operators (both public and privately owned), which have been granted exclusive rights of exploitation of a service,[9] regardless of their ascribed ownership. Within the utility procurement sphere, 'privatised utilities [can], in principle, [be] excluded from the procurement rules when a genuinely competitive regime within the relevant market structure would rule out purchasing patterns based on non-economic considerations'.[10] Such a competitive regime between utility operators themselves, pre-supposes self-regulation; inevitably discontinuing concurrent contracting authorities from the market. Notably however, the European Commission believes that such self-regulation through competitive markets is a long way down the road, as recently it has published the draft Directive for Utilities, which is expected to be implemented across Member States within 2014.

The term 'contracting authority', under the Public Procurement Directives, has been applied by the Court of Justice of the European Union ('CJEU' or 'the Court') so as to catch any authority that tries to hide behind *formal public structure*. Entities that are of both public and private structure will be trapped by the Public Procurement Directives if they fall within the criteria laid down by the CJEU. The applications of the *functionality* and *dependency* tests have also allowed the Court to effectively apply the Public Procurement Directives, preventing authorities escaping their remit. Clearly, the CJEU has been able to establish principles, allowing effective application of the Public Procurement Directives and limiting uncertainty.

STATE, REGIONAL AND LOCAL AUTHORITY: THE PRACTICAL ASPECT OF CONTRACTING AUTHORITIES

Conformity actions brought by the European Commission against Member States can effectively determine whether or not an entity falls within the Directives' definition of what amounts to a 'contracting authority' under public procurement law. For example, a practical way of identifying whether an entity is a contracting authority or not, is if under the circumstances the State can be held accountable for infringements of European Community law by public entities over which it exerts a level of control.[11] Such distinct accountability suggests a clear-cut causal link between the State and the relevant entities. It is a maintained conception that public interest operations are fragmented across a number of different undertakings, forming a 'loop-hole' within the very definition of the term contracting authorities; as *prima facie* they are not formally part of the State and fail to fall within the criteria for the definition of bodies governed by public law. Such circumstances arise where the entity is a non-governmental

[8] See Article 2(1)(b) of Directive 2004/17/EC, *op. cit.*

[9] Ibid.

[10] See C. Bovis, (fn. 1), at p. 64.

[11] See Article 228 of the Treaty of the Functioning of the European Union ("TFEU").

organisation, which functions under the 'umbrella' of the central/local government; and are accountable under the clear understanding that they operate under the public interest.[12]

Accordingly, the concept of the state is not confined to the 'administration',[13] but also covers bodies which do not, *prima facie*, form part of the traditional structures of the administration, have no *legal personality* of their own and carry out tasks that are normally the responsibility of the state administration.[14] Such a body may award public contracts or conclude framework agreements for works, supplies or services intended for contracting authorities.[15] In *Beentjes*, the CJEU had to decide whether the procurement Directive[16] applied to the award of public works contracts by a body with no *legal personality* of its own.[17] The Court conveyed 'the objective of [the] Directive [...] is to coordinate national procedures for the award of public works contracts concluded in member States on behalf of the State, regional or local authorities or other legal persons governed by public law'.[18] The CJEU further emphasised that the term 'the State', within the Directive should be interpreted in its 'functional terms' (functional test).[19] Hence, the Public Procurement Directives should ensure effective attainment of freedom of establishment to provide services in respect of public works contracts and although the body concerned is not formally a part of the State it has the ability to contract out.[20] Thus, a body whose composition and functions are laid down by legislation is regarded as falling within the notion of the State, regardless of its formal appearance.[21] It further holds where such an authority exercises a certain degree of control, there is clear connection between the state and the entities in question; for the purposes of the procurement Directives.[22]

Following the CJEU's application of the functional test in *Beentjes*, the Court was able to reiterate its interpretation, however, via a different standpoint. In *Teoranta* the CJEU interpreted the public procurement Directive, using the functional test in order to determine the nature of entities that have a distinctive public interest.[23] The latter case involved a private company set up by the State, created under national legislation; carrying out forestry activities and other related deeds, which was deemed as falling

[12] See C. Bovis, 'Public entities awarding procurement contracts under the framework of EC Public Procurement Directives', (1993) 1 *Journal of Business Law* 56–78.

[13] See Article 1(9) of Directive 2004/18/EC, *op. cit.*

[14] See Case C-31/87, *Gebroeders Beentjes BV v State of the Netherlands* [1988] ECR 4635.

[15] See C. Bovis, (fn. 1) at p. 191.

[16] Directive 71/305/EEC (OJ L 209, 24.7.1992, pp. 1–24) – now Directive 2004/18/EC, *op. cit.*

[17] See Case C-31/87, *Beentjes* (fn. 14), at paras. 2–4.

[18] Ibid., at para. 9.

[19] Ibid., at para. 11; Case C-470/99, *Universale-Bau and Others* [2002] ECR I-11617, at paras. 51–53; Case C-214/00, *Commission v Spain* [2003] ECR I-4667, at paras. 52 and 53; and Case C-283/00, *Commission v Spain* [2003] ECR I-11697, at para. 69.

[20] Ibid.

[21] See C. Bovis, (fn. 1), p. 192; Case C-249/81, *Commission v Ireland* [1982] ECR 4005; Case C-36/74 *Walrave and Koch v Association Union Cycliste International et al* [1974] ECR 1423.

[22] See Case C-24/91, *Commission v Kingdom of Spain* [1994] ECR I-1989; Case 247/89, *Commission v Portugal* [1991] ECR I 3659.

[23] See Case C-306/97, *Connemara Machine Turf Co Ltd v Coillte Teoranta* [1998] ECR I-8761.

within the notion of the State.[24] It was entrusted with specific tasks of public interest, such as managing national forests, as well as providing recreational, educational, scientific and cultural facilities.[25] More importantly however, it was under decisive administrative, financial and management control by the state. The Court held that the state had 'indirect' control over *Teoranta's* policies, thus, in functional terms it formed part of the state.[26] A similar outcome was enhanced by the Court in the case better known as *Vlaamese Raad*,[27] where it was held that the definition of the State encompasses all bodies which exercise legislative, executive and judicial powers, at both regional and federal levels.[28] Consequently, it fell within the definition of the state and held to be a contracting authority.[29] Notably, although the Belgian Government was not exercising any direct or indirect control relating to procurement policies over the *Vlaamese Raad*, it was deemed irrelevant by the Court on the grounds that a Member State "*cannot rely on provisions, practices or circumstances existing in its internal legal order in order to justify its failure to comply with the obligations and time-limits laid down by a directive*".[30]

A wider and flexible interpretation of the Public Procurement Directives, using the *functionality* approach, allows the Court to closer analyse the relationship between an entity and the State, regional or local authority.[31] Identifying aspects of management or financial control and the intention and function of establishment of the entity in question, are factors which the Court uses when establishing a positive link between the entity and the State. In other words, it allows the Court to look between the lines when assessing a relationship between an entity and the state; identifying its true function, purpose and full dimensions.

'BODIES GOVERNED BY PUBLIC LAW'

To be categorised as a contracting authority, for the functionality of the Directives, a body governed by public law must fall within the relevant cumulative criteria.[32] First, such a body is; (a) established for the specific purpose[33] of meeting needs in the general interest, not having an industrial or commercial character; (b) having legal personality; and (c) financed, for the most part, by the State, regional or local

---

24 Ibid., at paras. 19–21.

25 Ibid., at para. 19.

26 Ibid., at paras. 26–27.

27 See Case C-323/96, *Commission v Kingdom of Belgium* [1998] ECR I-5063.

28 Ibid., at paras. 11–14.

29 Ibid., at paras. 17–24.

30 Ibid., at para. 42; Case C-144/97, *Commission v France* [1998] ECR I-613, at para. 8.

31 See C. Bovis, (fn. 1) at p. 195.

32 See Case C-44/96, *Mannesmann Analagenbau Austria* [1998] ECR I-73, at para. 21.

33 See Cases C-223/ 99 & C-260/99, *Agora Srl v Ente Autonomo Fiera Internazionale di Milano; Excelsior Snc di Pedrotti runa & C v Ente Autonomo Fiera Internazionale di Milano* [2001] ECR I-3605, at para. 32; Case C-44/96, *Mannesmann Analagenbau Austria* [1998] ECR I-73, at paras. 20–29 and 37–41; Case C-306/97, *Connemara Machine Turf Co Ltd v Coillte Teoranta* [1998], ECR I-8761, at paras. 32–36.

authorities, or other bodies governed by public law; or subject to management supervision by those bodies; or having an administrative, managerial or supervisory board, more than half of whose members are appointed by the State, regional or local authorities,[34] or by other bodies governed by public law.[35] Lists of bodies and categories of bodies, governed by public law, which fulfil the three latter criteria, are set out in *Annex III* of the Directive.[36] It is also imperative that Member States *periodically* notify the Commission of changes to their lists and categories of bodies, so as not create future uncertainty.[37] The obligation of a 'body governed by public law' to comply with the Directive does not, however, depend on its prior inclusion in the list; it is under such an obligation as soon as it fulfils the criteria. Similarly, although a body may be on the list, it could be *exempted* from complying with the Directive if it no longer meets the cumulative criteria. With this in mind, the Court has expanded on the above criteria, exposing the definition of 'bodies governed by public law' under the Public Procurement Directives. Further to this, the Court has sought the opportunity to advance on the literal meaning of 'bodies governed by public law', creating thematic areas or tests, which reveal the true purpose of an entity.

(i) The Dependency Test

Ostensibly, this section relates to *any body* with legal personality under public or private law, whose operational choices and activities are or may be influenced by a 'contracting authority'[38] as a result of the links between them by virtue of one or more of the conditions that go to make up the third criterion (c).[39] Thus, the Court revealed that there is an intimate dependency of such entities on the State, in terms of corporate governance, management supervision and financing. In *OPAC*[40] it was held that entities providing social housing for people in France were held to be 'bodies governed by public law',[41] falling within the remit of the procurement Directives. Direct management supervision either by the State itself *or* other contracting authorities, conveyed state control over funds, governance and management.[42] The Courts have concluded that such bodies are heavily dependent on the state, relying on state management,

---

[34] See Case C-188/89, *Foster and others v British Gas plc* [1990] ECR I-3313.

[35] See Article 1(9) of Directive 2004/18/EC, *op. cit.*

[36] See Annex III of Directive 2004/18/EC, *op. cit.*

[37] Refer to: http://ec.europa.eu/internal_market/publicprocurement/index_en.htm (available 25 January 2016).

[38] See Case C-300/07, *Hans & Christophorus Oymanns GbR, Orthopädie Schuhtechnik v AOK, Rheinland/Hamburg* [2009] ECR I-4779; Case C-536/07, *Commission v Germany* [2009] ECR I-10355.

[39] See Case C-220/05, *Jean Auroux and Others v Commune de Roanne* [2007] ECR I-385.

[40] See Case C-237/99, *Commission v France* [2001] ECR I-939.

[41] Ibid., at paras. 94–97.

[42] Ibid., at paras. 31 and 36.

financing and supervision/monitoring,[43] nevertheless, such a presumption is not absolute.[44]

Conceivably, obtaining public finance from the state or a contracting authority is a distinct suggestion that an entity is most likely to be a body governed by public law. In the *Cambridge* case, the Court was faced with four questions as to whether the entity was dependent on the state: whether (i) awards or grants paid by one or more contracting authorities for the support of research work; (ii) consideration paid by one or more contracting authorities for the supply of services comprising research work; (iii) consideration paid by one or more contracting authorities for the supply of other services, such as consultancy or the organisation of conferences; and (iv) student grants paid by local education authorities to universities in respect of tuition for named students constitute public financing for the university.[45] First, the Court held that *only explicit payments* transferred to an entity by the state (or other public authorities), have the effect of creating or reinforcing a specific relationship and dependency.[46] Direct funding received in the form of grants/awards, by the state or other contracting authorities, as well as funding received in the form of student grants for tuition fees for named students, constitutes public financing, thus dependency.[47] However, if there is a *specific consideration* for the state to finance an entity, the Court suggested that the dependency ties are not sufficiently close to merit the entity financed by the state meeting the third criterion.[48]

Notably, within paragraph 25 of the Judgment the Court drew a positive correlation between public financing obtained by an entity and the receiving of subsidies.[49] Nevertheless, if there is a *specific consideration* for the state to finance an entity of choice, the Court advocated that dependency ties 'are *not* sufficiently close to merit the entity financed by the state meeting the third criterion of the term bodies governed by public law'.[50] Consequently, capital obtained by the University for research work, or consultancies, or conference organisation cannot be deemed as public financing. Lastly, the Court held that the proportion of public finances received by an entity must exceed 50 per cent to enable it to meet the third criterion.[51] Accordingly, there must be an annual evaluation of the (financial) status of an entity for the purposes of being considered a contracting authority.[52]

---

[43] See Case C-152/84, *Marshall v Southampton and South West Hampshire Area Health Authority* [1986] ECR 723.

[44] See Case C-380/98, *The Queen and HM Treasury, ex parte University of Cambridge* [2000] ECR I-8035.

[45] Ibid., at para. 13.

[46] Ibid., at paras. 11–26.

[47] Ibid., at paras. 34–36, 37–44.

[48] Ibid., at paras. 20–21 and 25.

[49] Ibid., at para. 25; See Case C-380/98 (fn. 44), Opinion of the Advocate General at para. 46.

[50] Ibid., at para. 26.

[51] Ibid., at para. 18. See also Aticle 1(9)(c) of Directive 2004/18/EC, *op. cit.*

[52] Ibid., at paras. 40 and 44.

(ii) Management Supervision of Entities

The Court has considered that management supervision essentially arises where one of the above alternative criteria under 'bodies governed by public law' is satisfied. As the Court has identified within previous case-law, management supervision would co-exist where the body in question is financed, for the most part, by the public authorities or where the latter appoint more than half of the members of its administrative, managerial or supervisory organs, enabling the public authorities to influence the decisions in relation to public contracts.[53] Such rationale stems from the notion that managerial supervision, per se, does not necessarily sanction public organisations to *directly* influence the relevant entity with regards to its contractual dealings.[54] In the case of *Adolf Truly*, the Court held that through the shareholders' agreement it expressly provided that the public authority was authorised to examine not only the annual accounts of the company but also its conduct from the point of view of proper accounting, regularity, economy, efficiency and expediency. It also allowed the public authority to inspect the company's business premises and facilities and to report the results of those inspections to the competent bodies and to the company shareholders and the City of Vienna.

Conclusively, it was held that such powers enabled the public authority in question to actively to control the management of that company.[55] In summary, the latter criterion is fulfilled where the public authorities in question administer the annual accounts of the relevant body and oversees its performance "*from the point of view of proper accounting, regularity, economy, efficiency and expediency and where those public authorities are authorised to inspect the business premises and facilities of that body and to report the results of those inspections to a regional authority which it holds, through another company, all the shares in the body in question*".[56]

(iii) Acting in the 'General Interest' and Meeting Needs of an Industrial or Commercial Nature

Bodies which are established in the 'general interest' and fulfil the other criteria, but are not regarded as contracting authorities by the Directive, are those set up for the specific purpose of meeting needs of an industrial or commercial nature, that is, economic activities in the industrial field that involve supplying goods/services on markets open to public/private operators under fully competitive conditions.[57] In assessing whether or not such a need in the general interest is present, account must be taken of all the relevant legal and factual elements, such as the circumstances prevailing at the time when the body concerned was established and the conditions under which it

[53] See Case C-237/99, *Commission v France* (fn.40), at paras. 48 and 49.

[54] See Case C-373/00, *Adolf Truley GmbH and Bestattung Wien GmbH,* [2003] ECR I-1931, at para. 70.

[55] Ibid., at para. 73.

[56] See Case C-373/00, *Adolf Truley* (fn. 54), at para. 74.

[57] See Case C-118/85, *Commission v Italy* [1987] ECR I-2599, at para. 7.

exercises its activity.[58] From this area of the Court's jurisprudence emanates the distinction between profit-making and public interest motives. It also highlights the clear intention of the Court to provide a clear and distinct formula when identifying the activities of bodies governed by public law.

As expected, the condition of non-commercial or industrial character of the needs in the general interest has produced problems; such as distinguishing certain commercial activities of public or private undertakings and whether they fall within the remit of the procurement Directives.[59] It is clear from the current case-law that the industrial or commercial nature of an entity rests on certain benchmark criteria, exposing the organisation's core involvement within the relevant industry. Thus, identifying whether a body governed by public law falls within the relevant criteria, is to reveal whether it is the organisation's intention to attain profitability and pursue its goals via commercially stimulated decisions. In particular, it must be ascertained whether the body in question carries out its activities in a competitive environment, since the existence of competition may, be an indication that a need in the general interest has an industrial *or* commercial character.[60] The requirement of the 'non-commercial/industrial character of needs in the general interest' has raised complications, as they carry out business equivalent to that of a private operator.

In *BFI,* the Court was able to clarify the element of non-commercial or industrial character. The first criterion of 'bodies-governed-by-public-law' was held to be an '*essential criterion*' when identifying contracting authorities and that there might be 'needs of general interest' having an industrial/commercial character.[61] The Court also highlighted that it is also possible that private undertakings can meet needs of a general interest which *do not* have an industrial and commercial character.[62] Moreover, in *Agora*[63] the question arose as to whether a body whose object is to carry on activities relating to the organisation of fairs, exhibitions and other similar initiatives, which is non-profit-making, but managed according to the criteria of performance, efficiency and cost-effectiveness, and which operates in a competitive environment, meets needs in the general interest, not having an industrial or commercial character.

First, the Court highlighted the conclusions reached in the *BFI* case which underlined that activities relating to the organisation of fairs, exhibitions and other similar initiatives meet needs in the general interest. However, the Court further held that a body whose object is to carry on activities relating to the organisation of fairs, exhibitions and other similar initiatives; which is *non-profit-making* but is managed according to the criteria of performance, efficiency and cost-effectiveness; and which

---

58 See C. De Koninck and T. Ronse, '*European Public Procurement Law: The European Public Procurement Directives and 25 Years of Jurisprudence by the Court of Justice of the European Communities: Texts and Analysis*', Kluwer Law International, (2008) at pp. 187–9.

59 See Case 118/85, *Commission v Italy* [1987] ECR 2599, at para. 7.

60 See Case C-360/96, *BFI Holding* [1998] ECR I-6821, at paras. 48–49; and Case C-373/00, *Adolf Truly* (fn. 54), at para. 61.

61 See Case C-360/96, *BFI Holding* (fn. 60), at paras. 31–36 and 53.

62 Ibid., at para. 53.

63 See Case C-223/99, *Agora Srl v Ente Autonomo Fiera Internazionale diMilano* [2001] ECR I-3605.

operates in a *competitive environment*, is *not* a 'body governed by public law'.[64] Nevertheless, market competitiveness and profitability cannot be complete determining factors for the commerciality or industrial nature of an activity, as they *do not* eliminate the possibility that a 'body-governed-by-public-law' may choose to be guided by considerations other than economic ones.[65] The absence of competition is not *necessarily* a condition to be taken into account in order to define a 'body governed by public law'.[66]

It has also been affirmed by the CJEU that an entity which was originally not established for the specific purpose of meeting needs in the general interest, however, which has consequently taken the obligation for fulfilling such needs in its present form and fulfils the condition required by the first indent of the second subparagraph of Article 1(9) of Directive 2004/18/EC,[67] is regarded as a body governed by public law for the purposes of the Directive.[68] The entity in question was a sewage treatment plant within the confines of Vienna called *Entsorgungsbetriebe Simmering GesmbH* ("EBS").[69] When EBS was established formally as a company, its original purpose was not to serve the needs of the general interest, but to operate purely on a commercial basis. It is clear that EBS's original activities were not reserved or allotted to the public sector and that there was no indication in the relevant statutes confirming that EBS was established for the specific purpose of meeting needs in the general interest, not having an industrial or commercial character.

However, in 1985 EBS entered into a lease with the city of Vienna, under which it started to manage the said sewage plant with staff supplied by the city of Vienna, which undertook to reimburse EBS the expenses occasioned by such personnel. Consequentially, in two contracts drawn up between the city of Vienna and EBS in 1996, the city of Vienna further covered the plant's operating expenses. On that note, it was apparent that EBS did not carry on that branch of its activities for profit motivations. It was in fact an activity of general interest which the city of Vienna delegated to EBS and which was managed in such a way as to cover the expenses; an activity not of an industrial or commercial character.[70] EBS (as did the Commission), submitted that under the circumstances it cannot be considered as a body governed by public law within the meaning of the second subparagraph of Article 1(9) of Directive 2004/18/EC, on the understanding that it is clear from the wording of the first indent of that provision that the sole deciding factor is the task which it was given at the date of its establishment.[71] Conversely, the Austrian and Netherlands Governments advocated that EBS's 'present' undertaking should be considered and not its original function when

---

[64] Ibid., at paras. 38, 42 and 43; and Case C-360/96, *BFI Holding* (fn. 60), at para. 49.

[65] See C. Bovis, (fn. 1), at p. 200.

[66] See Case C-223/99, *Agora Srl* (fn. 63), at para. 42.

[67] See Case C-44/96, *Mannesmann Analagenbau* (fn. 32).

[68] See Case C-470/99, *Universale-Bau AG, Bietergemeinschaft Hinteregger & Söhne Bauges. mbH Salzburg, ÖSTU-STETTIN Hoch- und Tiefbau GmbH, and Entsorgungsbetriebe Simmering GesmbH* [2002] ECR-11617.

[69] Ibid., at para. 32.

[70] Ibid., at para. 46.

[71] Ibid., at paras. 47 and 48.

EBS was formally created.[72] It was further conveyed by both Governments that only a functional interpretation of the term 'contracting authority' is able to preclude avoidance of entities, such as EBS, falling short of the Directive's remit.[73]

Subsequently, the CJEU held that for determining whether a body satisfies the condition set out in the first indent of the second subparagraph of Article 1(9) of Directive 2004/14/EC, it is necessary to consider the activities which it actually carries on.[74] Accordingly, the Court held that the effectiveness of the procurement Directive would not be fully upheld if the function of an entity which falls within the conditions set out in the second subparagraph of Article 1(9) could be omitted due to the fact that the tasks which it performs in the general interest having a character other than industrial or commercial, were not delegated to it at the time of its creation.[75] The Directive does not distinguish whether or not the national statutes of such an entity were or were not amended to reflect actual changes in its sphere of activity; the entity is still caught regardless.[76] The mere existence or even absence of needs in the general interest not having an industrial or commercial character must be evaluated objectively; 'the legal form of the provisions in which those needs are mentioned being immaterial in that regard'.[77] Irrespective of whether EBS's obligation to provide needs in the general interest not having an industrial or commercial character has not been officially contained within national statutes, it can still be objectively established through the written contract made with the city of Vienna.[78] In conclusion, a body which was not intentionally established to fulfil needs in the general interest not having an industrial or commercial character, but for some reason has consequently acquired accountability for such needs (which it has since actually satisfied), provided that it fulfils the conditions laid out in Article 1(9); and as long as its provision of needs in the general interest and so on can be established objectively, it is classified as a body governed by public law for the purposes of the Public Procurement Directives.

DIFFERING INTERPRETATION OF THE DIRECTIVES' DEFINITION 'BODIES GOVERNED BY PUBLIC LAW' UNDER UK NATIONAL LAW: THE *ALSTOM* CASE

An interesting case which was presented in early 2012 to the High Court within the UK, considered as a primary question whether Eurostar International Limited (EIL) fell within the definition of a 'contracting authority' for the purposes of the 'Public Contract Regulations' (PCR).[79] While it focused largely on the Utilities Contract Regulations 2006 (UCR) the judge gave detailed examination to the definition of

---

72 Ibid., at para. 49.
73 See Case C-237/99, *Commission v France* (fn. 41), at para. 43.
74 See Case C-44/96, *Mannesmann Analagenbau* (fn. 32), at para. 25.
75 See Case C-470/99, *Universale-Bau AG* (fn. 19), at paras. 57–59.
76 Ibid., at para. 61.
77 Ibid., at para. 60; Case C-360/96, *BFI Holding* [1998] ECR I-6821, at para. 63.
78 See Case C-470/99, *Universale-Bau AG* (fn. 19), at paras. 62 and 63.
79 See *Alstom Transport v Eurostar International Ltd* [2012] EWHC 28 (Ch).

'contracting authority'. The UCR and the Regulations give effect to the EU Procurement Directives in the UK and, although the implementing Regulations should be interpreted in the light of the Directives,[80] the two regimes are *mutually exclusive*. Therefore, under the UK Regulations, a 'contracting authority' can *only* be a body within the UK. The equivalent EU Directive, on the other hand, applies the definition to a body within any Member State.

With regards to the company's background, EIL is a joint venture between SNCF (wholly owned by the French government) 55 per cent, London and Continental Railways Ltd (LCR) (wholly owned by the British Secretary of State for Transport) 40 per cent and SNCB (wholly owned by the Belgian government) 5 per cent.[81] When the case was brought EIL still held a monopoly over rail services through the Channel Tunnel; Alstom Transport maintained that EIL was a body 'governed by public law', arguing that it has legal personality; it was established for the specific purpose of meeting needs in the general interest, not having an industrial or commercial character; and that it is subject to management supervision by other bodies subject to public law.

It is clear from the judgment that Alstom did not contend whether EIL had legal personality, as it was clear that this was satisfied. The question therefore was whether the activities were of an industrial or commercial nature. Through interpreting briefly the CJEU's case-law, the High Court examined the extent of competition within the given market.[82] As previously identified, the presence of extensive competition identifies the entity's activities as likely to have an industrial or commercial character.[83] On this issue, Alstom submitted that EIL was the sole operator through the Channel Tunnel, and was not directly open to competition. Alstom further relied strongly on the facts that EIL was not operating profitably and that very substantial State aid had to be provided from the UK government to enable it to recapitalise for restructuring, and indeed for it to afford the procurement of the next generation of trains. Receiving substantial amounts of State aid precludes an entity from having an industrial or commercial character within the terms of the Procurement Directives. Here the judge held that it is important to look to the 'commercial character' of the undertaking, not its profitability. The underlying rationale of this criterion is that it serves as an indication of whether the undertaking would be expected to take procurement decisions on economic grounds.

Although EIL may only have been able to continue in business as a result of State aid, that aid was being given precisely in order to enable it to operate for the future as a commercial entity. It was restructuring aid and part of a package of measures designed to restore EIL's long-term viability and make the company independently sustainable. That package further included a revised access charging system, reducing the charges so as to help attract new entrants to the market. The overall package involved a restructuring of LCR, separating its interest in Eurostar (through EIL) from the operation of the Channel link, with the consequence that EIL acquired more of an

[80] See Case C-106/89, *Marleasing*[1990] ECR I-415, at para. 8; and Cases C-397/01 to C-403/01, *Pfeiffer* [2004] ECR I-8835.

[81] See *Alstom Transport* (fn. 79), at para. 11.

[82] See Case C-18/01, *Korhonen* [2003] ECR I-5345, at para. 32.

[83] See Case C-360/96, *BFI Holding* (fn. 60), at paras. 48–49.

independent commercial character than beforehand, so that it could operate in a more competitive environment.

EIL argued that, while it was the sole operator through the Channel Tunnel, there were still many other options for crossing the Channel, that is, by coach, plane, car and ferry.[84] It was also the case that the market had been de-regulated[85] and that from 2013 *Deutsche Bahn* would be operating a train service through the Channel Tunnel.[86] Arguably, EIL was relying on the argument that they would be openly facing *future* competition from other companies. The High Court judge held that it was right to take the surrounding transport market across the Channel into consideration and the future in which competition would increase.[87] Roth J held that under such unrestricted commercial use of the infrastructure, it does not have the character of being protected from competition; as other competing operators may use the same infrastructure.[88] Roth J further held that EIL has no public service obligation: unlike the UK Franchised rail operators, it is not obliged to provide any particular level of service, capacity or frequency other than as a result of the contractual arrangements which it enters into, and it is run as a commercial entity. Thus, on that basis the court found that EIL's activities were of an industrial/commercial character, not falling within the definition of a body governed by public law and not a contracting authority for the purposes of the UK Statute and of the Utilities Directive.

Roth J further examined whether EIL was subject to management supervision by other bodies subject to public law. Clearly, as mentioned above all three of the joint venture partners – SNCF, SNCB and LCR were owned or controlled by the governments of Member States. Under the Directive this would be sufficient to show management supervision by other bodies subject to public law. The judge however took an idealistic view that the UK government had specifically implemented the Directive so that only UK bodies could be considered contracting authorities for the purposes of the PCR. Accordingly, under the Regulations as ratified within the PCR, but not under the Directive, a 'contracting authority' can only be a body within the UK; whereas Directive 2004/17/EC applies the definition to a body within any Member State. As soon as SNCF was taken out of the picture, it was not possible to argue that EIL was subject to management supervision by other bodies subject to public law.

The general purpose of the EU public procurement regime is to contribute to completion and operation of the internal market, so that the awarding of public contracts is not influenced by national preference but made on the basis of economic considerations.[89] The Directives' other purpose is to create uniformity and certainty across Member States, not a variety of interpretations. Roth J considered that the domestic definition of contracting authority should not be interpreted in accordance with the Directive and so it did not extend to non-English bodies, stating that "*in my*

---

84 See *Eurotunnel (No 3)* [1995] 4 CMLR 801, at paras. 64–66.
85 Directive 91/440 (OJ L 237 of 24.8.1991).
86 See *Alstom Transport* (fn. 79), at para. 26.
87 Ibid., at para. 66.
88 Ibid., at paras. 65–66.
89 See Case C-18/01, *Korhonen* [2003] ECR I-5345, at para. 32.

judgment, that would go beyond the bounds of a generous, purposive interpretation".[90] It is debateable whether Roth J made the correct decision in considering solely the UK statutes' definition of 'contracting authorities' and not the wider EU Directive definition[91] combined with the CJEU's functional and extensive interpretation of the applicable case-law.[92] It is likely the applicants will appeal the decision; however, it will be interesting to see if the Court of Appeal alters the current legal standing, in favour of a wider functional and effective interpretation of the CPR, in light of the Procurement Directives.

PRIVATE LIMITED COMPANIES MEETING A NEED IN THE GENERAL INTEREST

A clear question was submitted to the Court as to whether a limited company (Taitotalo) established, owned and managed by a regional or local authority was to be regarded as a contracting authority meeting a specific need in the general interest, not having an industrial or commercial character.[93] Taitotalo was essentially a limited company whose capital is wholly owned by the town of Varkaus (Finland), and whose objects were to buy, sell and lease real property and shares in property companies, and to organise and supply property maintenance services and other related services needed for the management of those properties and shares. The company's board had three members, who were officials of the town of Varkaus, appointed by the general meeting of the company's shareholders, at which the town had 100 per cent of the voting rights.

Taitotalo submitted to the Court that its sole objective was to promote the conditions for the exercise of the activities of specific undertakings, not for the exercise generally of economic activity in the town of Varkaus, while the fact that it was owned and financed by a contracting authority was of no relevance, since, in the case in the main proceedings, it met industrial or commercial needs. Further to this, Taitotalo maintained that it attained at market price the land needed for the building works at issue in the main proceedings and that the financing of the project would be taken in hand essentially by the private sector, by means of bank loans secured by mortgages.[94] Thus, contextually Taitotalo was stating that its activity could not be compared with those at issue in the *BFI Holding* and *Commission v France* cases; the leasing of premises for industrial or commercial use cannot in any case be regarded as within the prerogatives which by their very nature are part of the exercise of public powers.[95] On the other hand however, the Finish government disputed that Taitotalo's primary aim was not to

---

90 See *Alstom Transport* (fn. 79), at para. 93.

91 See Case C-165/91, *Van Munster* [1994] ECR I-4661, at para. 34; and Case C-262/97, *Engelbrecht* [2000] ECR I-7321, at para. 39.

92 See Case C-283/00, *Commission v Spain* (fn. 19), at paras. 48, 50 and 51.

93 See Case C-18/01, *Arkkitehtuuritoimisto Riitta Korhonen Oy, Arkkitehtitoimisto Pentti Toivanen Oy, Rakennuttajatoimisto Vilho Tervomaa andVarkauden Taitotalo Oy.* [2003] ECR I-5321, at para. 32.

94 Ibid., at paras. 35 and 36.

95 Ibid., at para. 37.

generate profits by its activity but to create favourable conditions for the development of economic activities in the territory of the town of Varkaus, which fitted in perfectly with the functions which regional and local authorities may assume by virtue of the autonomy guaranteed to them by the Finnish constitution. In addition, they submitted that the core and substantive objective of Directive 92/50 (now Directive 2004/18) would be compromised if such a company were not regarded as a contracting authority within the meaning of the directive, as municipalities might in that case by tempted to establish, in their traditional sphere of activity, other undertakings whose contracts would be outside the scope of the directive.[96] Effectively, the Finish government was attempting to show that Taitotalos's activity was seeking to meet a need in the general interest because of the strong incentive it gave to trade and the development of business activities in the territory of the town of Varkaus.

Subsequently, the Court held that Taitotalo met a 'demand' in the 'general interest', where it acquired services promoting the development of industrial/commercial activities on the territory of that regional/local authority.[97] To conclude whether that 'demand' has no industrial/commercial character, the national court is *obligated* to evaluate the circumstances *after* the company was set up and the conditions attached to its activity. Activities such as those carried on by Taitotalo were deemed as meeting needs in the general interest, in that they are likely to give a stimulus to trade and the economic and social development of the local authority concerned, since the location of undertakings on the territory of a municipality often has favourable repercussions for that municipality in terms of creation of jobs, increase of tax revenue and improvement of the supply and demand of goods and services.[98] The procurement Directives would not be entirely upheld if the application to a body satisfying the conditions,[99] could be omitted because the tasks in the 'general interest' having a character other than industrial/commercial which it carries out in practice, were *not* entrusted to it at the time of its establishment.[100] Nevertheless, the existence or absence of needs in the 'general interest' not having an industrial/commercial character *must* be evaluated objectively.[101] An entity not founded to satisfy explicit needs in the 'general interest' not having an industrial/commercial character, but which has subsequently taken responsibility for such needs, and which it has since actually satisfied, fulfils the condition required by Article 1(9)(a) is thus, regarded as a 'body-governed-by-public-law'.[102]

96 Ibid., at paras. 38–39.
97 Ibid.
98 Ibid., at para. 45.
99 See Article 1(9) of Directive 2004/18/EC, *op. cit.*
100 See C. Bovis, (fn. 1), at p. 203.
101 See Case C-360/96, *BFI Holding* (fn. 60), at para. 63.
102 See Case C-470/99, *Universale-Bau* (fn. 19).

THE CONCEPT OF DUAL CAPACITY OF CONTRACTING AUTHORITIES

The 'dual capacity' of a body as a public service provider/commercial undertaking, is an additional factor to consider when determining whether an entity is a 'body governed by public law'.[103] The concept of 'dual capacity' of contracting authorities was raised in *Strohal,* where it was submitted to the Court that if an entity's 'public service obligations' displace its commercial presence, it could be considered a 'body covered by public law'.[104] The entity concerned (*Österreichische Staatsdruckerei*) ("ÖS") was established in order to produce, on an exclusive basis, official administrative documents, some of which required secrecy or security measures, such as passports, driving licences and identity cards, whilst others were intended for the dissemination of legislative, regulatory and administrative documents of the State. According to the relevant legislation, the Court conveyed that ÖS was established for the purpose of meeting needs in the general interest, not having an industrial or commercial character. Such a conclusion was reached due to the fact that the documents which the ÖS produced were closely linked to public order and the institutional operation of the State; the majority of the shares in the ÖS were held by the Austrian State.[105] It was held immaterial that such an entity is free to carry out other activities in addition to its appointed task. The fact, raised by the Austrian Government in its written observations, that meeting needs in the general interest constitutes only a relatively small proportion of the activities actually pursued by the ÖS was also found irrelevant, provided that it continued to attend to the needs which it was specifically required to meet.[106]

Decisively, the wording within Article 1(9) of Directive 2004/18 does not exclude the possibility that a contracting authority may pursue other activities in addition to its specific task of meeting needs in the general interest, not having an industrial or commercial character. Authoritatively, if an entity's public service activities are minimal, then it falls foul of the procurement Directives' requirements of a 'contracting authority'.[107] The CJEU, on the principle of legal certainty, eliminated selective application of the Directives in the case of 'dual capacity contracting authorities'.[108] The Court further added that only the purpose for which an entity is founded is applicable in order to categorise it as body governed by public law and not the separation between public and private activities.[109] Nonetheless, the CJEU recognised 'dualism' in *Strohal*, by holding that 'contracting authorities' have the ability to carry out commercial activities as well as activities meeting the requirements of a 'general interest' not having industrial/commercial nature.[110]

[103] See Case C-44/96, *Mannesmann Analagenbau* (fn. 32).
[104] Ibid., at para. 16.
[105] Ibid., at para. 24.
[106] Ibid., at para. 25.
[107] Ibid., at paras. 17–35.
[108] Ibid., at paras. 34–35
[109] Ibid., at para. 31.
[110] Ibid.

Critically, with the question presented, the Court in *Strohal* confirmed the principle/possibility of dualism, allowing contracting authorities to execute a 'dual' range of activities. Effectively an entity is able to procure work and services for the public, as well as to jointly partake in commercial activities. More importantly, the Court emphasised that the proportion between activities pursued by an entity, which on the one hand aim to meet needs of general interest not having an industrial or commercial character, and commercial activities on the other is irrelevant for the characterisation of that entity as a body governed by public law.[111] A point which was reiterated again and again by the Court was that of the intention behind the establishment of the entity in question, that is, whether the entity carries the specific purpose of meeting needs in the general interest, not having an industrial or commercial character. Understandably, specificity does not signify exclusivity of purpose, but merely the intention of establishment to meet general needs.

Before the *Stohal* case, the Court had been unable to observe conjoint corporate relationships and the influence the procurement Directives had in this area. From the Judgment it is clear that the Court did not set a clear precedent with regard to such organisations; however it undoubtedly specified the essential conclusions/pointers for Member States' national courts, so that they are able to distinguish and identify public and private undertakings who are trying to avoid the remit of the public procurement Directives. Therefore, when a national court is examining such a relationship it should identify the actual purpose/function for which the entity in doubt has been created. It must be noted that the dual capacity of a contracting authority is immaterial as to the application of public procurement rules; for example: if a contracting authority assigns the rights and obligations of a public contract to an entity which is not a contracting authority, that entity is caught by the public procurement rules. *Ipso facto*, the concept of dual capacity prevents private and public entities operating within the public sector from hiding behind the curtain of commercialism.

THE NOTION OF PRIVATE 'BODIES' PERFORMING PUBLIC SERVICES

The *Foster* principle[112] established that state accountability could not embrace privatised enterprises. However, it is evident that an entity's private law 'status' does not exclude it from being branded as a 'contracting authority'.[113] The 'effectiveness' of the Public Procurement Directives would be minimal if such an entity could be omitted under Member States' national law by which it is bound, falling within the scope of private law.[114] An entity which is governed by private law but which, however, meets the relevant criteria of 'bodies governed by public law' within the first, second and third indents of the second subparagraph of Article 1(9) of Directive 2004/18 (and

[111] Ibid., at paras. 25 and 34.

[112] See Case 188/89, *Foster v British Gas* [1990] ECR I-1313.

[113] See Case C-214/00, *Commission v Spain*, (fn. 19), at paras. 54, 55 and 60.

[114] See C. Bovis, '*Developing Public Procurement Regulation: Jurisprudence and its influence on Law Making*' (2006) 43(2) *Common Market Law Review* pp. 461–495, at p. 472.

Article 2(1)(a) of Directive 2004/17) will be conclusively held to be a contracting authority for the purposes of the public procurement Directives. An important distinction to identify is that of the activities relating to public authority and those which fall within the private domain (although carried out by public persons). Such a distinction has been clearly reached by the Courts.[115]

The question of whether private bodies performing public services would fall within the cumulative criteria of bodies governed by public law was considered in the case of *Commission v Spain*.[116] Here the Commission brought an action against the Kingdom of Spain for failing correctly to transpose into its national legal system Council Directive 93/36/EEC (now 2004/18/EC). One of the Commission's three grounds for action claimed that following transposition of the procurement Directive into national law, it excluded the possibility of private entities which may satisfy the requirements of contracting authorities under the relevant cumulative criteria set out in Article 1(b) of Directives 93/36/EEC and 93/37/EEC. Further to this, the Commission asserted that the concept 'body governed by public law' is a Community-wide concept of an independent nature.[117] In addition, the Commission upheld the Court's jurisprudence,[118] submitting that a body governed by public law must be understood as a body which fulfils the three cumulative conditions set out in the second subparagraph of Article 1(b) of the relevant Directives, which must be interpreted purposefully, utilising the true function of the Directives.[119] As expected, the Spanish Government opposed the Commission's arguments, maintaining that a literal interpretation of the definition of 'body governed by public law' should be affirmed, disregarding private bodies falling with the Directives' remit.[120] The government further argued that the relevant Directives do not include commercial companies under public control, quoting Directive 93/38/EEC (now Directive 2004/17/EC) as a means for its defence.[121]

In response, the Court first upheld that according to settled case-law the definition of 'body governed by public law' is a concept of Community law which must be given a 'uniform' interpretation.[122] Whether a private law entity is to be labelled as a body governed by public law, it is essential only to ascertain whether the body in question satisfies the three cumulative conditions laid down in the second subparagraph of Article 1(b) of the procurement Directives.[123] The clear stance of the Court was to convey to the European Community that an entity's private law status does not impede

[115] See Case C-364/92, *SAT Fluggesellschafeten* [1994] ECR 1-43.

[116] See Case C-84/03, *Commission of the European Communities v Kingdom of Spain* [2005] ECR I-139.

[117] Ibid., at para. 23.

[118] See Case C-44/96, *Mannesmann Analagenbau* (fn. 32), at paras. 17–35.

[119] See Case 31/87, *Beentjes* (fn. 14); Case C-360/96, *BFI Holding* (fn. 59).

[120] See Case C-84/03, *Kingdom of Spain* (fn. 116), at para. 24.

[121] See Directive 93/38/EEC (OJ L 199, 9.8.1993, pp. 84–138) which coordinated the procurement procedures of entities operating in the water, energy, transport and telecommunications sectors. It distinguishes between the notion of 'body governed by public law', which is the same in the Public Contracts Directives, *op. cit.*, and 'public undertaking', whose definition corresponds to the definition of public commercial company.

[122] See Case C-84/03, *Kingdom of Spain* (fn. 116), at para. 27.

[123] Ibid., at para. 28.

or disqualify it from being classified as a contracting authority; express reference within the Directives is not needed to catch private entities. Finally, a private entity is not excluded from being incompatible with the requirement of non-industrial or commercial character of the general interest needs,[124] due to the fact that these aspects are anticipated to be evaluated independently of its legal title.

Companies which are directed by private law created for the explicit function of meeting needs in the general interest, not having industrial or commercial character, holding legal personality; are financed by public authorities or other 'entities governed by public law'; or are subject to supervision by the latter, or have an administrative/managerial board consisting of more than 50 per cent members appointed by public authorities or other entities governed by public law, are deemed to be 'contracting authorities' for the purposes of the Procurement Directives.[125] The CJEU has held that such organisations *could* be classified as 'bodies governed by public-law' if they fulfil three conditions within Article 1(9).[126] Such a *broad* interpretation by the CJEU captures all entities that fall within the above criteria, preventing Member State national law from excluding effective application of the Public Procurement Directives. However, the problematic concept of the specificity, reasoning the existence of the establishment to meet needs in the 'general interest', has been approached by reference to the reasons and the objectives *behind* its establishment.[127]

When deciding if a 'private' body is a 'contracting authority' under the procurement Directives, identifying whether the entity does not aim primarily at making a profit, the risks associated with the activity, and observation of any public financing of the activity in question is required.[128] More recently, in *Oymanns*, a statutory sickness-fund which was indirectly financed by the State, and without any consideration in return, received mandatory contributions set by law from employers and private individual members, was held to be a 'contracting authority' under the Directive.[129] Conclusively, the fund was found to be financed mostly by the State, as a result of the fixed conditions of contributions, and had the sole objective to perform interests in the 'general needs', with no industrial/commercial character.[130] Similarly, in *Bayerischer Rundfunk*,[131] it was deemed that compulsory fee contributions by private individuals to a broadcasting fund, the level of which were set by national law, constituted state financing of the relevant undertaking, consequently bringing the entity into the definition of 'body governed by public law' for the purposes of the Directive.

The cases *Adolf Truley* and *Korhonen* also held private entities to be contracting authorities, where a limited company established, owned and managed by a regional authority meets a need in the general interest which has not a commercial or an

---

[124] Ibid., at para. 29.

[125] See Case C-44/96, *Mannesmann Analagenbau* (fn. 32), at paras. 20–21.

[126] See Article 1(9) of Directive 2004/18/EC, *op. cit.*

[127] See Case C-223/99, *Agora Srl* (fn. 63); C-360/96, *BFI Holding* (fn. 60); and Case C-44/96, *Mannesmann Analagenbau* (fn. 32).

[128] See Case C-18/01, *Korhonen and Others* [2003] ECR I-5321, at para. 51; Case C-107/98, *Teckal Slr v Comune di Viano* [1999] ECR I-8121, at paras. 49–51.

[129] See Case C-300/07, *Hans & Christophorus Oymanns* (fn. 38).

[130] See Case C-337/06, *Bayerischer Rundfunk et al v GEWA* [2007] ECR I-11173.

[131] Ibid.

industrial character, where it acquires services for the development of business and commercial activities on the territory of that regional authority.[132] Specifically, *Korhonen* identified that 'contracting authorities' are able to set up legally independent entities, offering services to third parties under normal market conditions.[133] Irrefutably, entities which aim to make profit, bear the losses related to the exercise of their activities, and perform no public tasks are not classified as contracting authorities for the purposes of the Public Procurement Directives.[134]

Similarly, in *Commission v Spain*, the issue of whether private companies under state control fall within the definition of 'contracting authorities' under the Procurement Directives was considered.[135] Here a private Spanish company, SIEPSA, was contracted to build prisons for the Spanish government. SIEPSA performed transactions, such as locating and acquiring buildings to be fitted out as new prisons and the development and execution of preparatory and construction works. The Spanish Government firstly contended that; '*generally* [...] *Directive*[s] *93/37* [and] *93/36/EEC* [now Directive 2004/18], [do] *not include commercial companies under public control, such as SIEPSA, within the notion of bodies governed by public law*'. As previously contented by the Spanish government,[136] the latter point is supposedly supported by the fact that Directive 93/38 (now Directive 2004/17) illustrates a definite difference between the concept of a body governed by public law, and the notion of a public undertaking, the definition of which resembles that of a public commercial company.[137] While they upheld that SIEPSA satisfied the two last provisions under Article 1(b) of the Directive, accordingly, SIEPSA retained the characteristics of a commercial orientated company, meeting general-interest needs of a commercial character. It was the Government's belief that SIEPSA should encounter the same conduct as private undertakings supplying the gas, electricity or water sectors which satisfy essential social requirements and are governed by private law. It was also the Government's interpretation that the concept of 'body governed by public law' is dependent on the lists contained in Annex I (Annex III) to the Directive, suggesting that SIEPSA did not belong to any of those categories and was not an independent body.

The core mission of the company was to build new prisons for the needs of society, and consisted of a general interest condition of a commercial nature, acting in the general interest.[138] In addition, the Spanish government submitted that that company's activity could not be regarded as 'administrative' as it generated profits and that it was subject to free competition; although the absence of competition is not a condition necessarily to be taken into account in defining a body governed by public law.[139] It further contended that because such a company did not appear directly/indirectly within

[132] See Case C-373/00 *Adolf Truly* (fn. 54), at para. 66; and Case C-18/01 *Korhonen and Others* (fn. 128), at paras. 48 and 59.

[133] See Case C-18/01, *Korhonen and Others* (fn. 128), at para. 51.

[134] Ibid., at paras. 51–53.

[135] See Case C-283/00, *Commission v Spain* (fn. 19).

[136] See Case C-84/03, *Kingdom of Spain* (fn. 116), at para. 24.

[137] See Case C-283/00, *Commission v Spain* (fn. 19), at para. 37.

[138] See Case C-283/00, *Commission v Spain* (fn. 19), at para. 43.

[139] See Case C-360/96, *BFI Holding* (fn. 60), at para. 47.

the list[140] of 'bodies governed by public law', it fell outside of the Directives' definition of a 'contracting authority'. It rounded up its argument by submitting that subsequently, if the State assists the general interest and since it has a majority shareholding in State commercial companies, it is plausible to assume that such entities will, throughout their existence continue to be so consistently. "*If in order for the body to be classified as a contracting authority, it were sufficient that it should perform tasks in the general interest, such as contributing to the imposition of criminal penalties, then the condition that those tasks should not be industrial or commercial in character would be meaningless*".[141]

From the perspective of the Commission, SIEPSA fell within the relevant criteria and was a contracting authority under the relevant Directives. First, the Commission submitted that the Spanish government had clearly failed to implement the procurement Directives effectively into national law and that the functional interpretation of the notion 'body governed by public law' as interpreted through the Court's case-law implies that the latter notion covers commercial companies under public control. Further to this, the Commission highlighted the distinction between public undertaking and bodies governed by public law, in that bodies governed by public law are created specifically to meet needs in the general interest having no industrial or commercial character, whereas public undertakings act to satisfy needs of an industrial or commercial character.[142] The Government's argument relating to Annex 1 of the Directive was criticised by the Commission, holding that the lists are not exhaustive, leaving open the possibility for any entity to satisfy the cumulative criteria laid down in Article 1(b), which does not appear on the list.[143] Thus, according to the Commission, the interpretation favoured by the Spanish Government contradicts the fundamental objective of the Directive. Crucially, Article 1(9) of the Directive 2004/18 is not fundamentally concerned with the distinction between entities which are public or private, their legal form, but rather looks at the purpose or function for which the bodies in question were created. Further to this, the Commission added that SIEPSA was clearly established for the specific purpose of meeting needs in the general interest, not having an industrial or commercial character. The general interest is closely linked to public order and the institutional operation[144] of the State and by imposing penalties depriving persons of their liberty, does not per se hold an industrial or commercial character.

With regard to the Spanish Government's argument that SIEPSA operated under free competition, the Commission conveyed that, even though its core activities were not subject to competition, and even if it should be conceded that it carries out an activity subject to free competition, does not mean that it cannot be regarded as a contracting authority for the purposes of the Directives.[145] Finally the Commission reasoned that SIEPSA's activity cannot be compared with private-sector activity, that is, of a commercial nature. As the information was presented, SIEPSA did not offer prisons on the penal establishments market (there is no such market) but, however, acted as the

140 See Annex III of Directive 2004/18/EC, *op. cit.*

141 See Case C-283/00, *Commission v Spain* (fn. 19), at para. 49.

142 See Directive 93/38/EEC, *op. cit.*

143 See Case C-360/96, *BFI Holding* (fn. 60), at para. 50.

144 See Case C-44/96, *Mannesmann Analagenbau* (fn. 32), at para. 24.

145 See Case C-360/96, *BFI Holding* (fn. 60), at para. 47.

agent of the State government in order to lend a hand in the construction, management and selling of prison properties. On the conception of the separation of SIEPSA's activities by the Spanish Government, it was clear that the Court had previously answered this argument. It had declared that the collection and treatment of public waste[146] and the printing of official government documents[147] are needs in the general interest, not having an industrial or commercial character. The Court did not separate the entity's activities, it identified the organisation's core purpose/function and its links to the State. Even if the entities core objective is to make profit it is irrelevant if it serves the needs in the general interest, not having an industrial or commercial character.

After considering the facts and examining both party's opinions, the Court held that SIEPSA was clearly established for the specific purpose of meeting needs in the 'general interest', not having an industrial/commercial character and, consequentially, was held to be a 'contracting authority'.[148] The Court observed that, in accordance with established case-law, in light of the dual purpose of opening up competition and of transparency pursued by the Directive, the concept of 'body governed by public law' must be given an interpretation as functional as it is broad.[149] For the purposes of settling the issue of the classification of an entity governed by public law within the meaning of the second paragraph of Article 1(9) of the Directive, as previously held, it is necessary to establish only whether or not the body concerned fulfils the three conditions set out in that provision.

Importantly, the CJEU stated: 'for that body's status as a body governed by private law[150] does not constitute a criterion capable of excluding it from being classified as a contracting authority for the purposes of the Directive'.[151] Commercial companies under public control such as SIEPSA are not omitted from the *scope* of both the Spanish rules and the Community rules on procurement. According to the Court, Directive 93/38 was adopted for the purpose of extending the application of the Community rules regulating public procurement to the water, energy, transport and telecommunications sectors which were not covered by the procurement Directives; however, it encapsulated a functional approach similar to that of the other Directives. The contracting entities functioning in the areas regulated by Directive 93/38/EC were incorporated within its scope on condition that the entity fulfilled certain criteria, their legal personality and the rules under which they were moulded are held to be irrelevant. In addition, if a specific body does not appear in the list (Annex III, which is not exhaustive),[152] its legal and factual situation must be analysed individually, to see whether it meets a need in the 'general interest'.[153]

---

[146] Ibid.

[147] See Case C-44/96, *Mannesmann Analagenbau* (fn. 32).

[148] See Case C-44/96, *Mannesmann Analagenbau* (fn. 32), paras. 20–21 and 24–25; Case C-283/0 (fn. 19), at paras. 48, 50–51; Case C-470/99, *Universale-Bau* (fn. 19), at paras. 51–53; and C-373/00 *Adolf Truley* (fn. 54), at para. 43.

[149] See Case C-283/00, *Commission v Spain* (fn. 19), at para. 53.

[150] See C-237/99, *Commission v France* (fn. 40), at paras. 41–43; Case C-470/99, *Universale-Bau* (fn. 19), at paras. 51–53.

[151] See Case C-283/00, *Commission v Spain* (fn. 19), at paras. 54 and 55.

[152] See Case C-373/00, *Adolf Truley* (fn. 54), at paras. 39, 44.

[153] See Case C-18/01, *Korhonen*, (fn. 128), at paras. 48–49.

Establishing whether or not there exists a need in the general interest not having an industrial or commercial character full analysis of the relevant legal and factual circumstances, of the entity must take place, such as when the body concerned was formed and the conditions attached to its activity, the competition within the given market, whether its primary aim is not the making of profits, whether it bears the risks associated with the activity, and finally whether there is any public financing of the activity.[154] If the body operates in normal market conditions, aims at making a profit and bears the losses associated with the exercise of its activity, it is unlikely that the needs it aims at meeting are not of an industrial or commercial nature. It was held that the fact that SIEPSA conducts its activities for profit and even if its activities did generate profits (reported losses in 1997–98), it is implausible in the circumstances that it should be in itself the company's chief aim;[155] which is to support the execution of State prison policy. Finally, the Court conveyed that the imposition of criminal penalties is one of the rights and powers granted to the State. As a result there is *no official market* for the goods and services offered by SIEPSA in the planning and creation of prisons. Therefore, activities such as paying off the costs of and the setting up of prisons, (SIEPSA's primary objectives), are not subject to market competition; and are not entirely directed by economic factors.[156]

PUBLIC UTILITIES AND 'UNDERTAKINGS' AS BODIES GOVERNED BY PUBLIC LAW

Towards the end of 2012 the Council of the European Union published updated wording for the proposed Directive of the European Parliament and of the Council on procurement by entities operating in the water, energy, transport and postal services sectors. This draft Directive is intended to replace the Utilities Directive 2004/17/EC (the "Utilities Directive") which requires entities in certain sectors to follow rules of competitive procurement designed to ensure a single market in these sectors which have in the past been heavily dominated by state entities.

The concept of a public undertaking has always been different from that of a 'body governed by public law', in that the latter are created specifically to meet needs in the 'general interest' having no industrial/commercial character, whereas public undertakings act to satisfy needs of an industrial/commercial character.[157] Article 1(2) of the Utilities Directive forms another category of 'contracting authorities' namely, 'public undertakings'.[158] The Directive defines a 'public undertaking' as being an entity over which the State may exercise directly or indirectly a 'dominant influence' by having ownership of it (that is, it is the majority shareholder), financial influence (capital finance), or through legal instruments/regulations of the public undertaking (that is, the

[154] See C-373/00, *Adolf Truly* (fn. 54), at para. 66, and Case C-18/01, *Korhonen* (fn. 128), at paras. 48 and 59.

[155] See Case C-280/03, *Commission v Spain* (fn. 19), at para. 88.

[156] See Case C-373/00, *Adolf Truley* (fn. 54), at para. 42, and *Korhonen* (fn. 128), paras. 51–52.

[157] See Case C-118/85, *Commission v Italy*, [1987] ECR 2599.

[158] See Article 1(2) of Directive 93/38/EC, *op cit.*

power to appoint the board of directors).[159] Conclusively, 'public undertakings' are granted the exclusive rights to profits arising from their service; nonetheless, they are strictly controlled by the Utilities Directive. An entity governed by private law as a contracting authority is also compatible with the concept of public undertakings, in accordance with the Utilities Directive. It must be noted that fully privatised utilities can be excluded from the established procurement rules, where competition erases 'purchasing patterns based on non-economic considerations'.[160] Thus, self-regulation would inevitably unleash such contracting authorities from public procurement requirements. There are clear differences between the sectorial or utilities regime and the general regime. The general regime, which applies to a much wider range of bodies, is less flexible. This difference means that the field of application of the utilities regime is to be interpreted narrowly.[161]

Notably, with regard to private utility companies that are privatised, State accountability appeared to be minimal[162] until the enactment of the utilities Directives in the 1990s.[163] Such utilities bought under the Directives include the energy, telecommunications and water industries;[164] a substantive selection of the latter fall within the term 'bodies governed by public law'.[165] The Directive recognises such bodies as contracting entities, where the 'contracting authorities' exercise directly or indirectly a dominant influence by virtue of their ownership of them, their financial participation therein, or the rules which govern them.[166] Specifically, control is expanded beyond the 'dominant influence' notion found in the utilities Directive.[167] It also encapsulates undertakings which, although they are not contracting authorities or public undertakings, function on the basis of exclusive rights granted by a Member State through means of legislative, regulatory or administrative provisions.[168] As also noted earlier, under the test of dualism, is the ability of 'mixed-character' undertakings to be regarded as 'contracting authorities', provided that they pursue public interest functions of a non-industrial/commercial character.[169] Moreover, public undertakings cover utilities operators, which have been granted exclusive rights of exploitation of a service. Irrespective of their ownership, they are subject to the Utilities Directive in as much as the exclusivity of their operation precludes other entities from entering the relevant market under substantially the same competitive conditions.

159 See Article 1(2), 1(3) and 13 of Directive 93/38, *op. cit.*
160 See C. Bovis (fn. 1), at p. 193.
161 See Case C-393/06, *Ing. Aigner* [2008] ECR I-2339.
162 See Case C-188/89, *A. Foster and others v British Gas plc* [1990] ECR I-3313.
163 See Directives 90/531; 93/38; 98/4EEC, *op. cit.*
164 See Recital 2 of Directive 2004/17, *op. cit.*
165 See Article 1(1) of Directive 93/38, *op. cit.*
166 See Article 2(1)(b) of Directive 2004/17, *op. cit.*
167 Ibid.
168 See Article 2(3) of Directive 2004/17, *op. cit.*
169 See Case C-44/96, *Mannesmann Analagenbau* (fn. 32), at paras. 17–35.

IN-HOUSE PROCUREMENT ARRANGEMENTS IN RELATION TO 'CONTRACTING AUTHORITIES'

In-house contracts are contracts made between public authorities and are granted exemptions under the term 'contracting authority' of the procurement Directives[170] if they fulfil the required criteria.[171] The leading case, *Teckal*, established the non-applicability of the procurement rules to in-house relations.[172] First, the condition established by *Teckal* requires evidence of control similar to that which the contracting entity exercises over one of its own departments.[173] The concept of 'control' and the 'similarity' requirement constitute a comprehensive approach, including the company set-up and the contracting authority's shareholding majority.[174] Such corporate control indicates decisive influence over management actions, operational and strategic decisions; however, there is the possibility that minority shareholding capacity in corporations provides for rights enabling extended influence over prevailing decisions. 'Control' for the purposes of in-house exemptions, entails much more than 'dominant influence';[175] it should include individual management and operational decisions, combined with corporate control.

What is more, *Carbotermo* raised the question as to whether, the direct award of a contract for the supply of fuel for heating appliances in buildings owned by or within the competence of a public authority, and relating to operation, supervision and maintenance, to a joint stock company whose capital was jointly held by a joint stock company, of which the awarding authority was a public entity; and was the majority shareholder (99.98 per cent of the shares), or to a company (AGESP) in which a direct holding was owned not by the public authority but by another company (AGESP Holding), 99.98 per cent of whose capital was at that time owned by the public administration, compatible with Directive 93/36 (Directive 2004/18).[176] First, the Court noted that in accord with Article 1(a) of Directive 93/36/EC, it is satisfactory if a contract was concluded where the local authority exercises over the person concerned a control which is similar to that which it exercises over its own departments and, at the same time, that person carries out the essential part of its activities with the controlling local authority or authorities.[177]

The Court held that 'joint stock' public companies display similar control where a contracting authority holds, single-handedly or collectively, all the share capital in a single entity.[178] Nevertheless, if the controlling board comprises wide power control

---

170 See Case C-295/05, *Asociacion Nacional de Empresas Forestales (Asemfo) v Transformacion Agraria SA (Tragsa) and Administracion del Estado* [2007] ECR I-2999, at para. 65.

171 See Articles 1(3) and 13 of Directive 2004/17, *op. cit.*

172 See Case C-107/98, *Teckal Slr* (fn. 128).

173 Ibid., at paras. 11–15 and 49–51.

174 Ibid., at para. 50.

175 See C. Bovis, 'Public Procurement in the EU: Jurisprudence and Conceptual Directions' (2012) 49(1) *Common Market Law Review* 253; and Article 2(1)(b) of Directive 2004/17.

176 See Case C-340/04, *Carbotermo SpA, Consorzio Alisei v Comune di Busto Arsizio, AGESP SpA* [2006] ECR I-4137, at paras. 36–39; and Case C-231/03, *Coname* [2005] ECR I-7287, at paras. 25–30.

177 See Case C-340/04, *Carbotermo* (fn. 176), at para. 50.

178 Ibid., at paras. 36–39; and Case C-231/03, *Coname* (fn. 176), at paras. 5 and 28.

and there is no power to counter their decisions, the similarity of control is not present.[179] Accordingly, the relevant national statutes of AGESP Holding and AGESP granted the Board of Directors extensive powers for the general and particular management of the company. The statutes did not reserve for the Comune di Busto Arsizio (municipality of Busto Arsizio) any control or specific voting powers for limiting the powers conferred to the Boards of Directors. The control exercised by the Comune di Busto Arsizio was found to be considerably limited. Thus, the Court held that Directive 93/36 prevents the direct award of a public supply and service contract to a joint stock company whose Board of Directors has abundant managerial/decision making powers, which it may exercise autonomously and whose share capital is, at present, held entirely by another joint stock company whose majority shareholder is, in turn, the contracting authority.[180]

Similar control exercised by a contracting authority over an entity is principally the majority shareholders' rights granted[181] by Member States' company regulations; thus, such control cannot be classified as being similar to that exercised upon the contracting authority's own departments.[182] Conclusively, if an entity is jointly controlled, the control criterion in *Teckal* is fulfilled if the contracting authority has control over the relevant entity similar to that exercised over their own controlled departments;[183] and it is fulfilled if joint control is exercised by the majority of controlling contracting authorities.[184] The concept of control must bc understood in functional and not in formal terms.[185] The control exercised over an entity or an undertaking by a public authority must be similar to that which the authority exercises over its own departments, but not indistinguishable and must be effective; it need not be exercised individually.[186] In the case of inter-municipal mutual organisations, where its members are contracting authorities, if it is evidenced that joint control is employed by the majority of the leading contracting authorities, then it is sufficient for the similarity of control criterion to be met.[187]

In *Stadt Halle* a question arose as to whether the public procurement rules apply where a 'contracting authority' intends to conclude a public contract with a company governed by private law, legally distinct from the authority and in which it has a majority capital holding and exercises a certain control.[188] Here, the City of Halle awarded to RPL Lochau a contract to draw up a plan for the pre-treatment, recovery

179 See Case C-340/04, *Carbotermo* (fn. 176), at paras. 58–72.

180 Ibid., at para. 47.

181 See Case C-410/04, *Associazione Nazionale Autotrasporto Viaggiatori (ANAV) v Comune di Bari, AMTAB Servizio SpA* [2006] ECR I-3303.

182 See C. Bovis, (fn. 175), at p. 254.

183 See Case C-340/04, *Carbotermo* (fn. 176), at para. 57.

184 See C-324/07, *Coditel Brabant SA v Commune d'Uccle, Région de Bruxelles-Capitale* [2009] ECR I-8457.

185 See Case C-283/00, *Commission v Spain* (fn. 19), at para. 69.

186 See Case C-458/03, *Parking Brixen* [2005] ECR I-8612, at para. 62; and Case C-295/05, *Asemfo* [2007] ECR I-2999, at para. 57.

187 See Case C-324/07, *Coditel Brabant* (fn. 184).

188 See Case C-26/03, *Stadt Halle, RPL Recyclingpark Lochau GmbH* v. *Arbeitsgemeinschaft Thermische Restabfall- und Energieverwertungsanlage TREA Leuna* [2005] ECR I-1.

and disposal of its waste. RPL Lochau was a limited liability company with 75.1 per cent wholly owned by the City of Halle, and 24.9 per cent by a private limited liability company; thus, making it a 'semi-public entity'. It was argued that RPL Lochau was an emanation of the City of Halle, as it was subsequently controlled by it; and therefore maintained that it was an 'in-house operation' to which the Community rules on public procurement did not apply.

The Court subsequently held that joint public and private involvement cannot pursue public interest purposes, where private partaking has an effective role.[189] The relationship between a public authority which is a contracting authority and its own departments is governed by considerations and requirements proper to the pursuit of objectives in the public interest. Any private capital investment in an undertaking follows considerations appropriate to private interests and pursues objectives of a different kind.[190] Conclusively, participation, even as a minority, of a private undertaking in the capital of a company in which the awarding public authority is also a participant, excludes in any event the possibility of that public authority exercising over such a company a control similar to that which it exercises over its own departments.[191]

The procurement Directives are applicable in cases where a contracting authority plans to conclude a contract with an entity which is legally distinct from it, whether or not that entity is itself a 'contracting authority';[192] the public procurement rules are inapplicable where the contracting entity and the body with which it concludes a public contract are dependent on each other in terms of management and control.[193] *Mödling* held that if an in-house public contract was awarded, in line with the *Teckal* criteria, and within a short period the controlling contracting authority transferred shares to a private undertaking, intending to screen the award of public service contracts to other semi-public companies, this would weaken the effectiveness and the principles of the public procurement Directives.[194]

The recent case of *ANAV* further extends the *Teckal* criteria to companies limited by shares, averting abuse of the *Teckal* exception even when at the time of the award of an in-house public contract there is no private sector participation in the capital of the controlled entity.[195] Notably however, when shares in the contracting entity, which were formerly (wholly) owned by the contracting authority, are transferred to a private undertaking shortly after the award of a contract to that undertaking, the in-house exemption is not possible.[196] Therefore, in so far as the concessionaire is a company which is open, even in part, to private capital, that fact precludes it from being regarded as a structure for the 'in-house' management of a public service on behalf of the controlling local authority.[197] The CJEU, in both *ANAV* and *Parking Brixten* attempted

---

189 Ibid., at paras. 49–50.

190 Ibid., at para. 50.

191 Ibid., at para. 49; C-295/05, *Asemfo* (fn. 186), at para. 57.

192 See Case C-107/98, *Teckal Slr* (fn. 128), at paras. 50 and 51.

193 Ibid.

194 See Case C-29/04, *Commission v Austria* [2005] ECR I-563.

195 See Case C-410/04, *Associazione Nazionale Autotrasporto Viaggiatori (ANAV) v Comune di Bari, AMTAB Servizio SpA* [2006] ECR I-3303.

196 See Case C-29/04, *Commission v Austria* (fn. 194), at paras. 38–41.

197 See Case C-231/03, *Coname* (fn. 176), at para. 26.

to close loopholes preventing the abuse of the *Teckal* exception, even when at the time of the award of an in-house public contract there is no private sector participation in the capital of the controlled entity. However, it leaves certain questions unanswered with regard to future or potential privatisation of entities, where a contract is well past its initial performance date.[198]

The case of *Sea* appears to answer the latter question. The case involved a company called *Setco*, limited by shares and owned by a number of municipalities in the *Val Seriana*, the majority shareholder being the *Comune di Clusone*. *Sea* claimed, *inter alia*, that by awarding the service in question directly to *Setco*, the *Comune di Ponte Nossa* had infringed the relevant legislation, in so far as it did not exercise over *Setco* any control similar to that which it exercises over its own departments, as is required for the direct award of a service to an undertaking owned by the contracting authority. It has been confirmed that when several public authorities own a company to which they entrust the performance of one of their public service tasks, the control which those public authorities exercise over that entity may be exercised by them jointly.[199] With regard to a body that takes its decisions collectively, the procedure used for the taking of those decisions, in particular recourse to a majority decision, is irrelevant. The question that was presented to the Court was whether a contracting authority can exercise over a company in which it holds shares, and with which it means to conclude a contract, control similar to that which it exercises over its own departments in a situation in which it is possible for private investors to enter the capital of the company concerned, even though that has not in fact happened. The CJEU noted that where a contracting authority holds, together with other public authorities, all the share capital in a contractor company, it is likely that that contracting authority exercises over that company control similar to that which it exercises over its own departments;[200] unlike where this a minority holding.[201] It was held that it is necessary to take into account the fact that, when a contracting authority awards a contract to a company whose entire capital it holds, the national legislation applicable provides for the compulsory opening of that company, in the short term, to other capital.[202] When shares in the contracting company, previously wholly owned by the contracting authority, are transferred to a private undertaking shortly after the contract at issue has been awarded to that company, such an action is used as a scheme intended to avoid the relevant Community rules.[203]

Where the capital of the contracting company is wholly public and there is no actual sign of any impending opening of that company's capital to private shareholders, the mere fact that private persons may hold capital in that company is not enough to support the conclusion that the condition relating to control by the public authority has not been satisfied.[204] It is also apparent, that if a public authority becomes a minority

---

[198] See Case C-29/04, *Commission v Austria* (fn. 194), at paras. 38–41.

[199] See Case C-324/07, *Coditel Brabant* (fn. 184), at para. 50.

[200] See Case C-340/04, *Carbotermo* (fn. 176), at para. 37; and Case C-324/07, *Coditel Brabant* (fn. 184), at para. 31.

[201] See Case C-26/03, *Stadt Halle* (fn. 188), at para. 49; and Case C-324/07, *Coditel Brabant* (fn. 184), at para. 30.

[202] See Case C-458/03, *Parking Brixen* (fn. 186), at paras. 67 and 72.

[203] See Case C-29/04, *Commission v Austria* (fn. 194), at paras. 38–41.

[204] See Case C-573/07, *Sea Srl. v Comune di Ponte Nossa* [2009] ECR I-8127, at para. 51.

shareholder in a company limited by shares with wholly public capital for the purpose of awarding the management of a public service to that company, the control that the public authorities which are members of that company exercise over it may be classified as similar to the control they exercise over their own departments when it is exercised by those authorities jointly.

The second *Teckal* criterion stipulates that an essential part of the controlled entity's activities must be carried out for the benefit of the controlling contracting authority or authorities (operational dependency).[205] If the 'geographical area' of the activities is extended to the whole country/abroad, the essential part of the 'controlled entities' activities cannot be carried out for its benefit.[206] The 'essential part' principle correlates to a minimum proportion of the total activities performed by the controlled body.[207] *Carbotermo* provides the Court's view on 'operational dependency'; it declared that the 80 per cent rule of affiliated 'operational dependency'[208] cannot be imported into the public sector procurement because that provision is regarded as a restrictively interpreted exception, covering connected undertakings which are distinctively different from public sector procurement entities, being subject to a procedural notification regime which cannot be implemented.[209] Conclusively, an 'essential part' indicates a quantitative measure in relation to turnover or financial level of activities performed by the controlled entity, qualitative factors such as strategic services,[210] organisational planning, market analysis, the profitability of the entity and the market dynamics under which the controlled entity operates should be taken into account.[211] Account must be taken of *all* the activities which the undertaking carries, regardless of who pays for those activities, and irrespective of being the contracting authority itself or the user of the services provided, to be granted exemption.[212]

Notably, the case *Parking Brixen* underlined that 'control' is 'a potential power of decisive influence over both strategic objectives and significant decisions'.[213] The Court identified that the application of Directives 93/36/EC and 93/37/EC (Directive 2004/18) depends on the existence of a contract concluded between two distinct persons. Also, it was held not to be appropriate to apply the Community rules on public procurement or public service concessions in cases where a public authority performs tasks in the public interest for which it is responsible by its own administrative, technical and other means, without calling upon external entities.[214] Accordingly, in the field of public service concessions, the application of the rules set out in Articles 18, 49 and 56 TFEU, as well as the general principles of which they are the specific expression, was held to

---

[205] Ibid.

[206] See Case C-458/03, *Parking Brixen* (fn. 186).

[207] See Case C-573/07, *Sea Srl.* (fn. 203), at paras. 78–80.

[208] Ibid., at para. 65.

[209] See Case C-340/04, *Carbotermo* (fn. 176).

[210] See Case C-573/07, *Sea Srl.* (fn. 204); Case C-458/03, *Parking Brixen* (fn. 185), at paras. 67, 72; and Case C-410/04, *ANAV* (fn. 195).

[211] See Case C-573/07, *Sea Srl.* (fn. 204), at paras. 50–58.

[212] See Case C-458/03, *Parking Brixen* (fn. 186), at paras. 67 and 72.

[213] See Case C-458/03, *Parking Brixen* (fn. 186), at para. 65.

[214] See Case C-26/03, *Stadt Halle* (fn. 188), at para. 48.

be precluded if the control exercised over the concessionaire by the concession-granting public authority is similar to that which the authority exercises over its own departments and if, at the same time, that entity carries out the essential part of its activities with the controlling authority.[215]

The Court further held that it is appropriate to examine, first, whether the concession-granting public authority exercises a control over the concessionaire which is similar to that which it exercises over its own departments. Second, the examination must take account of all the legislative provisions and relevant circumstances. It must follow from that examination that the concessionaire in question is subject to a control enabling the concession-granting public authority to influence the concessionaire's decisions. In conclusion, the Court finally conveyed that control per se, must be a case of a power of decisive influence over both strategic objectives and significant decisions. Thus, the capacity to hold certain rights to give commands and rights to make arrangements, combined with confirmation that the supervisory powers specify the power to manipulate corporate behaviour and that such authority does not derive from statutory provisions alone is sufficient enough to show control.[216]

A public authority is able to perform the public interest tasks conferred on it by using its own resources, without requesting the aid of outside entities.[217] Recently, flexibility has been offered to contracting authorities relative to their freedom to organise and deliver public services.[218] Collaboration between independent contracting authorities in which no similar control is exercised to that over their own departments, touches the criteria for an 'in-house exception', as long as the public cooperation exists in relation to a public task or service identified under EU law, there is no intention to evade public procurement rules and the contractual relation is not based on any pecuniary interest consideration.[219] This principle has also been similarly affirmed where contractual relations exist between inter-municipal cooperative societies whose members are contracting authorities; these are deemed to be in-house.[220]

The new proposals for the updated Public Sector Directive clarify when contractual relations between public bodies are not subject to the public procurement rules (in-house procurement).[221] These conditions are drawn from European case-law: (i) the contracting authority must exercise control over the legal entity concerned similar to that which it exercises over its own departments; (i) more than 90 per cent of the legal entity's activities must be performed for the controlling authority; and (iii) there must be no private participation in the controlled legal entity. The proposals also define when contracting authorities should be deemed to exercise joint control over a legal entity, creating legal certainty and clear guidelines identifying contractual relations between public bodies.

---

215 See Case C-458/03, *Parking Brixen* (fn. 186), at para. 62.

216 See Case C-458/03, *Parking Brixen* (fn. 185), at paras. 69–70.

217 See Case C-26/03, *Stadt Halle* (fn. 187), at para. 48.

218 See Case C-480/06, *Commission v Germany* [2009] ECR I-4747.

219 Ibid., at paras. 45–46.

220 See Case C-324/07, *Coditel Brabant* (fn. 184).

221 http://eur-lex.europa.eu/LexUriServ/LexUriServ.do?uri=CELEX:52011PC0896:EN:NOT: Article 11 Relations between public authorities (available 25 January 2016).

3. Public contracts in public procurement regulation

Christopher Bovis

The existence of a public contract is a precondition to the application of the public procurement Directives.[1] Public procurement law has configured the meaning of a public contract. The determining factor of its nature is neither what and how it is described as a public contract in national laws, nor is the legal regime (public or private) that governs its terms and conditions, nor are the intentions of the parties. The crucial characteristics of a public contract, apart from the obvious written format requirement, are: (i) a pecuniary interest consideration given by a contracting authority; and (ii) in return of a work, product or service which is of direct economic benefit to the contracting authority.

THE PECUNIARY CONSIDERATION IN PUBLIC CONTRACTS

A functional application of the pecuniary interest consideration requirement by the Court brought in a variety of payment mechanisms such as direct or deferred payment by the contracting authority to the economic operator, commitment to lease-back an asset after its construction, asset swaps between the contracting authority and the economic operator or conferral to the economic operator of an exclusive right to collect third-party payments.

---

1 See Article 1(2)(a) of the Public Sector Directive. Public contracts are contracts for pecuniary interest concluded in writing between one or more economic operators and one or more contracting authorities and having as their object the execution of works, the supply of products or the provision of services. Article 1(2)(b) of the Public Sector Directive specifies as public works contracts, contracts which have as their object either the execution or both the design and execution, of works, or the completion, by whatever means, of a work corresponding to the requirements specified by the contracting authority. A work means the outcome of building or civil engineering works taken as a whole which is sufficient of itself to fulfil an economic or technical function. Article 1(2)(c) of the Public Sector Directive specifies as public supply contracts, contracts having as their object the purchase, lease, rental or hire purchase, with or without option to buy, of products. A public contract having as its object the supply of products and which also covers, as an incidental matter, placement and installation operations must be considered as a public supply contract. Article 1(2)(d) of the Public Sector Directive specifies as public service contracts, contracts other than public works or supply contracts having as their object the provision of services referred to in Annex II of the Directive. A public contract having as its object both products and services within the meaning of Annex II must be considered as a 'public service contract' if the value of the services in question exceeds that of the products covered by the contract.

In *Köln Messe*[2] leasing and sub-leasing arrangements between the City of Cologne and *Grundstücksgesellschaft Köln Messe* for the construction and use for 30 years of four exhibition halls, ancillary buildings and relevant infrastructure were regarded as pecuniary interest considerations. The pecuniary interest consideration requirement is also indissolubly linked with the ability of the contracting authority to specify the object of the public contract. Requirements specified by contracting authorities include measures which define the type of works or action on the part of contracting authorities which has decisive influence over the design of a project or the execution of works. The means of execution are irrelevant, in the sense that prime contracting or subcontracting could be utilised for the fulfilment of the contract's object with no effect on contractual obligations or liability issues arising from the public contract. Interestingly, the Court did not consider urban planning conditions as specifications by a contracting authority capable of attributing an immediate economic benefit, even if public interest is served by such conditions.

Interestingly, planning gain contracts or contractual arrangements emanating from planning decisions of contracting authorities are covered by the public procurements Directives, irrespective of the identity of the entity responsible for their execution. The Court in *Ordine degli Architetti* has ruled[3] that the conditions attached to planning permission to develop and deliver certain infrastructure requirements specified by a contracting authority as a result of its granting planning to a landowner are capable of generating contractual obligations which are conducive to public contracts. However, the relationship between the contracting authority and the landowner is not a public contract, since the contracting authority does not have any choice over who was to be responsible for the execution of the planning gain requirements, as the only person responsible could be the landowner. That relation is regarded as a *mandate* emanating from the contracting authority and obliges the landowner to treat planning gain requirements as public contracts.

THE NOTION OF PUBLIC SERVICE CONCESSIONS

The notion of a concession is based on the fact that no remuneration is paid by the granting entity to the concessionaire. The latter must therefore simply be given the right to economically exploit the concession, although this right may be accompanied by a requirement to pay some consideration to the grantor. The main distinctive feature of a concession includes three essential characteristics. First, the beneficiary of the service provided must be third parties rather than the awarding entity itself. Secondly, the subject of the service ceded must concern a matter which is in the public interest. Finally, the concessionaire must assume the economic risk related to the performance of the service at issue.[4]

2 See Case C-536/07, *Commission v Germany,* judgment of 29 October 2009.

3 See Case C-399/98, *Ordine degli Architetti and Others* [2001] ECR I-5409.

4 See Case C-324/98, *Telaustria Verlags GmbH and Telefonadress GmbH v Post & Telekom Austria AG,* judgment of 18 May 2000.

The Community legislature has viewed the absence of, at least full, consideration passing from the granting entity to the concessionaire as constituting the essence of a concession. The public works Directive 93/37 defines a public works concession as a contract of the same type as public works contracts, except for the fact that consideration for the works to be carried out consists either solely in the right to exploit the construction or in this right together with payment.[5] The above characteristic represents a fundamental feature of a concession whose importance is not limited to those which are concerned with public works. This feature finds expression in the fact that the concessionaire itself must bear the principal, or at least the substantive, economic risk attaching to the performance of the service involved. If the national court is satisfied that the economic burden or risk has effectively been passed to the concessionaire by the grantor of the concession, then there must be a very strong presumption that the arrangement concluded between them amounts to a concession rather than a contract.

The single most important indication of whether economic risk is to be borne by the concessionaire will emerge from examining the nature of the exploitation in which the supposed concession requires it to engage. *Arnhem and Rheden* provides a strong indication that the Court views the requirement to exploit the right ceded in order to obtain remuneration as the core of what constitutes a genuine concession.[6] Thus, where, for example, the public authorities effectively guarantee to indemnify the concessionaire against future losses, or where there is no effective exploitation by the concessionaire of the service whose performance is ceded, the arrangement at issue could not amount to a concession.[7]

However, there is no overriding definition of a public services concession. *Lottomatica* and *Arnhem and Rheden* reveal that where the remuneration is fixed or determinable the arrangement should be viewed as contractual and falling, *prima facie*, within the scope of the relevant procurement directive. In *Lottomatica*, the Italian State had published a contract notice for the purported concession of the computerization of the Italian Lotto and maintained that, as a concession to carry out a public service it was not covered by the public supplies Directive 77/62. The Court rejected this argument and held that the introduction of the computerized system in question does not involve any transfer of responsibilities to the concessionaire in respect of the various operations inherent in the lottery and that it was common ground that the contract at issue related to the supply of an integrated computerized system including in particular the supply of certain foods to the administration. The fact that the system was to become the property of the administration at the end of the contractual relationship

---

[5] See Article 1(d) of the public works Directive 93/37 and the fifth recital in the preamble to that Directive.

[6] See Case C-360/96, *Arnhem and Rheden* [1998] ECR I-6821 para 25. The Court implicitly agreed with the view of the Advocate General that an important feature of service concessions in the Community context is that the concessionaire automatically assumes the economic risk associated with the provision and management of the services that are the subject of the concession. See para 26 of the Opinion provided by Advocate General La Pergola.

[7] See European Commission interpretative communication of Community law on public procurement concessions, [2000] OJ C21/2, footnote 10.

with the tenderer was irrelevant, because the price for the supply took the form of an annual payment in proportion to revenue.

It is, therefore, necessary in each case to look at a number of factors which will indicate whether in reality the arrangement amounts to a written contract for a pecuniary interest in respect of the provision of services. In the case of a concession, the beneficiary of the service must be a third party unconnected with the contractual relationship[8] and the concessionaire effectively must obtain at least a significant proportion of its remuneration not from the granting entity but from the exploitation of the service. Therefore, a case-by-case approach should be adopted to the question of whether a contract amounts to a concession or a service contract which takes account of all indicative factors, the most important of which is whether the supposed concession amounts to a conferral of a right to exploit a particular service as well as the simultaneous transfer of a significant proportion of the risk associated with that transfer to the concessionaire. The likelihood that the concessionaire will be able beneficially to exploit the concession would not suffice to permit a national court or tribunal to conclude that there is no economic risk. A national court or tribunal would need to be satisfied to a high degree of probability that the possibility of loss was minimal or even non-existent.

However, the requirement that the service ceded must be of public interest is more complicated. Under Community law, the service that is the subject of a service concession must also be in the general interest, so that a public authority is institutionally responsible for providing it. The fact that a third party provides the service means that the concessionaire replaces the authority granting the concession in respect of its obligations to ensure that the service is provided for the community.[9] Nevertheless, *Data-processing* held that the development of the data-processing systems for the performance of certain public activities, as well as the supply of such systems was not in itself a public service activity, although they enabled the authorities to carry out their duties.[10]

It appears that the supposed relevance of the general interest nature of the service that is the subject of the concession derives from the definition proposed by the Commission in both its initial and amended proposals for a procurement directive concerning public service contracts, where it referred, at Article 1(h) in both cases, to the transfer by an awarding authority of the execution of a service to the public lying within its responsibility.[11] Although it is likely that there will be a public interest in most of the services that are awarded under a public service concession arrangement between a contracting authority and a private or a public undertaking, the Court held that the notion of a service to the public under a public service concession arrangement should not be construed as the same with the notion of general interest[12] or as a service of general economic interest in the sense in which that notion has been interpreted for

---

[8] See Case C-360/96, *Arnhem and Rheden* [1998] ECR I-6821 para 26.

[9] See Case C-360/96, *Arnhem and Rheden* [1998] ECR I-6821 paras 26–28.

[10] See Case C-3/88, *Commission v Italy (Data-processing)* [1989] ECR 4035 para 26.

[11] See [1991] OJ C23/1 and [1991] OJ C250/4.

[12] See Case C-324/98, *Telaustria Verlags GmbH and Telefonadress GmbH v Post & Telekom Austria AG*, judgment of 18 May 2000.

the purposes of applying Article 90 of the EC Treaty (now Article 86 EC).[13] It should rather refer to the fact that the typical intended beneficiaries of a genuine public service concession will be third-party members of the general public or a particular category of that general public.

THE HISTORIC EXCLUSION OF PUBLIC SERVICE CONCESSIONS FROM THE PUBLIC PROCUREMENT RULES

The legislative history of the public services Directive 92/50, as well as from consideration of the overall scope of all the public procurement Directives, reveals that the Council did not wish to include concessions within the material scope of the Community instruments on public procurement. The Council rejected the Commission's proposal to include concessions within the scope of the public services Directive 92/50.[14] The initial rationale given by the Commission for their inclusion, focused on a coherent regime between the public works and public services regimes so public service concessions should be covered equally by the public services Directive in the same way as public works concessions are regulated by the public works Directives. However, during the legislative process, the Council decided to eliminate all references to public service concession from the proposal.[15] The Commission also failed to include public service concessions in its proposal for the initial utilities Directive 90/531, as well as the consolidated utilities Directive 93/38.[16] The Council rejected such inclusion on the grounds that public service concessions in the water, gas and electricity sectors were not uniformly regulated in the Member States.[17]

---

[13] See Case C-67/96 *Albany International v Stichting Bedrijfspensioenfonds Textielindustrie* [1999] ECR I-4532 paras 102–107.

[14] See Proposal for Council Directive relating to the coordination of procedures on the award of public service contracts, COM(90) 372 final, [1991] OJ C23/1. Special rules dealing with the situation where a concessionaire is a contracting authority were set out in Article 3 of the proposal. See also the amended proposal for Council Directive relating to the coordination of procedures on the award of public service contracts, COM(91) 322 final, [1991] OJ C250/4.

[15] See Document No 4444-92-ADD-1 of 25 February 1992. The Council felt that the differences between the various national laws on such concessions were too great so that the impact of adopting the proposal would not be the same in all Member States. That opposition appears to have been motivated by the fact that in some Member States concessions were only granted by public or administrative acts which would therefore have fallen outside the Commission's proposed definition which was based on concessions being granted pursuant to consensual contracts governed by private law. This was recognized by the Commission itself in its communication to the European Parliament concerning the common position; see SEC(2) 406 final of 5 March 1992.

[16] See proposal for a Council Directive amending Directive 90/531/EEC on the procurement procedures of entities operating in the water, energy, transport and telecommunications sectors, COM(91) 347 final, [1991] OJ C337/1.

[17] See point 10 of Council Document No 5250/90 of 22 March 1990, MAP 7, PRO-COOP 28.

The Court has also explicitly recognized that public service concessions were not regulated by the utilities Directives.[18] It also maintained that a literal interpretation of the notion of public service concessions would not permit written agreements, where the consideration is obtainable whether wholly by exploitation or partly by both exploitation and payment from the awarding entity, to fall within the scope of public procurement Directives. Even if the legislative history of public service concessions were to be overlooked, a contextual construction of the notion of 'contracts for pecuniary interest concluded in writing', which would be necessary to trigger the applicability of the public procurement Directives, would exclude concessions.[19]

However, public service concessions should not be viewed as falling outside the scope of European Union Law, although they are excluded from the public procurement rules. Even if public service concessions fall outside the scope of the public procurement Directives, the awarding authorities are bound to respect the Treaty and in particular Articles 52 and 59 of the EC Treaty (now, after amendment, Articles 43 EC and 49 EC) which preclude all direct and indirect discrimination based on nationality. In other words, contracting authorities must respect the principle of equal treatment between tenderers. They must also ensure that no conditions are imposed on the tenderer that would amount to an infringement of Article 30 of the EC Treaty (now, after amendment, Article 28 EC) on the principle of free movement of goods. Entities awarding public service concessions are also under a more general obligation, which appears to derive from the objectives underlying Articles 30, 52 and 59 of the EC Treaty, to ensure the transparency of the award procedures.[20] *Unitron Scandinavia* concerned the obligations affecting a body other than a contracting authority, but upon which special or exclusive rights to engage in a public service activity have been granted by such an authority, when that body awards public supply contracts to third parties. The Court held that the principle of non-discrimination on grounds of nationality cannot be interpreted restrictively and that principle implies, in particular, an obligation of transparency in order to enable the contracting authority to satisfy itself that it has been complied with.

The Court also considered that substantive compliance with the principle of non-discrimination on grounds of nationality requires that the award of concessions respect a minimum degree of publicity and transparency. However, the publicity and transparency requirements for the award of public service concessions should not necessarily be equated with publication.[21] Thus, if the awarding entity addresses itself directly to a number of potential tenderers, and assuming the latter are not all or nearly all undertakings having the same nationality as that entity, the requirement of transparency would be respected. Transparency, in this context, is therefore concerned with ensuring the fundamental fairness and openness of the award procedures,

---

18 See Case C-360/96, *Arnhem and Rheden* [1998] ECR I-6821 para 26.

19 See Case C-324/98, *Telaustria Verlags GmbH and Telefonadress GmbH v Post & Telekom Austria AG,* judgment of 18 May 2000.

20 See Case C-275/98, *Unitron Scandinavia and Others v Ministeriet for Fødevarer, Landbrug og Fiskeri* [1999] ECR I-564 para 42.

21 See Case C-324/98, *Telaustria Verlags GmbH and Telefonadress GmbH v Post & Telekom Austria AG,* judgment of 18 May 2000.

particularly as regards potential tenderers who are not established in the Member State of the awarding authority. It does not, however, require the awarding entity to apply by analogy the provisions of the most relevant of the public procurement Directives.

SERVICE CONCESSIONS AS PUBLIC CONTRACTS

Telaustria[22] recognised that concession services are contracts which are excluded from the scope of public procurement Directives by the fact that the consideration provided by the contracting authorities to the concessionaire consists in the latter obtaining the right to exploit for payment its own service. Notwithstanding such exclusion, contracting authorities concluding concession services are bound to comply with the fundamental rules of the Treaty, in general and, in particular, the principle of non-discrimination on the ground of nationality and the duty of transparency. The latter is indented as verification of compliance with the relevant Treaty principles and consists in ensuring a degree of competitiveness in the award of such contracts, in conjunction with a review process of the award procedure.

Coname[23] held that the direct award by a municipality of a service concession does not comply with the transparency principle if, without necessarily implying an obligation to hold an invitation to tender, undertakings located in other Member States were precluded from having access to appropriate information with a view to expressing their interest in obtaining that service concession. The Court held that infringement of the duty of transparency triggers the potential infringement of the principles of free movement of services and the right of establishment.

In *Parking Brixen,*[24] the Court reiterated that public authorities concluding services concessions are responsible for complying with the principle of non-discrimination on grounds of nationality and the principle of equal treatment, which conceptually correspond to the principles of the right of establishment and the freedom to provide services.[25] The Court has suggested that the right of establishment and the freedom to provide services are specific expressions of the principle of equal treatment.[26] The prohibition on discrimination on grounds of nationality is also a specific expression of the general principle of equal treatment.[27] The Court stated that the principle of equal treatment in public procurement is intended to afford equality of opportunity to all tenderers, regardless of their nationality.[28] As a result, the principle of equal treatment is applicable to public service concessions even in the absence of discrimination on grounds of nationality. The principles of equal treatment and non-discrimination on grounds of nationality imply, in particular, a duty of transparency which enables the

---

[22] See Case C-324/98 *Telaustria and Telefonadress* [2000] ECR I-10745.

[23] See Case C-231/03, *Consorzio Aziende Metano (Coname) v Comune di Cingia de' Botti* [2005] ECR I-7287.

[24] See Case C-458/0,3 *Parking Brixen* [2005] ECR I-8612.

[25] See Case C-324/98, *Telaustria and Telefonadress* [2000] ECR I-10745 para 60, and Case C-231/03 *Coname* [2005] ECR I-7287 para 16.

[26] See Case C-3/88, *Commission v Italy* [1989] ECR 4035 para 8.

[27] See Case 810/79, *Überschär* [1980] ECR 2747 para 16.

[28] See Case C-87/94, *Commission v Belgium* [1996] ECR I-2043 paras 33 and 54.

concession-granting public authority to ensure that those principles are complied with and that a sufficient degree of competition for the award of the service concession is maintained. Finally, the transparency obligation ensures the imperative of reviewing the impartiality of procurement procedures.[29]

Recourse to Article 106(1) TFEU does not alter the requirement of contracting authorities to comply with the principle of transparency for service concessions, as the granting of special or exclusive rights by Member States must not contravene the Treaty rules on equal treatment and the competition provisions.[30]

The essence of the definition of public service concessions under the public procurement Directives is that a service concession is a contract which meets the definition of a service contract except for the fact that the consideration for the provision of services consists either solely in the right to exploit the service or in that right together with payment. That corresponds to the Court's criterion of remuneration which comes not from the public authority concerned, but from sums paid by third parties. However, in addition, the Court has stressed that an essential feature of a public service concession is that the concession holder assumes the risk of operating the services in question.[31]

The Court has given some further guidance on what kind and degree of transfer of risk is required for a contract to be categorised as a service concession. In *Eurawasser*,[32] it ruled that in relation to a contract for the supply of services, the fact that the supplier does not receive consideration directly from the contracting authority, but is entitled to collect payment under private law from third parties, is sufficient for that contract to be viewed as a service concession, where the service provider assumes all, or at least a significant share of the operating risk faced by the contracting authority, even if that risk appears limited.

The Court thus took the view that what matters is not that the operating risk should be significant in itself but that whatever risk is already assumed by the contracting authority should be transferred, either fully or to a significant extent, to the successful service provider. In *Eurawasser*, the Court expressly considered the fact that the limitation of the risk relevant to the contract derived from public regulations (common in the utilities sector) which were, on the one hand, beyond the control of the contracting authority and, on the other hand, such as to reduce the likelihood of any adverse effect on transparency or competition.

---

[29] See Case C-324/98 *Telaustria and Telefonadress*, *op.cit*, paras 61 and 62.

[30] See C. Bovis, 'The State, Competition and Public Services', Chapter 11 in Birkinshaw and Varney (eds), *The European Union Legal Order after Lisbon*, Alphen aan den Rijn: Kluwer, 2010.

[31] See Case C-382/05 *Commission v Italy* [2007] ECR I-6657, para 34, and Case C-437/07 *Commission v Italy* [2008] ECR I-153, para 29; see also European Commission Interpretative Communication on Concessions under Community Law, [2000] OJ C121/2.

[32] See Case C-206/08 *WAZV Gotha v Eurawasser Aufbereitungs* [2009] ECR I-8377.

SHADOW PAYMENTS IN CONCESSIONS

In the *Norma* case,[33] the provider of public bus services was given the right to operate such services and was paid by the users of those services in accordance with a fixed fare scale. However, the contracting authority provided for a system of reimbursement against future potential losses. The question whether an operation is to be classified as a 'service concession' or a 'public service contract' must be considered exclusively in the light of European Union law.[34] It is clear from the definitions of service contract and service concession, contained in Article 1(2)(a) and (d) and Article 1(3) of Directive 2004/17 respectively, that the difference between a service contract and a service concession lies in the consideration for the provision of services. A service contract involves consideration which is paid directly by the contracting authority to the service provider while, for a service concession, the consideration for the provision of services consists in the right to exploit the service, either alone or together with payment.[35]

In the case of a contract for the supply of services, the fact that the supplier is not remunerated directly by the contracting authority, but is entitled to collect payment from third parties, meets the requirement of consideration of a concession. While the method of remuneration is one of the determining factors for the classification of a service concession, it also follows from the case-law that the service concession implies that the service supplier takes the risk of operating the services in question. The absence of a transfer to the service provider of the risk connected with operating the service shows that the transaction concerned is a public service contract and not a service concession.[36] It is thus necessary to establish whether the service provider takes the risk of operating the service. While that risk may, at the outset, be very limited, it is necessary for classification as a service concession that the contracting authority transfers to the concession holder all or, at least, a significant share of the risk which it faces.

It is not unusual that certain sectors of activity, in particular sectors involving public service utilities are subject to rules which may have the effect of limiting the financial risks entailed. First, the detailed rules of public law, to which the economic and financial operation of the service is subject, facilitate the supervision of how that service is operated, and scale down the factors which may threaten transparency and distort competition. Secondly, it must remain open to the contracting authorities, acting in all good faith, to ensure the supply of services by way of a concession, if they consider that to be the best method of ensuring the public service in question, even if the risk linked to such an operation is limited.[37]

---

[33] See Case C-348/10, *Norma-A SIA, Dekom SIA v Latgales plānošanas regions* [2011] ECR I-0000.

[34] See Case C-274/09, *Privater Rettungsdienst und Krankentransport Stadler* [2011] ECR I-0000 para 23.

[35] See *Eurawasser, op.cit,* paras 39 and 51.

[36] See *Privater Rettungsdienst und Krankentransport Stadler, op.cit,* paras 40 and 26.

[37] See *Eurawasser, op.cit,* paras 72–74.

In circumstances where the contracting authority has no influence on the detailed rules of public law governing the service, it is impossible for it to introduce and transfer risk factors which are excluded by those rules. Moreover, it would not be reasonable to expect a public authority granting a concession to create conditions which were more competitive and involved greater financial risk than those which, on account of the rules governing the sector in question, exist in that sector. The risk linked to such an operation must be understood as the risk of exposure to the vagaries of the market, which may, in particular, consist in the risk of competition from other operators, the risk that supply of the services will not match demand, the risk that those liable will be unable to pay for the services provided, the risk that the costs of operating the services will not be met by revenue or also the risk of liability for harm or damage resulting from an inadequacy of the service. By contrast, risks such as those linked to bad management or errors of judgment by the economic operator are not decisive for the purposes of classification as a public service contract or a service concession, since those risks are inherent in every contract, whether it is a public service contract or a service concession. Although the risk of operating the service may, at the outset, be very limited by reason of the public law arrangements governing the organisation of the service, it is necessary for classification as a service concession that the contracting authority transfers to the concession holder all or, at least, a significant share of the operating risk which it faces.

In the *Norma* case, the national legislation provided that the contracting authority is to reimburse the service provider for operating losses and, in addition, by reason of the rules of public law and the contractual terms governing the provision of those services, the provider does not bear 'a significant share of the operating risk'. The mandating authority is to compensate, within the limit of the funds allocated to the State budget, for the losses related to the provision of transport services, engendered by such provision and for related costs once the operating receipts from the transport services have been deducted. Furthermore, the service provider is compensated for losses associated with performance of the contract as regards essential costs associated with performance of the public transport service contract which exceed the income obtained, costs incurred through application of the tariffs laid down by the mandating authority, lost revenue because the mandating authority has applied a reduction of the transport price for certain categories of passenger, and costs incurred in fulfilling the minimum quality requirements laid down after the public transport services began to be provided, if compliance therewith involves additional costs compared to the quality requirements previously laid down. The Court maintained that those terms and national law provisions cannot render that a significant part of the exposure to the vagaries of the market is borne by the successful tenderer. Therefore, such an operation should be regarded as a 'service contract' and not a 'service concession'.

DEFICIT CONTRACTS AS CONCESSIONS

A public service concession relating to works was not advertised on the grounds that concession was incapable of generating either substantial revenue or an undue advantage for the concessionaire or for the public contracting authority.[38] The contracting authority did not invoke any objective facts capable of explaining the lack of any transparency in the award of the concession. On the contrary, it maintained that the concession was not liable to interest undertakings located in other Member States, in so far as the concession granted to a cooperative was designed so as not to be capable of generating substantial net revenue for its beneficiary or an undue advantage for the latter or for the municipality.

However, the fact that a concession is not capable of generating substantial net revenue or an undue advantage for an undertaking or for a public body does not, in itself, support the inference that the concession is of no economic interest for undertakings located in Member States other than that of the contracting authority. In the context of an economic strategy to extend part of its activities to another Member State, an undertaking may take the tactical decision to seek the award in that State of a concession despite the fact that that concession is incapable as such of generating sufficient profit, since that opportunity could nevertheless enable the undertaking to establish itself on the market of that State and to make itself known there with a view to preparing its future expansion. The Court concluded that EU law does not preclude the award, without a call for tenders, of a public service concession relating to works, provided that that award is consistent with the principle of transparency, observance of which, without necessarily entailing an obligation to call for tenders, must make it possible for an undertaking located in the territory of a Member State other than that of the contracting authority to have access to appropriate information regarding that concession before it is awarded, so that, if that undertaking so wishes, it would be in a position to express its interest in obtaining that concession.

CROSS-BORDER INTEREST IN CONCESSIONS

In the *Ancona* case,[39] a municipality directly awarded to a third party a public service concession. The Court has held that the principles of equal treatment and of non-discrimination on grounds of nationality impose, particularly on the contracting authority, a duty of transparency, consisting in the duty to ensure, for the benefit of any potential tenderer, a degree of publicity sufficient to enable the award procedure to be opened up to competition and the impartiality of that procedure to be reviewed, without necessarily implying an obligation to call for tenders.[40] To the extent that a concession may also be of interest to an undertaking located in a Member State other than the Member State of the contracting authority, the award, in the absence of any transparency, of that concession to an undertaking located in the latter Member State amounts to a difference in treatment to the detriment of the undertakings located in other Member States. In the absence of any transparency, the undertakings located in those other Member States have no real possibility of manifesting their interest in

38 See Case C-388/12, *Comune di Ancona v Regione Marche* [2013] ECR I-0000.

39 Ibid.

40 See Case C-260/04, *Commission v Italy* [2007] ECR I-7083 para 24, and Case C-324/07 *Coditel Brabant* [2008] ECR I-8457 para 25.

obtaining the concession.[41] Unless justified by objective circumstances, such a difference in treatment, which operates mainly to the detriment of undertakings located in another Member State, amounts to indirect discrimination on grounds of nationality, which is prohibited under Articles 49 TFEU and 56 TFEU.[42] In the absence of legislation, the law applicable to service concessions must be assessed in the light of primary EU law and, more specifically, the fundamental freedoms of the European Union.[43]

EXCLUSIVE RIGHTS AS CONCESSIONS

A private undertaking cannot be regarded as a contracting authority or entity solely on the ground provided by its capacity as the exclusive holder of a public service concession. The mere fact that a private undertaking is the exclusive holder of a public service concession is not enough to merit the engagement of the public procurement Directives. Rather, it is necessary that that public service should be provided under the control of a public authority and that that undertaking should have special powers beyond those which result from the normal rules applicable in relations between individuals.[44]

A private undertaking which by means of exclusive rights based on law has been given responsibility by the state for providing a public interest service under the regulatory control of the state is considered as a concessionaire[45] when it has special powers going beyond those which result from the normal rules applicable in relations between individuals, such as expropriation rights or rights which reflect the exercise of power of the state.

VERTICAL PROCUREMENT

A functional approach to the concept of contracting authority under the public procurement Directives[46] might imply that the public procurement rules do not apply to a contracting authority which is a prospective supplier to another contracting authority. If a contracting authority, while trading as a supplier, subcontracts certain services to a third party, the selection of that subcontractor may well be based on non-economic

[41] See case C-231/03 *Coname* [2005] ECR I-7287 paras 17 and 18.

[42] See Case C-347/06, *ASM Brescia* [2008] ECR I-5641 para 60.

[43] See Case C-324/98, *Telaustria and Telefonadress* [2000] ECR I-10745 para 60.

[44] See Case C-157/02, *Rieser Internationale Transporte* [2004] ECR I-1477 paras 25–27.

[45] See Case C-425/12, *Portgás – Sociedade de Produção e Distribuição de Gás SA v Ministério da Agricultura, do Mar, do Ambiente e do Ordenamento do Território* [2014] 2 CMLR 30.

[46] See Case C-31/87, *Beentjes* [1988] ECR 4635, para 11; and Case C-360/96 *BFI Holding* [1998] ECR I-6821 para 62.

considerations, and it is also quite possible that, at some stage in the process, public funds will be used.[47] The fact that the matter of the subcontracting does not fall within the remit of the activities of the contracting authority[48] and might be also subject to competition[49] is immaterial.

Mannesmann Anlagenbau Austria[50] made no distinction between public contracts awarded by a contracting authority for the purposes of fulfilling its task of meeting needs in the general interest, and those which are unrelated to that task. It is immaterial that the activity in question may be unrelated to the body's task in the general interest, or may not involve any public funds. Where, under the terms of the public procurement Directives, a body ranks as a contracting authority, the Directives require the conduct of award procedures. Accordingly that rule applies even where the contracting authority itself is trading as a supplier on the market, and subcontracting certain parts of a contract to a third party. It is, after all, entirely possible that non-economic considerations might be involved in the selection of a subcontractor, just as it is possible that public funds might be used in the course of the operation.

Contracting authorities are free to set up legally independent entities if they wish to offer services to third parties under normal market conditions. If such entities aim to make profit, bear the losses related to the exercise of their activities, and perform no public tasks, they are not to be classified as public bodies and hence not as contracting authorities for the purposes of the public procurement Directives. Their activities will therefore not be subject to the provisions of the public procurement Directives. A body which aims to make a profit and bears the losses associated with the exercise of its activity will not normally become involved in an award procedure on conditions which are not economically justified.[51]

It could be argued that the public procurement Directives do not require 'tenders within tenders'. Article 7 of the utilities Directive 93/38 excludes contracts awarded for the purposes of resale or hire to third parties from the scope of that Directive by virtue of the fact that the purchase of the goods occurs in principle in a context of free competition, and the ensuing commercial discipline prevents a contracting authority from favouring particular tenderers on non-economic grounds. However, this provision cannot be applied by analogy to supplies, works or services public procurement contracts, as the relevant provisions stipulated in the public supplies, works and services Directives respectively establish a dividing line between their regimes and the

---

47 See Case C-126/03, *Commission of the European Communities v Federal Republic of Germany*, judgment of 18 November 2004 and the Opinion of Advocate General para 28.

48 See Cases C-107/98, *Teckal* [1999] ECR I-8121, and C-399/98, *Ordine degli Architetti and Others* [2001] ECR I-5409.

49 See Case C-360/96, *BFI Holding*, and Joined Cases C-223/99 and C-260/99, *Agorà and Excelsior* [2001] ECR I-3605.

50 See Case C-44/96, *Mannesmann Anlagenbau Austria AG v Strohal Rotationsdruck GmbH* [1998] ECR I-73.

51 See Case C-18/01, *Korhonen and Others* [2003] ECR I-5321 para 51.

regime of the utilities Directive[52] and do not extend the possibility of vertical procurement to contracting authorities in the public sector.[53]

SUBCONTRACTING

A provision in an invitation to tender which prohibits recourse to subcontracting for material parts of the contract is contrary to the public procurement Directives.[54] On the contrary, all Directives envisage the possibility for a tenderer to subcontract a part of the contract to third parties, as that provision states that the contracting authority may ask that tenderer to indicate in its tender any share of the contract which it may intend to subcontract.[55] Furthermore, with regard to the qualitative selection criteria, all public procurement Directives make express provision for the possibility of providing evidence of the technical capacity of the service provider by means of an indication of the technicians or technical bodies involved, whether or not belonging directly to the undertaking of that service provider, and which the latter will have available to it, or by indicating the proportion of the contract which the service provider may intend to subcontract.

The Court ruled[56] that a tenderer cannot be eliminated from a procedure for the award of a public service contract solely on the ground that that party proposes, in order to carry out the contract, to use resources which are not its own but belong to one or more other entities. This means that it is permissible for a service provider which does not itself fulfil the minimum conditions required for participation in the procedure for the award of a public service contract to rely, vis-à-vis the contracting authority, on the standing of third parties upon whose resources it proposes to draw if it is awarded the contract. However, according to the Court, the onus rests on a service provider which relies on the resources of entities or undertakings with which it is directly or indirectly linked, with a view to being admitted to participate in a tendering procedure, to establish that it actually has available to it the resources of those entities or undertakings which it does not itself own and which are necessary for the performance of the contract.[57] Nevertheless, the public procurement Directives do not preclude a prohibition or a restriction on the use of subcontracting for the performance of essential parts of the contract precisely in the case where the contracting authority has not been

---

[52] See Article 1(a)(ii) of the public services Directive 92/50 and the equivalent Articles in Council Directive 93/36 coordinating procedures for the award of public supply contracts [1993] OJ L199/1) and Directive 93/37 coordinating procedures for the award of public works contracts [1993] OJ L199/54).

[53] See Case C-126/03, *Commission of the European Communities v Federal Republic of Germany* judgment of 18 November 2004.

[54] See Case C-176/98 *Holst Italia* [1999] ECR I-8607.

[55] See Case C-314/01, *Siemens AG Österreich, ARGE Telekom & Partner and Hauptverband der österreichischen Sozialversicherungsträger,* judgment of 18 March 2004.

[56] See Case C-176/98, *Holst Italia* [1999] ECR I-8607 paras 26 and 27.

[57] See ibid para 29.

in a position to verify the technical and economic capacities of the subcontractors when examining the tenders.[58]

DELINEATION OF PUBLIC SERVICE CONTRACTS

A question often arises whether the purpose of a contract is relevant in determining the applicable regime and in particular, whether, for the award of a contract with a single object but which is composed of several services, those services must be classified individually in the categories provided for in Annex I A and I B to Directive 92/50 in order to determine the regime applicable to the contract in accordance with Articles 8 to 10 of the Directive, or whether on the contrary the main purpose of the contract must be identified, in which case the ancillary services are governed by the same regime as the service relating to the main purpose. The Court held that the determination of the regime applicable to public service contracts composed partly of services falling within Annex I A to Directive 92/50 and partly of services falling within Annex I B to the directive does not depend on the main purpose of those contracts and is to be made in accordance with the unequivocal test laid down by Article 10 of that Directive.[59]

The 21st recital in the preamble to Directive 92/50 states that the application of its provisions in full must be limited, for a transitional period, to contracts for services where its provisions will enable the full potential for increased cross-border trade to be realized, the contracts for other services during that period being subject only to monitoring. To that end Directive 92/50 makes a distinction between contracts for services referred to in Annex I A, which under Article 8 are awarded in accordance with the provisions of Titles III to VI, and those for services referred to in Annex I B, which under Article 9 are subject to the provisions of Articles 14 and 16. In Article 10, Directive 92/50 also provides that contracts which have as their object services listed in both Annex I A and Annex I B are to be awarded in accordance with the provisions of Titles III to VI where the value of the services listed in Annex I A exceeds the value of the services listed in Annex I B, and where this is not the case only in accordance with Articles 14 and 16.

The argument that the main purpose of a contract determines the regime applicable to it cannot be accepted, according to the Court. The public services Directive does not contain any definition of what constitutes the main purpose of a contract, whilst Article 10 explicitly acknowledges, on the contrary, that a contract may have as its purpose the provision of different services falling under different annexes to the directive. In that respect, the Court in *Tögel* held that the references in the annexes to Directive 92/50 to the CPC nomenclature were binding. It is thus contrary to the purpose of the directive to classify a contract composed of several services, referred to in different sections of the CPC nomenclature, according to only one of those services. The judgment in

[58] See Case C-314/01, *Siemens AG Österreich, ARGE Telekom & Partner and Hauptverband der österreichischen Sozialversicherungsträger,* judgment of 18 March 2004.

[59] See Case C-411/00, *Felix Swoboda GmbH v Österreichische Nationalbank*, judgment of 14 November 2002.

Gestion Hotelera Internacional,[60] in which the Court laid down the principle that the main purpose of the contract determined which directive was applicable to a given contract, provides little support. *Gestion Hotelera Internacional* is rather irrelevant in determining the applicable regime within the public services Directive in so far as, first, its purpose was to determine whether a contract constituted a contract for works or a contract of another type, and secondly, the criterion adopted by the Court in that judgment was the merely incidental nature of repair work in relation to the main purpose of the contract based on the express definition of public works contracts in accordance with the public works Directives. If in the context of that judgment the Court had taken the view that the determining factor for distinguishing between contracts for works and contracts for services was the predominant nature of a service in terms of value, it would have clearly so ruled, referring to Article 10 of Directive 92/50 and not to the 16th recital in the preamble thereto, which provides that when those works are incidental rather than forming the object of a contract, they do not justify treating the contract as a public works contract.

It follows from those provisions that in the context of Directive 92/50 the argument that the main purpose of a contract determines the regime applicable to it cannot be accepted. First, Directive 92/50 itself states, in the seventh recital in the preamble, that for the application of procedural rules and for monitoring purposes the field of services is best described by subdividing it into categories corresponding to particular positions of a common classification, in this case the CPC nomenclature. In paragraph 37 of the judgment in *Tögel*, the Court held that the reference made in Annexes I A and I B to Directive 92/50 to the CPC nomenclature was binding. Secondly, Article 10 of Directive 92/50 provides an unequivocal test for the determination of the regime applicable to a contract composed of several services, which is based on the comparison of the value of the services referred to in Annex I A to the directive with the value of the services referred to in Annex I B.

A further question arises whether in the award of a contract having one purpose but composed of several services, the classification of those services in Annexes I A and I B to Directive 92/50 deprives the directive of its effectiveness.[61] This question also leads to the uncertainty whether there is an obligation on the part of the contracting authority, if as a result of that classification the value of the services falling within Annex I B exceeds that of the services falling within Annex I A, to separate the services referred to in Annex I B from the contract in question and to award separate contracts in respect of them. The Court maintained that the award of a contract with a single object but composed of several services, the classification of those services in Annexes I A and I B to Directive 92/50, far from depriving it of its effectiveness, is in accordance with the system laid down by the directive. When, following the classification thus made by reference to the CPC nomenclature, the value of the services falling within Annex I B exceeds the value of the services falling within Annex I A, there is no

[60] See Case C-331/92, *Gestion Hotelera Internacional SA v Communidad Autonoma de Canarias*, [1994] ECR 1-1329.

[61] See Case C-411/00, *Felix Swoboda GmbH v Österreichische Nationalbank*, judgment of 14 November 2002.

obligation on the part of the contracting authority to separate from the contract in question the services referred to in Annex I B and to award separate contracts in respect of them.

The classification of services in Annexes I A and I B to Directive 92/50, even in the context of a contract with a single object, is in accordance with the system provided for by the directive as it appears, *inter alia*, in the seventh and 21st recitals in the preamble and in Articles 8 and 10, which envisage the application of the directive on two levels. Directive 92/50 must be interpreted as in no way requiring the separate award of a contract for the services referred to in Annex I B thereto when, in accordance with the classification made by reference to the CPC nomenclature, the value of those services exceeds, for the contract in question, the value of the services referred to in Annex I A. To require such a separation in that case would effectively deprive Article 10 of Directive 92/50 of any purpose.[62] Under the second sentence of Article 10 of the Directive the contract is subject only to Articles 14 and 16.

It would be the same if the contracting authority artificially grouped in one contract services of different types without there being any link arising from a joint purpose or operation, with the sole purpose of increasing the proportion of the services referred to in Annex I B to Directive 92/50 in the contract and thus of avoiding, by way of the second sentence of Article 10, the application of its provisions in full. Moreover, that conclusion is supported by the wording of Article 7(3) of Directive 92/50, from which it is clear that the choice of the valuation method is not to be made with the intention of avoiding the application of the directive. Although that article relates to a different situation (the artificial splitting up of the contract), the purpose which inspires it (the concern to avoid any risk of manipulation) also precludes a contracting authority from artificially grouping different services in the same contract solely in order to avoid the application in full of the directive to that contract.

The classification of services in Annexes I A and I B to Directive 92/50 is primarily a question of fact for the contracting authority to determine, subject to review by the national courts which eventually must decide the regime applicable to the contract forming the object of the procedure at issue in the main proceedings on the basis of Article 10 of Directive 92/50, in particular by verifying that the services which make up that contract and the reference numbers of the CPC nomenclature correspond. In any case, Category 20 of Annex I B to Directive 92/50 cannot be interpreted as also including land transport services themselves, as they are explicitly covered by Category 2 of Annex I A to the Directive.

ANNEX II B SERVICES CONTRACTS

For Annex II B Services Contracts, which are also referred to as non-priority public service contracts, the Community legislature assumed that contracts for such services are not, in the light of their specific nature, of cross-border interest such as to justify their award being subject to the conclusion of a tendering procedure in accordance with

[62] See the Opinion of the Advocate General, para 55 in Case C-411/00, *Felix Swoboda GmbH v Österreichische Nationalbank*, judgment of 14 November 2002.

the public procurement Directives. For that reason, the public sector Directive merely imposes a requirement of publicity after the award of such service contracts.

An Post[63] touched on contracts concerning services which fall under Annex II B of the public sector Directive. The contracting authorities are bound only by the obligation to define the technical specifications by reference to national standards implementing European standards which must be given in the general contract documents and to send a notice of the results of the award to the Publications Office of the EU. The other procedural rules provided for by the public sector Directive, including those relating to the award procedures and award criteria are, by contrast, not applicable to those contracts.

However, the limited advertisement requirements contained in the public sector Directive for contracts relating to services within the ambit of Annex II B cannot justify the absence of any transparency, especially when the relevant contract is of certain cross-border interest. The Court held[64] that if a contract of certain cross-border interest is awarded to an undertaking located in the same Member State as the contracting authority without any call for competition, this action would amount to a difference in treatment to the detriment of undertakings which are located in other Member States and might be interested in that contract. Such a difference in treatment, by excluding all undertakings located in other Member States, amounts to indirect discrimination on grounds of nationality[65] and contravenes the purpose of the public procurement Directives to eliminate barriers to intra-Community trade in accordance to the fundamental principles of Community law, and in particular the right of establishment and the freedom to provide services.[66]

INTER-ADMINISTRATIVE AGREEMENTS AS PUBLIC CONTRACTS

Exclusion of agreements between legally distinctive contracting authorities from the public procurement rules is contrary to the principles of the Directives.[67] In *Commission v Spain*, national law excluded from its scope cooperation agreements concluded either between the general State administration and Social Security, autonomous communities, local bodies, their autonomous bodies and any other public body, or between public bodies themselves. The Spanish government maintained that inter-administrative agreements are the normal way for bodies governed by public law to establish relations between each other and asserted that those relations are marginal to

---

[63] See Case C-507/03, *Commission v Ireland (An Post)* [2007] ECR I-9777.

[64] See Case C-324/98, *Telaustria and Telefonadress* [2000] ECR I-10745 paras 60 and 61, and Case C-231/03 *Coname* [2005] ECR I-7287 para 17.

[65] See Case C-231/03 *Coname* [2005] ECR I-7287 para 19.

[66] See Case C-380/98 *University of Cambridge* [2000] ECR I-8035 para 16; Case C-19/00, *SIAC Construction* [2001] ECR I-7725 para 32; and Case C-92/00 *HI* [2002] ECR I-5553 para 43.

[67] See Case C-84/03, *Commission of the European Communities v Kingdom of Spain* [2005] ECR I-139.

the concept of a contract. Furthermore, it suggested that the principle enshrined in Article 6 of the public services Directive 92/50 is implicitly included in the other directives on public contracts. Article 6 of the public services Directive provides for the inapplicability of the Directive to service contracts which are awarded to an entity which is itself a contracting authority within the meaning of the Directive on the basis of an exclusive right which is granted to the contracting authority by a law, regulation or administrative provision of the Member State in question.

The Commission argued that exclusion of inter-administrative agreements from the framework of the public procurement Directives constitutes an incorrect transposition of the Directives, as inter-administrative agreements are of the same kind as the public contracts covered by them and that this exclusion is not found in Directives 93/36 and 93/37. The Commission relied on the definition of a contract set out in Article 1(a) of Directives 93/36 and 93/37 and the case-law of the Court, according to which, in order to show the existence of a contract, it must be determined whether there has been an agreement between two separate persons.[68]

The Court held that according to the definitions given in Article 1(a) of Directives 93/36 and 93/37, public supply or public works contracts are contracts for pecuniary interest concluded in writing between a supplier or a contractor and a contracting authority within the meaning of Article 1(b) of the directives, for the purchase of products or the performance of a certain type of works. In accordance with Article 1(a) of Directive 93/36, it is sufficient, in principle, if the contract was concluded between a local authority and a person legally distinct from it. The position can be otherwise only in the case where the local authority exercises over the person concerned a control which is similar to that which it exercises over its own departments and, at the same time, that person carries out the essential part of its activities with the controlling local authority or authorities.[69]

Having regard to the fact that the elements constituting the definition of a contract in Directives 93/36 and 93/37 are identical, except for the purpose of the contract in question, the approach adopted in *Teckal* must be applied to inter-administrative agreements covered by Directive 93/37. Consequently, if national law excludes, *a priori*, from the scope of the public procurement Directives relations between public authorities, their public bodies and non-commercial bodies governed by public law, whatever the nature of those relations, such law constitutes an incorrect transposition of the public procurement Directives 93/36 and 93/37.

AGENCY ARRANGEMENTS AS PUBLIC CONTRACTS

Commission v France[70] touched upon agency or representation relations with the object of delegating project contracting between contracting authorities and entities district from them or their internal departments. Such relations are deemed public service contracts, provided a written agreement is concluded between the contracting authority

[68] See Case C-107/98, *Teckal* [1999] ECR I-8121 para 49.
[69] See ibid para 50.
[70] See Case C-264/03, *Commission v France* [2005] ECR I-8831.

and the agent or representative for pecuniary interest in return of agency or representation services, provided the agent or representative is responsible for signature, project authorisation or payments to third parties on behalf of the contracting authority and does not have sufficient autonomy in executive decisions to be considered as a beneficiary of the contract's objects.

Public contracts denote a demonstrable element of economic benefit or of risk directly attributable to the contracting authority. Features of direct economic benefit include ownership of asset by a contracting authority, a legal right over its use and future economic advantages enjoyed by the contracting authority or risks assumed by the contracting authority in relation to the materialisation of a project. In *Auroux*,[71] a dispute arose relating to a leisure centre in the French town of Roanne, the design and execution of which was entrusted to a semi-public urban development company without the prior issue of a call for tenders. The project had some specific features in as much as only certain parts of the proposed leisure centre, once constructed, were intended for the town itself, while other parts were to be disposed of by the urban development company directly to third parties, although the town was to contribute towards their financing, take over those parts not disposed of at the end of the project, and bear the full risk of any losses incurred. The Court held that an agreement by which a contracting authority entrusts another contracting authority with the execution of a work constitutes a public works contract, regardless of whether or not it is anticipated that the first contracting authority is or will become the owner of all or part of that work. Ownership of an asset is crucial only in determining work concession contracts, for it is deemed necessary as the means to grant an exclusive exploitation right to the concessionaire.

The Court thus maintained in *Auroux* that, even if national laws oblige the conclusion of a contract with certain undertakings which are themselves contracting authorities and are bound to use the provisions of the public procurement Directives to the award of any following subcontractual arrangements directly related to the former contract, contracting authorities must regard the initial contract as a public contract and apply the procurement Directives to its award in order to preserve legal certainty and eliminate the potential avoidance of the application of public procurement rules by division of subcontracts into lots below the relevant thresholds. It follows that the contractual relation between two, *ipso facto,* contracting authorities is to be regarded as a prime public contract, which is capable in demonstrating a clear element of economic benefit or of risk attributable to the contracting authority, irrespective of the obligation imposed upon the second contracting authority to apply the public procurement rules for the award of the relevant subcontracts.

Auroux, although reflecting obvious similarities with *Commission v Germany*[72] in the sense of public sector entities cooperating for the delivery of public projects, differs fundamentally in that the latter case introduced a genuine public-public partnership relation, where the contractual interface was not based upon pecuniary interest considerations nor any payment was materialised in return of the delivery of the contract's objects.

---

[71] See Case C-220/05, *Jean Auroux and Others v Commune de Roanne* [2007] ECR I-385.

[72] See Case C-480/06, *Commission v Germany, op.cit* fn. 53.

Auroux revealed that the legislative gap in procurement for public works contracts, in the sense that an analogous provision to Article 18 of the Public Sector Directive, which covers public service contracts awarded by a contracting authority to another contracting authority or an association of contracting authorities on the basis of an exclusive right based on law, regulation or administrative provision compatible with the Treaty, does not exist within the framework of the provisions relevant to public works contracts, can only be filled by the presence of the dependency test, that is, the *Teckal* criteria.

Auroux left open the issue of double tendering, as the Court did not address the issue of consecutive procurement of prime public contracts and subsequent subcontracts.[73] The Court, however, ruled that in order to determine the value of a public contract, account must be taken of the total value of the works contract from the point of view of a potential tenderer, including not only the total amounts to be paid by the contracting authority but also all the revenue received from third parties. In cases of mixed public contracts, a quantitative evaluation reflecting contract values is applicable to the services/supplies divide, whereas a qualitative evaluation reflecting the object of contract is conducive to the works/services divide. The object of contract, which also reflects on the requirements and specification of contracting authorities, represents that decisive classification factor for the works/services divide.

LAND AND REAL ESTATE CONTRACTS

The Court in *Helmut Müller*[74] held that the sale of assets or land by contracting authorities to economic operators or other contracting authorities are not deemed public contracts, as a public contract is based on a 'purchasing' capacity of contracting authorities and on the imperative of a contracting authority in being able to determine standards and specifications suitable to meet the conditions of immediate economic benefit. Thus, the sale of assets or land is not a public contract, unless a directly related public contract to that asset or land is imminent by the contracting authority or another contracting authority, in which case the land or asset sale and the consecutive public works should be viewed in their entirety as a public contract.

The Court in *Helmut Müller* reiterated that the concept of public works contracts does not require that the works which are the subject of the contract be materially or physically carried out for the contracting authority, provided that they are carried out for that authority's *immediate* economic benefit. The Court restricted the conditions which reflect the direct economic benefit to a contracting authority by inserting an element of functionality in the notion of public contracts, and rendered the ownership

[73] The European Commission in its Interpretative Communication on Public-Private Partnerships COM (2007) 6661 is against double tendering requirements in the case of Institutional Public Private Partnerships, by encouraging contracting authorities to consider *en bloc* the selection of a private partner and the subsequent award of works or services as a single contractual interface.

[74] See Case C-451/08, *Helmut Müller v Bundesanstalt für Immobilienaufgaben* [2010] 3 CMLR 18.

of assets irrelevant to the determination of direct economic benefit on the part of contracting authorities. In fact, the necessary conditions to satisfy an *immediate economic benefit* to contracting authorities reflect only on the legal right of a contracting authority over the use of an asset or on the future economic advantages enjoyed or risks assumed by the contracting authority in relation to the relevant asset.

Helmut Müller revealed that the immediate economic benefit from a concession contract to a contracting authority presupposes a significant assumption of operational or functional risks by the concessionaire and a different makeup of the pecuniary interest consideration, in that the concessionaire has the economic freedom to charge end-users or third parties for certain duration. The ability of an economic operator to obtain urban planning does not reflect operational risk and the unlimited duration of concessions could not be regarded as lawful.

PRE-LET CONTRACT ARRANGEMENTS AS PUBLIC CONTRACTS

A contract to let buildings which have not yet been constructed constitutes a public works contract despite having elements characteristic of a lease, and is not, therefore, covered by the exclusion referred to in Article 1(a)(iii) of Directive 92/50.[75] Whether a transaction constitutes a public works contract for the purposes of EU legislation is a question of EU law. The classification of the proposed contract as a 'lease' is not decisive in that regard.[76] Where a contract contains both elements relating to a public works contract and elements relating to another type of contract, it is necessary to refer to the main object of that contract in order to determine its legal classification and the applicable EU rules.[77]

If the main object of the contract is the creation of a building complex, for which the subsequent letting of the complex is presupposed,[78] in order for it to be classified as a 'public works contract', it is required that the execution of the planned work corresponds to the requirements specified by the contracting authority[79] or that the contracting authority has taken measures to define the characteristics of the work or, at the very least, has had a decisive influence on its design.[80]

The pre-let contract in the case *Impresa Pizzarotti* specified the various technical and technological characteristics of the planned work and, on the basis of a set of statistical data relating to judicial activity in the district of Bari (number of civil and criminal cases, number of hearings per week per court, number of judges or prosecutors, number of members of administrative staff, criminal investigation staff or security service staff, number of lawyers admitted to the Bari Bar), lists the specific requirements of each of

---

[75] See Case C-213/13, *Impresa Pizzarotti & C. SpA v Comune di Bari, Giunta comunale di Bari, Consiglio comunale di Bari*, judgment of 10 July 2014.

[76] See Case C-480/06, *Commission v Germany, op.cit*, para 54.

[77] See C-220/05, *Auroux v Commune de Roanne* [2007] E.C.R. I-385 para 37; Case C-412/04, *Commission v Italy* [2008] ECR I-619 para 47; and *Commission v Germany, op.cit*, para 57.

[78] See *Commission v Germany, op.cit*, para 56.

[79] See ibid, para 55.

[80] See Case C-451/08, *Helmut Müller* [2010] 3 CMLR 18 para 67.

the courts coming within that judicial district (number of offices and of courtrooms, conference rooms, meeting rooms and archive rooms required, surface area of rooms, methods of internal communication), along with certain common requirements, such as car park capacity. It follows that the contracting authority has a decisive influence on the design of the work to be constructed. The pre-let contract also included certain elements of a lease. However, the leasing payments amounted to a far less consideration when compared to the construction cost. The Court maintained that the decisive element for the purposes of the classification of the contract concerned is the main object of that contract, not the amount paid to the contractor or the arrangements for payment.[81]

SOCIAL HOUSING AS A RESULT OF PLANNING GAIN

The development of social housing units which are subsequently to be sold at capped prices to a public social housing institution, or with substitution of that institution for the service provider which developed those units, is covered by the concept of 'public works contract'.[82] Initially, it could be maintained that such arrangements are outside the thrust of public procurement rules. Two types of contracts entered into by contracting authorities do not fall within the scope of EU public procurement law. The first type are those contracts which are concluded by a public entity with a person who is legally distinct from that entity where, at the same time, that entity exercises over the person concerned a control which is similar to that which it exercises over its own departments and where that person carries out the essential part of its activities with the entity or entities which control it.[83] The second type of contracts are those which establish cooperation between public entities with the aim of ensuring that a public task that they all have to perform is carried out. In those circumstances, the EU rules on public procurement are not applicable in so far as, in addition, such contracts are concluded exclusively by public entities, without the participation of a private party, no private provider of services is placed in a position of advantage vis-à-vis competitors and implementation of that cooperation is governed solely by considerations and requirements relating to the pursuit of objectives in the public interest.[84]

However, the development of social housing units as a result of planning gain is regarded as a public contract, provided certain conditions are present. The existence of a contract concluded in writing between the contracting authority and the economic operator is required. The obligation to provide affordable housing at capped prices is usually imposed directly on developers by planning laws and is applicable merely because they own the land in relation to which they have applied for planning

---

[81] *See Commission v Germany, op.cit*, para 61.

[82] See Joined Cases C-197/11 and C-203/11, Libert *v Gouvernement Flamand* [2013] 3 CMLR 35.

[83] See Case C-480/06, *Commission v Germany* [2009] ECR I-4747 para 37; Case C-159/11, *Ordine degli Ingegneri della Provincia di Lecce and Others* [2012] ECR 0000 para 32.

[84] See Case C-480/06 *Commission v Germany* [2009] ECR I-4747 para 37; Case C-159/11, *Ordine degli Ingegneri della Provincia di Lecce and Others*, *op.cit*, paras 34 and 35.

permission. This requirement, on its own, is not sufficient to bring the obligation of the economic operator who is obliged to supply social housing as a result of a condition in the planning permission to develop land, into the realm of public contracts. The Court alluded that some type of contractual relationship, such as a development agreement, must exist between a contracting authority and a developer, where under such a development agreement the purpose of determining the work to be undertaken by the developer and the terms and conditions relating thereto must be established. The fact that the development of social housing units is a requirement imposed directly by national legislation and that the party contracting with the authorities is necessarily the owner of the building land does not preclude the existence of a contractual relationship between the authorities and the developer.[85] However, an administrative arrangement between the contracting authority and the developer who is obliged to develop social housing as a conditional requirement of the planning permission which does not regulate the relationship between the contracting authority and the economic operator concerned cannot be regarded as a contractual relation between them.

RESEARCH ACTIVITIES AS PUBLIC CONTRACTS

A research study and evaluation of the seismic vulnerability of hospital structures concluded between two public entities, one of which is a university, is a public service contract for pecuniary interest, even if the consideration does not exceed the costs incurred.[86] A contract cannot fall outside the concept of public contract merely because the remuneration remains limited to reimbursement of the expenditure incurred to provide the agreed service. The meaning of the phrase 'pecuniary interest' is to be interpreted widely, thus covering also cost-only remunerative contracts.

Thus, with regard to entities such as public universities, the Court has held that such entities are, in principle, entitled to take part in a tendering procedure for the award of a public service contract. The Court held that a contract for pecuniary interest concluded in writing between an economic operator and a contracting authority and having as its object the provision of services is a public contract. In that regard, first, it is immaterial whether that operator is itself a contracting authority.[87] It is also immaterial whether the body concerned is primarily profit-making, whether it is structured as an undertaking or whether it has a continuous presence on the market.[88]

If the estimated value of the contract reaches the required thresholds, public procurement rules apply. Otherwise, the fundamental rules and the general principles of the EU Treaty, in particular the principles of equal treatment and of non-discrimination on grounds of nationality and the consequent obligation of transparency, apply, provided that the contract concerned has a certain cross-border interest in the light,

---

[85] See Case C-399/98, *Ordine degli Architetti and Others* [2001] ECR I-5409 paras 69 and 71.

[86] See Case C-159/11, *Azienda Sanitaria Locale di Lecce, Università del Salento v Ordine degli Ingegneri della Provincia di Lecce and Others*, *op.cit.*

[87] See Case C-107/98, *Teckal* [1999] ECR I-8121, para 51.

[88] See Case C-305/08, *CoNISMa* [2009] ECR I-12129 paras 30 and 45.

inter alia, of its value and the place where it is carried out.[89] The criteria in order to determine whether an invitation to tender is mandatory or not are relevant both with regard to the interpretation of public procurement Directives and with regard to the interpretation of those rules and principles of the EU Treaty.[90] As an exemption from European Union public procurement law, the conclusion, without an invitation to tender, of a contract is permitted by which public entities establish cooperation among each other the purpose of such a contract is to ensure that a public task that those entities have to perform is carried out, where that contract is governed solely by considerations and requirements relating to the pursuit of objectives in the public interest or where it is such as to prevent placing a private provider of services in a position of disadvantage vis-à-vis his competitors.[91]

National law may regulate the activities of entities such as universities and research institutions and, *inter alia*, authorise or not authorise them to operate on the market, taking into account their objectives. However, if and to the extent that such entities are entitled to offer certain services on the market, they may not be prevented from participating in a tendering procedure for the services concerned.[92]

In the *Azienda Sanitaria Locale di Lecce* case, national law expressly authorised public universities to supply research and consultancy services to public or private entities provided that that activity does not impair their educational role. However, activities such as research and evaluation of the seismic vulnerability of hospital structures fall, either within the framework of research and development services covered by Annex II A, category 8, of Directive 2004/18 or within the framework of engineering services and related scientific and technical consulting services covered by category 12 of that annex.

If a contract contains a series of substantive aspects a significant or even major part of which corresponds to activities usually carried out by market operators under a competitive market environment, even though these aspects carry a public service or public function task, the cumulative requirements of horizontal public co-operation established by *Commission v Germany* cannot be met. In addition, a distortion of competition may occur, if external collaborators to a public body gain an unfair advantage over other providers as a result of such cooperation.

EMERGENCY AMBULANCE SERVICES AS PUBLIC CONTRACTS

The provision of urgent and emergency ambulance services, on a preferential basis, and by direct award, without any form of advertising, to the voluntary associations covered

---

[89] See Joined Cases C-147/06 and C-148/06, *SECAP and Santorso* [2008] ECR I-3565 paras 20, 21 and 31.

[90] See Case C-573/07, *Sea* [2009] ECR I-8127 paras 35–37.

[91] See Case C-480/06, *Commission v Germany* [2009] ECR I-4747.

[92] See *CoNISMa*, *op.cit*, paras 45, 48, 49 and 51.

by the agreements which, for the provision of those services, receive only reimbursement for the costs actually incurred for that purpose and a fraction of their fixed and ongoing costs is not to be considered as public service contracts.[93]

Urgent and emergency ambulance services are covered by Category 2 in Annex II A to Directive 2004/18 and Category 25 in Annex II B to that directive as regards the medical aspects thereof.[94] However, EU law does not preclude national legislation which provides that the provision of urgent and emergency ambulance services must be entrusted on a preferential basis and awarded directly, without any advertising, to the voluntary associations covered by the agreements, in so far as the legal and contractual framework in which the activity of those associations is carried out actually contributes to the social purpose and the pursuit of the objectives of the good of the community and budgetary efficiency on which that legislation is based.

If a system of agreements allow for public authorities to have recourse, by direct award, on a preferential basis to voluntary associations covered by the agreements to satisfy needs in that area, such legislation excludes for-profit entities from an essential part of the market concerned. According to the case-law of the Court, the award, in the absence of any transparency, of a contract to an undertaking located in the same Member State as the contracting authority amounts to a difference in treatment to the detriment of undertakings which might be interested in that contract but are situated in another Member State. Unless it is justified by objective circumstances, such a difference in treatment, which, by excluding all undertakings located in another Member State and operates mainly to the detriment of the latter undertakings, amounts to indirect discrimination on the basis of nationality, and as such is prohibited under Articles 49 TFEU and 56 TFEU.[95]

However, if the method of organising ambulance services is based upon the principles of universality, the good of the community, economic efficiency and suitability, the recourse on a preferential basis to the voluntary organisations covered by the agreement seeks specifically to ensure that that public service is provided in an economically balanced manner for budgetary purposes. In so far as it provides for the participation of voluntary associations in a public service and refers to the principle of the good of the community, a system of agreements allow for public authorities to have recourse, by direct award, on a preferential basis to voluntary associations is compatible with EU law.

In that connection, EU law does not detract from the power of the Member States to organise their public health and social security systems.[96] Member States may not introduce or maintain unjustified restrictions of the exercise of fundamental freedoms in the area of health care. However, in the assessment of compliance with that prohibition, account must be taken of the fact that the health and life of humans rank

[93] See Case C-113/13, *Azienda sanitaria locale n 5 'Spezzino' v San Lorenzo Soc coop sociale* [2015] 2 CMLR 9.

[94] See Case C-76/97, *Tögel* [1998] ECR I-5357 para 39.

[95] See *Commission v Ireland*, paras 30 and 31; *Commission v Italy*, para 64; and *Commission v Italy*, para 66.

[96] See Case C-70/95, *Sodemare SA v Lombardia* [1997] ECR I-3395 para 27; Cases C-570/07 and C-571/07, *Blanco Pérez and Chao Gómez*, [2010] 3 CMLR 37 para 43.

foremost among the assets or interests protected by the Treaty and it is for the Member States, which have a discretion in the matter, to decide on the degree of protection which they wish to afford to public health and on the way in which that degree of protection is to be achieved.[97] Moreover, not only the risk of seriously undermining the financial balance of a social security system may constitute per se an overriding reason in the general interest capable of justifying an obstacle to the freedom to provide services, but also the objective of maintaining, on grounds of public health, a balanced medical and hospital service open to all may also fall within one of the derogations, on grounds of public health in so far as it contributes to the attainment of a high level of health protection.[98] Thus, measures which aim, first, to meet the objective of guaranteeing in the territory of the Member State concerned sufficient and permanent access to a balanced range of high-quality medical treatment and, secondly, assist in ensuring the desired control of costs and prevention, as far as possible, of any wastage of financial, technical and human resources are also covered.[99]

In *Sodemare and Others*, the Court held that a Member State may, in the exercise of the powers it retains to organise its social security system, consider that a social welfare system for elderly people necessarily implies, with a view to attaining its objectives, that the admission of private operators to that system as providers of social welfare services is to be made subject to the condition that they are non-profit making. Therefore, a Member State, in the context of its discretion to decide the level of protection of public health and to organise its social security system, may take the view that recourse to voluntary associations is consistent with the social purpose of the emergency ambulance services and may help to control costs relating to those services. However, it must be observed that a system of organisation of the emergency ambulance services such as that at issue in the main proceedings, consisting, for the competent authorities, in recourse on a preferential basis to voluntary associations, must actually contribute to the social purpose and the pursuit of the objectives of the good of the community and budgetary efficiency on which that system is based. In that connection, the Court found that it is essential that, where they act in that context, the voluntary associations do not pursue objectives other than those mentioned in the previous paragraph of the present judgment, do not make any profit as a result of their services, apart from the reimbursement of the variable, fixed and on-going expenditure necessary to provide them, and do not procure any profit for their members. Furthermore, although it is permissible to maintain a workforce, for it would, without one, be almost impossible for those associations to act effectively in numerous domains in which the principle of the good of the community may naturally be implemented, the activities of those associations must strictly comply with the requirements laid down by national law. The activities of voluntary associations may be carried out by the workforce only within the limits necessary for their proper functioning. As regards the reimbursement of costs, it must be ensured that profit making, even indirect, cannot be pursued under the cover of a voluntary activity and that volunteers may be reimbursed

---

[97] See Case C-147/07, *Commission v Germany* paras 46 and 51 and Cases C-570/07 and C-571/07, *Blanco Pérez and Chao Gómez* paras 43, 44, 68 and 90.

[98] See Case C-444/05, *Stamatelaki* [2007] E.C.R. I-3185 paras 30 and 31.

[99] See *Commission v Germany*, para 61.

only for expenditure actually incurred for the activity performed, within the limits laid down in advance by the associations themselves. Assessments are required by national courts in order to verify whether the system of organisation of emergency ambulance services at issue in the main proceedings, as regulated by the applicable legislation and implemented by the regional framework agreements and the individual agreements which flow from there, actually contributes to the social purpose and the pursuit of the objectives of the good of the community and budgetary efficiency on which that system is based.

CONTRACTS BELOW THE THRESHOLDS OF THE DIRECTIVES

The Court's settled case law[100] has made clear that contracts below the stipulated thresholds of the Directives are excluded from their applicability. *Vestergaard*[101] ruled that although such contracts are excluded from the scope of public procurement Directives, contracting authorities are nevertheless bound to comply with the fundamental principles of the Treaty.[102] *Medipac-Kazantzidis*,[103] confirmed that contracts below the stipulated thresholds need to comply with the duty of transparency[104] as well as the principle of non-discrimination on grounds of nationality.[105] *Correos*[106] ruled that even in the absence of any discrimination on grounds of nationality, the principle of equal treatment is applicable to the award of public contracts below the stipulated thresholds.[107]

The principles of equal treatment and non-discrimination on grounds of nationality imply, in particular, a duty of transparency which enables contracting authorities to verify that those principles are complied with. The duty of transparency which is imposed on contracting authorities consists in ensuring a sufficient degree of advertising to enable the relevant public contract to be opened up to competition and the impartiality of procurement procedures to be reviewed.[108]

---

[100] See Joined Cases C-147/06 and C-148/06, *SECAP SpA* and *Santorso Soc. coop. arl,* [2008] ECR I-3565; Case C-412/04 *Commission v Italy* [2008] ECR I-619 para 65.

[101] See Case C-59/00, *Vestergaard* [2001] ECR I-9505.

[102] See Case C-324/98, *Telaustria and Telefonadress* [2000] ECR I-10745 para 60.

[103] See Case C-6/05, *Medipac-Kazantzidis AE v Venizelio-Pananio (PE.S.Y. KRITIS)* [2007] ECR I-4557.

[104] See Case C-324/98, *Telaustria and Telefonadress* [2000] ECR I-10745 paras 60 and 61; Case 59/00, *Vestergaard*, paras 20 and 21; Case C-231/03, *Coname* [2005] ECR I-7287 paras 16 and 17, and Case C-458/03, *Parking Brixen* [2005] ECR I-8585 paras 46 to 48.

[105] See Case C-324/98, *Telaustria and Telefonadress*, para 60; Case C-50/00, *Vestergaard*, paras 20 and 21; Case C-264/03, *Commission v France* [2005] ECR I-8831 para 32; and Case C-6/05, Medipac-*Kazantzidis* [2007] ECR I-4557 para 33.

[106] See Case C-220/06, *Asociación Profesional de Empresas de Reparto y Manipulado de Correspondencia v Administración General del Estado* [2007] ECR I-12175.

[107] See Case C-458/03, *Parking Brixen* [2005] ECR I-8585 para 48, and Case C-410/04, *ANAV* [2006] ECR I-3303 para 20.

[108] See Case C-458/03, *Parking Brixen* [2005] ECR I-8612 para 49, and Case C-410/04, *ANAV*, para 21.

However, the application of the fundamental principles of the Treaty to contracts below the stipulated thresholds is based on the assumption that the contracts in question are of certain cross-border interest.[109]

The parameters which could determine if a contract is likely to be of certain cross-border interest and therefore attract economic operators from other Member States comprise of the contract's estimated value in conjunction with its technical complexity or the location of its execution. It is in principle for the contracting authority concerned to assess whether there may be cross-border interest in a contract whose estimated value is below the threshold laid down by the procurement Directives. However, such assessment should be subject to judicial review.

It is permissible, nevertheless, for national legislation to lay down objective criteria, at national or local level, stipulating certain cross-border interest for public contracts which fall below the thresholds of the public procurement Directives. Such criteria could include, *inter alia*, the quantum of the monetary value of a contract, or its strategic importance to economic operators, in conjunction with the place where the work is to be carried out. The projected profitability to an economic operator from a sub-dimensional contract may also be part of such criteria to determine certain cross-border interest for public contracts. Where the financial returns in the relevant contracts are very modest,[110] the likelihood of a cross-border interest is considerably weakened. However, in certain cases, the geography and the particular location of the performance of a public contract could trigger cross-border interest, even for low-value contracts.

The Court held that exclusion of sub-dimensional public contracts of certain cross-border interest from the application of the fundamental rules and general principles of the Treaty could undermine the general principle of non-discrimination, could give rise to collusive conduct and anti-competitive agreements between national or local undertakings and finally could impede the exercise of freedom of establishment and freedom to provide services.[111]

CHANGES OF CIRCUMSTANCES IN PUBLIC CONTRACTS

A change in the terms and conditions of a contract which was previously awarded in accordance with the public procurement Directives may necessitate initiating fresh award procedures. In *Pressetext*,[112] various changes were introduced by the contracting authority, in particular instituting an internal re-organisation by transferring the contract to a subsidiary of the economic operator that was carrying out the contract and waving the right to terminate contract for three years. Additionally, a rebate increase from 15 to

[109] See Case C-507/03 *Commission v Ireland* [2007] ECR I-9777 para 29, and *Commission v Italy*, paras 66 and 67.

[110] See Case C-231/03, *Coname* [2005] ECR I-7287 para 20.

[111] See Case C-79/01, *Payroll and Others* [2002] ECR I-8923 para 26; Case C-442/02, *CaixaBank France* [2004] ECR I-8961 paras 12 and 13; and Case C-452/04, *Fidium Finanz* [2006] ECR I-9521 para 46.

[112] See Case C-454/06, *Pressetext Nachrichtenagentur* [2008] ECR I-4401.

25 per cent was set up to counterbalance the price conversion to Euro from the domestic currency and a clause was introduced to update price indices. The Court held that these changes were *not* sufficient to constitute a new award under the procurement Directives.

The key test appears to assert that amendments during the duration of an awarded public contract necessitate new award procedures when they are materially different in character from the original contract and therefore demonstrate the intention of the parties to re-negotiate the essential contractual terms. In practice, it is not easy to distinguish between material and non-material amendments in a public contract. An amendment may be regarded as material when it would have extended significantly the duration of the initial contract; when it would have allowed for admission of different bidders or selection of a different bid in the original tender; when it extends the scope of the contract considerably to encompass services not initially covered; or when it changes the economic balance of the contract in favour of the contractor.

However, if the change in terms and conditions was foreseen in the initial contract, such change is normally regarded as a variation of the execution of the contract, thus not meriting fresh award procedures.

In *Commission v Germany*[113] (Ambulances case) an extension of ambulance services contract to a new area increasing its value by 15 per cent was regarded as a material change. In *Wall*,[114] the change of subcontractor, even with the consent of the contracting authority and even if the possibility of such change was provided for in contract, amounts to a material change, requiring a re-tender, if the use of that subcontractor was a decisive factor in the award decision. In *Commission v Spain*,[115] contract changes effected in the period between the contract notification notice in the OJEU and the award of the contract are material when the final contract included additional works which were not mentioned in the OJEU notice or tender specifications and when they increase the value of the contract. The possibility of additional works not constituting material changes in the terms and conditions of a contract is only permitted if such additional works have been envisaged in the OJEU notice published by the contracting authority.

A post-award change in the financial make-up of a contract, which results it being de-classified as a concession is also to be regarded as material change. So, if the contracting authority alters the method of remuneration of the economic operator by substitution of the right to exploit the concession with direct payment, a significant reduction in operational risk is effected, which favours the concessionaire and takes away the two necessary criteria for concessions, namely the assumption of operational risk by the concessionaire and the total or partial payment by means of third-party or end user contributions based on the concessionaire's exclusive right of exploitation.

113 See Case C-160/08, *Commission v Germany,* judgment of 29 April 2010.

114 See Case C-91/08, *Wall AG v Stadt Frankfurt am Main*, judgment of 13 April 2010.

115 See Case C-423/07, *Commission v Spain*, judgment of 22 April 2010.

4. Public procurement and frameworks

Rick Canavan

INTRODUCTION

Framework agreements[1] have become an established feature of the public procurement landscape. Essentially a means of identifying a qualified supplier (or suppliers) with whom contracts might later be concluded on terms broadly identified by the framework, they represent a flexible tool deployed across a range of procurement activities, useful almost irrespective of scale and to some extent frequency of dealing. Such arrangements potentially offer a means of readily achieving administrative and price efficiencies, particularly in the context of repeat dealings in the same or similar types of goods and particularly for the acquisition of commodity goods.

The purpose of this chapter is to offer an exposition of the nature and purpose of the framework agreement at large and to then focus in on the framework agreement as it is defined and conceived for the purposes of European public procurement regime with a particular emphasis on the understanding of that regime in the UK. This chapter will consider the concept, definition and forms of framework agreement and how frameworks to which Directive 2004/18/EC[2] is applicable may be operated, established and breaches of them remedied. Finally, this chapter will turn to examine whether, notwithstanding their wide usage, frameworks are in fact capable in principle and in fact of delivering the efficiencies and cost benefits that they appear to herald while maintaining fairness and transparency.

THE NATURE AND PURPOSE OF THE FRAMEWORK AGREEMENT

Framework agreements have their origins in private sector procurement where they provide a convenient structure for a host of transactions ranging from the substantially peripheral, such as variable frequency purchases of relatively low value supplies and commodity items such as stationery, to being a central means by which a provider serves the needs of its client, for example in the context of a managed service provider (MSP) whose income derives substantially from providing subcontractors and so on, in response to call downs under a framework agreement to which it is party.

---

[1] Often referred to as umbrella agreements or in the US indefinite delivery, indefinite quantity (IDIQ) agreements.

[2] Hereinafter 'the Public Sector Directive' or 'the Directive', given effect in UK law by the Public Contracts Regulations 2006 and to a much lesser extent Directive 2004/17/EC, 'the Utilities Directive'.

Agreements may take a number of forms and may involve multiple suppliers and contracting authorities (acting collaboratively), a single contracting authority[3] dealing with a range of potential suppliers or an agreement between a single contracting authority and a single supplier. Certain framework agreements may also allow for the participating suppliers and entities to change over the course of the framework's life. In addition, the framework may be concluded by a third party and a range of potential suppliers with the intention that the framework then be 'let' to contracting authorities, allowing the task of identifying and qualifying suitable suppliers to be undertaken by an appropriately qualified and resourced body. In public procurement, these distinctions continue to be of note in the context of the Directives and have been particularly troublesome historically.

Function of Frameworks

At a 'commercial' level framework, agreements are apt to meet a range of needs on the part of the contracting authority. Whether that is flexibility in terms of the quantity and even the nature of what is to be supplied or by the range of parties capable of supplying it, a framework agreement allows a contracting authority to meet a range of often dynamic needs and ensure the inclusion of suppliers that might otherwise by excluded, while themselves having access (in principle) to more favourable terms and prices individually or by grouping with other procuring bodies to form a 'consortium' which collectively use the framework agreement all in the context of a relatively streamlined process. It is this streamlining (and consequent *cost* reduction), achieved by the obviation of the need to repeat the same or a similar tender process, which as much as potential *price* reductions is the real prize for contracting authorities utilising frameworks as it avoids the need to frequently repeat the same or similar tendering processes – with its attendant bureaucratic burden – by establishing, as Professor Arrowsmith identifies,[4] what essentially amounts to an approved supplier list, thereby reducing cost and the time required to obtain the requisite goods and services. With such a range of self-apparent benefits, or at least potential benefits[5] it is no surprise that such frameworks have been taken up and come also to be used in the public sector, indeed today can be regarded as a well-established feature of the public procurement landscape.

As a comparator to the exposition of the public sector regime which follows below, it is worth noting that in the private sector the operation of framework agreements is as unproblematic as it is unregulated. While behaviours and the extent of regulation varies across jurisdictions, private sector contracting authorities enjoy substantially unlimited freedom to contract with any supplier based on any criteria, via any process, with minimal requirements for fairness or transparency beyond those which they themselves

[3] As defined by Article 1(9) of the Public Sector Directive.

[4] S. Arrowsmith, *Framework Purchasing and Qualifications Lists Under the European Procurement Directives: Part II* (1999) 8 PPLR 161 at 172.

[5] It is questionable particularly in the context of commodity purchases whether the relatively cumbersome approach adopted by the Directive in reality negates any substantial savings.

specify and for a duration determined by commercial convenience.[6] In this context, the only question is whether or not the framework agreement can be regarded as a contract or merely an agreement to agree in the future. This is a question which falls to be determined largely by reference to the prevailing principles of contract formation and their application to the facts of any particular case. An analysis of the agreement concluded ought to reveal for example whether the parties intend it to be legally binding, whether it does in fact contain any obligations which are intended to be or are capable of enforcement, and so on. Generally, framework agreements themselves will not be regarded as contracts[7] as they predominantly serve only to sketch the shape of future contracts[8] whilst requiring no performance by either party. A contract is then formed in accordance with the procedure set out and on the terms contained in the framework when a call down is made. Even at this point the framework agreement itself cannot be said to crystallise into a contract serving merely as the continuing overarching transactional framework and repository of the parameters of contractual terms and the means by which contracts are to be later concluded. The only exception will be in cases of a single contracting authority/single supplier framework agreement where it is unambiguous that the identified supplier must supply when required or when the contracting authority commits to purchasing specific quantities over the life of the framework. In this circumstance, it is conceivable that the framework agreement could be regarded as being sufficiently certain but in the instance that for example that the supplier subsequently refused to supply, it is difficult to see that the argument that the framework agreement is a contract does much to practically advance the position of the contracting authority as the question of what remedy might then be awarded seems to yield only unappealing answers, an issue which will be considered in due course. Arrowsmith argues (writing in relation to framework agreements governed by the European procurement rules) that the question in principle of whether or not a framework agreement is a legally binding contract or not is in reality of any great moment as even if it is not, the contracts to which it does give rise will be governed by the Directive.[9]

---

[6] This is exemplified in the English Law context by cases such as *Blackpool and Fylde Aero Club Ltd v Blackpool Borough Council* [1990] 3 All ER 25, which while not a case concerned with the European regime and approached by Court of Appeal as a purely contractual matter, held that there was an obligation on the local authority to consider all tenders submitted in the prescribed form by the time and place stipulated for their submission.

[7] While most certainly not labelled as such, the IDIQ nature of a framework is apparent in classic cases such as *Foley v Classique Coaches* [1934] 2 KB 1 whereby a contract under which a 'vendor shall sell to the company and the company shall purchase from the vendor all petrol which shall be required by the company for the running of their said business at a price to be agreed by the parties in writing and from time to time', was held, notwithstanding the apparently binding nature of the obligation to buy and sell to be unenforceable.

[8] Price, quantity and (to a limited extent) duration being the main variables to be determined in the course of the contract, although the identity of the contracting parties will of course also be unknown in many instances and may even be unforeseeable (to some degree) in the context of dynamic purchasing systems.

[9] S. Arrowsmith, *The Law of Public and Utilities Procurement*, 2nd edn., London: Sweet & Maxwell, 2005, ch.11 at 11.35.

Transposition into the Public Sector

Almost irrespective of whether a framework is used in the public sector or the private sector, the reasons for its use are likely to be broadly similar, although in the public sector the use of the framework may also be used to further policy goals that would be unlikely to concern private sector contracting authorities such as utilising a framework to allocate lots specifically created to encourage the participation of small and medium-size enterprises (SMEs). It is here, however, that the similarity ends along with any further consideration of the operation of frameworks in private sector procurement. Public sector frameworks carry with them a substantial degree of additional concerns and requirements which manifest in a discrete body of legal rules which operate to control them. The broad reasons for this are clear. First, there is a need to inculcate the creation of frameworks with the values which pervade all public procurement activities in the EU, transparency, equality of treatment and non-discrimination. The nature of frameworks is that they isolate to more or less an extent (dependent upon the contracting behaviour of the contracting authority and whether they are party to binding or non-binding) a group of contracting authorities from the market at large for a fixed period. Far from ensuring efficient and competitive procurement, this may have the opposite effect. Furthermore, in the process of separating the contract authority from the market at large, the procurement process may be cloaked in a way that the award of a single contract would not be, while at the same time, the market remains static in the sense that it is also closed to new entrants.

In addition, the law is concerned with addressing particular issues raised by frameworks. The static 'micro-market' into which suppliers and contracting authorities are locked for a period of time may give rise to improper practices on the part of both suppliers and contracting authorities. On the part of suppliers, where contract terms are to be determined through the life of the framework, there may be the temptation to collude in order to ensure a particular division of contracts under the framework or to manipulate the price that is to be paid for the supplies by the contracting authority. The greater the duration of the framework, the greater the danger of this occurring. Such behaviours are of course prohibited under EU competition law[10] but their prohibition alone does ensure that they will not occur, nor that the perpetrator's actions will be discovered by a contracting authority.

The corollary of this is that a lock-in with a fixed group of suppliers may lead the contracting authority to believe that their conduct after the conclusion of the framework, as each subsequently formed contract is essentially a discrete internal matter, need not meet the standards that run as the red thread through all public procurement activities. Indeed, it is conceivable, particularly when duration is needlessly lengthy, that collusion between contracting authorities and suppliers could occur thereby reducing both the probity and transparency of the process and failing to realise value for the public purse.

The regime has had to adapt and grow to meet these challenges while others remain and have resulted from it. The regime supplements the pre-existing requirements in respect of advertising and the evaluation of tenders; to enter into a framework adds to

[10] In the example case of Article 101 TFEU.

the administrative burden, at least at the time of formation, for the contracting authority. It also requires as a result that suppliers must join perhaps several frameworks. While unlikely, it is conceivable that notwithstanding the investment of time and resource in doing so, no orders will ever be forthcoming. Many suppliers will also participate in private sector frameworks, which in terms of their operation are apt to carry a less onerous administrative burden. Participation in both public and private sector frameworks may be unattractive as a result and so the efforts to necessarily inculcate public sector frameworks with the values of the existing law may serve to reduce participation and consequently competition, countering the boost to competition and efficiency the framework is intended to bring about. Yet, the law does not provide any means by which a contracting authority's decision to utilise a framework may be questioned as such.[11]

This critique of framework agreements will be revisited in due course, augmented with the findings of empirical studies and economics literature which questions the ability of frameworks to deliver real price efficiencies through competition at all. What is apparent at this stage, however, is that the legal regime faces a great challenge to ensure effective competition, let alone to ensure the avoidance of maladministration.

Having sketched out the nature of the framework agreement and its function and alluded to some of its inherent weaknesses which have contributed to the shaping of the legal regime, it is necessary to turn to a consideration of the various forms of framework agreement and the legal regime applicable to them.

SPECIES OF FRAMEWORK AGREEMENT

Single Provider Frameworks

The single provider framework is concluded between a single contracting authority and a single supplier. Depending on the structure of the framework, it may have been of a type previously caught by the regime. Single provider frameworks take a number of forms.[12] The form chosen by a particular contracting authority will reflect the nature of the supplies to be procured and the nature of the relationship which the contracting authority desires to have with the supplier. A contracting authority will likely wish to tailor their contract taking into account whether or not they wish to be obliged to make purchases under the framework accepting that this may mean that a retainer is payable

---

11 However, this must be contrasted with the position where all procurement activity in respect of one class of supplies is governmentally mandated to be by framework agreement. In the Irish case of *Copymoore v Commission for Public Works* [2013] IEHC 230, Hogan J found that such a requirement in respect of printing services manifestly undermines and would serve to distort the entire procurement regime; however it is interesting to note that he did add that, 'The matter would have been entirely different if the request for tender for the MPS Framework Agreements had stipulated that the use of such Framework Agreements was mandatory for the entire public service', which would indeed ensure that all suppliers enjoyed a level playing field but potentially at tremendous economic cost.

12 Arrowsmith identifies five of the most used models of single-provider framework agreement, see Arrowsmith, *supra* n. 9, ch.11 at 2.1, pp. 671–2.

to the supplier in consideration of maintaining the capacity to meet this demand; whether they wish to bind themselves to using one framework or wish to maintain the flexibility to use a range of frameworks, although with the consequence that a supplier will likely offer less favourable terms as a result, and whether or not there is a pressing need to partner with a specific supplier in order to secure the supply of a scarce resource. In order to determine the balance of obligations (or not) the contracting authority must also carefully consider its likely future demands (and the likely supply and price) for the good or service in question. The agreements themselves will take many forms and the contracting authorities are free to conclude agreements which best reflect the balance of priorities and the nature of the supplies concerned. In common with most other framework agreements, for the reasons discussed above, single provider frameworks will seldom be regarded as legally enforceable contracts as they lack consideration; however, this will not be the case where a retainer is paid by the contracting authority in consideration of the supplier continuing to ensure their ability to fulfil the contracting authority's needs. In the majority of instances such a definitive obligation will be absent and the agreement will not be enforceable at common law.

Multi-provider Frameworks

Multi-provider frameworks are concluded between a contracting authority and a plurality of potential suppliers. The framework will either operate to establish the majority of the terms of subsequent call-offs or will leave some or the majority of terms to be determined at a later time meaning that to secure orders under the framework suppliers will be required to participate in a secondary competition or 'mini-tender' phase.

As with single-providers it will be for the contract authority to consider whether they wish to be bound to purchase all of their requirements for a particular class of supplies from the suppliers under the framework or whether it would be preferable to maintain the ability to 'shop around' knowing that in the process this may make the suppliers reluctant to guarantee their ability to supply and that to do so may cause the contracting authority to incur additional expense. In certain circumstances it may be preferable to create a framework which binds neither party to supply or undertake to supply under the framework. This latter arrangement is particularly suitable for central purchasing bodies where the framework will be let to other purchasers and where demand consequently is extremely difficult to forecast in terms of overall value or distribution of orders over the life of the framework.

A further variation of the multi-provider framework is the dynamic purchasing system (DPS).[13] This is a distinct form of public contract which is also regulated by the Public Sector Directive and differs in that it must operate exclusively electronically[14] but is primarily distinguished by the fluid nature of the participants. Rather than the suppliers being fixed at the conclusion of the award phase, qualifying suppliers may be added to the DPS at any stage in its life[15] and are entitled to have their suitability

[13] Defined by Article 1(6) of the Directive, elaborated by Article 33.

[14] Article 1(6).

[15] Article 33(2) & (4).

quickly determined. The flexible nature of the DPS, coupled with its exclusively online existence, offers obvious advantages over the more rigid framework agreements and is at the heart of the vision for a fully electronic regime for procurement but brings with it the need to comply in full with all the attendant rules on electronic procurement should this route be chosen, which may be undesirable or not cost effective from the perspective of either supplier or contract authority who is also bound to use only the open procedure for the award phase.[16]

THE LEGAL FRAMEWORK – HISTORICAL CONTEXT

Having considered in broad terms the nature, function and variety of framework agreements, this section will now continue to give an exposition of the key features of the over-arching legal framework which regulates framework agreements and which has moved from a position where framework agreements were at best on the periphery of what was permitted and left to be regulated (if they were permitted at all) by provisions that were not designed with frameworks in mind to the position under the current regime where they are explicitly recognised and specifically regulated.

Recognition of Frameworks – Utilities

In respect of utilities procurement, the legality of frameworks was never in question and it is explicitly recognised and defined by Article 5 of Directive 93/38 as, 'an agreement between one of the contracting entities defined in Article 2 and one or more suppliers, contractors or service providers the purpose of which is to establish the terms, in particular with regard to the prices and, where appropriate, the quantity envisaged, governing the contracts to be awarded during a given period'.

This provision is now obsolete and a consideration of the current definition follows below, what must be noted however is how distinct the approach in respect of utilities is. Article 5 offers an unambiguous acceptance of the framework agreement in sharp contrast to the position in respect of goods and public works where years of ambiguity hung over the provisions of Directive 93/37/EEC.

The Recognition of Framework Agreements – Public Works, Supplies and Services

Following the promulgation of the Public Sector Directive, by virtue of Articles 1(5) and 32 there is now no question as to the legality of framework agreements *per se*, although practical questions may persist as to what falls within the scope of the definition. However, this assent marks the end point of an interesting journey during which they were accepted in respect of utilities but apparently prohibited in respect of contracts for the supply of goods and public works on the grounds that they subvert the need for open, transparent procedures and yet were simultaneously regarded implicitly and explicitly as being important to the furtherance of the objectives of a now maturing

---

[16] Article 33(2).

common procurement policy. The journey towards recognition provides a good example of the sometimes contradictory forces that have shaped and continue to shape this still 'malleable' area of law.

Historical Uncertainty as to the Status of Frameworks

Before the current position brought about by the Public Sector Directive, the question of the legality of framework agreements was not a question that existed merely as a matter of principle.[17] Anecdotal evidence suggests that frameworks were already in widespread use in some Member States including the UK, France and Sweden (where the view was taken that they would likely be regarded as permissible under regulation 93/38/EEC), long before the Public Service Directive came into force. That they were in *widespread* use seems all the more likely as by 2011, framework agreements accounted for 11 per cent[18] of all contract notices in the Official Journal equating to 17 per cent[19] in terms of value. Such substantial figures while admittedly possible, particularly given year on year growth in the use of framework agreements estimated at 18 per cent per year,[20] it is suggested seem on balance more likely to have built up from a basis of use which was established before the promulgation of the Public Sector Directive.

That framework agreements were in use to some degree during the life of Directive 93/38/EEC was left beyond doubt by the fact that the Commission commenced infringement proceedings against the UK Government in 1997.[21] The proceedings against the UK government came in response to attempts by the Northern Ireland Department of the Environment to establish a framework for the procurement of a range of architectural and engineering works. The press release which announces the Commission's intention to pursue the UK Government makes clear that the establishment of the framework agreement is in contravention of Directives 92/50/EEC, 93/36/EEC and 93/37/EEC and is not justified by the UK Government's response. The tone of the press release is almost strident. The breach for which the UK is being pursued is set amongst a range of other ostensibly more serious breaches by fellow Member States and is preceded by an introduction making clear that such breaches of the Directive(s) will not be ignored. The context and tone of this press release suggests an implacable objection to the notion of framework agreements or at the very least an absolute reluctance to entertain the possibility that the relevant Directives might be

---

17 Aside from the fact that they were already permitted in the utilities sector by virtue of 83/38/EEC.

18 See I. Strand, et al. *Public Procurement in the EU – cost and effectiveness,* prepared for the European Commission by PWC, London Economics & Ecorys, March 2011, available 26 January 2016 at at p. 22.

19 Ibid.

20 Ibid at p. 5. Davis J., also notes evidence given as to the popularity of framework agreements in his judgment in *R (on the application of Denfleet International Ltd) v NHS Purchasing and Supply Agency* [2005] EWHC 55 (Admin) at para 12.

21 IP/97/1178 of 19/12/1997.

capable of accommodating them;[22] however, an explanation for the basis of the Commission's objection to the use of frameworks is absent, as is any nuance as to whether this is simply an objectionable framework or whether in fact all such frameworks are objectionable. It is worth considering precisely what the basis of the Commission's objection was at this time.

The Commission's Objections to Framework Agreements

The Commission had already sought some degree of clarification on the use of frameworks in its action against Greece,[23] the result of which suggested that only some frameworks failed to fall within the regime. The tender in that case concerned the purchase of bandages for use by the Greek military and civilian healthcare systems and concerned a framework agreement concluded between the Ministry for Industry, Energy and Technology and six suppliers which had not been advertised in the Official Journal. AG Lenz expressed the view that in the context of Directive 88/295/EEC such an agreement – where the individual call-offs left little or nothing of substance to be determined – must, 'be treated as a supply contract within the meaning of the Directive'. Regrettably in the judgment this issue is not further explored but this argument nonetheless adds weight to the view that such arrangements were lawful. In any case a distinction appears to be tentatively drawn here between frameworks that comprise substantive terms that may be lifted verbatim into contracts called-off from the framework, that is to say the framework agreement itself has the character of a contract caught by the Directive and 'inchoate' frameworks which leave a number of terms to be concluded under each framework.

The distinction is legally sustainable as contracts created under inchoate frameworks would clearly be something very different to the framework, a step in the procurement process in themselves, and consequently ought to be subject to an appropriately transparent procedure for their creation[24] but at a stroke the value of this type of framework, which is very commonly used, is lost. This distinction, as discussed below, has re-emerged in the Public Sector Directive. It may be that this is the distinction also hinted at in the open textured language of press release IP/97/1178 of 19/12/1997[25] but other possibilities are also open to exploration.

An alternative interpretation of the Commission's words/explanation of the action, may lie in a restrictive and somewhat 'revisionist' reading of the definition of 'contracts' deployed across Directives 92/50/EEC, 93/36/EEC and 93/37/EEC, placing almost all frameworks, however detailed and mutually binding in nature, outside of the scope of the regime. That is to say the Commission sought in commencing action to

---

[22] The press release sets out that, 'the use of such framework contracts is not authorised by the public procurement rules ...' although this, it must be acknowledged, could be interpreted as meaning the framework of the type used in this instance, however, the same press release also makes clear that this case, 'raises an important matter of principle', suggesting that the Commission's concerns lay with the legality of frameworks *per se*.

[23] Case C-79/94, *Commission v Greece* [1995] ECR I-1071, ECJ.

[24] As explained by Arrowsmith *supra* n. 9 at p. 677, n. 14.

[25] For the relevant text of which see *supra* n. 15.

seek clarification of the view that the majority of frameworks were outside of the regime for this reason.

The Directives defined any contract caught by the regime as a 'contract for pecuniary interest'.[26] Despite the ostensible circuity of the definition, there is clear insistence that the contracting authority must conclude a *contract*, as opposed to some other lesser form of agreement lacking (and presumably intended to lack) the attendant legal enforcement mechanisms, places the majority of frameworks clearly outside of the regime. While a framework agreement could of course be added to the category of *sui generis* agreements[27] that are treated as contracts notwithstanding such defects in formation, on the face of it, it would appear to fall well short of being a contract in the context of 'contract(s) for pecuniary interest'. Yet, when the opportunity to bring frameworks into this class of 'contracts' in *R (on the application of Denfleet International Ltd) v NHS Purchasing and Supply Agency*[28] no attempt was apparently made to do so. The issue of merely whether or not this is a 'contract' seems not to have been a cause of concern for the Commission. The position in *Denfleet* may be contrasted with the position adopted in *Henry Brothers (Magherafelt) Ltd v Department of Education for Northern Ireland*[29] when considering the remedies available under for the breach of a framework agreement and whether it amounted to a 'public contract' for such purposes. Considering the issue, the Court of Appeal of Northern Ireland held that a framework agreement could not be regarded as a contract in the true sense.

In domestic law the formative defect in these *sui generis* contracts is often an absence of consideration[30] (synonymous with an absence of pecuniary interest[31]) and it is this, which might also have been the real obstacle for the Commission. The notion of pecuniary interest is primarily intertwined with a profit (or intention to profit) from the transaction but can also include any instance where the contracting authority pays more than that which is required to simply reimburse the supplier for the cost of the provision.[32] Many frameworks, especially those that do not provide a framework for the

---

[26] Directives 92/50/EEC, 93/36/EEC 1(a) and 93/37/EEC Art 1(a).

[27] An example of which would be the rights of a beneficiary named under a letter of credit to whom the issuing bank owes a duty to make payment despite the beneficiary providing no consideration for this. Unfortunately, space does not permit a detailed examination of this interesting category of agreements and the extent to which a framework agreement could be regarded as part of it. It is suggested, however, that intention is the key here and so a framework would be regarded in fact as a member of the class of agreements (including 'honour clauses' (*Rose & Frank Co. v Crompton Bros* [1925] AC 445; *Jones v Vernon's Pools Ltd* [1938] 2 All ER 628), 'ex gratia' payments (*Edwards v Skyways Ltd* [1964] 1 WLR 349), letters of comfort (*Kleinwort Benson v Malaysia Mining Corporation* [1989] 1 WLR 379) which are recognised by law but which the law would not seek to enforce.

[28] [2005] EWHC 51 (Admin).

[29] [2011] NICA 59.

[30] The most obvious example being that of documentary credits.

[31] *R (on the application of Chandler) v Secretary of State for Children, Schools and Families* [2009] EWCA Civ 2011.

[32] As opposed to mere reimbursement of expenses but including, for example, a service paid for by subsidy see *Commission v Italy* [2007] ECR I-0000 and *Ordini degli Architetti delle Province di Milano e Lodi v Commune di Milano* Case C-399/98 [2001] ECR I-5409 and in the

pricing of what is to be supplied, only create the possibility of a speculative profit of uncertain size, dependent on future call-offs on the framework being made.

Viewing the definition through the common law prism, it would also suggest that the pecuniary interest must in fact be payable or become payable and be capable of being determined. However, as already noted, under a framework agreement, the price may be left to be determined, for example by subsequent mini-tenders, and in any case, it is not under the framework agreement that the obligation to perform (or the right to receive the payment) arises. This obligation becomes extant only when (and if) contracts are subsequently called off from it.

The real issue then was not with almost all frameworks but with frameworks that were not sufficiently definitive to be contracts of pecuniary interest, meaning that some frameworks fell within and others without, but with little certainty as to exactly where the line was drawn.[33]

Resolving the Ambiguity as to the Basis of the Commission's Objections

The actual substance of the Commission's objections did not ultimately emerge until 2000 when the position was partially clarified. By their press release of 13 July 2000[34] the Commission set out that,

> [I]f the terms of a framework agreement are sufficiently specific as to detail the key elements of any individual contracts to be awarded subsequently, and if these are set out in binding form, when those individual contracts are awarded it is not necessary to follow the detailed procedural requirements of the Directives. However, where the key terms and conditions of individual contracts are vague, or simply not specified at all [as in this case], they must be advertised in the Official Journal and follow the detailed procedural requirements of the public procurement Directives.

This clarity seems to have been forthcoming following pressure from some Member States where framework agreements were widely used. However, as noted above[35] the fundamental issue for the Commission appeared to be the use of frameworks *per se* whereas here the issue is framed as simply being one of the ways in which this particular agreement was cast and the lack of clarity as to the terms advertised. The difficulty with the Commission's approach here is that by its nature, the terms of the framework agreement are to be left to be fully agreed at a later stage, begging the question (even under the Public Sector Directive) of just how much definition is required for a framework to be lawful, an issue that will revisited in due course. Crucially, what became apparent here is that there had been a shift in the Commission's

---

domestic context, interpreting the Public Contracts Regulations 2006, *R (on the application of Chandler) v Secretary of State for Children, Schools and Families* [2009] EWCA Civ 2011.

[33] Later evidence for which can be found in Case C-399/98 *Ordine degli Architetti and Others* [2001] ECR I-5409 where the framework in question is concluded to be one concluded for a pecuniary interest and consequently unproblematic.

[34] European Commission, *Public Procurement: Commission Refers United Kingdom to Court*, IP/00/813. That this is the position is left beyond doubt by the Commission's explanatory note to the Public Sector Directive; see n. 39.

[35] See *supra* n. 16.

views on frameworks, a shift that would ultimately manifest in the acceptance of frameworks in the Public Sector Directive.

Such pressure ought not to have been necessary, however, as at the same time as announcing enforcement action against the UK, the Commission was also expounding a vision for public procurement in which frameworks played a central role adding a further layer of uncertainty as to the basis of the Commission's 1997 position. In the previous year the Commission's Green Paper *Public Procurement in the European Union: Exploring the Way Forward*[36] – which sketched out the now extant regime – clearly identified a number of policy objectives which would be furthered to a large extent by the use of framework agreements, *inter alia*, the greater use of electronic tendering and the increased participation of SME's.

The Commission was clear[37] that SME's ought to play a role in public procurement in proportion to their role in the economy at large but identified that there were substantial obstacles to this, including a:

> lack [of] practical information on contracts put out to tender in their sector ... lack ... [of] trained staff and technical assistance necessary to cope with prequalification procedures, particularly in the utilities sectors, and where appropriate, to prepare bids; they have problems in meeting quality certification requirements; and they are often too small in comparison with the contracts covered by the Directives and put up for competition at Community level. The problem of size is compounded by the difficulty in setting up effective and advantageous forms of partnership between SMEs.[38]

A further problem for SMEs is that to participate actively in public procurement activity requires entering into numerous contracts and thus numerous tendering procedures, which even when the supplier has experience still carry with them a substantial burden. Frameworks do not tackle the inherent complexity and particularity of procurements. However they are effective at addressing some of the barriers to participation by putting suppliers on an approved footing with numerous potential buyers. Frameworks also obviate the need for SMEs to be forced to act cooperatively in order to participate in a tender process, particularly where the framework is divided into lots which are suitable for individual SME suppliers. This negates the need to form partnerships (with its own inherent costs), which would in any case serve largely to reduce competition between the participants and amount to a subsidy of SMEs by the public purse.

Frameworks and particularly dynamic purchasing systems[39] are central to the Commission's still to be realised vision for electronic tendering. However, even when electronic tendering was very much in its infancy the potential benefits of it were

---

[36] COM(96) 583 final available 26 January 2016 at http://europa.eu/documents/comm/green_papers/pdf/com-96-583_en.pdf.

[37] As it had been for some time see for example, Commission Communications (COM (90) 166) of 7 May 1990 and (SEC (92) 722) of 1 June 1992.

[38] See *supra* n. 22 at 5.4, p. 30.

[39] For a description of which see above.

recognised.[40] Electronic procurement improves the extent of dissemination of information about existing or forthcoming tenders and allows ready access to information about past and future needs and behaviours of contracting authorities; electronic procurement further reduces the barriers to SME participation by providing ready access to material with the capability to submit and track the progress of tender documents online in real time. The use of dynamic purchasing systems, essentially a form of online framework agreement where qualifying participants can be added at any point substantially adds to the opportunities for SME participation.

Overall, it is clear that the Commission was both implicitly and explicitly committed to the furthering of policy goals in no small part through the use of framework agreements. The position therefore in the late 1990s was a curious one with the Commission simultaneously extoling the virtues of frameworks whilst arguing that in principle that they were incompatible with the law. A subsequent softening of position had already been noted and of course ultimately, governmental pressure led to the much needed recognition of framework agreements through the inclusion of specific provisions in the Public Sector Directive. A contracting authority can now be certain of the legality of the framework agreement into which it is entering and to this extent the proper recognition of frameworks must be applauded; however, turning to look at the substance of those provisions it becomes apparent that the regime still does not bring certainty and clarity to all aspects of framework agreements and may in fact have reduced the flexibility enjoyed by users of framework agreements prior to the Public Sector Directive.

THE CURRENT LEGAL FRAMEWORK

The law defining and regulating the establishment and use of framework agreements is to be found primarily in Articles 1(5) and 32 of the Public Sector Directive. This section will turn to analyse these provisions.

The Definition under the Public Sector Directive

The broad range of possible framework agreements and tremendous diversity of their subject matter naturally poses a challenge when seeking to formulate a workable definition. The Public Sector Directive defines a framework agreement as:

> [a]n agreement between one or more contracting authorities and one or more economic operators, the purpose of which is to establish the terms governing contracts to be awarded during a given period, in particular with regard to price and, where appropriate, the quantity envisaged.[41]

It is immediately apparent that in defining a framework merely as an agreement (as opposed to a properly constituted contract) and eschewing the need for a 'pecuniary

---

[40] See *supra* n. 22 at 4.17 p. 24.

[41] Article 1(5).

interest' that one of the main issues that existed previously, that of what amounts to a framework for the purposes of the regime, has been resolved by the definition set out here. No framework above the threshold can now be left outside of the regime with the risk that either the framework itself or subsequent call offs under it fall foul of the rules. All frameworks must therefore be established in accordance with the usual procedures for any other contract covered by the Directive.[42] This definition avoids from the outset the distinction discussed previously between frameworks whose terms are more or less 'filled out', thereby avoiding the creation of difficult borderline cases.

Framework Agreements and Framework Contracts

This remains a narrow definition in the sense that it defines frameworks as agreements whose purpose is merely to, 'establish the terms', of future contracts distinct from contracts for public works,[43] supplies[44] and services[45] which remain 'contracts for pecuniary interest ... for [X]', although this includes certain forms of framework where the terms including price are determined. What the Directive is doing therefore is to encompass all frameworks but to maintain distinct internal regimes dividing[46] frameworks[47] into 'framework contracts' and 'framework agreements'. This distinction is found in Article 32 along with all the substantial provisions relating to framework agreements.

The Commission's *Explanatory Note* defines frameworks agreements as frameworks which, '[do] not include certain terms or [do] not establish in a binding way all the terms necessary'[48] for the conclusion of subsequent contracts. By contrast to framework contracts in, 'which the terms applicable to any orders under this type of framework agreement are set out in a binding manner'.[49] Both forms of framework are governed by the regime set out in Article 32. That the framework contract is defined in this way does not mean that it can be treated as a conventional public contract, although it is conceivable that this could be a source of uncertainty, for example in relation to the limitation on the duration of the framework.

Indeed what the two species of framework have in common in contrast to the conventional public contract is that they are both defined in terms of having no absolute, compelling obligations in terms of the duty to supply or purchase, works, supplies or services, thereby preserving the fundamentally open-ended character of the framework. This of course contrasts with the ordinary contract for public works where such obligations would be defined and binding. The distinction therefore is 'binary'. In the context of the Directive, a framework agreement is not and cannot be a public

42 Public Sector Directive Article 32(2).

43 Public Sector Directive Article 1(2)(b).

44 Public Sector Directive Article 1(2)(c).

45 Public Sector Directive Article 1(2)(d).

46 In the manner suggest in *Commission v Greece* [1995] ECR I-1071, ECJ.

47 *Explanatory Note – Framework Agreements – Classic Directive* CC/2005/03_rev 1 of 14.7.2005 available 26 January 2016 at http://ec.europa.eu/internal_market/publicprocurement/docs/explan-notes/classic-dir-framework_en.pdf.

48 Ibid at 1.1, p. 3.

49 Ibid at 1.1, p. 3.

contract in the usual sense and vice versa. Such a clear distinction is helpful but this does not mean that all agreements fit neatly within it.[50]

For the purposes of regulating the award phase of the tender, Article 32 also draws further sub-distinctions for the purposes of setting out the regime for the conclusion of contracts called-off from framework agreements, distinguishing between: framework agreements between a single provider where the only option is to finalise the outstanding terms with the chosen supplier (or enter into contracts utilising the terms of the framework agreement);[51] framework agreements with multiple suppliers where the terms of the call-off contracts are established and the outstanding issue is how call-offs are to be allocated; and finally, framework agreements with multiple providers and incomplete terms where a further competition will be required to win call-off contracts.[52] For ease, unless the distinction is material, the phrase 'framework agreement' will continue to be used to refer both framework agreements and contracts.

Binding and Non-binding Frameworks

While a framework may or may not establish the terms of future contract and will not have the binding nature of a public contract (in the sense that it does not in itself create a binding agreement to purchase or supply), it can be binding in the sense that it obliges the contracting authority to make use of it to the exclusion of other frameworks. Occurrences of binding framework agreements are few as they restrict the freedom to consider the offerings of a wide range of suppliers that frameworks are apt to facilitate.

The majority of framework agreements will be non-binding and permit the contracting authority to use alternative frameworks. This reflects the practice of many contracting authorities being members of several consortia which form into 'buying clubs, and so on and in so far as it allows the ready comparison of terms and ultimately price is ostensibly beneficial. However, as will be discussed in more detail in due course, the ability to utilise a large number of frameworks may create inefficiencies. A plurality of frameworks operating to supply broadly the same types of goods and so on, to broadly the same contracting authorities will result in the needless duplication of the administrative burden of establishing and running the framework on the part of the procuring bodies and for suppliers, additional costs in tendering to participate in the framework. Numerous frameworks potentially serve to dilute demand and make anticipating demand more difficult; they also increase the risk for the supplier that they will receive no order under the framework. Taken together, the uncertainty of fewer, smaller orders, the risk of receiving none at all and the greater burden of participation on all sides will serve only to add to costs and simultaneously discourage the participation of the under-represented groups which frameworks are heralded as being capable of including in public procurement activity.

Contracting authority participation in numerous frameworks, even if this is apt to bring about inefficiencies in the procurement process is not seemingly prohibited by the Improper Use Rule set out in Article 32(2). The issue is one of balancing flexibility for

---

50 See below in relation to 'term contracts'.

51 Governed by Article 32(3).

52 Governed by Article 32(4).

the contracting authority with the commercial risk to which this exposes the supplier. This is a risk which to some extent the supplier alone can determine and decide whether or not to bear but the decision is made increasingly more informed if not any easier by the access that the supplier has to information such as that contained in prior information notices (PINs)[53] which indicate the future procurement plans of that particular contracting authority. The development of PINs is one strand of electronic procurement. Another, which may assist a supplier in determining the risk and/or commercial merit of a framework agreement is the buyer profile,[54] which while not mandated, is a repository for information on the contracting authorities previous contracting activities and behaviours – information which may prove invaluable to a potential supplier.

TERM CONTRACTS

The Procurement Lawyers Association[55] notes a problematic application of the definition of framework agreements to so called 'term contracts'. A term contract is an agreement usually between a single contracting authority and a single supplier for what are termed 'responsive works' such as repairs to social housing stock, repair of damaged road surfaces and so on, the need for and nature of which cannot be anticipated at the time the agreement is concluded. When a repair or other works are required, an order is then placed under the term contract.

Term contracts by their nature cannot anticipate when and crucially if such orders will be placed[56] and in any case, there is seldom any obligation on the contracting authority to ensure any level of usage of the term contract. The absence of an obligation to perform at the outset leaves the term contract as merely a repository for the terms of the orders that are subsequently placed. Term contracts it seems are likely to be caught by the definition set out in the Directive.

This is problematic because it potentially reinterprets what may have been intended to have been a public works contract as a framework agreement subjecting it in the process to rules with which the contracting authority or the supplier may not be familiar. This is unhelpful in itself, does little to encourage participation in tendering for public works and in subjecting the agreement to different rules means that it may inadvertently fall foul of them. This is likely to be particularly problematic for term contracts[57] as they are frequently concluded for a duration beyond the four years permitted for framework agreements by the Directive.[58]

[53] See Public Sector Directive and particularly Annex VII A.
[54] Public Sector Directive, Annex VIII.
[55] Procurement Lawyers' Association, *The Use of Frameworks in Public Procurement.*
[56] Generally these contracts are used only where a consistent flow of orders is anticipated to be forthcoming such as in the context of highway maintenance.
[57] Ibid at 3.20, p. 11.
[58] Article 32(2).

Valuation

The key determinant, aside from the subject matter of the procurement activity, of whether a contract is to regulated by the regime set out in the Public Sector Directive is whether or not it surpasses the value thresholds set out in Article 7. In a 'conventional' public contract the nature and quantity of the supplies will often be substantially determined before the tender process begins allowing the contracting authority to easily determine the value of the contract and consequently whether it is caught by the Directive. However, the nature of the framework with indeterminate quantities involved makes this very much more difficult.

By contrast to the relatively more complex formulae set out in Articles 9(7) and (8), which set out the rules for the valuation of 'conventional' public contracts, Article 9(9), which is addressed specifically to framework agreements, provides that,

> ... the value to be taken into consideration shall be the maximum estimated value net of VAT of all the contracts envisaged for the total term of the framework agreement or the dynamic purchasing system.

For a framework involving multiple suppliers and contracting authorities this may well be a difficult task; although the Directive does not require absolute accuracy or a minimum value to be specified, determining with some meaningful level of accuracy adds to the administrative burden of establishing a framework.

The problem is further exacerbated when a framework is to be let to a number of other users who must also consider their likely requirements under the framework; this also imposes a further burden on the lead authority who bears responsibility for the valuation. Yet another layer of difficulty is added where the framework in question is a term contract where the demand can only be estimated based upon previous patterns of usage or where the framework agreement is non-binding, making the process of valuation difficult to conclude with real certainty.

Clearly, in practice, the strict nature of the internal processes, which precede the tender process and serve to establish the need for the procurement exercise in the first place will often be informed by reliable data relating to current and past trends in demands for and usage of products, services and so on, and will allow contracting authorities to accurately value the goods and services to be called-off from the framework. However, that will not be an absolute guarantee that notwithstanding even very good information and forecasts as to future patterns, contracting authorities will not succumb to the temptation to over-value framework agreements. In itself such behaviour may not be problematic and reflects a desire to ensure compliance with the Directive but as a consequence the over-valuation may have a practical impact on the way in which the tender is advertised and an impact on the suppliers who subsequently seek to become party to the framework.

If an advertisement of a framework agreement contained seriously misleading statements as to the likely value of contracts to be awarded, this could breach the over-arching duty to ensure transparency in the procurement process.[59] The extent to

---

[59] Public Sector Directive Article 2.

which the contracting authority must err in its valuation so as to materially reduce transparency is difficult to determine with any real precision but it must be the case that if the behaviour of a potential supplier is materially changed by the valuation, that is to say it determines that it would be unable to participate or that it would be uneconomic to participate because of the misstated scale of the contract, or it is essentially disqualified from doing so because it would ostensibly be unable to meet the qualification criteria for the contract, the transparency of the process is compromised as the accurate valuation of the process is something in which a potential participant has a legitimate interest. A failure to arrive at an accurate valuation therefore could leave the process which has concluded the framework open to challenge[60] or at the very least form the basis of a legitimate complaint from a would-be participant.

Finally, it should be noted that Article 9(9) also implicitly requires that irrespective of whether or not a framework is divided into lots,[61] the advertised valuation must represent the aggregate value of all lots to be awarded under the framework.

Having considered the definition and valuation of frameworks, the two requirements which engage the substantive rules on their establishment and operation, these rules will now be considered.

ESTABLISHING AND OPERATING A FRAMEWORK

Bodies Capable of Establishing a Framework

As noted previously the Directive recognises two types of frameworks, those involving a single contracting authority and a single economic operator and those involving a number of contracting authorities. Any contracting authority[62] may enter into a framework agreement. By virtue of Article 11, framework agreements may also be established by central purchasing bodies.[63] Once a framework has been established, it is not possible to add to it further contracting authorities.[64] This is an ostensibly very restrictive provision; however, it is one that can be legitimately avoided by defining a

---

60 An interesting comparison (see *supra* n. 42 at 4.6, p. 16) has been drawn between the position in respect of valuation and the obligation to accurately code advertisements using the Common Procurement Vocabulary (CPV). Use of the CPV, which was established by Regulation 2195/2002 (as amended) is mandatory. It has been held that CPV codes and accurate CPV coding are things in which a potential supplier has a legitimate interest as inaccuracy will result in potential participants failing to discover the existence of the tender or being unable to reach sound conclusions as to their suitability as a bidder. A complaint (333/2009/(BEH)/KM) in respect of a failure by the European Air Safety Agency (EASA) to use accurate CPV codes (the EASA using only higher level codes and arguing the implicitly all sub-codes were to be included) has been upheld by the European Ombudsman.

61 Framework agreements, particularly those for a diverse range of supplies will often be divided into smaller, more appropriate lots as suppliers, particularly SME's may be unable or unwilling to economically supply the full range of supplies required under the framework. Division into lots which are simply smaller is also possible.

62 As defined by Article 1(9) and elaborated by Annex III of the Directive.

63 As defined by Article 1(10).

64 Article 32(4).

class of contracting authorities that will use the framework as opposed to individually naming those authorities[65] providing that the class of contracting authorities is defined in sufficient detail so as to comply with the over-arching requirement of transparency.

The Contract Notice

As with all procurement activities that fall to be regulated by the Directives, all pre-award procedures must be followed including the placing of a notice in the OJEU. The usual rules on notices set out in Articles 35 and 36 of the Directive apply to framework agreements as to any other public contract. However, Annex VIIA also includes specific stipulations in respect of framework agreements namely that the notice must make clear that it is a framework agreement that the contract authority is seeking to conclude,[66] the duration of the framework irrespective of whether or not the duration exceeds the default four year limit,[67] the number of participants[68] and the 'estimated total value of the supplies for the entire duration of the framework agreement and, as far as possible, the value and the frequency of the contracts to be awarded'.[69]

Determining the Participants

As with any other public contract, it is for the contracting authority to decide which procedure will be used to determine the qualifying tenders. The rules in respect of the open and restricted procedures, which are considered in detail elsewhere in this book, will then apply in the usual way. The obligations on the contracting authority are not modified merely because they are establishing a framework agreement nor is the standard of care. This is a point illustrated by the recent Scottish decision in *Healthcare at Home Ltd v Common Services Agency*[70] where the Court of Session drew no distinction whatsoever between a framework agreement and any other public contract when considering whether the respondent had discharged its duty under regulation 4[71] of the Public Contracts (Scotland) Regulation 2006, to treat potential suppliers equally, without discrimination and itself to act in a transparent and proportionate manner in considering the tender submitted by the respondent to supply drugs for the treatment of cancer and associated nursing services. The court held that the standard to be reached by the contracting authority in its approach to reviewing submitted tenders was unmodified and was comfortable to treat all stages of the tender in precisely the same manner as the equivalent step in respect of any other public contract tender; for

---

[65] This approach is outlined in the guidance published by the Commission, see *supra* n. 40 and previously by the Office for Government Commerce, see n. 57 below.

[66] Annex VIIA, *Contract Notices*, 3(c).

[67] Annex VIIA, *Contract Notices*, 18. Point 18 also requires a supplementary explanation if the framework is to operate for more than four years.

[68] Annex VIIA, *Contract Notices*, 18.

[69] Annex VIIA, *Contract Notices*, 6(b), third indent.

[70] [2013] CSIH 22.

[71] Public Sector Directive Article 2.

example, turning immediately to the established authorities in respect of the formulation of award criteria, invitation to tender and so on, and seeking to make no distinct or special case in respect of framework agreements.

The only additional requirement in relation to framework agreements is that set out in Article 32(4) which requires that a minimum of three qualified suppliers must be appointed to a multi-provider framework. This is a measure intended to ensure that the competitive element that is built in to the multi-provider model is preserved. The outstanding issue, once the framework agreement is concluded, is how the call-offs under it are to be divided.

The Award Phase

Despite the distinction drawn throughout between single and multi-provider frameworks, it will be apparent that many of the rules on framework apply equally to both; however, the distinction between the two is most important and apparent when considering Article 32(3) and Article 3(4) which set out the procedures for the awarding of binding contacts under the framework agreement. A very different regime will be seen for each. The reasons for this are apparent. Under the single provider framework, the terms of the contracts must be substantially complete and once the supplier has been chosen there is then no question as to with whom orders arising under the framework will be placed. By contrast, under a multi-provider framework, the questions of which provider will supply and on precisely what terms may both be left to be determined; all that has been established is that these suppliers are qualified to supply. Notwithstanding this bifurcation, Article 32(2) applies to both single and multi-provider frameworks and requires that in respect of both, the contracting authority[72] may not seek to substantially modify the award criteria after they have been advertised. The contracting authority is also obliged by Article 32(2) to indicate how the award will be made and if it is to be made on the basis of the most economically advantageous tender the criteria that will be considered and the weight that they will carry. Under a multi-provider framework, where the award of contracts is contingent upon a second round of tenders the way in which that second round of 'mini-tenders' will function must also be disclosed, although the contracting authority is not obliged to apply the same award criteria to the second phase as to the first. The award of contracts under each of the two main forms of framework will now be considered.

The award phase – single provider frameworks

Article 32(3) of the Directive sets out that in the case of a single-provider framework the contracts called-off must be concluded on substantially the same terms of those set out in original tender. The requirement to substantially transpose the terms does not absolutely preclude some degree of variation but it does severely (but entirely appropriately) limit the extent to which a procuring authority can vary the original tender, for example by seeking to change or extend the subject matter of the framework

[72] Which must be identified along with other potential users of the framework *per* Article 32(2), no parties not identified can utilise the framework.

agreement.[73] As Article 32(2) fixes the framework participants this will also mean that the contract authority cannot seek to add further suppliers to the framework thereby creating a multi-provider framework. Whether the contracting authority is obliged to place orders with the chosen supplier is a matter left to be determined by the framework agreement itself.

The award phase – multi-provider frameworks

As noted above, the method by which contracts are awarded under a multi-provider framework is contingent upon the extent to which the framework agreement furnishes the parties with a sufficiently complete set of contract terms or whether it leaves a number of matters outstanding to be resolved by a further competitive stage.

Where the terms are laid out sufficiently completely[74] so as not to require a further competitive stage, the issue is essentially one of how the contracts to call-offs are to be distributed between the winning suppliers. Clearly, despite all qualifying, some suppliers will have scored better than others in the first stage. It is therefore common for the top ranked supplier to be given preferential treatment and given 'first refusal' on all call-offs under the contract. When the preferred supplier is unwilling or unable to accept a contract, it is offered to the second highest ranking winner and so on. This is known as the cascade method and so far as any method is preferred this would appear to be regarded as the most desirable by the Commission.[75] If the cascade method is not to be used the contracting authority may instead decide to award call-offs on an entirely random basis, by offering them to all suppliers in sequence, irrespective of original ranking (the so-called 'cab rank' approach), by awarding them between suppliers in pre-determined percentages or by random selection. Beyond the Commission's suggestion that the cascade method is preferable, there is no absolute requirement that any one method be used, providing that the chosen method upholds the values of transparency and so on, required of the process as a whole.

For the award of a contract under a framework with terms sufficiently incomplete so as to require/contemplate a second round of competition the procedure is very different. Before considering the procedure, however, it must be noted that there is no absolute division between these two cases and no specific degree of 'completeness' is required.[76] In practice, the majority of terms will in fact be determined prior to the creation of the framework agreement, indeed prior to the commencement of the process when initial identification of need was undertaken, with the exception of price, which is effectively determined using a second stage and which the Commission has stated may be left to be determined at the call-off phase.[77] The corollary of this is that the contracting

---

[73] On determining what amounts to material variation see Case C-454/06, *Pressetext Nachrichtenagentur GmbH v Austria* [2008] ECR I-4401.

[74] Including details as to how the call-offs will be assigned.

[75] *Explanatory Note – Framework Agreements – Classic Directive* CC/2005/03_rev 1 of 14 July 2005, at n. 24, available 26 January 2016 at http://ec.europa.eu/internal_market/public procurement/docs/explan-notes/classic-dir-framework_en.pdf.

[76] Ibid at para. 2.2.

[77] Ibid. Note that this view is not uncontroversial, as the Directive can be interpreted as requiring that an award must be made on the basis of either price or a range of criteria which

authority may not simply re-open the tender, when sufficiently certain terms do exist, to attempt to extract more favourable terms from the suppliers.

Whatever thc dcgrcc of completeness, a competitive process will be required to complete the terms of the framework and fill them out so as to ensure they are sufficient to form a legally binding contract. This 'mini-tender' phase is governed by Article 34(4) which requires that the contracting authority shall consult with every supplier capable of performing the contract, that is to say all suppliers that are party to the framework.[78] Article 34(4) further requires that the contracting authority specify the time limit for the mini-tender process;[79] however, it offers no more detail leaving the contracting authority to determine the appropriate period, 'taking into account factors such as the complexity of the subject-matter of the contract and the time needed to send in tenders'.[80] The contracting authority is also obliged to maintain the confidentiality of submitted written tenders until the expiry of the submission period. The contracting authority is then obliged to award the contract 'to the tenderer who has submitted the best tender on the basis of the award criteria set out in the specifications of the framework agreement'.[81]

Duration

Article 32(2) makes clear that the duration of a framework agreement is strictly limited to four years although a framework may operate for a shorter period. Whatever the chosen duration, the contracting authority is under an obligation to ensure that this is stated accurately in the contact notice.

While the four year rule provides useful clarity, it is a restriction that did not exist in respect of the frameworks to which Directive 93/37 applied. Moreover it is clear to see that in some instances a four year framework may be unattractive. Such instances might include for example, a framework for the supply of certain materials for a substantial or lengthy building project, where a range of supplies will continue to be needed beyond the four year horizon and where call-offs may be on a 'spot' basis as opposed to long-term contracts for supply which persist beyond the expiry of the framework agreement. In such instances, Article 32(2) permits the contracting authority establishing the framework to exceed the four year limit if it can be argued that this is an 'exceptional case'.

The Directive offers no guidance as to what constitutes an exceptional case and the provision is simply reproduced verbatim in the Public Contracts Regulation 2006, although the Commission's Explanatory Note on Framework Agreements,[82] emphasising the fifth paragraph of Article 32(2) and the over-arching objectives of the Directive

---

comprise the most economically advantageous tender (MEAT). Whichever is chosen, the procedure for determining the price must arguably be set out in the framework agreement.

78 Article 34(4)(a).

79 Article 34(4)(b).

80 Article 34(4)(c).

81 Article 34(4)(d).

82 Ibid at p. 5.

set out in the second recital, suggests that a longer duration will be appropriate where it brings about, 'effective competition', for the supplies in question.

For public sector bodies establishing frameworks this raises two issues. First, the need to be mindful that there is clearly an interaction here with European competition policy and indeed that Article 32(2) paragraph 5 explicitly prohibits the use of frameworks so as to distort competition. Secondly, in a practical sense, that there is a need to carefully balance the desires to avoid the needless inconvenience and expense of repeating the framework tender process[83] and benefit from cost savings and efficiencies that may be achieved when a supplier can be reasonably well assured that orders will continue for some time and can spread the cost of 'tooling up' and so on, over a longer period, against the effect that any form of artificially closed market will have on competition in that market and the adverse impact that a longer duration of agreement may have on the value that can be extracted from the contracts called-off. A failure to properly balance these two objectives may amount to a breach of the other requirement set out in Article 32(2) paragraph 5 to refrain from the improper use of frameworks. Arrowsmith suggests that in some circumstances, paragraph 5 might in fact operate to limit the duration of a framework agreement to less than the maximum allowed in some circumstances.[84]

Contracts called-off from the framework may continue to subsist beyond the expiry of the framework under which they were created. The extent to which this is problematic is dependent upon the intention of the contracting authority in entering into that contract. If a call-off has been awarded with the intention, or having the effect of preserving the framework in another form beyond its inevitable expiry, for example by the conclusion of an unusually lengthy contract, this will be regarded as an attempt to breach the limits imposed on the duration of the framework itself. While it may not be good practice to award a contract which will run for a short period beyond the expiry of the framework this is unlikely to fall foul of the rules.

The now defunct Office of Government Commerce indicated[85] that it is preferable to ensure that all contracts called off from the framework agreement are coterminous with the expiry of the framework itself. However, by their nature, some frameworks will give rise to lengthy contracts and to suggest that for example a two-year contract must be conterminous with the framework under which it is created is clearly unhelpful; the position therefore is not a certain one, nor is it clear, where a lengthy contract is awarded close to the expiry of a framework, whether this could be found to distort competition and thus be an abuse of the framework by the contracting body. Yet the distorting effect of a single contract will almost always be far less than the distorting effect of the now extinct framework agreement which created it. It is perhaps therefore preferable to ensure that contracts do not dramatically overrun the expiry of a

---

[83] Which may in any case amount only to costly a 'renewal' of the framework agreement on the same terms, with the same participants, etc.

[84] Arrowsmith, *supra*, n. 9, ch.11 at 11.39.

[85] Office of Government Commerce, *Framework Agreements OGC Guidance on Framework Agreements*, Norwich, 2008 available 26 January 2016 from https://www.gov.uk/government/uploads/system/uploads/attachment_data/file/62063/ogc-guidance-framework-agreements-sept08.pdf.

framework agreement and that if they are likely to a longer period of framework is contemplated at the outset.

Improper Use of Frameworks

Article 32(2) imposes the generalised prohibition on contracting authorities using 'framework agreements improperly or in such a way as to prevent, restrict or distort competition'. This requirement appears to be an attempt to ensure that the inherently, potentially negative impacts of frameworks are avoided or at least ameliorated and to inculcate frameworks with the same explicit concerns for effective competition in public procurement activities that have long been manifested in the case-law.[86]

While there is no closed class of behaviours that will represent a violation of Article 32(2) it is clear that there are certain behaviours which could well be regarded as breaching it. The most obvious example of this will be an abuse of the duration requirement, particularly disregard for the four-year limitation purely for the purpose of continuing a relationship with an existing supplier.

Remedies

Following two decisions where uncertainty was entertained as to the applicability of the remedies regime to framework agreements and call-off contracts,[87] the position of frameworks in respect of remedies has now, in the domestic context at least, been remedied by the Public Contracts (Amendment) Regulations 2009.[88] The result is that where grounds for challenge are made out,[89] *per* regulation 47J a judge may now order that a framework or a contract awarded under that framework be declared ineffective,[90] ineffective and curtailed and/or a financial penalty incurred or an award of damages be made. Regulation 47O makes clear, however, that the finding that a framework agreement is ineffective will not in turn render a contract made under it similarly ineffective. In short, the regime applies to a framework agreement as it does to any other public contract, subject to some difficulties in how certain aspects of the regime translate.

The first difficulty concerns the balancing exercise to be undertaken should a contracting authority seek to have the automatic suspension on activity that takes effect on the commencement of proceedings lifted. The appropriate test remains that set out

---

[86] See for example the decision in C-247/02, *Sintesi SpA v Autorita per la Viglinaza sui Lavori Pubblici* [2004] ECR I-9215.

[87] *McLaughlin & Harvey Ltd v Dept for Finance & Personnel* [2008] NIQB 122; *Henry Brothers (Magherafelt) Ltd v Department of Education for Northern Ireland* [2011] NICA 59.

[88] SI 2009/2992.

[89] The grounds for challenge being essentially equivalent to those for any other public contract, modified where appropriate to the context of the framework e.g. award of a contract on different terms to those set out in a single-provider framework or the award of a contract under a multi-provider framework that is substantially different from the terms set out in the framework.

[90] See reg. 47K *Grounds for Ineffectiveness* subject to the usual 30 day time limit specific in reg. 47E.

in *American Cyanamid Co v Ethicom.*[91] The fundamental question is whether or not the balance of convenience favours the maintenance of the suspension or not[92] but the nature of the framework opens other issues to be considered, taking account, for example, of the consequences of contracts already operating under the framework concluded with other used of the framework and the possibility that they might needlessly be burdened with expense.[93]

The second difficulty concerns just how damages are to be calculated. Particularly under a multi-provider framework, structured so as to offer a supplier no guarantee of orders or even when orders are to be placed with a particular contractor the frequency is unknown or unknowable. The reality here is that the extent of the supplier's loss is almost impossible to calculate with any degree of accuracy. It could be argued that the supplier has wasted expenditure in seeking to join an ineffective framework in the first place but that argument becomes difficult to sustain if the supplier has previously been awarded contracts under the framework (unless some form of repayment of expenditure *pro rata* were considered) particularly as there is not necessarily any guarantee of further contracts. The position of the supplier may in fact not be prejudiced as a consequence of the finding.

If the supplier has not previously secured any contracts or has not had the opportunity to do so either because the contracting authority has wrongfully prevented their participation or because the framework has been challenged at a very early stage the question then becomes whether or not the supplier can seek damages for what amounts to the loss of a chance to participate which may have resulted in a profit. While domestic law has recognised that an individual can be compensated for loss of a chance[94] where there is a strong possibility that that chance would have manifested some actual benefit for the party concerned, the difficulty for a supplier is that this requires a court to potentially predict the outcome of a competition of potentially quite substantial complexity before it has even fully been designed and even then the quantum awarded will likely fail to reflect the profit anticipated from a transaction. This, however, offers little more assistance as the claim for a potential profit from a contract that may or may not have come to exist is at least as speculative and unlikely to be regarded as sufficiently foreseeable to be recoverable, although any such generalisation is very difficult to make without reference to particular facts which could have a transformative effect.

EVALUATION OF FRAMEWORKS

On the face of it, a process which is successful in establishing a pool of capable suppliers who can supply at a determined price and specification, under which call-offs can be made without any further substantive need for negotiation and so on, is ideal

---

91 [1975] AC 396.

92 Considered with the other two.

93 *Exel Europe Ltd v University Hospitals Coventry and Warwickshire NHS Trust* [2010] EWHC 3332 (TCC).

94 *Chaplin v Hicks* (1911) 2 KB 786.

and is provided by frameworks, which also ensure that each call-off can be made without a needless administrative burden. The benefits of framework agreements are therefore self-apparent but it must be noted that these benefits exist largely as benefits in principle; it is not clear whether, in practice, framework agreements simply add to transaction cost by adding in themselves a further cumbersome layer of bureaucracy to the procurement of commodity items and further and perhaps more importantly, whether the framework agreement really is in fact a mechanism capable of realising the best possible price that the market has to offer and even if this is possible, whether frameworks and the processes that they create are in fact designed so as to ensure this.

In bringing this chapter to a close the evidence for whether or not frameworks are inherently capable of delivering any real efficiencies or improvements and whether any cost savings and efficiencies manifest in reality will be considered.

Can Frameworks Deliver Value?

The use of frameworks can only be truly be justified when frameworks operate in a way the upholds the core values of public procurement activities and do so in a way that also furthers the broader objectives of procurement policy, such as improving the participation of under-represented groups and achieving this while at the same time reducing or, at least, not adding to the financial burden of participating in procurement activity – the two of course being closely intertwined. Further, frameworks can only be regarded as desirable if they are capable of doing this while ensuring that the goods supplied under them are supplied at the best possible price.

An emergent body of research, however, suggests that framework agreements may not be used with the intention of achieving anything beyond administrative convenience and in the process do little to encourage participation, reduce the cost of participation and reduce the ultimate cost of the supplies procured.[95]

It is argued[96] that frameworks are in fact often incapable of achieving best available prices because they create cost uncertainty. That is to say, because the supplier does not know exactly what they may be asked to supply in what quantity or when they are forced to bear the risk in fluctuations in the market for the goods or raw materials they require to meet the call-offs made under the framework. Price uncertainty will also arise when frameworks are used by a range of buyers. While the needs of each buyer under the framework will be in broad terms similar they may often manifest in ways that materially impact on the supplier.

For example, a supplier of office supplies to a number of schools in a region may incur comparatively much higher costs when a school at the farthest reach of the area served makes frequent call-offs of bulky or large items. The corollary of this of course is that the need to create effective competition in this latter situation might also be lost

---

[95] Europe Economics., Markt/2004/10/D, *Evaluation of Public Procurement Directives* (2006) at 5.17–5.28, available 26 January 2016 at http://ec.europa.eu/internal_market/public procurement/docs/final_report_en.pdf.

[96] Y. Gur et al., *Framework Agreements in Procurement: An Auction Model and Design Recommendations*, available 26 January 2016 at http://www8.gsb.columbia.edu/cbs-directory/sites/cbs-directory/files/publications/Framework%20Agreements.pdf

where only one supplier under the framework agreement is prepared to meet a particular call-off and therefore has the freedom to dictate price in a way that would not be possible if other participants in the framework were also interested in supplying the same good. The lack of competition that might arise here is clearly in contrast to the mandated[97] competition that arises when the framework agreement is established.

The relatively uncompetitive price achieved may also result from the fact that the framework is being run and led by an agency that does not in fact have the hands-on experience of negotiating for supplies of this type.

To some extent[98] through the type of contract chosen, that is, whether binding or not, and through the terms of the contract, for example requiring prices to be benchmarked against market prices as seen in *Denfleet*,[99] contracting authorities can ensure that some of these potential inefficiencies are avoided. Equally, these in themselves may bring with them additional costs such as the need to pay a form of retainer to the supplier if the supplier is to ensure capacity to deliver under the framework is to remain open at all times. Further, the inefficiencies that can result from the need to supply too great a diversity of products (even when they form part of a class such as 'office supplies') to too broad a range of contract authorities can be avoided or at least ameliorated by ensuring careful design of the framework before it is advertised and ensuring that when it is, potential suppliers can seek to make their own forecasts and assess the desirability of a particular framework by having access to the greatest possible volume of data on the contracting behaviours of the contracting authority in the past.

The structure of an individual contract however, is not sufficient to avoid the charge levelled by Yukins[100] that framework agreements 'carry risks to competition and efficiency … [and that] … at their worst, IDIQ contracts establish false, if temporary, oligopolies, sheltering just a few select suppliers from ongoing competition'.[101] As noted above, this is simply symptomatic of what occurs when a part of the market is separated off and in the process sheltered to some extent from prevailing market forces. Although it may be argued this is often not the case and that suppliers under the framework are left still to deal with uncertainties of the market, it is clear to see that there is scope for oligopolies or other forms of collusion, for example, avoiding competition at the call-off stage so as to maximise individual gains. This is a structural disadvantage that cannot be overcome entirely but to some extent, as Yukins makes clear, the lessons of poorly run framework agreements have already been learned by the US, and the European regime has built in safeguards which ought to prevent serious abuse, such as the default duration of only four years. This will still not address the potential for a poverty of competition in a closed market but does address it to some extent. Contracting authorities can also ensure the involvement of the widest possible range of suppliers to further prevent abuses. Yukins also endorses the competitive

[97] Public Sector Directive Article 32(4) requires that in a multi-provider framework, at least three parties must participate.

[98] As Gur, et al. *supra*, n.96 conclude.

[99] *R (on the application of Denfleet International Ltd) v NHS Purchasing and Supply Agency* [2005] EWHC 55 (Admin).

[100] C.R. Yukins, 'Are IDIQs Inefficient? Sharing Lessons with European Framework Contracting', (2008) 37(3) Pub. Cont. L.J. 545.

[101] Ibid at 555.

'value' of the second tender stage found in multi-provider frameworks as another means of ensuring a truly competitive process.[102]

Yet, as Albano and Sparro[103] conclude through their work, the competitive process, even its two stages, is not necessarily any guarantee of realising cost savings through greater competition unless the needs of the various participating contracting authorities are the same or at least similar; savings being lost rapidly when the suppliers are required to supply essentially differing goods to different participants each with their discrete requirements.

Notwithstanding the criticism of how frameworks *potentially* fail to deliver value as a consequence of inherent structural weaknesses, it must be borne in mind that what they fundamentally allow for is the completion of a number of procurement 'tasks' without the need and expense of repeating the tender process on each occasion. This, as was identified earlier, is the real perceived benefit of frameworks and the source of the most substantial savings which ought to be realised far more frequently.

Do Frameworks Deliver Value?

Empirical research[104] as to the efficiency savings generated by framework agreements is sparse. That which there is suggests that the majority of contracting authorities use frameworks simply because this makes it easier to comply with the requirements of the Directive,[105] although the same proportion,[106] if not necessarily the same respondents also cited perceived cost savings as a key motivation.[107] This would suggest that such savings must be routinely achievable.

A detailed, unique empirical study has been conducted on behalf of the Commission,[108] which while not studying directly the extent to which frameworks do in practice distort competition or fail to deliver cost savings because of the behaviours they encourage in suppliers,[109] does comprehensively consider the extent to which framework agreements bring about the savings in terms of set-up and running costs by comparison to running numerous, separate tender processes has found that frameworks are capable of delivering cost efficiencies but only when used to 'replace' individual procedures for a number of contracts.

---

102 Ibid at 560–2.

103 G.L. Albano and M. Sparro, 'A Simple Model of Framework Agreements: Competition and Efficiency', (2008) 8 J. Pub. Proc. 356 at 376.

104 See Strand, supra, n. 18

105 Europe Economics., Markt/2004/10/D, *Evaluation of Public Procurement Directives* (2006) at 5.17–5.28, available 26 January 2016 at http://ec.europa.eu/internal_market/public procurement/docs/final_report_en.pdf.

106 Ibid at 5.17(a).

107 Ibid at 5.17(b).

108 Strand, supra n. 18.

109 Ibid at p. 86; the report does note, however, that on average, a multi-provider framework will be concluded with 4.4 suppliers and in modelling to determine the cost, etc. of frameworks work on the basis that only half of participants, if it can be assumed that this is a reasonable estimate of participation it does little to suggest strong competition between the participants, although as noted, requirements that bids must be able to achieve market price or better may make this irrelevant.

Where a framework is used to satisfy only a small number of call-offs, the cost of the framework is higher than the cost of running separate competitions not least because the multi-provider framework comprises two competitive stages, meaning the average cost of a framework is 2 per cent of the total cost of the supplies procured, making it the most expensive of all types of competition, 0.6 per cent greater than the mean cost and 1.5 per cent greater than restricted procedures which are the least expensive of all procurement activities to run.[110] This is a very real concern and is compounded by the fact that, as the report notes, the average overall value of a framework is only twice the average call-off under a framework,[111] suggesting that there are likely many extant frameworks which will be incapable of realising any real cost savings. The latter apparent inefficiency is simply remedied by ensuring that the framework will yield a sufficient number of contracts so as to ensure the initial costs of establishing it are dispersed as widely as possible. This it seems is perhaps not hugely difficult providing that the contracting authority endeavours to ensure when contemplating the use of a framework, that it ensures that it is the most appropriate form of award and that it will attract a meaningful number of tenders who will then seek actively to participate in subsequent mini-tenders.

The costs incurred and savings available to the contracting authority, however, are only one consideration. The report favourably notes that when the costs incurred by both the contracting authorities and suppliers are added together, the overall cost of a competition to conclude a framework agreement is actually less than the mean – €23,000 rather than €28,000. However, as the report notes, this means that frameworks are overall only 'a bit cheaper' than other procedures and as has been shown here do not apparently, as they are currently used, offer compelling savings.

Overall, the report finds that '[f]ramework agreements appear to offer little savings but this is due to frameworks being most commonly used in high wage countries. This drives up the monetary cost estimate even if in terms of person-days they offer significant savings'.[112]

It is apparent that what is not offered here is a ringing endorsement of framework agreements as a means of delivering real value in public procurement, although they do not appear to damage the realisation of value and, it is suggested, many of the shortcomings reflect the instances in which frameworks are used, which unlike the basic model are capable of being remedied as is encouraging their use in low wage economies after their utility has been demonstrated in Northern Europe.

CONCLUDING REMARKS

The recognition of framework agreements following a period of uncertainty in which the Commission appeared to recognise the benefits of frameworks but not the concept of them in practice represented a positive evolution of European procurement law.

---

[110] Ibid, fig. 2.14 at p. 90.

[111] Ibid at p. 90. Somewhat confusingly, however, the report also notes (at p. 86) that under the average framework of three years duration fifteen call-offs would be expected.

[112] Ibid at p. 87.

While the precise nature of the framework may at times remain unclear, it is now clear that any such contract that falls within the broad definition provided by the Public Sector Directive will be subject to the same regime and can be said to embody the same strands of equality, transparency and non-discrimination that are embedded in the law relating to other regulated public contracts.

The regime that regulates the awards made under framework agreements would appear to be apt to ensure a balance between ensuring real competition for participation and call-offs while at the same time ensuring that suppliers are generally treated in accordance with the principles applicable to all public contracts. Yet the regime could not be said to be the most lucid or simple and is clearly not without problems in its application to framework agreements.

In respect of the effectiveness of frameworks, their widespread use and the speed with which they have become established serve as anecdotal evidence of their effectiveness and popularity to achieve administrative and thus at least to some extent real cost savings. Notwithstanding the many dangers inherent in shielding a group of approved suppliers from competition this appears to be surmounted by the Directive itself and by steps taken by individual contracting authorities; however, structural inefficiencies brought about by the very nature of framework agreements are difficult if not impossible to satisfactorily ascertain and quantify. What is clear, however, is that even if contracting authorities cannot always obtain the best price for supplies using frameworks, the framework itself does at least offer a potentially more cost effective way of conducting a competition; savings which, given the substantial usage of framework agreements, are apt to have a material impact on the efficient administration of public contracts, particularly as the use of frameworks spreads to Member States where they are currently little used; if indeed, frameworks continue to have a place in the face of the rise of dynamic purchasing systems.

5. Public procurement and award criteria

Roberto Caranta

1. INTRODUCTION

A procurement procedure is very much like a hurdle race or maybe, even better, like a board game (or a video game, for those even marginally younger than me). The competitors – called economic operators in EU English – must clear a number of obstacles such as meeting technical specifications and passing the qualification phase. Those fit enough to survive these stages may move to the final level of the game, that is the award phase. At this level one and only one economic operator will be chosen to be the contractor (unless of course the contract is awarded into lots or the procedure is either for the conclusion of framework agreements or to set up a dynamic purchasing system).

The usual flow of the procedure is captured by Article 44 of Directive 2004/18/EC ('Verification of the suitability and choice of participants and award of contracts') according to which contracts shall be awarded on the basis of the criteria provided in the directive, after the suitability of the economic operators not excluded has been checked by contracting authorities in accordance with the criteria of economic and financial standing, of professional and technical knowledge or ability.[1] Very shortly put, award criteria are those indicators allowing the contracting authorities to chose the contractor among the economic operators having made it to the final level of the game: and the winner is ...

In domestic law award procedures (and award criteria) have been designed to maximise the benefit contracting authorities can derive from any given contract. Under EU law, the additional concern about having a working internal market has to be added, because, as the Court of Justice has very often stated,

> the purpose of coordinating at Community level the procedures for the award of public contracts is to eliminate barriers to the freedom to provide services and goods and therefore to protect the interests of traders established in a Member State who wish to offer goods or services to contracting authorities established in another Member State.[2]

The rules of the game at this level are somewhat complicated. The Court of Justice has in most cases striven to iron out some of the issues left open by Directive 2004/18/EC. However, the new Classic Sector Directive is a real game changer, and a number of questions are sure to arise in its application. This chapter endeavours to map anew what

[1] See also Article 56 of the new Public Sector Directive, which is partly innovative in that allows Member States to provide for post-qualification under certain specific circumstances.

[2] Case C-470/99 *Universale Bau* [2002] ECR I-11617, para 51.

legal landscape has already been explored and to offer some educated guess on what might lie in the unknown.

The question of the permissible award criteria will be analysed first, and the individual award criteria next. Abnormally low tenders will then be considered. The conclusion will also raise the issue of the distinction or separation between different phases of the procurement procedure.

2. THE PERMISSIBLE AWARD CRITERIA AND THE CHOICE AMONG THEM

Before the transposition deadline of the new Public Sector Directive expired, award criteria were listed and regulated under Article 53 of Directive 2004/18/EC.[3]

Only two award criteria were allowed under this provision, either the lowest price or the most economic advantageous tender (MEAT).[4] This is explained in Recital 46 to the Directive, which links the choice to have two award criteria only to the need that contracts are awarded on the basis of objective criteria which ensure compliance with the general principles of the Treaty as developed starting with the well-known *Telaustria* case.[5] Other criteria, however, could have been consistent with the general principles of the TFEU and thus be permissible for contracts not covered or only partially covered by the 2004 directives.[6] The terminology has chanaged.

According to Recital 89 of the new Public Sector Directive:

> The notion of award criteria is central to this Directive. It is therefore important that the relevant provisions be presented in as simple and streamlined a way as possible. This can be obtained by using the terminology 'most economically advantageous tender' as the overriding concept as all winning tenders should finally be chosen in accordance with what the individual contracting authority considers to be the economically best solution among those offered. To avoid confusion with the award criterion that is currently known as the 'most economically advantageous tender' in Directives 2004/17/EC and 2004/18/EC, a different terminology should be used to cover that concept, the 'best price-quality ratio'.

---

[3] For no apparent good reason, the corresponding provision of Article 55 of Directive 2004/17/EC is drafted differently even if its content is usually considered to be equivalent: M. Franch and M. Grau, 'Contract Award Criteria' in M. Trybus, R. Caranta, G. Edelstam (eds), *EU Public Contract Law. Public procurement and beyond* (Brussels: Bruylant, 2013), 126.

[4] Franch and Grau, 'Contract Award Criteria' above fn. 3, 128; the alternative between these two criteria corresponds to an internationally widespread practice: S. Arrowsmith, J. Linarelli and D. Wallace, *Regulating Public Procurement* (The Hague: Kluwer, 2000), 702.

[5] Case C-324/98 *Telaustria* [2000] ECR I-10745; see R. Caranta, 'The Borders of EU Public Procurement Law', in D. Dragos and R. Caranta (eds) *Outside the EU Procurement Directives – Inside the Treaty?* (Copenhagen: DJØF, 2012), 25, and C. Risvig Hansen, *Contract not Covered or not Fully Covered by the Public Sector Directive* (Copenhagen: DJØF, 2012).

[6] Risvig Hansen, *Contract not Covered or not Fully Covered by the Public Sector Directive*, above fn. 5, 214.

Now, under Article 67 of the new Public Sector Directive, the most advantageous economic tender is no more one of the award criteria, it is the only award criterion which in turn is articulated in different award criteria.

One must have a quite weird understanding of clarity to think that it can be achieved by the label of the species becoming the label of the genus which itself is in some way re-christened, and the same happens to one of the species. And this made writing this chapter somewhat complicated. There were two options: either 'projecting' the new and unfamiliar names to the past, editing quotations from provisions and the case-law accordingly, or writing about an '(old) MEAT' and a '(new) MEAT'. To allow time for familiarisation with the new terminology the latter option was preferred here. In due time the other one could well look just as sensible.

Besides the usual safeguard for national laws, regulations or administrative provisions concerning the price of certain supplies or the remuneration of certain services,[7] Article 67(1) of the new Public Sector Directive now provides that 'contracting authorities shall base the award of public contracts on the most economically advantageous tender'. The categorisation of award criteria is now distinguished within the (new) MEAT. One could even question whether the (new) MEAT is strictly speaking an award criterion, or whether the term 'award criteria' is to be reserved for the different forms the (new) MEAT can take. A slight but still significant change from the text as approved by the Internal Market and Consumer Protection Committee of the European Parliament and the final provision – the word 'criterion' is dropped from Article 67(1) – would rather point to the latter solution.

This is only the beginning of the problems. Article 67(2), which should lay down the different award criteria, has been heavily redrafted a number of times during the procedure leading to the adoption of the new directive. The proposal of the Commission first echoed present Article 53(1) with 'cost' taking the place of 'price' in what should have become the 'lowest cost'. Lowest cost, in turn, could be based on either price or a cost-effectiveness approach, such as life-cycle costing.[8] The most advantageous tender was to include, in addition to price or cost, some of the criteria making up the old MEAT. The European Parliament proposed a radically new text providing for just one criterion, the MEAT. The Council moved back to the Commission's proposal of the traditional two award criteria, and added – in a way limiting the possible effects of the *Sintesi* case which will be discussed below – that Member States were allowed to make mandatory the use of the (old) MEAT for all or certain types of contracts.[9] The final text of Article 67(2) owes much to the text approved by the European Parliament, only if possible made more difficult to understand. The first part of the provision now reads:

> The most economically advantageous tender from the point of view of the contracting authority shall be identified on the basis of the price or cost, using a cost-effectiveness approach, *such as* life-cycle costing in accordance with Article 68, and *may* include the best

---

[7] But see also Recital 38aa, pointing out that it would normally be possible to assess value for money on the basis of factors other than the sole price or remuneration.

[8] See D. Dragos and B. Neamtu, 'Sustainable Public Procurement: Life Cycle Costing (LCC) in the New EU Directive Proposal' (2013) *Eur. Publ. Priv. Partnership Law Rev.* 19.

[9] Case 247/02 *Sintesi* [2004] ECR I-9231.

> price-quality ratio, *which* shall be assessed on the basis of criteria including qualitative, environmental and/or social aspects linked to the subject-matter of the public contract in question.[10]

Recital 90, which probably was not brought up to date with the changes made to the provision, points to cost as being distinguished in price only or cost-effectiveness. Article 67(2) instead distinguishes price and cost *and* equates cost and cost-effectiveness. From the point of language, however, the biggest problem is '*which*'. What is it that must be assessed on the basis of the criteria listed in the provision? Is it cost? Is it the best price quality ratio? If the latter, than we have three award criteria now: the resurrected (lowest) price, cost-effectiveness, and best price-quality ratio. The problem here becomes that this way cost-effectiveness will exclude the criteria listed in Article 67(2), which does not make much sense because, due to the appalling way these provisions have been drafted, the criteria listed in Article 67(2) immediately after the section quoted above overlap to a fair extent with those listed in Article 68 with reference to life-cycle costing. Just to take one instance, the environmental aspects are obviously relevant to both provisions. The same objections hold true with reference to a possible alternative reading, according to which cost-effectiveness could be structured in two variants: 'pure' cost-effectiveness, including life-cycle costing, and ('may') cost-effectiveness including price-quality ratio. The point is that distinguishing cost-effectiveness from price-quality ratio is highly artificial.

Article 67 has been tampered with too much (and too clumsily) in the process leading to the passing of the new Public Sector Directive. Considering that life-cycle costing has now been very much structured by Article 68, a reasonable assumption is that contract can be awarded either to (a) the lowest price; (b) the lowest life-cycle costing, (c) the best price-quality ratio, or (d) a combination of the latter two. True Article 67(2) seems to indicate that life-cycle costing is only one instance of cost-effectiveness. Honestly, however, I cannot think of an additional hypothesis of cost-effectiveness going beyond life-cycle costing plus the very broad criterion referred to as best price-quality ratio. So much for a provision presented in as simple and streamlined as possible way. Whichever is the criterion chosen, it implies an evaluation model structuring the contracting authority's discretion.[11]

Article 41 of the Public Concessions Directive is instead much more essential, basically recalling the general principles of EU law as a loose framework for the discretion left to the contracting authorities in designing award criteria 'linked to the subject-matter of the contract'.

---

[10] Emphasis added.

[11] See P. Bordalo Faustino, 'Evaluation Models in Public Procurement: A Comparative Law Perspective' in S. Treumer and M. Comba, *Award of Contracts in EU Procurements* (Copenhagen: DJØF, 2013) 331.

3. THE CHOICE AMONG THE CRITERIA

Even if the words in both the recitals and the provision have changed with the new Public Sector Directive, the same reasons spelled out in Recital 46 of Directive 2004/18/EC still militate for the conclusion that neither the Member States nor the contracting authorities can devise additional criteria to those provided in Article 67(2) of the new Public Sector Directive (at least in so far as public procurement contracts covered by the Directive are concerned).

In principle it was up to each contracting authority to choose the award criterion more appropriate to the procedure at issue among those two laid down in Article 53 of Directive 2004/18/EC. Basically, as will be argued later on, the lowest price is appropriate to the purchase of standard goods and services. Moreover, the lowest price would be easier to manage in open procedures when a large number of participants can be expected. However, since both award criteria are general criteria and neither of them is exceptional, contracting authorities are under no duty to give reasons as to their choice of one rather than the other criterion.

In *Sintesi* the Court of Justice addressed the question whether Member States have the power to restrict the discretion of contracting authorities.[12] The case arose from an Italian statute providing that works procurement contracts could only be awarded to the lowest price. According to the Italian government the provision had been enacted to fight corruption in the public works contracts sector by eliminating the administration's discretion in choosing the contractor. In theory this should be permissible, since EU law is rather suspicious of excessive discretion left to contracting authorities possibly leading to discrimination against non-national economic operators.[13] However in *Sintesi* the Court of Justice held that:

> the abstract and general fixing by the national legislature of a single criterion for the award of public works contracts deprives the contracting authorities of the possibility of taking into consideration the nature and specific characteristics of such contracts, taken in isolation, by choosing for each of them the criterion most likely to ensure free competition and thus to ensure that the best tender will be accepted.[14]

The Court of Justice recalled that the procedure at issue in front of the national court concerned a technically complex work so that the contracting authority could have profitably taken that complexity into account when choosing objective criteria for the award of the contract, such as those set out, by way of example, in provisions applicable to the (old) MEAT.[15]

The situation has somewhat changed with the new Public Sector Directive. Price has been suffering from bad press from different quarters, the case having been made that

---

12 Case 247/02 *Sintesi* [2004] ECR I-9231.

13 *Case C-513/99, Concordia Bus* [2002] ECR I-7213, para 61: 'an award criterion having the effect of conferring on the contracting authority an unrestricted freedom of choice as regards the award of the contract to a tenderer would be incompatible with'; this approach will be analysed later in this chapter.

14 Case 247/02 *Sintesi* [2004] ECR I-9231, para 40.

15 Paragraph 41.

referring to price both depresses quality, including in social services, and consequently and anyway it forestalls innovation. The 2011 Green Paper on *The modernisation of EU public procurement policy – Towards a more efficient European Procurement Market* launched the reform process by asking stakeholders and civil society to answer a number of questions.[16] Some of them focused on the desirability to cancel or limit the possibility to award to the lowest tender.[17] Under Article 31(1) of Directive 2014/24/EU, the lowest price criterion is not applicable to awards following an innovation partnership procedure.

The tension on the lowest price reflected itself in the proposal of the Commission, which referred to the 'cost' rather than to the 'price', and on some provision in the final text. According to the last phrase of Article 67(2) of the New Public Sector Directive, Member States may forbid contracting authorities to use price only or cost only, and this both generally or with reference to certain types of contracts.[18]

Moreover, under the last part of Article 76(2) Member States may also provide that the choice of the service provider in contracts for social and other specific services listed in Annex XIV shall be made on the basis of the best price-quality ratio taking into account quality and sustainability criteria for social services.

4. SOME GENERAL RULES ON AWARD CRITERIA

Article 67 of the new Public Sector Directive also provides some rules generally applicable to all award criteria. The directive has thus codified the case law and extended the scope of some rules previously applicable to the (old) MEAT only. The reference here is to the well-known *Concordia Bus* case.[19] This case is very relevant in that it made it clear that contracting authorities may refer to criteria not having an economical value, including environmental ones.[20] In proceedings aimed at outsourcing the urban transport bus network of the Municipality of Helsinki, the decision was taken to award the contract according to the (old) MEAT. Account had to be taken of three types of criteria, namely the overall price of operation, the quality of the (bus) fleet and the operator's quality and environment management. The second and third criteria are relevant here. Regarding the quality of the vehicle fleet, additional points were to be awarded for the use of buses having limited nitrogen oxide emissions and external noise, while in relation to the operator's quality and environment programme, additional points were to be awarded, *inter alia*, for a certified environment programme.

[16] COM/2011/0015 final.

[17] Question 70.1.1. asks whether it would be useful to change the existing rules to eliminate the criterion of the lowest price only, and question 70.1.2. enquiries on limiting the use of the price criterion or the weight which contracting authorities can give to the price.

[18] See also Recital 37; some legislation along these lines already exists for instance in Spain: see A. Sanchez Graells, 'Award Criteria and Award-Related Challenges under Spanish Public Procurement Law' in Treumer and Comba, *Award of Contracts in EU Procurements*, above fn. 11, 214 and 226 ff.

[19] Case C-513/99, *Concordia Bus* [2002] ECR I-7213.

[20] R. Caranta, 'Sustainable Public Procurement in the EU' in R. Caranta and M Trybus (eds) *The Law of Green and Social Procurement in Europe* (Copenhagen: DJØF, 2012), 22 ff.

Concordia Bus was not given points under the second criterion, while as to the third took less points than the successful bidder, who was awarded the contract even though the overall price it offered was higher. Advocate General Mischo strongly emphasised that 'an environmental criterion may be included in the criteria for the award of a public service contract',[21] provided that it is 'applied in conformity with the fundamental principles of Community law, in particular the principle of non-discrimination and the four freedoms, and with all the procedural rules laid down in the relevant directive, in particular the rules on advertising'.[22]

This approach was fully followed by the Court of Justice which in allowing environmental considerations in award criteria added that this was so provided that the criteria referred to, beside being linked to the subject-matter of the contract (an issue which will be tackled later), 'do not confer an unrestricted freedom of choice on the authority, are expressly mentioned in the contract documents or the tender notice, and comply with all the fundamental principles of Community law, in particular the principle of non-discrimination'.[23]

These requirements were fine-tuned a few years later in *EVN*.[24] The Republic of Austria had invited tenders for the supply of electricity in an open procurement procedure. Under the heading 'Award criteria', the invitation stated that the economically most advantageous tender was to be chosen according to different criteria, including the price and the 'effect of the services on the environment in accordance with the contract documents', which was weighted at 45 per cent. The supplier was to undertake to supply the Federal offices, so far as technically possible, with electricity from renewable energy sources and in any case not knowingly to supply electricity generated by nuclear fission. However, the supplier was not required to submit proof of his sources of supply. Moreover, in the introduction to the tender documents it was stated that the contracting authority was aware that for technical reasons no supplier could guarantee that the electricity he supplied to a particular customer had actually been generated from renewable sources. Unsurprisingly, an unsuccessful bidder brought an action in front of the national courts complaining that the environmental criterion breached then EC law. The case having been referred to the Court of Justice, Advocate General Mischo, while in principle ready to uphold the legality of environmental criteria, considered, *inter alia*, that only those award criteria which permit the accuracy of the information given by suppliers to be actually checked are admissible.[25]

Closely following *Concordia Bus*, the Court of Justice reiterated the principle stipulating that:

---

[21] Paragraph 91; as P. Charro, 'Case note to *Concordia Bus Finland*' (2003) 40 C.M.L.Rev. 181, points out, the Advocate General 'sees no reason why secondary considerations should be treated with greater suspicion than purely economic criteria'.

[22] Paragraph 123.

[23] Paragraph 69.

[24] Case C-448/01, *EVN and Wienstrom* [2003] ECR I-14527; see Th. Gliozzo, 'L'admissibilité d'un critère environnemental au regard de la réglementation communautaire des marchés' Act. Jur. Dr. Adm. 2004, 334.

[25] Paragraphs 40 ff.

> Community legislation on public procurement does not preclude a contracting authority from applying, in the context of the assessment of the most economically advantageous tender for a contract for the supply of electricity, a criterion requiring that the electricity supplied be produced from renewable energy sources, provided that that criterion is linked to the subject-matter of the contract, does not confer an unrestricted freedom of choice on the authority, is expressly mentioned in the contract documents or the contract notice, and complies with all the fundamental principles of Community law, in particular the principle of non-discrimination.[26]

On this basis the Court held that the principle of equal treatment implies 'that tenderers must be in a position of equality both when they formulate their tenders and when those tenders are being assessed by the contracting authority'.[27] As a consequence, 'where a contracting authority lays down an award criterion indicating that it neither intends, nor is able, to verify the accuracy of the information supplied by the tenderers, it infringes the principle of equal treatment, because such a criterion does not ensure the transparency and objectivity of the tender procedure'.[28] Recital 1 of Directive 2004/18/EC expressly referred to *Concordia Bus*, and recalled that environmental criteria are allowed provided, *inter alia*, that they do not confer an unrestricted freedom of choice on the contracting authority, are expressly mentioned and comply with the fundamental principles of EU public procurement law.

Article 67(4) of the new Public Sector Directive, even if does not refer to the general principles of the Treaty, may be said to have been upgraded from recital to actual provision to the *Concordia Bus* case law:

> Award criteria shall not have the effect of conferring an unrestricted freedom of choice on the contracting authority. They shall ensure the possibility of effective competition and shall be accompanied by specifications that allow the information provided by the tenderers to be effectively verified in order to assess how well the tenders meet the award criteria. In case of doubt, contracting authorities shall verify effectively the accuracy of the information and proof provided by the tenderers.

Finally, award criteria giving preferences to local or locally established economic operators, for instance awarding extra points to those having an office or a plant within a given distance from the place where a service has to be provided are inconsistent with the general principles of the Treaty and with the fundamental market freedoms.[29]

---

[26] Paragraph 34.

[27] Paragraph 47.

[28] Paragraph 51; see also, concerning another element of uncertainty in the tender invitation we do not need to discuss here, paras 56 ff.

[29] Case C-234/03, *Contse* [2005] ECR I-9315, paras 49 ff; the Court of Justice was not sure whether the latter case was not a service concession, but the qualification was not material since the general principle of non discrimination was applied; see also Case C-315/01, *GAT* [2003] ECR I-6351, paras 71 ff (this was an above the threshold supply contract).

5. THE (LOWEST) PRICE

As it has been rightly remarked, '[t]his criterion is self-explanatory'.[30] The lowest price criterion has not attracted significant litigation at EU level. Its operation is easy, and as a criterion is rather dumb and as a matter of good procurement management its use should be limited to simple procurement.[31] In some Member States, however, concerns about corruption are a major reason for favouring the lowest price.[32]

Legislation in a number of Member States shows that the price criterion refers both to the overall price and to the sum of the prices for estimated quantities.[33] The possibility to refer to estimated quantities can be inferred from the judgement of the Court of Justice in *SIAC*.[34] The case concerned a measure-and-value contract, under which the quantities estimated for each item were set out in the bill of quantities; the tenderer completed the bill of quantities by filling in a rate for each item and a total price for the estimated quantity; the price actually payable was determined by measuring the actual quantities on completion of the work and valuing them at the rates quoted in the tender.[35]

The problem is the extent to which deviance from the estimated quantities might imply such a variation of the contractual terms to require re-tendering under the *pressetext* case-law. As is well known, the Court of Justice held that, in order to ensure transparency of procedures and equal treatment of tenderers, amendments to the provisions of a public contract during its currency constitute a new award of a contract when they are materially different in character from the original contract.[36] An amendment may be regarded as being material in three situations: (a) when it introduces new conditions which, 'had they been part of the initial award procedure, would have allowed for the admission of tenderers other than those initially admitted or would have allowed for the acceptance of a tender other than the one initially accepted', (b) when it extends the scope of the contract considerably to encompass subject matter not initially covered, and (c) when it changes the economic

---

[30] P. Trepte, *Public Procurement in the EU*, 2nd edn, (Oxford: Oxford University Press, 2007) 463.

[31] E.g. Arrowsmith, *The Law of Public and Utilities Procurements*, 3rd edn, London, Sweet and Maxwell, 2014, vol1, 736; F. Lichère, 'Award of Contracts Covered by the EU Public Procurement Rules in France' in Treumer and Comba, *Award of Contracts in EU Procurements*, above fn.11, 72 f, and Franch and Grau, 'Contract Award Criteria' above fn. 3, 134; with reference to the difference jurisdictions making up the UK see P. Telles, 'Awarding of Public Contracts in the United Kingdom' in Treumer and Comba, *Award of Contracts in EU Procurements*, above fn. 11, 255 ff.

[32] P. Bordalo Faustino, 'Evaluation Models in Public Procurement', above fn. 11, 339, also for further references.

[33] E.g. Article 17 of the French *Code des marchés publics*; Article 82 of the Italian *Codice dei mercati pubblici*; total price is instead preferred in Romania: D. Dragos, B. Neamtu and R. Suciu, 'The Theory and Practice of Award Criteria in the Romanian Procurement Law' in Treumer and Comba, *Award of Contracts in EU Procurements*, above fn. 11, 184.

[34] For a different reading see however P. Trepte, *Public Procurement in the EU*, above fn. 30, 464.

[35] Case C-19/00, *SIAC Construction* [2001] ECR I-7725, para 5; see Franch and Grau 'Contract Award Criteria' above fn. 3, 144.

[36] Case C-454/06, *pressetext Nachrichtenagentur* [2008] ECR I-4401, para 34.

balance of the contract in favour of the contractor in a manner which was not provided for in the terms of the initial contract.[37]

The matter is to be more regulated by the detailed provisions of Article 72 of the new Public Sector Directive which also refers to price revision clauses. Price may also be indexed according to formulas spelt out in the contract documents which were advertised.[38] For instance, Article 18 of the French *Code des marches publics* indicates that overall price has normally to be indexed for contracts of long duration.[39]

6. THE (OLD) MEAT AND ITS TRANSFIGURATION IN THE NEW PUBLIC SECTOR DIRECTIVE

'The buyer often cares about both the price and other non-monetary attributes, including various measures of quality'.[40] This is an economic truism which, as has already been remarked, in EU legal jargon translates into the MEAT. Economists tend to write about 'scoring rules'.[41] The old MEAT was defined as the sum of a number of criteria – with the unfortunate terminological consequence of a criterion made up of criteria. As already recalled, Article 53(1)(a) of Directive 2004/18/EC codified the case-law and more specifically *Concordia Bus*. In that case the Court of Justice had made it clear both that the list in the corresponding provisions of the older directives was not exhaustive,[42] and that, and possibly more important, the provisions on the (old) MEAT cannot be interpreted as meaning that each of the award criteria used by the contracting authority to identify the economically most advantageous tender must necessarily be of a purely economic nature. It cannot be excluded that factors which are not purely economic may influence the value of a tender from the point of view of the contracting authority.[43]

To counterbalance this generous reading of the possible criteria making up the (old) MEAT, and to limit the risk of abuse, in *Concordia Bus* the Court of Justice also spelt out a number of conditions to the legality of award criteria not having a purely economic nature, the first one being the link to the subject matter of the contract.[44] The Court referred to a line of precedents beginning with *Beentjes* stating that award criteria must be aimed at identifying the economically most advantageous tender to conclude that 'Since a tender necessarily relates to the subject-matter of the contract, it follows

---

37 Paragraphs 35 ff.

38 Case C-454/06, *pressetext Nachrichtenagentur* [2008] ECR I-4401, paras 68 ff.

39 See generally Lichère, 'Award of Contracts Covered by the EU Public Procurement Rules in France' above fn. 31, 72 ff.

40 F. Dini, R. Pacini and T. Valletti, 'Scoring Rules' in N. Dimitri, G. Piga and G. Spagnolo, *Handbook of Procurement* (Cambridge: Cambridge University Press, 2006), 295.

41 Ibidem.

42 Case C-513/99, *Concordia Bus* [2002] ECR I-7213, para 54, referring to Case C-19/00, *SIAC Construction* [2001] ECR I-7725, para 35.

43 Paragraph 55; 'value' does not however mean 'measurable in economic terms': differently Franch and Grau 'Contract Award Criteria' above fn. 3, 148.

44 See also the discussion in C. Bovis, *EC Public Procurement: Case Law and Regulation* (Oxford, Oxford University Press, 2006), 431 ff.

that the award criteria which may be applied in accordance with that provision must themselves also be linked to the subject-matter of the contract'.[45]

In *EVN* the Court of Justice considered an award criterion which referred to the provision of energy from renewable sources to users from the general public rather than specifically to the contracting authority not to be linked to the subject matter of the contract.[46] This requirement has been much clarified by the *Max Havelaar* judgment.[47] The province of North Holland had set an award criterion consisting of the fact that the ingredients to be supplied were to bear the Eko and/or Max Havelaar labels. The Commission brought an infringement proceedings against the Netherlands lamenting, *inter alia*, that the link to the subject-matter of the contract was absent since those labels do not concern the products to be supplied themselves, but the general policy of the tenderers (especially in the case of the Max Havelaar label). This was consistent with the Commission's approach according to which reference to a specific production process is possible only if it helps in specifying the 'visible or invisible' characteristics of the product or service purchased.[48] This approach was rejected by the Advocate General reasoning that the Eko label directly concerns the product characteristics – more precisely the environmental characteristics – of the ingredients to be supplied. While not defining any product characteristics in the strict sense, it does, however, provide information on whether or not the goods to be supplied were traded fairly.[49] The conclusions were fully followed by the Court of Justice, holding that contracting authorities are 'authorised to choose the award criteria based on considerations of a social nature, which may concern the persons using or receiving the works, supplies or services which are the object of the contract, but also other persons'.[50]

It is submitted that the *Max Havelaar* judgment clearly indicates that anything taking place during the life cycle of a product or service is linked to the subject-matter of the contract. *Max Havelaar* clearly impacted the drafting of the new Public Sector Directive. The Council added to the Commission's proposal what has now become Article 67(3):

> Award criteria shall be considered to be linked to the subject-matter of the public contract where they relate to the works, supplies or services to be provided under that contract in any respect and at any stage of their life cycle, including factors involved in:
>
> (a) the specific process of production, provision or trading of those works, supplies or services, or
> (b) a specific process for another stage of their life cycle, even where such factors do not form part of their material substance.

---

[45] Paragraph 59; see also, expressly referring to *Beentjes*, Case C-19/00, *SIAC Construction* [2001] ECR I-7725, para 36.

[46] Case C-448/01, *EVN and Wienstrom* [2003] ECR I-14527, paras 67 ff; the case is discussed by Bovis, *EU Public Procurement Law* above fn. 44, 281 ff.

[47] Case C-368/10, *Commission v Netherlands* [2012] ECR I-0000.

[48] COM(2001) 274 final, point II.1.2.; see also COM(2001) 566 final, point 1.2.

[49] Paragraphs 109 ff.

[50] Paragraph 85; see also para 91: 'there is no requirement that an award criterion relates to an intrinsic characteristic of a product'.

No more do we need the assistance of psychics to divine the 'visible or invisible' characteristics of products or services or their 'material' or 'immaterial' substance. Reference to the life cycle is now sufficient. The question is why we still need the 'link to the subject matter of the contract' since this is equivalent to the less metaphysically connoted and therefore presumably clearer notion of life cycle? The answer might possibly be that the 'link to the subject matter of the contract' is still relevant for those criteria which can hardly be said to be part of the life cycle, such as for instance aesthetic characteristics. Here too the notion seems, however, more a liability than an asset, the general principles of EU law being a more elegant tool to strike down criteria which are incongruous as it shown in *EVN*.[51]

Among the permissible criteria listed in Article 53(1)(a) of Directive 2004/18/EC, a few were quite generic, like quality, technical merit, aesthetic and functional characteristics, and environmental characteristics; others were easier to assess, such as running costs, cost-effectiveness, after-sales service and technical assistance, delivery date and delivery period or period of completion.

Article 53(2) of Directive 2004/18/EC – with a provision which is largely replicated in Article 67(4) of the new Public Sector Directive – laid down a duty on contracting authorities to specify in the procurement documents the criteria they intended to refer to, the relative weighting given to each of the criteria chosen, possibly by providing for a range with an appropriate maximum spread.[52] Along with the scoring method, weightings inform the potential tenderers of the relative importance of different criteria or sub-criteria.[53] In case contracting authorities think the weighting not possible for objective reasons, they must indicate the criteria in descending order of importance.[54] This is obviously quite seldom if ever the case, as it is shown by the German experience.[55]

The Court of Justice gave the rationale for this provision holding that it is intended to inform potential tenderers of the features to be taken into account in identifying the economically most advantageous offer. All the tenderers are thus aware of the award criteria to be satisfied by their tenders and the relative importance of those criteria. Moreover, that requirement ensures the observance of the principles of equal treatment of tenderers and of transparency.[56]

---

[51] Case C-448/01, *EVN and Wienstrom* [2003] ECR I-14527.

[52] In the case law for instance Case C-470/99, *Universale Bau* [2002] ECR I-11617, paras 97 ff. See also S. Arrowsmith, J. Linarelli and D. Wallace, *Regulating Public Procurement* (The Hague: Kluwer, 2000) 721 ff, with reference to the rules applicable in different jurisdictions.

[53] Bordalo Faustino, 'Evaluation models in public procurement', above fn. 11, 333 ff; Trepte, *Public Procurement in the EU*, above, fn. 30, 472 f.

[54] See also Article 40(5).

[55] M. Burgi, 'Awarding of Contracts in German Procurement Law' in Treumer and Comba, *Award of Contracts in EU Procurements*, above fn. 11, 108; see also, with reference to Romania, Dragos, Neamtu and Suciu, 'The Theory and Practice of Award Criteria in the Romanian Procurement Law' above fn. 33, 193.

[56] Case C-87/94, *Commission v Belgium* [1996] ECR I-2043, para 88; the directive applicable to that case was 90/531/EEC.

In the new Public Sector Directive the old MEAT has been somewhat dissolved into two distinct criteria, cost-effectiveness, and best price-quality ratio, spreading the criteria previously listed in Article 53(1)(a) between the two.

6.1 The Lowest Life-cycle Costing

According to the definition in Article 2(20) of the new Public Sector Directive:

> 'life cycle' means all consecutive and/or interlinked stages, including research and development to be carried out, production, trading and its conditions, transport, use and maintenance, throughout the existence of a product or a works or the provision of a service, from raw material acquisition or generation of resources to disposal, clearance and end of service or utilisation.[57]

Life-cycle costing is a tool to evaluate the costs of a good or service taking into account not just price (the upfront cost, usually incorporating production costs) but all costs which will accrue with operation and maintenance and finally disposal. When externalities are included, life-cycle costing becomes 'an environmentally-relevant methodology'.[58]

As Recital 96 of the same directive recalls, life-cycle costing is a key instrument in fostering innovation and achieving the goals of sustainable development laid down in the Europe 2020 Strategy.[59] In its proposal, later shared by the Council, the European Commission classified life-cycle costing as an instance of lowest cost, along with lowest price. This is why we write about the 'lowest life-cycle costing'. The Commission's approach can be explained by the determination to limit the discretion of contracting authorities which could be abused to discriminate against non-national economic operators. Again Recital 96, after pointing out that methods used in life-cycle costing can also include costs imputed to environmental externalities, such as pollution caused by extraction of the raw materials used in the product or caused by the product itself or its manufacturing, requires that these costs may be monetised and monitored. Morevoer, the methods used for assessing costs imputed to environmental externalities should be 'established in advance in an objective and non-discriminatory manner and be accessible to all interested parties'. Whatever the level these methods are established at, 'they should, to avoid distortions of competition through tailor-made methodologies, remain general in the sense that they should not be set up specifically for a particular public procurement procedure'.

As a result, Article 68 of the new Public Sector Directive has very much structured life-cycle costing. Article 68(1) recasts the definition in Article 2(20) breaking down life-cycle costing into the different phases of a product or service life, from acquisition

---

57 See also Recitals 40 f.

58 Dragos and Neamtu, 'Sustainable Public Procurement' above fn. 8, 20 (also for references to some existing life-cycle costing methodologies).

59 See also M. Burgi, 'Can Secondary Considerations in Procurement Contracts be a Tool for Increasing Innovative Solutions?' in G.S. Ølykke, C. Risvig Hansen and C.D. Twarnø (eds), *EU Procurement Directives – Modernisation, Growth and Innovation* (Copenhagen: DJØF, 2012) 264.

to end of life. The life-cycle costing can include the costs accrued in all phases or only in some of them. According to the provision, this should depend on 'the extent relevant'. These are rather empty words, and the costs covered in any life-cycle costing method will depend on the level of commitment of and the amount of information available to those developing those methods. Costs are also distinguished depending on who is shouldering them: the contracting authority or other users on the one hand and the environment on the other. The reason for the distinction is that it will be possible to refer to environmental externalities only if 'their monetary value can be determined and verified'. Other costs obviously can and shall, so no specific provision is necessary. This approach makes it close to impossible to refer to social and employment criteria in life-cycle costing (but they could still be relevant under the best price-quality ratio which will be discussed below).[60]

Article 68(2) first lays down a duty of transparency. The contracting authority shall indicate in the procurement documents both the data to be provided by tenderers and the method that will be used to determine the life-cycle costing. This method must have three cumulative characteristics: (a) it must be 'based on objectively verifiable and non-discriminatory criteria'; it must, however, be recognised that the science of life-cycle costing is still far from perfect;[61] moreover, 'where it has not been established for repeated or continuous application, it shall not unduly favour or disadvantage certain economic operators'; the Commission, and later the Council, had made a requirement that the method be established for repeated or continuous application to limit the risk that life-cycle methodologies are used to favour some tenders;[62] the final version corresponding to the more liberal approach of the Parliament safeguards against discrimination had to be spelt out; (b) it is accessible to all interested parties, and (c) 'the data required can be provided with reasonable effort by normally diligent economic operators, including operators from third countries party to the Agreement or other international agreements by which the Union is bound'; the 'Agreement' is the Government Procurement Agreement which is a plurilateral agreement of the WTO to which the EU is a party. The GPA can be construed as prescribing a canon of proportionality as to the documents tenderers are required (for example, Article VIII, on qualification), while the reference to a 'reasonable effort by normally diligent economic operators' offsets the deletion from what was the original Commission's proposal of the possibilities for tenderers to avail themselves of self-declarations.[63]

Finally, and tautologically, under Article 68(3), when a common method has been made mandatory, it shall be applied. More sensibly, to avoid the proliferation of life-cycle costing methods, the Commission sought to make reference to methods developed in the EU legislation or on the basis of EU legislation the only option

[60] See critically Dragos and Neamtu, 'Sustainable Public Procurement' above fn. 8, 24.

[61] Dragos and Neamtu, 'Sustainable Public Procurement' above fn. 8, 27.

[62] See A. Semple, 'Reform of the EU Procurement Directives and WTO GPA: Forward steps for sustainability?' available 26 January 2016 at http://papers.ssrn.com/sol3/papers.cfm?abstract_id=2089357, at 17.

[63] Which would have allowed a wider competition but would have made more difficult to manage the procurement procedure: Dragos and Neamtu, 'Sustainable Public Procurement' above fn. 8, 22.

available to contracting authorities wishing to use such a method. As the provision reads today, it would seem that a contracting authority can reject methods developed but not made compulsory by the EU institutions and develop their own methods, provided, of course, that they comply with Article 68(2).

Annex XIII lists Directive 2009/33/EC on the promotion of clean and energy-efficient road transport vehicles.[64] This Directive:

> aims to stimulate the market for clean and energy-efficient road transport vehicles, and especially – since this would have a substantial environmental impact – to influence the market for standardised vehicles produced in larger quantities such as passenger cars, buses, coaches and trucks, by ensuring a level of demand for clean and energy-efficient road transport vehicles which is sufficiently substantial to encourage manufacturers and the industry to invest in and further develop vehicles with low energy consumption, CO_2 emissions, and pollutant emissions.[65]

As made plain in its Article 1 the directive 'requires contracting authorities, contracting entities as well as certain operators to take into account lifetime energy and environmental impacts, including energy consumption and emissions of CO_2 and of certain pollutants ... with the objectives of promoting and stimulating the market for clean and energy-efficient vehicles and improving the contribution of the transport sector to the environment, climate and energy policies of the Community'. When purchasing road transport vehicles, procuring entities must take into account the operational lifetime energy and environmental impacts of the vehicles. Under Article 5(3), this may be done 'by setting technical specifications for energy and environmental performance in the documentation for the purchase of road transport vehicles on each of the impacts considered, as well as any additional environmental impacts'; as an alternative to setting technical specifications for energy and environmental performance, procuring entities may either use environmental impacts as award criteria or monetise them for inclusion in the purchasing decision, according to the methodology for the calculation of operational lifetime costs set out in Article 6. The impacts considered concern at least the energy consumption, the emissions of CO_2, and the emissions of NOx, NMHC and particulate matter. One could say that in this case reference to a life-cycle costing method is semi-compulsory in that contracting authorities may choose whether to adapt their technical specifications or their award criteria.

Developing more life-cycle costing methodologies at the EU level would certainly help their adoption by contracting authorities. However, as it has been pointed out, 'It is extremely difficult to define one-size-fits-all methodologies for life-cycle costing, and efforts towards harmonisation should not be at the expense of those authorities who are already applying successful LCC approaches for specific contracts'.[66]

In more than one way, life-cycle costing finds itself closer to the lowest price than to the best price-quality ratio in that it presupposes a monetisation method which can be applied on the basis of data to be provided to the contracting authority. As has been rightly remarked, 'the price remains the only criterion for award, so all externalities

---

64 Dragos and Neamtu, 'Sustainable Public Procurement' above fn. 8, 21.

65 Recital 11.

66 Semple, 'Reform of the EU Procurement Directives and WTO GPA', above fn. 62, 22.

have to be incorporated and monetized as elements of the price'.[67] The contracting authority may enjoy some discretion when deciding to adopt a given method or to develop one, but once the method is chosen its application is almost automatic. This makes the criterion quantitative rather than qualitative.[68]

6.2 Best Price-quality Ratio

The best price-quality ratio is the natural heir to the (old) MEAT. The award criterion ceases to be quantitative and become qualitative. Criteria making up the best price-quality ratio still need to be 'objectively quantifiable'. This does not mean, however, that they are measurable (or that they may be monetised) as is the case with life-cycle costing.[69] Supposing, as seems more convincing, that the 'which' in Article 67(2) refers to the best price-quality ratio, the provision can be read as follows: the best price-quality ratio shall be assessed on the basis of criteria including qualitative, environmental and/or social aspects linked to the subject-matter of the public contract in question. Note that if we take the (new) MEAT as the award criterion, we have come here to something like 3rd degree criteria: criteria in a criterion (best price-quality ratio) in a criterion (the MEAT). Think of an EU award criteria matryoshka doll.[70]

As is stated in Recital 92, 'Contracting authorities should be encouraged to choose award criteria that allow them to obtain high-quality works, supplies and services that are optimally suited to their needs'. Contracting authorities enjoy a wide discretion in choosing the criteria which make up the (old) MEAT in any given case (provided of course that they are linked to the subject-matter of the contract).[71] They have been free both to choose the criteria *and* to give to each criterion chosen the weight they consider appropriate.[72] This mirrors the freedom contracting authorities normally enjoy in defining the subject matter of the contract.[73] They decide what to buy, including by

---

[67] Dragos and Neamtu, 'Sustainable Public Procurement' above fn. 8, 22.

[68] See also Bordalo Faustino, 'Evaluation models in public procurement', above fn. 11, 335 ff and 347 f (with reference to the attitude of domestic courts in the review of these choices).

[69] The difference between 'quantifiable' and 'measurable' is quite clear in Arrowsmith, *The Law of Public and Utilities Procurements*, above fn. 31, 767; as Trepte, *Public Procurement in the EU*, above fn. 30, 471, quite rightly remarks, '[s]ome of the permitted award criteria are, by definition incapable of being objectively quantified (aesthetic merit)'; for some interesting cases see Dragos, Neamtu and Suciu, 'The Theory and Practice of Award Criteria in the Romanian Procurement Law', above fn. 11, 191 ff.

[70] On the notion of criteria see Bordalo Faustino 'Evaluation models in public procurement', above fn. 11, 332 ff.

[71] See Franch and Grau, 'Contract Award Criteria' above fn. 3, 141, and the Green paper on *The modernisation of EU public procurement policy – Towards a more efficient European Procurement Market* COM/2011/0015 final, at 37. In the case law see Case C-448/01, *EVN and Wienstrom* [2003] ECR I-14527, para 37; Case C-19/00 *SIAC Construction* [2001] ECR I-7725, para 36.

[72] See also Bordalo Faustino, 'Evaluation models in public procurement' above fn. 11, 337 s.

[73] M. Burgi, 'Specifications' in Trybus, Caranta and Edelstam, (eds) *The EU Law of Public Contracts*, above fn. 3, 39.

setting what for them is the appropriate price/quality ratio.[74] Here again contracting authorities need to keep in mind the link with the subject-matter of the contract, in that the weight attributed to different criteria must be proportionate to the object of the contract.[75]

However, as already recalled, an award criterion having the effect of conferring on the adjudicating authority an unrestricted freedom of choice as regards the awarding of the contract in question to a tenderer would be today in breach of Article 67(4) of the new Public Sector Directive which has restated the case-law.[76] This means that the criteria must be capable of objective – but again not necessarily quantitative – evaluation.[77] Article 67(2) of the new Public Sector directive lists three instances – expressly qualified as such – of criteria which might referred to in awarding a contract to the best price-quality ratio; those criteria are in turn specified in a number of sub-criteria.[78]

The first criterion is quality. It includes 'technical merit, aesthetic and functional characteristics, accessibility, design for all users, social, environmental and innovative characteristics, trading and its conditions'. Some of these were already listed in Article 53(1) of Directive 2004/18/EC. Others are new entries, at time related to the novel emphasis on strategic objectives. Anyway, here again we do not have a closed list, since it has 'including' as its incipient and anyway the whole exercise is about 'instances'.

The real innovation is the second criterion: 'organisation, qualification and experience of staff assigned to performing the contract, where the quality of the staff employed can significantly impact the level of performance of the contract'. A long line of cases going back to *Beentjes* had introduced a very rigid segregation of qualification and award criteria.[79] This case-law was reaffirmed in *Lianakis*, a case concerning a call for tenders for a contract to carry out a project in respect of the cadastre, town plan and implementing measure for a small hamlet in Greece.[80] The contract notice listed as award criteria the proven experience of the expert on projects carried out over the last three years; the firm's manpower and equipment; and its ability to complete the project by the anticipated deadline, together with its commitments and its professional potential. Referring to *Beentjes* the Court of Justice, while accepting that EU law does not in theory preclude the examination of the tenderers' suitability and the award of the

---

74 See Case C-448/01, *EVN and Wienstrom* [2003] ECR I-14527, para 39: 'provided they comply with the requirements of Community law, contracting authorities are free not only to choose the criteria for awarding the contract but also to determine the weighting of such criteria, provided that the weighting enables an overall evaluation to be made of the criteria applied in order to identify the most economically advantageous tender'.

75 Case C-448/01 *EVN and Wienstrom* [2003] ECR I-14527, para 42.

76 Case C-19/00, *SIAC Construction* [2001] ECR I-7725, para 37 (referring to then Article 29 of Directive 71/305/EEC); Case C-513/99, *Concordia Bus* [2002] ECR I-7213, para 61; Case C-448/01 *EVN and Wienstrom* [2003] ECR I-14527, para 37.

77 Case C-513/99, *Concordia Bus* [2002] ECR I-7213, para 60.

78 See also Recital 38.

79 Case 31/87, *Beentjes* [1988] ECR 4635.

80 Case C-532/06 *Lianakis and Others* [2008] ECR I-251.

contract from taking place simultaneously, stressed that the two procedures are nevertheless distinct and are governed by different rules.[81]

This approach met with well grounded criticism. The quality of the performer is obviously relevant in many cases and may justify a higher contract price.[82] As it has rightly been stressed '[t]he experience of the proposed staff to provide the services may be used as a proxy for measuring the means for managing the risk of under-performance of the contract'.[83]

While the Commission's proposal was ready to relax the separation of qualification and award criteria for service contracts and for contracts involving the design of works, quite sensibly the Parliament introduced the less stringent reference to a significant effect on the performance of the contract. Finally, Article 67(2) lists a number of miscellaneous award criteria which were already present in Article 53(1) of Directive 2004718/EC, such as after-sales service and technical assistance, delivery conditions such as delivery date, delivery process and delivery period or period of completion.

Article 67(2) also empowers contracting authorities to set a fixed price or cost on the basis of which economic operators will compete on quality criteria only. Most of the rules spelt out with reference to the (old) MEAT obviously apply to the best price-quality ratio, since both are qualitative in nature and call for special care to avoid criteria being abused to either discriminate or favour some economic operators. The criteria must be formulated in such a way as to allow all reasonably well-informed and normally diligent tenderers to interpret them in the same way.[84] The same rule, with different words, is now cast in Article 67(2) of the new Public Sector Directive. Additionally, the obligation of transparency also means that the adjudicating authority must interpret the award criteria in the same way throughout the entire procedure,[85] which *a fortiori* rules out the legality of any change not just to the criteria themselves but to their weightings and sub-weightings as well once the tenders are known to the jury charged with selecting the best tender.[86] Finally, when tenders are being assessed, the award criteria must be applied objectively and uniformly to all tenderers.[87]

What is not yet fully clear is the extent to which the jury charged with awarding the contract or the person who has to choose the best tender can specify the criteria which have been published.[88] According to *ATI EAC* a breach of EU law would be established in any of the following three situations: (a) when the decision applying such weighting altered the criteria for the award of the contract set out in the contract documents or the

---

[81] Paragraph 26.

[82] See S. Treumer, 'The Distinction between Selection and Award Criteria in EC Public Procurement Law: A Rule without Exception?' (2009) *Public Procurement L. Rev.* 111.

[83] Bordalo Faustino, 'Evaluation models in public procurement', above fn. 11, 335.

[84] Case C-19/00, *SIAC Construction* [2001] ECR I-7725, paras 40 ff; Case C-448/01, *EVN and Wienstrom* [2003] ECR I-14527, para 57.

[85] Paragraph 43.

[86] Case C-226/09, *Commission v Ireland* [2010] ECR I-11807, paras 57 ff; for a discussion of this case see also Risvig Hansen, *Contract not Covered or not Fully Covered by the Public Sector Directive*, above fn. 5, 20 ff.

[87] Paragraph 44; Case C-448/01 *EVN and Wienstrom* [2003] ECR I-14527, para 48.

[88] See, with reference to the practice in a number of Member States, Bordalo Faustino, 'Evaluation models in public procurement', above fn. 11, 346 f. See also Case C-46/15 Ambsig, ECLI:EU:C:2015:2014.

contract notice; (b) when the decision contains elements which, if they had been known at the time the tenders were prepared, could have affected that preparation, and (c) when the jury adopted the decision to apply weighting on the basis of matters likely to give rise to discrimination against one of the tenderers.[89] These conditions, and especially the second one, are potentially quite restrictive since in principle every bit of additional information is liable to push potential tenderers to reorient their tender.[90] True, if the burden of proof concerning the materiality of those conditions is put on the claimant they will probably end up being less stringent. However, in *Lianakis*, a case where the criteria were only listed in the contract notice and subsequently weighted by the jury, the Court of Justice distinguished *ATI EAC*, holding that the jury is allowed to specify the weighting factors to be applied to sub-criteria, and this before the tenders are opened, while it is unlawful to stipulate both the weighting factors and the sub-criteria after opening the applications expressing interest.[91]

Provided that the distinction between criteria and sub-criteria is not set in stone but depends very much from a choice made by the contracting authority when drafting the criteria, it may be in practice difficult to distinguish between allowed specifications and unlawful changes to the award criteria.

6.3 Combination of Life-cycle Costing and Best Price-quality Ratio

Finally, life-cycle costing and best price-quality ratio may well be combined. For instance we can have an award based on lowest life-cycle costing and 'organisation, qualification and experience of staff'. Article 68 will be applicable to the lowest life-cycle costing component, while Article 67(2) to (5) will rule the best price-quality ration and the combined operation of the two components.

This is confirmed by Article 67(2) under which 'The cost element may also take the form of a fixed price or cost on the basis of which economic operators will compete on quality criteria only'.

7. BELOW THRESHOLD CONTRACTS AND CONTRACTS FOR SOCIAL AND OTHER SPECIFIC SERVICES

In the well-known *Telaustria* case the Court of Justice held that even if some contracts (in that case, a service concession) fall without the scope of the procurement directives, still contracting entities awarding them are 'bound to comply with the fundamental

---

[89] Case C-331/04, *ATI EAC and Viaggi di Maio and Others* [2005] ECR I-10109, paras 26 ff.

[90] It is therefore difficult to understand how Case C-226/09 *Commission v Ireland* [2010] ECR I-11807, para 48, could claim that 'the relative weighting of the award criteria communicated to the members of the evaluation committee in the form of a matrix would not have provided potential tenderers, had they been aware of that weighting at the time the bids were prepared, with information which could have had a significant effect on that preparation'.

[91] C-532/06, *Lianakis and Others* [2008] ECR I-251, paras 42 ff.

rules of the Treaty, in general, and the principle of non-discrimination on the ground of nationality, in particular'.[92]

Once the deadline for implementation of the new directives has expired, concession contracts are regulated by a specific directive; the general principles will however still be relevant for below the threshold contracts. Concerning contracts for social and other specific services, Article 76 of the new public Sector Directive expressly refers to the general principles of EU law providing that Member States shall put in place national rules for the award of these contracts in order to ensure contracting authorities comply with the principles of transparency and equal treatment of economic operators.

Reference to the general principle implies that the core rules discussed above will also apply to below the thresholds contracts and to contracts for social and other specific services.[93] In an infringement procedure against Ireland the Court of Justice considered the rules on award criteria as requirements designed to ensure transparency of procedures and equal treatment of tenderers.[94] However, it also held that the scope of the principle of equal treatment and the obligation of transparency do not extend to requiring that the relative weighting of criteria used by the contracting authority is to be determined in advance and notified to potential tenderers when they are invited to submit their bids.[95] Moreover, as already recalled, under Article 76(2) Member States may provide that 'the choice of the service provider shall be made on the basis of the most economically advantageous tender, taking into account quality and sustainability criteria for social services' and thus possibly ruling out award to the lowest price.

8. ABNORMALLY LOW TENDERS

Tenders may be considered to be abnormally low when the price they quote is so low or the quality promised is so high when linked to the price component as to be unrealistic.[96] The rationale for the EU rules on abnormally low tenders is now spelt out in Recital 103 of the new Public Sector Directive: '[t]enders that appear abnormally

---

92 Case C-324/98, *Telaustria* [2000] ECR I-10745, para 60.

93 See also the Commission interpretative communication on the 'Community law applicable to contract awards not or not fully subject to the provisions of the 'Public Procurement' Directives' 2006/C 179/02, on which see, beside the contributions in the previous volume of this series: Dragos and Caranta (eds), *Outside the EU Procurement Directives – Inside the Treaty?*, above fn. 5, and Risvig Hansen, *Contract not Covered or not Fully Covered by the Public Sector Directive*, above fn. 5, A. Brown, 'Seeing Through Transparency: the Requirement to Advertise Public Contracts and Concessions Under the EC Treaty' [2007] *PPLR* 1.

94 Case C-226/09, *Commission v Ireland* [2010] ECR I-11807.

95 Paragraph 43.

96 See generally G.S. Ølykke, *Abnormally Low Tenders – with an Emphasis on Public tenderers* (Copenhagen: DJØF, 2010); A. Sanchez Graells, 'Rejection of Abnormally Low and Non-compliant Tenders in EU Public Procurement: A Comparative View on Selected Jurisdictions' in Treumer and Comba, *Award of Contracts in EU Procurements*, above, fn. 11, 267.

low in relation to the works, supplies or services might be based on technically, economically or legally unsound assumptions or practices'.[97]

The old directive did not give any indication as how to define an abnormally low tender. The Commission's reform proposal sought to set a percentage threshold to define abnormally low tenders, while the text proposed by the Council was again silent on this and additionally left to the discretion of Member States and contracting authorities whether or not to ask for explanations.[98]

In the end, Article 69(1) of the new Public Sector Directive is very much on the same lines of Article 55(1), providing instead that contracting authorities shall require economic operators to explain the price or costs proposed in tenders which appear to be abnormally low. It is therefore up to Member States to give a definition of abnormally low tenders. In case domestic legislation also keeps silent, contracting authorities will tackle the issue on a case-by-case basis.[99] Generally speaking, when an abnormally low tender is spotted, it shall be investigated.[100]

8.1 Procedural Safeguards

The main rule in Article 55(1) of Directive 2004/18/EC is that a contracting authority confronted with a tender which appears to be abnormally low shall, before it may reject it, request in writing details of the constituent elements of the tender which it considers relevant.[101] As has quite rightly been remarked, the directive lays down procedural guarantees to the benefit of tenderers who must be given the 'the opportunity to demonstrate that their tenders are genuine' thereby preventing possibly arbitrary decisions by contracting authorities.[102]

Already in *Transporoute* the Court of Justice held that the contracting authority may not in any circumstances reject an abnormally low tender without even seeking an explanation from the tenderer, since the aim of Article 29(5) of Directive 71/305/EEC (then in force), which is to protect tenderers against arbitrariness on the part of the

---

97 But the rationales for these rules may be different: see G.S. Ølykke, 'How Should the Relation between Public Procurement Law and Competition Law be Addressed in the New Directive?' in Ølykke, Risvig Hansen and Twarnø (eds), *EU Procurement Directives*, above fn. 59, 67.

98 The Commission's proposal did: for a discussion see Ølykke, 'How Should the Relation between Public Procurement Law and Competition Law be Addressed in the New Directive?' above fn. 97, 68 ff.

99 Franch and Grau, 'Contract Award Criteria' above fn. 3, 134 ff; see also Sanchez Graells, 'Rejection of Abnormally Low and Non-compliant Tenders in EU Public Procurement', above fn. 96, 270, and 276 ff, who also reports that most Member States leave the identification of abnormally low tenders to the contracting authorities.

100 For a discussion of the Commission's proposal see Ølykke, 'How Should the Relation between Public Procurement Law and Competition Law be Addressed in the New Directive?' above fn. 97, 69 f.

101 Bovis, *EU Public Procurement Law* above fn. 44, 286.

102 See, also for further references, Sanchez Graells, 'Rejection of Abnormally Low and Non-compliant Tenders in EU Public Procurement' above fn. 96, 270.

authority awarding contracts, could not be achieved if it were left to that authority to judge whether or not it was appropriate to seek explanations.[103]

EU institution had a long fight before finally coercing Italy to comply with these rules. In an earlier phase, the Court of Justice held that (then) EEC law forbade Member States from introducing provisions which require the automatic exclusion from procedures for the award of public works contracts of certain tenders determined according to a mathematical criterion, instead of obliging the awarding authority to apply the examination procedure laid down in the Directive.[104]

In *Impresa Lombardini* the applicable Italian legislation provided that every tender had to be accompanied, at the time of submission, by explanations of the most significant price components representing at least 75 per cent of the basic value of the contract in question. According to the Court of Justice, however, each tenderer suspected of submitting an abnormally low tender should:

> have the opportunity effectively to state his point of view in that respect, giving him the opportunity to supply all explanations as to the various elements of his tender at a time – necessarily after the opening of all the envelopes – when he is aware not only of the anomaly threshold applicable to the contract in question and of the fact that his tender has appeared abnormally low, but also of the precise points which have raised questions on the part of the contracting authority.[105]

According to the Court, a step by step approach to abnormally low tender is mandated by EU law, so that a contracting authority is under a duty, 'first, to identify suspect tenders, secondly to allow the undertakings concerned to demonstrate their genuineness by asking them to provide the details which it considers appropriate, thirdly to assess the merits of the explanations provided by the persons concerned, and, fourthly, to take a decision as to whether to admit or reject those tenders'.[106]

In the more recent *SAG* case, the Court of Justice has somewhat elaborated the same idea holding that the existence of a proper exchange of views, at an appropriate time in the procedure for examining tenders, between the contracting authority and the tenderer, to enable the latter to demonstrate that its tender is genuine, constitutes a fundamental requirement of EU law 'in order to prevent the contracting authority from acting in an arbitrary manner and to ensure healthy competition between undertakings'.[107] This means that 'the contracting authority must set out clearly the request sent to the tenderers concerned so that they are in a position fully and effectively to show that their tenders are genuine'.[108]

---

[103] Case 76/81, *Transporoute* [1982] ECR 417, para 18; see also Joined Cases C-285/99 and C-286/99, *Impresa Lombardini* [2001] ECR I-9233, para 44.

[104] The leading case is Case 103/88, *Fratelli Costanzo* [1989] ECR 1839, paras 19 and 21; see also Case C-295/89, *Donà Alfonso* [1991] ECR I-2967 (Summary publication), paras 1 and 2 of the operative part.

[105] Joined Cases C-285/99 and C-286/99, *Impresa Lombardini* [2001] ECR I-9233, para 53.

[106] Paragraph 56; see also the discussion in Bovis, *EC Public Procurement: Case Law and Regulation*' above fn. 44, 442.

[107] Case C-599/10, *SAG ELV Slovensko* [2012] ECR I-0000, para 29.

[108] Paragraph 31; according to the Court of Justice it is up to the national courts to review 'whether the request for clarification enabled the tenderers concerned to provide a sufficient

Coming back to the circumstances of the *Impresa Lombardini* case, obviously at the time when an economic operator submits his tender he cannot be aware of the precise aspects of his tender which will be suspected of being abnormal, so that he is not really in a position to supply useful and complete explanations in support of the various elements constituting his tender.[109] This notwithstanding, the Court of Justice considered those explanations alone might be sufficient to convince the contracting authority that, although the tender appears abnormally low, it is serious and may be accepted, so that this rule contributes to accelerating the procedure for verifying tenders.[110]

Moreover, since the Directive does not define the concept of an abnormally low tender and, *a fortiori*, does not determine the method of calculating an anomaly threshold, the Member States may design their own method of calculation, including mathematical ones based on the average price offered, provided that they are objective and non-discriminatory.[111] The mere fact that the anomaly threshold is not known at the time when the tenders are submitted – since it is not determined until all the tenders have been submitted – is in any event 'not capable of affecting its compatibility with the Directive. At that stage of the procedure, all the tenderers, like the contracting authority itself, are unaware of what that threshold will be'.[112]

The last – so far – case in this saga arose from a provision in the Italian legislation concerning below the threshold public works contracts according which tenders considered to be abnormally low were to be automatically excluded without affording the economic operators concerned the opportunity to show that their tender made commercial sense.[113]

Asked by the *Consiglio di Stato*, the highest administrative court of the land, whether such arrangement is consistent with the fundamental principles of EU law, the Court of Justice reiterated that the specific provisions of the directive do not apply to below the threshold contracts.[114] However, it also affirmed that the fundamental rules of the Treaty and the principle of non-discrimination on the ground of nationality in particular do apply,[115] provided that the contracts in question are of certain cross-border interest.[116]

On this basis, the Court of justice held that

> Indeed, the application of the rule requiring the automatic exclusion of tenders considered to be abnormally low to contracts of certain cross-border interest may constitute indirect discrimination since, in practice, it places at a disadvantage operators from other Member

explanation of the composition of their tender' (para 32); it is submitted that both the Commission and the Court of Justice are to oversee the way this power is used by the national courts.

109 Joined Cases C-285/99 and C-286/99, *Impresa Lombardini* [2001] ECR I-9233, para 59.

110 Paragraph 62.

111 Paragraphs 67 ff; see also Sanchez Graells, 'Rejection of Abnormally Low and Non-compliant Tenders in EU Public Procurement' above fn. 96, 275 ff, and Franch and Grau, 'Contract Award Criteria' above fn. 3, 134 ff.

112 Joined Cases C-285/99 and C-286/99, *Impresa Lombardini* [2001] ECR I-9233, para 70.

113 Joined Cases C-147/06 and C-148/06, *SECAP* [2008] ECR I-3565.

114 Paragraph 19.

115 Paragraph 20; see also the opinion by AG Colomer, paras 23 ff.

116 Paragraph 21.

> States which, as they have different cost structures, may benefit from significant economies of scale or, intending to cut their profit margins in order to enter the market in question more effectively, would be in a position to make a bid that was competitive and at the same time genuine and viable but which the contracting authority would not be able to consider as a result of that legislation.[117]

Automatic exclusion would only exceptionally be possible in case of below the threshold contracts having cross-border interest when this is justified by the unduly large number of tenders.[118]

8.2 Grounds for Justification and Exclusion

Article 55(1) of Directive 2004/18/EC listed five possible grounds an economic operator may rely on in order to show that his is not abnormally low,

(a) the economics of the construction method, the manufacturing process or the services provided;
(b) the technical solutions chosen and/or any exceptionally favourable conditions available to the tenderer for the execution of the work, for the supply of the goods or services;
(c) the originality of the work, supplies or services proposed by the tenderer;
(d) compliance with the provisions relating to employment protection and working conditions in force at the place where the work, service or supply is to be performed;
(e) the possibility of the tenderer obtaining State aid.

Article 69(2) of Directive 2014/24/EU is almost identical; only compliance with the applicable legislation is more articulated since the new provision refers to compliance with obligations referred to in Article 18(2) ('obligations in the fields of environmental, social and labour law established by Union law, national law, collective agreements or by the international environmental, social and labour law provisions listed in Annex X'), and in Article 71 (the same obligations but with reference to subcontracting.[119]

---

117 Paragraph 26; see also para 28: 'the application of the rule requiring the automatic exclusion of abnormally low tenders to contracts of certain cross-border interest could deprive economic operators from other Member States of the opportunity of competing more effectively with operators located in the Member State in question and thereby affect their access to the market in that State, thus impeding the exercise of freedom of establishment and freedom to provide services, which constitutes a restriction on those freedoms'.

118 Paragraph 32.

119 See also Recital 14c, according to which '... this should in no way prevent the application of terms and conditions of employment which are more favourable to workers. The relevant measures should be applied in conformity with the basic principles of European Union law, notably with a view to ensure equal treatment. Such relevant measures should be applied in accordance with Directive 96/71/EC of the European Parliament and of the Council of 16 December 1996 concerning the posting of workers in the framework of the provision of services and in a way that ensures equal treatment and does not discriminate directly or indirectly against economic operators and workers from other Member States'; see also Recital 14f.

In *Impresa Lombardini* the Court of Justice held that such provision simply gives the contracting authority the possibility of basing its decision on certain types of objective explanation of the price proposed by a given tenderer, without imposing upon it any obligation to do so.[120] This must be understood in the sense that an economic operator must be able to submit in support of his tender all the explanations, and in particular (but not only) those listed above, which, bearing in mind the nature and characteristics of the contract in question, he considers appropriate, 'without any limitation in that respect'.[121] Otherwise said, 'the Directive does not establish an exhaustive catalogue of explanations that are capable of being submitted, but merely gives examples of explanations which the tenderer may provide in order to demonstrate the genuineness of the various price elements proposed. *A fortiori*, the provision in question does not authorise the exclusion of certain types of explanation',[122] such as those relating to 'any elements for which minimum values are laid down by law, regulation or administrative provision or for which minimum values can be ascertained from official data'.[123]

This approach has been affirmed in the later case-law, the Court of Justice holding that although the list is not exhaustive, 'it is also not purely indicative', meaning that neither the Member States nor the contracting authorities can disregard any of the relevant factors listed in the directive.[124]

As to the powers of contracting authorities when faced with what appear on their face to be abnormally low tenders, Article 55(2) of Directive 2004/18/EC was content with providing that the contracting authority 'shall verify those constituent elements by consulting the tenderer, taking account of the evidence supplied'. Article 69(3) of the new Public Sector Directive is more 'directive' in that it provides that the contracting authority 'may only reject the tender where the evidence supplied does not satisfactorily account for the low level of price or costs proposed, taking into account the elements referred to in paragraph 2'. The problem here is that taken literally the provision would mean that economic operators may avail themselves only of the grounds of justification referred to in paragraph 2, the list thus becoming an 'exhaustive catalogue'. There is, however, no reason why the lawmaker should have contradicted the case law referred above, and in any case paragraph 2 indicates that the list is not exhaustive by introducing it with words 'in particular'.

Under Article 69(5) of the new Public Sector Directive information concerning for instance laws, regulations, universally applicable collective agreements or national technical standards may be obtained by way of administrative cooperation any from the Member State where the economic operator is established. Administrative cooperation is ruled under Article 86, to which the Commission's proposal expressly referred. More generally, as it is indicated by Recital 40f, the verifications necessary to assess whether a tender is abnormally low must be carried out in accordance with the rules on selection, in particular those governing means of proof and self-declarations. Since the

---

120 Joined Cases C-285/99 and C-286/99, *Impresa Lombardini* [2001] ECR I-9233, para 79.

121 Paragraph 82.

122 Paragraph 83.

123 Paragraph 85.

124 Case C-292/07, *Commission v Belgium* [2009] ECR I-59, para 159; Case C-599/10, *SAG ELV Slovensko* [2012] ECR I-0000, para 30.

explanations expressly referred to in the old as well as in the new directive also refer to elements which rather pertain to the technical specifications Articles 41 and following should also apply.

Article 55(3) of Directive 2004/18/EC and Article 69(4) of the new Public Sector Directive similarly provide that a contracting authority can reject a tender when the tenderer has obtained State aid only where the tender is unable to prove that the aid in question was granted legally. If so, the contracting authority shall also inform the Commission of that fact.[125] EU law allows the granting of State aids in a number of circumstances, and through a number of funds and programs the EU itself acts as a grantor. It would defeat the legitimate policies behind these grants if the beneficiaries were then not allowed to seek public contracts. As the Court of Justice held in *ARGE*:

> the mere fact that a contracting authority allows bodies receiving subsidies of any kind, whether from that contracting authority or from other authorities, which enable them to submit tenders at prices appreciably lower than those of the other, unsubsidised, tenderers, to take part in a procedure for the award of a public service contract does not constitute either covert discrimination or a restriction contrary to [then] Article 59 of the Treaty.[126]

The legality of the aid may be proven by showing either that it complied with the requirements of one of the general exemptions – something which strictly speaking should not be a matter for imposing a burden of proof on the recipient – or that it had been the object of a positive clearance decision by the Commission. It is not in the powers of contracting authorities to reject a tender because a legal State aid has been abused.[127]

Other EU competition law concerns, focusing for instance on agreements in restraint of trade or market abuses might also be relevant, the question here being how well are contracting authorities equipped to deal with this kind of situation.[128] Article 69(3) of the new Public Sector Directive also provides that '[c]ontracting authorities shall reject the tender, where they have established that the tender is abnormally low because it does not comply with applicable obligations referred to in Article 18(2)'.[129]

In all cases where a tender is rejected because it is deemed to be abnormally low, the contracting authority shall include the reasons for the rejection in the written report provided for in Article 43(1)(d) of Directive 2004/18/EC and in Article 84(1)(c) of the new Public Sector Directive.[130] Tenders having been found by a contracting authority to be abnormally low are among those which shall be considered as being irregular, thus empowering the same contracting authority to award a contract using a competitive

---

125 See Trepte, *Public Procurement in the EU*, above, fn. 30, 474 f.

126 Case C-94/99 *ARGE* [2000] ECR I-11037, para 32; for a discussion see Bovis, *EU Public Procurement Law* above fn. 44, 288.

127 Sanchez Graells, 'Rejection of Abnormally Low and Non-compliant Tenders in EU Public Procurement' above fn. 96, 274 f.

128 See the analysis by Ølykke 'How Should the Relation between Public Procurement Law and Competition Law be Addressed in the New Directive?' above fn. 97, 70 f.

129 See also Recital 44a.

130 Sanchez Graells, 'Rejection of Abnormally Low and Non-compliant Tenders in EU Public Procurement' above fn. 96, 269.

procedure with negotiation or a competitive dialogue under Article 26(4)(G) of the new Public Sector Directive.

9. CONCLUSIONS

The effort to modernise EU public procurement law is quite apparent in the provisions on award criteria. New ideas have been taken abroad, the most egregious being life-cycle costing. The case law following Directive 2004/18/EC has been either incorporated – as is the case with *Max Havelaar* – or departed from – as with *Lianakis*.

Interpreting the new provisions on award criteria is, however, going to be quite difficult. Concepts have bumped into each other, are collapsed one on the other. The underlying tension between the desire to promote strategic procurement and the fear that social and environmental considerations might be abused does feel very much in the provisions as they were finally drafted. The recitals, far from helping, do not just bear witness to this tension, but at times make the problems worse because of a lack of last minute coordination between them and the provisions.

It is sumitted that the reversal of *Lianakis* should lead to a generally less rigid division among the different stages of the procurement cycle:[131] technical specifications, selection criteria, award criteria, and performance conditions as discrete entities pertaining to different phases of the procedure. This might well have been so in the past.[132] Now it is suggested that the picture is much more nuanced or, to be more precise, the different phases of the procedure still deserve to be distinguished, but they do not refer to ontologically different things. Only, what may be the same 'thing' is treated – in a way, processed – differently, in different phases. It is now written in the black letters of the law that 'organisation, qualification and experience of staff assigned to performing the contract' can be referred to in award criteria as well as in qualification provided that 'the quality of the staff employed can significantly impact the level of performance of the contract'. Other instances of possible plural relevance of the same 'thing' in different contract stages may also be found (such as prescriptions as how a service has to be delivered might be relevant in both technical specifications and contract performance conditions). What is to be stressed is that the past rigidities stood in the way of achieving best value for money, so that changes here are most welcome.[133]

---

131 Please see R. Caranta, 'Award Criteria under EU Law (Old and New)' in Treumer and Comba, *Award of Contracts in EU* Procurements, above fn. 11, 21 ff.

132 The distinction between qualification and award criteria was already laid down in Case 31/87, *Beentjes* [1988] ECR 4635, para 15.

133 See, with reference to the *Lianakis* case, S. Treumer, 'The Distinction between Selection and Award Criteria in EC Public Procurement Law: A Rule without Exception?' (2009) *Public Procurement L. Rev.* 111.

6. Sub-dimensional public procurement in the European Union

Dacian C. Dragos

1. INTRODUCTION

The EU Public Procurement Directives (Public Sector Directive and Utilities Directive[1]), cover only a part of the public procurement contracts; those that are not covered by the directives make up more than 80 per cent of the entire procurement market.[2] This demands an effort to investigate the legal regime applicable to such contracts.[3] They include 'sub-dimensional procurement' (below thresholds contracts), excluded contracts and concessions, but in this chapter only the regime for contracts below thresholds and non-priority services will be analyzed extensively.

In terms of the number of procedures, based on an estimate provided by DG MARKT, less than 10 per cent of public procurement procedures are subject to the provisions of EU public procurement directives. Moreover, 90 per cent of the procedures recorded in national statistics are for amounts falling below the thresholds laid down in EU legislation. Even when considering the value of contracts, procurement subject to EU legislation is estimated to be greater than procurement below EU thresholds. One must keep in mind, though, that this is not due to the obligation to apply the directives, but to Member States' voluntary expansion of the coverage of the directives. In addition, a significant part of public expenditure on the acquisition of goods, works and services is made through other mechanisms than the award of public contracts (for example, payment structures in health, education) or involves procurement which is exempt from the provisions of EU procurement legislation (for example, services concessions).[4]

In terms of values, data presented by the European Commission reveals that only 20 per cent of total public expenditure on goods and services is covered by the EU

[1] Directive 2014/24/EU of the European Parliament and of the Council of 26 February 2014 on public procurement and repealing Directive 2004/18/EC; Directive 2014/25/EU of the European parliament and of the Council of 26 February 2014 on procurement by entities operating in the water, energy, transport and postal services sectors and repealing Directive 2004/17/EC.

[2] European Commission, Internal Market and Services, *EU public procurement legislation: delivering results. Summary of evaluation report,* available 27 January 2016 at http://ec.europa.eu/internal_market/publicprocurement/docs/modernising_rules/executive-summary_en.pdf.

[3] The chapter is a development of the article previously published by Dacian C. Dragos and Roxana Vornicu, *Public Procurement below Thresholds in the European Union. EU Law Principles and National Responses*, EPPPL 3|2015, p. 187 ff.

[4] European Commission, Internal Market and Services, *EU public procurement legislation: delivering results. Summary of evaluation report*, above, fn. 2.

Directives, which means that the bulk of total public expenditure on goods, services, and works is not organized in accordance with EU procurement legislation. Alternative forms of expenditure include: (a) providing health, education and social services (over 6 per cent of EU GDP), which is not covered by the directives; (b) public contracts below the EU thresholds – estimated at around €250 billion in 2008 or around 2 per cent of EU GDP; and (c) exemptions for expenditure on fuel, water and defence equipment (covered by a separate Directive).[5]

This chapter focuses on contracts that fall outside the ambit of the Public Sector Directive – the sub-dimensional public procurement. The analysis applies also to contracts above and below the thresholds set out for Annex XVI services (non-priority services), the latter being only in part subjected to EU law rules anyway. The exclusions from the Public Sector Directive that are covered by the Utilities Directive as well as those covered by Directive 2009/81/EC on the coordination of procedures for the award of certain works contracts, supply contracts and service contracts by contracting authorities or entities in the fields of defence and security will not be examined here. Reference to concession contracts[6] and excluded contracts will be made only in so far as they can help addressing issues connected with the sub-dimensional public procurement.

In principle, sub-dimensional contracts are left at the whim of the national legislators; however, the Court of Justice of the European Union (CJEU) has stimulated a different conception, by asserting the inclusion of such contracts into the scope of EU primary law and its principles. This chapter dwells on the characteristics of the legal regime of sub-dimensional contracts; it carries out a comparative analysis of practices employed by selected Members States and the way in which the general principles of law upheld by the CJEU are observed in those jurisdictions. The analysis investigates the novelties and the foreseeable impact of the new 2014 Directives by referring back to national practices regarding contracts falling under the thresholds set up previously in Directive 2004/18/EC (the public sector directive) and Directive 2004/17/EC (the utilities directive).

2. THE SCOPE OF SUB-DIMENSIONAL PUBLIC PROCUREMENT

2.1 Thresholds

The thresholds are currently set forth in Article 4 of the 2013 Directive:

(a) €5,186,000 for public works contracts,
(b) €134,000 for public supply and service contracts awarded by central government authorities and design contests organized by such authorities; where public supply

[5] European Commission, Internal Market and Services, *EU public procurement legislation: delivering results. Summary of evaluation report,* section 3.3, above, fn. 2, p. 9.

[6] Directive 2014/23/EU of the European Parliament and of the Council of 26 February 2014 on the award of concession contracts.

contracts are awarded by contracting authorities operating in the field of defence, that threshold shall apply only to contracts concerning products covered by Annex III;

(c) €207,000 for public supply and service contracts awarded by sub-central contracting authorities and design contests organized by such authorities; this threshold shall also apply to public supply contracts awarded by central government authorities that operate in the field of defence, where these contracts involve products not covered by Annex III;

(d) €750,000 for public contracts for social and other specific services listed in Annex XVI.[7]

The threshold for work contracts is the same as in the previous Directive; this legal provision will continue to leave 70 per cent of all works contracts below the threshold. The Commission's evaluations suggest that in order to go above the threshold, purchasers resort as a practice to aggregation of contracts, for which the combined value exceeds the thresholds, or just follow the EU procedures voluntarily.[8] The last conclusion renders Member States as main promoters of the Common Market, instead of the EU legislator.

The reasoning behind the decision to maintain the system of different thresholds for central and sub-central contracting authorities, with higher thresholds for sub-central ones is not evident from reading the Directive. In its appraisal of the state of the field before the new Directive proposal, the Commission has acknowledged the fact that the degree of centralization varies enormously across Member States and there is a significant amount of procurement carried out by bodies providing specific public services which are neither central nor local government administrations. It is obvious that in devolved administrations but not only there, large cities carry out procurement worth of billions of euros while central authorities may never have to resort to procurement covered by the Directives. Moreover, most of the smaller authorities may never make a purchase large enough to fall within the scope of the Directives.[9] Figure 6.1 illustrates how confusing it is to resort to dichotomies such as central and sub-central authorities in this field.

The previous Directives did not offer any explanation for the existence of thresholds, they just affirmed the effect of their existence: the fact that full assistance of EU law is offered only to contracts above the thresholds. The thresholds were to be defined and then revised on a regular basis.[10]

---

[7] In the initial Proposal, the threshold for social services was set at €500,000.

[8] European Commission, Internal Market and Services, *EU public procurement legislation: delivering results. Summary of evaluation report*, above, fn. 2, p. 12 .

[9] European Commission, Internal Market and Services, *EU public procurement legislation: delivering results. Summary of evaluation report*, above, fn. 2, p. 9 .

[10] For a history of the thresholds, see R. Caranta and D. Dragos, *Outside the EU Procurement Directives – Inside the Treaties?* European Law Series, vol. 4, Copenhagen: DJOF Publishing, 2012.

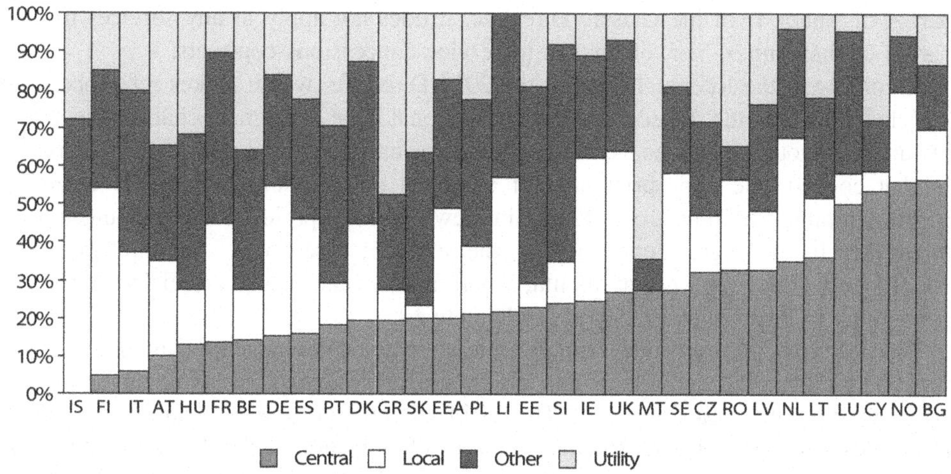

Source: European Commission, Internal Market and Services, *EU public procurement legislation: delivering results. Summary of evaluation report*, p. 9.

Figure 6.1 Breakdown of total value of contracts awarded by type of Authority (2006–2009)

The WTO Government Procurement Agreement (GPA)[11] was mentioned in the 2004 Directives as a source of obligations for the European Union. The 2014 Directive reiterates the bound competence of the EU when it comes to deciding on the thresholds: 'an increase of the thresholds set in the Agreement should be explored during the next round of negotiations' (Recital 18).

The GPA is an important international instrument when it comes to opening the markets up for competition. It is also the main international agreement relating to public procurement. The current version, was updated in 2012.[12] At Community level, the GPA was approved by Council Decision 94/800/EC of 22 December 1994.[13] The then applicable Public Procurement Directives were adapted through Directives 97/52/EC164 and Directive 98/4/EC165 to ensure that contracting authorities and entities would act in conformity with the GPA when following the (thus modified) Directives and applying these to economic operators from third countries which are signatories to the GPA.

The thresholds in the GPA (expressed in SDR – special drawing rights) applicable to the EU were replicated in the 2014 Directives. There are different thresholds for parties to the agreement, but the majority of parties have agreed to roughly the same thresholds as the EU. The GPA only applies to service contracts for (most of) the services listed in

---

[11] *European Commission, Internal Market and Services, EU public procurement legislation: delivering results. Summary of evaluation report*, p. 38, available 27 January 2016 at http://ec.europa.eu/internal_market/publicprocurement/modernising_rules/evaluation/index_en.htm.

[12] See for details http://www.wto.org/english/tratop_e/gproc_e/thresh_e.htm, last accessed 27 January 2016.

[13] [1994] OJ L336/1.

part A of Annex II of the Classic Directive. It does not apply to any services listed in part B of that Annex, nor, of course, to service concessions contracts.

According to the Recital 134(b) of the 2014 Directive, which makes reference to the Article XXII(7) of the Agreement, the international legal instrument shall be the subject of further negotiations three years after its entry into force and periodically thereafter. In that context, the appropriateness of the level of thresholds should be examined, bearing in mind the impact of inflation in view of a long period without changes of the thresholds in the Agreement; in case the level of thresholds should change as a consequence, the Commission should, where appropriate, adopt a legislative proposal amending the thresholds set out in the Directive.

The full applicability of the Directives was always a declaration of intention for the future, as the period for which thresholds and other exceptions were regulated was taken to be only 'transitional'.[14] The 2014 directive promises again to revise the thresholds when appropriate. Recital 56a links this revision to the developments within the GPA. Article 6 Revision of the thresholds also brings new details as to the process of revision, imposing on the Commission to verify every two years starting with 30 June 2013, that the thresholds set out in points (a), (b) and (c) of Article 4 correspond to the thresholds established in the GPA and to revise them where necessary.

The Commission was also granted extra powers as to the establishment of thresholds and their publicity. Thus, every two years from 1 January 2014, the Commission shall determine the values, in the national currencies of the Member States which are not participating in monetary union, of the thresholds referred to in Article 4. The revised thresholds (in euros and national currencies) shall be published by the Commission in the Official Journal of the European Union at the beginning of the month of November following their revision.[15]

The Directive gives the Commission the power to adopt delegated acts to adapt the methodology for calculation of thresholds to any change in the methodology provided in the Government Procurement Agreement and for the determination of the thresholds in the national currencies of the Member States not participating in monetary union; when there is urgency in such revisions, the Commission can resort to Article 90 providing for an expedited procedure for the entry into force of such delegated acts.[16]

Recital (17) of the 2004 Directive also explained the need for just one band of thresholds at the EU level, as multiple thresholds for applying the coordinating provisions would complicate matters for contracting authorities.

2.2 Non-priority Services

Apart from contracts falling below thresholds, the new Directive continues to regulate lightly a list of services that are considered to be too 'subjective' to stand for a full objective award procedure. They mostly relate to services to persons but they are not confined to that (Annex XVI): social and health services, administrative social, educational, healthcare and cultural services, religious services, hotel and restaurant

---

14 2004 Directive, Recital (19).

15 Article 6 para 3 of the 2014 Directive.

16 Article 6 paras 5 and 6 of the 2014 Directive.

services, legal services, to the extent not excluded pursuant to Article 10(ca), services to the community, prison related services, public security and rescue services to the extent not excluded pursuant to Article 10(ga), postal services, international services, investigation and security services, other community, social and personal services including services furnished by trade unions, political organizations, youth associations and other membership organization services, miscellaneous (tyre remoulding, blacksmith services).

These services are awarded according to the so called 'light regime', as it entails the award of a contract with minimum transparency requirements: publishing notices of intent and then notices of contract award (if the contract exceeds the threshold of €750,000).[17] Member States have freedom in providing further detailed rules for above the threshold contracts, in order to ensure that contracting authorities comply with the principles of transparency and equal treatment of economic operators. The procedural rules are needed as long as such rules allow contracting authorities to take into account the specificities of the services in question. The Directive recommends also that regulations provide that the choice of the service provider shall be made on the basis of the most economically advantageous tender, taking into account quality and sustainability criteria for social services. The real explanation for the exclusion (partial or totally) of non-priority services is not the lack of market potential, as it may seem, but the desire of Member States not to open some of their markets to competition.[18]

2.3 Rules of Calculation of the Contract Value

In Article 5, the Directive provides rules for calculation of the estimated value of the contract. This is central to ensuring that contracts that would otherwise be covered by the Directive do not escape its application.

The calculation of the estimated value of a contract shall include the total amount payable, net of VAT, as estimated by the contracting authority, including any form of option and any renewals of the contracts as explicitly set out in the procurement documents. The organization of public authorities has an important bearing on the evaluation of the value:[19] only operational units that have independent responsibilities to conduct public procurement may evaluate their own needs separately; other units must aggregate their needs under the umbrella of the higher authority.

The division into lots poses new problems.[20] In principle, the total value of the lots is taken into account when deciding whether the contract falls under the Directive or not. However, the new directive allows the award of different lots under different legal regimes. Thus, the principle remains that the value of a contract divided into lots is estimated by taking into account the aggregated value of the lots.

However, a new provision allows contracting authorities to award lots that are falling below the thresholds of €80,000 for supplies or services or €1 million for works

[17] Chapter I of the Title III of the 2014 Directive, arts 74–76.

[18] R. Caranta, 'The Borders of EU Public Procurement Law', in Caranta and Dragos, *Outside the EU Procurement Directives – Inside the Treaties?* above, fn. 10, p. 28.

[19] Article 5 para 1a of the 2014 Directive.

[20] Article 5 para 7 of the 2014 Directive.

without applying the procedures provided for under the Directive; nonetheless, the value of the lots should not exceed 20 per cent of the aggregated value of the procurement.[21]

2.4 Mixed Contracts

The directive promotes several scenarios for dealing with mixed contracts:[22]

(a) For mixed contracts that pertain to procurement covered by the Public Sector Directive – a combination of works, services or supplies, a combination of priority and non-priority services, or procurement based both on the Public Sector directive and on the Utilities Directive, the higher value is the criteria to decide the main object of the contract and thus assign the legal regime.
(b) For mixed contracts that involve defence and security issues, the solution is leaning towards these special regimes.
(c) For mixed contracts containing elements of *dimensional* procurement and *sub-dimensional* procurement, or excluded contracts – for instance, supply, works or service contracts and concessions, pre-eminence is given to the application of the Directive, providing the element covered by it has the higher value.[23]

In all the above cases, the contracting authority may decide to award separate contracts, if they are objectively separable. The Recital 11 of the Directive tries to give additional (although not sufficient) guidance as to the way in which contracting authorities may decide the severability of the contract, stating that the determination should be carried out on a case-by-case basis, in which the expressed or presumed intentions of the contracting authority to regard the various aspects making up a mixed contract as indivisible should not be sufficient, but should be supported by objective evidence capable of justifying them and of establishing the need to conclude a single contract, and that it should be clarified that the need to conclude a single contract may be due to reasons both of a technical and of an economic nature.

The provisions of Article 3 mention only mixed contracts where the component parts are procurement, either covered or excluded from its coverage. It leaves out the issue of mixed contracts where a part is procurement and a part is something entirely different – a privatization, for instance, or a sale of shares.

The situation is not regulated by the procurement directives but was at the centre of several cases in the Court of Justice. Thus, in *Loutraki* (2010),[24] the Court of Justice considered the danger mentioned in the Green Paper on public-private partnerships (PPPs),[25] namely whether a capital transaction does not in reality conceal the award to a private partner of contracts which might be termed public contracts or concessions. In

---

[21] Article 5 para 9 of the 2014 Directive.

[22] Article 3 of the 2014 Directive.

[23] Article 3 para 4 of the 2014 Directive.

[24] Joined Cases C-145/08 and C-149/08, *Club Hotel Loutraki* [2010] ECR I-4165.

[25] Green Paper on public-private partnerships and Community law on public contracts and concessions (COM(2004) 327 final), 61, point 69.

this case, the Greek government's intention to privatize a casino led to the imminence of a contract that combined the selling of 49 per cent of state shares in the company that was managing the casino to a 'single purpose limited company' (AEAS) set up by the winner, an agreement between the seller and the AEAS for some investments in the casino and for the management of the casino, and a clause of compensation based on which the new company was to be shielded from competition from other casinos that were to be established (lawfully) in the same geographical area during the period of validity of the contract (10 years).

Both the referring court and the Court of Justice were of the opinion that this was a mixed contract composed of a sale of shares, supply of services (managing the casino) and performance of works (refurbishment and development of the casino). The Court held that:

> A mixed contract of which the main object is the acquisition by an undertaking of 49% of the capital of a public undertaking and the ancillary object, indivisibly linked with that main object, is the supply of services and the performance of works does not, as a whole, fall within the scope of the directives on public contracts.

It is rather clear that the *higher value* method referred to in Article 22 of the previous Directive (2004/18) and restated in Article 3 of the 2014 Directive with reference to such criteria have no significance here. The only criterion on account of which the regime of such contracts is determined – PPP or public procurement – is the pre-eminence of one or another of the different objects of the contract. The main object (feature) gives the legal qualification of the contract. In this case, the privatization aspect was predominant, and the other aspects were considered inseparable from the main object of the contract.

In another case, *Mehiläinen Oy*,[26] the Oulu City Council in Finland decided to set up a joint venture with its private partner, to be governed the legislation on limited companies. The capital of the joint venture was divided equally between the two partners and its management was shared. The joint venture's activity was to consist in providing occupational health care and welfare services and the two partners intended its activities to be chiefly and increasingly, focused on private clients. However, for a transitional period of four years, they undertook to purchase from the joint venture the health services they were required, as employers, to provide for their staff in accordance with national law. The joint venture's estimated turnover was approximately €90 million during the transitional period, €18 million of which represented the value of services that it was to provide to its staff. The two partners were to transfer to the joint venture, as a capital contribution, their respective units responsible internally for providing occupational health care services to their employees in accordance with the applicable national law. The Law on public procurement required the City to put out to tender its occupational health services once they had become the responsibility of the joint venture. During the transitional stage, however, the City justified continuing its customer relationship with the joint venture on account of the fact that the arrangement would safeguard the position of staff transferring from the City (the City's current

[26] Case C-215/09, *Mehiläinen Oy* [2010] ECR I-13749.

contract is favourable and competitive), and the joint venture would begin its operations in favourable conditions.

The reference was made in the course of proceedings between Mehiläinen Oy and Terveystalo Healthcare Oy, limited companies incorporated under Finnish law, and the City of Oulu, concerning the legal classification, from the point of view of the EU rules on public procurement, of a contract concerning the creation of a joint enterprise. The court decided that where a contracting authority concludes with a private company independent of it a contract establishing a joint venture in the form of a share company, the purpose of which is to provide occupational health care and welfare services, the award by the contracting authority of the contract relating to the services for its own staff, the value of which exceeds the threshold laid down by that directive, and which is severable from the contract establishing that company, must be made in accordance with the provisions of that directive applicable to the services in Annex II B thereof.

3. RATIONALE FOR THE DIVISION OF PUBLIC PROCUREMENT INTO DIMENSIONAL AND SUB-DIMENSIONAL AND ITS CRITIQUE

Public Procurement Directives have always excluded some contracts from their ambit, either on account of their value or because of their nature.[27] As a result of the application of the *de minimis* principle, EU Public Procurement Directives cover only public procurements above certain thresholds. This is a general exclusion from the scope of the Public Procurement Directives, and such contracts are subjected in principle to national law.

The reasoning behind the general exclusion from the Directives seems to be the presumption that there is not enough cross-border interest in these contracts, which are of low value or, in case of non-priority services, are intrinsically national.

The logical explanation for leaving some contracts outside the EU procurement directives would be that these are of lesser importance for the common market. Another rationale behind the division of the public procurement regime into *dimensional* and *sub-dimensional* categories according to the thresholds has to do with a supposition that contracts above the thresholds could cover the majority of the public procurement in Member States, and that little will be left to contracts under the thresholds.

A 'scape goat' is also the GPA, which is invoked in order to explain the impossibility of amending the thresholds due to obligations assumed by the EU under the GPA and that those thresholds should be the result of international negotiations.

None of the above assumptions or explanations is safe from criticism. Evidence from the practice of public procurement in Member States shows that sub-dimensional procurement overwhelmingly surpasses dimensional public purchasing in size, thus rendering the application of the Directives only partly responsible for the integration of

---

[27] For the succession of Directives and contracts excluded from their application, see Caranta, 'The Borders of EU Public Procurement Law', above, fn. 18, p. 25 ff.

public markets in the EU.[28] Research data shows that in all EU Member States the award of public procurement contracts falling below the EU thresholds is of significant importance and represents a large share of total procurement. In 2006 and 2008, for instance, evaluations commissioned by the European Commission concluded that only about 20 per cent of the total amount of public procurement was covered by the detailed rules of the Directives, while the remainder falls under exceptions to the Directives – defence procurements and below-threshold procurement.[29] Against this background, the way in which national governments design procurement policies and rules for the award of these contracts bears an obvious importance for the effectiveness of the public procurement system as a whole. However, a forthright explanation for exclusions would be that they are exempt basically due to the resistance of some Member States to open the corresponding markets to EU-wide competition.[30]

The rationale for exclusion is different for concessions – in *Telaustria*,[31] the Court of Justice argued that the consideration provided by the contracting authorities to the concessionaire consists in the latter obtaining the right to exploit for payment its own service and this is the reason for exclusion. As for Annex XVI Services, the assumption is that the specificity of such contracts keeps them outside the cross-border interest. This is the reason why the Public Sector Directive imposes only some degree of publicity after the award of such service contracts.

The 2014 Directive brings about a (slight) change on this matter: based on the results of the *Evaluation on the Impact and Effectiveness of EU Public Procurement Legislation*,[32] which suggested that the exclusion of certain services from the full application of the Directive should be reviewed, and that the full application of the Directive will be extended to a number of services.

Evidently, certain categories of services by their very nature are likely to incite a limited cross-border interest; consequently they are left to be provided within a particular context that varies widely amongst Member States, and are influenced by different cultural traditions. Such services are known as 'services to the person', and include mainly social, health and educational services. A specific regime is therefore imposed only for public contracts with a higher threshold of €750,000. Services to the person that fall under these values are presumed not to be of interest to providers from other Member States, unless there are concrete indications to the contrary, such as Union financing for trans-border projects. Recital 114 of the 2014 Directive states that contracts for services to the person above the threshold should be subject to Union-wide transparency.

---

[28] C.H. Bovis, *EU Procurement Law*, Cheltenham, UK and Northampton, MA, USA: Edward Elgar, 2007, p. 70.

[29] OECD, 'Public Procurement in EU Member States: The Regulation of Contract below the EU Thresholds and in Areas not covered by the Detailed Rules of the EU Directives', Sigma Paper 45, 2010, p, available 27 January 2016 at http://dx.doi.org/10.1787/5km91p7s1mxv-en.

[30] R. Caranta and S.Treumer, *Foreword by the editors of the European Public Procurement Law Series*, in Dragos and Caranta (eds), *Outside the EU Procurement Directives, inside the Treaty?* above, fn.11, p. 2.

[31] Case C-324/98*Telaustria and Telefonadress* [2000] ECR I-10745.

[32] SEC(2011) 853 final, 27 June 2011.

4. THE CASE LAW OF THE CJEU AND THE SHAPING OF THE SUB-DIMENSIONAL REGIME

The CJEU has played an important role in shaping the regime of sub-dimensional public procurement. *Unitron Scandinavia*[33] is considered to be the first case on this matter.[34] In this case, an obligation to ear-tag pigs in order to enable their provenance to be determined, derived from a Council Directive, was supplemented in practice by an obligation, under Danish legislation and implementing measures, to buy the tags from a certain private undertaking, which in turn procured the tags from the market. Unitron and another producer challenged this arrangement, claiming that the Danske Slagterier was a procuring entity under the meaning of Procurement Directive 93/36/EEC then in force.

The questions referred to the Court of Justice regarded whether the agreement between the Danish ministry and Danske Slagterier should have included a duty for the private undertaking to follow public procurement procedures. Although the Court of Justice concluded that no such obligation stemmed from the Directive, it also recalled that under Article 2(2) of the Directive, 'where a contracting authority grants to a body which is not a contracting authority special or exclusive rights to engage in a public service activity, the only requirement is that the measure whereby that right is granted must stipulate that, in relation to the public supply contracts which it awards to third parties in the context of that activity, the body in question must comply with the principle of non-discrimination on grounds of nationality'. Further interpretation gave the principle of non-discrimination on grounds of nationality a wide scope, in the sense that it should imply an obligation of transparency in order to enable the contracting authority to make sure the principle was complied with.

Another point of reference in this development is considered to be the *Telaustria* case,[35] where the Court has emphasized the possibility that some contracts falling outside the ambit of the Directives could still be of certain cross-border interest and thus at least the general principles of EU law, in particular the non-discrimination principle complemented with an obligation of transparency, should be observed.

In *Telaustria*, which dealt with service concessions, the Court of Justice commented for the first time on the obligation of transparency as part of a broader endeavour to comply with the principle of non-discrimination, in cases not covered by the Public Procurement Directives. This jurisprudence has become the standard for all contracts falling outside Public Procurement Directives.

The questions were raised in proceedings between Telaustria Verlags GmbH (Telaustria) and Telefonadress GmbH (Telefonadress), on the one hand, and Telekom Austria AG (Telekom Austria), on the other, concerning the conclusion by Telekom Austria of a concession contract with Herold Business Data AG (Herold) for the production and publication of printed and electronically accessible lists of telephone subscribers (telephone directories).

---

33 Case C-275/98, *Unitron Scandinavia and 3-S A/S, Danske Svineproducenters Serviceselskab v Ministeriet for Fødevarer, Landbrug og Fiskeri* [1999] ECR I-8291.

34 Caranta, 'The Borders of EU Public Procurement Law', above, fn. 18, p. 32.

35 C-324/98, *Telaustria and Telefonadress* [2000] ECR I-10745

Upon declaring the concession contract to be outside the remit of Directive 93/98, the Court tackled nevertheless the obligations stemming from the general principles of the Treaties. Thus, contracting entities concluding such contracts are, nonetheless, bound to comply with the fundamental rules of the Treaty, in general, and the principle of non-discrimination on the ground of nationality, in particular, that principle implying, in particular, an obligation of transparency in order to enable the contracting authority to satisfy itself that the principle has been complied with. The transparency required needs to assure a degree of advertising sufficient to enable the services market to be opened up to competition and the impartiality of procurement procedures to be reviewed.[36]

The application of the general principle of non-discrimination to contracts not covered by the public procurement directives was reiterated in *Commission v France*.[37] The court declared that reserving the task of delegated project contracting to 'an exhaustive list of legal persons under national law, by which the contracting authority may, by an agreement in writing and for remuneration, appoint an agent to fulfil, in its name and on its behalf, all or any of certain of its responsibilities' fails to fulfil both obligations under Directive 92/50 in force at the time and those stemming from Article 49 EC as regards public service contracts outside the scope of Directive 92/50.

The imposition of new legal obligations in this field has generated controversy in the doctrine.[38] Some authors maintain that despite several important judgments that have been delivered by the Court of Justice since *Telaustria*, it is still very much uncertain which duties apply for contracts covered by this regime.[39] Some Member States have reacted with criticism as well. Germany has brought a case against the very policy promoted by the Commission, with the backing of other Member States and of the European Parliament. In *Germany v Commission*,[40] the Court replied that the Communication does not contain new rules for the award of public contracts which go beyond the obligations under Community law, so it does not produce binding legal effects liable to affect the legal situation of the Federal Republic of Germany and the interveners, and the action must therefore be dismissed as inadmissible.

---

36 *Telaustria*, paras 61 and 62.

37 Case C-264/03, *Commission v France* [2005] ECR I-8831.

38 P. Braun, 'A Matter of Principle(s): the Treatment of Contracts Falling Outside the Scope of the European Public Procurement Directives' [2000] PPLR 39; S. Treumer and E. Werlauff, 'The Leverage Principle: Secondary Community Law as a Lever for the Development of Primary Community Law' [2003] ELR 124; E. Pijnacker Hordijk and M. Meulenbelt, 'A Bridge Too Far: Why the European Commission's Attempts to Construct an Obligation to Tender Outside the Scope of the Public Procurement Directives should be Dismissed' [2005] PPLR 123 and S. Arrowsmith, *The Law of Public and Utilities Procurement*, 2nd edn., London: Sweet & Maxwell, 2005 at 197.

39 Caranta, 'The Borders of EU Public Procurement Law', above, fn. 18, p. 28.

40 Case T-258/06, *Germany v Commission* [2010] ECR II-2027; see also, for a commentary, Z. Petersen, 'Below-threshold Contract Awards under EU Primary Law: Federal Republic of Germany v Commission (T-258/06)' [2010] *PPLR* NA215.

In later cases, the Court has demarcated the scope of the obligation to apply EU treaty principles, emphasizing the distinction between legislative policy and administrative policy. Thus, in *Commission v Italy*[41] the Commission claimed in its complaint against Italy that national laws should guarantee, by way of express provisions, that principles of transparency and equal treatment enshrined in the EC Treaty must be observed even if the estimated value of the contract is below the threshold for application of the Directive. The Court has on one hand refused to interfere with the legislative choices of Member States in areas not covered by the Community law, reiterating on the other hand that the EU law principles are not put into question in the case. In other words, the principles are applicable when there is cross-border interest in the contract, even though the national law does not stipulate itself this obligation. The matter is left at the appraisal of contracting authorities, which are entirely responsible for deciding whether there is a cross border interest in the contract.

However, there are authors arguing that in cases where 'the national statute at issue is not just implementing a directive, but purports to lay down all the rules applicable to public contracts. In this situation, not having actual provisions to the same effect as the Treaty principle, will mean by implication that contracting authorities will feel free to follow any procedure – if any – they like'.[42]

Another relevant case is *Coname*,[43] where the Court of Justice analyzed a direct award by a municipality of a service concession – the management of the public gas-distribution service – to a public controlled company. After concluding that for contracts falling outside the Directives there is still an obligation of transparency, the court has duly explained that the requirement of transparency does not necessarily imply an obligation to hold a formal invitation to tender. The advertisement may even be limited to a short description of the contract to be awarded and of the award method together with an invitation to contact the contracting entity, completed if necessary by additional information available on the internet or to be obtained upon request from the contracting authority. The transparency test set out by the court should enable an undertaking located in the territory of another Member State to have access to the information regarding that concession, so that it could express an interest in obtaining the concession. The Court held that infringement of the duty of transparency has an effect on the principles of free movement of services and the right of establishment.

The case *Bent Mousten Vestergaard*[44] dealt with the obligation to treat tenders equally even in that regard including in the general conditions of the contract, a clause requiring the use in carrying it out of a product of a specified make, where that clause does not include the words 'or equivalent', the possibility of using similar products while carrying out the contract. Mr Vestergaard claimed that by requiring in the call for tenders the use of a specified product for the outside doors and windows, Spøttrup Boligselskab had infringed the Treaty, by not having an option of delivering similar

[41] Case C-412/04, *Commission v Italy* [2008] ECR I-619. See also Case C-507/03, *Commission v Ireland* [2007] ECR I-9777.

[42] Caranta, 'The Borders of EU Public Procurement Law', above, fn. 18, p. xx.

[43] Case C-231/03, *Consorzio Aziende Metano (Coname) v Comune di Cingia de' Botti* [2005] ECR I-7287, para 21.

[44] Case C-59/00, *Vestergaard v Spottrup Boligselskab* [2001] ECR I-9505.

products of other producers as represented by additional words 'or equivalent' in the tender specification.

The Review Board analyzing the plea considered that contracts of value below the thresholds are of no importance to the Community context and complying with requirements of the Directive would be too costly for this level of contracts. It also considered that *Commission v Ireland*, invoked by the claimant, concerned a large-scale project whose value exceeded the threshold laid down in Council Directive 71/305/EEC – since repealed and replaced by Directive 93/37 – so that that judgment was of no relevance for the application before it.

However, the Court of Justice held that (then) Article 30 of the EC Treaty precludes a contracting authority from including in the contract documents for a public works contract which does not fall under the Public Procurement Directive in force at the time a provision requiring the use of a product of a specified brand, without giving the possibility of substituting an equivalent. Such specifications may deter some economic operators using systems similar to that product from participating in the procedure, and thus may impede the flow of imports in intra-Community trade.

In another case, *Parking Brixen*, the Court reiterated the conclusions in *Telaustria* and *Coname* that when awarding contracts outside the Directives, such as services concessions, contracting authorities must comply with the principle of non-discrimination on grounds of nationality and the principle of equal treatment, which are closely linked to the principles of the right of establishment and the freedom to provide services. The case was about Parking Brixen challenging the award to Stadtwerke Brixen AG of the management of the two car parks, arguing that the Municipality of Brixen should have applied the public procurement provisions. Stadtwerke Brixen, a special undertaking owned by that municipality, has been converted in regard to its areas of activity, its geographical coverage – from local to national – and its management. It was endowed with legal personality and corporate autonomy and it constituted a municipal body, the specific function of which is the uniform and integrated provision of local public services. The Municipality of Brixen denied that there was any obligation to proceed by way of a public call for tenders, as it completely controlled Stadtwerke Brixen AG and that there was therefore no award of a contract to a third party.

The Court held that 'although the Directives do not apply to service concessions, articles 43 EC and 49 EC and the principles of equal treatment, non-discrimination and transparency, are to be interpreted as precluding a public authority from awarding, without putting it out to competition, a public service concession to a company ...' and then went on to describe the legal situation of Stadtwerke. The Court disregarded the allegation by the municipality that the issue was purely local/national as both undertakings were Italian, arguing first, that according to its previous jurisprudence, the prohibition on discrimination on grounds of nationality is a specific expression of the general principle of equal treatment,[45] then that in the field of public procurement the principle of equal treatment of tenderers is intended to afford equality of opportunity to all tenderers when formulating their tenders, regardless of their

[45] Case 810/79, *Überschär* [1980] ECR 2747, para 16.

nationality,[46] and, finally, that the principle of equal treatment of tenderers is to be applied to public service concessions even in the absence of discrimination on grounds of nationality.[47]

Finally, the considerations expressed in the case law of the Court regarding procurement by European Institutions should be mentioned. This is a separate development from the one taking place in Member States, but it is nevertheless relevant for the construction of principles of equal treatment (with its corollary, the principle of transparency) among tenders. The leading case is *Succhi di frutta*,[48] where the Commission had bound itself by Regulation[49] to award competitively the free supply of agricultural products to the peoples of Georgia, Armenia, Azerbaijan, Kyrgyzstan and Tajikistan; during the procedure the Commission changed the conditions for the remuneration originally foreseen for the contract by allowing successful tenderers to take as payment for their supplies products other than those specified in the notice of invitation to tender and, in particular, peaches instead of apples and oranges. The Court of First Instance and then the Court of Justice rightly declared that when a contracting entity had laid down prescriptive requirements in the contract documents, observance of the principle of equal treatment of tenderers requires that all the tenders must comply with them so as to ensure objective comparison of the tenders, and that the principle of equal treatment implies an obligation of transparency in order to permit verification that it has been complied with.

In a similar case, *Evropaïki Dynamiki*,[50] the Court held that the principle of transparency, which is a corollary of the principle of equal treatment, is essentially intended to preclude any risk of favouritism or arbitrariness on the part of the contracting authority. Moreover, the Court explained that this requirement means that all the conditions and detailed rules of the award procedure must be drawn up in a clear, precise and unequivocal manner in the contract notice or tendering specifications. Consequently, all technical information relevant must be made available as soon as possible to all the undertakings taking part in a public procurement procedure. The 'reasonably well-informed and normally diligent tenderers' should thus be able to understand their precise scope and to interpret them in the same manner. Moreover, this would enable the contracting authority actually to verify whether the tenderers' bids meet the criteria of the contract in question'.[51]

---

[46] Case C-87/94, *Commission v Belgium* [1996] ECR I-2043, paras 33 and 54.

[47] Case C-458/03, *Parking Brixen GmbH v Gemeinde Brixen*, [2005] ECR I-8612, para 48.

[48] Joined Cases T-191/96 and T-106/97, *CAS Succhi di Frutta SpA* v *Commission*, [1999] ECR II-3184.

[49] Commission adopted Regulation (EC) No 2009/95 of 18 August 1995 laying down detailed rules for the free supply of agricultural products held in intervention stocks to Georgia, Armenia, Azerbaijan, Kyrgyzstan and Tajikistan pursuant to Regulation No 1975/95 ([1995] OJ L196/4).

[50] Case T-50/05, *Evropaïki Dynamiki – Proigmena Systimata Tilepikoinonion Pliroforikis kai Tilematikis AE v European Commission* [2010] ECR II-1071, paras 55–59, 61.

[51] Paragraph 59.

In *Strong Segurança*,[52] the reference was made in the context of a dispute between a security company and Município de Sintra (Sintra Municipal Council, Portugal) concerning the award of a contract for surveillance and security services for the installations of that municipality. The Court ruled that Directive 2004/18/EC does not create an obligation for Member States to apply Article 47(2) to contracts which have as their object services referred to in Annex II B thereto. However, that directive does not preclude Member States and, possibly, contracting authorities, from providing for such application in, respectively, their legislation and the documents relating to the contract. Roberto Caranta[53] observed that in *Strong Segurança* the Court of Justice wished to draw a line against a 'broad approach' to the applicability of the principle of equal treatment which could lead to the application to non-priority service contracts of other essential provisions of Directive 2004/18/EC, and that it is hard to reconcile *Strong Segurança* with *Telaustria* and *SECAP* (see below), where the Court of Justice was far less prudish in spelling obligations to be followed by contracting authorities.

In the *Medipac-Kazantzidis* case,[54] the principles of equal treatment and transparency were invoked by the Court in order to preclude the exclusion from a sub-dimensional award procedure of surgical sutures that were allegedly inadequate, although they bore the EC marking. The reasoning behind the decision was that technical requirements for the said products had been subject to harmonization and certification could only be challenged through a special safeguard procedure. Since that procedure can be initiated only by competent national authorities, the contracting authority may suspend the procedure until the matter is decided. However, if delays are jeopardizing the functioning of a public hospital, the contracting authority may decide proportional interim measures.

Special attention must be given to *SECAP*,[55] because it deals with national legislation on sub-dimensional procurement and its compliance with general principles of EU law. The Italian law authorizing the automatic exclusion of abnormally low tenders without an opportunity to justify the offer was considered to be infringing on the said principles, including (indirect) non-discrimination, since it placed at a disadvantage operators from other Member States which, as they have different cost structures, may benefit from significant economies of scale or, intending to cut their profit margins in order to enter the market in question more effectively, would be in a position to make a bid that was competitive and at the same time genuine and viable but which the contracting authority would not be able to consider as a result of that legislation.[56]

Commission v Ireland[57] provides useful (albeit general) criteria indispensable for identifying the rules from the Directives that may be expanded to sub-dimensional procurement. Thus, in an infringement procedure against Ireland occasioned by a translation services contract (which is a list B service), the Court held that, in order to

---

[52] Case C-95/10, *Strong Segurança SA v Município de Sintra, Securitas-Serviços e Tecnologia de Segurança* [2011] ECR I-1865, para 35.

[53] Caranta, 'The Borders of EU Public Procurement Law', above, fn. 18, p. 51.

[54] Case C-6/05, *Medipac-Kazantzidis* [2007] ECR I-4557.

[55] Joined Cases C-147/06 and C-148/06, *SECAP* [2008] ECR I-3565.

[56] Paragraph 26.

[57] Case C-226/09, *Commission v Ireland* [2010] ECR I-0000, para 41.

be applicable to B list services (similarly, to concessions and sub-dimensional procurement), the rules contained in the Directive must constitute a direct consequence of the fact that the contracting authorities are required to comply with the principle of equal treatment and the consequent obligation of transparency. In this case, the relative weights given to the award criteria were not advertised properly and moreover, the weighting was changed during the procedure, after a number of tenders had already been examined. Two different situations were distinguished here: not providing clear weighting criteria beforehand may be permitted under the equal treatment principle, but changing the weighting after bids were already opened is not. Contracting authorities have a duty to interpret the award criteria in the same way throughout the procedure.

Recent cases also may be mentioned here. In a judgment from 2013 – *Belgacom*,[58] the CJEU dealt with an agreement concluded by public entities of one Member State and an undertaking of that Member State, regarding the transfer of their television provision activities and, for a fixed period, the exclusive right to use their cable networks. The absence of any invitation to tender was justified by the existence of an earlier agreement between the two parties, which was disputed. The transaction concluded between the parties intended to put an end to litigation concerning the interpretation of that agreement. In this context, the Court rejected the argument that avoidance of litigation could be considered a valid 'overriding reason in the public interest' justifying a direct award of a concession contract. In determining compliance with EU primary law requirements it is of no importance that the award of the services concession forms part of a settlement agreement. What mattered most was that the concession was *of* certain cross-border interest. The Court gave pre-eminence to transparency to the detriment of the discretion of contracting authorities as regards alternative dispute resolution in the field of public contracts.

However, as Albert Sanchez Graells[59] has observed, the practical effects of the *Belgacom* Judgment may be relatively limited once the future 2014 Directives are adopted, as they expressly regulate contract modification and set clear limits that will trigger the obligation to retender the contract (see Article 72 of the new Public Sector Procurement Directive and Article 89 of the new Concessions Directive).

Finally, the quantitative approach to the division between concessions covered by the 2014 Concessions Directive and those outside its remit may be put into question by the judgement of 14 November 2013 in case *Comune di Ancona*,[60] and this may also have a spillover effect on sub-dimensional procurement. The new Directive on concessions applies only to contracts above €5 million, and these contracts are supposed to be the only ones which bear cross border interest. The case regarded a concession for the management of a European Regional Development Fund (ERDF)-supported port infrastructure (a slipway) directly awarded by the Comune di Ancona to the local fishermen cooperative. The conditions of the concessions excluded a profit for either of the parties, so the justification provided for the direct award was that 'it was not necessary, for the purposes of granting a concession for management of the slipway, to

[58] Case C-221/12, ECLI:EU:C:2014:736.

[59] See A. Sanchez Graells' analysis at http://howtocrackanut.blogspot.co.uk/2013/11/cjeu-rejects-avoidance-of-litigation-as.html#! (accessed 28 January 2016).

[60] C-388/12 Comune di Ancona v Region Marche, ECLI:EU:C:2013:734.

publish a call for tenders, in so far as no operators apart from the Pescatori cooperative were interested in that concession'.[61]

However, the Court has held that the fact that a concession is not capable of generating substantial net revenue or an undue advantage for an undertaking or for a public body does not, in itself, support the inference that the concession is of no economic interest for undertakings located in Member States other than that of the contracting authority. In the context of an economic strategy to extend part of its activities to another Member State, an undertaking may take the tactical decision to seek the award in that State of a concession despite the fact that that concession is incapable as such of generating sufficient profit, since that opportunity could nevertheless enable the undertaking to establish itself on the market of that State and to make itself known there with a view to preparing its future expansion.

What are the implications of this judgement for the application of the Concessions Directive? I agree with Albert Sanchez Graells that 'a dual legal regime will persist between "Directive concessions" and "*Ancona* concessions", where the CJEU will continue pointing out the potential existence of cross-border interest for concessions with a value below €5mn (or in the excluded and preferential sectors, such as water or social services)'. And this may not be a development that will simplify the interpretation of the new Directives.[62]

5. FROM CASE-LAW TO SOFT LAW: THE 2006 COMMUNICATION

Following the developments in the case-law, in 2006 the European Commission issued an Interpretative Communication[63] that synthesized the jurisprudence of the Court and made recommendations for Member States pertaining to contracts below thresholds. The Communication sheds light on the Commission's understanding of the Court of Justice case-law and suggests best practices in order to help the Member States to reap the full benefit of the internal market. The document has the same relevance after the 2014 Directives enter into force as before their enactment.

In the Communication, the European Commission places the responsibility for deciding whether an intended contract award might potentially be of interest to economic operators located in other Member States on the individual contracting authorities. This decision has to be based on the individual circumstances of each case, taking into consideration factors such as the subject matter of the contract, its estimated value, the size and structure of the particular market, commercial practices and the geographic location of the place of performance.

---

[61] C-388/12, at para 16.

[62] See also A. Sánchez Graells, 'What Need and Logic for a New Directive on Concessions, Particularly Regarding the Issue of Their Economic Balance?' (2012) 2 *European Public Private Partnerships Law Review* 94–104.

[63] Commission Interpretative Communication on the Community law applicable to contract awards not or not fully subject to the provisions of the Public Procurement Directives [2006] OJ C179/02.

The European Commission identified certain basic standards that are to be followed by contracting authorities related to 'advertising', 'contract award' (that is, the impartiality of procedures relating to contract award) and 'judicial protection'. It also expresses its view of what compliance with the basic standards means in practice. The obligation to provide adequate advertising presupposes a degree of advertising sufficient to enable the market to be opened up to competition, and ensures that an undertaking located in another Member State has the appropriate information regarding the contract before it is awarded in order to be in a position to express its interest in obtaining that contract. The Communication also offers examples of adequate and commonly used means of publication: internet, national official journals, local newspapers or even the Official Journal of the EU. Local means of publication are advisable only for small contracts for which there is only a local market.

As to the principles applying to contract awards, the Commission expressed a strong opinion towards awards being in line with the rules and principles of the Treaty so as to guarantee fair competition to all economic operators interested in the contract and impartial procedures for award. The measures envisaged to be taken in order to ensure compliance with the principles of the Treaty include non-discriminatory descriptions of the subject matter of the contract; equal access for economic operators from all Member States; mutual recognition of diplomas, certificates and other evidence of formal qualifications; the use of appropriate time limits; and the use of a transparent and objective approach.[64]

The final aspect covered by the Communication regards judicial protection. Member States have an obligation to ensure impartial and effective review mechanisms of the award procedure. The Communication was the most important instrument in the hands of the Commission in its attempts to forge a sort of harmonization of sub-dimensional public procurement in spite of the opposition of the Member States.[65] The Communication, being a soft law tool, is still applicable after the entering into force of the new Directive. However, it is often overlooked that the Recitals of the directives have the same effect as the Communication. Thus, in *Germany v Commission*[66] the Court observed that the Communication is not alone in referring to the principles of EU law, but the Recitals of the 2004 Directives ascertain their importance as well.

6. PRINCIPLES APPLICABLE TO SUB-DIMENSIONAL CONTRACTS

Directive 2004 in Recital 2, proclaimed from the outset that, generally, the award of public contracts by Member States is subject to the respect of the principles of the Treaty, and that, as a 'special precaution', provisions for the coordination of national

---

[64] Commission Interpretative Communication, section 2.

[65] See for doctrinarian discussions U. Neergard, 'Public Service Concessions and Related Concepts – the Increased Pressure from Community Law on Member States' Use of Concessions' [2007] PPLR 387; A. Brown, 'Seeing Through Transparency: the Requirement to Advertise Public Contracts and Concessions Under the EC Treaty' [2007] PPLR 1.

[66] Case T-258/06, *Germany v Commission* [2010] ECR II-0000.

procedures for the award of contracts above certain values are necessary in order to ensure the effects of the above mentioned principles and to guarantee the opening-up of public procurement to competition.

The same paradigm is reiterated in Recital 1 of the 2014 Directive, which places on all awards of public contracts by or on behalf of Member States' authorities the duty to comply with the principles of the Treaty on the Functioning of the European Union, and in particular the free movement of goods, freedom of establishment and the freedom to provide services as well as the principles deriving therefrom, such as equal treatment, non-discrimination, mutual recognition, proportionality and transparency.

The principles invoked in the Recital seem to overlap, but they are nevertheless distinct. Thus, the Tribunal in *Germany v Commission*[67] stated that the principle of equal treatment derives from the cumulative application of other related principles: the obligation of transparency; the principle of freedom to provide services; and the principle of free competition; it consequently does not create new obligations.

The principle of non-discrimination entails, according to the Commission's Communication and based on the case-law of the Court of Justice (*Bent Mousten Vestergaard*, described above), the non-discriminatory description of the subject-matter of the contract. Such description of the characteristics required of a product or service should not refer to a specific make or source, or a particular process, or to trade marks, patents, types or a specific origin or production unless such a reference is justified by the subject matter of the contract and accompanied by the words 'or equivalent'.[68] In any case, it would be preferable to use more general descriptions of performance or functions.[69]

According to the 2006 Communication, non-discrimination entails equal access for economic operators from all Member States. Consequently, any conditions causing direct or indirect discrimination against potential tenderers in other Member States, such as the requirement that undertakings interested in the contract must be established in the same Member State or region as the contracting entity must be avoided. The only derogation regards the requirement that the successful tenderer should establish certain business infrastructure at the place of performance if this is justified by the specific circumstances of the contract.

There is debate in the scholarly literature whether the principle of equal treatment has the same implications as the principle of non-discrimination,[70] or whether the latter has a narrower scope.[71] The Court has invoked the equal treatment principle, for instance, in cases relating to procurement organized by EU institutions, because in

---

67 Ibid para 131.

68 Paragraph 109. See also Commission interpretative communication on facilitating the access of products to the markets of other Member States, [2003] OJ C265/2 ('Interpretative communication').

69 Interpretative communication, p. 5.

70 Caranta, 'The Borders of EU Public Procurement Law', above, fn. 18, p. 37.

71 Pijnacker Hordijk and Meulenbelt, *A Bridge Too Far: Why the European Commission's Attempts to Construct an Obligation to Tender outside the Scope of the Public Procurement Directives should be Dismissed*, above, fn. 38; S. Arrowsmith and P. Kunzlik, *Social and Envirnomental Policies in EC Procurement Law*, Cambridge: Cambridge University Press, 2009, p. 86.

those cases there is a general assumption that EU institutions do not discriminate on a nationality basis. In cases referred by national courts, on the other hand, the distinction may be justified, as equal treatment means more than just non-discrimination based on nationality. In the same vein, the related principle of mutual recognition refers to diplomas, certificates and other evidence of formal qualifications that tenderers are required to submit in writing. The principle entails that documents from other Member States offering an equivalent level of guarantee have to be accepted by the contracting authorities.[72]

The principle of *proportionality* is not explained in the Interpretative Communication, and there is only one reference to it in the specific case-law. However, the reference to appropriate time-limits may be considered an expression of the proportionality principle. Thus, without any reference to case-law, the Communication advises Member States to use time-limits for expression of interest and for submission of offers that are long enough to allow undertakings from other Member States to make a meaningful assessment and prepare their offer.[73] As to the case-law, in *SECAP*,[74] after concluding that automatic exclusion for abnormally low tenders was in the case at hand not consistent with EU law, the Court conceded that national or local legislation or even the contracting authorities themselves would be entitled to set a reasonable threshold for the automatic exclusion of abnormally low tenders.

Both the Court of Justice[75] and the Directives[76] refer to a principle of transparency in itself rather than being merely a corollary of the principle of equal treatment. In some cases, the Court uses also the concept of 'obligation of transparency', which follows from the principle of equal treatment. This means that basically all participants must be able to know the applicable rules in advance and must have the certainty that these rules apply to everybody in the same way.[77]

---

72 Interpretative communication, p. 5.

73 Interpretative communication, p. 6.

74 Joined Cases C-147/06 and C-148/06, *SECAP* [2008] ECR I-3565, para 32.

75 See for instance *Commission v Ireland*, paras 26 and 29–31; Case C-95/10, *Strong Segurança SA v Município de Sintra, Securitas-Serviços e Tecnologia de Segurança* [2011] ECR I-01865, para 35.

76 Recital 1 of the 2014 Directive.

77 For two rather recent and interesting studies that tackle the limits of the general principles (transparency, equal treatment and non-discrimination) and their existence within and beyond 'the completion of the common market as a sole warrant for their application', see S. de Mars, 'The Limits of General Principles: A Procurement Case Study' (2013) 38(3) E.L. Rev. 316–34 and J. Howell, 'Is there a General Principle Requiring Transparency about How Decisions will be Taken?' (2011) 16(4) *Judicial Review* 322–35. The latter has particularly analyzed English courts' reaction to such a possible interpretation of the principle of transparency. Furthermore, the issue is also dealt with (although indirectly and within the framework of a different analysis) by Sanchez Graells whilst describing the common goals of competition law and public procurement law. Also, see a very interesting academic debate on the subject matter between A. Sanchez Graells, Prof. S. Arrowsmith and Prof. P. Kinzlik ('The Purpose of the EU Procurement Directives: Ends, Means and the Implications for National Regulatory Space for Commercial and Horizontal Procurement Policies' (2011–2012) 14 *Cambridge Yearbook of European legal studies* 1–47. Sanchez Graells's reply is available at: http://howtocrackanut.blogspot.it/.

Limitations as to the number of participants in the procedure must be also be transparent. Contracting entities may rely on the previous experience of the applicants in the sector concerned, the size and infrastructure of their business, their technical and professional abilities or other objective factors. The recourse to lots, either exclusively or in combination with other selection criteria is also an option.[78]

An alternative method for selection is to draw a list of qualified operators in a transparent and non-discriminatory way, and then select the operators to be invited to submit an offer from the list of qualified operators (for example, by drawing them in rotation from the list).

A practice that flourishes unabated all over Europe is to individually invite a number of potential contractors to bid for sub-dimensional contracts. This practice is not in line with the Communication and with the case-law, as it does not entail a 'sufficiently accessible advertisement prior to the award of the contract'.[79] Transparency must be observed before the procedure is initiated, because it cannot be covered afterwards.[80]

An application of the transparency principle was attempted in *Impresa Portuale di Cagliari*, a case that was not adjudicated in the end by the Court because the preliminary reference was withdrawn, but where Advocate General Jacobs indicated that transparency requirements applicable to technical specifications in contracts relating to non-priority services may be fulfilled by making the general documents readily available to all interested undertakings in sufficient time and on equal conditions.[81]

7. NATIONAL RESPONSES TO THE LIMITED APPLICATION OF THE DIRECTIVES

The exclusion of sub-dimensional procurement from the ambit of the Directives should have made national jurisdictions a playground for the principles of EU law. However, Member States (and contracting authorities) had employed different techniques in order to cope with the discretion given by the Directives: extension of the rules of the Directives to sub-dimensional procurement (either fully or partially), or the application

78 Interpretative communication, p. 6.

79 Interpretative communication, p. 6, para 2.1.2.

80 Case T-258/06, *Commission v Germany* [2010] ECR II-0000, paras 76 ff; Case C-231/03, *Coname* [2005] ECR I-7287, para 21, is referred to; see also para 79: 'It follows from that case-law that the obligation of transparency in terms of adequate advertising thus presupposes a form of advertising that takes place before the award of the public contract in question: in other words, prior publication of an advertisement …'; see also M. Trybus 'Public Contracts in European Union Internal Market Law: Foundations and Requirements' in R. Noguellou and U. Stelkens (eds) *Droit comparé des contrats publics*, Brussels: Bruylant, 2010, p. 103.

81 Opinion of Advocate General Jacobs delivered on 21 April 2005, Case C-174/03, *Impresa Portuale di Cagliari Srl v Tirrenia di Navigazione SpA*, available 28 January 2016 at http://curia.europa.eu/juris/document/document.jsf;jsessionid=9ea7d2dc30d577525dd616d047b48a41e4107f00e510.e34KaxiLc3qMb40Rch0SaxuSbhb0?text=&docid=58134&pageIndex=0&doclang=en&mode=lst&dir=&occ=first&part=1&cid=105479.

of general public or private law rules. National courts and review bodies have contributed as well to the shaping of the legal regime for such contracts.

Under the previous Directives (2004), the Member States had the same power to decide on the rules and procedures to be applied for sub-dimensional contracts as they have now, under the 2014 Directive. The consistency of such rules with the principles of the Treaty is assured in cases where the rules of the Directives were extended beyond their ambit, because the award procedures are in principle transparent and non-discriminatory. The issue becomes more complex where the strict delineation between dimensional and sub-dimensional procurement is respected (as in the UK, for instance). However, even in the first hypothesis, there are still areas not covered by these extensions (direct procurement under a national threshold).

A short survey of the rules and practices employed by the Member States is useful for understanding the conceivable developments (if any) in the sub-dimensional procurement regime at the national level following the adoption of the 2014 Directives.

Thus, a study put together by OECD in 2010[82] concluded that the majority of Member States regulate public procurement above and below EU thresholds within the same legislative act, and require that contracts below the EU thresholds be based on open, fair and competitive procedures. These procedures essentially have similar features to those applicable under the EU Directives, whilst those Member States that have no regulation still promote the use of competitive tendering below the EU thresholds.

There are obvious differences in regulatory approaches employed by the Member States. They may be explained by different traditions governing national administrative systems, but may also be the direct influence of the law in place at the time of EU accession. The tactic of new EU entrants (2004 and 2007) was generally to expand the detailed provisions for dimensional procurement to sub-dimensional contracts as well, out of fear of corruption. This tendency is not limited though to Eastern Member States – France, Italy and Spain for instance follow the same pattern. In some countries from Western Europe, on the other hand, as the resistance to the regime imposed by case-law and soft law reveals, the discretion of contracting authorities as regards contracts not covered by the Directives was guarded more effectively (Germany, Denmark, the UK).

Many Member States (for instance, Italy, Spain, Romania, Poland, are advocates of a practice called 'gold plating' – defined by the European Commission as 'exceeding the requirements of EU legislation when transposing Directives into national law'.[83] This

[82] OECD (2010), 'Public Procurement in EU Member States – The Regulation of Contract Below the EU Thresholds and in Areas not Covered by the Detailed Rules of the EU Directives', Sigma Papers, No. 45, OECD Publishing, available 28 January 2016 at http://dx.doi.org/10.1787/5km91p7s1mxv-en.

[83] See the Commission's definition in: 'Communication from the Commission to the European Parliament, The Council, Economic and Social Committee and the Committee of the Regions Review of the "Small Business Act" for Europe' Brussels, COM(2011) 78 final, 23 February 2011, point 7.

practice, fairly widespread,[84] increases complexity in the national legislation implementing EU Directives, often laying the blame for the introduction of new rules on the EU, which in reality are not imposed by European legislation.[85]

In the procurement context, gold plating means that application of EU Directives is extended to contracts below the thresholds, leaving only 'minor contracts' to direct procurement. This practice is frowned upon by the Commission, although not necessarily in public procurement, as there is no express prohibition of gold plating in the Public Procurement Directives. The fact that in other Directives the Commission has expressly indicated that gold plating is prohibited[86] may lead to the conclusion that where not specified, such an approach is tolerated or even welcomed. It may also be inferred from this that in the field of public procurement, the stricter rules for dimensional procurement are considered a better guarantee for the correctness of the award procedure, and the failure of the Commission to bring down the thresholds during the process of adopting the Directives may be the reason to consider gold plating as a good practice when employed by some Member States on their own motion.

In France, public procurement contracts are regulated either by Procurement Contracts Code adopted in 1964 and last amended in 2006, or by the Ordinance of 6 June 2005, which transposes the Directives. Contracts below the European thresholds are divided between those regulated in a way similar to that provided for in the EU Directives (above domestic thresholds) and those not regulated at all (below domestic thresholds). Several pre-existing thresholds were kept when the EU Directives were transposed. Also, the option not to extend the application of the Directives' rules to all and every public contract is subject to circumstantiating remarks: the publicity above a domestic threshold currently set at €90,000 was regulated as well. The contracts falling below the European thresholds are mostly public contracts, subject to the review of administrative courts.

Spain is also an example of limited extended implementation, as the procedures below thresholds do not benefit from remedies associated with the public procurement regime above thresholds. The main provisions in the Law on Public Sector Contracts on below thresholds contracts are substantially identical to those applicable to contracts subject to EU rules – with exceptions related to publicity, remedies and the so-called 'minor contracts'.

---

[84] See for instance R.K.A. Morris, 'The Application of the Habitats Directive in the UK: Compliance or Gold Plating? (2011) 28(1) *Land Use Policy* 361–369; J.H. Jans and L. Squintani, 'Gold Plating of European Environmental Measures?' (2009) 6(4) *Journal of European Environmental & Planning Law* 417–35.

[85] M.E. Comba and S. Richetto, "Minor Contracts': Outside the Directives and Outside the Treaties? Comparative analysis on public procurement below the thresholds in Europe' in Dragos and Caranta, *Outside the EU Procurement Directives, Inside the Treaty?* above, fn. 10, p. 360.

[86] Commission Directive 2006/73/EC of 10 August 2006, implementing Directive 2004/39/EC of the European Parliament and of the Council as regards organizational requirements and operating conditions for investment firms and defined terms for the purposes of that Directive, Recital 7: 'Member States and competent authorities should not add supplementary binding rules when transposing and applying the rules specified in this Directive, save where this Directive makes express provision to this effect.'

The same division into three layers is to be found in Poland and Romania as well. In Poland, the same PPL provisions apply both to the procurement contracts above and below the EU-thresholds, with the exception of some technical specifications, procedural award provisions and a narrower access to remedies. Below the national threshold of €14,000, the Civil Code takes over. The development of the current public procurement legal framework has taken place in the context of Romania's accession to the EU and of the legislative harmonization. Thus, Emergency Governmental Ordinance no. 34/2006 has transposed the EU Directives on public procurement using almost the same wording and expanding its realm beyond the thresholds established in the Directives. Consequently, only minor value contracts (below €15,000) are subjected to direct award, the remaining being covered by the provisions of the legislation transposing the Directives. Certain distinctions exist based on the value of the contract (some of them introduced in December 2011) and they concern the applicable procedure (type of procedure, publicity rules, and time limits).

Going back to the specifics of the legal regime for sub-dimensional procurement, it has to be noted that national procedures for sub-dimensional procurement are usually simplified. Although the degree of simplification varies between the Member States, it normally includes shorter time limits for submission of applications or tenders (further shortened in the case of electronic submission) and less demanding rules for publication and selection of tenderers. Data compiled by the OECD shows that around 18 per cent of all contracts published in Tenders Electronic Daily (TED) have values below the €125,000 threshold while 30 per cent of sub-central contracts are below €193,000.[87] Time limits may vary between 10 and 25 days. Rules on technical specifications, selection and award criteria and the right to file complaints are basically the same for sub-dimensional contracts as for dimensional contracts,[88] and the choice of award criteria in the Directive (either the lowest price or the most economically advantageous tender) is expanded by most Member States for below threshold contracts.

8. DIRECT PROCUREMENT

Direct procurement is permitted when a very modest economic interest is at stake, based on the assumption that a contract award would be of no interest to economic operators located in other Member States. Taking stock of the case-law of the CJEU which has, indirectly, given the go ahead for the establishment of *national thresholds*, on top of the EU ones, many Member States allow direct procurement under ceilings that range between €5,000 and €50,000 – for instance Spain has €50,000 for works and €18,000 for services and supplies, France and Poland €15,000, Italy €40,000, Romania €100,000 for works and €30,000 for services and supplies. Denmark goes as high as €67,000.

87 Idem.

88 OECD above, fn. 82, p. 7.

In other Member States (UK and Germany,[89] for instance) there is no national threshold, but devolved local authorities may establish similar thresholds. For these contracts, Member States mostly exclude the application of any procedural rule, leaving the award procedure to the complete discretion of the contracting authority, as if they were private contracts.[90] The award is devoid of any competitive procedures and without any obligation of publicity. Other examples of simplified procedures include requesting quotations from a specified number of tenderers without prior publication of an advertisement or advertisement on a national portal but using a simplified procedure.[91]

In order to understand the procedures applicable for different value-related bands, I will refer to Romania, where contracts up to a value of €30,000 can be directly procured, contracts up to the EU thresholds can be awarded using simplified procedures (request for tenders), that involve transparency – the publication of the notice on a central web portal but in a simplified manner, shorter time limits and shorter standstill; finally, contracts above the EU thresholds are awarded using the procedures provided for by the Directives.

The legal regime of contracts below the national thresholds raises the question whether it falls in line with the TFEU principles of transparency and non-discrimination – especially where the value of the thresholds is higher, such as is the case in Italy, Spain, Romania and Denmark.

The question here is whether the value of the contract is the only criteria for deciding on the legal regime, or it may be supplemented with other considerations that need to be assessed on a case-by-case basis. The Court of Justice held in *SECAP* that national legislation may lay down objective criteria indicating that there is certain cross-border interest. Such criteria could be, *inter alia*, the fact that the contract in question is for a significant amount, in conjunction with the place where the work is to be carried out. The possibility of such an interest may also be excluded in a case, for example, where the economic interest at stake in the contract in question is very modest.[92]

However, such an assessment is hardly ever carried out by the contracting authorities. There is also a lack of data concerning such contracts and their share in overall public procurement. Generally, Member States can offer only data for contracts that are awarded following some degree of publicity. Consequently, no reliable data exists concerning 'minor contracts' because they are awarded without any formalities and the absence of transparency leaves them unknown to competitors.

---

89 See for details M. Burgi and F. Koch, 'Contracts Below the Thresholds and List B Services from a German Perspective'; L.R.A. Butler, 'Below Threshold and Annex II B Service Contracts in the United Kingdom: A Common Law Approach' both in Caranta and Dragos, *Outside the EU Procurement Directives, Inside the Treaty?* above, fn. 10.

90 Comba and Richetto, "Minor Contracts': Outside the Directives and Outside the Treaties? Comparative analysis on public procurement below the thresholds in Europe', above fn. 85, p. 361.

91 OECD – SIGMA, Brief 15 Public Procurement – Below Threshold Contracts, available 28 January 2016 at http://www.sigmaweb.org/publications/Threshold_Contracts_Public_Procurement_2011.pdf, p. 4.

92 See, to that effect, Case C-231/03, *Coname* [2005] ECR I-7287, para 20.

9. THE 'CROSS BORDER INTEREST' TEST

The ultimate test for the application of EU law principles to sub-dimensional public procurement is the 'cross border interest' assessment. It entails an evaluation performed by each contracting authority in order to determine whether the projected contract would be of interest for tenderers outside the Member State in which the procedure is conducted.

This evaluation should look at different relevant aspects to the individual circumstances of the case. Thus, the 2006 Communication enumerates the subject-matter of the contract, its estimated value, the specifics of the sector concerned (size and structure of the market, commercial practices, and so on) and the geographic location of the place of performance.[93] I would say that previous experiences with similar contracts are also relevant, as well as the intentions already expressed by prospective economic operators.

The assessment is reviewable by the competent national review bodies or courts[94] and by the CJEU in preliminary ruling procedures. Having in mind review procedures, one irrefutable argument for the cross border interest would be the fact that a foreign operator challenges the award procedure based on lack of proper advertisement.

The question here is whether the cross border interest should be presumed to be lacking in all sub-dimensional procurement or the contrary. The first presumption would have as a consequence the fact that the burden to argue the contrary falls with the presumable interested tenderers. The latter in many cases have no way of finding out about the tendering process anyway, so this is a complicated matter.

The above interpretation may follow from the fact that in infringement procedures, the Court considered that is up to the Commission to demonstrate that a contract passed without complying with the non-discrimination and transparency principles was of 'certain cross-border interest'.[95] The Commission has not succeeded yet in demonstrating this interest.[96] Notwithstanding the fact that in the beginning the Court construed

[93] Paragraph 1.1.

[94] E.g. Joined Cases C-147/06 and C-148/06, *SECAP* [2008] ECR I-3565, para 30.

[95] See Case C-507/03, *Commission v Ireland* [2007] ECR I-9777, para 32 ff; in Case C-195/04, *Commission v Finland* [2007] ECR I-3351, para 25, the action was found even more wanting, the heads of claim as formulated in the application being ambiguous and not enabling the Court to identify clearly and precisely the misconduct which the Commission imputes to the Republic of Finland; in Case C-532/03, *Commission v Ireland* [2007] ECR I-11353, para 37, the Court was not satisfied the Commission had proven there was a contract; see A. Brown 'The Commission Loses another Action against Ireland Owing to Lack of Evidence: A Note on Case C-532/03 Commission v Ireland' in (2008) PPLR NA92.

[96] In Case C-507/03, *Commission v Ireland* [2007] ECR I-9777, para 34, the Court held that 'A mere statement by [the Commission] that a complaint was made to it in relation to the contract in question is not sufficient to establish that the contract was of certain cross-border interest and that there was therefore a failure to fulfil obligations'; see also see also Case C-119/06, *Commission v Italy* [2007] ECR I-168, paras 58 and 62; the latter case is analyzed by A. Brown, 'Application of the Directives to Contracts to Non-for-profit Organisations and Transparency under the EC Treaty: A Note on Case C-119/06 Commission v Italy' [2008] PPLR NA96.

the test by using precisely the cases initiated by the Commission,[97] so in a way the Commission had no way of knowing how to approach the case, it can be argued, on the other hand, that the Recitals of the directives, which refer to EU law principles as well, should have been taken into consideration.[98]

Looking at other cases (not confined to the rules of infringement procedures like those referred to above), it may seem that at least some degree of transparency is always advisable, because the cross border interest may be constantly present. Thus, in *Coname* the Court of Justice argued that unless it is justified by objective circumstances, the absence of any transparency amounts to indirect discrimination on the basis of nationality; the Court observed that it was not apparent from the file that, because of special circumstances, it could reasonably be maintained that an undertaking located in a Member State other than Italy would have no interest in the concession at issue and that the effects on the fundamental freedoms concerned should therefore be regarded as too uncertain and indirect to warrant the conclusion that they may have been infringed.[99]

This leaves the circumstance where there is 'very modest economic interest at stake' referred to in *Coname* as the only truly safe justification for not total lack of transparency.

In *SECAP* the Court of Justice provided further indications as to how to perform the cross border interest test. It was argued that the cross border interest of a works contract could be derived from its estimated value in conjunction with its technical complexity or the fact that the works are to be located in a place which is likely to attract the interest of foreign operators. Member States are encouraged to go further and establish objective criteria, at national or local level, indicating that there is certain cross-border interest. Such criteria could be, *inter alia*, the fact that the contract in question is for a significant amount, in conjunction with the place where the work is to be carried out. Upon reiterating that such an interest may be excluded if the economic interest at stake in the contract in question is very modest, the Court however warned that 'in certain cases, account must be taken of the fact that the borders straddle conurbations which are situated in the territory of different Member States and that, in those circumstances, even low-value contracts may be of certain cross-border interest'.[100]

An unexpected (although in a reverse thinking logical) conclusion was drawn for service contracts in *Strong Segurança*[101] and for service concessions in *Wall*,[102] where the decision of a contracting authority to voluntarily advertise a contract at EU level gave way to the assumption that the contract was of 'certain cross-border interest'. It is, however, evident that such an initiative may lead to the widening of the circle of

---

97 Case C-507/03, *Commission v Ireland* [2007] ECR I-9777, para 25.

98 Case T-258/06, *Federal Republic of Germany v European Commission* [2010] ECR II-2027, para 66.

99 Case C-231/03, *Coname* [2005] ECR I-7287, paras 19 ff; see, to that effect, Case C-69/88, *Krantz* [1990] ECR I-583, para 11; Case C-44/98 *BASF* [1999] ECR I-6269, para 16; and the order in Case C-431/01, *Mertens* [2002] ECR I-7073, para 34.

100 Joined Cases C-147/06 and C-148/06, *SECAP* [2008] ECR I-3565, paras 24 and 31.

101 E.g. Case C-95/10, *Strong Segurança* [2011] ECR I-0000, para 38.

102 Case C-91/08, *Wall* [2010] ECR I-0000, para 35.

interested undertakings, as showcased in *Commission v Ireland*, where three of the tenderers participating in the procedure were established in a Member State other than Ireland.[103]

Regardless of the indications given by the Court of Justice, in the national jurisdictions the situation is pretty much straightforward: the test is not performed either because as a result of gold plating, the application of the Directives was expanded to cover sub-dimensional procurement as well (for instance in Spain, Italy and Romania), or because it is presupposed that contracts not covered by the Directives have no cross border interest. There is no documented case-law in the Member States on the cross border interest test.[104]

Although, if one comes to think about it, this is not at all surprising, because the percentage of cross border public procurement is small even above the EU thresholds. Data compiled by the European Commission shows that only a small proportion of contracts are awarded for firms from another Member State. Direct cross-border procurement accounted for 1.6 per cent of awards or roughly 3.5 per cent of the total value of contract awards published in TED during 2006–2009. In addition to direct cross-border procurement, indirect cross-border procurement – firms that bid for contracts through their foreign affiliates or subsidiaries – accounted for 11.4 per cent of awards published in TED and 13.4 per cent by value during 2006–2009.[105]

10. REMEDIES AVAILABLE FOR SUB-DIMENSIONAL PROCUREMENT

Considering the fact that the Remedies Directives[106] covers only contracts falling within the scope of the Public Procurement Directives, the sub-dimensional procurement is subjected to national procedural rules, which in turn have to comply with the principles of equivalence and effectiveness.[107] The majority of countries analyzed in the OECD study adopt the same approach to remedies for both above and below threshold contracts.[108] Direct procurement is governed by the national rules of redress – judicial review with or without prior administrative appeal.

Again, case-law was of utmost importance in the development of a legal regime for sub-dimensional procurement. In *Telaustria* the CJEU stressed the importance of

[103] Case C-226/09, *Commission v Ireland* [2010] ECR I-0000, para 33.

[104] Treumer, comparative in OUTSIDE.

[105] European Commission, DG Internal Market and Services, Final report Cross-border procurement above EU thresholds, March 2011, available 28 January 2016 at http://ec.europa.eu/internal_market/publicprocurement/docs/modernising_rules/cross-border-procurement_en.pdf.

[106] Directive 89/665/EEC, [1989] OJ L395/33 and Directive 92/13/EEC, [1992] OJ L76/14.

[107] See R. Caranta 'Many Different Paths, but Are They All Leading to Effectiveness' in S. Treumer and F. Lichère (eds), *Enforcement of the EU Public Procurement Rules*, Copenhagen: DJØF, 2011, pp. 57 ff. For the case law, see Case C-50/00, *Unión de Pequeños Agricultores* [2002] ECR I-6677, para 39 and Case 222/86, *Heylens* [1987] ECR 4097, para 14. More generally, Cases C-46/93 and C-48/93, *Brasserie du Pêcheur* [1996] ECR I-1029, para 83 and Case C-327/00, *Santex* [2003] ECR I-1877, para 55.

[108] OECD SIGMA, above, fn. 91, p. 7.

providing a review mechanism for the impartiality of the procedure. The Commission has then recommended that decisions adversely affecting a person having or having had an interest in obtaining the contract, such as any decision to eliminate an applicant or tenderer, should be subject to review for possible violations of the basic standards derived from primary Community law.[109] An effective review presupposes an obligation for contracting authorities to state the grounds for their decisions.[110]

The recent *Wall* case, decided by the Grand Chamber of the Court of Justice, could be read as disproving the above considerations.[111] The case concerned subsequent amendments to a service concession, that is, a contract excluded from the coverage of the 2004 directives. The Court held that the change of a highly qualified subcontractor could be considered to be a substantial alteration to the contract, so much that 'If need be, a new award procedure should be organised'.[112] However, and somewhat contradictorily, when asked whether the national court was under a duty to terminate the contract, the Court of Justice held that 'the principles of equal treatment and non-discrimination on grounds of nationality enshrined in Articles 43 EC and 49 EC and the consequent obligation of transparency do not require the national authorities to terminate a contract or the national courts to grant a restraining order in every case of an alleged breach of that obligation in connection with the award of service concessions'.[113]

This judgment in no way contributes to clarifying a potentially contentious issue (so much so that a number of Member States intervened in the proceedings). At no point of the reasoning does the Court refer to the infringement judgment against Germany which – as it will be shown – led to the establishment of the duty to terminate long-term concession contracts directly awarded.[114]

Similarly troubling is a short passage in the *Loutraki* case.[115] Having considered a mixed contract in which a privatization component was pre-eminent to fall outside the coverage of the procurement directives, the Court conceded that that arrangement could still fall under the basic rules and general principles of the Treaty, but did not consider it fit to address the problem since a positive answer 'could in no way lead to a finding that Directive 89/665 applies'.[116]

An alternative take on this in *Wall* could suggest that in the end it only decided that ineffectiveness does not follow from all and every breach.[117] This is not mind-boggling.

---

109 Interpretative communication on the 'Community law applicable to contract awards not or not fully subject to the provisions of the "Public Procurement" Directives', para 2.3.2.

110 A. Brown 'EU Primary Law Requirements in Practice: Advertising, Procedures and Remedies for Public Contracts outside the Procurement Directives' [2010] PPLR 178.

111 Case C-91/08, *Wall* [2010] ECR I-0000. See Treumer and Lichère, (eds), *Enforcement of the EU Public Procurement Rules*, above, fn. 107, § 4.2.

112 Paragraph 43.

113 Paragraph 65.

114 Case C-503/04, *Commission v Germany* [2007] ECR I-6153; see S. Treumer, 'Towards an Obligation to Terminate Contracts Concluded in Breach of the EC Public Procurement Rules: the End of the Status of Concluded Public Contracts as Sacred Cows' [2007] PPLR 371.

115 Joined Cases C-145/08 and C-149/08, *Club Hotel Loutraki* [2010] ECR I-0000.

116 Paragraph 63.

117 A. Brown, 'EU Primary Law Requirements in Practice', above fn 112, p. 180.

Even after the modifications introduced in 2007, the remedies directives stopped short of making ineffectiveness the general rule. If the Court of Justice had held that the general principles of the Treaty require ineffectiveness to follow from all and every breach of procurement rules the limits found in the remedies directives would no longer make sense.[118]

The implementation Directive 2007/66/EC has only harmonized to a limited extent the remedies in public procurement.[119] As in the case of other aspects of public procurement regime, the sub-dimensional procurement was left to the discretion of the Member States. Inevitably they had several options at hand: (1) to expand the remedies regime of the above thresholds contracts to below the thresholds ones; (2) to devise less detailed remedies or rules for below thresholds regimes; or (3) to leave it altogether to the pre-existent national law, be it public or private. Out of the three options described above, two have often been used by the jurisdictions of the Member States.

10.1 Expansion of Remedies System to below Thresholds and/or List B Services, with or without a National Threshold

In some jurisdictions, the legal regime established by the Directives was expanded to cover, more or less, all public contracts, which brings about an assimilation of contracts below thresholds with contracts above thresholds. In Italy, France, Poland and Romania, contracts outside the scope of the Remedies Directives are given (almost) the same protection as the ones covered by the Directives.[120] The limitations refer to different standstill provisions and deadlines.

In countries where there are national thresholds, the expansion of remedies stops at this threshold, thus not covering minor contracts. In Poland, below the national threshold of €14,000, there are public or private law provisions (Civil Code, for instance) which limit the freedom of awarding authorities to arrange the procurement procedures not covered by the scope of Public Procurement Law (PPL), providing also for remedies in case of breaching the rules. Apart from these legal provisions, public authorities have developed their own rules regarding the details of the procurement regime under the national threshold. These rules are binding for their issuers, and the private contractors may accept them based on a contractual basis.[121] Though it can happen that these rules are similar to those above thresholds, it is argued that a general 'opt in' clause, which would extend the application of the PPL to the 'low value' procurement, is ineffective. In Romania, minor contracts under €30,000 and List B

---

[118] See also Treumer and Lichère 'Enforcement (EU)', and C. Risvig Hansen, *Contract not Covered or not Fully Covered by the Public Sector Directive*, Copenhagen: DJØF, 2012, pp. 287 ff.

[119] R. Caranta, 'Many Different Paths, but Are They All Leading to Effectiveness?' in Treumer and Lichère (eds), *Enforcement of the EU Public Procurement Rules*, above, fn. 107, pp. 57 ff.

[120] F. Cassella and M. E. Comba, 'Public Procurement Below the Thresholds in Italy'; F. Lichère, 'Public Procurement Contracts Below EU Thresholds and Annex II. B Services in France'; and P. Szwedo and M. Spyra, 'Public Procurement Below the Thresholds in Poland', all in Caranta and Dragos, *Outside the EU Procurement Directives, Inside the Treaty?* above, fn. 10.

[121] Ibidem.

services below thresholds are not subject to the remedies system established by the Directives, but subjected to the General Law on Judicial Review of Administrative Acts no. 544/2004.[122]

10.2 Remedies Regulated by the National Public or Private Law

The other approach is to subject remedies for below thresholds contracts entirely to national law, already in place when the Directives were transposed. In *Denmark*, for instance, the Remedies Directive 2007/66/EC was implemented with the new Act on Enforcement of the Public Procurement Rules, which bore no changes to the legal regime for contracts below the EU thresholds and List B services, covered by the Tender Act.[123] However, some provisions of the Remedies Directive apply also to sub-dimensional procurement – the standstill period, for instance, and the award of damages. Apart from these two remedies, there are no specific effective remedies provided for in the Tender Act for below thresholds contracts. Danish courts rely on the principle of effectiveness and on the case law from the Court of Justice on Member State liability.

The German procurement system provides for two different sets of rules for contracts above and below the EU thresholds. The difference between the two regimes is dramatic: the whole range of remedies provided by the Directives is available only for above the thresholds contracts, where subjective rights can be enforced.[124] Thus, the award procedures covered by the Directives give rise to subjective rights with external effect and effectively enforceable by a special review regime, in front of specialized procurement tribunals, followed by appeals to one of the procurement senates within the appellate courts. For contracts not falling within the domain of the Directives, the situation is different, as the special review system is not applicable. A duplication of the review system for below thresholds contracts is also unacceptable, at least in the opinion of the Federal Administrative Court. Consequently, issues relating to public contracts in general are decided upon by ordinary courts based solely upon civil law, as the State is considered to be just a consumer on the market when buying services or products, as opposed to the position in which it is fulfilling public tasks. The German Procedural Act (ZPO) is applicable as it regards the procedure.

As noted by German legal scholars, the 'common civil law review regime is not fully designed to appropriately review complex award decisions',[125] if only for the lack of specialization of judges and the huge number of courts that can decide differently on the same issue. Another argument comes from the fact that tenderers asking review of the contracts below the thresholds are faced also with uncertainty about the appropriate

---

[122] See generally D.C. Dragos, B. Neamtu and R. Veliscu, 'Remedies in Public Procurement in Romania' in Treumer and Lichère (eds) *Enforcement of EU Public Procurement Rules*, above fn. 107, p. 155.

[123] S. Treumer, 'On the Development of a Danish Public Procurement Regime outside the Scope of the EU Public Procurement Directives: EU Principles of Law do not Come Easy' in Caranta and Dragos, *Outside the EU Procurement Directives, Inside the Treaty?* above, fn. 10.

[124] See for details Burgi and Koch, 'Contracts Below the Thresholds and List B Services from a German Perspective', above, fn. 89.

[125] Ibidem.

basis for claim. Public notices establishing an intention to award a contract may lead to a quasi-contractual claim for injunctive relief or compensation, but this solution is wildly debated in both the doctrine and the jurisprudence. All available forms of review are performed *before* the award of the contract, and the most incisive remedy is the interdiction to award the contract; consequently there are no mechanisms to declare the contract ineffective. The standstill period is also ignored when it comes to contracts under the secondary procurement regime. The burden of proof is reversed when compared with administrative law regime: the onus is with the tenderer, who has no right to inspect files and does not benefit from investigation *ex officio* by the court.[126]

Unsurprisingly, in the United Kingdom, in the absence of specific national legislation the redress for illegal award procedures not covered by the EU law fairly limited.[127] However, some rules exist on how to complain about allegedly irregular procedures. The administrative appeal to the awarding authority is the first instance review, in terms of cost effectiveness and speed. Alternative dispute resolution can be used, but is only optional. Finally, tenderers can lodge a court action.

In recent years, the implied contract doctrine has been applied in this field, with tenderers claiming the breach of an 'implied tender contract' (*Blackpool* jurisprudence).[128] This is a noteworthy remedy, as it can cover cases outside the reach of Directive remedies. However, based on an examination of the relevant jurisprudence following *Blackpool*, there have been authors claiming that 'whilst there is support for the view that an implied (below-threshold) contract may give rise to an implied duty to act fairly, this issue is not definitively settled'.

By contrast, List B Services, although only half way subjected to the Public Sector and Remedies Directives, in certain circumstances benefit from the remedy system established thereby. Thus, even though the Remedies Directive allows Member States to circumvent a standstill period in situations where prior publication of a contract notice in the Official Journal is not necessary (such as List B services), and the UK has not regulated the standstill outside the Directive, it is noteworthy that contracting authorities voluntarily observe the standstill period.[129] Moreover, in a case from 2009,[130] the court has argued that the standstill obligation derives from the general principles of EU law, and that an award procedure may be subject to requirements

---

[126] Ibidem.

[127] For a useful overview of the United Kingdom public procurement review and remedies system for contracts above threshold, see M. Trybus, 'An Overview of the United Kingdom Public Procurement Review and Remedies System with an Emphasis on England and Wales' in Treumer and Lichère (eds) *Enforcement of EU Public Procurement Rules*, above fn. 107, pp. 201–34.

[128] See for details Butler, 'Below Threshold and Annex II B Service Contracts in the United Kingdom: A Common Law Approach', above, fn. 89.

[129] See for instance, Office of Government Commerce, Implementation of the Remedies Directive: OGC Guidance on the 2009 Amending Regulations at 21, para. 87 referenced in Butler, 'Below Threshold and Annex II B Service Contracts in the United Kingdom: A Common Law Approach', above, fn. 89.

[130] *Federal Security Services Ltd. v Chief Constable of Northern Ireland and Resource Group Ltd* [2009] NICH 3, [2009] Eu. LR. 774, in Butler, 'Below Threshold and Annex II B Service Contracts in the United Kingdom: A Common Law Approach', above fn. 89.

which exceed the minimal obligations to which it is subject under the Directives and implementing Regulations.

In Spain, recent developments include amendments to the remedies system required by the European Commission in order to comply with the Remedies directive. The two remedies available for above the threshold procedures – ineffectiveness (annulment) and special procurement review procedures can be brought before the Central Administrative Tribunal of Contractual Appeals. They are not available in the case of contracts below EU thresholds. The legal doctrine is unanimous in criticizing this shortcoming of the Spanish remedies system,[131] the argument being that it leaves important contracts without effective remedies.

In this context, remedies that apply to below thresholds contracts come from the general administrative law. There are Spanish authors that argue that the current system is in breach of the European principle of effective protection, as the remedies are limited: the general administrative law has narrow conditions for standing, lengthy procedures, and no automatic interim relief. Taking into account the relevance of below thresholds procurement (around 90 per cent in number of contracts, and 20 per cent in value), it was also argued that a revision of current rules would improve the effectiveness of public procurement in Spain.[132]

The whole remedies regime for sub-dimensional contracts is subjected to debates. In the UK, for instance, it has been questioned whether the intrusion of the courts, invoking EU law principles, into the realm of below thresholds contracts is justified in light of a traditional judicial and legislative policy of minimal intervention in low value contract awards. Answering to the Commission on its Green Paper on Modernization, local government groups in the UK stressed the fact that the public procurement regime should ensure only a basic level of fair competition in line with Treaty principles and not over-regulate or micro-manage procurement arrangements within Member States.[133] Notwithstanding such an approach there are voices in the English procurement literature that also point out the fact that such a position may be defensible for low

---

[131] M. Molina, 'La Ley 34/2010 y la adaptación en España' (27–8); J. M. Baño León, 'El contencioso precontractual: las insuficiencias de la tutela jurisdiccional' in G. Ferrer (ed), *Comentarios a la Ley de contratos de las administraciones públicas* (Civitas 2004) 329, 348 and ff; J. Tornos Mas, 'Novedades en la regulación de los recursos en materia de contratos de las Administraciones Públicas' (2006) 59 *Contratación administrativa práctica: revista de la contratación administrativa y de los contratistas* 45, 51; M. López-Contreras González, 'El control de la adjudicación de los contratos públicos. En particular, el recurso especial y las medidas cautelares' in J.A.M. Molina (ed), *La Ley de contratos del sector público y su aplicación por las entidades locales* (CEMCI – Diputación de Granada 2008) 289, 305; and B. Noguera de la Muela, 'El recurso especial en materia de contratación y las medidas cautelares en la Ley 30/2007, de 30 de octubre, de contratos del sector público, a la vista de la Directiva 2007/66/CE, por la que se modifica la Directiva 89/665/CEE' (2008) *Revista Aragonesa de Administración Pública* [monográfico: El derecho de los contratos del sector público] 295, 329; all cited in A. Sánchez Graells, 'Public Procurement Below Thresholds in Spain' in Caranta and Dragos, *Outside the EU Procurement Directives, Inside the Treaty?* above, fn. 10.

[132] A. Sanchez Graells, 'Public Procurement Below Thresholds in Spain' in Caranta and Dragos, *Outside the EU Procurement Directives, Inside the Treaty?* above, fn. 10

[133] See for details Butler, 'Below Threshold and Annex II B Service Contracts in the United Kingdom: A Common Law Approach', above, fn. 89.

value contracts but this argument cannot be made in relation to a major works contract below the EU threshold.

The regime and remedies applicable to contracts below the thresholds have been analyzed in France as well and authors dealing with the argument have described the situation of public procurement contracts outside the scope of the EU Directives as being somewhat paradoxical, as EU rules were simply added on top of national rules, which are complicating the regime. Francois Lichère for example proposes a solution according to which domestic thresholds should disappear and clearer guidelines should be formulated.[134]

In the same vein, the need for an adequate system of remedies for below thresholds contracts has been intensely debated in *Germany*, as 90 per cent of contracts fall within this category. The arguments for maintaining the current system, which is constitutional,[135] based, *inter alia*, on the fear of a 'landslide of applications' is counterbalanced by the reality that tenderers seeking review are few because undertakings are not normally interested in risking valuable future business chances by initiating litigation. It is noteworthy that the German legislator at the level of the Bund is not allowed to establish a new review system for contracts below the thresholds at all, so only the *Länder* can do it. In the end, especially in times of economic crisis, the necessity of having a well-oiled and functioning system seems to take priority over effective protection of tenderers seeking review, as long as the EU allows such discretion to Member States.[136]

In Romania, from the outset, the reasoning behind an almost identical regime applicable to all public procurement contracts regardless of the thresholds was a precautionary approach in the context of widespread corruption, the intention being to allow as little discretion as possible to contracting authorities. Later on, the pressure of absorption of EU structural funds has led to a relaxation of the rules for low value contracts (direct procurement) as well as for contracts below the EU thresholds (simplified procedures).[137]

11. FINAL CONSIDERATIONS

The low impact of public procurement legislation on the principle and objectives of transparency in European public markets can be explained by resorting to three scenarios:[138]

Sub-dimensional public contracts escape applicability of the Directives. Member States do not properly enforce the rules that prohibit intentional division of contracts

---

[134] See Lichère, 'Public Procurement Contracts Below EU Thresholds and Annex II. B Services in France', above, fn. 120.

[135] BVerfG of 13.6.2006, 1 BvR 1160/03, NZBau 2006, p. 791, cited by Burgi and Koch, 'Contracts Below the Thresholds and List B Services from a German Perspective', above, fn. 89.

[136] Burgi and Koch, 'Contracts Below the Thresholds and List B Services from a German Perspective', above, fn. 89

[137] See for details Dragos, Neamtu and Veliscu, 'Public Procurement outside EU Directives in Romania: Is Voluntary Compliance Leading to Effectiveness?' above, fn. 122.

[138] Bovis, above fn. 28, p. 71.

into lots, which gives contracting authorities room for manoeuvre when deciding on the value of the contract to be tendered. Up to the time of writing, there has been no case or complaint before national courts or before the European Court of Justice relating to the intentional division of contracts into lots with lower thresholds in order to avoid the application of the Directives.

The relevant thresholds which are subject to the mandatory publication requirement clearly result in a segmentation of public markets in quantitative terms by creating a dimensional forum which is subject to the rigorous legal regime. A *de minimis* rule applies to contracts below the thresholds, which exempts them from the provisions of the Directives. Sub-dimensional public procurement is only subject to the principle of non-discrimination at European level, whereas at domestic level, national tendering rules regulate the award of these contracts.

Direct cross-border procurement has not increased as much as was anticipated, although it is commonplace in smaller Member States. Many economic operators still appear to be deterred from competing for tenders in other Member States by a combination of competitive, structural and legal or administrative factors. The regulatory guarantees established by the Directives may be a necessary but not a sufficient condition to break down the barriers to cross-border participation in public procurement markets.[139]

The creation of new law on the basis of vague legal basis was considered controversial by the doctrine.[140] Some authors maintain that despite several important judgments that have been delivered by the Court of Justice since *Telaustria*, it is still very much uncertain which duties apply to contracts covered by this regime.[141]

Some Member States have reacted with criticism as well. Germany has brought a case against the very policy promoted by the Commission, with the backing of other Member States and of the European Parliament.[142] Import penetration in the public sector remains significantly lower than in the private sector. In 2005 public sector import penetration stood at 7.5 per cent, compared to private sector import penetration of 19.1 per cent.[143] The gap between public and private sector import penetration has narrowed slightly in the period 1995–2005.

The low level of public sector import penetration can be explained in large part by the nature of the goods and services that the public sector consumes. Public administration, education, health and social services make up more than 60 per cent of public

---

139 Commission Staff Working Paper Evaluation Report Impact and Effectiveness of EU Public Procurement Legislation Part 1 SEC(2011) 853 final, p. xix.

140 P. Braun, 'A Matter of Principle(s): the Treatment of Contracts Falling Outside the Scope of the European Public Procurement Directives', [2000] PPLR 39; S. Treumer and E. Werlauff, 'The leverage principle: secondary Community law as a lever for the development of primary Community law' above fn. 38; Pijnacker Hordijk and Meulenbelt, 'A Bridge Too Far: Why the European Commission's Attempts to Construct an Obligation to Tender Outside the Scope of the Public Procurement Directives should be Dismissed', above, fn. 38 and Arrowsmith, *The Law of Public and Utilities Procurement*, above, fn. 38, p. 197

141 Caranta, *The Borders of EU Public Procurement Law,* above, fn. 18, p. 28.

142 Case T-258/06, *Germany v Commission* [2010] ECR II-2027.

143 Commission Staff Working Paper Evaluation Report Impact and Effectiveness of EU Public Procurement Legislation Part 1 SEC(2011) 853 final, p.xiii.

sector expenditure (25.3, 14.3 and 21.2 per cent respectively in 2005). These sectors have import penetration close to zero (0.1 per cent). In markets for public contracts which are the specific focus of EU public procurement legislation, only a small proportion of contracts are awarded for firms from another Member State. Direct cross-border procurement accounts for 1.6 per cent of awards or roughly 3.5 per cent of the total value of contract awards published in TED during 2006–2009. In addition to direct cross-border procurement, however, there is a considerable volume of indirect cross border procurement. For example firms can bid for contracts through their foreign affiliates or subsidiaries. This channel accounted for 11.4 per cent of awards published in TED and 13.4 per cent by value during 2006–2009. It seems that direct procurement is lacking any form of transparency, and this is a 'pragmatic solution'[144] which acknowledges that the majority of very low value contracts are unlikely to be of relevance to the internal market and that there is a need to ensure that the process used to procure contracts is proportionate to the contract being procured.

[144] SIGMA OECD, above, fn. 91, p. 4.

PART 2

STRATEGIC PROCUREMENT

7. Innovative and sustainable procurement: framework, constraints and policies

Oana S. Pantilimon Voda

1. INTRODUCTION

In cases where no solutions yet exist on the market, innovative procurement enables public purchasers to get technologically innovative solutions developed according to their specific needs.[1] By steering product development upstream in the product development process, public purchasers are better positioned to improve the quality, effectiveness and efficiency of their public services, while the private business sector operates within an increasingly competitive environment. Such an approach contributes to achieving better value for money as well as wider economic, environmental and societal benefits in terms of generating new ideas, translating them into innovative products and services and thus promoting sustainable growth.[2]

European competitiveness in the global marketplace is a top priority for Europe. The European Union strongly supports the public procurement of innovative and sustainable solutions through a number of policy documents linked to the Europe 2020 strategy for smart, sustainable and inclusive growth.[3] Instrumental in achieving this objective is to enhance European innovation. A renewed emphasis on innovation as an instrument of industrial policy was developed at the end of the 20th century as a result of an increasingly competitive nature of the international economic arena and the correlated structural changes.[4] Furthermore, in the context of the now-obsolete Lisbon Agenda, the European Union undertook the goal of becoming the most competitive and dynamic knowledge-based economy worldwide.[5] It is in this context that the importance of the

---

[1] Public purchasers may procure research and development services from undertakings through both exclusive development and pre-commercial procurement procedures. See the Communication and associated staff working document – Communication from the Commission to the European Parliament, the Council, the European Economic and Social Committee and the Committee of the Region, 'Pre-commercial procurement: driving innovation to ensure sustainable high quality public services in Europe', COM(2007) 799 final, 14 December 2007.

[2] See Recital 47 of the Directive 2014/24/EU of the European Parliament and the Council of 26 February 2014 on public procurement and repealing Directive 2004/18/EC.

[3] Communication COM (2010) 2020 final, *Europe 2020, A strategy for smart, sustainable and inclusive* growth. See also the Europe 2020 flagship Innovation Union Initiative, available 28 January 2016 at www.bit.ly/innovation-union-initiative.

[4] L. Georghiou, 'The UK Technology Foresight Programme', (1996) 28(4) *Futures*, 359–77.

[5] Presidency Conclusions, Lisbon European Council, 23 and 24 March 2000, available 28 January 2016 at http://www.europarl.europa.eu/summits/lis1_en.htm.

demand-side instrument of public procurement was presented as a key component for this strategy and a potential solution to pulling innovation from the market.[6]

Public authorities and utility companies have the obligation to provide citizens (tax payers) with services of public interest of the best possible quality. At the same time, however, there seems to be a 'market failure' in the sense that, on one hand, the demand is not able to encourage the market to answer its needs by failing to give the right signals, while on the other hand, the offer is not known.[7] A collaborative approach whereby the combination of skills and the sharing of costs and risks are correlated with government support to compensate for market failure[8] is needed. This is where the public purchasing power can play a role to make a difference.[9] Market uptake of innovative and sustainable products and services could be enhanced by employing innovative public procurement practices.

2. INSTITUTIONAL FORCES PAVING THE GROUND FOR PUBLIC PROCUREMENT OF INNOVATION

2.1 State of Play in the European Union

At the European level, the legal framework for public procurement of innovative and sustainable solutions is defined by the provisions of the Treaty for the Functioning of the European Union ('TFEU') and by the EU Procurement Directives, namely Directive 2004/18/EC of the European Parliament and of the Council on the coordination of procedures for the award of public works contracts, public supply contracts and public services contracts ('Old Procurement Directive') and Directive 2004/17/EC of the European Parliament and of the Council coordinating the procurement procedures of entities operating in the water, energy, transport and postal services sectors ('Old Utilities Directive'). More recently, new procurement directives were passed ('New Procurement Directives').[10] While safeguarding the requirements of transparency, equal treatment, competition and non-discrimination, the New Procurement Directives open

---

[6] L. Georghiou et al. (2003), Raising EU R&D Intensity: Improving the Effectiveness of Public Support Mechanism for Private Sector Research and Development: Direct Measures 2003, EUR 20716; Business Decisions Limited (2003), The Power of Customers to Drive Innovation, Report to the Enterprise Directorate General; European Commission Wilkinson R. et al, Public procurement for research and innovation, DG Research, September 2005, EUR 21793. E. Aho, J. Cornu, L. Georghiou, and A. Subira. (2006) Creating an Innovative Europe. Report of the Independent Expert Group on R&D and Innovation, rapporteur: Luke Gheorghiou.

[7] See Public Procurement – Public purchasers as First customers, available at http://ec.europa.eu/enterprise/policies/innovation/policy/public-procurement/index_en.htm.

[8] Ibid 4.

[9] Ibid 4.

[10] Directive 2014/24/EU of the European Parliament and of the Council on public procurement and repealing Directive 2004/18/EC ('New Public Sector Directive') and Directive 2014/25/EU of the European Parliament and of the Council of 26 February 2014 on procurement by entities operating in the water, energy, transport and postal services sectors and repealing Directive 2004/17/EC ('New Utilities Directive').

new opportunities for the public procurement of innovative solutions, provided they are conducted proportionately and that compliance with the new State Aid Framework for research and development and innovation ('R&D&I')[11] is ensured. Innovative and sustainable procurement entails innovative approaches in both practices and procedures.[12] Both dimensions are equally addressed in the New Procurement Directives which encourage the employment of innovation-friendly approaches including, *inter alia*, the conduct of market consultations, the possibility to include social and environmental considerations in the tender specifications, the use of a life-cycle costing approach, the use of the most economically advantageous tender criteria ('MEAT') as award criteria and the acceptance of variant offers. In addition to mentioning Pre-commercial Procurement in the recitals of the New Procurement Directives, new procurement procedures have been added, specifically the innovation partnership[13] and the competitive procedure with negotiation, of particular relevance for public purchasers envisaging the purchase of innovative products. Moreover, Small and Medium Enterprises ('SMEs') are ensured better access to tender procedures through a number of changes to selection processes and documentation requirements. Additionally, new explicit rules on joint procurement are aimed at facilitating cooperation between public purchasers, encouraging risk and benefit-sharing for innovative projects and demand pooling. Consequently, the New Procurement Directives set the scene for a more strategic approach by public purchasers towards public procurement as a means to identify and support innovation and deliver better solutions to their needs.

2.2 International Trade Playing Field

The New Procurement Directives specifically mention the WTO Government Procurement Agreement ('WTO GPA')[14] and the obligation incumbent upon contracting authorities to accord to the works, supplies, services and economic operators of the signatories to this agreement treatment no less favourable than the treatment accorded to the works, supplies, services and economic operators of the Union.[15] Procurement-wise, the WTO GPA is an international agreement between several signatory parties which have agreed to open their public procurement markets towards each other, in full compliance with the principles of non-discrimination, equal treatment and fairness and

---

11 Commission, 'Framework for state aid for research and development and innovation' (2014 State Aid Framework) C(2014) 3282.

12 Lieve Bos, Stephan Corvers, 'Pre-commercial Public Procurement. A missing link in the European Innovation Cycle. Public Needs as a driver for innovation', *Tijdschrijft Aanbestendingsrecht* (2006).

13 The innovation partnership procedure provided for under article 31 of the New Public Sector Directive needs to be distinguished from the European Innovation Partnerships (EIPs). See http://ec.europa.eu/research/innovation-union/index_en.cfm?pg=eip (available 28 January 2016).

14 Available 28 January 2016 at http://www.wto.org/English/tratop_e/gproc_e/gp_gpa_e.htm.

15 See Article 25 of the New Public Sector Directive.

the procedural rules agreed to this end.[16] When a public institution does the procurement from a GPA signatory country,[17] this institution may be mandated to allow competition from other signatory countries. This depends on whether the respective public institution is covered by the GPA, the value of the procured contract and whether the object of the contract falls within the scope of the GPA. According to the GPA, the European Union is not restricted in regulating its own internal market, but rather in complying with certain obligations towards non-EU parties to the GPA. In this respect, the European Union did not draft separate rules to be applied for non-EU GPA signatories, but suggests the application of the EU public procurement directives to both EU and GPA bidders.[18]

In addition to already embedded demand side policies regarding the promotion of innovation through public procurement or the increased implementation of Green Public Procurement approaches, Corporate Social Responsibility ('CSR') and increased sustainability awareness have recently developed as paramount milestones to be considered in any procurement strategy. The basis for implementing these new policies is mainly grounded in the CSR instruments. The core set of internationally recognized principles and guidelines regarding CSR comprises the OECD Guidelines, ISO 26000 and the UN Global Compact together with the United Nations Guiding Principles on Business and Human Rights and the International Labour Organization's ('ILO') Conventions. They have a common normative basis as all aim to stimulate responsible business practices. Without going into too much detail on these international instruments, it is worth mentioning that they are all sets of voluntary recommendations and guidance for corporations in the fields of labour, human rights, the environment, economic aspects and other corporate responsibility issues they need to account for in their daily business conduct. Whereas the main issues covered by these instruments are equally addressed in each of them, differences exist in terms of applicability, outreach and enforcement mechanisms, legal status and government endorsement.[19]

---

16 The procedural rules are laid down in the Annexes to the GPA.

17 The GPA consists of 15 parties covering 43 WTO members (the European Union and its 28 Member States are covered by the Agreement as one party). Another 28 WTO members and four international organizations participate in the GPA Committee as observers. For more information, see http://www.wto.org/english/tratop_e/gproc_e/memobs_e.htm (available 28 January 2016).

18 Article 25 of the New Public Sector Directive.

19 For a comprehensive comparison of these instruments, see M. Theuws and M. van Huijstee, 'Corporate Responsibility Instruments: A Comparison of the OECD Guidelines, ISO 26000 & the UN Global Compact', SOMO (December 2013).

3. WHAT IS PUBLIC PROCUREMENT OF INNOVATIVE SOLUTIONS? DESIGNING INNOVATIVE AND SUSTAINABLE PROCUREMENT METHODOLOGIES – RELATIONSHIP BETWEEN SUPPLY AND DEMAND

Legally, Public Procurement of Innovation (PPI) is an approach for implementing a public procurement process according to applicable European and national legislation, in which public procurers, possibly in cooperation with additional private buyers, act as early adopters by procuring innovative solutions that are new arrivals on the market but not yet available on a large-scale basis.[20] In addition to meeting the needs of individual public sector players by the conduct of individual procurements, there is also the potential for PPI to be cooperative and to be conducted jointly. Cooperative procurement is intended to provide an innovative solution of interest for both public purchasers and end-users.[21] Four key aspects have been identified in relation to the design of co-operative public procurement strategies promoting innovation,[22] namely: the relationship between public and commercial demand; the reasons for public intervention; the kind of innovation involved; and the choice of modalities.

3.1 The Relationship between Public and Commercial Demand: Co-operative Procurement and Market Consultations

The relationship between public and commercial demand plays an important role, in terms of how public demand influences commercial demand and the other way around. Three categories of modes of interaction have been identified: a public purchaser could conduct a procurement procedure to fulfill an unmet unique need of its own ('direct procurement'); to develop an innovative solution of interest to both the procuring entity and the end users ('co-operative procurement'); or to develop a solution aimed at achieving a public goal of the contracting authority ('catalytic procurement').[23] This matter should also be regarded from the perspective pertaining to the interaction between users and producers, fundamental to product innovation and the modes of interaction in public procurement of innovation.[24] The three modes of intervention are generally described by reference to three parameters: interactive learning, which is

---

20 L. Bos and S. Corvers, 'Pre-commercial Public Procurement. A Missing Link in the European Innovation Cycle. Public Needs as a Driver for Innovation.', *Tijdschrijft Aanbestendingsrecht* (2006).

21 C. Edquist and L. Hommen, 'Public Technology Procurement and Innovation Theory' in C. Edquist et al (eds), *Public Technology Procurement and Innovation* (The Hague: Kluwer 2000).

22 J. Cave and E. Frinking, 'Public Procurement and R&D: Short Analysis of the Potential and Practices'. Chapter 1 in J.P. Gavigan (ed.) *Public procurement and R&D: A JRC/IPTS-ESTO fast track working paper*. European Commission Joint Research Centre – Institute for Prospective Technological Studies – European Science and Technology Observatory. 11–44 (2003).

23 The concepts are explained in more detail in Edquist and Hommen, 'Public Technology Procurement and Innovation Theory', above, fn. 21.

24 B. Lundvall, 'Product Innovation and User-producer Interaction', Aalborg: Aaalborg University Press, 1985.

deemed to occur in various contexts and within different networks; demand structure, in which user-producer communication plays an important role to promote innovation; and the needs addressed, namely the ultimate aim of the procurement. It was argued that 'when public procurement of innovation addressed this wide range of actors, needs and interests, coordination becomes essential. It becomes necessary to maximize complementarity of diverse initiatives through close interaction of firms, consumers and public authorities'.[25]

Several authors have argued that the combination of public and private demand to stimulate private sector innovation is a pre-eminent rationale for cooperative procurement.[26] Cooperative procurement takes place in a horizontally extended knowledge network, in a market with oligopsony structure, where congeneric need are addressed.[27] In order to ensure the best outcome, a broad consultation, taking the form of a structured dialogue (market consultation) with the widest possible cross-section of experts and stakeholders in the concerned field is needed. Market consultation is a powerful instrument that helps to bridge the gap between supply and demand and is vital as a means to create and increase awareness of the market relating to the needs of public authorities, by bringing all relevant stakeholders to the same table. The Old Procurement Directive was rather sketchy in providing guidance on the opportunity for public authorities to conduct market consultations. The New Public Sector Directive however, contains specific provisions regarding the conduct of market consultations,[28] which are used to provide knowledge on whether a specific product/technology is already available on the market or still needs to undertake development or whether a product requires customization which was not previously performed. They also shed light on several paramount issues for the success of a project, including project feasibility, the ability of the market to accomplish what is needed, the capacity of the market to achieve it in a time and cost efficient manner. It is most suitable to address these issues at the pre-tendering phase.

Various methods to engage the market exist, including market surveys, 'meet the buyer' events, industry days, or the organization of industry platforms. Several things need to be kept in mind when organizing market consultations, including: pro-active

[25] F. Meyer-Krahmer, 'Industrial Innovation and Sustainability – Conflicts and Coherence' in D. Archibugi and B.-A. Lundvall (eds), *The Globalizing Learning Economy*, Oxford/New York: Oxford University Press, 2001.

[26] R.J. Brody, 'Effective partnering: A report to congress on federal technology partnerships.' U.S Department of Commerce, Office of Technology Policy. Washington, D.C. (1996); Y. Fukasaku, 'Public-private partnerships for developing environmental technology.', OECD *STI Review 23* (1999).

[27] L. Hommen and M. Rolfstan, 'Classifying Public Procurement of Innovation: A Taxonomy', *Tijdschrijft Aanbestendingsrecht* (2006).

[28] Article 40 under the New Public Sector Directive states: 'Before launching a procurement procedure, contracting authorities may conduct market consultations with a view to preparing the procurement and informing economic operators of their procurement plans and requirements. For this purpose, contracting authorities may for example seek or accept advice from independent experts or authorities or from market participants. That advice may be used in the planning and conduct of the procurement procedure, provided that such advice does not have the effect of distorting competition and does not result in a violation of the principles of non-discrimination and transparency.'

communication by the demand side of its needs to potential suppliers; the participation of a previously consulted company must not affect competition within the future tender procedure and this should also translate into a clear separation between the market dialogue and the tender procedure itself; any information which a company may receive as result of its prior involvement must be shared with other participants; provision of legal assurances that suppliers' intellectual property rights ('IPRs') will be protected, or that compensation in case of breach is available; ensuring compliance with the principles of transparency, non-discrimination and equal treatment. A well conducted market consultation will provide the necessary basis for the initiation of the procurement process and the drafting of the technical specifications.

3.2 Reasons for Public Intervention – from Conventional EU GPP Criteria towards Increased Environmental and Social Responsibility

In drafting the technical specifications, the European Green Public Procurement ('EU GPP') criteria developed since 2007[29] serve as a guideline for contracting authorities purchasing sustainable products and services. However, the EU GPP do not always encompass the full life cycle socio-economic and environmental impacts of products, services or works to be procured, thus lagging behind the latest promoted demand side policies arguing in favour of increased innovation, CSR and sustainability awareness in public procurements. In the context of the CSR framework aforementioned, sustainability issues should focus on the social, environmental and economic impacts ('People, Planet, Profit') during the whole life cycle of products, services or works.[30] In a nutshell, first, social sustainability and ethical considerations cover issues regarding compliance with labour standards in terms of working age and labour conditions (which is often questionable in the case of home-based workers and unskilled workers in developing countries).[31] Secondly, environmental issues differ throughout the life-cycle of the products, services or works (ranging from production, to maintenance and end-of-life disposal processes).[32] An all-inclusive approach should cover all of these environmental impacts. Thirdly, economic sustainability issues concern the business efficiency, productivity and profit. These sustainability issues all need to be properly addressed in the market dialogue conducted with all project stakeholders in order to deliver a clear understanding of the purchasing bodies' needs and, respectively, the options available from the industry side. This approach will ensure clear, well-defined and comprehensive parameters designing the output based specifications to form the basis for the tender procedure. Outcome based specifications will give the suppliers the

[29] See EU GPP criteria for textiles, available 28 January 2016 at http://ec.europa.eu/environment/gpp/pdf/criteria/textiles.pdf.

[30] Case study: Introducing innovation procurement methods: Rawicz County Hospital, Poland, available 28 January 2016 at http://lowcarbon-healthcare.eu/cms/resources/uploads/File/Case%20Study_Rawicz.pdf. Also see M. Kautsch, 'Innovative public procurement of a bio-based product: Poland', paper presented in Krakow in 2013.

[31] See http://sustainabilityskills.net.au/sustainability-skills-resources/sustainability-sector-guides/sustainability-issues-clothing/ (available 28 January 2016).

[32] Ibid 30.

opportunity to respond on quality, durability, functionality and life cycle costs and avoid rounding their proposals on price solely.[33]

3.2.1 Setting clear requirements and technical specifications based on the market consultation outcome

The European procurement legislation does not contain any limitations as regards the definition of a contract subject matter. Contracting authorities enjoy a great freedom to choose what they wish to procure. The only limitations provided for under the applicable legislation are in regard to the way in which the desired products, services or works are procured, in order to ensure compliance with the principles of transparency, non-discrimination, equal treatment, proportionality and fair competition. In defining the subject matter of the contract to be awarded, the contracting authorities will conduct the market consultation described above in order to identify innovative solutions to minimize, for example, the environmental impact of the products, services or works. The market consultation will offer a clear image of what the market can offer.

Selection criteria should focus, in addition to the economic and financial standing of the bidders, on their ability to perform the contract. The Old Procurement Directive provides that 'the selection of bidders be done in accordance with objective rules and criteria which are available to interested economic operators'.[34] Nevertheless, in recent projects, some public purchasing bodies have decided that, for example, addressing ethical/CSR matters by including them under selection criteria in a tender procedure may prove less effective than including them in the award criteria[35] and thus opted for the second solution. The decision was grounded on the fact that 'using a selection criterion would be a less effective way of ensuring a commitment to social responsibility, as all potential suppliers were to found either their own code of conduct, a supply management system or a certificate proving compliance with CSR instruments'. Consequently, bidders were evaluated on the merits of each system and were required to provide a statement on how they built and implemented a system to verify social standards within the supply chain.[36]

To ensure clarity and avoid any doubt regarding what the contracting authorities envisage when including them in tender documentation, technical specifications[37] should be formulated by reference to European, international or national standards[38]

---

33 Ibid 30.

34 See Article 48 of the Old Procurement Directive.

35 ICLEI – Local Governments for Sustainability, 'The Landmark Project – Moving towards socially responsible procurement, Success stories in socially responsible public procurement: using public spending to drive improvements for workers in global supply chains' (2014).

36 Ibid 35.

37 Technical specifications serve a dual purpose: (i) they are used to describe the contract to the market in order to allow potentially interested bidders to decide whether it is of interest to them or not, whether they have the required capability and capacity to perform the object thereof and also help determine the level of competition and (ii) they provide measurable requirements against which tenders can be evaluated, provided they are clear, correct and conveyed in such a way as to ensure understanding thereof by the bidders.

38 Standards can take several forms, from full European standards (ENs) to European or national technical approvals, common or national technical specifications, international standards

and/or in terms of performance or functionality.[39] Technical specifications may also refer to appropriate specifications that are defined in eco-labels.[40] In order to encourage innovation, it is important not to be over prescriptive in demands. Functional specifications give the opportunity to the suppliers to differentiate their products on factors other than price.[41] Thus, requirements should be framed in terms of performance and not be technically descriptive. This approach will allow suppliers to provide innovative and creative solutions to meet performance targets, possibly expressed in several variants of the same offer. In fact, the use of variants is also encouraged in innovative procurements[42] as a means to introduce greater flexibility in the specifications of the procedure. Last but not least, the European legislation allows the formulation of technical specifications in terms of environmental performance of a material, product, supply or service.[43] Notwithstanding the above, the obligation of transparency incumbent upon contracting authorities in the conduct of tender procedures implies that technical specifications and the fact that variants are accepted are always clearly indicated in the contract notice and the tender documentation.[44]

3.2.2 Award criteria

Under the Old Procurement Directive, contracting authorities could compare offers on the basis of the lowest price or could choose to award the contract to the most economically advantageous offer. The New Procurement Directives mention only the MEAT award criteria, in an attempt of the legislator to ensure better value for money and higher quality of the products, works or services procured.[45] Award criteria must, however, be linked to the subject matter of the contract and must not confer a restricted freedom of choice. It must also be suitable of objective, transparent, proportionate and non-discriminatory evaluation, comply with Community law and must not qualify as selection criteria. When variants are allowed, MEAT criteria should always be used.

---

and other technical reference systems established by European standard bodies. Reference to technical standards can be included directly in the specification defining the contract subject matter. When reference to a standard is used, it must be accompanied by words 'or equivalent'. See Article 23 (3) of the Old Procurement Directive and Article 42 of the New Public Sector Directive.

[39] See Article 23 of the Old Procurement Directive and Recital 74 of the New Public Sector Directive, according to which performance-based specifications are appropriate means to favour innovation in public procurements.

[40] See Recital 29 of the Old Procurement Directive and Article 43 of the New Public Sector Directive.

[41] Ibid 35.

[42] Recital 48 of the new Public Sector Directive.

[43] Annex VI of the Old Procurement Directive.

[44] See Case 225/98 *Commission v France* [2000] ECR I-7445, in which technical specifications defined solely by reference to classifications in French legislation were found to be indirectly discriminatory.

[45] Recital 37 and Article 18(2) of the New Public Sector Directive.

3.3 Kinds of innovation involved – combining circular and life cycle costing approaches

As regards the kind of innovation involved, it is important to stress the forms of innovations (that is, product innovation and/or process innovation) and the relationship between them.[46] Product innovation is required to meet the need to develop a sustainable, innovative product, whereas process innovation translates into undertaking a circular approach[47] (see Figure 7.1 below) to meet the aforementioned primary need. Both approaches are built upon the circular approach of the sustainability dimensions occurring throughout the life cycle of a product development.

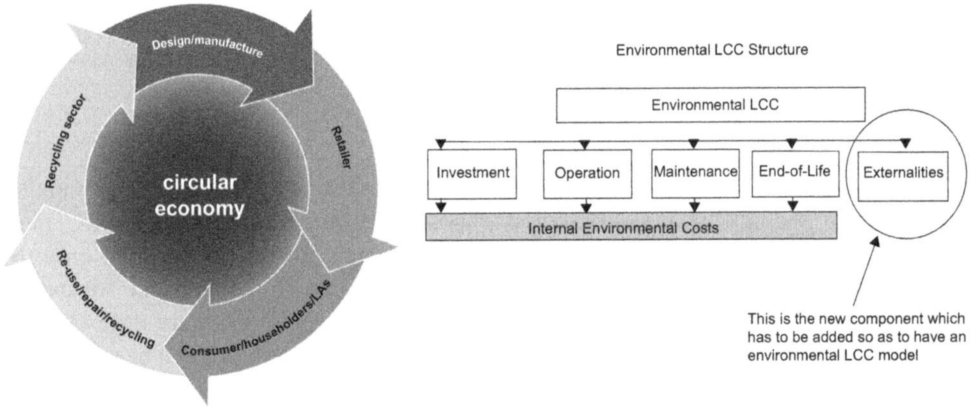

Figure 7.1 Circular economy[1] and life cycle costing structure[2]

Notes:
1. http://www.waste-management-world.com/articles/2013/02/reuse-recycing-targetef-by-circular-economy-100.html.
2. A potential approach to employ LCC could be found in the environmental LCC structure available at http://ec.europa.eu/environment/gpp/lcc.htm.

The circular economy approach should be complemented by a Life Cycle Costing ('LCC') approach. There is no specific legislation in Europe requiring LCC to be taken into account in procurement procedures, but the MEAT mechanism introduces it in the New Procurement Directives. While maintaining existing instruments (technical specifications expressed in terms of functional requirements, variants and so on), the New Procurement Directives encourage companies to develop their capacity for innovation. Thus, all procedures may take account of the total life cycle cost of purchases when

[46] Ellen MacArthur Foundation, available 28 January 2016 at http://www.ellenmacarthurfoundation.org/circular-economy/circular-economy/towards-the-circular-economy.

[47] Commission, 'Communication from the Commission to the European Parliament, the Council, the European Economic and Social Committee and the Committee of the Regions: Towards a circular economy: A zero waste programme for Europe', COM(2014) 398 final.

tenders are being evaluated and innovative bids may be awarded more points in the light of their long-term financial benefits.

LCC, also known as whole-life costing, is a methodology for assessing the total cost performance of a product over time, including the acquisition, maintenance and disposal costs.[48] This means internal costs (costs borne by the contracting authority or other users), as well as costs related to environmental factors.[49] In other words, internal costs include costs for research and development, acquisition, production, transport, consumption of energy, maintenance and end-of-life disposal, where externalities may include the emission of greenhouse gases, pollution caused by the extraction of raw materials used in the product or caused by the product itself or its manufacturing. At the level of the European Union it was argued that the LCC brings significant benefits as it is a key element in the assessment of environmental sustainability of products, it provides a tool for economic evaluation of alternative sustainability options unveiling different capital, operating costs or resource usage, it provides methods for evaluating the cost benefits of incorporating more sustainable options into the development of innovative products, it improves awareness of total costs and it helps evaluating competing options.[50]

As regards the stages in the procurement process when the LCC methodology could be employed, it could be argued that it can be used either at the specification phase, or at the award stage. In the first case, we note that both the Old and the New Procurement Directives allow the use of performance specifications, as well as of sustainability and environmental issues to be included in the technical specifications. These specifications can also include requirements for low or optimum levels of life cycle costs. Alternatively, at the award stage, LCC methodology is relevant in case the MEAT criteria are used.[51] The award criteria is better suited to include LCC in the award process and this could be achieved by including quality and life cycle costing requirements as main criteria in the award process. According to the New Procurement Directives, when contracting authorities assess the costs using a life-cycle costing approach, they shall indicate in the procurement documents the data to be provided by the bidders and the method which will be used to determine the life-cycle cost on the basis of those data.

The application of the LCC methodology is a rather complex task and the lack of trained and qualified professionals within the contracting authority could hinder the knowledgeable and successful employment of a LCC method. Another thing to consider is the need to agree on the components of a LCC calculation (which the contracting authority must be able to check objectively) in order to have an effective model, especially in complex projects aimed at the development of sustainable products where a circular approach is envisaged. Consequently, the effectiveness of using a LCC

---

48 See Article 68 of the New Public Sector Directive.

49 See http://ec.europa.eu/environment/gpp/lcc.htm (available 28 January 2016).

50 See 'Towards a common European methodology for Life Cycle Costing (LCC) – Guidance Document', available 28 January 2016 at http://ec.europa.eu/growth/sectors/construction/support-tools-studies/index_en.htm.

51 Ibid 52.

approach should be given due consideration, by employing a joint appraisal thereof from legal, economic and financial perspectives.

3.4 Choice of Modalities

As a general rule, different possibilities could be contemplated as regards the conduct of innovative procurement. Accordingly, in case of procurement of innovative solutions that require R&D, a Pre-commercial Procurement procedure could be employed, falling outside the Procurement Directives, followed by the conduct of a PPI, fully covered thereby.[52] Alternatively, in case of procurement of innovative solutions that do not require R&D, a PPI taking the form of procurement procedures under the Procurement Directives shall be conducted, whereby specific tactics could be employed to ensure an innovative approach. Last but not least, the recently adopted public procurement legal package has introduced a novel procedure, namely the Innovation Partnership, which will be given due consideration herein below.

3.4.1 Pre-commercial procurement followed by PPI – does it answer procurers' needs?

(i) General considerations In the above mentioned general context, public procurement of innovation in the form of Pre-commercial Procurement ('PCP')[53] was suggested as one way to kick-start innovation in the European Union.[54]

PCP has been designed as a demand-side instrument to deliver cutting-edge technologies or services to the market for which there is demand but which the market nevertheless fails to deliver due to various causes of market failure (for example, lack of information, lack of funding and so on). Whereas initially designed to be applied in the Information and Communication Technologies ('ICTs') sector, it is now promoted as an innovation support tool in a wide range of sectors (for example, healthcare, energy efficiency, social services).

PCP is an approach for procuring R&D services, which enables the public demand side to identify the best value for money solutions on the market to address a specific procurement need. In the innovation cycle designing the transformation of an idea into a marketable product or service, PCP entails the use of competitive development in phases, risk-benefit sharing under market conditions, and a clear separation between the

---

[52] B. Wert, 'Driving Innovation Through Public Procurement – Future European Support', presentation given during the European High Level Events on: Supporting Public Procurement of Innovation, Launching Events of the European projects Financed by the Competitiveness and Innovation Programme, 29 November 2012, London.

[53] Commission, 'Pre-commercial Procurement: Driving innovation to ensure sustainable high quality public services in Europe' ('PCP Communication') COM (2007)799 final. See also Commission, 'Example of a possible approach for procuring R&D services applying risk-benefit sharing at market conditions, i.e. pre-commercial procurement' (PCP Staff Working Document) SEC (2007) 1668.

[54] National IST Research Directors Forum Working Group on Public Procurement in support of ICT Research and Innovation, Pre-commercial Procurement of Innovation: A Missing Link in the European Innovation Cycle, March 2006.

procurement of R&D services and the potential public procurements of innovative solutions focusing on deployment of commercial volumes of end-products. Whereas the latter will always be subject to the provisions of the European procurement legal framework, the PCP is based on the exemption from the procurement directives of R&D services. According to the PCP Communication, the conditions that this exemption applies are:

(a) The scope of the PCP is limited to *R&D services only*, namely activities such as solution exploration and design, prototyping, up to the original development of a limited volume of first products or services in the form of a test series.[55] R&D does therefore not include commercial development activities such as quantity production, supply to establish commercial viability or to recover R&D costs integration, customization, incremental adaptations and improvements to existing products or processes.[56]
(b) A *risk-benefit sharing* approach is required, according to which the public purchaser does not reserve the R&D results exclusively for its own use but public authorities and the industry share risks and benefits of the R&D needed to develop new innovative solutions that outperform the ones already available on the market.[57]
(c) A *competitive procurement designed to exclude state aid* is required, translated in the need to organize the risk sharing and to conduct the entire procurement process 'in a way to ensure maximum competition, transparency, openness, fairness and pricing at market conditions' in order to identify the best possible solutions available from the supply side.[58]

PCPs that are implemented in line with these key prerequisites fall outside the scope of the EU public procurement directives, the WTO Government Procurement Agreement,[59] and the 2014 State Aid Framework. However, the main parties to the WTO

---

[55] According to the WTO GPA, 'Original development of a first product or service may include limited production or supply in order to incorporate the results of field testing and to demonstrate that the product or service is suitable for production or supply in quantity to acceptable quality standards'.

[56] See the PCP Communication.

[57] Ibid 55.

[58] Ibid 55.

[59] Procurement-wise, the WTO Government Procurement Agreement ('WTO GPA') is an international agreement between several signatory parties which have agreed to open their public procurement markets towards each other, in full compliance with the principles of non-discrimination, equal treatment and fairness and the procedural rules agreed to this end. When a public institution does the procurement from a GPA signatory country, this institution may be mandated to allow competition from other signatory countries. This depends on whether the respective public institution is covered by the GPA, the value of the procured contract and whether the object of the contract falls within the scope of the GPA. According to the GPA, the European Union is not restricted in regulating its own internal market, but rather to comply with certain obligations towards non-EU parties to the GPA. In this respect, the European Union did not draft separate rules to be applied for non-EU GPA signatories, but suggests the application of the EU public procurement directives to both EU and GPA bidders.

GPA including the EC have excluded R&D services[60] from the scope of the GPA (that is, from the national treatment[61] and the non-discrimination obligation). Except for the EEA and Stabilization and Association Agreements with partner countries of the European Neighborhood Policy, the EU has no national treatment and non-discrimination obligations vis-à-vis other parts of the world for the procurement of R&D services, but it does for supplies. As PCP regards R&D services, public purchasers are free to decide on a case-by-case basis on the possibility to open the competition worldwide, taking into account the full potential of the European Research Area.[62]

A PCP refers to innovation up to and including a first pre-commercial volume batch of products and / or services validated via field test.[63] It is usually designed as a three-phase process, with evaluation sessions after phase 1 and phase 2 (see Figure 7.2 below).[64]

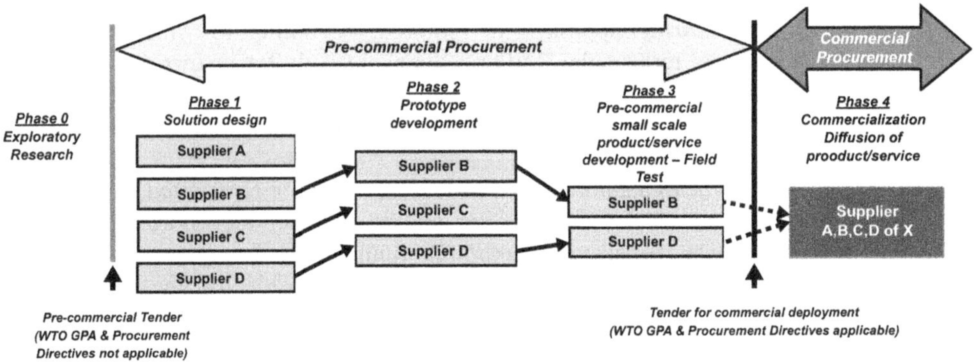

Figure 7.2 PCP process overview – A phased shared risk/shared benefit approach

Phase 1 involves solution exploration, the scope thereof being 'to verify the technical, economic and organizational feasibility of the proposal against the pros and cons of potential alternative solutions, as well as its ability to solve the problem of public interest. The output includes a technology evaluation, as well as an organizational plan and an estimated economic impact of the proposed solution'.[65] Phase 2 entails the development of a prototype by the best suppliers selected based on the R&D results achieved during phase 1. The output of phase 2 should include product specifications, a tested prototype,[66] a production plan and a business plan. Phase 3 covers test series

---

60 Annex IV of the WTO GPA.

61 The national treatment obligation implies that Member States do not operate discriminatory measures between domestic services or service suppliers and foreign ones.

62 COM(2007)161, Green Paper on ERA.

63 Ibid 12.

64 PCP Communication.

65 Ibid 12.

66 A prototype is an original model constructed to include all the technical characteristics and performances of the new product. It is built with the aim to test the characteristics and performances of the product and to use the testing results for further improvements. See Frascati

conducted by the best suppliers (minimum two) selected based on the results of phase 2, the production of a first batch of products/services, the testing thereof in relevant environments and the incorporation of the results of the field testing in a limited series of products, meant to demonstrate the suitability for large scale production, taking the form of classic public procurement. The outputs of this phase are refined production and business plan.[67]

Note should be made that when designing the three-stage PCP procedure in one tender, the PCP Communication assumes that the total value of the R&D services over all phases exceeds the value of products purchased through the contract.[68] Arguably, in case the value of the products (prototypes) purchased through the contract is higher than the one of the R&D services, the contract would qualify as an R&D supply contract and would thus be subject to the procurement directives.[69]

(ii) Legal analysis – compliance of PCP with state aid regulation and competition rules; IPR arrangements in PCP

(A) COMPLIANCE WITH STATE AID AND COMPETITION RULES – PCP AS EU INNOVATION CYCLE'S MISSING LINK As a general note, the PCP in Europe was intended to be a successful European replication of the US programme of 'Small Business Innovation Research' ('US SBIR'),[70] which was identified as one of the main mechanisms leading to innovation progress in the United States ('US') and placing the US ahead of Europe in this regard. Despite intended similarity between the two approaches, they differ in some major respects regarding, *inter alia*, the mandatory employment of the PCP approach[71] or the risk-benefit sharing.[72] Another difference between the two approaches rests in the fact that, unlike the European PCP approach the direct purchase of the solutions developed within SBIR is encouraged. Accordingly, in the US, companies

Manual, Proposed Standard Practice for Surveys on Research and Experimental Development, OECD (2002), p. 42.

67 National IST Research Directors Forum Working Group on Public Procurement in support of ICT Research and Innovation, 'Pre-commercial Procurement of Innovation: A Missing Link in the European Innovation Cycle' (2006).

68 Ibid 12.

69 Ibid 12.

70 The US Small Business Innovation and Research (SBIR) program has been applied in the Unite States since 1982, with the aim to provide a home market to innovative domestic firms in specifically identified areas in which the US aspired to become a global leader. The US believed that small businesses have the potential to be more innovative than large businesses and that the federal funds were insufficient to support them. See National IST Research Directors Forum Working Group on Public Procurement in support of ICT Research and Innovation, Pre-commercial Procurement of Innovation: A Missing Link in the European Innovation Cycle, March 2006.

71 In Europe, conducting PCP is left to the full discretion of the public purchasers, whereas in the US, all federal agencies are obliged to set aside budgets for SBIR calls.

72 The PCP Communication recommends the payment of a market price for R&D services, reflecting the sharing of benefits between the contracting authority and the R&D service providers, where in the US the federal agencies conducting SBIR procedures undertake the entire R&D costs plus a profit margin amounting to 7%.

which complete the feasibility and prototype stages of the SBIR scheme may be granted a 'Phase III status', which provides them with a preference in winning a contract with the federal agency.[73]

The main differences between the US SBIR and the European PCP model are grounded mainly in the desire of the European Commission to ensure PCP compliance with the European state aid regulations, which specifically prohibit the favouring of certain economic operators or the production of certain goods by state subsidies[74] and the overall competition rules in the Single Market. The EU state aid rules contribute to forming the basis underlying a European Union concept, namely the development of a market-based economy in which companies are rewarded according to their innovativeness and efficiency. It was argued that unwarranted support provided by Member States to some national companies may lead to the exclusion from the market of the most competitive companies, also triggering economic negative effects such as increased prices, lower quality, or less innovation.[75] PCP was thus deemed to fill the funding gap for innovative firms occurring after the materialization of the internal market and the disappearance of national champions and state-owned giants.[76]

In this line of reasoning, the European Commission considers that the direct procurement of PCP results has the potential of foreclosing competition due to the fact that at the moment the PCP process ends, it is not yet clear whether the PCP participants will be able to develop suitable products to meet the specific needs of the contracting authority. Consequently, such an approach could qualify as illegal state aid.

As regards the recommendation to pay a market price for the R&D services, this is an additional measure aimed at strengthening compliance with state aid rules. A market price in the context of the PCP translates into less than the total cost of the R&D that should be paid by the contracting authority, thus reflecting the market value of the benefits received by the PCP participants (for example, commercialization opportunities) and the risks assumed thereby (for example, IPR).[77] This means that the contracting authority needs to identify the maximum price it is willing to pay in the PCP process. According to the European Commission, the maximum price should be calculated by deducting from the total cost of the R&D activities[78] the market 'present value' of the benefits retained by the R&D service provider (namely, the commercialization opportunities).[79]

---

[73] See National Research Council (2008), An Assessment of the SBIR Program.

[74] Such an approach is deemed to affect trade among Member States. See Article 107(1) TFEU.

[75] See COM(2005) 107 final, State Aid Action Plan: Less and better targeted state aid: a roadmap for state aid reform 2005-2009 (Consultation document), Brussels, 7 June 2005.

[76] Ibid 12.

[77] SEC(2007) 1668, Commission Staff Working Document, Example of a possible approach for procuring R&D services applying risk-benefit sharing at market conditions, i.e. pre-commercial procurement, 14 December 2007. ('PCP Staff Working Document')

[78] All the costs incurred by the technology vendor, for example, the market value of the salaries of researchers/developers in a certain sector and the costs of R&D material required to perform the work, plus a reasonable margin. See FAQ Cordis, question no. 8. Available 28 January 2016 at ftp://ftp.cordis.europa.eu/pub/fp7/ict/docs/pcp/faq-sv7clean_en.pdf.

[79] See PCP Staff Working Document.

Furthermore, according to the 2014 State Aid Framework, no state aid within the meaning of Article 107(1)[80] of the TFEU is deemed to be awarded to undertakings delivering relevant services as long as an open or restricted procedure for the public procurement is carried out in accordance with the provisions of the New Procurement Directives. The same applies when public purchasers procure innovative solutions from a preceding R&D procurement, or non-R&D products and services that are delivered to a performance level requiring a product, process or organizational innovation. In all other cases, including Pre-commercial Procurement, the Commission will consider, *a priori* that, in principle, no state aid is awarded to undertakings where the price paid for the relevant services fully reflects the market value of the benefits received by the public purchaser and the risks taken by the participating providers.[81] The 2014 State Aid Framework voices the European Commission's intent to propose new measures to further promote R&D&I, ensure consistency with the Europe 2020 strategy which identifies R&D&I as key driver for achieving the objectives of smart, sustainable and inclusive growth, boost competitive markets and properly address market failures, cover financial gaps and promote risk-taking and experimentation. However, the European Commission does not provide a recommendation regarding a methodology for calculating the value of these commercialization opportunities, especially because they concern a product which has not yet been developed.

As a general rule, the public procurement legal framework does not allow the direct uptake of the solutions developed following the conduct of a PCP procedure, as the PCP covers only the applied R&D part of the typical innovation cycle. As an exception to this rule, both the Old[82] and the New[83] Procurement Directives contain provisions which could be argued to justify the direct purchase of the innovative products/services

---

[80] 'Save as otherwise provided in the Treaties, any aid granted by a Member State or through State resources in any form whatsoever which distorts or threatens to distort competition by favouring certain undertakings or the production of certain goods shall, in so far as it affects trade between Member States, be incompatible with the internal market.'

[81] Several additional conditions need to be met, including: the conduct of R&D services procurements via open, transparent and non-discriminatory procedures, based on objective selection and award criteria provided upfront in the tender documentation; the upfront provision of contractual arrangements describing all rights and obligations of the parties, including with regard to Intellectual Property Rights (IPR); strictly avoiding giving any of the participant providers any preferential treatment in the supply of commercial volumes of the final products or services to a public purchaser in the Member State concerned. Additionally, it is required that all results which do not give rise to IPR be widely disseminated and any IPR are fully allocated to the public purchaser. Alternatively, any service provider to which results giving rise to IPR are allocated is required to grant the public purchaser unlimited access to those results free of charge, and to grant access to this parties, for example by way of non-exclusive licenses, under market conditions.

[82] Article 31(1)(b) of the Old Procurement Directive.

[83] Article 32(2)(b) of the New Public Sector Directive specifically states that: 'The negotiated procedure without prior publication may be used for public works contracts, public supply contracts and public services contracts … where the works, supplies or services can be supplied only by a particular economic operator for any of the following reasons: (i) the aim of the procurement is the creation or acquisition of a unique work of art or artistic performance; (ii) competition is absent for technical reasons; (iii) the protection of exclusive rights, including intellectual property rights. The exceptions set out in points (ii) and (iii) shall only apply when

resulting from PCP. Accordingly, the contracting authority may follow a negotiated procedure without the prior publication of the contract notice in case this is necessary for the protection of exclusive rights, including IPR. Nevertheless, the scope of application of these provisions is rather restrictive and, according to applicable jurisprudence developed by the European Court of Justice, the 'simple possession of IPR would not justify direct negotiations with one specific participant, unless the contracting authority can show that there are no other substitutes to the PCP solution on the market'.[84]

Moreover, whereas in case of PCP, support to procurers' calls for R&D services comes from grants provided to encourage industry and academic researchers to take more risks in developing innovative solutions, processing new technologies and their applications, PPI is mainly driven by the demand of public customers, targeting the development of readily applicable solutions to meet their needs.[85] In this context, PCP and PPI are separate but complementary procurements where PPI does not cover the procurement of R&D. A split between PCP and PPI allows companies that have developed products through other means than a Pre-commercial Procurement (e.g., through SME funding instruments, other R&D grants, own company R&D resources) to still compete for PPI deployment contracts, avoiding issues of foreclosing of competition and crowding out of private R&D investments. PCP thus provides the link between R&D and the commercialization stages of the innovation cycle.

(B) IPR ARRANGEMENTS IN PCP In a PCP, the public purchasers, as technologically demanding first buyers, share with private sector suppliers the risks and benefits of moving research developments from their early stages to products ready for commercialization (that is, co-financing of the R&D and the award of IPRs to the private PCP supply side participants while the contracting authority could be granted a free license to use the developed product and the right to mandate the PCP participants from the supply side to license to subsequent suppliers under reasonable conditions[86]). This approach differs substantially from the exclusive development in which the public purchaser reserves all the results and benefits of the development for its own use, including the IPRs, the companies having developed the product/service being banned from reusing them for other potential customers and the overall price paid by public authorities for the developed results being incrementally higher.[87]

Note should be made that when benefits shared include IPRs, special attention need be paid to the way in which IPRs are assigned to companies having participated in the PCP procedure in order not to provide them with an unfair competitive advantage potentially affecting wide competition in future procurements. The 2007 PCP Communication is very clear in this regard and provides that this approach could be

no reasonable alternative or substitute exists and the absence of competition is not the result of an artificial narrowing down of the parameters of the procurement'.

84 Case C-394/02, *Commission v Greece* 2 June 2005; Case C-385/02, *Commission v Italy*, 14 September 2004.

85 Procurement of Innovation Platform, 'Guidance for public authorities on Public Procurement of Innovation' (2014), available 28 January 2016 at www.innovation-procurement.org.

86 In line with the FRAND terms (Fair, Reasonable and Non-Discriminatory).

87 PCP Communication.

implemented, for example, by the public purchaser requiring participating companies to license IPRs to third parties under fair and reasonable market conditions. The public purchaser could also demand a free license to use R&D results for internal use.[88] Another possible scenario could also be that public purchasers are given the ownerships of their generated IPRs, participating companies will enjoy the full ownership of their own generated IPRs and jointly generated IPRs are jointly owned. Last but not least, other variations on IPR arrangements could also be possible, depending on the sector of activity contemplated.

(iii) To conclude … In light of the above, the purchase of the solution developed following a PCP procedure needs to undergo a procedure conducted in full compliance with the procurement legal framework. Whereas this approach is grounded by the desire to preserve EU-wide competition in the procurement markets and also ensure compliance with the WTO GPA rules, it may also be a disincentive for public purchasers to conduct PCPs.[89]

In order to address this pitfall, the New Procurement Directives grants public purchasers more discretion in order to stimulate their engagement in the procurement of R&D and boost the uptake thereby of innovative solutions to societal problems. To this end, the new procedure regulated by the New Procurement Directives is the Innovation Partnership, which allows for the direct purchase of products/services developed within the framework of an R&D public private partnership.[90] We will further develop on the characteristics of the innovation partnership, as well as on the pitfalls under the New Procurement Directives as regards the regulation of this new procedure.

3.4.2 Innovation Partnership – the answer to promote innovation uptake?

(i) General considerations The New Procurement Directives provide for and regulate a new procedure aimed at offering contracting authorities a tool to act as demanding customers and early adopters of desired innovation, namely the Innovation Partnership. This new procedure allows the set-up of a structured, long term partnership by the contracting authority with one or several private undertakings, with the aim to concurrently perform R&D activities and the subsequent purchase of commercial volumes of resulting products, services or works (large deployment), provided they correspond to initially agreed levels of quality and costs.[91]

As regards the procedure to be followed, the New Procurement Directives provide that the Innovation Partnership shall be structured in successive phases following the sequence of steps in an R&D process, which may include the manufacturing of the products, the provision of the services or the completion of works. However, it is not clarified whether these steps correspond to the R&D phases in a PCP process and no

---

[88] Ibid 89.

[89] Anca Ramona Apostol, 'Pre-commercial Procurement in Support of Innovation: Regulatory Effectiveness?' (2012) 6 *Public Procurement Law Review* 213–25.

[90] Article 31 of the New Public Sector Directive.

[91] Article 31 (1) and (2) of the New Public Sector Directive.

definition of R&D is provided. Furthermore, the Innovation Partnership must set intermediate targets to be attained by the partners and provide for payment of the remuneration in appropriate instalments. It is based on these targets that the contracting authority may decide, after each phase, to terminate the innovation partnership with several partners or to reduce the number of partners by terminating individual contracts, subject to clearly mentioning these possibilities in the tender documentation.

The establishing of an Innovation Partnership follows the design of the competitive procedure with negotiation. The conduct of negotiations could occur in stages. The contracting authority shall negotiate with the bidders the initial and subsequent tenders submitted thereby, except for the final tender, fully observing the equal treatment, non-discrimination, proportionality and transparency principles.

Whereas the Innovation Partnership seems to be an alternative to the PCP procedure, the two are quite different in scope and effects. First, whereas PCP falls outside the scope of the procurement legislation, the Innovation Partnership falls within its scope and the contract must be awarded in accordance with the rules for a competitive procedure with negotiation. Additionally, unlike PCP, the Innovation Partnership allows the purchase of the products, services or works resulting from the conduct of the R&D activities, thus allowing the large scale deployment of solutions within the same procedure. Moreover, it could be argued that the provisions regulating Innovation Partnerships are rather poorly drafted[92] as they are limited to mentioning that the estimated value of supplies, services or works shall not be disproportionate in relation to the investment required for their development, without providing any information as to what is considered to be disproportionate. In the absence of more clarifications, the proportionality test will most probably be assessed by the European Court of Justice on a case-by-case basis. Besides, this subsequent purchase is not limited in time or to first products or services, but the law seems to encourage large deployments thereof, on a long term basis and, potentially, harm competition as the contracting authorities will no longer be stimulated to act as first customers and pull innovative products or services to the market.[93] Additionally, the New Procurement Directives do not specify in case of partnerships concluded with several industry players, what solution should be employed in case more operationally viable products are developed and whether a competition among the companies having successfully developed such products should be carried out. Lastly, we note that the provisions under the New Procurement Directives regarding Innovation Partnerships are silent as regards whether the contracting authority should encompass a single entity or could include several entities. Nevertheless, the New Procurement Directives expressly regulate the possibility of two or more contracting authorities agreeing to perform certain specific procurement jointly.[94] In the absence of specific provisions under the article regulating Innovation Partnerships in this respect, it could be argued that such provisions could be read in conjunction with the ones covering joint procurement.

---

92 Ibid 91.
93 Ibid 91.
94 Article 38 of the New Public Sector Directive.

In addition to the above mentioned pitfalls in the regulation of innovation partnerships, major concerns are raised from the perspective of compliance thereof with state aid regulations, competition rules and the arrangements applicable to IPR.

(ii) Legal analysis – compliance of the Innovation partnership with state aid regulation and competition rules; IPR arrangements in PCP

(A) COMPLIANCE WITH STATE AID AND COMPETITION RULES As a general note, Article 107(1) TFEU qualifies as incompatible with the common market any aid granted by a Member State or through state resources in any form whatsoever which distorts of threatens to distort competition by favouring certain undertakings or the production of certain goods, as long as it affects trade between Member States. In order to qualify as state aid and thus be subject to the prohibition aforementioned, four cumulative conditions must be met: (i) the measure has to be granted out of State resources; (ii) the measure needs to confer an economic advantage to certain undertakings; (iii) the advantage needs to be selective and distort competition; and (iv) the measure has to affect the trade between Member States.[95] In so far as the interplay between public procurement and state aid regulations is concerned, it could be argued that most of the above conditions could easily be met by certain public procurement activities.[96] Accordingly, public contracts are financed from State resources, the award thereof is selective and the effect on trade between Member States could be significant. It remains that the one thing that requires additional analysis is whether the public contracts awarded pursuant to public procurement procedures confer an economic advantage to the contractor which it would not receive under normal market conditions.[97]

The official position of the European Commission is that as long as a public contract is awarded in compliance with public procurement rules, it cannot amount to the grant of state aid, as compliance with procurement rules objectivizes the award of the contract and thus excludes the element of undue economic advantage.[98] This position is based on the case-law emanating from the European Court of Justice that the European Commission established a presumption that no state aid incompatible with the TFEU exists where the award of the contract (i) is a pure procurement transaction and (ii) the procurement procedure is compliant with the EU public procurement directives and suitable for achieving best value for money – inasmuch as no economic advantage which would go beyond normal market conditions will usually arise under these circumstances.[99] Consequently, in the EU Commission's view, compliance with public

---

[95] A. Sanchez Graells, 'Public Procurement and State Aid: Reopening the Debate?', available 28 January 2016 at http://ssrn.com/abstract=2037768.

[96] S. Arrowsmith, *The Law of Public and Utilities Procurement*, 2nd edn., London: Sweet and Maxwell, 2005.

[97] A. Doern, 'The Interaction between EC Rules on Public Procurement and State Aid', (2004) 3 *Public Procurement Law Review* 97–129.

[98] Ibid 97.

[99] See Case C-280/00, *Altmark Trans GmbH* [2003] ECR I-7747. See also P. Dethlefsen, 'Public Services in the EU – Between State Aid and Public Procurement', (2007) 3 *Public Procurement Law Review* NA53–64.

procurement regulations rules out incompatibility with state aid provisions. Nevertheless, such conclusion could be rather debatable in light of the new public procurement package promoting the innovation partnership procedure. Whereas the New Procurement Directives are aimed at increasing flexibility, modernization and simplification of the procurement rules, the risks triggered by this approach have been duly recognized in the Green Paper on the modernization of EU public procurement policy: 'The possible advantages of more flexibility and potential simplifications must be weighed against the increased risks of favouritism and, more generally, of overly subjective decisions arising from the greater discretion enjoyed by contracting authorities in the negotiated procedure. Such subjectivity would in turn make it harder to show that the resulting contract did not involve State aid.'[100] The same Green Paper highlights concerns regarding the use of State aid in innovation-promoting mechanisms under the New Procurement Directives. Whereas PCP is referred to as a mechanism which 'enables public authorities to share the risks and benefits of designing, prototyping and testing a limited volume of new products and services with suppliers, without involving States aid',[101] major concerns appear in relation to the newly introduced innovation partnership procedure.

As currently drafted, the 2014 State Aid Framework seems to cover not only Pre-commercial Procurement, but also the Public Procurement of Innovation and the Innovation Partnership, the new procedure under the New Procurement Directives.[102] Whereas the 2014 State Aid Communication is saluted by all relevant stakeholders in the innovation world, we note that failure to meet the relevant requirements would lead to the conclusion that the undertakings delivering the relevant services do not fall outside the state aid exemption rule and will thus be subject to notifying the Commission accordingly or to facing the consequences for failing to comply with state aid regulations.

The main sources of increased risk as regards compliance of the Innovation Partnership with state aid and competition rules are triggered by (i) the increased scope for negotiations which ultimately increases the discretion and subjectivity of the contracting authority; and (ii) the public finance of R&D projects followed by large deployments of the resulting products/services through this procedure. As noted above, the innovation partnership is to be structured in successive phases and the contracting authorities shall negotiate with tenderers the initial and all subsequent tenders submitted by them, except for the final tender, to improve the content thereof.[103] This increased flexibility introduced under the new public procurement package accounts for a significant policy shift from previous restrictive approaches to negotiations with tenderers prior to the award of the contract.[104] Under the new procurement rules,

---

100 See European Commission, *Green Paper on the modernization of EU public procurement policy – Towards a more efficient European Procurement Market* COM(2011) 15 final, available at http://eur-lex.europa.eu/LexUriServ/LexUriServ.do?uri=CELEX:DKEY=556316:EN:NOT.

101 Ibid 102.

102 This is only applicable in case the open or restricted procedures are used.

103 Article 31 of the New Public Sector Directive.

104 See the Statement concerning Article 7(4) of Council Directive 93/37/EEC of 14 June 1993 concerning the coordination of procedures for the award of public works contracts [1993] OJ L199/54: 'in open and restricted procedures all negotiations with candidates or tenderers on

contracting authorities enjoy greater freedom to choose the competitive procedure with negotiation. Accordingly, it could be argued that contracting authorities are given almost unlimited discretion to choose this procedure, provided they offer some motivation for their choice.[105] Whereas the New Procurement Directives include specific provisions aimed at minimizing the risk of distorting competition,[106] the increased flexibility and discretion which the contracting authorities now enjoy could pose a significant risk of coordination of public procurement and competition law and it would be highly recommendable that the choice of procedure to be followed should be carefully considered on a case-by-case basis, in order to avoid an artificial narrowing of competition.

Additionally, public spending should target growth-promoting policies and should make use of joined efforts towards common European objectives.[107] However, public spending in the form allowed by the Innovation Partnership procedure seems to have the potential to lead to a misuse of public resources, while also endangering competition within the Single Market.

In the same line of thinking, it was argued that when a procuring entity funds R&D relating to future procurement, this approach can generate anti-competitive conduct, in particular with regard to state aid rules.[108] Consequently, the main issue requiring consideration in this respect as regards the regulatory effectiveness of innovation partnership is whether an economic advantage is conferred to the private entities which they would not otherwise receive under normal market conditions, the more so in cases in which the goods, services or works developed thereunder are not for the exclusive use of the procuring entity.[109]

The risk that Article 107 TFEU is breached is higher in the case of Innovation Partnerships. The main characteristic of these partnerships is that they allow the development of an innovative product, service or work funded with public funds and the subsequent purchase of the resulting supplies, services or works. Such an approach could prevent effective competition in the private sector, 'by killing the competitive capacity of other competing SMEs which, due to the lack of similar state support, face abnormal competitive pressure'.[110] The immediate effect of this approach is the foreclosing of the market, which contravenes the scope of Recital 49 of the New Public

---

fundamental aspects of contracts, variations in which are likely to distort competition, and in particular on prices, shall be ruled out; however, discussions with candidates or tenderers may be held but only for the purpose of clarifying or supplementing the content of their tenders of the requirements of the contracting authorities and provided this does not involve discrimination.'

105 Ibid 91.

106 See Recital 49 of the New Public Sector Directive provides that 'Contracting authorities should not use innovation partnerships in such a way as to prevent, restrict or distort competition' ; and Article 18 which states that 'the design of the procurement shall not be made with the objective ... of artificially narrowing competition'. Also see Recital 59 of the New Utilities Directive.

107 Commission, Communication from the Commission, EU State Aid Modernization (SAM) COM(2012) 209 final.

108 P. Cerqueira Gomes, 'The Innovative Innovation Partnerships under the 2014 Public Procurement Directive' (2014) 23(4) *Public Procurement Law Review* 211–18.

109 Ibid 217.

110 Ibid 217.

Sector Directive and, respectively, of Recital 59 under the New Utilities Directive, advocating for the role of the innovation partnership to provide a market pull of innovative solutions. The current legal framework does not limit the commercial purchase of the innovative products to 'first products or services'. Consequently, a contracting authority may purchase R&D results even after their placing on the market. In such a case, the contracting authority will not be encouraged to act as first customer and 'pull' onto the market innovative products/services but, instead, it will be allowed to create long-term obstacles to competition that also could lead to favouring national based technology vendors and the industry.

(B) IPR ARRANGEMENTS In an attempt to address industry's concerns regarding the leakage of business information, the New Procurement Directives impose upon the contracting authority the obligation to preserve the confidential information communicated by a bidder participating in the negotiations unless express consent for the sharing of information is provided by the latter. In the same line of reasoning, specific provisions regarding the safeguarding of IPR rights have also been included. Accordingly, the contracting authority must define the arrangements applicable to IPR rights in the procurement documents. Specifically in case of a partnership with several partners, the contracting authority must not reveal to the other partners solutions proposed or other confidential information communicated by a partner in the framework of the partnership without the former's express consent.

However, contrary to the detailed provisions regarding the arrangements pertaining to IPRs triggered by the R&D in a PCP, the New Procurement Directives are rather sketchy as regards regulating the method to be employed and used to design how the relevant IPRs should be acquired once the Innovation Partnership comes to an end. The only provision under the New Procurement Directives in this respect states that 'in the procurement documents, the contracting authority shall define the arrangements applicable to intellectual property rights'.[111] However, the terms of acquisition of the IPRs are totally left to the discretion of the contracting authority. Provided that Member States do not share a common approach towards the regulation of the ownership of IPR,[112] the lack of more in-detail provisions in this respect under the Directive contributes to the increasing debates regarding the regulatory efficiency of the Innovation Partnership procedure. Consequently, it is rather arguable as to what is the best option to consider: should the private technology vendors keep the IPRs and provide the public purchaser a free license, should the IPRs fully accrue to the public purchaser or should they be jointly shared by the technology vendor and the public purchaser? In trying to answer this debate, note should be made that the ultimate scope of the Innovation Partnership is to respond to the public need for an innovative product, service or work and be structured in such a way as to provide the necessary 'market-pull', incentivizing the private sector to develop innovative solutions.[113] In this

---

[111] See Article 31(6) of the New Public Sector Directive and Article 49(6) of the New Utilities Directive.

[112] Cerqueira Gomes, 'The Innovative Innovation Partnerships under the 2014 Public Procurement Directive', above fn. 108, 217.

[113] See Recital 49 of the New Public Sector Directive.

line of thinking, it seems only feasible to allow the private companies to keep their IPRs, thus giving them adequate incentives and allowing them the opportunity to compete on equal chances. It is only in this way that the intended market-pull could be obtained.

(iii) To conclude … In light of the above, whereas the Innovation Partnership may appear appealing to public authorities which are now able to directly purchase the innovative results of the R&D effort without the need to organize a new competitive procedure to this end, the implementation thereof as currently regulated may pose a significant threat to the good functioning of the internal market and the compliance with fair competition principles among vendors active in the market.

The main threats potentially jeopardizing the effectiveness of Innovation Partnerships and allowing room for distortion of competition within the internal market include the likely lack of competitive pressure during the R&D stages by creating a 'closed user group', the possibility for the contracting authority to enter into a long term partnership with only one supplier from which the former would be bound to buy large volumes of products and the possibility to purchase the developed products long after they have been developed and even commercialized.

Making the Innovation Partnership a mandatory default procedure for acquiring the development and deployment of innovative solutions across all Member States represents thus significant dangers and drawbacks, especially since there is evidence that reopening of competition for deployment contracts after the R&D phase is better from a competition and public sector budget optimization point of view. Evidence from US defence procurements shows that compared to long term vendor partnerships that provide up front commitment for procuring R&D and large scale deployment, significantly higher quality products and on average 20 per cent cost savings on the first deployments are obtained when reopening competition after PCPs by tendering out the large deployment contracts separately (remaining competition for the deployment contracting phase is what keeps companies focusing on producing best value for money products and avoids supplier lock-in).[114] The lack of clearer provisions may pose a high risk on the practical implementation of the innovation partnership and the need for soft law explaining the mechanism appears more stringent than ever.

4. CONCLUSIONS AND FUTURE DEBATES

Public procurement of innovative solutions aims at closing the gap between revolutionary technology and processes and the public sector purchasers or users benefiting therefrom. Sharing risks, costs and gains are all important parts of the PPI, whereas a number of available options to structure the partnerships between the public and the private sectors in this regard are provided under the procurement legal framework.

[114] J. Gansler, 'Competitive Dual Sourcing', 7 October 2007; 'Annex G, "International Armaments Cooperation in a era of coalition security", report US Defense Science Board, August 1996', for more information see http://www.dtic.mil/cgi-bin/GetTRDoc?AD=ADA49 4656 (available 28 January 2016).

Nevertheless, the question arises whether the new procurement and concessions package adopted at the European level provides the necessary basis for increased use of innovative procurement approaches by public bodies and where is it to be expected that we will see more innovative solutions in procurement taking place? We will draft these conclusions based on the statement made at the very beginning of this chapter, namely that innovative procurement entails innovative approaches in both practices and procedures.

From a legal perspective, as mentioned above, the New Procurement Directives seem to encourage the employment of innovative approaches by several means, including: the express regulation of market consultations, the possibility to include social and environmental considerations within tender specification, the drafting of technical specifications by reference to standards and/or eco-labels, the use of the life-cycle-costing approach, the use of MEAT awarding criteria, the express regulation of public-public cooperation or the introduction of new tender procedures aimed at promoting the procurement of innovative and sustainable solutions (that is, the innovation partnership, the competitive procedure with negotiation[115]). However, whereas the new rules have been adopted by the European legislature bearing in mind the need for increased transparency, flexibility, fairness and efficiency, debates have been reopened regarding the clash between public procurement principles and their interplay with state aid, competition and IPR protection related issues, as we have pointed out above. These legal complexities, coupled with the novelty of the innovation-oriented procedures introduced by the New Procurement Directives, the limited experience on the side of public procurers in employing such approaches and the lack of case-law interpreting the new legal provisions could have a limiting effect on the quick uptake of innovative procurement approaches. When looking at the New Procurement Directives from a different angle, namely from a practical perspective, it results that whereas the New Utilities Directive applies to a limited category of contracting authorities and entities due to its specific scope, the New Public Sector Directive has a broader scope and it would therefore seem more likely that a higher number of innovative projects will be implemented under its regime.

Additionally, Directive 2014/23/EU of the European Parliament and the Council of 26 February 2014 on the award of concession contracts (the 'Concessions Directive') regulates for the first time the awarding of works and services concessions. The Concessions Directive has been thought of as an answer to the need for a regulatory regime for concession contracts, aimed at providing increased legal certainty and thus avoiding the arbitrary granting thereof. However, the Concessions Directive seems to allow even more freedom and flexibility to contracting bodies in the award of concession contracts when compared to the New Procurement Directives. Accordingly, while it does not provide any specific procurement procedures to be implemented for the award of concession agreements, it limits itself to setting out procedural guarantees of transparency, consistency and objective criteria which contracting bodies must fulfill when granting a concession (that is, the description of the concession, the provisions of technical specifications, award criteria and minimum requirements to be included in all

---

[115] We note that this procedure is only included in the New Public Sector Directive and not in the New Utilities Directive.

tender documentation). Whereas it could be argued that the increased flexibility is a basic condition to support the uptake of innovative solutions, it could also be argued that it translates into variable application of the governing principles and the Concession Directive throughout the Member States. This result, coupled with the insufficient legal certainty surrounding concessions arising also from limited and sometimes contradictory case-law in this field emanating from the Court of Justice of the European Union,[116] leads to the conclusion that the pull of innovative solutions by means of concessions is rather challenging, if not questionable.

In light of the above, it could be concluded that, whereas the new legal package regulating public procurement and concessions seems to encourage the uptake of innovative solutions, the occurrence thereof is expected to happen at a low pace due to the legal challenges aforementioned. Nevertheless, innovative solutions in procurement will have to be called for, especially in sectors which require them the most, such as healthcare, Information Communication Technologies, smart transportation networks or waste and water management, triggered by the need and duty incumbent upon public bodies to provide public services of increased quality and efficiency.

[116] Only 26 cases have been decided by the CJEU since 2000. See Michael Burnett, 'Directive on the award of concession contracts – 2014/23/EU', presentation held at the EIPA in Maastricht, Netherlands, April 2014.

8. Innovative public-private partnerships

Marta Andrecka

1. INTRODUCTION

Europe as well as any other region is faced with important societal challenges such as ensuring high quality and accessible health care, the fight against climate change and improving energy efficiency. Addressing these challenges often requires new and better solutions.[1] As research and innovation play a central role in the Europe 2020 strategy for smart, sustainable and inclusive growth, the procurement of innovation is of high value.[2] Furthermore, in its original form, the aim of Public-Private Partnerships (PPP) was to create and introduce new innovative methods, techniques, solutions, incentives, as well as new types of cooperation and investment to create a better value for money.[3] Therefore, one form of an innovation delivery may be through a PPP contract.

At the beginning of 2014, the European Parliament and the Council adopted the new Directive 2014/24/EU on public procurement.[4] The new act is a greater codification of the provisions, and there are more decisions for the contracting authorities to make. The Public Sector Directive puts greater emphasis on promotion of innovation than its predecessors. It manifests it among others by introducing a new procedure called the innovation partnership.[5] The availability of the new provisions may be valuable particularly from the perspective of complex contracts such as Public-Private Partnerships, which are characterised as mixed contracts.[6] This is because the innovation partnership has the potential to enable a contracting authority to procure complex

[1] Communication from the Commission to the European Parliament, the Council, The European Economic and Social Committee and the Committee of the Regions on pre-commercial procurement: Driving innovation to ensure sustainable high quality public services in Europe, Brussels, 14 December 2007 COM (2007) 799 final (further: Communication on pre-commercial procurement).

[2] Commission's Communication, Europe 2020 on a strategy for smart, sustainable and inclusive growth, Brussels, 3 March 2010, COM (2010) 2020 final.

[3] Tvarnø, 'Why the EU Public Procurement Law should contain Rules that allow Negotiation for Public Private Partnerships. Innovation calls for negotiating opportunities' in Ølykke, Risvig and Tvarnø, *EU-Public Procurement – Modernisation Growth and Innovation Discussions on the 2011 proposals for Procurement Directives* (Copenhagen: DJØF Publishing, 2012) p. 215; see also: Abdel, 'Successful Delivery of Public–Private Partnerships for infrastructure Development' (2007) 133(12) *Journal of Construction Engineering and Management* 918.

[4] Directive 2014/24/EU of the European Parliament and of the Council of 26 February 2014 on public procurement and repealing Directive 2004/18/EC ('Public Sector Directive').

[5] Article 31 of the Public Sector Directive.

[6] Joined Cases C-145/08 and C-149/08, *Club Hotel Loutraki* [2010] ECR I-4165; Case C-215/09, *Oulun kaupunki* (2010); Andrecka, 'Institutionalised Public-Private Partnership as a Mixed Contract under the Regime of the New Directive 2014/24/EU' (2014) 3 EPPPLR 174–86.

contracts with more than one subject matter regarding development of innovation and its delivery. However, both delivery of innovation and procurement of PPP contracts bring specific legal challenges, which need to be considered.

In this chapter the author will identify and analyse what are the available ways in which to procure innovative Public-Private Partnerships under the Public Sector Directive. To achieve this aim, first, the scene for the analysis will be set by a presentation of background information. This will include an introduction of the Public-Private Partnership concept and a description of how the innovation is defined in the new Public Sector Directive. Secondly, two methods of procuring the innovation will be discussed: the pre-commercial tender and delivery of an innovation by using procurement procedures such as the competitive dialogue procedure, the competitive procedure with negotiation and finally the newly introduced innovation partnership. Thirdly, particular attention will be given to the innovation partnership's provision in the new Public Sector Directive. Focus will be given to the proposed procedure and structure of the partnership. Fourthly, the answer will be given to the question what new the innovation partnership introduces. Finally, the last section will conclude the discussion.

2. WHAT IS A PUBLIC-PRIVATE PARTNERSHIP?

In recent decades the Public-Private Partnership (PPP) has become a very popular phrase used to describe all sorts of public-private collaborations.[7] In the widest sense a PPP may be described as a form of long-term contractual collaboration between a contracting authority and one or more economic operators, based on a cooperation with the objective to achieve public policies through a concluded contract.[8]

There are two main reasons for establishing PPPs. First, the fact that in the era of the world economic crisis public budgets are struggling to cover public activities, when the demand of citizens to receive good quality service increases every year. Therefore, private financing may be the only possibility for contracting authorities to carry out complex, high-value projects.[9] Secondly, there is a commonly held opinion that private involvement in public projects has the potential to deliver the best value for money over the life of the contract.[10] Value for money should not be understood as the lowest price, but rather as a combination of life-cycle cost[11] and quality to meet the users' needs.[12]

---

[7] In the UK – Private Financial Initiative (PFI); in Poland – Partnerstwo Publiczno Prywatne; in Denmark – Offentlig-private partnerskaber (OPP); Burnett, *Public-Private Partnerships (PPP) – A decision maker's guide* (European Institute of Public Administration 2007) p. 7.

[8] See: European Commission's Green Paper on Public-Private Partnerships and Community Law on Public Contracts and Concessions COM(2004) 327 final, Brussels 30 April 2004 at 3 (further: Green Paper on PPPs).

[9] Arrowsmith, 'Public Private Partnerships and the European Procurement Rules: EU Policies in Conflict?'(2000) 37 CMLR 710.

[10] Ibid.

[11] Article 68 of the Public Sector Directive.

[12] Burnett, 'The Current Private Finance Initiative (PFI) Reform in the United Kingdom – How should it be measured?' (2012) 2 EPPPL 119 referring to the UK Treasury.

Besides the initial costs of design and construction, whole-life (or life-cycle) costs include the costs of service, maintenance and repair of the asset, user support and training as well as the supply of materials and disposal costs.[13]

Traditionally the delivery of public services, works or supplies takes place in the following manner: the necessary payments are made up-front by the contracting authority, which then takes an ownership of the assets provided and uses them to provide the particular public work, supply, or service.[14] For example, when the city of Aarhus (Denmark) needs a new school, traditionally it will pay an economic operator to build it, and afterwards the city would manage the school and provide education. The additional services such as cleaning, maintenance, catering and security would be provided by the in-house service providers of the contracting authority, or they would be contracted out to private providers, often different ones.[15]

The PPP scheme[16] can deliver the same school project in a more efficient and innovative way. The contracting authority normally establishes a long-term contract – often for more than 20 years, depending on the subject of the contract – with an economic operator. The latter will not only design and build the school, but will also operate it and provide the additional services (mentioned above) during the duration of the PPP contract.

The financial scheme of the project is also different from the traditional procurement delivery, as the contracting authority does not pay up-front for the construction of the school. Rather the contracting authority pays the economic operator throughout the term of the PPP contract, or payments are made by the end users of the service (in case of a concession contract), or by combination of both forms.

In the demonstrated manner PPPs were initially introduced as vehicles for the realisation of transport infrastructure projects such as tunnels, roads, and bridges, but throughout the years the application of PPP contracts has spread to diverse sectors. These includes: the education and health sectors, where PPPs became a 'go to' form of project implementation, waste management, urban development, information technology service, construction and operation of prisons and schools and traffic control, innovation development and delivery.[17]

---

[13] Article 68 of the Public Sector Directive; See Burnett, 'The Current Private Finance Initiative (PFI) Reform in the United Kingdom – How Should it be Measured?' (2012) 2 EPPPL 119.

[14] S. Arrowsmith, *The Law of Public and Utilities Procurement*, 2nd edn. (London: Sweet and Maxwell, 2005), p. 26.

[15] Ibid.

[16] There is no authoritative definition of PPPs, therefore the concept may vary between Member States. See more on the lack of a PPP definition in Burnett, *Public-Private Partnerships (PPP) – A decision maker's guide* (European Institute of Public Administration 2007) p. 8; Tvarnø, 'A Critique of the Commission's Interpretative Communication on Institutionalized Public-Private Partnerships' (2009) 1 PPLR 11–23NA.

[17] Burnett, 'Current Private Finance Initiative (PFI) Reform in the United Kingdom – How should it be measured?' (2012) 2 EPPPL 118–19.

Despite the fact that PPPs are widely used and promoted by the Commission,[18] there is no clear agreement on what exactly PPPs are.[19] That may be due to the fact that there is no legal definition of PPPs at the European Union level.[20] The reason for this lack of legal definition of PPPs may be rooted in its historical development, as PPPs were 'born' in practice and not established by the law itself.

2.1 Aims and Benefits of Public-Private Partnerships

The aims of a PPP contract are to establish a close collaboration between parties built on trust, transparency, and sharing of the benefits and responsibilities. Such established PPP collaborations aim at generating efficiency, and securing value for money. The latter is understood as the optimum combination between the increase in the quality of the public work/service/supply and the whole life cost of the contract. It is argued that PPPs have the potential to be better at delivering value for money than the traditional procurement contracts, as they can reduce the cost of the projects. That is due to the fact that the price, risks of failures and responsibilities are shared in PPP contracts.[21] The benefits of PPPs are the same as for any other type of contracting out. However, there are certain capacities for efficiency gains that are specifically crucial for PPP contracts.[22] These may include the fact that PPPs have a potential to fill in the gap between the contracting authority's financing needs in regard to the implementation of essential policies and the available public funds.

Furthermore, PPP schemes may be beneficial for contracting authorities as skills and assets of each sector (public and private) are shared for the benefit of citizens. One of such benefits is an increase in the service quality, and that is due to the fact that the PPP form is strongly customer orientated. Also, the contracting authority can exploit a private party's ability to manage a project more efficiently and effectively plus – as empirical evidence shows – PPPs are able to provide on-time project delivery.[23] This is achieved due to simple logic, that is, the sooner a project is finished the sooner the payment stream can commence, and this of course motivates private partners.[24]

---

[18] Communication of the European Commission to the Council, to the European Parliament, to the Economic and Social Committee and to the Committee of the Regions on Public-Private Partnerships in Trans-European Network Projects COM(97) 453.

[19] IMF Financial Affairs Department, Public-Private Partnerships, March 2004, p. 6; Hodge and Greve, *The Challenge of Public-private Partnerships: Learning from International Experience* (Cheltenham, UK and Northampton, MA, USA: Edward Elgar, 2005), p. 1; Badcoe (ed.), *Public Private Partnership and PFI* (London: Sweet & Maxwell, 1999) looseleaf, at 1.00; Fischer, 'ACT4PPP – A Transnational Initiative to Promote Public-Private Cooperation in Urban Development' (2010) 2 EPPPL 107.

[20] Green Paper on PPPs at 5; Tvarnø, 'A critique of the Commission's interpretative communication on Institutionalized Public-Private Partnerships' (2009) 1 PPLR 11–23NA.

[21] Tvarnø et al, *Public-Private Partnership: an international analysis – from a legal and economic perspective,* (Asia Link Project, 2010) pp. 27–28, available 29 January 2016 at: http://www.unpcdc.org/media/142722/ppp%20book[1].pdf.

[22] Arrowsmith, *The Law of Public and Utilities Procurement*, p. 27.

[23] See Report of the Comptroller and Auditor-General, 'PFI: Construction Performance', HC 371 Session 2002–2003, February 2003, p. 3.

[24] Bovis, 'Risk and Public-Private Partnerships' (2012) 1 EPPPL 44.

Additionally, in the traditional public contract delivery, the contract's specification is based on demands and a specific description of these, opposite to a PPP contract, which is designed to focus on needs and functions. Such an approach challenges traditional ways of project delivery, as it provides greater opportunities for innovation. This may be due to the fact that the private partner is responsible for all elements of the PPP project.[25] The incentive of innovation goes hand in hand with the fact that borrowing money from a financial institution (private loans) is generally cheaper for a public authority than for a private party. Therefore, PPPs have potential to gain more beneficial loans, which may be used to deliver better quality solutions or to invest in developing new innovative solutions.

However, what is important to remember is that PPP contracts are not a miracle solution for organising collaborations between the contracting authorities and economic operators. It needs to be examined on a case-by-case basis, whether the PPP is the best possible solution. It needs to be noted that there are some public activities, which are not suitable for PPPs or at least controversial to be delivered in a PPP form, for example national defence, public law and order, diplomatic missions and maintenance of internal security.

2.2 IPPP as an 'Extended' Form of a Mixed Contract

An appropriate classification of a PPP's material scope is crucial, as it will decide whether the contract is excluded from the regime of procurement law or not.[26] Public contracts are usually easy to classify, but in the majority of PPPs the classification is not as obvious. This is due to the fact that PPPs usually consist of several elements, such as: work, supply and service as well as other matters not covered by the Public Sector Directive including the establishment of a common entity and possibly also sale of shares or development of an innovation.

The Public Sector Directive includes the definition of a mixed contract, which classifies complex public contracts under one set of provisions.[27] A mixed contract must be classified as either a public work, supply or service contract, as a specific contract cannot fall within more than one set of provisions.[28] In order to determine which rules must be used, two measures are applied: the main purpose of a contract and the value of the individual elements of a contract.[29] The former was developed by the European Court of Justice (ECJ) due to the absence of accurate and explicit rules in the Public Sector Directive.[30] The key element to a proper classification of the contract in regard to the concept of main purpose is an adequate distinction between what the main purpose of the contract is and the incidental activities that must take place to

[25] Arrowsmith, *The Law of Public and Utilities Procurement*, p. 27.

[26] Article 3 of the Public Sector Directive.

[27] Ibid.

[28] Arrowsmith, *The Law of Public and Utilities Procurement*, p. 331.

[29] See Case C-331/92, *Gestion Hotelera International SA* [1994] ECR I-1329; Joined Cases C-145/08 and C -149/08, *Club Hotel Loutraki* [2010] ECR I-4165.

[30] Bovis, *Public Procurement in the European Union* (Basingstoke: Palgrave Macmillan, 2005), p. 192.

deliver the main contract's objective.[31] The need for such a distinction is especially necessary due to the fact that in some cases, parties are interested in grouping various purchases together. The reason for this can be found in the regulation of threshold values. While dealing with a contract which involves service as the main object, but also certain incidental work, a party may be interested in qualifying the specific project as a work contract, since the threshold value is much higher than for service contracts.[32]

The question is how to decide which objective is the contract's main purpose. The answer is not clear. In the *Gestion Hotelera* case[33] the contract was challenged with the claim that it was a work contract; not a service contract. In this case the contract documents stated that it was a contract on managing a casino and hotel and extensive work activities.[34] However, works, which should be carried out or provisions for remuneration of the works were nowhere specified. In the light of these circumstances, the ECJ ruled that the works were only 'incidental', and the main objective of the contract was service. Nevertheless, the ECJ did not explain exactly what it meant by 'incidental', and how incidental actions should be characterised. It seems reasonable to consider what percentage of the economic value the incidental action has compared to the rest of the contract, and also if it would be possible to deliver the contract's objective without that element. If so it could be arguable that such an element is incidental. Such a line of argument is supported by the Commission's interpretative communication, which states that the test of main purpose is the preferable manner to distinguish between the aim of the contract and the incidental elements.[35] However, the communication does not elaborate on which characteristics such a test should have.

The fact is that a vast amount of mixed contracts include both supply of goods and services (usually the services will be linked to the goods). Such contracts need to be classified on the basis of the individual value of the contract's elements.[36] Services or supplies covered by a contract must be valued separately to decide which one represents the highest value and thereby defines the whole contract. The value is determined on the basis of the remuneration excluding VAT.[37] Even though this is a mandatory task, it can be a very difficult one. However, a contracting authority needs to be able to prove that it carried out all necessary investigations to obtain information on the objective value of a contract, especially if it comes to the conclusion that the value does not exceed the threshold value stipulated in the Public Sector Directive.[38]

In the majority of cases, PPP contracts will fulfill the characteristics of a mixed contract, as they will include different variations of a public contract. However, at the same time PPPs will also include aspects which are not regulated by the procurement regimes, such as development of an innovation. Therefore, until recently it was argued

---

31 Case C-220/05, *Jean Auroux v Commune de Roanne* [2007] ECR I-385.

32 Article 4 of the Directive.

33 Case C-331/92, *Gestion Hotelera International SA* [1994] ECR I-1329.

34 Ibid.

35 Commission's Interpretative Communication on Concessions under Community law, [2000] OJ C121/2, pp. 4–5.

36 Article 3 of the Directive.

37 Article 4 of the Directive.

38 Ibid.

that PPPs constitute an 'extended' mixed contract, where the non-procurement related contractual elements will not only have an impact on the PPP contract's classification, they will also make the procurement process even more complicated.[39] This argument has found its validation not only in the ECJ rulings, but also in the new Public Sector Directive. The provision regarding mixed contracts has been changed, and the changed wording now identifies that in the case of mixed contracts, which include elements covered by the Public Sector Directive as well as elements which are not, the contracting authorities may choose to award separate contracts for the separate parts or to award a single contract.[40] Where contracting authorities choose to award separate contracts for separate parts, the decision as to which legal regime applies to any one of such separate contracts shall be made on the basis of the characteristics of the separate part concerned.

3. INNOVATION PPPS AND ITS PROCUREMENT

Innovation is a time-consuming, planned process, where involved parties work together in a close collaboration with the intent to develop something new.[41] Until now there has not been any legal definition of innovation in EU public procurement law, and this could potentially cause some uncertainties and challenges. Among others it was unclear how to procure a contract including innovation and how to classify such a contract, especially since it is often difficult to specify the subject matter of an innovation contract. With the introduction of a new Public Sector Directive a legal definition of an innovation was also introduced in Article 2(22):

> 'innovation' means the implementation of a new or significantly improved product, service or process, including but not limited to production, building or construction processes, a new marketing method, or a new organisational method in business practices, workplace organisation or external relations inter alia with the purpose of helping to solve societal challenges or to support the Europe 2020 strategy for smart, sustainable and inclusive growth.

There are several problems with this definition – in particular – the question of how we should understand the concept of 'significantly improved'. In this respect, Recital 47 of the Public Sector Directive states that innovation should improve efficiency and quality; and that it should contribute to achieving best value for public money as well as wider economic, environmental and societal benefits. Therefore, it seems that the requirement for significant improvement should refer to these elements. The innovation should allow a contracting authority to deliver better public contracts in terms of quality, life-cycle cost, and enable the contracting authority to incorporate better environmental and societal considerations and standards. In addition, other elements of the definition can be criticised. First, it is unclear why the legislator would establish a definition,

---

[39] Green Paper on PPPs at 5.

[40] Article 3(4) of the Public Sector Directive.

[41] Steinicke, 'The Public Procurement Rules and Innovation' in Ølykke, Risvig and Tvarnø, *EU-Public Procurement – Modernisation Growth and Innovation Discussions on the 2011 proposals for Procurement Directives*, pp. 259–74.

which will become out-dated in five years, as the definition refers to the Europe 2020 strategy. Secondly, the definition is too complex. It might be better to refer simply to implementation of a new or significantly improved product, service or process, including but not limited to production, building or construction processes.

Having in mind the limits on the disclosure of information, the competitive environment including a number of tenderers, the ban on post-tender negotiation and issues regarding ownership of the IP rights in a majority of public procurement procedures, it needs to be noted that there are limits to the possibility of developing an innovation or innovative solution within the procurement process *per se*.[42] These limits are connected mainly with the fact that the procurement process should be quick, competitive and transparent, and an innovation process is not. The inflexibility and detail of the procurement framework makes it difficult to deliver innovation in the public tender.[43]

There are several ways in which the contracting authority can encourage the introduction of innovation in the procurement process. Among others are variants,[44] design contests[45] and a functional description of the subject matter.[46] Nevertheless, these options may increase risks and confusion as to how to make sure that the contracting authority is not comparing apples with oranges. Also, when these tools are used in open or restricted procedures they are not traditional innovation processes, as dialogue between contracting authorities and bidders is not allowed.

In the current legal framework, a procurement of innovation PPPs may be carried out in the following two ways. Firstly, the procurement of innovation may be carried out in a two-stage process: starting with a pre-commercial procurement when Research and Development (R&D) service is awarded, and followed by a procurement procedure of the already developed innovative solution (works, services, goods) on a commercial market.[47] Both a pre-commercial and a commercial tender may be conducted through the competitive dialogue procedure and by using the competitive procedure with negotiations.[48] Secondly, the whole process, including the pre-commercial and the commercial tender, may be combined into one procedure and be procured throughout the competitive dialogue procedure, competitive procedure with negotiation or the newly introduced innovative partnership.[49]

---

[42] Commission's Green Paper on the modernisation of EU public procurement policy towards a more efficient European Procurement Market, COM (2011) 15 at section 4.3.

[43] Steinicke, 'The Public Procurement Rules and Innovation', p. 273; See for other perspective Burgi, 'Can Secondary Considerations in Procurement Contracts be a Tool for Increasing Innovative Solutions?' in Ølykke, Risvig and Tvarnø, *EU-Public Procurement – Modernisation Growth and Innovation Discussions on the 2011 proposals for Procurement Directives*
pp. 275–90.

[44] Recital 48 and Article 45 of the Public Sector Directive.

[45] Article 78 of the Public Sector Directive.

[46] Article 42 of the Public Sector Directive.

[47] Communication on pre-commercial procurement, p. 1.

[48] Articles 29, 31(2)(a) and in Article 30(1)(d) of the Public Sector Directive; see also Steinicke, 'The Public Procurement Rules and Innovation', p. 265.

[49] Articles 29, 31(2)(a) and in Article 30(1)(d) of the Public Sector Directive; see also Steinicke, 'The Public Procurement Rules and Innovation', p. 265.

4. PRE-COMMERCIAL PROCUREMENT

The aim of a pre-commercial procurement is to award a PPP contract with the objective to develop an invention (further: innovation PPP), whereas the subsequent delivery of the already developed innovation will be procured on the commercial market. The Commission refers to the innovation as a Research and Development service (further: R&D), which will cover activities such as solution exploration and design, prototyping, and development of limited volume of test series.[50]

In regard to pre-commercial procurement the starting point is that such R&D services will normally be subject to the full procedural obligation of the Public Sector Directive. However, there is an exclusion of the applicability of the Public Sector Directive for the R&D services other than those where:

> … the benefit accrues exclusively to the contracting authority for its use in the conduct of its own affairs and, (b) the service provided is wholly remunerated by the contracting authority[51]

On the basis of the exception, the contracting authority is obliged to conduct a public tender only if it pays entirely for the service and also keeps the results solely for itself. In all other cases when, for example, the contracting authority will decide to share some of the R&D results, it may conduct an innovation PPP with an exclusion from the Public Sector Directive's requirements, which allows for a wide spectrum of flexibility. That is due to the fact that in such a scenario, the contracting authority does not reserve R&D results exclusively for its own usage, but the partners of the PPP share both risks and benefits of the R&D innovation. It is important to emphasise that there is only exclusion for the R&D service, not for the R&D works or supply.

4.1 The Structure of Pre-commercial Procurement

According to the Commission's communication a pre-commercial procurement can take the form of a single public procurement contract for the R&D managed in three stages.[52] The first stage is a solution exploration phase, which is followed by the second stage evolving around prototyping and, lastly, the third stage, which is a test series. The latter stage covers the development of a first lot of pre-commercial pre-products. However, nothing prevents Member States from developing different pre-commercial procurement schemes, as there is no European specific procedure, which would bind Member States. After the pre-products are tested, the commercial

---

50 Communication on pre-commercial procurement, p. 2.

51 Article 14 of the Public Sector Directive.

52 Communication on pre-commercial procurement, pp. 2–3; see also Apostol, 'Pre-commercial Procurement in Support of Innovation: Regulatory Effectiveness?' (2012) 6 PPLR 215–16.

development of the innovation starts, in the other words, at this point the pre-commercial phase transfers into the commercial procurement. The commercial development of the innovation will include volume production of the end product, or supply to create commercial validity or to recover the money invested in R&D costs.[53]

4.2 Challenges of Pre-commercial Procurement

Pre-commercial procurement on different markets has already proven to be extremely successful and has delivered the Internet Protocol technology and the Global Positioning System and more in the United States.[54] Nonetheless, in Europe there is still little experience with the pre-commercial procurement form proposed by the Commission. That might be because innovation delivery in the model of pre-commercial framework proposed by the Commission is tremendously complex and includes certain pitfalls. It is divided into three phases, involving many tenderers throughout an extended period of time. On the one hand, such an approach stretched over a period of time potentially secures transparency and equality and ensures competition between companies and the creation of multiple options. On the other hand, it bears some challenges and risks. To these may be added; extensive costs and time of handling multiphase procurements, the possibility of many changes of partners during the process and a lack of stability and legal certainty and the challenges of choosing the appropriate procurement procedure. The Commission acknowledges these issues, but until recently there was a strong belief in the Commission that the quality-price ratio and success rate will counteract these challenges.[55]

From the perspective of a PPP's private partner, the proposed process is more than complex – there are no guarantees and guidelines on how the private partner should proceed to ensure that he would be able to deliver the innovation service, which was his idea in the first place. Moreover, because of the division of the pre-commercial and commercial phase, the private partner has no warranty that he will be the one who will also deliver the innovation to the contracting authority, and it is most often the commercial part of the innovation development where the money lies.[56]

There is a fair argument to separate phases of the R&D and commercial procurement; since the risk exists that technological success will not always be the case.[57] However, a steady environment for R&D is an important factor in achieving the goals set. This should be taken into consideration as well as the fact that in the case of PPP contracts negotiation, trust and collaboration are crucial elements to achieve the established goals. If the private partner of the innovation PPP project changes often during the innovation process, not only time and money will be spent, but also such a scenario will attract legal challenges. The latter may include issues regarding IP rights,

---

[53] Communication on pre-commercial procurement, pp. 2–3; see also Apostol, 'Pre-commercial Procurement in Support of Innovation: Regulatory Effectiveness?' pp. 215–16.

[54] EURAB Report: 'US defence R&D spending: an analysis of the impact', PREST, 2004; see also: Mazzucato, *The Entrepreneurial State: Debunking Public vs Private Sector Myths* (London: Anthem Press, 2013), chapter 4.

[55] Communication on pre-commercial procurement, p. 9.

[56] Steinicke, 'The Public Procurement Rules and Innovation', p. 269.

[57] Ibid.

problems with the confidentiality of the provided solution by the previous PPP partner as well as claims for damages and uncertainties on how much information the contracting authority can disclose to the new PPP partner. Also, dividing a project into lots may be a type of 'cherry picking'[58] as every step of the way the public partner has the possibility to choose the best solution provided. This is beneficial for the contracting authority, but can be controversial for private market shareholders. Of course, it is debatable whether the contracting authority would be interested in changing partners all the time due to the financial and legal restraints. Nevertheless, the author's point here is to show that in theory such an approach may bring those risks mentioned above.

Even though the Public Sector Directive's requirements will not be applicable in the majority of pre-commercial procurements, if any procedure is required at all,[59] a good practice should be provided. Furthermore, the procedures should be concluded in a fair and non-discriminatory manner. It could be questioned, if there was a need for a procedure in the first place, why not just use a regular tender procedure? The answer is that the traditional procurement procedures have many detailed requirements which make them fairly inflexible, costly, and time-consuming. Hence, when the contracting authority wants to provide good practice, it will be keen to apply general EU law principles rather than the Public Sector Directive's provisions. This gives the contracting authority more flexibility and a larger scope of discretion in awarding the innovation PPP contract.

4.3 Exclusive Development

To ensure that the development of an innovation may proceed further, even in a case where the PPP's partner will need to be changed, the contracting authorities may opt for exclusive development of the innovation. The latter means that the contracting authority reserves all the rights, results and advantages coming from the R&D for itself.[60] In such circumstances companies which have developed an innovation or innovative solution, cannot reuse it for other potential customers. Exclusive development of the innovation, of course, will have its consequence in a higher price of the R&D.[61] While in some cases the importance of exclusive development is understandable (defence and security projects), in a majority of cases it is not indispensable in the experts' opinion.[62] Often, there is no reason to bear the high costs and risks of exclusive

58 See Andrecka, 'Institutionalised Public-Private Partnership as a Mixed Contract under the Regime of the New Directive 2014/24/EU' (2014) 3 EPPPLR 174–86.

59 The requirement to use a tender procedure for a pre-commercial stage of the innovation development is more based on state aid considerations than procurement law. For more on the issue see Bos and Corvers, 'Pre-commercial Public Procurement – A missing link in the European Innovation Cycle Public Needs as a driver for innovation' (2006) 5 *Tijdschrift Aanbestedingsrecht* 198–218.

60 Communication on pre-commercial procurement, p. 5.

61 Communication on pre-commercial procurement, p. 5.

62 The Wilkinson Report, Report of the Independent Expert Group lead by DTI – conducted for DG RTD, 'Public Procurement for research and innovation: Developing procurement practices favourable to research and innovation' September 2005 at 5 ('Wilkinson Report').

development. If the IP right will be shared as well as the R&D results, the other risks and benefits will be shared as well.[63]

4.4 Violation of Equal Treatment

One important element of non-exclusive development of the innovation is the fact that the contracting authority needs to make sure that the PPP's private partner will not be given unfair advantage in the possible subsequent commercial procurement, as such a situation would constitute a violation of the equal treatment principle.[64] To escape this risk the contracting authority may require for the PPP private partner to license IP rights to third parties. This should be done on fair and reasonable market conditions.

However, there is no legal basis in European Union law allowing Member State legislators to establish a general prohibition for participation in a commercial tender of a PPP's private partner who was involved in a pre-commercial tender that has helped with the establishment of the specification, or in any other way. In the *Fabricom* case[65] the ECJ clearly stated that establishing a total prohibition on participation of parties who had been involved in a preparation of a tender (the case concerned participating in a technical dialogue, but *per analogiam* a pre-commercial stage of the innovation development would most likely be treated the same way) is disproportionate and such a provision goes beyond what is necessary to secure transparency and equal treatment.[66] However, the contracting authority may place the burden of proof on the party seeking to participate in the tender to show that there is no unfair competition.[67]

As pointed out in previous paragraphs, the problem with distinguishing between the pre-commercial and commercial procurement is that the PPP's private partner who first was awarded the contract for the R&D innovative product/method/service in the pre-commercial stage needs to compete in multiple procurements for the award of (a) the potential next phase of R&D; and (b) the commercial delivery of innovation, will be at risk of being excluded from the commercial tender on the basis of having an unfair competitive advantage over other bidders.[68] Such an approach is not satisfactory for many private companies, which usually are interested not only in development of a new innovative idea, but also or even mainly in its delivery. From the above-mentioned reasons, the contracting authority will often try to combine the pre-commercial and commercial process of developing an innovation PPP into one tender procedure.

---

63 Communication on pre-commercial procurement, at 7.

64 The Wilkinson Report at 7.

65 Joined Cases C-21/03 and C-34/03, *Fabricom SA v Belgian State* (2005) ECR I-1559.

66 Ibid at paras 33–35.

67 See Article 24 of the Public Sector Directive.

68 Apostol, 'Pre-commercial procurement in support of innovation: regulatory effectiveness?' p. 220; See also: 'Trends and Challenges in Demand – Side Innovation Policies in Europe', Thematic Report 2011 under Specific Contract for the Integration of INNO Policy Trend Chart with ERAWATCH (2011–2012) 26 October 2011 p. 18.

5. THE INNOVATION PPP DELIVERY THROUGH THE PROCUREMENT PROCESS

As pointed out in the introductory remarks, besides procuring innovation PPP in a two-stage process of pre-commercial and commercial tender, the contracting authority may decide to combine all stages of the innovation development into one procurement procedure. For the purpose of such joint innovation procurement the following procedures are available: the competitive dialogue procedure, the competitive procedure with negotiation and the newly introduced innovation partnership procedure.[69]

5.1 Competitive Dialogue and Procurement of Innovation PPP

Article 26 of the Public Sector Directive sets up grounds for usage of both the competitive dialogue and the competitive procedure with negotiation. It states that these procedures may be used in regard to works, supplies or services when:

(i) the needs of the contracting authority cannot be met without adaptation of readily available solutions;
(ii) they include design or innovative solutions;
(iii) the contract cannot be awarded without prior negotiations because of specific circumstances related to the nature, the complexity or the legal and financial make-up or because of the risks attaching to them;
(iv) the technical specifications cannot be established with sufficient precision by the contracting authority …'[70]

Also the procedures may be used if in response to an open or a restricted procedure, only irregular or unacceptable tenders are submitted. According to the Public Sector Directive the 'irregular tenders' should be understood as tenders, which do not comply with the procurement documents, which were received late, where there is evidence of collusion or corruption, or which have been found to be abnormally low by the contracting authority.[71] Further, the 'unacceptable tenders' are perceived as these tenders, which are submitted by tenderers that do not have the required qualifications, and tenders where the price exceeds the contracting authority's budget as determined and documented prior to the launching of the procurement procedure.[72]

Recital 42 of the Public Sector Directive points out that over the past years the use of the competitive dialogue has significantly increased in terms of contract values, and the procedure is particularly fitted for innovative projects. Therefore, it is worth considering what challenges will accompany the procurement of a PPP contract involving an innovation in the framework of the competitive dialogue procedure.

Potential issues may be analysed on the following example: the contracting authority in Randers, Denmark, wants to establish a PPP contract in which a private partner will develop new innovative beds and cleaning system for them, and afterwards it will

[69] Steinicke, 'The Public Procurement Rules and Innovation', p. 265.
[70] Article 26 of the Public Sector Directive.
[71] Article 26(4) (b) of the Public Sector Directive.
[72] Article 26(4) (b) of the Public Sector Directive.

deliver them to a hospital.[73] Such a project would probably be classified as a mixed type of contract including innovation, supply and service.

The question is what the main purpose of this PPP contract is. If it is the innovation service, the process falls outside of the EU procurement framework on the basis of Article 14 of the Public Sector Directive (under the condition that the contracting authority does not demand the exclusive development right). However, in such a scenario the contracting authority will be obliged to create a tender for the delivery of the newly developed beds and cleaning service, like in the case of the pre-commercial tender. Therefore, the same issues as in the procurement divided into pre-commercial and commercial stages will occur.

On the other hand, if to classify the delivery of the beds or delivery of the cleaning service as the main purpose of the PPP contract, the aim of the contract could potentially be met, even if the innovation is not achieved, or not achieved to the extent that the contracting authority would want it to be. Furthermore, such a simple delivery of beds or cleaning service could be tendered through the open or restricted procedures. In such an approach the innovation would need to be treated as an 'incidental' element of the PPP contract, according to the theory of mixed contracts.[74] The problem is that the aim of the described project will not be achieved, if there is no innovation, as it is not just any delivery of beds or ordinary cleaning service that the contracting authority is interested in, but the delivery of *'the specific beds and cleaning service'* (emphasis added) which will be innovative. Therefore, the innovation will need to be developed first.

Besides the contract qualification the particular example of a PPP contract will also pose challenges from a procedural perspective. The open and restricted procedures are not suitable, as some scope of the negotiation is needed to establish who will be the best partner to the PPP and who will present the best approach to the effective delivery of the project. In the case of the competitive dialogue procedure it seems that the contract would meet the complexity requirements laid down in Article 26(4) of the Public Sector Directive. On the one hand, the technical complexity of the project would be satisfied, as the contracting authority's needs cannot be satisfied by any existing solution. Therefore, the contract focuses on developing an innovation. On the other hand, as the example contract is PPP collaboration, it will most probably include a complex financial structure, which would need to be established and negotiated. It would not be possible to establish the price of the delivery of one bed at the start of the procurement process, since the price is dependent on the level of the innovation's success. Also, if the innovation is not delivered, the contracting authority could not be obliged to pay for the delivery of beds of any kind or regular cleaning services. Also, the legal complexity of this particular PPP contract would be guaranteed, as the issue of the IP right would need to be settled.

---

[73] Telles, 'Competitive Dialogue: Should Rules be Fine-tuned to Facilitate Innovation?' in Ølykke et al, *EU-Public Procurement – Modernisation Growth and Innovation Discussions on the 2011 proposals for Procurement Directives*, p. 231, proposing to add innovation as a ground for availability of the competitive dialogue procedure.

[74] See Andrecka, 'Institutionalised Public-Private Partnership as a Mixed Contract under the Regime of the New Directive 2014/24/EU' pp. 174–86.

If applying the competitive dialogue procedure, the supply of the beds would need to be qualified as the main purpose of the contract or maybe the cleaning service. The problem is that the element of the contract defined as its main purpose would be very briefly elaborated on in the dialogue stage of the procedure, when the main focus would need to be on the innovation part of the project.

Furthermore, in Article 30(3) of the Public Sector Directive the provision defines that the contracting authority should open:

> ... a dialogue the aim of which shall be to identify and define the means best suited to satisfying their needs.

In fact, such a solution is not possible in this particular PPP contract, as the innovation would not be developed in the dialogue stage of the competitive dialogue procedure, but after the award of the contract. In fact, the innovation would be developed in the implementation phase of the PPP contract. The legal and financial makeup of the process could be developed, but not the innovation in itself.

From the provisions, it appears that such a dialogue should be continued until the solution is identified.[75] However, in reality no economic operator will be willing to participate in a process, which takes extensive time and resources without any guarantee of winning it or being reimbursed for the participation in other ways.[76]

In this approach, a procurement process, which is required – from the perspective of an obligation to procure the delivery of supply and service – in fact would not have much to do with delivery itself, as mainly it would be connected to the part of the PPP contract regarding the innovation.

5.2 Competitive Procedure with Negotiations

Besides the competitive dialogue procedure the innovation PPP may be procured using the competitive procedure with negotiations,[77] which is a successor to the negotiated procedure with prior notice.[78] As mentioned in the previous section the basis for usage of the competitive dialogue and competitive procedure with negotiation is the same under the new Public Sector Directive. It makes both procedures extremely similar. Therefore, it is debatable why they both are present in the new Directive.

The competitive procedure with negotiation is a competitive process, where negotiations are to be carried out with all the bidders still in the procurement process. The major change from the previous negotiated procedure with prior notice is that following negotiation on submitted tenders there is a formal end to the negotiating and bidders are invited to submit a revised tender (very much like the tender phase in the competitive dialogue procedure).[79] The procedure provision specifies the extent to

75 Article 29(5) of the Public Procurement Directive.

76 Article 30(8) of the Public Sector Directive gives the possibility to pay participants of the competitive dialogue for the participation in the tender. However, in practice that happens extremely rarely.

77 Article 29 of the Public Sector Directive.

78 Article 30 of the Directive 2004/18/EC.

79 Article 29(3) of the Public Sector Directive.

which the contracting authority can change its requirements during the process. The Public Sector Directive specifically precludes a contracting authority from amending: the description of the procurement, the part of the technical specifications, which define the minimum requirements and the award criteria. However, it acknowledges the right to make changes to other parts of the specification provided that bidders are given sufficient time to make an adequate response.

The new competitive procedure with negotiations has much in common with the competitive dialogue. What distinguish them is that, in the competitive dialogue the first phase solutions are developed until the contracting authority considers that it has identified one or more bidders capable of meeting its needs and then seeks to formalise positions in a tender, whereas in the new competitive procedure with negotiation tenders are submitted initially, are then subject to negotiation and then resubmitted to finalise positions.

From the perspective of the innovation PPP it needs to be noted that under the competitive procedure with negotiations the subject matter must be clearly and sufficiently precisely identified and described.[80] Consequently, it seems that the procedure should be used in situations where the requirement is well developed and full tender documents can be produced and submitted, but it is felt that there may be advantage in retaining the ability to hold negotiations, if there are certain aspects which bidders raise. Having in mind the level of unknown in the PPP with innovation aspects of subject matter would be described in quite a vague manner making it probably more appropriate for competitive dialogue procedure. Nevertheless, the scope for negotiations is broad, and there is no requirement similar to that of the competitive dialogue procedure providing that the solution should be identified and developed in the negotiation phase.

5.3 Innovation Partnership

The third option for procuring innovation PPP under the rules of the Public Sector Directive is to use a newly introduced procedure called innovation partnership.[81] The innovation partnership must aim at the development of an innovative product, service or works that does not exist on the market and consequently requires research and a long-term partnership for its development, and the subsequent purchase of the resulting supplies, services or works.[82] The basis for the application of the innovation partnership suggests that it is, in fact, a type of a PPP contract, as the basic and most common characteristics of PPPs are the contract's complexity and lengthy duration.

On the one hand, the innovation partnership combines both a pre-commercial and a commercial stage of procurement, as its subject matter is both an innovation development (pre-commercial stage) and a subsequent purchase of the innovation (commercial stage). The latter is under the condition that the innovation corresponds to the performance levels and maximum costs agreed between the contracting authorities and

[80] Article 29(1) of the Public Sector Directive.
[81] Article 31 of the Public Sector Directive.
[82] Article 31 of the Public Sector Directive.

the bidders.[83] Thus, it could be argued that the major challenge of the above mentioned innovation procurement methods such as risks of the conflict of interest or unequal treatment are overcome. On the other hand, the establishment of the innovation partnership may be seen not only as an answer to existing challenges, but also as a new way of realising the objective of a smart, sustainable and inclusive growth that characterises the Europe 2020 strategy.[84]

According to Recital 49 of the Public Sector Directive, the innovation partnership may be applied, if the authority has a need to procure an innovative product, service or work that does not exist on the market and consequently requires research and a long-term partnership for its development. Unfortunately, the wording of Article 31 regarding the innovation partnership is vague and uncertain posing some challenges. One of these is the challenge in assessing which projects may be considered sufficiently innovative. Article 2(22) of the new Public Sector Directive states that the project must result in a 'new or significantly improved' product, service, or method,[85] which is a rather vague wording. Nevertheless, addition of the legal definition of innovation to the Public Sector Directive is an improvement of the preliminary directive proposal,[86] as to some degree it limits the possibilities of abuse of the innovation partnership procedure. In particular, the rules prevent the use of the innovation partnership, when innovation is purely incidental. Nevertheless, the risk of abuse of the innovation partnership is quite small in practice, because of the detail of regulation of the stages after the conclusion of the procurement agreement, and the fact that applicable rules are quite costly, time-consuming and extensive.[87]

There are differences between the original proposal for the directive[88] and the Public Sector Directive itself, particularly in regard to guidance on how the innovation partnership shall be awarded. The proposal was limited to stating that: any bidder may submit a request to participate in response to a contract notice with a view to establishing the innovation partnership, to be awarded in accordance with the rules for a competitive procedure with negotiations.[89] In accordance with the latter, only invited bidders could submit offers, and the award of the innovation partnership contract was to be based solely on the most economically advantageous tender.

The Public Sector Directive elaborates more on the procedure, and includes more details regarding exactly how such a process should be concluded. In the procurement documents, the contracting authority shall identify the need for an innovative product,

---

83 Article 31(2) of the Public Sector Directive.

84 See Commission's Communication Europe 2020 on a strategy for smart, sustainable and inclusive growth, Brussels COM(2010) 2020 final; Melo et al, 'The New Public Procurement Directives and the PPC: Practical Implications of EU Law on the Portuguese Public Procurement Code' (2012) 7 EPPPL 106.

85 Article 2(22) of the Public Sector Directive.

86 Proposal for a Directive of the European Parliament and of the Council on public procurement, Brussels, 20 December 2011 COM(2011) 896 final ('the Proposal').

87 See more on the potential risk that the innovation partnership may bring to the competition in Graells, 'Public Procurement and State Aid: Reopening the Debate?' (2012) 21 PPLR 211.

88 The Proposal.

89 Article 29 of the Proposal.

service or works that cannot be met by purchasing products, services or works already available on the market. It shall indicate which elements of this description define the minimum requirements to be met by all tenders. These minimum requirements are those conditions and characteristics (particularly physical, functional and legal) that any tender should meet or possess in order to allow the contracting authority to award the contract in accordance with the chosen award criteria.[90] The information provided in the procurement documents shall be sufficiently precise to enable bidders to identify the nature and scope of the required solution and decide whether to request to participate in the procedure. It needs to be acknowledged that, unless the needs of the contracting authority are defined broadly enough, there could be a risk of material change to the terms of the contract once entered into, giving rise to a risk of a procurement challenge.[91] Therefore, the first challenge for the contracting authority is to define its needs broadly enough for the procurement process not to be challenged, but precisely enough for the potential bidder to make an informed decision on participation.

Another new addition to the adopted form of the Public Sector Directive is that the contracting authority may decide to set up the innovation partnership with one partner or with several partners conducting separate research and development activities.[92] Also, in the proposal, Member States were given the choice of implementing the innovation partnership procedure in national law or not, whereas now it is mandatory. As well as, the wording of the award criteria is changed from 'most economically advantageous tender' to 'the best price-quality ratio'[93] (the terminology used in the 2014 Public Sector Directive for awards that include non-price elements).

The innovation partnership procedure has two stages: the selection of participants and the bidding phase. In selecting bidders, contracting authorities shall pay particular attention to criteria concerning the bidders' capacity in the field of research and development, and developing innovative solutions.[94] Requirements of the selection criteria may potentially pose some challenges, as they need to be read in conjunction with Article 58(c)(4) of the Public Sector Directive regarding technical and professional ability. As the objective of an innovation partnership is an innovation, it is difficult to prove definitively that the bidder possesses the 'necessary human and technical resourses and experience'.[95] This can only be proved on the basis of similar projects, and if the innovation is ground-breaking, there is a chance that similar projects were not undertaken in the past. To deal with this issue, the experience of the bidder in different innovation processes should be taken into consideration.

It seems appropriate to state that to a large extent, an innovation partnership will need to be established on the basis of very general criteria. At the same time, it is important to add that besides innovative research and development experience, the

---

[90] Recital 45 of the Public Sector Directive.
[91] Article 72 of the Public Sector Directive.
[92] Article 31(1) of the Public Sector Directive.
[93] Article 31(1) of the Public Sector Directive.
[94] Article 30(6) of the Public Sector Directive.
[95] Article 58(c)(4) of the Public Sector Directive.

bidder should also possess the ability to produce and deliver the developed goods/services/works.

5.3.1 'Cherry-picking' in the innovation partnership

The introduction of changes to the technical specification and other procurement documentations after a round of negotiation, during the bidding stage of an innovation partnership, signals a possibility of 'cherry-picking' (a possibility first referred to by the Commission in proposing Directive 2004/18/EC introducing the competitive dialogue procedure).[96] 'Cherry-picking' is a practice of selecting all or some of the aspects of various candidates' solutions and including them as the basis for the final tender of other candidates.[97]

From the contracting authority's perspective, 'cherry-picking' from the proposed solutions could be the most beneficial in developing an innovation. Therefore, the limited confidentiality of the dialogue stage of the competitive dialogue procedure was proposed, by allowing the contracting authority to define its technical specifications for the tender phase, either by including one of the solutions presented by one of the bidders in it, or by combining the presented solutions and asking all the bidders to submit their final tenders on this basis.[98] This proposal was met with strong objections from the private market as this threatened the protection of confidential information as well as the bidder's competitive advantage in proposing an innovative solution.[99] Thus Directive 2004/18/EC limited 'cherry-picking' by requiring agreement from participating tender bidders for such a practice.[100] Nevertheless, since the introduction of the competitive dialogue in 2004 it was identified that in practice this procedure was concluded in different ways, which could be grouped in four models. Authors have identified that in some of these models 'cherry-picking' occurs, where the participants share their solutions and try to influence as much as possible what will be included in the technical specification.[101] That is due to the fact that in such a way these bidders will have a larger chance of winning the tender.

How is this issue treated in the new Public Sector Directive and particularly in the context of the innovation partnerships? Article 31 states that during negotiation, the contracting authority may discuss all aspects (with the exception of the minimum

---

[96] Commission's Proposal for a Directive of the European parliament and of the council on the coordination of procedures for the award of public supply contracts, public service contracts and public works contracts, COM(2000) 275 final.

[97] Arrowsmith and Treumer, 'Competitive Dialogue in EU Law: A Critical Review' in Arrowsmith and Treumer, *Competitive Dialogue in EU Procurement* (Cambridge: Cambridge University Press, 2012), chapter 1, p. 64.

[98] Ibid.

[99] Rubach-Larsen, 'Competitive Dialogue' in Nelsen and Treumer, *The New EU Public Procurement Directives* (Copenhagen: DJØF Publishing, 2005) p. 76.

[100] Article 29 (3) of Directive 2004/18/EC.

[101] Arrowsmith, Treumer, 'Competitive dialogue in EU law: a critical review' pp. 72–8; Telles, *Competitive Dialogues in Portugal and Spain*, PhD thesis 2010 Nottingham University, pp. 260–4; Racca and Casalini, 'Implementation and Application of Competitive Dialogue: Experience in Italy', paper presented at the Global Revolution V conference in Copenhagen, September 2010.

requirements) of the innovation partnership contract with the bidders. However, throughout this discussion, the contracting authority is obliged to treat all participants equally and in particular must not provide information in a discriminatory manner.[102] For example, the contracting authority is not allowed to provide information to one bidder and not to others, and it is prohibited from informing selected bidders about certain tender requirements ahead of time. As well as this, the contracting authority cannot reveal confidential information communicated by a bidder participating in the negotiations to the other participants without the bidder´s agreement. Such an agreement shall not take the form of a general waiver, but shall be given with reference to the intended communication of specific information.[103] At first glance it seems that the situation regarding 'cherry-picking' in the innovation partnership looks very similar to before – prohibited unless given approval by the bidder.

However, in the previous Directive 2004/18/EC besides the confidential information it was prohibited to share the proposed solution with others. This rule needed to be read in conjunction with the old Article 29(6) of Directive 2004/18/EC, which implied that the contracting authority must ask bidders to submit their final tenders on the basis of the solution or solutions that were developed during the dialogue stage.[104]

In the current provisions on the innovation partnership it is stated that in the case of an innovation partnership with several partners, the contracting authority shall not, in accordance with Article 21, reveal to the other partners solutions proposed or other confidential information communicated by a partner in the 'framework of the partnership' without that partner's agreement. This part of the provision is placed in the second part of Article 31, which regulates the structure of the innovation partnership not the bidding process *per se*. The question may be posed; should that provision be read in the context of the bidding stage or the implementation stage of the innovation partnership? If the latter interpretation is correct, potentially some scope for 'cherry-picking' without the agreement of the relevant bidders would be allowed during the bidding stage. This argument is supported by the fact that it is allowed for the contracting authority to change the technical specification as well as other procurement documents after a round of negotiations. In addition, the contracting authority is required to give an adequate amount of time to bidders to allow them to be able to modify and re-submit amended tenders. Also, the provision in Article 31(4) of the Public Sector Directive prohibits sharing confidential information, but not the solutions proposed in the tender. There is no reference similar to those in the competitive dialogue procedure[105] requiring bidders to submit their final tenders on the basis of the solutions presented in the dialogue. Therefore, it could be argued that bidders are allowed to submit their final tenders on the basis of the solution identified and developed during the round of negotiations.

Contrary to the above view, it could be argued that the bidder in such a case would try to classify all aspects of his solution as confidential information, the sharing of which he does not agree to. Therefore, it could be argued that it is only permitted to use

---

[102] Article 31(4) of the Public Sector Directive.
[103] Article 31(4) of the Public Sector Directive.
[104] Treumer, 'Competitive dialogue' (2004) 23 PPLR 181–2.
[105] Article 30(6) of the Public Sector Directive.

parts of solutions which are not classified as confidential information, or which the bidders agree to share, and on which basis the technical specifications or other procurement documents are changed.

A different interpretation would be that all paragraphs need to be read in conjunction with each other and the prohibition on sharing solutions without agreement of the relevant bidders, which cannot be provided in the form of a general waiver, is applicable to the whole process, including bidding.[106] The way that the wording in the Public Sector Directive was 'tightened' from 2004 to 2014 indicates that this is probably the correct interpretation. This may be supported by the fact that both paragraphs (4) and (6) of Article 31 refer to the requirement of the confidentiality established in Article 21. Additionally it is worth noting that contracting authorities will face a difficult task of redesigning the procurement documents and being able to include changes, as they will need to ensure that the confidentiality of specific information is granted and respected.

One way for the contracting authority to share solutions or information could be to include the promise of reimbursement for sharing of the bidders' knowledge in the tender process. This option is clarified in the competitive dialogue procedure,[107] where it is possible to specify prices and payments in return for the participants' consent.[108] In addition, in the innovation partnership procurement documents the contracting authority must define the arrangements applicable to IP rights, where it could be argued the reimbursement could be included.[109] The price should reflect the time invested in the procedure, and the fact that a bidder is willing to share his 'know-how' (and all its future consequences) in the competition for a specific contract.[110]

Until recently it was debated whether, alternatively, the contracting authority could simply set a requirement of information sharing in the contract notice.[111] In Article 31(4) of the new Public Sector Directive it is expressly stated that it is prohibited to reveal confidential information communicated by a candidate or tenderer to the other participants without the tenderer's agreement, which cannot be provided in the form of a general waver – this seems to imply that a waiver cannot be either general, or automatic, since agreement must be given for each item of information.[112] Consequently, it seems that under the Public Sector Directive an establishment of a general entry condition of information sharing is most probably not permitted. It is worth considering what alternatives (if any) would be possible under the new regime. Would it be possible to set as an entry requirement for sharing of specific information that way to escape the prohibition of general character of a waiver? If so what legal qualification would such a requirement have?

---

106 Arrowsmith, *The Law of Public and Utilities Procurement*, 3rd edn. (London: Sweet and Maxwell, 2014) chapter 9.

107 Article 30 (8) of the Public Sector Directive.

108 Arrowsmith and Treumer, 'Competitive Dialogue in EU Law: A Critical Review' pp. 131–5; Arrowsmith, *The Law of Public and Utilities Procurement*, para 8-124.

109 Articles 31 of the Public Sector Directive.

110 Treumer, 'Competitive dialogue', p. 182.

111 Commissions's explanatory note on competitive dialogue in the classic sector, January 2006, p. 7.

112 Arrowsmith, *The Law of Public and Utilities Procurement*, pp. 1057–8.

Some authors have argued that an entry condition of sharing information is to be classified as a selection criterion and therefore is not permitted as this type of selection criterion is not contemplated in the Public Sector Directive.[113] According to Rubach-Larsen, if the acceptance of any type of *'cherry-picking'* assumes a different legal character than that of a condition for participation in the tender, it would be difficult to argue for its validity and consequently that the contracting authority would not have any means to enforce such a condition.[114]

However, it could be argued that the requirement of specific information sharing is not a selection criterion, but simply a procedural rule for participation akin to rules on, for example, the required formats of bids.[115] The ruling in the *Beentjes* case[116] may support this line of argument, which strongly suggests that a tender, which is non-compliant with the stated requirements, may be rejected.[117] However, whether such an approach is allowed under the new 'tightened' regime is unclear. What is more than certain is that requiring information sharing of any kind general or specific might deter bidders from participating.[118]

5.3.2 Structure of the innovation partnership

The innovation partnership is a new type of procurement in that it deals not only with the award procedure, but also with the structure of the innovation partnership and the position after conclusion of the contract.

The innovation partnership must be structured in consecutive stages, following the research process and possibly, but not necessarily up to the manufacturing of the supply or the provision of the work or services, involving intermediate targets to be achieved by the partner and providing for payments in appropriate parts.[119] Based on those targets, the contracting authority may decide to terminate the innovation partnership after each phase or, in the case of an innovation partnership with several partners, to reduce the number of partners by terminating individual contracts, provided that the contracting authority has indicated those possibilities and the conditions for their use in the procurement documents. However, in the Public Sector Directive there is a lack of definition or guidance on how certain terms used should be understood. Firstly, there is lack of explanation of what a 'research process' is. As Apostol correctly points out, it is unclear whether the consecutive stages of the innovation partnerships correspond to the

---

113 Rubach-Larsen, 'Competitive Dialogue' in Nelsen and Treumer, *The New EU Public Procurement Directives*, p. 76; Sołtysińska, *Europejskie Prawo Zamówień Publicznych. Komantarz*, 2nd edn. (Warszawa: Lex Wolters Kluwer, 2012) p. 202; Treumer, 'Competitive dialogue', p. 182.

114 Rubach-Larsen, 'Competitive Dialogue' p. 77.

115 Arrowsmith and Treumer, 'Competitive Dialogue in EU Law: A Critical Review', p. 66.

116 Case C-31/87, *Gebroeders Beentjes BV* [1988] ECR 4635.

117 See Trepte, *Public Procurement in the EC A Practitioner's Guide* 2nd edn. (Oxford: Oxford University Press, 2007) p. 301.

118 Arrowsmith and Treumer, 'Competitive Dialogue in EU Law: A Critical Review', p. 66; Treumer, 'Competitive dialogue' pp. 181–2.

119 Article 31(2) of the Public Sector Directive.

stages of pre-commercial procurement, that is, solution exploration, prototyping and field-testing.[120] It seems as if this matter is left open.

The structure of the innovation partnership requires the contracting authority to (a) define the arrangements applicable to intellectual property rights; and (b) have the right to terminate the innovation partnership after each of the agreed stages, provided that the possibility and conditions for such termination have been specified in the procurement documents.[121] In regards to the IP rights it is not specified by the Public Sector Directive who should own the resulting IP rights.[122] If the supplier should own the IP rights it could be argued that he would be paid twice – first, for development of innovation and secondly, by keeping the IP rights in the end. Therefore such a situation may trigger state aid issues. However, there are high stakes when considering the option of contracting authority ownership of the IP rights (allowing the authority to appoint another partner to supply the outcome of the innovation), as the authority may not be an expert in development, and may risk being liable for issues about which it knows little. Another option in practice is for the contracting authority and the supplier to have a shared ownership of the IP rights; in that way they could share all the risks and benefits.

Lastly, in regard to the structure of the innovation partnership the Public Sector Directive requires that the partnership agreement should include information on how long the contract will last, the scope of the financial remuneration for the private partner and a description of how the progress should be documented.[123] It can be noted that some authors[124] already had identified that the wording of the provision in the original proposal for the new Public Sector Directive was poorly drafted, especially in regard to price and subsequent purchase of the developed goods/works/services. It seems that the adopted version of the Directive did not resolve these issues.

In Article 31(7) it states:

> The estimated value of supplies, services or works shall not be disproportionate in relation to the investment required for their development.

It is not clear why the costs of development should necessarily affect the price of the purchasing contract. These seem to be incorporated into an earlier stage of the innovation partnership. Indeed, Article 31(2) of the Public Sector Directive states:

---

[120] Apostol, 'Pre-commercial Procurement in Support of Innovation: Regulatory Effectiveness?' p. 219.

[121] Article 31(2) & (6) of the Public Sector Directive.

[122] On IP rights see Arrowsmith, *The Law of Public and Utilities Procurement*, vol 1, para 9-143; Gomes, 'The Innovative Innovation Partnerships under the 2014 Public Procurement Directive' (2014) 4 PPLR 2014 (4) 211–18; Graells, *Public Procurement and the EU Competition Rules* (Oxfrod: Hart Publishing 2011), pp. 362–4; Telles, 'Competitive Dialogue: Should Rules be Fine-tuned to Facilitate Innovation?' Paper presented at Public Procurement Days conference in Copenhagen, 10 February 2012.

[123] Article 31(7) of the Public Sector Directive.

[124] Apostol, 'Pre-commercial Procurement in Support of Innovation: Regulatory Effectiveness?', p. 220; Steinicke, 'The Public Procurement Rules and Innovation', p. 271.

> The innovation partnership shall set intermediate targets to be attained by the partners and provide for payment of the remuneration in appropriate instalments.

To argue otherwise one would need to acknowledge that bidders might be unwilling to take part in the innovation partnership, if there is a risk of being excluded from later stages without being proportionally remunerated for the incurred costs.[125] However, Arrowsmith argues that the contracting authority enjoys a discretion in deciding what and when should be paid.[126] She argues that the directive does not necessarily require all the development work to be remunerated directly at full market rates, but that it gives the contracting authority flexibility to remunerate the supplier for the development through later purchases, if the contracting authority will find it most beneficial.[127] It seems that as long as principles of transparency and equal treatment are respected, it should not be of importance whether the private partner would be remunerated at the stage of the development or during the purchasing stage. What is crucial in practice, however, is not to underestimate the costs of the development for large innovation projects. These may be a lot bigger than the actual supply order for one single supplier.

The practical challenge for the contracting authority will be to ensure that it uses the innovation partnership in compliance with competition rules. Thus it must ensure that the contracting authority is purchasing commercial quantities of innovation, the value of which is not disproportionate to the acquired investment for its development, rather than crossing the border into purchasing innovation that is already commercialised (that is, no longer operating as a 'first customer' and motivating innovative solutions).[128] Such a practice would violate the rule that contracting authorities must not use the innovation partnerships in such a way as to prevent, restrict or distort competition.[129]

Another challenge in the innovation partnership may arise when the research is truly novel and innovative and, during the course of the research the PPP parties working in a partnership will potentially discover that the successful bidder is lacking certain expertise to more fully develop or deliver the service that he has promised. In such a situation issues may arise concerning the change in the identity of the winning bidder. Procurement law permits change in consortium members or changes in key subcontractors but only within strict parameters.[130] To escape this risk it could be argued that it would be beneficial to conclude the innovation partnership with several partners, so that another PPP partner could step in and take over the development of the innovation in this scenario, However, the principle of confidentiality may preclude the contracting authority from providing the 'stepping-in' partner with the information that he needs. Further, it is not in any case clear that procurement law allows this kind of 'stepping-in' when it is due to a lack of certain expertise of the primary chosen bidder. It could be argued that the scope of the service provision awarded to this partner is

---

125 Steinicke, 'The Public Procurement Rules and Innovation' p. 271.

126 Arrowsmith, *The Law of Public and Utilities Procurement* pp. 1056–7.

127 Arrowsmith, *The Law of Public and Utilities Procurement* pp. 1056–7.

128 Apostol, 'Pre-commercial Procurement in Support of Innovation: Regulatory Effectiveness?' p. 220.

129 Recital 49 of the Public Sector Directive.

130 See Article 72 of the Public Sector Directive; Treumer, 'Contract Changes and the Duty to Retender Under the New EU Public Procurement Directive' (2014) 23(3) PPLR 148–55.

extended without opening competition, given that this PPP partner was chosen to deliver a 'different' part of the innovation development. Thus it may be necessary to conduct a new procurement procedure.

6. WHAT IS NEW?

Looking at the innovation partnership provisions it may be noticed that for the first time a procurement directive regulates post-procurement, contractual issues relating to a structure of a partnership. However, in regard to the procedural rules for conducting the award process these are similar to the negotiated procedure with prior notice from Directive 2004/18/EC and the competitive procedure with negotiations in the new Public Sector Directive. Therefore, the question is whether it was necessary to establish a whole new procedure.

To answer this question it is worth considering how the procurement of an innovation partnership would look under the previous regime of Directive 2004/18/EC. The procurement rules would often apply. First, they would apply to the procurement of exclusive development of innovation. Secondly, if the development was to be non-exclusive, the classification of the contract would be based on rules applicable to mixed contracts: the contract would include both elements covered by Directive 2004/18/EU (that is, works, supplies and services) and elements not covered by that Directive (that is, establishment of institutionalised partnerships in the form of a semi-public company and development of an innovation). Consequently, one of the available procedures of Directive 2004/18 may need to be applied to that award. It seems that the procedures available here would be, as previously mentioned competitive dialogue – on the basis of the complexity of the contract – and the negotiated procedure with prior notice – in case of services, on the overall pricing grounds or the ground that no specification can be set.

As was pointed out in the previous sections the appropriateness of the competitive dialogue procedure is debatable or at least its use would pose some challenges. However, it seems that if available, the negotiated procedure with a prior notice would allow enough flexibility and discretion for the contracting authority to establish a successful innovation partnership and facilitate innovation. Therefore, as Arrowsmith has argued,[131] it can be contended that from the outset of the procedure everything that can be done under innovation partnership could be done using the negotiated procedure with a prior notice under the Directive 2004/18/EC. However, according to the Commission, the negotiated procedure with prior notice was an exceptional procedure to be applied only in specific and limited circumstances. Consequently, the question may be posed, whether to these exceptional cases could be included all innovative procurements of the type falling under the new innovation partnership procedure, given that the type for which the innovation partnership is used are very rare in practice. It seems reasonable to argue that yes they would, particularly under governance of the old Article 30(1)(b) which points out that negotiated procedure could be used, when the nature of the works, supplies, or services or the risks attaching thereto do not permit

[131] Arrowsmith, *The Law of Public and Utilities Procurement* Vol.1, paras 9-125–9-130.

prior overall pricing. Having in mind the subject matter of the innovation partnership (innovation PPP), it can be seen that the pricing will depend on the level of achieved technological development. In the research and development process there are no guarantees that the innovation goal will be achieved, or if it will be achieved to the level expected by the contracting authority. Therefore, it could be impossible or at least extremely difficult to predict the overall pricing of the contract.

Consequently, if the outset as well as grounds of the use of the innovation partnership could be achieved under the negotiated procedure with prior notice, it is debatable whether it was necessary to introduce a whole new procedure, particularly because the availability of the competitive procedure with negotiation (successor of the negotiated procedure with prior notice) has been extended in the new Public Sector Directive.

7. CONCLUSION

The new Public Sector Directive introduces changes to the procurement regime, which allow wider access to procurement procedures. That includes a revamped version of an old procedure (competitive procedure with negotiation) and introduction of a brand-new 'hybrid solution' (the innovation partnership). For these reasons it seems that procurement of PPP projects and particularly these including innovation has the largest legal support ever. The question is, however, whether the legislator missed the chance of simplifying the procurement regime and instead actually made it more complex and confusing, particularly by introducing the innovation partnership. Yet another procedure, which is complex, time consuming and some of its provisions are defective in places as they introduce uncertainty and confusion. Finally it needs to be noted that the innovation partnership does not introduce anything new to the procurement of PPP projects. At the outset of the procedure everything that can be done under innovation partnership could be done while procuring innovation PPP using the negotiated procedure with a prior notice in the Directive 204/18/2004 and under new competitive procedure with negotiation.

Perhaps a better approach would be to have one flexible procedure allowing among others procurement of innovation PPP projects instead of three similar procedures (competitive dialogue, innovation partnership and competitive procedure with negotiations). Such an approach would add more flexibility to the development of innovation, and at the same time safeguard procurement principles.

9. Strategic EU public procurement and small and medium size enterprises

Spyros Panagopoulos

A. PUBLIC PROCUREMENT IN THE EU: STATE OF PLAY AND STRATEGIC ROLE

Public procurement, the process by which governments and regional and local public authorities or bodies governed by public law purchase products, services and public works, represents large volumes of public spending each year.

According to recent surveys, within the OECD, public procurement accounted for an average of roughly one-third of all general government expenditure in 2011.[1] Furthermore, estimates made by the European Commission put the total value of expenditure by general government and utilities on public works, goods and services in the European Union (EU) in 2011 at €2.406 billion, some 19 per cent of the Union's GDP, and a large part of this purchasing is subject to public procurement rules, either national or EU regimes. Public contracts under the latter – normally purchases above a set of value thresholds set in EU public procurement secondary law – accounted for about €425 billion in 2011 (3.4 per cent of EU GDP), showing a substantial growth over the past decade.[2] Based on these figures, public procurement is of tremendous economic significance for the Union's economy.

Given its economic significance, public procurement has the potential to influence the market in terms of production and consumption trends in favour of environmentally friendly, socially responsible and innovative products and services on a large scale. In recent years, public procurement has been widely recognized as an instrument offering possibilities that go beyond its fundamental objectives, that is, the efficient utilization of public funds when acquiring works, services or goods. Public procurement is now considered as a lever that can assist both the European Union Institutions and the Member States (MS) to develop and implement secondary policies that serve the pursuit of objectives aiming to promote sustainable economic growth targets across the Union.[3] The gradual evolution of this trend led to the development of the doctrine for the strategic use of public procurement.

[1] OECD (2013): Government at a Glance. Available 29 January 2016 at http://dx.doi.org/10.1787/gov_glance-2013-en.

[2] PwC/ICF/GHK/Ecorys (2014): 'SMEs' access to public procurement markets and aggregation of demand in the EU.' Available 29 January 2016 at http://ec.europa.eu/internal_market/publicprocurement/docs/modernising_rules/smes-access-and-aggregation-of-demand_en.pdf.

[3] Bovis, 'The Regulation of Public Procurement as a Key Element of European Economic Law' (1998) 4(2) *European Law Journal* 220–42; McCrudden, *Buying Social Justice. Equality, Government Procurement & Legal Change* (Oxford: Oxford University Press, 2007); Scherrer,

The term 'strategic use of procurement' indicates that procurement (also referred to as sustainable procurement) is about more than just pursuing efficiency in public purchasing and rational use of public funds. Other important interests such as social, environmental and secondary economic considerations can be promoted through public procurement. According to the recent developments in EU public procurement policy and regulation, decision makers and contracting authorities in the various MS are given the opportunity to develop policies and practices that promote the better use of public procurement in support of such wider societal goals. Thus, the MS may use their purchasing power to procure works, goods and services that foster innovation, comply with environmental requirements and goals, while at the same time improving employment, public health and social conditions. However, the objective of the procurement rules is primarily to strengthen the Single Market and the EU's competitiveness.[4]

As has been mentioned above, the strategic use of public procurement is considered as an efficient instrument for meeting other sustainable development objectives. The desire to integrate such other policies into public procurement is already widespread throughout Europe, and the European Commission also attributes considerable importance to this issue as a key measure for implementing the 'EU 2020' strategy.[5] Among these, regional development and the fostering of certain types of industries were not the least. With a focus on public procurement as a means to influence regional development and economic out-comes as well as to foster employment and innovation, the potential role of Small and Medium Enterprises (SMEs) springs to mind.[6]

The aim of this chapter is to improve the understanding of SMEs' involvement in public procurement in the EU. The study provides an overview of EU public procurement policy with regard to the facilitation of a wider SMEs' involvement and a description and analysis of the barriers SMEs face in entering the public procurement market and the available countermeasures.

- Section A gives an introduction of procurement state of play in EU and the strategic aspects of public procurement.
- Section B looks into SMEs' access to the EU public procurement market.
- Section C describes the main barriers that deter SMEs from tendering for public contracts and illustrates the countermeasures available to decision makers and contracting authorities, taking into account the recent development in EU public procurement law and the related best practices.
- In the last part of the study (Section D) the main findings and conclusions are summarized.

Hänlein, Heig and Hofmann (2010): 'Stärkung von Arbeiterinteressen durch soziale Vergabekriterien im öffentlichen Beschaffungswesen' in: Clement, Nowak, Scherrer and Ruß (eds), *Public Governance und Schwache Interessen* (Wiesbaden: VS, 2010), pp. 111–126.

[4] Hettne, 'Strategic Use of Public Procurement–Limits and Opportunities' (2013) 7 *European Policy Analysis* 1.

[5] Available 29 January 2016 at http://eur-lex.europa.eu/LexUriServ/LexUriServ.do?uri=COM:2010:2020:FIN:EN:PDF.

[6] Bovis; McCrudden, *op.cit.*

B. SMES AND PUBLIC PROCUREMENT

According to the standing EU definition,[7] 'Small-Medium Enterprises' are independent enterprises or groups of enterprises with less than 250 employees, and with total annual turnover not exceeding €50 million, or a balance sheet not exceeding €43 million.[8]

SMEs are considered the backbone of the European economy. The approximately 20.8 million SMEs registered in the EU represent 99.8 per cent of all enterprises and produce more than half of European GDP. SMEs represent a vast majority of all enterprises and account for roughly two-thirds of all jobs in the EU.[9] Given the above, SMEs are held as key drivers for European economic growth, competitiveness, innovation, employment and social integration.

Due to their significance, SMEs are also in the prime focus of European public policy, with a host of corresponding initiatives focusing on identifying SMEs' specific challenges and on promoting a favourable business environment for them. Main policy initiatives from recent years include the European Charter for Small Enterprises (2000),[10] the re-launched Lisbon Programme (2005)[11] and the Communication on implementing a 'Modern SME Policy for Growth and Employment' (2005),[12] the European Small Business Act (SBA) (2008),[13] and the European Small Business Portal (2010).[14]

SME policy extends also over the area of public procurement. Creating an even playing field for SMEs, facilitating their wider access to public contracts is an explicit policy objective of the EU. This choice is supported by data collected though a series of surveys on the subject, which produced figures that demonstrate that SMEs are somewhat underrepresented in above-threshold public procurement, compared to their overall weight in the economy.[15]

---

[7] See Commission Recommendation 2003/361/EC. Available 29 January 2016 at http://eur-lex.europa.eu/LexUriServ/LexUriServ.do?uri=OJ:L:2003:124:0036:0041:EN:PDF.

[8] SMEs are further broken down to three nested categories: (a) 'Micro': Less than 10 employees and total annual turnover < €2 million, or a balance sheet < €2 million; (b) 'Small': Less than 50 employees and total annual turnover < €10 million, or a balance sheet < €10 million, (c) 'Medium': Less than 250 employees and total annual turnover < €50 million, or a balance sheet < €43 million.

[9] Data sourced from Eurostat's SBS database: http://ec.europa.eu/eurostat.

[10] See the original document, best practices and additional information at http://ec.europa.eu/growth/smes/business-friendly-environment/small-business-act/.

[11] Communication from the Commission on 'Common Action for Growth and Employment: The Community Lisbon Programme' (COM/2005/330).

[12] Communication from the Commission on 'Implementing the Lisbon Programme: Modern SME Policy for Growth and Employment' (COM/2005/551).

[13] Communication from the Commission 'Think Small First: A Small Business Act for Europe' (COM/2008/394).

[14] http://ec.europa.eu/small-business/index_en.htm.

[15] For surveys focusing on barriers in accessing the public contracts market, see, among others: EIM (2004): The access of SMEs to public procurement contracts, available 29 January 2016 at: http://www.europarl.europa.eu/hearings/20070508/imco/eim_summary_en.pdf; GHK (2007) Evaluation of SMEs' access to public procurement markets in the EU, available online: http://ec.europa.eu/growth/tools-databases/newsroom/cf/itemdetail.cfm?item_id=1135&

Furthermore, looking at the SMEs' position in public tendering, they are faced with specific hindrances and challenges in participation as well as certain disadvantages compared to larger enterprises that make it difficult for them to bid for, and win, public contracts. Thereby, specific limitations SMEs face are strongly related to public tendering practices. Against this background, it comes as no surprise that creating an even playing field for SMEs, where all actors have equal access to information, and enjoy equal opportunities has been a prime goal in the EU agenda, already appearing in the previous Directives of 2004 governing public procurement above EU-thresholds.[16]

Recent years have seen renewed efforts from the European Commission, as well as various MS, in addressing particular barriers preventing SMEs from successfully competing for public contracts in Europe. Related initiatives have been included in the European Small Business Act (and corresponding good practices from similar initiatives). Furthermore, the new Public Sector Procurement Directive 2014/24/EU ('New Classic Directive'), which forms part of the recent legislative package for the reform of the EU Public Procurement Law[17], put significantly more emphasis on this objective.

In the next section we highlight the main hindrances for SME involvement in public procurement and debate on the possible countermeasures in the form of specific initiatives and best practices, taking into account the recent development in EU public procurement policy and regulation.

C. FOSTERING SMES' INVOLVEMENT IN PUBLIC PROCUREMENT: CHALLENGES AND OPPORTUNITIES

While some problems that arise in procurement are common to all enterprises, regardless of their size, some of them seem to affect SMEs more. SMEs, due to their limited size, encounter a rather specific situation regarding public tendering: On the one hand, the volume and diversity of public procurement across the EU means that this specific market segment constitutes an attractive field of business activity, especially during times of recession. On the other hand, their ability to participate in public

lang=en&title=Evaluation-of-SMEs%27-Access-to-Public-Procurement-markets-in-the-EU, and PWC/ICF/GHK/Ecorys (2014), *op.cit.*

[16] Directive 2004/17/EC of the European Parliament and of the Council coordinating the procurement procedures of entities operating in the water, energy, transport and postal services sectors ([2004] OJ L134/1); Directive 2004/18/EC of the European Parliament and of the Council on the coordination of procedures for the award of public works contracts, public supply contracts and public service contracts ([2004] OJ L134/114).

[17] Directive 2014/23/EU of the European Parliament and of the Council of 26 February 2014 on the award of concession contracts ([2014] L134/1); Directive 2014/24/EU of the European Parliament and of the Council of 26 February 2014 on public procurement and repealing Directive 2004/18/EC ([2014] L94/65); Directive 2014/25/EU of the European Parliament and of the Council of 26 February 2014 on procurement by entities operating in the water, energy, transport and postal services sectors and repealing Directive 2004/17/EC ([2014] L94/243).

tenders is restricted by limited resources compared to larger companies. In this context, certain specific problems arise for SMEs.[18]

Within this framework, easier acccss to public procurement is a topic of special interest in the 'Small Business Act'. Several European studies[19] tried to identify the factors influencing SMEs' share in winning public contracts. Public consultations with stakeholders have surfaced the significant difficulties SMEs face in accessing the public procurement market and mapped the typical barriers to successful SMEs participation in public procurement. Building on these findings, the 'European Code of Best Practices'[20] has highlighted and developed a number of practices within the former EU regulatory framework (Directive 2004/18/EC), which optimize chances for the participation of SMEs, ensure equal opportunities and also propose a series of solutions to the aforementioned problems encountered and reported by SMEs.[21]

The issue of fostering an increased participation of SMEs in public procurement across the EU was high on the agenda of the Commission's initiative for modernization of EU public procurement law[22] that led to the adoption of the New Classic Directive in March 2014. The new Directive introduces new rules and provides for administrative practices that are intended to serve this objective. The main barriers to SMEs' involvement and the respective countermeasures, in line with the recent developments in Union law are presented and discussed briefly below:

1. Large Contract Volumes and Broad Capabilities Required

SMEs interested in public contracts often complain that they are excluded from large-scale contracts simply because they do not have the capacity to tender for the full range of the contracts.[23] In fact, the larger the contract volume and value the lesser the likelihood that an SME will win that contract. What is more, if one considers that the centralized procurement in the EU is on the rise and that the New Classic Directive

---

[18] Sarter, Sack and Fuchs, 'Public Procurement as Social Policy? An introduction to social criteria in public procurement in Germany' in Working Paper Series 'Comparative Governance', No.1 (2014) Universität Bielefeld. Available 29 January 2016 at www.unibielefeld.de/soz/powi.

[19] Evaluation of SME Access to Public Procurement Markets in the EU, DG Enterprise and Industry, September 2011. Available 29 January 2016 at http://ec.europa.eu/enterprise/entrepreneurship/public_procurement.htm; Synthesis report of the SBA public consultation closed on 30 March 2008, available online: http://ec.europa.eu/enterprise/entrepreneurship/docs/sba_consultation_report_final.pdf and European Network for SME Research (ENSR) 1999 survey, available online: http://ec.europa.eu/enterprise/enterprise_policy/analysis/doc/ensr_6th_report_en.pdf

[20] European Commission: 'European Code of Best Practices Facilitating Access by SMEs to Public Procurement Contracts' (SEC/2008/2193).

[21] See also: 'SMEs access to public procurement' in *European Charter for Small Enterprises*: 2009, Good Practice Selection.

[22] Green Paper on the modernization of EU public procurement policy: Towards a more efficient European Procurement Market (COM/2011/0015 final).

[23] For large scale tendering constituting a key obstacle for SMEs see among others: Bovis, *op.cit*; Loader and Kim, 'Supporting SMEs through government purchasing activity' (2005) 8(3) *International Journal of Entrepreneurship and Innovation* 17–26; Morand: 'SMEs and public procurement policy' (2003) 8(3) *Review of Economic Design* 301–18.

promotes centralized purchasing activities,[24] one must feel a growing fear that asymmetric treatment against small-medium sized firms will slowly increase over time if not tackled with appropriate instruments.[25]

While the characteristics of a large contract may justify the award to a single contractor, the following possibilities can always be considered in order to overcome difficulties relating to the size of the contracts:

1.1 Sub-dividing contracts into lots

Directive 2014/18/EC allowed contracts to be awarded in the form of separate lots.[26] The sub-division of public purchases into lots clearly facilitates access by SMEs, both quantitatively (the size of the lots may better correspond to the productive capacity of the SME) and qualitatively (the content of the lots may correspond more closely to the specialized sector of the SME). Furthermore, sub-dividing contracts into lots and thereby further opening the way for SMEs to participate, broadens competition, which is beneficial for the contracting authorities, provided that this is appropriate and feasible in the light of the respective works, supplies and services concerned, so it does not impair fair competition and guarantees equal treatment and non-discrimination.

Against this background, the New Classic Directive addresses this issue by explicitly stating that aggregation and centralization of purchases should be carefully monitored in order to avoid excessive concentration of purchasing power and collusion, and to preserve transparency and competition, as well as market access opportunities for SMEs.[27] To that end and in order to enhance competition, provisions are introduced that aim to foster SME participation in the market by promoting the division of contracts into lots. Such division could be done on a quantitative basis, making the size of the individual contracts better correspond to the capacity of SMEs, or on a qualitative basis, in accordance with the different trades and specializations involved, to adapt the content of the individual contracts more closely to the specialized sectors of SMEs or in accordance with different subsequent project phases.[28]

More specifically, contracting authorities are encouraged to divide contracts into separate lots when procuring contracts and may decide the size and subject matter of such lots.[29] As with other provisions in the Directive referring directly to the conduct of contracting authorities, it appears that the effect of this provision is not just to clarify that contracting authorities may do this when permitted by their MS, but that the latter may not prevent contracting authorities from splitting procurements into lots if they wish so.[30]

---

24 Recital 69 Directive 2014/24/EU.

25 Fana and Piga: 'SMEs and Public Contracts, an EU Based Perspective' in *EU Procurement Directives, modernization, growth & innovation- Discussions on the 2011 Proposals for Public Procurement Directives* (Copenhagen: Djøf Publishing. 2012).

26 Article 9(5) Directive 2004/18/EC.

27 Recital 59 Directive 2014/24/EU.

28 Recital 78 Directive 2014/24/EU.

29 Article 46 Directive 2014/24/EU.

30 Arrowsmith, *The Law of Public and Utilities Procurement*, 3rd edn. (London: Sweet & Maxwell, 2012), Vol.1, p. 470, para 6–118.

Secondly, where the procurement of a contract could have been divided into lots but has not been, the contracting authority will be required to provide explanation for their decision not to sub-divide the contract into lots, either in the procurement documents or in the report of the procurement that is required by the Directive.[31] Such reasons could for instance be that the contracting authority finds that such a division could risk restricting competition, or risk rendering the execution of the contract excessively technically difficult or expensive, or that the need to coordinate the different contractors of the lots could seriously risk undermining the proper execution of the contract.[32]

This measure is expected to facilitate increased SME participation in competitions for public contracts by enabling SMEs to bid for a part or parts only of a contract in circumstances where the entire contract would otherwise be beyond their capacity. However, some authors question if such a requirement will lead many authorities to change their practices, and given that many contracts are not suitable for awarding in lots because of the administrative cost and need for integration of different parts, this requirement may impose a disproportionate burden on contracting authorities.[33]

It is also provided that the contracting authority may accept tenders for one, several or all of the lots and/or limit the number of lots that may be awarded to one tenderer, even though the best tenderer for the lot in question has the capabilities and resources to deliver all the lots.[34] This provision shall create more opportunities for SMEs, who may not be able to perform the entire contract.

1.2 Fostering of SMEs' co-operation

In the context of large-scale contracts, joint bidding may be considered apt to provide a meaningful way to foster SMEs' abilities to actively participate in tendering procedures. When a contract covers a range of deliverables that an individual SME might not be able to fulfill on its own, joint bidding of several SMEs might be an option to still be able to participate. Therefore, consortia could provide a means for small firms to enhance their capacity.[35]

Directive 2004/18/EC[36] allowed a tenderer to rely on economic and financial capacities and on technical abilities of other entities, regardless of the legal nature of their links, in order to prove compliance with the level of capacities or abilities required

---

31 Article 46(1) Directive 2014/24/EU: 'Contracting authorities shall, except in respect of contracts whose division has been made mandatory pursuant to paragraph 4 of this Article, provide an indication of the main reasons for their decision not to subdivide into lots, which shall be included in the procurement documents or the individual report referred to in Article 84.'

32 Recital 78 Directive 2014/24/EU.

33 Arrowsmith, *op.cit*, p. 470, para 6-118.

34 Article 46(2) Directive 2014/24/EU: 'Contracting authorities shall indicate, in the contract notice or in the invitation to confirm interest, whether tenders may be submitted for one, for several or for all of the lots. Contracting authorities may, even where tenders may be submitted for several or all lots, limit the number of lots that may be awarded to one tenderer, provided that the maximum number of lots per tenderer is stated in the contract notice or in the invitation to confirm interest […].'

35 Loader and Kim: 'Are public sector procurement models and practices hindering small and medium suppliers?' (2011) 31(4) *Public Money & Management* 287–94.

36 Articles 47(2)(3), 48(3)(4) and 52(1) Directive 2004/18/EC.

by the contracting authority. The tenderer had to prove, nonetheless, that it would have at its disposal the resources necessary for the performance of the contract. In the case of joint bidding, the group of bidders could rely on the capacities of all its members and also on capacities of other entities.

The New Classic Directive includes provisions which clarify the rules on relying on the capacities of third parties or group members.[37] Clarity in terms of facilitating the use of capacities of third parties or the sharing of capacities between bidders who form consortia will stimulate the co-operation between them and thus allow SMEs to enter the market, either at a secondary level (primarily as subcontractors) or through joint-bidding.

In addition, contracting authorities may, subject to national legislation, provide in the contract documents that main contractors must not deal with their subcontractors on less favourable terms than those agreed between the contracting authority and the main contractor.

2. Restricting Market Access through Framework Agreements/Dynamic Purchasing Systems

Contracting authorities frequently use framework agreements improperly or in such a way that it restricts or distorts competition, usually in long lasting agreements with one economic operator. This practice often leads to the establishment of a closed system where no other economic operator may enter for a given period, thus reducing the scope of SMEs' participation in public procurement. In order to promote the proper use of framework agreements, in line with the objective of the SMEs' wider involvement in the public procurement market, the following countermeasures are discussed.

2.1 Making use of the possibility to conclude framework agreements with several economic operators

Directive 2004/18/EC offered contracting authorities the possibility to conclude a framework agreement with several economic operators[38] and to organize 'mini-competitions' between the framework agreement parties as purchasing needs arose for

---

[37] Article 63 Directive 2014/24/EU: 'Reliance on the capacities of other entities: 1. With regard to criteria relating to economic and financial standing as set out pursuant to Article 58(3), and to criteria relating to technical and professional ability as set out pursuant to Article 58(4), an economic operator may, where appropriate and for a particular contract, rely on the capacities of other entities, regardless of the legal nature of the links which it has with them. With regard to criteria relating to the educational and professional qualifications as set out in point (f) of Annex XII Part II, or to the relevant professional experience, economic operators may however only rely on the capacities of other entities where the latter will perform the works or services for which these capacities are required. Where an economic operator wants to rely on the capacities of other entities, it shall prove to the contracting authority that it will have at its disposal the resources necessary, for example, by producing a commitment by those entities to that effect ... Under the same conditions, a group of economic operators as referred to in Article 19(2) may rely on the capacities of participants in the group or of other entities'.

[38] Article 32 Directive 2004/18/EC.

the contracting authority. The same model is adopted in the New Classic Directive.[39] In comparison to a traditional tendering arrangement, where a contracting authority advertises for one supplier to execute the contract, which may favour larger undertakings, the former possibility may give SMEs a chance to compete for contracts which they are in a position to perform. This is particularly the case where a framework agreement will include a high number of economic operators and is itself sub-divided into lots, or where contracts based on such framework agreements are awarded in the form of lots.

In any event, contracting authorities need to ensure, especially by keeping selection criteria proportionate, that SMEs, who often believe that the scope of a framework agreement precludes their involvement and that the bidding procedure is more complex and prolonged, are not deterred from taking part.

Finally, the new Directive explicitly stipulates that the term of a framework agreement shall not exceed four years, save in exceptional cases duly justified, in particular by the subject of the framework agreement. This provision aims to deter market closure by excessively lengthy framework agreements, a practice that denies SMEs the opportunity to explore and infiltrate new markets.

Based on the above, contracting authorities should carefully plan their framework agreements strategy and practice, especially in terms of structure and life-span of the frameworks, with a view of conciliating the advantages of framework procurement (less red tape, more speed, economies of scale and so on) with the need to foster SMEs' participation in the framework agreements.

2.2 Participation in large-scale dynamic purchasing systems

In order to further the possibilities of SMEs to participate in large-scale dynamic purchasing systems (DPS),[40] for instance one that is operated by a central purchasing body, the contracting authority may articulate the system in objectively defined categories of products, works or services. Such categories should be defined by reference to objective factors, which might for instance include the maximum allowable size of specific contracts to be awarded within the category concerned, or a specific geographic area in which specific contracts are to be performed. Where a DPS is divided into categories, the contracting authority should apply selection criteria that are proportionate to the characteristics of the category concerned.[41] The aforementioned measures may strengthen the participation of SMEs in DPS and thus foster their wider involvement in public procurement.

3. Disproportionate Technical and Financial Qualification Levels

Overly demanding requirements concerning technical capacity and financial standing frequently constitute an unjustified obstacle to the involvement of SMEs in public procurement. Setting proportionate selection criteria, as discussed below, can surpass these obstacles:

---

39 Article 33(1), (4) Directive 2014/24/EU.

40 Article 34 Directive 2014/24/EU.

41 Recital 66 Directive 2014/24/EU.

3.1 Keeping selection criteria proportionate

Directive 2004/18/EC stipulated that the criteria on financial standing and on technical abilities need to be related and proportionate to the subject matter of the contract.[42]

Keeping selection criteria proportionate is of core importance for SMEs, since contracting authorities that require overly high financial and technical capacity levels exclude de facto a considerable number of SMEs from participating in tender procedures. Consequently, it is of the utmost importance that the selection criteria are clear, non-discriminatory and proportionate to the kind of procurement involved and its value.

In the case of technical and professional capacity, the contracting authority should opt for selection criteria, which enable it to determine whether a tenderer has the capacity required for the contract in question, rather than the general capacity of tenderers. However, care should be taken that this does not unduly narrow down the field of eligible applicants.

Despite the provisions of Directive 2004/18/EC, the level of the financial capacity requirements set by contracting authorities, especially in terms of minimum turnover, has often been proven prohibitive for SMEs. Acknowledging this persistent problem, the New Classic Directive restricts the contracting authorities from setting disproportionately high turnover requirements, save for cases where this is justified by the special nature of the contract in question.[43] More specifically, contracting authorities are not allowed to require economic operators to demonstrate a minimum annual turnover that would be disproportionate to the subject matter of the contract. This requirement should normally not exceed at the most twice the estimated contract value. However, in duly justified circumstances, it should be possible to apply higher minimum turnover requirements. Such circumstances might relate to the high risks attached to the performance of the contract or the fact that its timely and correct performance is critical, for instance because it constitutes a necessary preliminary for the performance of other contracts.[44]

3.2 Combining forces to meet selection criteria

As already indicated above (item 1.2), the New Classic Directive offers the possibility for economic operators to rely on the economic and financial standing and technical capacity of other undertakings or members of a group, in the case of joint bidding. This

---

[42] Article 44(2) Directive 2004/18/EC.

[43] Recital 83 Directive 2014/24/EU: 'Overly demanding requirements concerning economic and financial capacity frequently constitute an unjustified obstacle to the involvement of SMEs in public procurement. Any such requirements should be related and proportionate to the subject matter of the contract. In particular, contracting authorities should not be allowed to require economic operators to have a minimum turnover that would be disproportionate to the subject-matter of the contract; the requirement should normally not exceed at the most twice the estimated contract value …'

[44] Article 58(3) Directive 2014/24/EU: 'Selection criteria: The minimum yearly turnover that economic operators are required to have shall not exceed two times the estimated contract value, except in duly justified cases such as relating to the special risks attached to the nature of the works, services or supplies …'

possibility can obviously help SMEs cope with high qualification levels and financial requirements.

3.3 Requiring only proportionate financial guarantees

Disproportionate financial guarantees, such as participation or performance bonds, required by contracting authorities constitute an obstacle to the participation of SMEs in public procurement, since the latter face certain restrictions in obtaining such guarantees from competent institutions, due to their low credit rates and limited financing levels. This results in SMEs being unable to participate in many tenders. At the same time, unjustified high requirements in guarantees further restrict SMEs' liquidity and access to financing. The factors clearly undermine the wider SMEs' participation in public procurement.

For the same reasons, unjustified and prolonged retention of the resources (for example, participation bonds) of the economic operators should be avoided and a decrease of financial guarantees according to the progress of the performance of the contract should be encouraged. Besides, contracting authorities might consider not requiring financial guarantees automatically, but on a case-by-case basis, depending on considerations relating to a detailed assessment of the risks inherent to the given contract.

4. Over Emphasis on Price and Costly Industry Standards and Certifications

Another set of obstacles that deter SMEs' wider participation in public procurement across the EU includes, first, the prevailing practice of contracting authorities to emphasize the economic aspects of the bid when awarding the contract and secondly the determination of technical specifications by using costly industry standards and certifications. The European Public Procurement rules include provisions that allow for alternative, more sophisticated practices, which may correspond better to SMEs features and foster their participation in public procurement procedures.

4.1 Award of the contract on the basis of MEAT criterion

Directive 2004/18/EC offered the possibility to award contracts either on the basis of the lowest price or on the basis of the most economically advantageous tender (MEAT).[45] This latter option allowed contracting authorities to take account of various bid elements relating to the subject-matter of the contract, such as quality, technical merit, functional characteristics, running costs, cost-effectiveness, after-sales service and technical assistance and so on. However, contracting authorities would usually award the contract on the basis of the criterion of the lowest price, either because of their focus on maximizing cost savings or because of the complexity of the MEAT method. Even when using MEAT criterion, the price would be sometimes so dominant and quality criteria so fragmented to a large number of sub-criteria, that even large quality differences in certain key areas do not have any influence on the evaluation outcome. This practice is deemed to undermine SME's participation in public procurement, since they in principle are in no position to compete against larger enterprises in terms of pricing, although they may offer goods or services of better quality.

---

[45] Article 53(1) Directive 2004/18/EC.

The New Classic Directive allows for more scope for promoting qualitative solutions by rendering mandatory the award of public contracts on the basis of the economically most advantageous tender thus allowing for more flexibility when assessing the financial and qualitative aspects of the bid.[46] Furthermore, the provisions of the Directive on award criteria clarify and expand the definition of the most economically advantageous tender from the point of view of the contracting authority, which shall be identified on the basis of the price or cost, using a cost-effectiveness approach, and may include the best price-quality ratio, which shall be assessed on the basis of criteria, including qualitative, environmental and/or social aspects, linked to the subject-matter of the public contract in question (for example, quality, technical merit, social, environmental and innovative features, after sales technical support, delivery time and conditions and so on). The cost element may also take the form of a fixed price or cost on the basis of which economic operators will compete on quality criteria only.[47] On the other hand, the contract award decision shall not be based on non-cost criteria only. Qualitative criteria shall always be accompanied by a cost criterion that could, at the choice of the contracting authority, be either the price or a cost-effectiveness approach such as life cycle costing.[48]

This approach is closely related to the 'value for money' concept, which is defined as 'the optimum combination of whole life costs and quality' and gives contracting authorities the opportunity to evaluate not only the direct costs of a purchase, but also its life-cycle costs.[49] At the same time, the said approach gives economic operators an incentive to provide real added value to the contracting authority and has a positive impact on innovation, as it represents an incentive for economic operators to develop better and sustainable products or services. This is particularly important for the SME sector, which is a source of innovations and important R&D activities.

At first glance, the awarding of contracts on the basis either of the cost-effectiveness rather than the lowest price or on the basis of the best price/quality ratio, including the competition only on quality criteria against a fixed price/cost may benefit SMEs, which sometimes struggle to compete on price alone against larger, more established enterprises. The new, more refined approach on bid evaluation and award in the New Classic Directive is expected to give SMEs a better chance to place competitive bids that will score high in the evaluation matrix due to their superior qualitative elements or efficient life-cycle costing. However, although this provision could encourage more sustainable and better value procurement in the long term, it should be noted that

---

46 Article 67(1) Directive 2014/24/EU.

47 Article 67(2) Directive 2014/24/EU.

48 Recital 92 Directive 2014/24/EU.

49 Article 68 Directive 2014/24/EU: 'Life-cycle costing:

> 1. Life-cycle costing shall to the extent relevant cover parts or all of the following costs over the life cycle of a product, service or works: (a) costs, borne by the contracting authority or other users, such as: (i) costs relating to acquisition, (ii) costs of use, such as consumption of energy and other resources, (iii) maintenance costs, (iv) end of life costs, such as collection and recycling costs. (b) Costs imputed to environmental externalities linked to the product, service or works during its life cycle, provided their monetary value can be determined and verified; such costs may include the cost of emissions of greenhouse gases and of other pollutant emissions and other climate change mitigation costs …'

contracting authorities may mitigate the advantageous approach by insisting on applying the most economically advantageous tender criterion considering price as the sole or decisive criterion for the award of the contract. In order to avoid this risk, the new Directive stipulates that MS may provide that contracting authorities may not use price only or cost only as the sole award criterion or restrict their use to certain categories of contracting authorities or certain types of contracts.[50]

4.2 Fostering of innovation by defining technical specifications in terms of performance or functional requirements and allowing variants

SMEs often face difficulties in meeting the technical specifications defined in the tender documents, by reference to standards, since the obtaining of these certifications requires considerable investment in time and money. While contracting authorities should dispose of full freedom to procure the goods and services that best meet their needs, they should take care not to limit the possibilities of participation by enterprises that provide new, innovative solutions, which may offer better value for money.

The New Classic Directive explicitly states that the technical specifications drawn up by public purchasers need to allow public procurement to be opened up to competition. To this end, it must be possible to submit tenders that reflect the diversity of technical solutions according to the nature and the specific characteristics of the subject matter of the contract in question. Accordingly, it must be possible to draw up the technical specifications in terms of functional performance and requirements, and, where reference is made to the European standard or, in the absence thereof, to the national standard, tenders based on equivalent arrangements must be considered by contracting authorities.[51] This output-oriented approach, adopted by the New Classic Directive,[52] enables contracting authorities to concentrate on their actual purchasing needs and it also grants tenderers the freedom to develop new, innovative goods or services which might better correspond to the actual needs of the contracting authority.

In addition, the new Directive, acknowledging the importance of innovation, requires the MS to encourage the contracting authorities to allow variants as often as possible.[53]

---

50 Article 67(2) Directive 2014/24/EU.

51 Recital 74 Directive 2014/24/EU.

52 Article 42(3) Directive 2014/24/EU: '3. Without prejudice to mandatory national technical rules, to the extent that they are compatible with Union law, the technical specifications shall be formulated in one of the following ways:

> (a) In terms of performance or functional requirements, including environmental characteristics, provided that the parameters are sufficiently precise to allow tenderers to determine the subject-matter of the contract and to allow contracting authorities to award the contract;
> (b) …
> (c) In terms of performance or functional requirements as referred to in point (a), with reference to the technical specifications referred to in point (b) as a means of presuming conformity with such performance or functional requirements;
> (d) By reference to the technical specifications referred to in point (b) for certain characteristics, and by reference to the performance or functional requirements referred to in point (a) for other characteristics.'

53 Recital 48 Directive 2014/24/EU.

The possibility for variants existed also in Directive 2004/18/EC.[54] Accordingly, the New Classic Directive explicitly provides for contracting authorities to allow tenderers to submit variants.[55] As contracting authorities might not always have an up-to-date knowledge of what goods and services the market may offer, the authorization of variants may also allow tenderers, especially SMEs, to come forward with innovative solutions. In this case, contracting authorities making use of this possibility have to state in the contract documents what are the minimum requirements to be met by the variants and any specific requirements regarding how to present them.

The efficient utilization of the aforementioned tools, that is, opting for output specification and allowing variants, is reasonably expected to foster the participation in public procurement of SMEs and, in particular, innovative SMEs who might face difficulties in meeting the technical specifications approved by the recognized standards bodies, but who produce supplies, provide services or use materials, methods or techniques of high technical and/or environmental value and are able to meet the performance or functional requirements laid down by the contracting authorities by alternatives means.

5. Insufficient Information about Opportunities

Large companies use in general more information sources, as compared to smaller ones, which face more difficulties in obtaining information, due to the fact that they are unable to allocate sufficient resources to information collection. Ensuring early and easy access to all the relevant information on business opportunities in public procurement is of key importance for SMEs.

5.1 Improvements offered by widening the use of e-procurement

The New Classic Directive stipulates that public authorities must ensure they provide, free of charge, full electronic access to the complete set of procurement documentation related to every contract. Electronic means of information and communication can greatly simplify the publication of contracts, increase the efficiency and transparency of procurement processes, promote competition and greatly enhance SMEs' possibilities to participate in procurement procedures across the internal market.

E-procurement offers free access to contract notices and tender documentation reduces the costs of participating in public tenders and enables quick communication (for example, downloading the tender documents without incurring copying or mailing costs). Moreover, SMEs can more easily identify tenders relevant for them and thus expand their business opportunities.

For that purpose, publication of procurement notices in electronic form on the Tenders Electronic Daily (TED) database[56] and national public procurement portals, electronic availability of the procurement documents and communication by electronic means at all stages of the procedure, including the electronic transmission of requests

[54] Article 24 Directive 2004/18/EC.

[55] Article 45(1) Directive 2014/24/EU: '1. Contracting authorities may authorise or require tenderers to submit variants. …'

[56] http://ted.europa.eu/TED/main/HomePage.do.

for participation and, in particular, the transmission of the tenders will be made mandatory by April 2016.[57]

Additionally, the obligation to use the Common Procurement Vocabulary (CPV)[58] for any references to nomenclatures in the context of public procurement[59] is expected to improve the traceability and facilitate the easier detection of business opportunities.

The extensive use of electronic communication means should improve access to public procurement, especially for SMEs. Recent Eurostat figures show that nearly 99 per cent of SMEs have access to the Internet. Moving towards e-procurement therefore means SMEs will better access the whole EU public procurement market and hence obtain significant opportunities to pursue a larger market share by participating in more tenders.[60]

5.2 Information centers

Personalized assistance can be very helpful for SMEs. At European level, SMEs can enjoy easy access to advice and support from the members of the Enterprise Europe Network (EEN).[61]

The Enterprise Europe Network already: (i) provides services to SMEs to participate in tenders across borders; (ii) organizes matchmaking events for private enterprises either through visits or during leading fairs; and (iii) has a – rarely used – mandate to assist public enterprises in their innovation efforts. These are the basic elements upon which additional activities could be built at low cost. Opening relevant existing events for public buyers, specifically approaching them for participation and targeting them with new services/event types might significantly increase the knowledge about existing and upcoming innovative solutions for the procurers and give information on demand to the suppliers.

Such initiatives with a view to enhancing the flow of information on public procurement opportunities, creating new markets and networking between public and private stakeholders, foster substantially the infiltration of the public procurement markets by SMEs that were hesitant or unable to get actively involved.

---

57 Recital 52 Directive 2014/24/EU: 'Electronic means of information and communication can greatly simplify the publication of contracts and increase the efficiency and transparency of procurement processes. They should become the standard means of communication and information exchange in procurement procedures, as they greatly enhance the possibilities of economic operators to participate in procurement procedures across the internal market. For that purpose, transmission of notices in electronic form, electronic availability of the procurement documents and – after a transition period of 30 months – fully electronic communication, meaning communication by electronic means at all stages of the procedure, including the transmission of requests for participation and, in particular, the transmission of the tenders (electronic submission) should be made mandatory. Member States and contracting authorities should remain free to go further if they so wish. …'

58 Regulation (EC) No 2195/2002 of the European Parliament and of the Council of 5 November 2002 on the Common Procurement Vocabulary (CPV) ([2002] L340/1).

59 Article 23(1) Directive 2014/24/EU.

60 http://europa.eu/rapid/press-release_MEMO-14-20_en.htm.

61 Detailed information on EEN's SME orientated activities and services available 29 January 2016 at http://een.ec.europa.eu/

6. Lack of Knowledge about Procedures/Limited Tendering Skills and Experience

Contracting authorities usually lack training and guidance on how to design an award procedure in a way that ensures that SMEs can participate on an equal footing with large enterprises. The lack of sufficient, relevant and clear information means that it is not easy for economic operators to understand the needs of the contracting authority and to formulate the right bid. What is more, SMEs usually do not dispose of specialized administrative capacities and are not well acquainted with public procurement language and procedures.

Improving the quality and understanding of the information provided needs to be taken into account at the drawing up of their tenders, and constitutes a key measure in order to facilitate SMEs' successful participation in award procedures. Investing in guidance and training of all stakeholders could meet these objectives. For example:

6.1 Training and guidance for contracting authorities

Issues that could usefully be dealt with in this context might include not only how to apply the existing legal framework in a way which ensures that SMEs can participate in award procedures on an equal footing with big businesses, but also management issues, such as how to deal with more complex bidding procedures and contractual relations where contracts or framework agreements are sub-divided into lots.

6.2 Training and guidance for SMEs

The majority of MS organize conferences, seminars and training sessions, provide guidelines and other support materials for tenderers and maintain helpdesk services. However, there appears to be a need for further promotion and development of ad hoc guidance and training tailored to the specific needs of SMEs regarding their participation in public procurement procedures.

The need for developing more targeted and consistent guidance is explicitly acknowledged by the New Classic Directive[62] that obliges the MS to ensure that:

(i) Information and guidance on the interpretation and application of the EU public procurement law is available free of charge to assist contracting authorities and economic operators, in particular SMEs, in correctly applying the Union public procurement rules; and
(ii) Support is available to contracting authorities with regard to planning and carrying out procurement procedures.

7. Insufficient Time to Prepare Bids

SMEs typically have limited, if any, specific administrative capacity to deal with the preparation of bidding documents in a timely fashion. Contracting authorities need to be aware of this fact when setting time limits, by allowing sufficient time to draw up tenders, so that they can maintain the broadest possible basis for SMEs' participation.

---

62 Article 83(4) Directive 2014/24/EU.

Directive 2004/18/EC offered the possibility to use prior information notices (PIN) on a voluntary basis in order to allow potential tenderers to prepare themselves to bid in time for the contracts advertised.[63] This is particularly important in the case of large and complex contracts, where SMEs might need time to find partners for joint bidding.

When contracting authorities make use of the possibility to reduce time-limits for the submission of bids or applications, following the publication of a PIN, they should take care to ensure that the prior information notice is sufficiently detailed to actually allow economic operators to prepare for the forthcoming tender.

The New Classic Directive has also introduced a provision that encourages contracting authorities to set the appropriate time limits allowing sufficient time for the preparation of the tenders.[64] Furthermore, it provides contracting authorities with the possibility to publish PINs, in order to prepare the market for future procurements and by giving economic operators enough time to prepare for bidding.[65]

8. Insufficient Information Exchange and Poor Feedback

Facilitating dialogue between procurers and vendors is often seen as a key factor in implementing successful public procurement schemes and fosters transparency and visibility of the procedures. However, this approach has not yet been incorporated in the contracting authorities' purchasing culture to the desired extent. Moreover, poor understanding of crucial elements of the contract to be procured at an early stage, prior to the commencement of the procurement process, represents a disadvantage for any kind of tenderer but especially for SMEs that try to enter new markets and need time to adapt their operational and pricing processes in order to have a fair chance in winning the tender. In addition, insufficient exchange of information during the procurement process often leads to elimination of tenderers due to their misunderstanding of the tender conditions, a problem that mostly affects SMEs.

Furthermore, contracting authorities do not always provide tenderers with adequate information about the rejection of the bids. The understanding of the reasons for their elimination from the tender process is vital for the SMEs' effective adaptation and performance improvement that will grant them better chances of winning in subsequent tenders.

In order to overcome the aforementioned obstacles, the following countermeasures are available:

8.1 Preliminary market consultations

The idea of exchange of views between purchasers and economic operators was hesitantly approached in Directive 2004/18/EC that accepted the use of a 'technical

---

[63] Article 35(1) Directive 2004/18/EC.

[64] Article 47(1) Directive 2014/24/EU: 'Setting time limits: 1. When fixing the time limits for the receipt of tenders and requests to participate, contracting authorities shall take account of the complexity of the contract and the time required for drawing up tenders, without prejudice to the minimum time limits set out in Articles 27 to 31 …'

[65] Article 48(1) Directive 2014/24/EU: 'Contracting authorities may make known their intentions of planned procurements through the publication of a prior information notice …'

dialogue' between the buyer and the market.[66] The New Classic Directive for the first time introduces specific provisions that make progress in this field,[67] which are expected to broaden the room for preliminary consultations with a view to predetermining certain characteristics of the contract and clarifying key aspects of the procurement procedure prior to its commencement.

Early engagement with the market is considered as an essential component of intelligent procurement as it enables the procurer to understand and identify what is available and whether alternative solutions exist. The new rules on preliminary market consultations enable contracting authorities to launch market sounding prior to tendering with a view to determining their exact needs, defining the technical specifications, mapping the competitive landscape and setting up the conditions for the award and performance of the contract in the tender documents. At the same time, it facilitates the better understanding of the key elements of the forthcoming contract by the private sector stakeholders, thus allowing them to draft compliant and competitive tenders. Additionally, this procedure allows the contracting authorities to inform the economic operators of their short/long term procurement plans and requirements and reassure the market's response to the relevant procurement procedures. What is more, the dialogue with the market may prove to be useful in cases where the contracting authorities are unable to define the means of satisfying their needs or assessing what the market can offer in terms of technical solutions. It should be noted, however, that such initial consultation with the market shall safeguard the principles of equal treatment and non-discrimination of economic operators and should not have the effect of precluding or distorting competition. To ensure transparency, any information provided by the buyer during this process should be circulated to any potential tenderer.

8.2 Questions and answers on the tender procedure

Clear communication and exchange of sufficient information during the tendering phase with bidders and responding to specific questions raised by them is essential in order for them to understand the requirements and to draw up appropriate and potentially successful tenders. In order to address this need, the New Classic Directive obliges the contracting authorities to supply all tenderers with additional information relating to the specifications and any supporting documents in good time.[68] Moreover, unclear or insufficient information on the tendering process frequently leads to the elimination of bids on formal errors or minor omissions or deviations from the conditions set in the tender documents. In order to tackle this problem, the new Directive introduces a mechanism for rectifying these types of bid defects, by allowing

[66] Recital 8 Directive 2004/18/EC.

[67] Article 40 Directive 2014/24/EU: 'Before launching a procurement procedure, contracting authorities may conduct market consultations with a view to preparing the procurement and informing economic operators of their procurement plans and requirements.

For this purpose, contracting authorities may for example seek or accept advice from independent experts or authorities or from market participants. That advice may be used in the planning and conduct of the procurement procedure, provided that such advice does not have the effect of distorting competition and does not result in a violation of the principles of non-discrimination and transparency.'

[68] Article 53(2) Directive 2014/24/EU.

for the bidder to supplement, clarify or complete the relevant information or documentation within an appropriate time limit, provided that the principles of equal treatment and transparency are preserved.[69] These rules are expected to significantly improve both the compliance of SMEs with the conditions set in the tender documents as well as the conformity and quality of their bids.

8.3 Post award debriefing

In addition to ensuring easy access to all the relevant information on business opportunities, giving feedback to economic operators who have participated in an award procedure is also essential. In order to prepare for future bids, it is very helpful for a tenderer to see which aspects of its bid were considered strong by the contracting authority and what were the weaknesses. This is especially important for SMEs, which try to enter new segments of the market and need to evolve their practices in order to meet the specific requirements.

The New Classic Directive explicitly stipulates that on request from a candidate or tenderer, the contracting authority shall inform the former of the reasons for the rejection of its application/tender, of the characteristics and relative advantages of the tender selected as well as the name of the successful tenderer as well as of the conduct and progress of negotiations and dialogue with tenderers. Such post award debriefing constitutes a very useful tool that can facilitate transparency and cultivate cooperation between contracting authorities and economic operators, by improving the understanding of the unsuccessful bidders regarding the reasons why their tender was not selected.[70]

9. Excessive Administrative Burden

The production and gathering of bulky paperwork when compiling their tender dossiers is a rather time-consuming task that raises bidding cost. Thus the excessive administrative burden is among the most common complaints voiced by SMEs. Therefore, as SMEs normally do not have large and specialized administrative capacities and plenty resources, keeping administrative requirements to a minimum is essential. In that respect, the following considerations may be taken into account in order to alleviate the administrative burden.

Directive 2004/18/EC provided that contracts shall be awarded after the suitability of economic operators has been checked by contracting authorities against the personal situation of the candidates or tenderers, their capability to pursue the professional activity concerned, and their technical or professional capacities.[71]

---

[69] Article 56(3) Directive 2014/24/EU: 'General principles: Where information or documentation to be submitted by economic operators is or appears to be incomplete or erroneous or where specific documents are missing, contracting authorities may, unless otherwise provided by the national law implementing this Directive, request the economic operators concerned to submit, supplement, clarify or complete the relevant information or documentation within an appropriate time limit, provided that such requests are made in full compliance with the principles of equal treatment and transparency …'

[70] Article 55 Directive 2014/24/EU.

[71] Article 44 Directive 2004/18/EC.

As regards verification of the suitability of candidates and tenderers to pursue the professional activity concerned, and examination of their technical or professional capacities, the Directive also set limits within which these verifications were carried out. However, in all cases, it was up to the MS to specify, in accordance with their national law, the implementing conditions of those exclusion and suitability checks and to decide on the details of the documentary evidence to be submitted by candidates and tenderers in the context of public procurement procedures, including on how and when such documentary evidence should be submitted to the contracting authorities before the contract award.

Within this framework, the 'European Code of Best Practices Facilitating Access by SMEs to Public Procurement Contracts'[72] has encouraged MS to invite candidates or tenderers to 'self-declare' on their honour that they fulfill each and every condition required and only the tenderer who has placed the winning bid shall be required to issue all the relevant original certificates within a fixed time-limit. However, for such a formula to ensure that the contract will only go to a suitable tenderer, national rules must provide for an effective, proportionate and dissuasive penalty system to be applied in all cases where the tenderer who made the best offer is ultimately unable to furnish the relevant documentary evidence before the deadline or, worse, is found not to fulfil one or more of the conditions required from suitable candidates or tenderers. In any event, if the tenderer who made the best offer fails to produce the relevant documentary evidence, the contract would not be awarded to him, but could be awarded to the tenderer who submitted the next best offer, if this latter possibility was mentioned in the tender documents.

Besides, contracting authorities may usefully be allowed to waive the obligation for candidates or tenderers to submit part or all of the documentary evidence required if such evidence has already been submitted to them recently within the framework of another procurement procedure and provided that the relevant documents were issued within a fixed reasonable time period and are still valid. In such cases, the candidate or tenderer concerned could be invited to declare on his honor that the documentary evidence has already been provided in a previous procurement procedure and to confirm that there has been no change in the situation. In this case, too, MS must provide for an effective, proportionate and dissuasive penalty regime to be applied in cases where the tenderer who made the best offer was ultimately shown not to have provided the relevant documentary evidence.

In addition, short and simple standardized forms and certificates, elimination of the requirement to submit official translations and documents already submitted in the past, retrieval of documents kept by public services or agencies directly by the contracting authorities, electronic submission of tenders and use of electronic tools, will definitely help SMEs to provide the relevant information in less time and at a lower cost.

Inspired by the aforementioned recommendations, the New Classic Directive acknowledges that all bidders, including SMEs, consider as a major obstacle to their participation in the EU public procurement procedures the overwhelming administrative burdens deriving from the need to produce a substantial number of certificates or

72 Ibid.

other documents related to exclusion and selection criteria.[73] Therefore, the new Directive introduces measures aimed at simplifying tender participation and reducing the administrative burden associated with the tendering procedure.

In particular, the requirement of the bidders to provide full documentation that they are eligible to perform the given contract at the time of the bid submission is eliminated, and is replaced by a standard form of self-declaration, the 'European Single Procurement Document' (ESPD).[74] Therefore, at the time of submission of applications/tenders, contracting authorities will be required to accept a completed ESPD from each bidder as *prima facie* evidence of satisfaction of the core selection criteria and confirmation that he does not fall within any of the mandatory grounds for exclusion. The ESPD should also provide the relevant information in respect of entities on whose capacities a bidder relies, so that the verification of the information regarding such entities can be carried out together with and on the same conditions as the verification in respect of the main bidder.[75]

Subsequently, only the winning bidder will be required to submit the full set of the formal evidence to verify the information provided in the ESPD. However, the contracting authority may ask tenderers and candidates at any moment during the procedure to submit all or part of the supporting documents where this is necessary to ensure the proper conduct of the procedure.[76]

Moreover, with a view to further reducing administrative burden, the new Directive relieves the winning bidder from the obligation to produce supporting documents and other documentary evidence, in cases when the contracting authority already possesses the evidence required or has the possibility to obtain the certificates or the relevant information directly by accessing a national database in any Member State that is

---

73 Recital 84 Directive 2014/24/EU.

74 According to Article 59(2) Directive 2014/24/EU, the ESPD shall be provided exclusively in electronic form based on a standard form issued by the Commission by means of implementing acts adopted in accordance with Article 89(3).

75 Article 59(1) Directive 2014/24/EU: 'European Single Public Procurement Document: At the time of submission of requests to participate or of tenders, contracting authorities shall accept the European Single Procurement Document (ESPD), consisting of an updated self-declaration as preliminary evidence in replacement of certificates issued by public authorities or third parties confirming that the relevant economic operator fulfills the following conditions: (a) it is not in one of the situations referred to in Article 57 in which economic operators shall or may be excluded; (b) it meets the relevant selection criteria that have been set out pursuant to Article 58; (c) where applicable, it fulfills the objective rules and criteria that have been set out pursuant to Article 65.

Where the economic operator relies on the capacities of other entities pursuant to Article 63, the ESPD shall also contain the information referred to in the first subparagraph of this paragraph in respect of such entities.

The ESPD shall consist of a formal statement by the economic operator that the relevant ground for exclusion does not apply and/or that the relevant selection criterion is fulfilled and shall provide the relevant information as required by the contracting authority. The ESPD shall further identify the public authority or third party responsible for establishing the supporting documents and contain a formal statement to the effect that the economic operator will be able, upon request and without delay, to provide those supporting documents …'

76 Article 59(4) Directive 2014/24/EU.

available free of charge, such as a national procurement register, a virtual company dossier, an electronic document storage system or a prequalification system.[77]

Finally, in order to further simplify the handling of evidence, MS are required to keep up to date with the e-Certis database established by the European Commission,[78] the aim of which is to facilitate the exchange of certificates and other documentary evidence frequently required by contracting authorities in different MS.[79] It should be noted, however, that recourse to e-Certis will be made mandatory at a later stage.[80]

The aforementioned measures are expected to reduce significantly the administrative burden caused by participation requirements and may result in considerable simplification to the benefit of both contracting authorities and bidders, especially SMEs, that are most affected by complex and cumbersome administrative requirements.

10. Late Payments/Risk of No Payment

Long payment terms (as set out in contracts) and delays in payments (not meeting contractual obligations for deadlines) are two frequent problems encountered in public procurement that can have severe consequences especially for SMEs, taking into account their lower liquidity levels and restricted financing capability.[81] In particular, the risks and market distortions created by extended payment periods jeopardize the ability of these enterprises to take advantage of the Single Market opportunities. Furthermore, long payment periods strain cash flow and fuel uncertainty. They prevent SMEs from adequate and timely investment in research and development, technology and the labour force. As a result, long payment periods impede the development, competitiveness and profitability of SMEs, and even endanger their survival. Thus, ensuring that payments are made on time is of the utmost importance for the well operation of SMEs and their involvement in public procurement. The above thoughts were confirmed by the responses of several stakeholders in recent surveys. Based on these findings, the EU adopted the following countermeasures:

---

[77] Article 59(5) Directive 2014/24/EU.

[78] e-Certis database is accessible through the EUROPA server at http://ec.europa.eu/markt/ecertis/login.do

[79] Article 61 Directive 2014/24/EU: 'Online repository of certificates (e-Certis):

1. With a view to facilitating cross-border tendering, Member States shall ensure that the information concerning certificates and other forms of documentary evidence introduced in e-Certis established by the Commission is constantly kept up-to-date.
2. Contracting authorities shall have recourse to e-Certis and shall require primarily such types of certificates or forms of documentary evidence that are covered by e-Certis.
3. The Commission shall make available all language versions of the ESPD in e-Certis'.

[80] Recital 87 Directive 2014/24/EU.

[81] OECD SME (2002) in: 'Successes and Challenges for SMEs' (2003), the SME Union observes that payment delays caused by big companies are twice as frequent as those caused by SMEs.

10.1 New rules on late payment

The continuing irregularities in the form of delays of payment or no payments have triggered the review of the provisions of Directive 2000/35/EC.[82] The evaluation of the effectiveness of the EU legislation on late payments revealed that there is room for improvements to the aforementioned Directive, as some of its provisions do not match its ambitious goals. For instance, some provisions would benefit from being strengthened, penalties for late payments should constitute real deterrents, reimbursable recovery costs should be clearly defined and payment periods should be fixed.[83]

The response of the Commission came with the adoption of the new Directive 2011/7/EU[84] on combating late payment in commercial transactions, which strengthens businesses' rights to prompt payment.

The main provisions of the Directive include:

(i) Harmonization of period for payment by public authorities to businesses: Public authorities have to pay for the goods and services that they procure within 30 days or, in very exceptional circumstances, within 60 days.
(ii) Businesses are automatically entitled to claim interest for late payment and are also able to obtain a minimum fixed amount of €40 as a compensation for recovery costs. They can claim compensation for all remaining reasonable recovery costs.
(iii) The statutory interest rate for late payment in the MS should be increased to at least 8 percentage points above the ECB's reference.

In addition, the Commission has adopted further administrative measures that aim at assisting SMEs in receiving timely payments, such as (i) the 'Late Payment Help-Desk', that informs businesses about the implementation and application of the late payment Directive in the 28 MS, allows citizens to share information concerning the application of the Directive in their own countries, and to send any evidence of problems experienced when applying the rights conferred by the Directive;[85] and (ii) a dedicated Guide that is intended to support SMEs in enforcing cross-border claims by describing measures an entrepreneur can take from as early as the point of submitting a quotation up to the point of initiating European proceedings to prevent and avoid bad debt and measures available to an entrepreneur should an actual case of bad debt come about.[86]

---

[82] Directive 2000/35/EC of the European Parliament and of the Council of 29.6.2000 on combating late payment in commercial transactions ([2000] OJ L200/35).

[83] Hoche-Demolin, Brulard and Barthelemy (2006): 'Study on the effectiveness of EC legislation on combating late payment', p. 14. Available online: http://ec.europa.eu/enterprise/policies/single-market-goods/files/late_payments/doc/finalreport_en.pdf

[84] Directive 2011/7/EU of the European Parliament and of the Council of 16 February 2011 on combating late payment in commercial transactions (L 48/1/23.2.2011).

[85] The Late payments Help-Desk can be contacted at ENTR-LATE-PAY-E-DESK@ec.europa.eu.

[86] European Commission, DG Enterprise and Industry: 'Guide to cross-border credit and claims management: Supporting SMEs in enforcing cross-border claims' (EU Publications Office, 2013).

10.2 Direct payments to subcontractors

The New Classic Directive introduces a new option for MS that may facilitate further reduction of late-payment occurrences, by providing for direct payments to subcontractors. This development is especially important for SMEs, which frequently get assignments at the secondary public procurement market as subcontractors to main contractors that are larger companies.

Subcontractors are highly vulnerable to delayed payments, as they may perform the assigned task on schedule and according to specification and yet be subject to slow payment for completed assignments. Taking into account these difficulties that subcontractors encounter, and in order to prevent bidders from suffering of delayed payments and insolvency, the new Directive gives MS the option to provide in the national transposition law that contracting authorities pay subcontractors directly where the subcontractor requests so[87] or even to require contracting authorities to pay subcontractors directly without them having to make a request.[88] Direct payment is subject to the right of the main contractor to object to any undue payments.

The effective transposition and practical application of the aforementioned rules of Directives 2011/7/EU and 2014/24/EU by the MS is expected to streamline the cash flow to subcontractors and thus encourage SMEs to participate in the secondary public procurement market.

D. CONCLUSIONS

Both the EU Institutions as well as MS decision makers have sought to strategically use their purchasing power in order to promote the accomplishment of secondary objectives related to sustainable development. In the recent years, the issue of fostering SMEs' participation in the public procurement markets has attracted considerable attention, since SMEs are a highly important part of the economy accounting for a vast majority of all businesses as well as a majority of the jobs in the EU.

Two types of reasons can be put forward in order to justify the need for increased participation of SMEs in the public procurement market. The first relates to the advantages for the procuring authority and the general public interest: The rationale is that due to their organizational simplicity and lack of bureaucratic structures, they are more able to develop innovative capacities, flexibility and immediate response to the markets' needs. Secondly, if the SMEs' participation in the large and lucrative public

---

[87] Article 71(3) Directive 2014/24/EU: 'Subcontractors: 3. Member States may provide that at the request of the subcontractor and where the nature of the contract so allows, the contracting authority shall transfer due payments directly to the subcontractor for services, supplies or works provided to the economic operator to whom the public contract has been awarded (the main contractor). Such measures may include appropriate mechanisms permitting the main contractor to object to undue payments. The arrangements concerning that mode of payment shall be set out in the procurement documents.'

[88] Article 71(7) Directive 2014/24/EU: '7. Member States may provide for more stringent liability rules under national law or to go further under national law on direct payments to subcontractors, for instance by providing for direct payments to subcontractors without it being necessary for them to request such direct payment …'

contracts market is increased, they are likely to boost their profitability and economic sustainability, which in turns leads to job creation and local economic growth and social cohesion.[89]

The main concern put forward is that despite the fact that SMEs constitute the backbone of the European economy, their share of winning public contracts is not analogous to their total share of the overall economic activity in the Single Market. What is more, due to their limited capacities and resources, they are faced with certain barriers and challenges in entering the public procurement market as well as certain disadvantages compared to larger enterprises. In particular, SMEs encounter certain specific hindrances in tendering for public contracts and their chances of being awarded public contracts are majorly influenced by governmental policies and purchasing attitudes.

Against this background, it comes as no surprise that an impressive series of policy initiatives has taken place over the years and across the Union, aiming to foster SMEs' performance through a 'strategic' use of public procurement. The promotion of SMEs' participation in public tendering is a longstanding point of concern in strategic public procurement planning both at EU and MS level, with a view to facilitating SMEs' involvement in public tendering on equal terms with larger enterprises. Enabling SMEs to participate in tendering was initially laid down as a strategic target in the 2004 EU public procurement Directives and has gained importance ever since. The need of promoting SMEs' access has also been acknowledged in the New Classic Directive, which provides for increased monitoring at national level and requires MS to submit to the Commission every three years a monitoring report on the level of SMEs' participation in national award procedures.[90]

EU public procurement rules relating to SMEs are not oriented towards preferential awarding schemes but focus on an SME friendly procurement process. Such process is largely based on key measures to foster SMEs by tackling the hindrances they encounter. As discussed in detail under Section C, the measures put forward to promote SME participation in public contracts by the European regulatory framework fall under the following three categories: (a) those which facilitate access of SMEs to award procedures (for example, full observance of the principles and disciplines of the EU public procurement regime, division of larger contracts into lots, encouragement of association or cooperation between SMEs to bid for larger contracts, greater recourse to subcontracting parts of contracts by large companies to SMEs, review of the legal and fiscal conditions under which SMEs participate in public contracts and so on); (b) those which reduce administrative costs and burdens in public procurement (for example, simplification and streamlining of award procedures, increased use of electronic procurement tools, information services, reduction of delays in payment and so on) and

[89] Social cohesion is a core Union target, referred to the Declaration on Article 126 TFEU as such: 'Within this framework, the Conference also reaffirms its commitment to the goals of the Lisbon Strategy: job creation, structural reforms, and social cohesion.'

See also O'Brien, 'Public Procurement and the Small or Medium Sized Enterprise'(1993) PPLR 82.

[90] Article 83(3) Directive 2014/24/EU.

(c) those which prepare SMEs for effective participation in award procedures (for example, development of information channels, guidance, training and so on).

Whereas in other parts of the globe support to SMEs through procurement takes the form of bid preferences, set asides and liquidity support,[91] the EU approach explicitly excludes the possibility of set asides or preferences in public procurement,[92] and is heavily oriented towards simplification policies to reduce the burden of SMEs for participating in tenders. The reason is that these practices are in immediate contrast with the EU established doctrine,[93] which 'is not in favour of reserving markets to specific undertakings. Such actions would also be in contradiction with the principles of equal treatment and non-discrimination, a fundamental pillar of the EU public procurement regime anchored by the CJEU in the Treaty freedoms'.[94] All in all, the EU public procurement policy and practice does not tolerate reserving specific contracts for SMEs, but is oriented in facilitating access to public procurement for SMEs and larger enterprises on an equal footing,[95] thus providing incentives for contracting authorities to make the best possible use of the available instruments for SME-friendly procurement.

That being so, a crucial aspect that policy makers and contracting authorities should take into account is that public procurement law is part of the *Acquis Communautaire* that safeguards the free movement of goods and services in the internal market. Within this framework, one cannot help but agree that the prime objective of the public procurement rules is to strengthen the Single Market and the EU's competitiveness and facilitate efficient public purchasing and rational use of public funds.[96] As a consequence, all other policy objectives need to be reconciled with this primary goal. What is more, they must respect the EU fundamental public procurement principles of equal treatment and non-discrimination, genuine competition, mutual recognition and proportionality.

Therefore, the strategic use of public procurement, which aims to encourage SME participation, is subject to inherent limitations related to the accomplishment of the best value for money procurement. Whereas providing wider access to public procurement markets is regarded as an important driver to unlock the growth and innovation potential of SMEs, its economic and competitiveness benefits are still debated. Indeed, the use of public procurement as an SME policy leverage needs to be weighted against the costs incurred by its incorporation in the procurement process, bearing in mind that it can potentially result in price increase. For example, the promotion of the division of

---

91 Fana and Piga, 'SMEs and Public Contracts, an EU Based Perspective', *op.cit.*

92 See 'Think small first: A Small Business Act for Europe' (COM/2008/394 final).

93 Bovis (1998), *op.cit*; Jureík (2013): 'Small and Medium Size Enterprises (SME) and public procurement' in Lorca and Popescu (eds), *Recent Researches in Applied Economics & Management. Business Administration and Financial Management.* Vol.1. Proceedings of the 5th International Conference AEBD. Business and Economics Series 9, (WSEAS Press, 2013), p. 335–9.

94 Green Paper on the modernization of EU public procurement policy, *op.cit.*

95 European Commission, Communication to the Council: Promoting SME participation in public procurement in the Community (COM/90/166 final, p. 2).

96 Article 173 TFEU (ex Article 157(1) TEC) entrusts the EU and MS with securing the conditions for the competitiveness of EU industry.

large contracts to smaller lots is one absolutely lawful option. However, before resorting to it, the contracting authority needs to ensure that such a practice complies with the aggregation rules and the contract does not end up being burdened with excessive or disproportionate administrative costs. In any case, the initiatives to improve access of SMEs in the market of public procurement reach their limitations when they end up preventing undertakings that have the required capacity to participate in the award procedure and win the contract.

To sum up, due to the fact that public procurement is an area of high political influence and economic importance, by which many goals may be pursued, public authorities may be tempted to adopt measures which compromise value for money in order to discriminate in favour of SMEs against larger enterprises. However, this is a tendency that should definitely be avoided.[97] Contracting authorities should by all means refrain from the use of set asides and preference schemes while ensuring that measures which facilitate participation of smaller firms in the procurement market do not go as far as discriminating against larger enterprises or distorting competition.

As a general conclusion, it may be stressed that what is most needed in order to facilitate SMEs' access to public procurement is not so much a reform of the EU regulatory framework, but rather a change in the contracting authorities' purchasing mentality.

Since it is still early to venture an assessment of the actual benefits of SMEs promoting measures, an SME performance review would be highly anticipated in the forthcoming years.

---

[97] Hatzis, 'The Legality of SME Development Policies under EC Procurement Law', in Arrowsmith and Kunzlik (eds), Social *and Environmental Policies in EC Procurement Law: New Directives and New Direction* (Cambridge: Cambridge University Press, 2009), p. 367.

10. Public procurement and services of general economic interest

Sarah Schoenmaekers

1. INTRODUCTION

Public Services (generally identified as Services of General Economic Interest or SGEIs) occupy a vital role in the shared values of the Union: they promote social and territorial cohesion, foster the well-being of people across the EU and make an important contribution to Europe's economic development.[1] Examples range from large commercial services that are provided to the entire population at affordable conditions (network industries such as postal services, energy security of supply, electronic communication services or public transport) to a wide range of health and social services (such as care for elderly or disabled people). These services are of great importance since they deliver outcomes in the overall public good that would not be supplied – or would be supplied under different conditions in terms of objective quality, safety, affordability, equal treatment or universal access – by the market without public intervention. This definition of SGEIs, which was delivered by the Commission in its 2013 Quality Framework,[2] cannot be found in the EU treaties or in secondary legislation even though the concept appears in Articles 14 and 106(2) TFEU, Protocol No 26 to the TFEU, Article 36 of the Charter of Fundamental Rights of the European Union as well as in numerous Commission decisions, cases decided by the Court of Justice and the two SGEI Packages of the Commission.

When a public contract to provide SGEIs is awarded to a company, State aid comes into play. Indeed, public contracts are directly or indirectly attributable to public bodies and are generally financed through state resources. Since their award is by nature selective, they may generate competitive distortions which often have an appreciable effect on intra-EU trade. This chapter aims to explain the role of public procurement in the financing of SGEIs by focusing on the link between the application of the State aid rules and the public procurement framework. The central question that will be answered is: Does the application of a public procurement procedure entail that the financing of a SGEI does not constitute State aid?

---

[1] Communication from the Commission to the European Parliament, the Council, the European Economic and Social Committee and the Committee of the Regions, *Reform of the EU State Aid Rules on Services of General Economic Interest,* COM(2011) 146 final, 23 March 2011, p. 2.

[2] European Commission, Quality Framework set out in the Guide to the application of the EU rules on State aid, public procurement and the internal market to SGEI of 29 April 2013, p. 21.

2. THE CONCEPT OF 'SERVICES OF GENERAL ECONOMIC INTEREST'

Certain goods and services are by nature so essential for the well-being, health and fundamental rights of European citizens, European economic, social and territorial cohesion and sustainable development, that they deserve a special and adapted treatment in the face of free market forces in order to ensure that everyone can enjoy a high level of quality, safety and affordability of these services based on equal treatment.[3] These goods and services are known as Services of General Interest (SGIs). They can be considered as the backbone of the European economy as they provide essential infrastructures such as transport, energy or social services for both people and business and are an important aspect of the welfare State that is characteristic of most of the EU Member States.[4] SGIs are related to public markets. Public markets have monopsony structure tendencies – the State and its organs often appear as the sole outlet for an industry's output – and demand in such markets is institutionalized and operates mainly under budgetary considerations rather than price mechanisms.[5] In public markets the public interest substitutes profit maximization.

SGIs can be economic (SGEIs) or non-economic in nature (NESGIs). Member States are fully in charge when it comes to the regulation of NESGIs, as long as the general EU principles (equal treatment, non-discrimination, proportionality and transparency) are respected. This follows from Article 2 of Protocol 26 of the TFEU which indicates that the provisions of the Treaties do not affect in any way the competence of Member States to provide, commission and organise NESGIs. SGEIs on the other hand, can be characterised as economic activities that public authorities identify as being of particular importance to citizens that would not be supplied – or would be supplied under different conditions – by the market without public intervention. An economic activity is defined as any activity consisting in offering (not just purchasing) goods and services on a market, regardless of whether this is for the purpose of generating profit or non-profit.[6] As held by the Court of Justice of the EU (CJEU), SGEIs exhibit special characteristics as compared with the general economic interest of other economic activities since they comprise a general or public interest.[7] It follows that these services have a dual nature: they belong to the market, but other non-market values are applied

[3] Centre of Employers and Enterprises providing public services, *The Acquis Communautaire for Services of General Economic Interest,* 2013, p. II, available 29 January 2016 at http://www.ceep.eu/images/stories/ceep_acquis_glossary.pdf.

[4] Ibid, p. 1.

[5] C.H. Bovis, *Public Procurement, State Aid and Services of General Economic Interest,* speaker's contribution for ERA Academy of European Law, 23–24 May 2011, p. 2, available 29 January 2016 at http://www.era-comm.eu/UNCRPD/kiosk/speakers_contributions/111DV67/Bovis_paper.pdf

[6] Case C-343/95, *Diego Calì & Figli Srl v Servizi ecologici porto di Genova SpA (SEPG)* [1997] ECR I-1547, §23.

[7] Case C-179/90, *Merci convenzionali porto di Genova SpA v Siderurgica Gabrielli SpA* [1991] ECR I-5889, §27; Case 172/80, *Züchner* [1981] ECR 2021, §7; Case 7/82, *GVL v Commission* [1983] ECR 483, §§31–32; Commission, 25 April 2012, State aid SA.25051 Germany – Aid to Zweckverband Tierkörperbeseitigung, §160.

to them since they are subject to specific public service obligations (PSO[8]).[9] It is held that SGEIs are in the middle of a clash between the antagonistic interests of competition versus welfare and social goals.[10]

Whether a service should be labelled as a SGEI has to be determined on a case-by-case basis. The processing of waste, which is not only economic in nature but also deals with an environmental problem, electricity distribution, the transportation of sick persons and the basic postal services, services that bring about considerable investment costs, have all been qualified as SGEIs by the CJEU.[11] Social Services of General Interest (SSGIs) on the other hand are only covered by internal market rules as soon as they constitute an economic activity.[12] This broad approach entails that activities that intrinsically form part of the prerogatives of official authority and are performed by the State, such as the army or the police, air navigation safety and control, maritime traffic control and safety, anti-pollution surveillance, the organisation, financing and enforcement of prison sentences, activities in the area of social security including health care if based on the principle of solidarity and public education, do not constitute economic activities.[13]

The Lisbon Treaty recognises the essential role of SGEIs and, at the same time, their diversity in the European model of society.[14] As stated by Article 14 TFEU, 'Without

---

[8] PSO and SGEI are treated as interchangeable concepts for the purposes of this chapter.

[9] A. Jones and B. Sufrin, *EC Competition Law. Text, Cases and Materials* (Oxford: Oxford University Press, 2007) 621.

[10] J. Kociubiński, 'Services of General Economic Interest – Towards a European Concept of Public Services' (2011) 1(2) *Wroclaw Review of Law, Administration & Economics* 49. See also the 2004 White Paper of the European Commission on SGEIs in which it is held that the concept 'SGEI' has a community meaning which entails that it cannot be interpreted with reference to existing national definitions.

[11] See e.g. Case C-393/92, *Almelo* [1994] ECR I-1477; Cases C-320/91, *Corbeau* [1993] ECR I-2533; and C-203/96, *Chemische Afvalstoffen Dusseldorp BV and Others v Minister van Volkshuisvesting, Ruimtelijke Ordening en Milieubeheer* [1998] ECR I-4075. The management of waste deals with an environmental problem.

[12] SGIs is an umbrella term for economic/market services which are subject to competition rules (unless the derogations encapsulated in Article 106(2) TFEU apply) and non-economic services which are beyond the scope of EU competition law. See Communication from the Commission to the European Parliament, the Council, the European Economic and Social Committee and the Committee of the Regions, of 20 November 2007, accompanying the Communication on 'A single market for 21st century Europe' – Services of general interest, including social services of general interest: a new European commitment ((2007) 725 final).

[13] Communication from the Commission on the application of the European Union State aid rules to compensation granted for the provision of services of general economic interest (hereinafter: SGEI Communication), [2012] OJ C8, §§16—30. See also Joined Cases C-264/01, C-306/01, C-354/01 and C-355/01, *AOK Bundesverband and Others v Ichtyol-Gesellschaft Cordes, Hermani & Co. and Others* [2004] ECR I-2493, §63; Case 107/84, *Commission* v *Germany* [1985] ECR 2655, §§14–15; Case C-364/92, *SAT Fluggesellschaft* [1994] ECR I-43, §30.

[14] Communication from the Commission to the European Parliament, the Council, the European Economic and Social Committee and the Committee of the Regions, *Reform of the EU State Aid Rules on Services of General Economic Interest,* COM(2011) 146 final, 23 March 2011, p. 2.

prejudice to Article 4 of the Treaty on European Union[15] or to Articles 93,[16] 106 and 107 of this Treaty, and given the place occupied by services of general economic interest in the shared values of the Union as well as their role in promoting social and territorial cohesion, the Union and the Member States, each within their respective powers and within the scope of application of the Treaties, shall take care that such services operate on the basis of principles and conditions, particularly economic and financial conditions, which enable them to fulfil their missions'.[17] Since both Member States and the Union play an essential role regarding the proper functioning of these services, there is a shared competence for decision making in the field of SGEIs. In light of the principle of subsidiarity, however, the Union will not take action, unless this would be more effective than action taken at national, regional or local level. So far, the Commission has not proposed any legislation on the basis of Article 14 TFEU. Given the strategic importance of the sectors, the provision of SGEIs depends on policy choices that are generally taken at national level so that Member States enjoy a wide margin of discretion in defining a given service as a SGEI. Hence, the definition of such services by a Member State is generally rubber stamped by the European Commission and can only be questioned in the event of manifest errors.[18] Member States can decide to entrust to provision of a SGEI through a public contract (public procurement or service concession), but can also opt for specific regulation (a legal act falling outside the definition of public contract), authorisation schemes, exclusive rights or internal performance by the public authority (own division or in collaboration with other public authorities or a separate public entity (quasi in-house)). They can thus decide to reserve a given service to an emanation of the State. Nevertheless, as indicated above, Member States may not exercise their discretionary powers contrary to the provisions of the Treaty rules on internal market and competition.

The Lisbon Treaty also added Protocol 26 to the TFEU, specifically reflecting the essential yet diverse role of SGEIs in the EU. As stated by Article 1 of this Protocol, 'The shared values of the Union include, in particular, the essential role and the wide discretion of national, regional and local authorities in providing, commissioning and organising services of general economic interest as closely as possible to the needs of the users; the diversity between various services of general economic interest and the differences in the needs and preferences of users that may result from different geographical, social or cultural situations; a high level of quality, safety and affordability, equal treatment and the promotion of universal access and of user rights'. In addition, reference to SGEIs is also made in Article 36 of the Charter of Fundamental Rights which indicates that the Union recognises and respects access to SGEIs in order

[15] This article lays down the principle of constitutional respect of SGIs at local level.

[16] According to Article 93 TFEU, aids shall be compatible with the Treaties if they meet the needs of coordination of transport or if they represent reimbursement for the discharge of certain obligations inherent in the concept of a public service.

[17] Article 16 EC also highlighted the specific place occupied by SGEIs in the Member States and the EU.

[18] This is only different with regard to harmonised sectors such as the telecom or postal sector. Case T-17/02, *Fred Olsen v Commission* [2005] ECR II-2031, §175. See also Article 4(1) of Directive 2014/23/EU.

to promote the social and territorial cohesion of the Union. This entails that access to SGEIs is recognised as a true fundamental right.

SGEIs are often entrusted by the State acting as a public authority to a private undertaking,[19] for budgetary or technical reasons. As held by the Court in *BUPA*,[20] in order to be classified as a SGEI, a service needs to be of universal and compulsory nature, assume a general or public interest and be entrusted to an operator by a public authority act. While the universal nature entails the right of everyone to access these services,[21] the compulsory nature imposes obligations on service providers to offer defined services according to specified conditions, including complete territorial coverage at an affordable price.[22] This entails that the service provider is obliged to contract the other party *or* that special or exclusive rights are granted.[23]

It follows that a PSO is imposed on the provider by way of an entrustment which implies the supply of services which, if it were considering its own commercial interest, an undertaking would not assume or would not assume to the same extent or under the same conditions.[24] In this regard, the Commission held, for example, with regard to geothermical heat distribution in Germany, that although alternative heat distribution could also be and is actually ensured by private companies, this does not preclude that the provision of geothermical heat distribution may constitute a genuine SGEI, since there is no evidence that market forces would be able to provide this kind

---

19 An undertaking is every entity engaged in an economic activity, regardless of the legal status and the way in which it is financed. See Case C-41/90, *Höfner* [1991] ECR I-1979, §21. See also Case C-475/99, *Ambulanz Glöckner* [2001] ECR I-08089, §57 in which the Court held that also non-profit-making entities can be qualified as undertakings.

20 Case T-289/03, *BUPA and others v Commission* [2005] ECR II-2031, §187.

21 As held above, this right exists since these services are considered as essential. It is neither hampered by the fact that it is offered only in a restricted area or to a restricted group of people nor by the fact that this service is being reimbursed.

22 White Paper on Services of General Economic Interest (COM(2004)374 final). See also Article 3 of Directive 2002/22/EC of the European Parliament and of the Council of 7 March 2002 on universal service and users' rights relating to electronic communication networks and services (Universal Service Directive); Article 3(3) of Directive 2003/54/EC of the European Parliament and of the Council of 26 June 2003 concerning common rules for the internal market in electricity and repealing Directive 96/92/EC; Article 4(2) of Directive 2008/6/EC of the European Parliament and of the Council of 20 February 2008 amending Directive 97/67/EC with regard to the full accomplishment of the internal market of Community postal services.

23 The recognition of an SGEI mission does not necessarily presume that the operator entrusted with that mission will be given an exclusive or special right to carry it out. It is merely the instrument, possibly justified, which allows that operator to perform an SGEI mission. Case T-289/03, *BUPA and others v Commission* [2005] ECR II-2031, §179.

24 A PSO can thus not be attached to an activity which can be provided satisfactorily and under conditions, such as price, objective quality characteristics, continuity and access to the service, consistent with the public interest as defined by the State, by other undertakings under normal market conditions. See Communication from the Commission on the application of the European Union State aid rules to compensation granted for the provision of services of general economic interest, 2012/C 8/02 (SGEI Communication), [2012] OJ C8, § 48. See e.g. also Case T-79/10, *Colt Télécommunications France v European Commission* [2013], not yet published.

of service under the conditions specified by the responsible bodies in Germany.[25] This leads to the conclusion that the Commission does not always merely rubber stamp the decisions of the Member States. When it verifies whether there is a market failure with regard to the specific service it is using its powers more firmly. It follows that if applied strictly, the market failure requirement could significantly limit the scope for Member States to introduce SGEIs.[26] It may disrupt the Member State's prerogative to determine whether or not a service is in the general interest. There is thus an inherent tension between the provisions that seek to preserve the public service traditions of the Member States based on the subsidiarity principle on the one hand and the competition rules, which belong since the entry into force of the Lisbon treaty to the exclusive competence of the EU, on the other hand.[27]

3. SGEIS, STATE AID AND PUBLIC PROCUREMENT

3.1 Introduction

The TFEU only expressly covers two particular types of *public* anti-competitive behaviour: the granting of State aid as meant in Articles 107–109 TFEU and the granting of special or exclusive rights to undertakings, particularly to those providing SGEIs (Article 106 TFEU).[28]

Whenever a private company provides a SGEI, the competition rules including the State aid provisions may be applicable. Indeed, the granting of a SGEI may lead to the distortion of competition and State aid may come into play whenever a company is financed through public resources to provide a SGEI. As indicated above, Article 14 TFEU indicates explicitly that the EU and the Member States have to take care that SGEIs operate 'without prejudice to Articles 106 and 107 TFEU'. Article 107 TFEU is the well-known general article that specifically forbids State aid if certain conditions are fulfilled. It is applicable to all sectors of the economy and is not limited to public services. Article 106(2) TFEU on the other hand is specifically applicable to SGEIs and provides for an exception to the application of the competition rules to SGEI by providing that:

> Undertakings entrusted with the operation of services of general economic interest or having the character of a revenue-producing monopoly shall be subject to the rules contained in the Treaties, in particular to the rules on competition, in so far as the application of such rules does not obstruct the performance, in law or in fact, of the particular tasks assigned to them.

---

[25] European Commission, Case SA.31261 Municipal Guarantee for Loan for Geothermal Heat Distribution Network, § 29.

[26] W. Devroe and D. Gabathuler, 'The Evolving Treatment of Services of General Economic Interest under EU Law', in S. Schoenmaekers, W. Devroe and N. Philipsen, *State Aid and Public Procurement in the European Union* (Antwerp: Intersentia, 2014), p. 51.

[27] Ibid p. 47.

[28] A. Sanchez Graells, *Public Procurement and the EU Competition Rules* (Oxford: Hart Publishing, 2011), p. 117.

> The development of trade must not be affected to such an extent as would be contrary to the interests of the Union.

Article 106(2) TFEU reflects the balance between the internal market and free competition on the one hand and Member States and EU regulations intervening in the market in order to safeguard the public interest on the other hand.[29] The application of EU competition law is thus the rule and the compensation granted by public authorities for the performance of a SGEI is in principle subject to State aid scrutiny. Only if the application of the competition rules would obstruct the provision of the service, an exception can be made and the public interest shall prevail. Despite the lack of direct effect, Article 14 TFEU represents thus a significant step in the concretising of non-economic concerns in both the psyche and legal hierarchy of the European Union since it upgraded SGEIs from a mere defence in Article 106(2) TFEU to a fundamental value shared by the whole Union.[30]

3.2 Articles 107 and 106(2) TFEU

As stated by Article 107(1) TFEU, 'Save as otherwise provided in the Treaties, any aid granted by a Member State or through State resources in any form whatsoever which distorts or threatens to distort competition by favouring certain undertakings or the production of certain goods shall, in so far as it affects trade between Member States, be incompatible with the internal market'. Undertakings entrusted with the provision of SGEIs are exempted from this prohibition by Article 106(2) TFEU if the application of Article 107(1) would obstruct the provision of the services. As stated by the Court in *Corbeau*, Article 106(2) TFEU thus permits Member States to confer on undertakings to which they entrust the operation of SGEIs, exclusive rights which may hinder the application of the rules of the Treaty on competition in so far as restrictions on competition, or even the exclusion of all competition, by other economic operators are necessary to ensure the performance of the particular tasks assigned to the undertakings possessed of the exclusive rights.[31] Indeed, since the pursuit of a public interest may render the service in question less competitive than comparable services provided by other private undertakings, State aid is usually granted for the compensation of the provision of public services. Compensation granted to an undertaking is also subject to State aid control also where the market has been reserved for this single undertaking, including an in-house provider.[32] As stated in *Albany*,[33] disadvantages arising from public service obligations can justify exclusive rights or compensation payments. Of

---

29 Centre of Employers and Enterprises providing public services, *op. cit*, p. 4.

30 Kociubiński, *op. cit*, pp. 54–55; Leo Flynn, 'Competition Policy and Public Services in EC Law after Maastricht and Amsterdam Treaties' in David O'Keeffe and Patric Twomey (eds), *Legal Issues of the Amsterdam Treaty* (Oxford: Oxford University Press, 1999) p. 185; Hans W. Micklitz, 'Universal Services: Nucleus for a Social European Private Law' in Marise Cremona (ed.), *Market Integration and Public Services in the European Union* (Oxford: Oxford University Press, 2011) p. 95.

31 Case C-320/91, *Corbeau* [1993] ECR I-2533, §14.

32 SGEI Communication, §33.

33 Case C-67/96, *Albany* [1999] ECR I-5863, §86.

course, since any exemption from the competition rules needs to be proportionate to the legitimate aim pursued and limited to what is absolutely necessary, State aid is only considered compatible with the internal market if it is proportionate to clearly defined objectives of general interest. Nevertheless, even though exceptions should in principle be interpreted strictly, the Court held in *Corbeau* that Article 106(2) TFEU can be invoked whenever normal competition rules 'obstruct' the performance in law or in fact, of the particular tasks assigned to the undertaking.[34] It follows that a mere obstruction is already enough. Normal performance of the tasks should not necessarily have become impossible.

EU rules and practices on State aid have been further developed in secondary legislation and case-law. Specific rules for State aid granted to SGEIs can be found in the Commission's Monti-Kroes and Almunia Package as well as in case-law. These will be discussed in the following paragraphs.

3.3 Competing Views on Whether Compensation for SGEIs Amounts to State Aid

To determine whether the financing of a SGEI constitutes State aid, one has to take into account the *effect* of the measure and verify whether competition is distorted or can be distorted when a certain undertaking or the production of certain goods is favoured and this affects trade between Member States. The reasons or motives for granting State aid are thus irrelevant. Nevertheless, competing views on the issue have been developed by the case-law of the Commission and the Court.[35]

As held by the *State aid approach*, financial compensation for SGEI operators constitutes State aid within the meaning of Article 107(1) TFEU[36] which may, however, be justified by Article 106(2) TFEU provided that the conditions are fulfilled and the funding complies with the proportionality principle.[37] Since the reasons for compensation are not relevant, it does not matter in principle that the aid is granted to compensate for the PSO that is imposed on the undertaker. It follows that authorities that want to grant aid, have to notify the Commission and wait for its approval while new aid cannot be implemented until the Commission has declared it compatible with Article 106(2) TFEU. The State aid approach, which was, for example, confirmed in *Chronopost*,[38] does not apply the private investor principle since it assumes that the emergence and delivery of SGEIs do not take place in a normal, private market and take place in a separate, *sui generis* market.[39] The non-economic character of state intervention renders the private operator test immaterial for the reason that profitability,

---

34 Case C-320/91, *Corbeau* [1993] ECR I-2533, §13.

35 See for an extensive overview Bovis, *op.cit.*

36 Cases T-106/9,5 *FFSA* [1997] ECR II-229, §167; Case T-46/97, *Sociedade Independente de Comunição (SIC) SA v Commission of the European Communities* [2000] ECR II-2125, §84.

37 Case C-387/92, *Banco de Crédito Industrial S v Ayuntamiento de Valencia* [1994] ECR I-902.

38 Joined Cases C-83/01 P, C-93/01 P and C-94/01 P, *Chronopost v Ufex and Others* [2003] ECR I-6993.

39 P. Nicolaides and S. Schoenmaekers, 'Public Procurement, Public Private Partnerships and State Aid Rules: A Symbiotic Relationships' (2014) 1 *European Public Private Partnership Law Review* 16.

the *raison d'être* of private investment, is not present.[40] As suggested by Bovis, this lacunae is filled by the application of the public procurement regime since it sanitizes public subsidies as legitimate contributions towards PSOs and SGEIs.[41] This will be further discussed later.

The State aid approach was challenged by the Court in *ADBHU*[42] where it held that transfers representing payments for performance of public service obligations did not amount to an 'advantage' to the undertaking and therefore did not constitute State aid under Article 107(1) TFEU.[43] Indeed, according to the *compensation approach*, the compensation is not regarded as State aid, provided that it does not exceed the normal, appropriate remuneration for the costs of the service in question.[44] Hence, it also does not have to be notified to the European Commission. The compensation approach introduces an applicability threshold of State aid regulation and that threshold is determined by the perceived market price, terms and conditions for the delivery of the relevant service.[45] A problem with the compensation approach, which also accepts the *sui generis* character of SGEIs, is that one assumes that the 'appropriate' remuneration – the base line – can be found by a public procurement procedure. Nevertheless, when a contract is awarded by reference to the most economically advantageous tender (MEAT) criterion, it is very well possible that the market price is not at all equal to the price the contracting authority is willing to pay for the procurement of the relevant service, product or work.[46] The mere existence of a public procurement procedure cannot, therefore, reveal the necessary element of the compensation approach: the market price which will determine the 'excessive' State intervention and introduces State aid regulation.[47]

The *quid pro quo approach*, as developed by Advocate General Jacobs in his Opinion in the *GEMO*[48] case, is held to be the middle way between the other approaches. When applying this approach, the Court distinguishes between two categories of situations. The first comprises cases in which there is a direct and manifest link between the State financing and clearly defined PSOs.[49] Such link can be demonstrated by the existence of a public contract concluded in accordance with the public procurement directives. The contract then defines the obligations of the undertakings entrusted with the provision of the SGEIs and the remuneration they receive in return. In those cases the sums paid by the State to the recipient undertaking do not constitute State aid but merely the consideration for the public service obligations assumed by the undertaking. Cases falling into this category should be analysed according to the compensation

---

[40] Bovis, *op.cit*, p. 26.

[41] Ibid, pp. 26 and 33.

[42] Case T-240/83, *Procureur de la République v Association de défense des brûleurs d'huiles usagées (ADBHU)* [1985] ECR 531, §27.

[43] Kociubiński, *op.cit*, p. 60.

[44] Case C-44/96, *Mannesman* [1998] ECR I-73.

[45] Bovis, *op.cit*, p. 28.

[46] Nicolaides and Schoenmaekers, *op.cit*, p. 16.

[47] Bovis, *op.cit.*, p. 30.

[48] Case C-126/01, *GEMO* [2003] ECR I-13769, §§117–129.

[49] Case C-5/01, *Belgium v Commission* [2002] ECR I-3452.

approach.[50] The second category of situations covers cases without a direct and manifest link between the State financing and the PSOs, as well as cases where those obligations are not clearly defined. This amounts to verifying that there are laws, regulations or contractual provisions which specify the nature and content of the undertaking's obligations. In those cases the sums paid by the public authorities do constitute State aid which as such is subject to the procedural obligations laid down in Article 108(3) TFEU. The quid pro quo approach which puts procedural requirements at the heart of the appraisal, presents a major shortcoming, however, since it introduces elements of the *nature* of public financing into the process of determining the legality of aid while according to State aid jurisprudence, only the *effects* of the measure are to be taken into consideration.[51] In State aid jurisprudence, the nature of the measure is only relevant with regard to the assessment of the compatibility of the aid in line with the exemption provisions of the Treaty.

In the landmark case *Altmark*[52] the Court took the opportunity to reconcile these approaches. This case will now be discussed.

3.4 *Altmark*

In its *Altmark* judgement, the Court set out four specific criteria that had to be met for compensation granted for the provision of SGEIs that affects trade between Member States to escape qualification as State aid:

- First, the recipient undertaking must actually have a *PSO* to discharge, and this obligation must be *clearly defined.* This entails that the PSO needs to be assigned to the provider of the service by an official and binding act of entrustment[53] so that it creates an obligation for the operator to provide it. Generally this occurs if the service is not fully or not adequately provided by the market in terms of price, quality or frequency which is mainly due to the market's focus on profit. In this regard it should be noted, however, that there is no SGEI which is not at all provided by the market.[54] Indeed, every SGEI provider offers a service that has some characteristics or is offered in some geographic markets which are supplied by the market and is made available to some consumers who are also served by the market. For this reason, the Commission will have to examine whether the public service delegation contract is necessary and proportionate to a 'real public service need' manifested by a shortage of the specific type of service in a

---

50 Bovis, *op.cit*, p. 23.

51 Ibid.

52 Case C-280/00, *Altmark* [2003] ECR I-7747.

53 § 12 of the 2005 SGEI Framework contains some minimum criteria that have to be satisfied by this act, such as criteria relating to the content and the duration of the PSO, the undertaking and the territory concerned and the nature of any exclusive rights assigned to the undertaking.

54 Nicolaides and Schoenmaekers, *op.cit*, p. 14.

situation of free competition.[55] It should thus be determined whether there is a gap in the market that warrants intervention by the state.

- Second, the *parameters* on the basis of which the compensation is calculated must be established *in advance* in an *objective* and *transparent* manner. In this regard it should be noted that only the costs that are directly linked to the provision of the PSO can be taken into account while any revenue has to be deducted. With this requirement, the CJEU seeks to avoid a situation whereby the undertaking accumulates losses and is subsequently compensated for its losses, irrespective of whether these actually relate to the operation of the SGEI.[56] This would hamper efficiency. The establishment of parameters constitutes an *ex post* control mechanism for Member States and the European Commission.
- Third, the compensation *cannot exceed what is necessary* to cover all or part of the costs incurred in the discharge of PSOs, taking into account the relevant receipts and a *reasonable profit*. This criterion, which is a reflection of the proportionality test applied within the framework of Article 106(2) TFEU, is important to determine whether the compensation is not providing an economic advantage to the undertaking. The compensation (for example, monopoly rights, financial support, free rent) that is granted to the undertaking has to be related to the burden that is placed on it in the public interest (quality, affordability, continuity, consumer protection) to provide the SGEI and cannot go further. Since the Commission does not look at the lowest offer a private operator makes but at what a reasonable profit would be, the third *Altmark* criterion is rather objective. To determine whether a profit is reasonable, the Commission uses a case-by-case approach by comparing the respective profit with the profit which is common in the respective economic sector.[57] The Commission performs thus a full review of the actual costs *ex post*. The third Altmark criterion reflects the compensation approach.
- Fourth, where the undertaking which is to discharge PSOs in a specific case is not chosen pursuant to a *public procurement procedure* which would allow for the selection of the tenderer capable of providing those services at the least cost to the community, the level of compensation needed must be determined on the basis of an analysis of the costs which a *typical, well run and adequately equipped undertaking* would have incurred in discharging those obligations, taking into account the relevant receipts and a reasonable profit for discharging the obligations.[58] The reference to this procedural element indicates the link between this criterion and the quid pro quo approach as discussed above.

---

55 Commission Decision 2013/435 on state aid implemented by France in favour of Société Nationale Maritime Corse-Méditerranée [SA.22843].

56 M. Klasse, 'The Impact of *Altmark:* The European Commission Case Law Responses', in E. Szyszczak and J.W. van de Gronden (eds.), *Financing Services of General Economic Interest* (The Hague: Asser, 2013), p. 41.

57 See e.g. Commission, 16 November 2004, State Aid N 381/2004 Broadband Infrastructure Project Pyrénées-Atlantiques, paras 76 ff, para 82.

58 The *Altmark* case specifically referred to situations in which the EU public procurement legislation is applicable. In case a contract is not covered by EU legislation (e.g. if the threshold is not reached), there should be compliance with national procurement legislation or at least

If all these criteria are fulfilled the compensation for the PSO is not State aid and is thus not caught by Article 107(1) TFEU. It follows that it also does not have to be notified to the Commission.[59] This entails that the scope of application of State aid law is limited by the *Altmark* judgment. This is not consistent with the overall structure of competition law as such criteria normally serve as exemption grounds at best.[60] Nevertheless, since the Commission applies these criteria very strictly, scarcely any public service compensation granted by Member States has met all criteria and been regarded as aid-free.[61] Indeed, if one of the criteria is considered not to be fulfilled, the SGEI in question is potentially State aid and requires *ex ante* notification to the Commission. The compensation is then also subject to the standstill obligation as laid down in Article 108(3) TFEU. Nevertheless, even if the *Altmark* criteria are not fulfilled and the compensation in question could possibly be qualified as State aid, the aid can still be declared compatible under Article 107(2) and (3) TFEU. Furthermore, Article 106(2) TFEU can provide for an exemption.[62] This later aspect will be discussed in more detail in paragraph 3.5.

When it comes to the application of the criteria, the fourth criterion specifically has gained much attention. First of all, it is important to stress that State aid law does not impose an actual obligation on contracting authorities to tender a SGEI. Nevertheless, to be relieved from the State aid qualification, the compensation offered must be either the result of a public procurement procedure or the result of a benchmarking exercise with a typical well-run undertaking criterion. In this regard the Commission and the CJEU are of the opinion that a public procurement procedure allows for the selection of the undertaking providing the service at the least cost to the community and does not entail excess compensation. At least there is a presumption that the transaction will necessitate the least costs for the State. Compliance with public procurement rules thus objectivises the award of the contract and hence, excludes the element of an undue economic advantage as meant in Article 107(1) TFEU.[63] Important to note is however that the fourth *Altmark* criterion specifically refers to a public procurement procedure which allows for *the selection of the tenderer capable of providing those services at the least cost to the community*. Hence, a public procurement procedure as such does not necessarily include the selection of the tenderer with the lowest costs. In this regard it should first be noted that the 'lowest cost' aspect does not entail that one can only take into account the undertaking providing the service at the lowest price. In a public procurement procedure, the Most Economically Advantageous Tender criterion (MEAT) can also be used as an award criteria provided that the award criteria are

---

certain general principles like transparency and equal treatment (and the treaty principles if there is a transboundary effect) in order to achieve best value for money.

[59] Member States are competent to decide whether a PSO qualifies as State aid.

[60] Devroe and Gabathuler, *op.cit*, p. 75.

[61] Klasse, *op.cit*, p. 36.

[62] Commission Decision of 16 December 2003, *CADA Ireland* (N 475/2003) Commission Staff Working Document, Guide to the application of the EU rules on State aid, public procurement and the internal market to SGEI of 29 April 2013, p. 39 [2004] OJ C34/7.

[63] A. Sanchez Graells, 'Enforcement of State Aid Rules for Services of General Economic Interest before Public Procurement Review Bodies and Courts' (2014) 10(1) *Competition Law Review* 6.

closely related to the subject matter of the services to be provided and allow for the most economically advantageous offer to match the value of the market.[64] This is even encouraged by the Commission. Specifically with regard to SGEI and their importance for the community, wider quality, environmental and social goals are relevant when assessing tenders. It follows that also quality and social and environmental criteria can be taken into account as long as they are defined in advance to allow for effective competition. Indeed, a procurement procedure needs to allow for competing bids which provide for credible alternatives to be assessed.[65] Nevertheless, it seems that the fourth criterion indicates that not all public procurement procedures will lead to the selection of the tenderer that can provide the service *at the lower cost.* In order to verify whether a specific procedure actually allows for this, the Commission has indicated that it needs to undertake a 'material analysis' going beyond the mere consideration of the applicable public procurement rules.[66] Such material analysis may come to the conclusion that the tender does not suffice to meet the fourth criterion (first limb), or even where it does, the resulting compensation cannot per se be considered necessary (within the meaning of the third criterion).[67] In accordance with the Court's ruling in *Land Burgenland*, it can be held that where a public authority buys a product by way of a tender procedure, it can be presumed that the market price corresponds to the lowest bid (objective element), provided that it is established, first, that that bid is binding and credible and secondly, that the consideration of economic factors other than the price is not justified (subjective elements).[68] This presumption can be rebutted however. According to *Altmark*, it then has to be demonstrated that, *despite* having complied with procurement rules, the economic operator did not actually receive an economic advantage because the terms of the contract did not reflect normal market conditions.[69] It follows that contracting authorities that fully complied with the rules on public procurement may still have to notify the award as State aid. Even though in the absence of a clear disproportion between the obligations imposed on the economic operator and the consideration paid by the public buyer (which needs to be assessed in light of such complex criteria as the risks assumed by the contractor, technical difficulty, delay for implementation, prevailing market conditions, and so on) State aid rules impose a very

---

64 Commission Staff Working Document, Guide to the application of the EU rules on State aid, public procurement and the internal market to SGEI of 29 April 2013, p. 48. Of course, such award criterion may give rise to favouritism more easily.

65 Commission Decision 2013/435 on state aid implemented by France in favour of Société Nationale Maritime Corse-Méditerranée [SA.22843], §173.

66 Commission, 16 December 2003, State aid N 475/2003 *Security of supply Ireland (CADA)*; Klasse, *op.cit*, p. 47. This is specifically the case if a specific SGEI market is immature or where there are few similarities to the service required in the private sector.

67 Klasse, *op.cit*, p. 47.

68 Joined Cases C-214/12P, C-215/12P and C-223/12P, *Land Burgenland, Grazer Wechselseitige Versicherung AG and Republic of Austria v European Commission* [2013] ECR n.y.r. See also P. Nicolaides and S. Schoenmaekers, 'The Concept of 'Advantage' in State Aid and Public Procurement and the Application of Public Procurement Rules to Minimise Advantage in the New General Block Exemption Regulation' (2015) *European State Aid Law Quarterly* forthcoming.

69 Sanchez Graells (2011), *op.cit*, p. 121.

limited constraint on the development of anti-competitive public procurement,[70] this is rather unsatisfactory and does not contribute to making the rules easier to apply.

The benchmark for compensation in the absence of public procurement that is based on the costs which a typical undertaking, well run and adequately provided, bears, could be 'market remuneration' (comparison with the costs on the market) or 'analytical ratios representative of productivity' such as turnover to capital employed, total cost to turnover, turnover per employee, value added per employee or staff costs to value added.[71] In this regard the Commission will verify whether the price paid actually corresponds to the costs of a well-managed undertaking that provides comparable services in the same sector on the market. According to the Commission, statistical data based on the actual cost in a sector cannot be considered sufficient proof that an average of these costs represents the costs of an efficient undertaking, and hence does not suffice to meet the fourth criterion.[72] The benchmark is the would-be price, had the public service been assigned by way of a competitive tender.[73] Of course such assessment is only possible if there are suitable and genuine benchmarks that allow for comparison. Only in very exceptional circumstances, this benchmarking exercise has been successful. Indeed, many Member States have as part of their austerity measures privatized some public sector organisations that previously held a monopoly position.[74] The lack of competition in the market suggests that by entrusting a SGEI to a new undertaking little or no benchmark data will be available to determine if it is well run and therefore if the level of compensation is appropriate.[75] With regard to compensation paid in the bus transport sector in the Austrian Lienz District for example, the Commission held that since the sector was dominated by monopolies and since contracts were awarded without tenders for a long time, comparisons could not be made so that an undertaking operating in this market is not necessarily a well-managed undertaking. In *Chronopost*, the CJEU held that in the absence of any possibility of comparing the situation of La Poste with that of a private group of undertakings not operating in a reserved sector, 'normal market conditions', which are necessarily hypothetical, must be assessed by reference to the objective and verifiable elements which are available.[76]

It can be concluded that the *Altmark* conditions provide a link between the *compensation* and the *quid pro quo* approach. While on the one hand the parameters of the compensation approach are accepted, the need for a public procurement procedure (or benchmarking exercise) is of importance for reasons of transparency and in order to

---

[70] Ibid.

[71] E. Szyszczak, 'Introduction', in E. Seyszcak and J.W. van de Gronden, 'Financing Services of General Economic Interest' (The Hague: Asser, 2013), p. 22. See also SGEI Framework, §34.

[72] Commission, 26 November 2008, State aid C 3/08 *Southern Moravia Bus Companies* [2009] OJ L 97/14, paras 82, 83; Klasse, *op.cit*, p. 49.

[73] Commission, 26 November 2008, State aid C 3/08 *Southern Moravia Bus Companies* [2009] OJ L 97/14, paras 82, 83; Klasse, *op.cit*, p. 49.

[74] I. Clarke, 'The Role of Procurement and SGEI after *Altmark*' in Seyszcak and van de Gronden 'Financing Services of General Economic Interest', *op.cit*, p. 76.

[75] Ibid.

[76] Joined Cases C-83/01 P, C-93/01 P and C-94/01 P, *Chronopost* [2003] ECR I-6993.

verify whether there is true competition and to authenticate market prices. However, it is not simple to determine whether in a given case the *Altmark* criteria are fulfilled. It is often claimed that the ruling raised more questions than it provided answers. In an attempt to clarify the application of State aid rules, the Commission adopted the *Altmark* or Monti-Kroes package in 2005[77] in which it specified under which conditions public service compensations can be considered compatible with primary law. Since this package did not address all questions raised by the *Altmark* ruling, it was modified and updated in 2011 by the Almunia package. The most important features of this last package will now be discussed.

3.5 The Almunia Package

The principles of the 2012 Almunia package, also called 'the second *Altmark* package' are a clarification of the case-law and a simplification in terms of an exemption for social services and proportionality (stricter rules for certain sectors and for compensation above €15 million).[78] It aims to clarify key State aid principles and introduces a diversified and proportionate approach with simpler rules for SGEIs that are small, local in scope or pursue a social objective while taking competition considerations for large cases into account. These new State aid rules have been introduced against a backdrop of economic uncertainty across Europe with many Member States implementing challenging austerity measures which include privatisation and restructuring public service delivery.[79] The most important features of this package will now be discussed.

The package consists of:

1. **An interpretative Communication** that clarifies key concepts related to State aid for SGEIs and the meaning of the four *Altmark* conditions.[80] This Communication is a non-binding document issued by the European Commission in which the Commission confirms that if the *Altmark* criteria are fulfilled, there is no State aid so that the Commission should not be notified. As the Communication aims to clarify certain concepts, it puts much emphasis on the definition of 'economic activity' by referring to the case-law of the CJEU in order to determine whether the service concerned is a SGEI. In this regard, the liberalisation of markets and the fact that services can also be provided in-house raise particular challenges.[81]

[77] The *Altmark*-package consists of a Decision exempting SGEI in certain sectors (Commission Decision of 28 November 2005 on the application of Article 86(2) of the EC Treaty to State aid in the form of public service compensation granted to certain undertakings entrusted with the operation of services of general economic interest, [2005] OJ L312/67) and a Community Framework for State aid in the form of public service compensation, [2005] OJ C297/4.

[78] It should be noted that the package does in principle not apply to certain sectors, such as the transport sector.

[79] Clarke, *op.cit*, p. 71.

[80] Communication from the Commission on the application of the European Union State aid rules to compensation granted for the provision of services of general economic interest, [2012] OJ C8/4.

[81] Devroe and Gabathuler, *op.cit*, p. 56.

In so far as a public entity exercises an economic activity which can be separated from the exercise of its public powers, that entity, in relation to that activity, acts as an undertaking, while, if that economic activity cannot be separated from the exercise of its public powers, the activities exercised by that entity as a whole remain activities connected with the exercise of those public powers.[82] If an authority wishes to provide a service in-house, this does not thus entail that the provision of this service is not an economic activity. The SGEI Communication confirms the link with public procurement. As stated in §5, where a public authority chooses to entrust a third party with the provision of a service, it is required to comply with Union law governing public procurement, stemming from Articles 49 to 56 of the Treaty, the Union Directives on public procurement and sectoral rules. Even if the Directives are wholly or partially inapplicable (for example, if the threshold is not reached) the award may nevertheless have to meet Treaty requirements of transparency, equality of treatment, proportionality and mutual recognition. Furthermore, §37 specifically indicates that the decision to provide a SGEI by methods other than through a public procurement procedure that ensures the least cost to the community may lead to distortions in the form of preventing entry by competitors or making easier the expansion of the beneficiary in other markets. Of course a benchmarking exercise can also be accepted.[83] Of strategic importance is that with regard to the first limb of the fourth *Altmark* criterion, the Communication indicates that not every award procedure provided for in the procurement directives will satisfy State aid rules. Interestingly, it holds that an open procedure that is in line with the requirements of the public procurement rules is acceptable, but also a restricted procedure, unless interested operators are prevented to tender without valid reasons.[84] Nevertheless, since a competitive dialogue or a negotiated procedure with prior publication confer a wide discretion upon the adjudicating authority and may restrict the participation of interested operators, the increased use of negotiations in these procedures may lead to disguised State aid.[85] Therefore, they can only be deemed sufficient to satisfy the fourth *Altmark* criterion in exceptional cases.[86] Since the negotiated procedure without publication of a contract notice cannot ensure that the tenderer capable of providing those services at the least cost to the community is selected for there is no competitive selection possible, this procedure may only be allowed if only one operator is able to provide the service.[87] This is also laid down in the

[82] Case C-113/07 P, *SELEX Sistemi Integrati v Commission* [2009] ECR I-2207, §72 et seq.

[83] SGEI Communication, §62.

[84] SGEI Communication, § 66.

[85] See also Commission Decision N 282/2003 *Cumbria Broadband, Project Access, Advancing Communication for Cumbria and Enabling Sustainable Services*, Brussels, 10 December 2003, C(2003)4480fin.

[86] Commission Decision N 381/04 – *France, Projet de réseau de télécommunications haut débit des Pyrénées-Atlantiques*, and Commission Decision 382/04 – *France, Mise en place d'une infrastructure haut débit sur le territoire de la région Limousin (DORSAL).*

[87] Commission Decision SA.33054: *UK Post Office Compensation for net costs incurred to keep a non-commercially viable network*, §41.

SGEI Quality Framework[88] in which the Commission holds that full compliance with open or restricted public procurement procedures awarded on the basis of either the lowest price or, under certain conditions, the MEAT criterion means that the contract is awarded at the least cost to the community as required by the Court as one of the conditions for excluding the existence of State aid.

It follows that by only fully approving some procurement procedures the public procurement exemption regarding the existence of State aid is significantly reduced by the European Commission. This is rather peculiar, since this goes against the spirit of the new procurement package that was proposed by the same institution and adds additional flexibility for contracting authorities to negotiate and explicitly allows for these procedures if certain conditions are fulfilled. Indeed, the new public procurement package specifically allows for the use of the competitive dialogue and the negotiated procedure with prior publication if recourse to an open or negotiated procedure with prior publication would either be impossible or not useful. As suggested by Carranta, the suspicion the Communication is showing towards these procedures is probably unwarranted, since the same law maker has avowed that 'a greater use of these procedures is likely to increase cross-border trade, as the evaluation has shown that contracts awarded by a negotiated procedure with prior publication have a particular high success rate of cross-border tenders'.[89] In any case, to date, the content of the Communication does not appear to have led in practice to reluctance on the part of awarding authorities to use the competitive dialogue procedure or the negotiated procedure with prior publication because of the risk that the transaction might not be compliant with the EU State aid regime.[90] Caution is warranted however, since additional restrictions can make the provision of SGEIs more difficult.

In any case, taking into account what has been mentioned in the preceding paragraph, the fourth *Altmark* criterion will not be satisfied by procurement procedures that appear to be open or competitive but do not result in actual competition between credible bids which allow for choosing the tenderer capable of providing the services at the lowest cost. With regard to the benchmarking option, the Communication clarifies that it should be ensured that the high costs of an inefficient undertaking are not taken as the benchmark. As regards the comparison with a 'well run undertaking', Member States should apply objective criteria that are economically recognised as being representative of satisfactory

---

88 Communication from the Commission to the European Parliament, the Council, the European Economic and Social Committee and the Committee of the Regions, A Quality Framework for Services of General Interest in Europe, 20 December 2011, COM(2011) 900 final, p. 6.

89 R. Carranta, 'General report' in U. Neergaard, C. Jacqueson and G. Skovgaard Ølykke, '*Public Procurement Law: Limitations, Opportunities and Paradoxes, The XXVI Fide Congress in Copenhagen, 2014, Congress Publications Vol. 3' (Copenhagen:* DJØF Publishing, 2014), p. 148. See also recital 42 of Directive 2014/24/EU.

90 M. Burnett, 'The New European Directive on the Award of Concession Contracts – Promoting Value for Money in PPP Contracts?' (2014) 2 *European Public Private Partnership Law Review* 17.

management. Simply generating a profit is not a sufficient criterion for deeming an undertaking to be 'well run'.[91]

2. **A Decision**, which is in fact a binding block exemption Regulation, indicating that Member States are exempted to notify specific categories of public service compensations that constitute State aid to the Commission – although notification is still allowed – since they are held to be compatible with the internal market, more specifically with Article 106(2) TFEU.[92] SGEIs are exempted provided the compensation amount is less than an annual amount of €15 million.[93] Important to note, however, is that this compensation should only cover the net costs for carrying out the PSO which are estimated on the basis of the precisely defined parameters contained in the act of entrustment, including a reasonable profit. Social services are exempted from the obligation of notification to the Commission, regardless of the amount of the compensation received if they meet 'social needs as regards health and long term care, childcare, access to and reintegration in the labour market, social housing and the care and social inclusion of vulnerable groups'.[94] There are also exemptions for certain air or maritime links to islands and for certain SGEIs as regards airports and ports. Important to note is that the Decision is only applicable to SGEIs that make reference to it in the formal entrustment Act and have a maximum duration of ten years. Next to the fact that it contains reporting requirements it indicates in recital 29 that it applies without prejudice to the Union provisions in the field of public procurement.
3. **A Framework** with criteria for compensation payments, which will be the tool for assessing large compensation amounts granted to providers which are not exempted under the Decision.[95] The Framework, which is a non-binding document, will apply a more favourable regime to aid which in principle falls within the scope of application of the Decision but does not fulfil all of its conditions (such as the act of entrustment or the risk of overcompensation). While the compensation amounts should be qualified as State aid, they can be declared compatible with the internal market on the basis of Article 106(2) TFEU. In this regard, the Framework contains a set of criteria that have to be fulfilled for a positive compatibility assessment. First of all, the Framework leads to a systematic investigation of SGEIs from the perspective of public procurement rules.[96] Indeed, as stated in §19, aid will be considered compatible with the internal market on the basis of Article 106(2) TFEU only where the responsible authority,

---

[91] SGEI Communication, § 71.

[92] Commission Decision of 20 December 2011 on the application of Article 106(2) of the Treaty on the Functioning of the European Union to State aid in the form of public service compensation granted to certain undertakings entrusted with the operation of services of general economic interest, [2012] OJ L7/3.

[93] There are exceptions if the compensation related to transport and transport infrastructure.

[94] Article1(c) of the Decision.

[95] Communication from the Commission – European Union framework for State aid in the form of public service compensation, [2012] OJ C8/15, hereinafter: Framework. The Framework will be applicable to SGEIs of large dimensions apart from social SGEIs and to those of a medium scale

[96] Carranta, *op.cit*, p. 150.

when entrusting the provision of the service to the undertaking in question, has complied or commits to comply with the applicable Union rules in the area of public procurement.[97] This includes any requirements of transparency, equal treatment and non-discrimination resulting directly from the Treaty and, where applicable, secondary Union law.[98] It should be noted, however, that it does not ensue from the wording of Article 106(2) TFEU or the case-law of the Court that a general interest task may be entrusted to an operator only as a result of a tendering procedure.[99] For this reason, it can be held that by establishing a criterion of compliance with the applicable public procurement rules for State aid to be found compatible, the Commission seems to be transgressing the limits of its broad discretion in shaping the application of Article 106(2) TFEU.[100]

Furthermore the Framework contains some provisions on how to calculate the amount of compensation and a reasonable profit.[101] It contains some detailed provisions on the 'net avoided cost methodology'[102] to calculate the net cost necessary, or expected to be necessary to discharge the public service obligations and refers to calculations based on a swap rate[103] or the rate of return on capital that would be required by a typical company regarding the calculation of profit.[104] This will not be further discussed within the scope of this chapter. In any case, the Framework, which includes reporting requirements, obliges Member States to introduce incentives for the efficient provision of SGEIs of a high standard, unless they can duly justify that it is not feasible or appropriate to do so. Indeed, mechanisms for incentivising efficiency improvements contribute to reducing the risk of overcompensation. They should be based on objective and measurable criteria set out in the entrustment act and be subject to transparent *ex post* assessment carried out by an entity independent from the SGEI provider.[105]

4. **A *de minimis* Regulation** specifically applicable to SGEIs, stating that under the threshold of €500,000 for over a period of three fiscal years, compensations do not fall under State aid scrutiny.[106] This is based on the assumption that

[97] §10 Framework indicates that it is applicable without prejudice to requirements imposed by Union law in the field of public procurement.

[98] Aid that does not comply with such rules and requirements is considered to affect the development of trade to an extent that would be contrary to the interests of the Union within the meaning of Article 106(2) TFEU.

[99] N. Fiedziuk, 'Putting Services of General Economic Interest Up for Tender: Reflections on Applicable EU Rules' (2013) 50 *Common Market Law Review* 99. See also Case T-17/02, *Olsen v. Commission* [2005] ECR II-2031.

[100] Ibid.

[101] Framework, §§21–22.

[102] Framework, §§24–25.

[103] Framework, §36.

[104] Framework, §33.

[105] Framework §§39 and 42.

[106] Commission Regulation (EU) No 360/2012 of 25 April 2012 on the application of Articles 107 and 108 of the Treaty on the Functioning of the European Union to *de minimis* aid granted to undertakings providing services of general economic interest, [2012] OJ L114/8. It should be noted that this Regulation is only applicable to transparent aid which is defined as aid of which the gross grant equivalent can be calculated *ex ante* without the need to undertake a risk assessment.

> compensation that falls below this threshold is not likely to affect trade between Member States and/or have an appreciable effect on competition. Since the undertaker has to be compensated for the extra costs incurred in providing a public service, the threshold is higher than the one in the general *de minimis* Regulation.[107] Aid that exceeds the threshold will have to be investigated under the Decision and, failing that, under the Framework.[108] As stated by recital 21 of the Regulation, it is applicable without prejudice to the requirements of Union law in the area of public procurement.

It can be concluded that while the *Altmark* judgment establishes when a measure comes within the scope of the concept of State aid (Article 107(1) TFEU), the Decision and the Framework establish the conditions under which compensation constituting State aid is compatible with the internal market. It follows that if a public procurement procedure is in line with the fourth *Altmark* criterion and the other *Altmark* criteria are fulfilled as well, there is no State aid so the Decision or the Framework cannot be applied and there is no need to examine the compensation under Article 106(2) TFEU. As a consequence, whenever the *Altmark* test is not satisfied, the test is to be repeated under Article 106(2) TFEU.[109] Hence, the obligation to follow a tender procedure (or benchmarking exercise) imposed by public procurement rules may be overridden by the SGEI objectives inscribed in the provision of Article 106(2) TFEU.[110] Nevertheless, important to note in this regard is that the Almunia package, and specifically §19 of the Framework, also mandates compliance with public procurement rules as a condition for exemption of the aid granted to the undertaking entrusted with the SGEI. It follows that on the one hand it can be argued that failing to comply with the public procurement requirements will imply that compensation granted to an undertaking cannot be exempted under Article 106(2) TFEU.[111] On the other hand, it can be claimed that it does not ensue from the wording of Article 106(2) TFEU or the case-law of the Court that a general interest task may be entrusted to an operator only as a result of a tendering procedure.[112] In this regard it should be noted that tendering is not a miraculous remedy for all the ills of SGEIs and in many cases it may, in fact, be

---

107 Regulation No 1407/2013 of 18 December 2013 on the application of Articles 107 and 108 of the Treaty on the Functioning of the European Union to *de minimis* aid, [2013] OJ L352/1.

108 E. Szyszczak, 'Modernising State Aid and the Financing of SGEI' (2012) 3(4) *Journal of European Competition Law & Practice* 332.

109 Klasse, *op.cit*, p. 38.

110 N. Fiedziuk, 'Putting Services of General Economic Interest Up for Tender: Reflections on Applicable EU Rules' (2013) 50 *Common Market Law Review* 89.

111 Sanchez Graells (2014), *op.cit*, p. 18.

112 Fiedziuk, *op.cit*, p. 99. See also Case T-17/02, *Olsen v Commission* [2005] ECR II-2031. According to the Commission, the Decision does not set efficiency requirements and the amount of the compensation does not necessarily have to be determined through a public procurement procedure or benchmarking exercise. See Commission Staff Working Document, Guide to the application of the EU rules on State aid, public procurement and the internal market to SGEI of 29 April 2013, p. 61.

undesirable to follow tendering rules.[113] As suggested by Fiedziuk, 'if Member States have to follow a public procurement procedure, this has a negative impact on their high level of discretion which may in turn have a negative impact on the proper functioning of the public service. Furthermore, as opposed to direct awards, tendering procedures generate high transaction costs for both the contracting authority as the undertaker. In addition, tenderers often have to make high investments which may impose a disproportionate risk with regard to short-term contracts while a long-term contract may render the authority becoming 'locked-in' to an inefficient service provider for the period of the contract'.[114]

In any case, while *Altmark* allows for a self-assessment by Member States of public service compensations, the assessment of whether compensation that qualifies as State aid meets the requirements for compatibility under Article 106(2) TFEU is a matter for exclusive competence of the Commission.[115] As suggested by Klasse, in its practice, the Commission has had the tendency to find that the state-financing of public service missions does not comply with the *Altmark* criteria, thereby bringing it within the ambit of Article 107(1) TFEU, and then, subsequently, declaring it compatible with the common market on the basis of Article 106(2) or Article 107(3) TFEU.[116] So far, there is no case-law on the issue of derogation to a SGEI under Article 106(2) TFEU.

3.6 Public Procurement

3.6.1 Introduction

State aid law and public procurement law both want to ensure fair competition in the internal market. Indeed, both sets of regulation are based on the same economic principle – that, in the long term, competitive markets generate the most efficient outcomes and contribute to social welfare and are oriented towards correcting similar market failures – and so, both focus on curbing the undesirable market behaviour of different market agents.[117] However, both fields use different mechanisms to reach this aim. State Aid law aspires to achieve more competition by creating a level playing field for all the undertakings active in the internal market and ensure that they do not obtain an unwarranted advantage. Public procurement law aims to enhance competition by opening up national procurement markets and creating better value for money for public authorities. Public authorities wishing to set up a SGEI should therefore comply with the State Aid rules and the rules relating to the award of public contracts or concessions. While the State aid rules apply from the moment that an undertaking is financed, the mere financing of an activity is usually not covered by the public procurement rules which mainly focus on the award of the contract that contains an obligation to provide a service. Another difference between both areas of law is that while in State aid law, economic considerations always have priority, public procurement law is increasingly focusing on social and environmental concerns and connects

113 Fiedziuk, *op.cit*, p. 93.
114 Ibid, p. 95.
115 Klasse, *op.cit*, p. 50.
116 Ibid.
117 Sanchez Graells (2011), *op.cit*, p. 110.

the activities of the state with the pursuit of public interest. On the one hand this entails that both areas of law can pursue conflicting interests. On the other hand it may mean that specifically with regard to the tendering of SGEIs, there may be similar objectives since by definition public interest concerns are of great importance when it comes to SGEIs.

As has been demonstrated above, in principle the financing of SGEIs when channelled through public procurement reflects market value. A breach of public procurement rules will, in a significant number of cases (and almost in all cases involving SGEI) imply the existence of (potential) unlawful State aid. Public contracts should thus not be considered as potential instruments for granting disguised illegal State aid. However, while EU State aid law tries to incentivize tendering of SGEIs by providing for less rigorous treatment when the award of a contract is preceded by a public procurement procedure, public procurement law disregards the significance of the SGEI concept and adopts its own standards on when an agreement should follow a public procurement procedure and whether it merits derogation.[118] Indeed, SGEIs are as such not regulated by the procurement Directives. The general procurement Directive 2014/24/EU only indicates that it does not deal with the liberalisation of SGEIs and that Member States are free to define SGEIs, their scope and the characteristics of the services to be provided, including any conditions regarding the quality of the service, in order to pursue their public policy objectives. Furthermore, the Directive is without prejudice to the power of national, regional and local authorities to provide, commission and finance SGEIs in accordance with Article 14 TFEU and Protocol No 26. It also does not deal with the funding of SGEIs or with systems of aid granted by Member States, in particular in the social field, in accordance with Union rules on competition.[119] It follows that only if Member States decide to outsource the provision of SGEIs, public procurement law may apply. Member States are indeed not obliged to contract out or externalise the provision of services that they wish to provide themselves or to organise by means other than public contracts.[120]

Until now the Court has not explicitly acknowledged whether and how Article 106(2) TFEU would apply in the context of EU public procurement rules. As suggested by Fiedziuk, in *Commission v Ireland* Advocate-General Stix-Hackl indicated in her opinion that Article 106(2) TFEU could, in principle, be relied on by Member States if the application of the provisions on public procurement would have obstructed the performance, in law or in fact, of the tasks assigned to it.[121] This view seems to be correct since Article 106(2) TFEU, as opposed to other Treaty exemptions which are mostly domain-specific, is holistic in nature which entails that it has a capacity to derogate, as indicated by its wording, from 'the rules contained in the Treaties'.[122] It

118 Fiedziuk, *op.cit*, p. 88.

119 Recitals 6 and 7 and Article 1(4) of Directive 2014/24/EU. See also Article 4(1) of Directive 2014/23/EU on concession contracts.

120 Recital 5 Directive 2014/24/EU; Case C-107/98, *Teckal* [1999] ECR I-8121.

121 Opinion of A.G. Stix-Hackl of 14 September 2006 in *Commission v Ireland* [2007] ECR I-11353; Fiedziuk, *op.cit*, p. 112.

122 Fiedziuk, *op.cit*, pp. 110–11.

can thus also be invoked with regard to the internal market rules and the general principles of law which form the legal basis of the procurement Directives.

In the following paragraphs some aspects of public procurement law that deserve specific attention in the light of Article 106(2) TFEU will be briefly discussed. It concerns the existence of service concessions, the in-house provision of SGEIs and the concept of 'contracting authority' and the focus on flexibility in the new procurement package.

3.6.2 Service concessions

As stated by Article 106(1) TFEU, in the case of public undertakings and undertakings to which Member States grant special or exclusive rights, Member States shall neither enact nor maintain in force any measure contrary to the rules contained in the Treaties, in particular to those rules provided for in Article 18 and Articles 101 to 109. Public contracts do not generate significant exclusionary effects on market competition as meant in this Article. For this reason, Article 106(1) TFEU is not really relevant with regard to public contracts, except for concessions. Indeed, concessions have inherent exclusivity and quasi-monopolistic features which have a negative impact on (or completely exclude) the ability of other tenderers to compete with the concessionaire in the same geographical area under substantially equivalent conditions during the lifespan of the concession contract; thus resulting in a special or exclusive right for the purposes of Article 106(1) TFEU.[123] It follows that if a special or exclusionary right has been provided, Member States cannot enact or maintain in force any measure contrary to the Treaties.

Concessions are generally used to award SGEIs. Since they concern large contracts of long duration, they often require considerable infusions of public money even though in many Member States the provision of SGEIs has recently been privatised.[124] It follows that privatisation was often only in form and concessions have generally been awarded to domestic undertakings without advertisement at EU level.[125] In this regard it should be noted that even though traditionally service concessions were not regulated by the public procurement directives, the fundamental principles of EU law (equal treatment, non-discrimination, transparency) and Treaty provisions have always been applicable, at least if there is some cross-border interest. The new public procurement package that was adopted in parallel to the adoption of the new SGEI package contains a Directive[126] that specifically concerns the award of concession contracts.

Article 106(2) TFEU is an exception to Article 106(1) TFEU. This entails that in cases where Article 106(1) TFEU applies, Article 106(2) TFEU can be invoked to set aside the application of public procurement rules if this would jeopardise the performance of the specific SGEI. However, as suggested by Sanchez Graells, since

---

123 Sanchez Graells (2011), *op.cit*, p. 123.

124 R. Carranta, 'The Changes to the Public Contract Directives and the Story They Tell about how EU Law Works' (2015) 52(2) *Common Market Law Review* 391–459.

125 See the results in the report by the College of Europe available 29 January 2016 at http://ec.europa.eu/internal_market/consultations/docs/2010/concessions/college_europe_en.pdf.

126 Directive 2014/23/EU of the European Parliament and of the Council of 26 February 2014 on the award of concession contracts, [2014] OJ L94/1–64.

compliance with public procurement rules and principles concerns the contracting authority (not the undertaker) and must take place before the undertaking starts rendering the SGEI, it does not obstruct the performance, in law or in fact, of the particular tasks (which at the time of conducting the procurement process still do not exist) assigned to them as meant in Article 106(2) TFEU.[127] It follows that the award of the special or exclusive right to provide SGEIs in breach of public procurement rules will hardly ever fulfil the conditions of Article 106(2) TFEU. On the other hand it has been held that the reliance on Article 106(2) TFEU could become a viable option to overcome the new regime of Directive 2014/23/EU and restore public authorities' freedom to choose the most suitable mode of public service provision.[128] In this regard it should be noted, however, that since many concession contracts are of long duration, it might be wise to look for alternative ways to prevent corruption, such as more costly but effective monitoring.[129]

3.6.3 'In-house' provision of SGEIs and the concept of 'contracting authority'

As held above, SGEIs are often entrusted by the State acting as a public authority to a private undertaking. This can be done by way of a public procurement procedure. The procurement directives establish rules on the procedures for procurement by *contracting authorities* with respect to public contracts.[130] Contracting authorities include the State, regional or local authorities, bodies governed by public law or associations formed by one or more such authorities or one or more such bodies governed by public law.[131] Bodies governed by public law are established for the specific purpose of meeting needs in the general interest, not having an industrial or commercial character. Even though there might be needs of general interest, which have an industrial and commercial character and even though it is possible that private undertakings can meet needs of general interest which do not have industrial and commercial character, the acid test for needs in the general interest not having an industrial or commercial character is that the state or other contracting authorities choose themselves to meet these needs or to have a decisive influence over their provision.[132] As held above, in public markets the public interest substitutes profit maximisation. The fact that a body must have been established for the 'specific' purpose of meeting needs in the general interest does not mean that it should be entrusted only with meeting such needs.[133] The procurement directives do not make a distinction between public contracts awarded by a contracting authority in the general interest and those which are unrelated to that task.[134] In assessing whether or not a need in the general interest is present, account

---

[127] Sanchez Graells (2011), *op.cit*, p. 127.

[128] Fiedziuk, *op.cit*, p. 105.

[129] Ibid, p. 96.

[130] See e.g. Article 1(1) Directive 2014/24/EU.

[131] Article 2(1) Directive 2014/24/EU.

[132] Bovis, *op.cit*, p. 5.

[133] Case C-44/96, *Mannesmann* [1998] ECR I-73, §26.

[134] The applicability of the directives cannot be excluded owing solely to the fact that the tasks in the general interest having a character other than industrial or commercial which it carries out in practice were not entrusted to it at the time of its establishment. See Case C-470/99, *Universale-Bau AG* [2002] ECR I-11617.

must be taken of all the relevant legal and factual elements, such as the circumstances prevailing at the time when the body concerned was established and the conditions under which it exercises its activity, taking account in particular of the fact that it does not aim primarily at making a profit, the fact that it does not bear the risks associated with the activity, and any public financing of the activity in question.[135] In this regard, the existence of significant competition does not, of itself, allow the conclusion to be drawn that there is no need in the general interest, not having an industrial or commercial character.[136] However, it is an indication that it is highly likely that the respective entity is not a body governed by public law.[137] The key issue is whether the organisation primarily intends to achieve profitability. It follows that the concept 'body governed by public law' includes commercial companies under public control who fulfil the requirements of Article 2(1) of the Directive.[138] In this regard it should be avoided that the application of the Directives is circumvented by contracting authorities who use private undertakings under their control to award contracts. If the realisation of a project does not contribute to the aims and objectives of an undertaking, it is assumed that the project in question is awarded 'on behalf' of another undertaking, and if the latter beneficiary is a contracting authority under the framework of public procurement law, then the relevant Directives should apply.[139] An entity's private law status does thus not constitute a reason to exclude it from being classified as a contracting authority.

Important to note is that the procurement directives are not applicable to in-house situations.[140] A public contract awarded by a contracting authority to a legal person governed by private or public law falls outside the scope of the Directive where all of the following conditions are fulfilled: (a) the contracting authority exercises over the legal person concerned a control which is similar to that which it exercises over its own departments; (b) more than 80 per cent of the activities of the controlled legal person are carried out in the performance of tasks entrusted to it by the controlling contracting authority or by other legal persons controlled by that contracting authority; and (c) there is no direct private capital participation in the controlled legal person with the exception of non-controlling and non-blocking forms of private capital participation required by national legislative provisions, in conformity with the Treaties, which do not exert a decisive influence on the controlled legal person.[141] It follows that if the entity becomes market-oriented or in case of participation, even as a minority shareholder, of a private undertaking in the capital of a company in which a contracting

---

135 Case C-18/01, *Korhonen* [2003] ECR I-5321, §59.

136 Case C-373/00, *Adolf Truley* [2003] ECR I-1931, §66.

137 Case C-223/99, *Agora* [2001] ECR I-3605, §42.

138 It should be noted that the Court uses a functional test to assess the relationship between an entity and the state. In addition to the element of management or financial control the Court also considers factors such as the intention and purpose of establishment of the entity in question and as such approaches the issue in a flexible manner. See Bovis, *op.cit*, p. 21 and Case C-306/97, *Teoranta* [1998] ECR I-8761.

139 Bovis, *op.cit*, p. 8.

140 Case C-107/98, *Teckal* [1999] ECR I-8121.

141 Article 12(1) of Directive 2014/24/EU.

authority is also a participant, the dependency/control criterion is not met and the Directives will be applicable.[142]

With regard to the provision of SGEIs in particular, it has to be repeated in this regard that if the one of the *Altmark* criteria is not fulfilled, the compensation for the PSO in question is potentially State aid and requires *ex ante* notification to the Commission. This is also the case if the funding is provided to an in-house body within the meaning of the rules on public procurement which provides SGEIs. It follows that if a situation is not covered by the EU public procurement rules, this does not automatically entail that it is also excluded from the State aid rules.[143] As held above, the application of the competition rules does not depend on the legal status of the body providing the SGEIs but on the economic character of the activity performed.

3.6.4 The focus on flexibility in the new public procurement package

As has been mentioned above, the new public procurement package puts a lot of emphasis on flexibility and has emphasised the use of negotiations in this regard. As held by Article 26(4) of Directive 2014/24/EU, Member States should be able to provide for the use of the competitive procedure with negotiation or the competitive dialogue in various situations where open or restricted procedures without negotiations are not likely to lead to satisfactory procurement outcomes. This is, for example, the case if the needs of the contracting authority cannot be met without adaptation of readily available solutions or if those needs include design or innovative solutions. As already indicated, this clashes with the statements of the Commission in §66 of its SGEI Communication.

Moreover, Article 72 of Directive 2014/24/EU provides for the modification of contracts during their terms without the need for a new tender procedure as long as these modifications are not substantial and Article 72(2) even introduces a *de minimis* threshold of substantiality.[144] Given that the contractual conditions can be altered after award, those changes, while compliant with EU procurement law, could be a form of disguised State aid if they were not justified by the operative needs of the implementation of the contract or resulted in excessive (supra-competitive) compensation to the public contractor.[145]

As held by Sanchez Graells, the increased flexibility both at award phase and during the execution of public contracts imposes the need to adopt a new method in order to find an infringement of the State aid rules (or *rectius*, in order to reverse the presumption that compliance with public procurement rules excludes the existence of any undue economic advantage).[146] It is thus necessary to determine whether, despite having (formally) complied with procurement rules, the economic operator actually

---

[142] Case C-26/03, *Stadt Halle* [2005] ECR I-1.

[143] Commission Staff Working Document, Guide to the application of the EU rules on State aid, public procurement and the internal market to SGEI of 29 April 2013, p. 39.

[144] Sanchez Graells (2014), *op.cit*, p. 8.

[145] Ibid.

[146] Ibid.

received an economic advantage because the terms of the contract (either originally, particularly if negotiated or as amended) do not reflect normal market conditions.[147]

4. CONCLUSION

When a public authority externalises the provision of a public service, the private service provider will have to be motivated through a financial compensation from the public purse. Public authorities wishing to set up SGEIs must comply with the State Aid rules and the rules on the award of public contracts or concessions. As held by the Court in *Altmark*, several conditions have to be fulfilled before compensation paid for the provision of a public service is not considered to be State aid under Article 107(1) TFEU. One of these conditions is the selection of the undertaking that will discharge the PSO by means of a public procurement procedure that allows for the selection of the tenderer capable of providing the services at least cost to the community or a benchmarking exercise (fourth *Altmark* criterion). In this way, public procurement has emerged as an essential component in the process of determining the parameters under which public subsidies and state financing of public services constitute State aid.

Nevertheless, even though there is a tendency to incentivize tendering of SGEIs to ensure they are provided at the least cost, a tender procedure is not in itself sufficient to exclude over-compensation and cannot always depict the true status of the market.[148] It is, for example, possible that even the lowest bid turns out to be too high, for example, as a result of agreements, decisions or concerted practices within the meaning of Article 101 TFEU. Contracting authorities should thus always check whether a certain bid is credible which is not an easy task. Furthermore, there can be circumstances where a procurement procedure cannot allow for the least cost to the community as it does not give rise to a sufficient open and genuine competition. This can, for example, happen in the case of existing intellectual property rights or necessary infrastructure owned by a particular service provider or in procedures where only one bid is submitted.[149] It follows that even if a contracting authority has complied with the rules on public procurement and conducted a public procurement procedure, the award might still have to be notified as State aid.

The Commission's Almunia or SGEI package, which is a confirmation of the indissoluble link between State aid and public procurement, was designed to clarify key issues of State aid. It held that the fourth *Altmark* criterion is not fulfilled by procedures that appear to be open or competitive but do not result in actual competition between credible bids. In its SGEI Communication the Commission stated that a

---

[147] Ibid, p. 9; Opinion of AG Jacobs in Case C-126/01, *GEMO*, [2003] ECR I-13769, 122. See also Opinion of AG Fennelly in Case C-251/97, *France v Commission* [1999] ECR I-6639, §19.

[148] See e.g. Commission, 16 May 2006, State Aid N 604/2005 *Busverkehr Landkreis Wittenberg*, §60 and the subsequent decision clearing the measure as State aid free: Commission, 15 September 2009, State Aid N 207/2009; Commission Decision 2014/197, *Mutliarena Copenhagen,* as published in [2014] OJ L152.

[149] SGEI Communication, §68.

competitive dialogue or a negotiated procedure with prior publication confer a wide discretion upon contracting authorities and may restrict the participation of interested operators so that they only satisfy the *Altmark* ruling in exceptional cases.

If not all *Altmark* criteria are fulfilled, compensation for a PSO that is regarded as State aid might still be exempted under Article 106(2) TFEU. This is not an automatic exemption, however, as it is limited to situations in which the application of the Treaty would obstruct the performance of the particular tasks assigned to the undertakings entrusted with the provision of the SGEI. In this regard, §19 of the SGEI Framework indicates that aid will be considered compatible with the internal market on the basis of Article 106(2) only where the responsible authority, when entrusting the provision of the service to the undertaking in question, has complied or commits to comply with the applicable Union rules in the area of public procurement. It thus seems that failing to comply with the public procurement requirements implies that compensation granted to an undertaking cannot be exempted under Article 106(2) TFEU. It does not ensue from the wording of Article 106(2) TFEU or the case-law of the Court, however, that a general interest task may be entrusted to an operator only as a result of a tendering procedure. Since there is no case-law on the issue of derogation to a SGEI under Article 106(2) TFEU, there is thus no legal certainty on the relationship between the rules on public procurement and those on SGEIs and thus on the tendering of SGEIs. The question 'Should we tender public services?' is thus still open and will probably have to be answered on a case-by-case basis.

PART 3

JUSTICIABILITY IN PUBLIC PROCUREMENT

11. Judicial activism and public procurement

Christopher Bovis

1. INTRODUCTION

Judicial activism represents the most influential factor in the evolution of the public procurement *acquis,* which has been experiencing conceptual and regulatory vagueness, limited interoperability with legal systems of Member States and continuous market-driven modality changes in financing and delivering public services.[1] The jurisprudence of the Court of Justice of the European Union (CJEU) has been instrumental in developing and honing the concepts of the public procurement *acquis* and in providing for clarity and certainty to its decentralised application and enforcement. The current reform agenda of public procurement is guided by doctrines developed by the Court which attempt to fuse the underlying principles of public procurement regulation with the fundamental principles enshrined in the EU Treaties by supplementing the deficiencies of the public procurement Directives with primary EU law. Public procurement is viewed by both EU Institutions and Member States as an instrument for growth and competitiveness in the light of the European 2020 Strategy.

Public procurement law has been moulded by the instrumental role of the CJEU,[2] which has provided intellectual support to the efforts of the European institutions to strengthen the fundamental principles which underpin public procurement regulation.[3] The impact of the Court's jurisprudence has been in developing the public procurement *acquis* by submitting the conceptual themes of public procurement Directives to the doctrines which the Court established and had recourse to in its attempt to develop public procurement law as the conduit for the delivery of public services in EU Member States. Judicial activism in public procurement to expose *exhaustive harmonisation* as the main shortcoming of public procurement law and the cause of significant porosity in the procurement Directives, has resulted in a legal *lacuna* and a recurrent danger of limiting the effectiveness of the public procurement *acquis*. The way the porosity of the public procurement Directives has been treated by the Court is focused on the application of the transparency principle and its surrogate principle of equality in an attempt to fortify the public procurement Directives by supplementing their thrust with legal principles enshrined in primary European law.

1 See C. Bovis, 'Public Procurement in the EU: Jurisprudence and Conceptual Directions' (2012) 49 CMLRev 1–44.

2 See C. Bovis, 'Recent Case Law Relating to Public Procurement: A Beacon for the Integration of Public Markets' (2002) 39 CMLRev 1025–56.

3 See C. Bovis, 'The Effects of the Principles of Transparency and Accountability on Public Procurement Regulation' Chapter 11 in H. Hoffman and A. Turk (eds), *Legal Challenges in EU Administrative Law* (Cheltenham, UK and Northampton, MA, USA: Edward Elgar, 2009) pp. 288–321.

1.1 Judicial Activism and the Side Effects of Public Procurement Regulation

A first sight of the Court's judicial activism has been the *de lege ferenda* interpretation of public procurement Directives in order to provide a platform upon which Member States can effectively implement the *acquis* into domestic legal systems. The Court recognised the deficiencies and conceptual limitations of the public procurement Directives, and its jurisprudence has pointed towards the strategic goal of arming the regime with direct effect, in order to enhance access to justice at national level, to improve compliance and to streamline public procurement regulation by introducing an element of uniformity in its application.

The most pronounced deficiency of the public procurement Directives is their porosity which is caused by exhaustive harmonisation. The porosity of the public procurement Directives undermines their effectiveness by preventing their applicability to certain contractual situations and as a result restricting a *de lege ferenda* extension of their provisions.

Exhaustive harmonisation excludes *de lege lata* from the scope of the public procurement Directives public contracts below certain thresholds and certain contractual relationships which reflect inter-administrative interfaces in the public sector or contractual relations based on dominant influence between utilities and affiliated undertakings and in particular, service concessions, public contracts based on exclusive rights, public contracts in pursuit of services of general economic interest, in-house contracts, and non-priority services contracts. Exhaustive harmonisation reflects the mutual exclusivity of the public sector Directive and the Utilities Directive[4] as well as their non-applicability in cases of public contracts awarded pursuant to international rules,[5] or secret contracts and contracts requiring special security measures or contracts related with the protection of Member States' essential interests.[6] In addition, the public sector Directive also does not cover public contracts whose object is to provide or exploit public telecommunications networks;[7] contracts for the acquisition or rental or land; contracts related to broadcasting services; contracts related to financial securities, capital raising activities and central bank services; employment contracts; and research and development contracts which do not benefit the relevant contacting authority.[8] The Utilities Directive does not apply to contracts awarded in a third country;[9] contracts awarded by contracting entities engaged in the provision or operation of fixed networks for the purchase of water and for the supply of energy or of fuels for the production of energy;[10] contracts subject to special arrangements for the exploitation and exploration of oil, gas, coal or other solid fuels;[11] contracts and framework agreements awarded by central purchasing bodies;[12] contracts of whose object activity is directly exposed to

---

4 See the Utilities Directive 2004/17, [2004] OJ L134/1.

5 See Article 15 of the Public Sector Directive and Article 22(a) of the Utilities Directive.

6 See Article 14 of the Public Sector Directive and Article 21 of the Utilities Directive.

7 See Article 13 of the Public Sector Directive.

8 See Article 16 of the Public Sector Directive.

9 See Article 20(1) of the Utilities Directive.

10 See Article 26(a) of the Utilities Directive.

11 See Article 27 of the Utilities Directive.

12 See Article 29(2) of the Utilities Directive.

competition on markets to which access is not restricted[13] and contracts related to works and service concessions.[14]

Exhaustive harmonisation in *lex specialis* legal instruments such as the public procurement Directives cannot impose limits on the application of primary EU law to supplement their legal thrust. The Court has recognised the *lacuna* in the limited effectiveness of the procurement Directives and particularly in areas which cannot *de lege ferenda* be conducive to regulatory control and the need for conformity with EU law. Although the application of primary European law is not precluded in the presence of exhaustive provisions of secondary law,[15] the Court explicitly recognised that the *lex specialis* character of the procurement Directives aims at complementing fundamental freedoms of EU law.[16] The Court responded to and treated the porosity of the procurement Directives by signalling the necessity of supplementing their remit with *acquis* deriving from fundamental principles of EU law. Thus, the supplementary applicability of primary EU law intends to close the gap that exists in contracts falling outside the procurement Directives, such as service concessions and sub-dimensional contracts[17] and in contracts which fall within the remit of the Directives, but escape from the full thrust of the principles enshrined therein, such as non-priority services contracts.[18] The Court, also, manifested the need to increase compliance of contracting

---

[13] See Article 30(1) of the Utilities Directive.

[14] See Article 30(6) third indent of the Utilities Directive.

[15] See Cases C-37/92, *Vanacker and Lesage* [1993] ECR I-4947, para 9; C-324/99, *DaimlerChrysler* [2001] ECR I-9897, para 32; and C-322/01, *Deutscher Apothekerverband* [2003] ECR I-14887, para 64.

[16] See P. Craig, 'The Legal Effect of Directives: Policy, Rules and Exceptions' (2009) 34 ELRev 349.

[17] See Cases C-231/03, *Coname* [2005] ECR I-7287, para 16, and C-264/03, *Commission v France* [2005] ECR I-8831, para 32.

[18] See Cases 45/87, *Commission v Ireland* [1988] ECR I-4929, para 27, where the Court held that the inclusion in the contract specification of a clause stipulating exclusively the use of national specifications infringe Article 30 EC; C-243/89, *Commission v Denmark (Storebælt)* [1993] ECR I-3353, where the Court found that contract clauses concerning preference to national specifications and nominated subcontractors infringe Articles 30, 48 and 59 EC; C-158/03 *Commission v Spain* and C-234/03, *Contse and Others* [2005] ECR I-9315, where the content of tendering specifications, and in particular sub-criteria for the award of contracts ran contrary to Article 49 EC; C-92/00, *HI* [2002] ECR I-5553, para 42, where the Court ruled that contracting authorities' decisions are subject to fundamental rules of Community law, and in particular to the principles on the right of establishment and the freedom to provide services; C-244/02, *Kauppatalo Hansel Oy* [2003] ECR I-12139, paras 31 and 33, where the Court confirmed the principle under which primary law is to be taken into account in a supplemental capacity for evaluating the effectiveness of the public procurement Directives; C-57/01, *Makedoniko Metro and Mihaniki* [2003] ECR I-1091, para 69, where the Court held that even if the Community directives on public procurement *do not contain specifically applicable provisions*, the general principles of Community law … govern procedures for the award of public contracts; C-275/98, *Unitron Scandinavia* [1999] ECR I-8291, para 30 *et seq.*, where the Court held that Community law principles such as the principles of transparency and the prohibition of discrimination on grounds of nationality must embrace the remit of the public procurement Directives.

authorities by promoting the objectivity of the procurement Directives and enhancing their justiciability, whilst in parallel limiting their inherent flexibility.

The Court treated further the porosity of the public procurement Directives by relying on the principle of transparency for their interpretation and application. The principle of transparency is surrogate to the principle of equal treatment and both principles encapsulate the fundamental EU law principles which underpin public procurement, such as the free movement of goods, the right of establishment and the freedom to provide services, as well as the principle of non-discrimination. The Court's case-law shows the conceptual link between transparency and the principle of equal treatment. Transparency intends to ensure the effectiveness of equal treatment in public procurement by guaranteeing the conditions for genuine competition. As the principle of equal treatment is a general principle of EU law, Member States are required to comply with the duty of transparency, which constitutes a concrete and specific expression of that principle. The Court has viewed that the duty of transparency represents a concrete and specific expression of the principle of equal treatment,[19] which assumes that similar situations should not be treated differently unless differentiation is objectively justified.[20]

The Court had the opportunity to define the scope of the principle of equal treatment in the context of public procurement in *Commission v Denmark*[21] and *Commission v Belgium*.[22] The Court held that compliance with the principle of equal treatment requires an absence of discrimination on grounds of nationality and a duty of transparency which enables contracting authorities to ensure that that principle is complied with. The Court then defined the scope of the duty of transparency in *Telaustria*[23] and *Parking Brixen*.[24] Accordingly, the duty of transparency is intended to preclude any risk of favouritism or arbitrariness on the part of contracting authorities by ensuring a sufficient degree of advertising, which would result in opening up the market to competition and by guaranteeing effective review mechanisms of the impartiality of the procurement procedures. The duty of transparency also implies that all the conditions and detailed rules of the award procedure must be drawn up in a clear, precise and unequivocal manner in the notice or contract documents in order to enable all reasonably informed tenderers their significance and to allow unequivocally their interpretation. The duty of transparency must also enable contracting authorities to ascertain whether the tenders submitted satisfy the award criteria applied to the relevant contract.[25]

---

19 See Joined Cases C-117/76 and C-16/77, *Ruckdeschel and Others* [1977] ECR 1753, para 7.

20 See Joined Cases 201/85 and 202/85, *Klensch and Others* [1986] ECR 3477, para 9, and Case C-442/00, *Rodríguez Caballero* [2002] ECR I-11915, para 32.

21 See Case C-243/89, *Commission v Denmark* [1993] ECR I-3353, paras 37–39.

22 See Case C-87/94, *Commission v Belgium* [1996] ECR I-2043, in particular paras 51–56. See also Case C-496/99 P, *Commission v CAS Succhi di Frutta* [2004] ECR I-3801, para 108.

23 See Case C-324/98, *Telaustria and Telefonadress,* [2000] ECR I-10745.

24 See Case C-458/03, *Parking Brixen* [2005] ECR I-8612.

25 See European Commission Interpretative Communication on the Community Law applicable to contract awards not or not fully subject to the provisions of the Public Procurement Directives, [2006] OJ C179/02. The Commission drew up best practice by recommending means

1.2 Doctrinal Judicial Activism through a Rule of Reason

A second glimpse of the Court's judicial activism reveals an approach based on a *rule of reason.* Such approach is reflected in the establishment of a number of doctrines which have guided the application of the public procurement rules by defining essential legal concepts such as public contracts,[26] contracting authorities,[27] the remit of selection and qualification criteria,[28] and the parameters for contracting authorities to use environmental and social considerations[29] as award criteria and which have

---

of adequate and commonly used publication of notices in the Member States such as the internet, the contracting authority's website, or specific portal websites, national official journals and other means of publication including a voluntary submission to the OJEU/Tenders Electronic Daily for larger value contracts.

[26] See Cases C-399/98, *Ordine degli Architetti and Others* [2001] ECR I-5409; C-324/98, *Telaustria and Telefonadress* [2000] ECR I-10745; C-59/00, *Vestergaard* [2001] ECR I-9505; C-26/03 *Stadt Halle and RPL Lochau* [2005] ECR I-1; C-264/03, *Commission v France* [2005] E.C.R. I-8831; C-231/03, *Consorzio Aziende Metano (Coname) v Comune di Cingia de' Botti* [2005] ECR I-7287; C-507/03, *Commission v Ireland,* (An Post) [2007] ECR I-9777; C-231/03, *Coname* [2005] ECR I-7287; C-458/03, *Parking Brixen* [2005] ECR I-8585; C-264/03, *Commission v France* [2005] ECR I-8831; C-412/04, *Commission v Italy* [2008] ECR I-0000; C-295/05, *Asociación Nacional de Empresas Forestales (Asemfo) v Transformación Agraria SA (Tragsa) and Administración del Estado* [2007] ECR I-2999; C-220/05, *Jean Auroux and Others v Commune de Roanne* [2007] ECR I-385; C-382/05, *Commission v Italy* [2007] ECR I-6657; C-6/05, *Medipac-Kazantzidis AE v Venizelio-Pananio (PE.S.Y. KRITIS)* [2007] ECR I-4557; C-480/06, *Commission v Germany* [2009] ECR I-04747; C-148/06, *SECAP SpA* and *Santorso Soc. coop. arl* [2008] ECR I-3565; C-220/06, *Asociación Profesional de Empresas de Reparto y Manipulado de Correspondencia v Administración General del Estado* [2007] ECR I-12175; C-324/07, *Coditel Brabant SA v Commune d'Uccle, Région de Bruxelles-Capitale,* [2009] 1 CMLR 29; C-437/07, *Commission v Italy* [2008] ECR I-0000; C-147/06, *Commission v Ireland* [2007] ECR I-0000; C-206/08, *WAZV Gotha v Eurawasser Aufbereitungs* [2009] ECR I-8377.

[27] See Cases C-31/87, *Beentjes* [1988] ECR 4635; C-343/95, *Diego Cali et Figli* [1997] ECR 1-1547; C-44/96, *Mannesmann Anlagenbau Austria* [1998] ECR I-73; C-360/96, *BFI Holding* [1998] ECR I-6821; C-360/96, *Gemeente Arnhem Gemeente Rheden v BFI Holding BV* [1998] ECR 6821; C-380/98, *University of Cambridge* [2000] ECR I-8035; C-107/98 *Teckal* [1999] ECR I-8121; C-470/99 *Universale-Bau and Others* [2002] ECR I-11617; C-237/99 *Commission v France* (OPAC) [2001] ECR I-939; C-223/99, *Agora Srl v Ente Autonomo Fiera Internazionale di Milano* and C-260/99 *Excelsior Snc di Pedrotti runa & C v Ente Autonomo Fiera Internazionale di Milano* [2001] ECR 3605; C-373/00, *Adolf Truley* [2003] ECR-193; C-26/03, *Stadt Halle, RPL Recyclingpark Lochau GmbH v Arbeitsgemeinschaft Thermische Restabfall- und Energieverwertungsanlage TREA Leuna* [2005] ECR I-1; C-18/0,1 *Korhonen and Others* [2003] ECR I-5321.

[28] See Cases C-176/98, *Holst Italia* [1999] ECR I-8607; C-324/98, *Telaustria and Telefonadress,* [2000] ECR I-10745; C-399/98, *Ordine degli Architetti and Others* [2001] ECR I-5409; C-285/99 and C-286/99, *Lombardini and Mantovani* [2001] ECR I-9233; C-315/01, *(GAT) and Österreichische Autobahnen und Schnellstraßen AG (ÖSAG),* ECR [2003] I-6351; C-314/01, *Siemens and ARGE Telekom & Partner* [2004] ECR I-2549; C-57/01, *Makedoniko Metro and Mikhaniki* [2003] ECR I-1091; C-126/03, *Commission v Germany* [2004] ECR I-11197.

[29] See Cases C-31/87, *Gebroeders Beentjes B.V. v State of Netherlands* [1988] ECR 4635; C-225/98, *Commission v French Republic (Nord-Pas-de-Calais)* [2000] ECR 7445; C-513/99, *Concordia Bus Filandia Oy Ab v Helsingin Kaupunki et HKL-Bussiliikenne,* [2002] ECR 7213; C-448/01, *EVN AG, Wienstrom GmbH and Republik Österreich,* [2003] ECR I-14527.

influenced public procurement law making.[30] The Court's influence on the interpretation and application of the procurement *acquis* has positioned public procurement regulation as an instrument which creates compliance safeguards by authenticating established principles of European Union law[31] and which verifies compatibility links with European policies.[32]

The Court's jurisprudence reveals the following doctrines which have been utilised to construct the concepts of the public procurement Directives. First, the doctrine of *objectivity,* intends to provide a restrictive interpretation of rules governing selection procedures (quantitative and qualitative suitability criteria) and award procedures, in particular negotiated procedures as well as with the support of the test of *equivalence*, eliminate non-tariff barriers in the fields of technical standards, product specification and standardization. Secondly, the doctrine of *effectiveness* has been applied through the tests of *functionality* and *dependency* in order to define the notion of contracting authorities and also with a view to meeting the requirements of swift dispute resolution at national level and of enforceability of decisions of national courts or tribunals. Thirdly, the doctrine of *flexibility* which is defined through the tests of *dualism*, *commercialism* and *competitiveness* has been applied in order to determine the remit and thrust of public procurement rules, particularly in relation to the concept of contracting authorities and through the test of *compatibility* of socio-economic and environmental policies with the economic approach to public procurement regulation, to verify public procurement as a policy instrument of the European integration process. Fourthly, the doctrine of *procedural autonomy*, depicted through the wide discretion afforded to Member States to create the appropriate *fora* to receive complaints against decisions of contracting authorities and utilities, as well as actions for damages. Fifthly, the doctrine of *procedural equality*, expressed through the explicit obligation conferred to Member States to avoid introducing review procedures for public procurement disputes, as well as procedures for actions for damages which differ, in a discriminatory context, from other review procedures and procedures for actions for damages under national law.

2. THE CONCEPT OF REDRESS IN PUBLIC PROCUREMENT

The effectiveness of the substantive public procurement rules envisaged by the enactment of the Supplies, Works and Services Directives, as well as the Utilities

---

30 See Directive 2004/18, [2004] OJ L134 on the coordination of procedures for the award of public works contracts, public supply contracts and public service contracts and Directive 2004/17, [2004] OJ L134 coordinating the procurement procedures of entities operating in the water, energy, transport and postal services sectors. See C. Bovis, 'The New Public Procurement Regime of the European Union: A Critical Analysis of Policy, Law and Jurisprudence' (2005) 30 ELRev 607–30.

31 See P. Craig, 'Specific Powers of Public Contractors' in R. Noguellou and U. Stelkens (eds), *Comparative Law on Public Contracts* (Brussels: Bruylant, 2010).

32 See C. Bovis, 'Financing Services of General Interest, Public Procurement and State Aids: The Delineation between Market Forces and Protection' (2005) 11(1) ELJ 79–109.

Directives[33] would have been compromised without a legal framework which could provide a system of effective protection of interested parties in cases of infringements of their provisions.

Since the inspection of the first generation of public procurement Directives as legal instruments in need of incorporation within Member States,[34] the role of the CJEU has been instrumental. The main influence of the CJEU can be traced in important jurisprudence on the definition of contracting authorities,[35] the use of selection and qualification criteria,[36] and the possibility for contracting authorities to use environmental and social considerations[37] as criteria for the award of public contracts.

Under Article 267 TFEU which regulates the judicial co-operation between national judiciaries and the CJEU, in excess of 100 preliminary rulings during the last 30 years have shed light on the correct interpretation of the substantive public procurement Directives by pronouncing the direct effect of their provisions, declaring the incompatibility of national laws with the spirit and letter of the Directives and the underlying principles of EU law and finally offered to national judiciaries the necessary inferences

---

[33] See Directive 2004/18, [2004] OJ L134 on the coordination of procedures for the award of public works contracts, public supply contracts and public service contracts and Directive 2004/17, [2004] OJ L134 coordinating the procurement procedures of entities operating in the water, energy, transport and postal services sectors.

[34] See the Public Supplies Directive 93/36/EC, [1993] OJ L199, as amended by Directive 97/52/EC, [1997] OJ L328 and Directive 2001/78/EC, [2001] OJ L285; The Public Works Directive 93/37/EC, [1993] OJ L199, amended by Directive 97/52/EC [1997] OJ L328 and Directive 2001/78/EC, [2001] OJ L285; The Utilities Directives 93/38/EC, [1993] OJ L199, amended by Directive 98/4/EC [1998] OJ L101; The Public Services Directive 92/50/EEC, [1992] OJ L209, amended by Directive 97/52/EC [1997] OJ L328 and Directive 2001/78/EC, [2001] OJ L285;

[35] See Cases C-237/99, *Commission v France* [2001] ECR I-939; C-470/99, *Universale-Bau and Others* [2002] ECR I-11617; C-373/00, *Adolf Truley* [2003] ECR-193; C-84/03, *Commission v Spain* [2005] ECR I-139; C-44/96, *Mannesmann Anlagenbau Austria* [1998] ECR I-73; C-31/87, *Beentjes* [1988] ECR 4635; C-360/96, *BFI Holding* [1998] ECR I-6821; C-223/99, *Agora Srl v Ente Autonomo Fiera Internazionale di Milano* and C-260/99, *Excelsior Snc di Pedrotti runa & C v Ente Autonomo Fiera Internazionale di Milano* [2001] ECR 3605; C-360/96, *Gemeente Arnhem Gemeente Rheden v BFI Holding BV* [1998] ECR 6821; C-343/95, *Diego Cali et Figli* [1997] ECR I-1547; C-380/98, *University of Cambridge* [2000] ECR I-8035; C-237/99 *Commission v France* [2001] ECR I-939; C-26/03, *Stadt Halle, RPL Recyclingpark Lochau GmbH v Arbeitsgemeinschaft Thermische Restabfall- und Energieverwertungsanlage TREA Leuna* [2005] ECR I-1; C-107/98, *Teckal* [1999] ECR I-8121; C-18/01, *Korhonen and Others* [2003] ECR I-5321; C-237/99 *Commission v France* (OPAC) [2001] ECR I-939.

[36] See Cases C-315/01, *(GAT) and Österreichische Autobahnen und Schnellstraßen AG (ÖSAG)* [2003] ECR I-6351; C-21/03 and C-34/03, *Fabricom SA v État Belge* [2005] ECR I-1559; C-285/99 and C-286/99, *Lombardini and Mantovani* [2001] ECR I-9233; C-324/98, *Telaustria and Telefonadress* [2000] ECR I-10745; C-126/03, *Commission v Germany* [2004] ECR I-11197; C-176/98, *Holst Italia* [1999] ECR I-8607, para 29; C-399/98, *Ordine degli Architetti and Others* [2001] ECR I-5409, para 92; C-314/01, *Siemens and ARGE Telekom & Partner* [2004] ECR I-2549, para 44; C-57/01 *Makedoniko Metro and Mikhaniki* [2003] ECR I-1091.

[37] See Cases C-31/87, *Gebroeders Beentjes B.V. v State of Netherlands* [1988] ECR 4635; C-225/98, *Nord-Pas-de-Calais Commission v French Republic* [2000] ECR 7445; C-513/99, *Concordia Bus Filandia Oy Ab v Helsingin Kaupunki et HKL-Bussiliikenne* [2002] ECR 7213.

to comprehend the concepts and doctrines of public procurement regulation within the remit of EU law.

In addition to the reference procedures under Article 267 TFEU, the European Commission may bring actions against Member States before the CJEU by virtue of Article 258 TFEU. The action is a compliance procedure against Member States and their contracting authorities which breach the substantive public procurement Directives. It may initiate proceedings, on its own initiative[38] or in response to a complaint, against a defaulting Member State for failure to fulfil its obligations under the Treaty. Existence of specific legal interest is not required[39] as a condition of the admissibility of the action, since it is in the general interest of the Commission to observe, supervise and ensure the correct application of EU law. During the past 30 years, there have been in excess of 100 rulings from the CJEU. Although their high profile is evident, the rulings under the compliance procedure of Article 258 TFEU have limited effectiveness, as they have mainly declaratory character on the part of the defaulting Member State of the failure to comply with EU law.

The inadequacy of existing remedies at national level to ensure compliance and enforcement of the public procurement *acquis* was highlighted by their inability to correct infringements and ensure a correct application of the substantive public procurement rules. In order to facilitate a decentralised enforcement of the public procurement Directives, European institutions enacted the Remedies Directive on the harmonization of laws, regulations and administrative provisions relating to the application of review procedures in the award of public works and public supply contracts[40] which was extended to embrace the utilities procurement rules, by its sister Utilities Remedies Directive[41] on remedies and review procedures to the water, energy, transport and telecommunication sectors.

The scope and thrust of the Remedies Directives focused on the obligation of Member States to ensure effective and rapid review of decisions taken by contracting authorities which infringe public procurement provisions. Undertakings seeking relief from damages in the context of a procedure for the award of a contract should not be treated differently under national rules implementing EU public procurement legislation and under other national rules. This meant that the measures to be taken concerning the review procedures should be similar to national review proceedings, without any discriminatory character. Any person having or having had an interest in obtaining a particular public supply or public works contract and who has been or risks being harmed by an alleged infringement of public procurement provision shall be entitled to seek review before national courts. This particular obligation is followed by a stand-still provision concerning the prior notification by the person seeking review to the contracting authority of the alleged infringement and of his intention to seek review. However, with respect to admissibility, there is no qualitative or quantitative definition

[38] Individuals cannot force the European Commission to bring a State before the Court under Article 169 EC procedure. See Case C-48/65, *Alfons Luttucke GmbH v Commission* [1966] ECR 19.

[39] See Case C-167/73, *Commission v France* [1974] ECR 359.

[40] See Directive 89/665, [1989] OJ L395.

[41] See Directive 92/13, [1992] OJ L76/7.

of the interest of a person in obtaining a public contract. As to the element of potential harm by an infringement of public procurement provisions, it should be cumulative with the first element, that of interest. The prior notification should intend to exhaust any possibility of amicable settlement before the parties have recourse to national courts. A novelty in the Remedies Directive of the Utilities sectors[42] was deemed to be the introduction of the *attestation procedure*. Member states were required to give the contracting entities the possibility of having their purchasing procedures and practices *attested* by persons authorised by law to exercise this function. Under the attestation mechanism, possible irregularities in the award of a public contract may be identified in advance and provide for the opportunity to contracting authorities to correct them. The latter may include the attestation statement in the notice inviting tenders published in the Official Journal (OJ). The system appeared in principle flexible and cost-efficient and could potentially have prevented wasteful litigation. The attestation procedure under Directive 92/13/EC was deemed the essential requirement for the development of EU standards of attestation.[43]

The extra-territoriality of the legal regime regulating the public procurement of the Member States of the European Union has been achieved by virtue of the special inter-governmental agreements concluded between the EU and member/signatories to the GATT Agreement. It was initially the GATT Agreement on Government Procurement (AGP), which was concluded during the Tokyo Round of negotiations that provided third-country contractors access to EU public markets. The AGP was amended by virtue of the WTO Government Procurement Agreement (GPA) during the Uruguay Round. In principle, access to the public sector markets of the Member States has been guaranteed, as far as the framework of provisions in relation to procedural and substantive stages of public procurement is concerned. However, even the most comprehensive set of rules would be ineffective, if its enforcement appeared not sufficient. Access to justice for third-country providers under the GATT/WTO agreements is thus equally important with the principles of access to the public markets of the EU Member States.

Both the WTO Government Procurement Agreement and its predecessor (the GATT AGP) are considered inter-governmental instruments which are addressed to States and do not intend to confer rights and duties upon individuals as such. Irrespective of the clearness and precision, the unconditionality of their provision and the lack of discretion reserved to States for their implementation, international agreements are not deemed to produce direct effect,[44] thus depriving individuals from taking advantage of directly effective provisions in litigation before national courts. The Decision of the European Council which incorporates the WTO GPA into Community law specifically stipulates that the provisions of the GPA do not have direct effect. However, there is apparently a contradiction between the difficulties arising from applying the theory of direct effectiveness to the GPA provisions and the spirit and wording of the agreement. Express provision of remedies for aggrieved providers is made under Article XX of the

---

[42] See Directive 92/13, [1992] OJ L76/7.

[43] See Article 7 of EC Directive 92/13.

[44] See Cases 21-24/72, *International Fruit Co NV v Produktschap voor Groenten en Fruit* [1972] ECR 1236. Also Case C-280/93, *Germany v Council* [1993] ECR I-3667.

GPA, where the remedies provided should be as favourable as those conferred upon Community contractors. Also, Article III of the GPA stipulates that signatories to the agreement should not be treated in a less favourable manner than national providers or providers from other parties. How in practice these provisions concerning access to justice at national level for third-party providers will operate remains to be seen.

As with its predecessor, the WTO Government Procurement Agreement has created an inter-governmental mechanism for settling disputes arising from its application. The mechanism is referred to as the *Understanding on Rules and Procedures Governing the Settlement of Disputes* (DSU) and is attached to Annex II of the Agreement. The mechanism provides for a dispute settlement procedure between parties to the Agreement, that is states and not individuals. The DSU apparently elevates the pre-contractual or the contractual dispute between a third-party provider and a contracting authority to a grievance of an inter-governmental dimension. To invoke the DSU, a state must first exhaust all possible ways of settling the dispute in an amicable manner by means of direct consultation and negotiations with the State allegedly in breach. If settlement cannot be reached, the State then may request the WTO Dispute Settlement Body for a Panel to be established in order to hear the case. The Panel is appointed in consultation with the parties and comprised of persons with experience in the area of government procurement. The Panel has as its task the provision of a report to the parties concerned, which is then adopted by the Dispute Settlement Body. The latter would then request the state in breach to repeal all the measures which contravene the principles of the WTO GPA. Failing to do so, the Dispute Settlement Body may authorise *unilateral suspension* of the application of the GPA or any other agreement under the WTO in the territory of the state affected by the violation.

This chapter aims to project the concepts of the Remedies Directives in public procurement and reflect on the insights of the CJEU in making public contracts redress as effective as possible with a view to facilitating the decentralised application of the substantive public procurement Directives.

3. THE PRINCIPLES OF THE REMEDIES DIRECTIVES

The Remedies Directives have been based on three fundamental principles; the principle of effectiveness, the principle of non-discrimination and the principle of procedural autonomy. In both Directives, effective review of decisions or acts of contracting authorities is the essential requirement of compliance with the substantive public procurement rules. The principle of effectiveness includes two individual features; first, the swift resolution of disputes and secondly the enforceability of decisions. In particular, the Remedies Directives stipulate that Member States must take any measures necessary to ensure that decisions taken by the contracting authorities may be reviewed effectively and as rapidly as possible and can be effectively enforced[45] on the grounds that such decisions have infringed EU law in the field of public procurement or national implementing laws.

[45] See Article 2(7) of Directive 89/665 and Article 2(8) of Directive 92/13.

There is an explicit obligation conferred on Member States to avoid introducing review procedures for decisions of contracting authorities and utilities, as well as procedures for the recovery of damages which differ, in a discriminatory context, from review procedures for other administrative acts and procedures for the recovery of damages under national law.[46] Finally, the Remedies Directives leave Member States with wide discretion as to the creation of the appropriate forum to receive complaints and legal actions against decisions of contracting authorities and utilities, as well as action for damages in public procurement cases.[47]

4. CONCEPTS IN LEGAL REDRESS IN PUBLIC PROCUREMENT CONTRACTS

The spectrum of redress in public procurement contracts reflects on three pivotal concepts for remedies available to aggrieved parties. First, interim protection, secondly, set aside and annulment of decisions of contracting authorities and finally, actions for damages.

4.1 The Concept of Interim Protection

4.1.1 Interim measures and their admissibility

The most important function of interim measures in public procurement is the ability to suspend an award procedure, particularly prior to the conclusion of the contract. The suspensory character of interim measures is a demonstrable factor of the ability of aggrieved tenderers to review decisions of contracting authorities and utilities or any other act or measure which forms part of the procurement process, without necessarily having recourse to an action for damages, which, in all Member States, appears as the only possible remedy available after the conclusion of the contract. It is widely accepted that a public contract, once concluded, is not subject to any set aside or annulment actions. The courts in most Member States apply a balance of interest test, where the complainant may have to show, *prima facie,* that he is likely to suffer serious and possibly irreparable harm if interim measures are not granted. Harm that must outweigh the inconvenience or any harm or damages which the interim order would cause both to the awarding authority and to the public interest at large.[48] The complainant might also have to show that the harm which he is likely to suffer could not be adequately compensated through financial damages. Interim measures against not only definitive acts but also procedural acts, should be admissible, if they determine, directly or indirectly, the substance of the case, bring an end to the award procedures of a public contract, or cause irreparable harm to legitimate rights of interested parties.[49] The Remedies Directives do not provide for any derogation

46 See Article 1(2) of Directive 89/665 and Article 1(2) of Directive 92/13.

47 See Article 2(2) of Directive 89/665 and Article 2(2) of Directive 92/13.

48 See Article 2(4) of Directive 89/665 and Article 2(4) of Directive 92/13.

49 See Cases C-214/00, *Commission of the European Communities v Kingdom of Spain* [2003] ECR I-4667; C-236/95, *Commission v Greece* [1996] ECR I-4459.

regarding the possibility of appealing against procedural acts, or administrative measures which do not bring administrative proceedings to an end.[50] However, national legislation which restricts interim judicial protection to proceedings for suspension of the operation of an administrative act and made the suspension conditional on bringing an action for the annulment of the contested act, contravene the spirit of the public procurement *acquis*.[51]

Interim measures represent an autonomous legal remedy which is to remain unconditional to any other judicial review process. Their objective is to correct the alleged infringement or to prevent further damage to the interests concerned, to suspend or ensure the suspension of the procedure for the award of a public contract and finally to suspend or ensure the suspension of the implementation of any decision taken by the contracting authority. Interim measures are granted with reference to a balance test which takes into consideration the likely consequences of such measures for all parties liable to be harmed on the one hand and the public interest on the other hand.

The CJEU examined[52] the conditionality of an application for interim measures upon a prior action to set aide or annul an act or a decision of a contracting authority and ruled against such a requirement on the grounds that it restricts interim judicial protection by making the suspension of an administrative act procedurally conditional on bringing an action for the annulment of the contested act.[53] The Court maintained that not only actions against definitive acts but also procedural acts should be allowed to be suspended by the application of interim measures, if they determine, directly or indirectly, the substance of the case, or bring an end to the award procedures for a public contract, or cause irreparable harm to legitimate rights of interested parties. The Remedies Directives do not provide for any derogation regarding the possibility of appealing against procedural acts, or administrative measures which do not bring administrative proceedings to an end.[54]

National provisions concerning the possibility of applying for interim measures against acts or decisions of contracting authorities must not be specific to the award of public contracts, but apply equally to all procedures.[55] National legislation which restricts judicial protection in public procurement disputes through the conditional

---

[50] See Case C-81/98 *Alcatel Austria and Others* [1999] ECR I-7671. The conception of precluding the review of procedural acts is embedded in Community case-law. See case C-282/95 P *Guérin automobiles v Commission* [1997] ECR I-1503. The Court has also held that the preparatory nature of the act against which the action is brought is one of the grounds of inadmissibility of an action for annulment, and that that is a ground which the Court may examine of its own motion, see Case 346/87, *Bossi v Commission* [1989] ECR 303.

[51] See Case C-236/95, *Commission v Greece* [1996] ECR I-4459.

[52] See Cases C-214/00, *Commission of the European Communities v Kingdom of Spain* [2003] ECR I-4667; C-236/95, *Commission v Greece* [1996] ECR I-4459.

[53] See Case C-236/95, *Commission v Greece* [1996] ECR I-4459.

[54] See Case C-81/98, *Alcatel Austria and Others* [1999] ECR I-7671. The conception of precluding the review of procedural acts is embedded in Community case-law. See Case C-282/95, P *Guérin automobiles v Commission* [1997] ECR I-1503. The Court has also held that the preparatory nature of the act against which the action is brought is one of the grounds of inadmissibility of an action for annulment, and that that is a ground which the Court may examine of its own motion, see Case 346/87, *Bossi v Commission* [1989] ECR 303.

[55] See Case C-236/95, *Commission v Greece* [1996] ECR I-4459.

application of interim measures, that interested parties must bring an action for the annulment of the contested act of a contracting authority first, is in contradiction with the principle of procedural equality.

4.1.2 Pre-judicial stages in review procedures

Making access to the review procedures, which are provided for by the Public Sector Procurement Review Directive 89/665/EC, conditional on prior application to a body which has no judicial character, such as a conciliation commission, is contrary to the aims and objectives of the Remedies Directives and in particular the objective of speed and effectiveness in the judicial review of acts or decisions of contracting authorities. First, prior application to a non-judicial body which has the aim to conciliate disputes arising between contracting authorities and aggrieved tenderers inevitably has the effect of delaying the initiation of the review procedures which Directive 89/665/EC requires Member States to establish. Secondly, a non-judicial review body such as a conciliation commission has none of the powers which Article 2(1) Directive 89/665/EC requires Member States to grant the bodies responsible for carrying out those review procedures, so that referral to it does not ensure the effective application of the Directives on public procurement.[56]

Even though Member States are free to determine the detailed rules according to which they must make the review procedures provided for in that Directive available to any person having or having had an interest in obtaining a particular public contract and who has been or risks being harmed by an alleged infringement,[57] they cannot interpret the term 'interest in obtaining a public contract' strictly.[58] Thus, a person who has participated in a contract award procedure, but subsequently failed to initiate pre-judicial proceedings, such as conciliation or mediation proceedings, to review an act or decision of a contracting authority must not be regarded as having lost his or her interest in obtaining the contract and therefore being precluded from lodging an action to contest the legality of the contract awarding decision or any decision of the contracting authority.[59]

4.2 The Set Aside and Annulment of Decisions

The principle of effectiveness of review procedures under the Remedies Directives covers the ability of aggrieved tenderers to initiate proceedings for the set aside decisions of contracting authorities taken unlawfully or to remove discriminatory technical, economic or financial specifications in the invitation to tender, the contract documents or in any other document relating to the contract award procedure. Set aside procedures are deemed as legitimate conditional remedies for the award of damages.

---

56 See Case C-230/02, *Grossmann Air Service, Bedarfsluftfahrtunternehmen GmbH & Co. KG and Republik Österreich* [2004] ECR I-1829.

57 See Case C-327/00, *Santex* [2003] ECR I-1877, para 47.

58 See Case C-410/01, *Fritsch, Chiari & Partner and Others* [2003] ECR I-11547, paras 31 and 34.

59 See Case C-230/02, *Grossmann Air Service, Bedarfsluftfahrtunternehmen GmbH & Co. KG and Republik Österreich* [2004] ECR I-1829.

The powers of national courts or administrative tribunals to set aside or annul acts of contracting authorities aim at nullifying the decision of the contracting authority or utility awarding a contract, prior to its conclusion. A set aside or annulment order cannot attack the contract itself, as the latter represents a pact between the contracting authority and a third party. In most legal orders, a set aside or annulment order will be reached after the application of a balance of interest test. However, many legal systems rely predominantly on the mere lawfulness of the administrative act of the contracting authority or the utility and do not involve any test which weights interests and potential harm and damages. The Remedies Directives also stipulate that national courts or administrative tribunals must be given the power to set aside or annul acts of contracting authorities.

The set aside or annulment of decisions of contracting authorities aims at nullifying administrative acts to award public contracts before the conclusion of the relevant contract. The nature of set aside or annulment orders is such as to prevent them contesting the legality of a concluded contract between a contracting authority and a third party. In most legal orders of the EU Member States, a set aside or annulment order will be successfully granted by the competent court after the application of the *balance of interest test*, in a similar manner to the application of the test in interim measures cases. However, some legal systems rely on the examination of the lawfulness of the administrative act of the contracting authority to award a public contract and do not apply any balance of interest test which weights interests and potential harm to aggrieved parties.[60]

4.2.1 Locus standi and interest to review acts

Persons to whom review procedures must be available must include, at least, any person having or having had an interest in obtaining a public contract[61] who has been or risks being harmed by an alleged infringement.[62] The formal capacity of tenderer or candidate is not thus required.[63] The CJEU maintained that an assessment of an aggrieved tenderer's interest in reviewing a decision or an act of a contracting entity should be examined on the face that he did not participate in the contract award procedure, as well as he did not appeal against the invitation to tender before the award of the contract.

According to Article 1 of the Public Sector Remedies Directive 89/665/EC and Article 1 of the Utilities Remedies Directive 93/13/EC, Member States shall ensure effective and rapid review of decisions taken by contracting authorities which infringe public procurement provisions. Undertakings seeking relief from damages in the context of a procedure for the award of a contract should not be treated differently under national rules implementing EU public procurement legislation and under other

---

[60] See Bovis, *EU Public Procurement, Case Law and Regulation* (Oxford: Oxford University Press, 2006), Chapter 14.

[61] See Case C-26/03, *Stadt Halle, RPL Recyclingpark Lochau GmbH v Arbeitsgemeinschaft Thermische Restabfall und Energieverwertungsanlage TREA Leuna,* [2005] ECR I-1.

[62] See Case C-212/02, *Commission v Austria,* judgment of 24 June 2004.

[63] See Case C-230/02, *Grossmann Air Service, Bedarfsluftfahrtunternehmen GmbH & Co. KG and Republik Österreich* [2004] ECR I-1829.

national rules. This means that the measures to be taken concerning the review procedures should be similar to national review proceedings, without any discriminatory character.

Any person having or having had an interest in obtaining a particular public supply or public works contract and who has been or risks being harmed by an alleged infringement of substantive public procurement law shall be entitled to seek review before national courts. This is laid down in the third paragraph of Article 1 Directive 89/665/EC and Article 3 Directive 92/13/EC. In both cases this is followed by a stand-still provision concerning the prior notification by the person seeking review to the contracting authority of the alleged infringement and of his intention to seek review. However, with respect to admissibility aspects, there is no qualitative or quantitative definition of the interest of a person in obtaining a public contract. As to the element of potential harm by an infringement of public procurement provisions, it should be cumulative with the first element, that of interest. The prior notification should intend to exhaust any possibility of amicable settlement before the parties have recourse to national courts.

Fritsch Chiari[64] precludes the conditionality of *locus standi* upon prior participation of aggrieved tenderers in conciliation procedures as incompatible with the effectiveness principle, thus recognizing the autonomous and unconditional character of judicial review procedures in public procurement. Even though Member States are free to determine the detailed rules according to which they must make the review procedures provided for in the Remedies Directive available to any person having or having had an interest in obtaining a particular public contract and who has been or risks being harmed by an alleged infringement,[65] they cannot interpret the term interest in obtaining a public contract strictly.[66] Thus, a person who has participated in a contract award procedure, but subsequently failed to initiate pre-judicial proceedings, such as conciliation or mediation proceedings, to review an act or decision of a contracting authority must not be regarded as having lost his interest in obtaining the contract and therefore being precluded from lodging an action to contest the legality of the contract awarding decision or any decision of the contracting authority.[67]

Grossmann[68] confirmed the existence of interest in obtaining a contract where no bid has been submitted. The CJEU held that it must be possible for an undertaking to seek review of discriminatory specifications before submitting a bid and without waiting for the contract award procedure to be terminated, but a refusal to acknowledge interest in obtaining a contract of a person who has not participated in the contract award procedure or has not sought review against the invitation to tender does not impair the effectiveness of the Remedies Directives.

---

[64] See Case C-410/01, *Fritsch, Chiari & Partner, Ziviltechniker GmbH and Others and Autobahnen- und. Schnellstraßen-Finanzierungs-AG. (Asfinag),* ECR [2003] I-11547.

[65] See Case C-327/00, *Santex* [2003] ECR I-1877, para 47.

[66] See Case C-410/01, *Fritsch, Chiari & Partner and Others* [2003] ECR I-11547, paras 31 and 34.

[67] See Case C-230/02, *Grossmann Air Service, Bedarfsluftfahrtunternehmen GmbH & Co. KG and Republik Österreich* [2004] ECR I-1829.

[68] See Case C-230/02, *Grossmann Air Service, Bedarfsluftfahrtunternehmen GmbH & Co. KG and Republik Österreich* [2004] ECR I-1829.

Espace Trianon,[69] recognised the existence of both collective and individual interest in obtaining a contract in cases of consortia participation in public procurement procedures and the CJEU held that not only all the members of a consortium without legal personality which has participated in a procedure for the award of a public contract and has not been awarded that contract, acting together, may bring an action against the decision awarding the contract, but *locus standi* is recognised even where only one member of the consortium seeks review. Interestingly, if the application of one of the consortium members is held inadmissible, *locus standi* of the other members of the consortium is not affected.

Elisoccorso/Elilombarda[70] repeated the *Espace Trianon* ruling by confirming the existence of individual interest and reaffirming the eligibility of an aggrieved individual member of a consortium without legal personality to contest a decision or an act of a contracting authority in relation to the award of a public contract.

4.2.2 The failure to participate in the contract award procedure

Under Article 1(3) of the Public Sector Remedies Directive 89/665/EC, the Member States are required to ensure that the review procedures provided for are available at least to any person having or having had an interest in obtaining a particular public contract and who has been or risks being harmed by an alleged infringement of EU public procurement law or national rules transposing that law. It follows that Member States are not obliged to make those review procedures available to any person wishing to obtain a public contract, but instead, require that the person concerned has been or risks being harmed by the alleged infringement.[71]

In that sense, participation in a contract award procedure may, in principle, with regard to Article 1(3) Directive 89/665/EC, validly constitute a condition which must be fulfilled before the person concerned can show an interest in obtaining the contract at issue or that he or she risks suffering harm as a result of the allegedly unlawful nature of the decision to award that contract. If he or she has not submitted a tender it will be difficult for such a person to show that he or she has an interest in challenging that decision or that he or she has been harmed or risks being harmed as a result of that award decision. However, where an undertaking has not submitted a tender because there were allegedly discriminatory specifications in the documents relating to the invitation to tender, or in the contract documents, which have specifically prevented it from being in a position to provide all the services requested, it would be entitled to seek review of those specifications directly, even before the procedure for awarding the contract concerned is terminated.

It is maintained that, on the one hand, it would be excessive to require an undertaking allegedly harmed by discriminatory clauses in the documents relating to the invitation to tender to submit a tender, before being able to avail itself of the review

[69] See Case C-129/04, *Espace Trianon SA and Société wallonne de location-financement SA (Sofibail) v Office communautaire et régional de la formation professionnelle et de l'emploi (FOREM)* [2005] ECR I-7805.

[70] See Case C-492/06, *Consorzio Elisoccorso San Raffaele v Elilombarda Srl and Azienda Ospedaliera Ospedale Niguarda Ca' Granda di Milano* [2007] ECR I-8189.

[71] See Case C-249/01, *Hackermüller* [2003] ECR I-6319, para 18.

procedures provided for by Directive 89/665/EC against such specifications, in the award procedure for the contract at issue, even though its chances of being awarded the contract are non-existent by reason of the existence of those specifications. On the other hand, it is clear from the wording of Article 2(1)(b) Directive 89/665/EC that the review procedures to be organised by the Member States in accordance with the Directive must, in particular, set aside decisions taken unlawfully, including the removal of discriminatory technical, economic or financial specifications. It must, therefore, be possible for an undertaking to seek review of such discriminatory specifications directly, without waiting for the contract award procedure to be terminated.

Member States are not obliged to make review procedures available to any person wishing to obtain a public contract, but instead, require that the person concerned has been or risks being harmed by the alleged infringement.[72] In that sense, participation in a contract award procedure may validly constitute a condition which must be fulfilled before the person concerned can show an interest in obtaining the contract at issue or that he or she risks suffering harm as a result of the allegedly unlawful nature of the decision to award that contract.

4.2.3 Absence of proceedings against the invitation to tender

National courts sought to ascertain whether Article 1(3) of the Public Sector Remedies Directive 89/665/EC must be interpreted as meaning that it precludes a person who not only has not participated in the award procedure for a public contract but has not sought any review of the decision of the contracting authority determining the specifications of the invitation to tender either, from being regarded as having lost his interest in obtaining the contract and, therefore, the right of access to the review procedures provided for by the Directive. The CJEU examined the absence of proceedings against the invitation to tender in the light of the purpose of Directive 89/665/EC and in particular its intentions to strengthen the existing mechanisms, both at national and EU level, to ensure the effective application of the EU public procurement directives, in particular at a stage when infringements can still be remedied. To that effect, Article 1(1) Directive 89/665/EC requires Member States to guarantee that unlawful decisions of contracting authorities can be subjected to effective review which is as swift as possible.[73]

It must be pointed out that the fact that a person does not seek review of a decision of the contracting authority determining the specifications of an invitation to tender which in his or her view discriminate against him or her, in so far as they effectively disqualify him or her from participating in the award procedure for the contract at issue, but awaits notification of the decision awarding the contract and then challenges it before the body responsible, on the ground specifically that those specifications are discriminatory, indicates a conduct which is incompatible with the spirit and objective of the Public Sector Remedies Directive. Such conduct, in so far as it may delay,

---

[72] See Case C-249/01, *Hackermüller* [2003] ECR I-6319, para 18.

[73] See Cases C-81/98, *Alcatel Austria and Others* [1999] ECR I-7671, paras 33 and 34; C-470/99 *Universale-Bau and Others* [2002] ECR I-11617, para 74; and C-410/01 *Fritsch, Chiari & Partner and Others* [2003] ECR I-6413, para 30.

without any objective reason, the commencement of the review procedures which Member States were required to institute by Directive 89/665/EC impairs the effective implementation of the EU public procurement Directives.

In those circumstances, a refusal to acknowledge the interest in obtaining the contract in question and, therefore, the right of access to the review procedures provided for by Directive 89/665/EC of a person who has not participated in the contract award procedure, or sought review of the decision of the contracting authority laying down the specifications of the invitation to tender, does not impair the effectiveness of the Public Sector Remedies Directive. Therefore, once a public contract has been awarded, an aggrieved tenderer may be regarded as having lost his right of access to the review procedures provided for by the Directive if he did not participate in the award procedure for that contract on the ground that he was not in a position to supply all the services for which bids were invited, because there were allegedly discriminatory specifications in the documents relating to the invitation to tender, but he did not seek review of those specifications before the contract was awarded.

The CJEU examined the material scope of Article 1(3) Public Sector Remedies Directive 89/665/EC with a view to determining the persons to whom review procedures must be available and providing a definition of interest in obtaining a public contract.[74] It also pointed out that the fact that Article 1(3) Directive 89/665/EC expressly allows Member States to determine the detailed rules according to which they must make the review procedures available to any person having or having had an interest in obtaining a particular public contract and who has been or risks being harmed by an alleged infringement nonetheless does not authorise them to give the term interest in obtaining a public contract an interpretation which may limit the effectiveness of that Directive.[75] Thus, Article 1(3) Directive 89/665/EC precludes an undertaking which has participated in a public procurement procedure from being considered as having lost its interest in obtaining that contract on the ground that, before bringing review procedures for setting aside or annulling an act or a decision of a contracting authority, it failed to exhaust pre-judicial proceedings.

The CJEU also examined the scope of Article 1(3) of the Public Sector Remedies Directive 89/665/EC in respect of review procedures concerning the award of public contracts and the *locus standi* of persons that are eligible to bring such review procedures before the competent national forum.[76] The Court pointed out that, under Article 1(3) Directive 89/665/EC, Member States are required to ensure that the review procedures laid down by the Directive are available at least to any person having or having had an interest in obtaining a particular public contract and who has been or risks being harmed by an alleged infringement of EU public procurement law or the national rules implementing that law. Therefore, it is apparent that the provision does not oblige the Member States to make those review procedures available to any person wishing to obtain a public contract but allows them to require, in addition, that the

---

[74] See Case C-410/01, *Fritsch, Chiari & Partner, Ziviltechniker GmbH and Others and Autobahnen- und Schnellstraßen-Finanzierungs-AG (Asfinag)* [2003] ECR I-11547.

[75] See Case C-470/99, *Universale-Bau and Others* [2002] ECR I-11617, para 72.

[76] See C-249/01, *Werner Hackermüller and Bundesimmobiliengesellschaft mbH (BIG), Wiener Entwicklungsgesellschaft mbH für den Donauraum AG (WED)* [2003] ECR I-6319.

person concerned has been or risks being harmed by the infringement he or she alleges. The Court concluded that Article 1(3) Directive 89/665/EC does not preclude the review procedures laid down by the Directive being available to persons wishing to obtain a particular public contract only if they have been or risk being harmed by the infringement they allege.

The national court also sought to ascertain whether a tenderer seeking to contest the lawfulness of the decision of the contracting authority not to consider his bid as the best bid may be refused access to the review procedures laid down by Directive 89/665/EC on the ground that his or her bid should have been eliminated at the outset by the contracting authority for other reasons and that, therefore, he or she neither has been nor risks being harmed by the unlawfulness which he alleges. The Court reiterated that Directive 89/665/EC is intended to strengthen the existing mechanisms, both at national and EU level, to ensure the effective application of the EU public procurement Directives, in particular at a stage when infringements can still be remedied. To that effect, Article 1(1) Directive 89/665/EC requires Member States to guarantee that unlawful decisions of contracting authorities can be subjected to effective review which is as swift as possible.[77] The full achievement of the objective of Directive 89/665/EC would be compromised if it were permissible for a body responsible for the review procedures provided for by the Directive to refuse access to them to a tenderer alleging the unlawfulness of the decision by which the contracting authority had not considered its bid as being the best bid, on the ground that the same contracting authority was wrong not to eliminate that bid even before making the selection of the best bid. The CJEU pointed out that there can be no doubt that a decision by which the contracting authority eliminates the bid of a tenderer even before making that selection is a decision of which it must be possible to seek review under Article 1(1) Directive 89/665/EC, since that provision applies to all decisions taken by contracting authorities which are subject to EU public procurement law,[78] and makes no provision for any limitation as regards the nature and content of those decisions.[79] Therefore, if the tenderer's bid had been eliminated by the contracting authority at a stage prior to that of the selection of the best bid, he or she would have had to be allowed, as a person who has been or risks being harmed by that decision to eliminate his or her bid, to challenge the lawfulness of that decision by means of the review procedures provided for by Directive 89/665/EC.

In those circumstances, if a review body were to refuse access to those procedures to a tenderer, the effect would be to deny him or her not only his or her right to seek review of the decision he or she alleges to be unlawful but also the right to challenge the validity of the ground for exclusion raised by that body to deny him or her the status of a person who has been or risks being harmed by the alleged unlawfulness. Admittedly, if in order to mitigate that situation the tenderer is afforded the right to

---

[77] See Case C-81/98, *Alcatel Austria and Others* [1999] ECR I-7671, paras 33 and 34, and Case C-470/99 *Universale-Bau and Others* [2002] ECR I-11617, para 74.

[78] See Case C-92/00, *Hospital Ingenieure* [2002] ECR I-5553, para 37, and Case C-57/01 *Makedoniko Metro and Michaniki* [2003] ECR I-1091, para 68.

[79] See Case C-81/98, *Alcatel Austria and Others* [1999] ECR I-7671, para 35 and Case C-92/00 *Hospital Ingenieure* [2002] ECR I-5553, para 49.

challenge the validity of that ground of exclusion in the review procedure he or she instigates in order to challenge the lawfulness of the decision by which the contracting authority did not consider his or her bid as being the best bid, it is possible that at the end of that procedure the review body may reach the conclusion that the bid should actually have been eliminated at the outset and that the tenderer's application should be dismissed on the ground that, in the light of that circumstance, he neither has been nor risks being harmed by the infringement he alleges. However, if the contracting authority has not taken a decision to exclude the tenderer's bid at the appropriate stage of the award procedure, the method of proceeding described in the previous paragraph must be regarded as the only one likely to guarantee the tenderer the right to challenge the validity of the ground for exclusion on the basis of which the review body intends to conclude that he or she neither has been nor risks being harmed by the decision he or she alleges to be unlawful and, accordingly, to ensure the effective application of the EU public procurement Directives at all stages of the award procedure.

The CJEU concluded that Article 1(3) Directive 89/665/EC does not permit a tenderer to be refused access to the review procedures laid down by the Directive to contest the lawfulness of the decision of the contracting authority not to consider his bid as the best bid on the ground that his bid should have been eliminated at the outset by the contracting authority for other reasons and that therefore he neither has been nor risks being harmed by the unlawfulness which he alleges. In the review procedure thus open to the tenderer, he or she must be allowed to neither challenge the ground of exclusion on the basis of which the review body intends to conclude that he neither has been nor risks being harmed by the decision he alleges to be unlawful.

4.2.4 The meaning and content of decisions for judicial review

The CJEU verified that any remedies available to interested parties against decisions of contracting authorities extends also to decisions taken outside a formal award procedure and decisions prior to a formal call for tenders,[80] such as decisions on whether a particular contract falls within the personal and material scope of the public procurement Directives, a question discussed in detail in Chapter 1 of this book, as well as decisions to withdraw invitations to tender and abort public procurement procedures.[81] The Remedies Directives preclude national legislation from limiting review of the legality of the withdrawal of an invitation to tender to mere examination of whether this was arbitrary. However, the Court has defined the scope of the obligation to notify reasons for abandoning the award procedure of a contract,[82] which must be limited to exceptional cases or must necessarily be based on serious grounds.[83] Although a contracting authority is required to notify candidates and tenderers of the grounds for its decision if it decides to withdraw the invitation to tender for a public contract, there

80 See Case C-26/03, *Stadt Halle, RPL Recyclingpark Lochau GmbH v Arbeitsgemeinschaft Thermische Restabfall und Energieverwertungsanlage TREA Leuna*, [2005] ECR I-1.

81 See Case C-92/00 *Hospital Ingenieure* [2002] ECR I-5553, para 55.

82 See [1993] OJ L199/54.

83 See Case C-27/98, *Fracasso and Leitschutz v Salzburger Landesregierung* [1999] ECR I-5697, paras 23 and 25.

is no implied obligation on that authority to carry the award procedure to its conclusion.

The broad meaning of the concept of a decision taken by a contracting authority is confirmed by the Court's case law. The CJEU has held that there is no restriction with regard to the nature and content of the decisions taken by contracting authorities.[84] Nor may such a restriction be inferred from the wording of the Remedies Directives. Moreover, a restrictive interpretation of the concept of a decision amenable to review would be incompatible with the requirement of Member States providing for interim relief procedures in relation to any decision taken by the contracting authorities.[85] On the other hand, decisions or acts of contracting authorities which constitute a mere preliminary study of the market or which are purely preparatory and form part of the internal reflections of the contracting authority with a view to a public award procedure are not reviewable.[86] The CJEU has held that the contracting authority's decision prior to the conclusion of the contract as to the tenderer to whom the contract will be awarded must in all cases be open to review, regardless of the possibility of obtaining an award of damages once the contract has been concluded.[87]

4.2.5 Time limits to enact review proceedings

Member States have wide discretion to establish the procedural framework for review procedures and the logistics for its operation. The existence of national legislation which provides that any application for review of decisions of contracting authorities must be commenced within a specific time-limit and that any irregularity in the award procedure relied upon in support of such application must be raised within the same period is compatible with public procurement *acquis*,[88] provided that, in pursuit of fundamental principle of legal certainty, such specific time limits are reasonable.[89]

The duration to assess the legality of acts or decisions of contracting authorities[90] remains within the discretion of Member States, subject to the requirement that the relevant national rules are not less favourable than those governing similar domestic actions.[91]

In *Universale Bau*,[92] Austrian procurement rules stipulated limitation periods within which certain allegedly unlawful decisions had to be challenged. The CJEU declared that the Remedies Directives do not provide for any specific limitation periods and that

---

[84] See Case C-81/98, *Alcatel Austria and Others* [1999] ECR I-7671, paras 32–35.

[85] See Case C-92/00, *Hospital Ingenieure* [2002] ECR I-5553, para 49.

[86] See the Opinion of Advocate-General Stix-Hackl in Case C-26/03, *Stadt Halle, RPL Recyclingpark Lochau GmbH v Arbeitsgemeinschaft Thermische Restabfall und Energieverwertungsanlage TREA Leuna,* points 23-29, delivered on 23 September 2004.

[87] See Case C-81/98, *Alcatel Austria and Others* [1999] ECR I-7671, para 43.

[88] See Case C-470/99, *Universale-Bau AG, Bietergemeinschaft* [2002] ECR I-11617.

[89] See Case C-261/95, *Palmisani* [1997] ECR I-4025, para 28, and Case C-78/98 *Preston and Others* [2000] ECR I-3201, para 33.

[90] See Case C-92/00, *Hospital Ingenieure Krankenhaustechnik Planungs- GmbH (HI) and Stadt Wien,* [2002] ECR I-5553.

[91] See Case C-390/98, *Banks v Coal Authority and Secretary of State for Trade and Industry* [2001] ECR I-6117, para 121; Case C-453/99 *Courage and Crehan* [2001] ECR I-6297, para 29.

[92] See Case C-470/99, *Universale-Bau and Others* [2002] ECR I-11617.

in absence of EU rules, Member States are free to provide procedural rules if they are coherent with fundamental principles of the Treaty. The Court considered a two-week limitation period in principle consistent with principles of effectiveness and equivalence and reflecting an element of appropriateness in the light of their overall objective.[93]

In *Sanetex*,[94] Italian law provided that an invitation to tender or clauses thereof must be challenged within the limitation period of 60 days; when that period has expired, a challenge is no longer possible. An aggrieved bidder did not contest a specific and potentially discriminatory clause because the contracting authority led him to believe that the disputed clause would be interpreted in a non-discriminatory manner. After the elapse of the time limitation period, the contracting authority excluded the bidder from the tender procedure on basis of the potentially discriminatory clause. The Court considered that the 60 days limitation period is reasonable but held that the conduct of the contracting authority had rendered the exercise of the rights conferred on the tenderer excessively difficult. Therefore, despite the elapse of the limitation period, the aggrieved party could challenge the act of the contracting authority. The latter assertion by the Court gives reasonable guidance to national courts to interpret national laws on limitation periods in a functional manner in which if redress for challenging public contracts is rendered excessively difficult, the relevant limitation periods may not apply or may be extended to allow for effective access to justice.

In *Lämmerzahl*,[95] the CJEU dealt with an application for review being deemed inadmissible where no complaint is raised about infringements that are identifiable in the contract notice by, at the latest, the end of the period for submission of bids. The Court held that a contract notice lacking any information as to the estimated contract value followed by evasive conduct of the contracting authority must, in view of the limitation period, be seen as rendering excessively difficult the exercise by the tenderer concerned of rights conferred on him by EU law.

In *Uniplex*[96] the CJEU confirmed that any periods laid down for bringing proceedings start to run only from the date on which the claimant knew or ought to have known of the alleged infringement and requires the contracting authority to notify unsuccessful candidates of the relevant reasons, at least a summary of its decision in relation to the award of a public contract. The Court had the opportunity to rule on the compatibility of United Kingdom law which provides that:

> ... proceedings must be brought promptly and in any event within three months from the date when grounds for the bringing of the proceedings first arose unless the Court considers there is a good reason for extending the period within which proceedings may be brought.[97]

---

[93] See Case C-231/96, *EDIS* [1998] ECR I-4951.

[94] See Case C-327/00, *Santex SpA v Unità Socio Sanitaria Locale n. 42 di Pavia* [2003] ECR I-1877.

[95] See Case C-241/06, *Lämmerzahl GmbH v Freie Hansestadt Bremen* [2008] 1 CMLR 462.

[96] See Case C-406/08, *Uniplex (UK) Ltd v NHS Business Services* Ltd [2010] ECR I-0000.

[97] See Regulation 47(7)(b) of the Public Contracts Regulations 2006 and regulation 45(6)(b) of the Utilities Contracts Regulations 2006 which implement Article 2c of Directive 89/665/ EEC, as amended by Directive 2007/66/ EC and article 2c of Directive 92/13/ EEC, as amended by Directive 2007/66/EC respectively.

The Court held that the United Kingdom provisions give rise to legal uncertainty as the limitation period the duration of which is at the discretion of the competent court is not predictable in its effects. Moreover, national courts are bound to interpret national law that transposes a directive in the light of the wording and purpose of the directive, that is, in a way that the period begins to run from the date on which the claimant knew or ought to have known infringement. If national law does not arrive at such an interpretation the national court is bound to extend the period for bringing proceedings in relation to the award of public contracts.

The CJEU upheld the *Uniplex* ruling in *Commission v Ireland*,[98] where national law provided that application for review of a decision to award a contract shall be made:

> ... at the earliest opportunity and in any event within three months from the date when grounds for the bringing of the proceedings first arose unless the Court considers that there is good reason for extending such period.

The Court maintained that the national limitation periods are to be interpreted by national courts as to apply not only to the final decision to award the contract but also to preparatory acts or interim decisions and that national rules need to be unequivocally clear and beyond doubt as to the time from which the limitation period starts to run.

The principle of effectiveness underpinned *Commission v Germany*,[99] where the Court confirmed that the Commission, as guardian of the TFEU has absolute discretion to initiate compliance proceedings for failure to implement EU law against a Member State even if limitation periods under national law have expired.

4.2.6 *Ex proprio motu* investigation of the unlawfulness of decisions

National courts responsible for hearing review procedures in actions brought by aggrieved tenderers, with the ultimate aim of obtaining damages, may declare on their own motion the unlawfulness of a decision of the contracting authority other than the one contested by the tenderer.[100] However, a tenderer harmed by a decision to award a public contract, the lawfulness of which he or she is contesting, cannot be denied the right to claim damages for the harm caused by that decision on the ground that the award procedure was in any event defective owing to the unlawfulness, raised *ex proprio motu*, of another decision of the contracting authority. Therefore, national courts cannot dismiss an application for damages on the ground that, owing to the unlawfulness raised of the courts' own motion, the award procedure was in any event unlawful and that the harm which the tenderer may have suffered would therefore have been caused even in the absence of the unlawfulness alleged by the tenderer.

4.2.7 Obligation to allow sufficient time between contract award and contract conclusion

Member States are required to provide for a review procedure so that an applicant may apply for the set aside of a decision of a contracting authority to award a public

---

98 See Case C-456/08, *Commission v Ireland* [2010] ECR I-0000.

99 See Case C-17/09, *Commission v Germany,* [2010] ECR I-4.

100 See Case C-315/01, *Gesellschaft für Abfallentsorgungs-Technik GmbH (GAT) and Österreichische Autobahnen und Schnellstraßen AG (ÖSAG),* [2003] ECR I-6351.

contract to a third party, prior to the conclusion of the contract.[101] That right of review for tenderers must be independent of the possibility for them to bring an action for damages once the contract has been concluded.[102] A national legal system that makes it impossible to contest the award decision because of the award decision and the conclusion of the contract occurring at the same time deprives interested parties of any possible review in order to have an unlawful award decision set aside or to prevent the contract from being concluded. Complete legal protection requires that a reasonable period must elapse between the decision which awards a public contract and the conclusion of the contract itself, as well as a duty on the part of contracting authorities to inform all interested parties of an awarding decision.

4.2.8 The standstill period

The standstill period is viewed as the answer to prevent a race to sign a public contract and as the mechanism to allow interested parties to launch review procedures 10 calendar days from the day following the day of the award decision if fax or electronic means are used, or 15 calendar days from the day following the day of the award decision if other means of communication are used, or 10 calendar days from the day following the date of the receipt of the contract award decision.

4.2.9 The notion of ineffectiveness

The threat of ineffectiveness is a deterrent factor in the award of public contracts in breach of the relevant Directives and offers a considerable margin of discretion to the national legislator. Ineffectiveness may result in retrospective cancellation of contractual obligations, or reduction of contractual obligations or appropriate penalties in the sense of fines levied on contracting authorities or shortening of concluded public contracts. Grounds for deviation from ineffectiveness reflect overriding reasons relating to a general interest and must be subject to alternative penalties.

Overriding reasons are economic interests, in exceptional circumstances, which manifest the conclusion of the contract due to the disproportionate consequences arising from its ineffectiveness. Economic interests directly linked to the contract such as costs resulting from the delay in the execution of the contract, costs resulting from the launching of a new procurement procedure, costs resulting from the change of the economic operator and costs of legal obligations resulting from the ineffectiveness are not deemed overriding reasons.

Member States may provide that application for review regarding ineffectiveness of contracts must be made before 30 calendar days after publication of the contract award notice, provided that the decision of the contracting authority to award the contract without prior publication of a contract notice was justified or in any case before expiry of period of at least six months after conclusion of the contract.

---

101 See Case C-212/02, *Commission v Austria*, judgment of 24 June 2004.

102 See Case C-81/98, *Alcatel Austria and Others* [1999] ECR I-7671, para 43.

5. DAMAGES

The public procurement Directives do not require the provision of a remedy for the award of damages when there is a breach of a directly effective provision. The reasons for that absence vary: in some cases a national court has held that the authority in breach of EU law did not owe any obligation directly to the plaintiff or that the plaintiff's losses were the result of foreseeable economic risk; in others, the award of damages was seen as an unacceptable restraint on the freedom of authorities to enact legislative measures or administrative rules in good faith, pursuant to their general duty to safeguard the public interest. Damages in public procurement may be available as a consequence of breaches of provisions of national law which make a national authority liable to compensate for the breach of its obligations. However, in the context of the Remedies Directives, a pattern has emerged where a complainant seeking damages must prove that the contracting authority has committed an infringement of the procurement rules and as a direct result and consequence of that infringement, he or she has suffered harm or loss. In some legal orders, the complainant does not have to prove a breach of procurement rules on the part of the contracting authority, if a previous set aside or annulment judgment of an administrative court or tribunal had declared the award decision unlawful. In most Member States, the burden of proof concerning damages is set at a relatively high level. The mere presence of a breach of procurement procedures, which could be proved by the applicant or through a previous set aside or annulment order of the award decision of a contracting authority would be a sufficient ground to trigger the award of damages relating to bid costs and costs necessary for the preparation and submission of a tender. However, the recovery of damages relating to losses of profit is subject to the complainant proving that, in the absence of the alleged breach, he would have been awarded the contract.[103]

Article 2(1)(c) in both Remedies Directives provides for the award of damages to persons harmed by an infringement of public procurement law. The purpose behind this provision is to mobilise interested stakeholders in order to supervise the application of the EU public procurement Directives. However, the most important issue emerging from actions for damages in the legal systems of Member States relates to the burden of proof on the part of the aggrieved tenderer seeking damages. In most legal orders, the recovery of damages relating to losses of profit is subject to the complainant proving that, in the absence of the alleged breach, he would have been awarded the contract. The public sector Remedies Directive 89/665/EC is silent on this issue, whereas Directive 92/13/EC provides some clarification as regards the recovery of bid costs as against utilities. Directive 92/13/EC provides that where an aggrieved tenderer establishes that an infringement deprived him of a real chance of winning the contract, he is entitled (at least) to damages covering his bid costs. General principles and

[103] The public sector Remedies Directive 89/665 is silent on this issue, whereas Directive 92/13 provides some clarification as regards the recovery of bid costs as against utilities. Directive 92/13 provides that where an aggrieved tenderer establishes that an infringement deprived him of a real chance of winning the contract, he is entitled (at least) to damages covering his bid costs. For more details, see chapter 11 in Bovis, *EC Public Procurement: Case Law and Regulation* (Oxford: Oxford University Press, 2006).

relevant case-law in a number of Member States suggest that this real chance test would apply more generally to any claim for damages under either Remedies Directive.

Award of damages in public procurement is limited to persons economically harmed by an infringement on the part of the contracting authority. After the conclusion of the contract, damages represent the only remedy available. The amending Remedies Directive[104] has introduced contract ineffectiveness as a new type of remedy to restore equilibrium after the conclusion of an illegally awarded public contract.

The Remedies Directive contains no further requirements, as to the burden of proof nor the method of calculation of damages. The national legislator is free to decide; it must however comply with the principle of equivalence and the principle of effectiveness. The degree of the effective award of damages in breach of public procurement law varies enormously within the legal orders of the Member States. Some national courts may award punitive damages on the grounds of likelihood of harm; others, in order to award damages for breaches of public procurement law, require proof that the contract would have been awarded to the claimant. Difficulties also arise in cases where no bid was submitted or in cases of direct awards, where the award criteria did not require that in cases where no notice was published or no tender procedure was carried out.

Commission v Germany,[105] recognised that the principle *pacta sunt servanda* and the prospect of litigation for damages for termination of illegally awarded contracts cannot act as a defence for contracting authorities. German municipalities concluded service contracts for a term of at least 30 years without publishing notices in the Official Journal of the EU. The conclusion of the contracts and the threat of damages arising from potential termination of the contracts were used as arguments for not rescinding illegally awarded contracts. Germany argued that any breach of public procurement law was cured by the conclusion of the relevant contracts and after that time, there is no actual breach. The Court held that the effects of unlawful contract awards go beyond the conclusion of the contract because of its long duration and any breach of obligations under the public procurement Directives and EU law in general remain as long as the unlawfully concluded contract is valid.

In *Wall v Frankfurt*,[106] the Court held that the principles of equal treatment and non-discrimination and the consequent obligation of transparency do not require the national authorities to terminate a contract or grant a restraining order in every case of an alleged breach of that obligation in connection with the award of service concessions. But it is for the national law to regulate the legal procedures for safeguarding the rights which individuals derive from the transparency obligation in such a way that those procedures are no less favourable than similar domestic procedures according to the principle of equivalence and they do not make the exercise of those rights practically impossible or excessively difficult according to the principle of effectiveness.

In *Commission v Portugal*,[107] the conditionality of procedures related to the award of damages upon proof of fraud or fault on the part of the contracting authority was found

---

[104] See Directive 2007/66/EC, [2007] OJ L335/31.

[105] See Joined Cases C-20/00 and C-28/01, *Commission v Germany,* [2003] ECR I-3609.

[106] See Case C-91/08, *Wall AG v City of Frankfurt* [2010] ECR I-2815.

[107] See Case C-275/03, *Commission v Portugal* and Case C-70/06, *Commission v Portugal* [2004] ECR I-0000.

to contravene the Remedies Directives. Portuguese law made the award of damages to persons harmed by a breach of EU procurement law conditional on proof of fault or fraud conditions which substantially reduced the likelihood of aggrieved tenderers in obtaining damages.

In *Aktor ATE v ESR*,[108] the CJEU expanded *de lege ferenda* the coverage of the Remedies Directives to bodies which are not contracting authorities but their decisions are capable of having a certain effect on the outcome of a procurement procedure. The Court found that the national law did not comply with principles of equivalence and effectiveness, as it rendered impossible to seek annulment of a decision and to obtain compensation for any damage incurred, whereas this was not the case in other areas by virtue of national law applicable to damages incurred by virtue of unlawful acts of public authorities. As a result, those bodies should be deemed as contracting authorities, by applying the functionality test, and their decisions or acts in relation to public procurement procedures must be subject to review procedures to satisfy the effectiveness principle of the Remedies Directives. The Court reiterated that in the absence of EU rules governing damages it is for each Member State to designate the courts having jurisdiction and to lay down detailed procedural rules governing actions for safeguarding rights which individuals derive from EU law as long as they are not less favourable than those governing similar domestic actions in accordance with the principle of equivalence.

6. CONCLUSIONS

The EU Remedies Directives and the implementing regimes of the domestic legal orders of the Member States aim at decentralising the application and enforcement of the EU public procurement *acquis* and rest upon a fundamental conceptual principle, the principle of effectiveness of national remedies to avail redress to aggrieved parties. Although in relative terms public procurement jurisprudence of the CJEU has been limited over the past 30 years, it is encouraging to see an increasing flow of cases before national courts that underpin the concepts of the Remedies Directives. Decentralisation in the enforcement and application of public procurement law will definitely increase litigation before the competent national *fora* and result in an acceptable degree of compliance of Member States and contracting authorities; it will enhance transparency and accountability in the award of public contracts and it will improve the justiciability of public contracts redress. The key question is if the increased levels of justiciability will result in speculative litigation with the adverse side effects of delaying procurement processes, making contracting authorities more reluctant in engaging with the private sector and finally, increasing the cost of procurement as a result of the potential of contractual ineffectiveness and damages to aggrieved parties.

---

108 See Case C-145/08, *Club Hotel Loutraki AE and Others v Ethnico Symvoulio Radiotileorasis and Ypourgos Epikrateias* and Case C-149/08 *Aktor Anonymi Techniki Etaireia (Aktor ATE) v Ethnico Symvoulio Radiotileorasis* [2010] ECR I-0000.

12. The Remedies Directive in public procurement

Emanuela Matei

INTRODUCTION

The initial Remedies Directives suffered from serious shortcomings, in the sense that their provisions did not provide for effective review procedures between the stages of contract award and contract conclusion respectively. This gave rise to direct awards and the so-called race to sign the relevant contract to assume immunity from any redress based on the *pacta servanta sunt* principle. In addition, at both pre-contractual and post-contractual stages there were no effective deterrents for breach of either procedural or substantive public procurement laws.

The European institutions examined carefully two options: first, to entrust the enforcement of the *acquis* through compliance procedures to the European Commission and secondly to promote the establishment of national independent authorities to monitor compliance of public contracts awards with the *acquis*. The preferred solution was to introduce a consolidated Directive as a single amending instrument, based on the principles of subsidiarity and proportionality, in an attempt to rectify the shortcomings of the Remedies Directives.

The amending Remedies Directive[1] is based on the previous instruments but it introduced new themes such as a clear divide between pre-contractual and post-contractual stages, a balance between effective review of public contracts and need for efficient public procurement, a strict standstill requirement for contract conclusion, including direct awards by contracting authorities, extensive communication and monitoring requirements and a substantial refocus of the corrective mechanism. The amending Remedies Directive repealed the attestation and conciliation procedures which were laid down by their predecessors and extended their coverage to countries of the European Economic Area (EEA).

The weaknesses of the original Remedies Directives reflected in particular the absence of a period allowing an effective review between the decision to award a contract and the conclusion of the contract in question. This has often resulted in contracting authorities and contracting entities who wish to make irreversible the consequences of the disputed award decision proceeding very quickly to the signature of the contract. In order to remedy this weakness, which is a serious obstacle to effective judicial protection for aggrieved tenderers and especially those who have not been definitively excluded from the procurement process, a minimum standstill period during which the conclusion of the contract in question is suspended appears as the best solution, irrespective of whether conclusion occurs at the time of signature of the contract. The duration of the standstill period should take into account different means

[1] See Directive 2007/66/EC [2007] OJ L335/31.

of communication. If rapid means of communication are used, a shorter period can be provided for than if other means of communication are used. The new Remedies Directive only provides for minimum standstill periods. Member States are free to introduce or to maintain periods which exceed those minimum periods. Member States are also free to decide which period should apply, if different means of communication are used cumulatively.

In order to eliminate the illegal direct contract awards the need for effective, proportionate and dissuasive sanctions is paramount. Therefore a contract resulting from an illegal direct award should in principle be considered ineffective. The ineffectiveness should not be automatic but should be ascertained by or should be the result of a decision of an independent review body. Ineffectiveness as a concept introduced by the amending Remedies Directive is the most appropriate way to restore competition and to create new business opportunities for those economic operators which have been deprived illegally of their opportunity to compete. Direct contract awards should include all contract awards made without prior publication of a contract notice or in accordance with a procedure without prior call for competition.[2] Contracts that are concluded in breach of the standstill period or automatic suspension should therefore be considered ineffective in principle if they are combined with other infringements to the extent that those infringements have affected the chances of the tenderer applying for review to obtain the contract. In the case of other infringements of formal procedural requirements, Member States might consider the principle of ineffectiveness to be inappropriate. In those cases Member States should have the flexibility to provide for alternative penalties which should be limited to the imposition of fines to be paid to a body independent of the contracting authority or entity or to a shortening of the duration of the contract.

Economic interests in the effectiveness of a contract may only be considered as overriding reasons if in exceptional circumstances ineffectiveness would lead to disproportionate consequences. However, economic interests directly linked to the contract concerned should not constitute overriding reasons. Furthermore, the need to ensure over time the legal certainty of decisions taken by contracting authorities and contracting entities requires the establishment of a reasonable minimum period of limitation on reviews seeking to establish that the contract is ineffective.

The amending Remedies Directive should not exclude the application of stricter sanctions in accordance with national law. The objective to be achieved where Member

---

[2] Possible justifications for a direct award within the meaning of this Directive may include the exemptions in Articles 10 to 18 of Directive 2004/18/EC, the application of Article 31, Article 61 or Article 68 of Directive 2004/18/EC, the award of a service contract in accordance with Article 21 of Directive 2004/18/EC or a lawful 'in-house' contract award following the interpretation of the Court of Justice. The same applies to contracts which meet the conditions for an exclusion or special arrangements in accordance with Article 5(2), Articles 18 to 26, Articles 29 and 30 or Article 62 of Directive 2004/17/EC, to cases involving the application of Article 40(3) of Directive 2004/17/EC or to the award of a service contract in accordance with Article 32 of Directive 2004/17/EC. In exceptional cases the use of the negotiated procedure without publication of a contract notice is permitted immediately after the cancellation of the contract. If in those cases, for technical or other compelling reasons, the remaining contractual obligations can, at that stage, only be performed by the economic operator which has been awarded the contract, the application of overriding reasons might be justified.

States lay down the rules which ensure that a contract shall be considered ineffective is that the rights and obligations of the parties under the contract should cease to be enforced and performed. The consequences resulting from a contract being considered ineffective should be determined by national law. National law may therefore, for example, provide for the retroactive cancellation of all contractual obligations (*ex tunc*) or conversely limit the scope of the cancellation to those obligations which would still have to be performed (*ex nunc*). This should not lead to the absence of forceful penalties if the obligations deriving from a contract have already been fulfilled either entirely or almost entirely. In such cases Member States should provide for alternative penalties as well, taking into account the extent to which a contract remains in force in accordance with national law. Similarly, the consequences concerning the possible recovery of any sums which may have been paid, as well as all other forms of possible restitution, including restitution in value where restitution in kind is not possible, are to be determined by national law.

However, in order to ensure the proportionality of the sanctions applied, Member States may grant the body responsible for review procedures the possibility of not jeopardising the contract or of recognising some or all of its temporal effects, when the exceptional circumstances of the case concerned require certain overriding reasons relating to a general interest to be respected. In those cases alternative penalties should be applied instead. The review body independent of the contracting authority or contracting entity should examine all relevant aspects in order to establish whether overriding reasons relating to a general interest require that the effects of the contract should be maintained.

The most important changes brought by the adoption of Directive 2007/66/EC refer to the standstill provisions, the remedy of ineffectiveness and the alternative sanctions meant to complement or replace the solution of rendering a contract ineffective.[3] Settled case-law shows that the purpose of the EU directives coordinating procedures for the award of public contracts is to avoid the risk of preference being given to national tenderers, whenever a contract is awarded by the contracting authorities and the possibility that a body financed or controlled by the State, regional or local authorities or other bodies governed by public law may choose to be guided by non-economic considerations.[4]

The main objective of the supranational public procurement law is to ensure that the economic actors in all 28 Member States of the EU as well as Iceland, Norway and Liechtenstein have full and equal access to contract awards throughout the EEA area, ensuring a level playing field within the public procurement market. The substantive

[3] /*SEC/2006/0557*/ The most important problems identified during the consultation process and in case law were (i) the lack of effective Remedies against the practice of illegal direct awards of public contracts (i.e. public contracts awarded in a non-transparent and non-competitive manner to a single tenderer) and (ii) the race to signature of public contracts by Awarding Authorities which actually deprives economic operators participating in formal tender procedures of the possibility to bring Remedies actions effectively, i.e. at a time when infringements can still be corrected.

[4] See, in particular, Case C-380/98, *University of Cambridge* [2000] ECR I-8035 para 17, Case C-237/99, *Commission v France* [2001] ECR I-00939 para 42, and Case C-470/99, *Universale-Bau and Others* [2002] ECR I-11617 para 52.

directives apply to all contracts above certain thresholds.[5] The CJEU has emphasised the principal objective of the supranational rules in this legal field, namely the free movement of services and the opening-up to the widest possible undistorted competition in all Member States.[6]

Based on the principle of non-discrimination and preserving a liberalisation pact, a bilateral agreement between the EU and Switzerland was signed in order to secure reciprocal access to purchases of products and services, including construction services, by telecommunications operators, railway operators, entities active in the field of energy other than electricity and private utilities of both parties.[7] Through its bilateral relations the Union advocates within the context of the WTO an ambitious opening of international public procurement markets of the Union and its trading partners, in a spirit of reciprocity and mutual benefit.

The objectives of the EU directives coordinating the award procedures would nevertheless be unattainable, if the economic operators were unable to effectively ensure that the rights granted by the Union procurement law were observed everywhere in the EU. Directives 89/665/EEC[8] and 92/13/EEC[9] were consequently adopted as flanking measures in order to guarantee access to rapid and effective procedures for seeking redress in cases where the economic operators have reasons to believe that a public contract has been unfairly awarded.

On 21 June 2007 the European Parliament, having regard to the Commission proposal and Article 47 of the Charter approved the proposal for a new remedies directive. For ease of reference I will use two generic nominations: 'substantive directives' for the rules on coordinated procedures for the award of public contracts and 'procedural directives' for the rules on coordinated review procedures. Directive 2007/66/EC (hereinafter referred to as the 'Remedies Directive') was adopted on 15 November 2007 by the European Council at first reading with a view to adoption by means of codecision procedure. On 11 December 2007 the named codecision procedure took place and the directive was published on 20 December 2007.

An improved access of the economic operators established in the EU to public procurement markets of certain third countries protected by restrictive procurement measures and the preservation of equal conditions of competition within the internal

---

[5] Commission Regulation (EU) No 1251/2011 of 30 November 2011 amending Directives 2004/17/EC ([2004] OJ L134/1–113), 2004/18/EC ([2004] OJ L134/114–240) and 2009/81/EC ('substantive directives') of the European Parliament and of the Council in respect of their application thresholds for the procedures for the awards of contract Text with EEA relevance, [2011] OJ L319/43–44.

[6] Case C-26/03, *Stadt Halle and RPL Lochau* [2005] ECR I-1 paras 44 and 47.

[7] Agreement between the European Union and the Swiss Confederation on certain aspects of government procurement, [2002] OJ L114/430.

[8] Council Directive of 21 December 1989 on the coordination of the laws, regulations and administrative provisions relating to the application of review procedures to the award of public supply and public works contracts, [1989] OJ L395/33–35.

[9] Council Directive of 25 February 1992 coordinating the laws, regulations and administrative provisions relating to the application of Union rules on the procurement procedures of entities operating in the water, energy, transport and telecommunications sectors, [1992] OJ L76/14–20.

market require the harmonisation of the rules governing the treatment of third-country goods and services not yet covered by specific international commitments of the Union.[10]

I. THE DEFINITION OF DECISIONS FOR JUDICIAL REVIEW

The provisions of the Remedies Directive apply to all decisions taken by contracting authorities who are subject to the rules of Union law on public procurement[11] and no limitation regarding the nature and content of those decisions is allowed.[12] The directive lays down nevertheless only the minimum conditions to be satisfied by the review procedures established in domestic law in order to ensure compliance with the requirements of Union law on public procurement.[13] Where one activity carried out by a body falls within the scope of the public procurement directives, all the other activities carried out by that body, irrespective of their possible industrial or commercial character, are also covered by those directives.[14]

It must be said also that the system established by the Union legislature for contracts relating to non-priority services, that is, services falling within the ambit of Annex II B of the substantive directives, endorses the application of the principles deriving from Articles 49 TFEU and 56 TFEU or, therefore, of the requirements designed to ensure transparency of procedures and equal treatment of tenderers, if such contracts are nevertheless of certain cross-border interest.[15] The previously established distinction between priority and non-priority services should nevertheless be abolished according to the Commission proposals for new substantive directives on public procurement.[16]

The obligation to provide effective and rapid remedies against decisions taken by contracting authorities includes the decisions taken outside a formal award procedure and the decisions prior to a formal call for tenders, in particular the decision on whether a particular contract falls within the personal and material scope of the substantive directives. The possibility of review shall not depend on the fact that the public procurement procedure in question has formally reached a particular stage. The expression of will formulated in a manner capable of producing legal effects must

---

[10] Proposal for a Regulation on the access of third-country goods and services to the Union's internal market in public procurement and procedures supporting negotiations on access of Union goods and services to the public procurement markets of third countries COM(2012) 124 final 2012/0060 (COD) Brussels, 21 March 2012.

[11] See *inter alia* Case C-92/00, *HI* [2002] ECR I-5553 para 37, and Case C-57/01, *Makedoniko Metro and Michaniki* [2003] ECR I-1091 para 68.

[12] Case C-81/98, *Alcatel Austria* [1999] ECR I-07671 para 35, and *HI*, cited supra footnote 11, para 49.

[13] See, *inter alia*, Case C-327/00, *Santex* [2003] ECR I-1877 para 47, and Case C-315/01, *GAT* [2003] ECR I-6351 para 45.

[14] Case C-44/96, *Mannesmann Anlagenbau,* [1998] ECR I-73 paras 25 and 26.

[15] Case C-226/09, *Commission v Ireland* [2010] ECR I-11807 paras 29, 31.

[16] COM/2011/0895 final – 2011/0439 (COD) and COM/2011/0896 final – 2011/0438 (COD) The EESC is in favour of maintaining the difference between A and B Services under the condition of legal certainty and the possible extension of cross-border contracts of B Services.

be open to review.[17] An invitation to tender and its allegedly unlawful clauses must be made subject to review.[18] The withdrawal of an invitation to tender also must be open to review and its examination cannot be reduced to determining whether the decision to withdraw was arbitrary.[19]

Decisions of other public authorities than the contracting authorities themselves can be made subject to review under public procurement law. The exclusion of the tenderer in *Club Hotel Loutraki* resulted from a decision taken by a Greek public authority, ESR, whose activities were in principle not governed by the review system laid down by the procedural directives. However the decisions of ESR could lead to the exclusion of a tenderer, who individually was characterised by one or another of the incompatibilities stipulated by the relevant national rules. Therefore the decisions of ESR were not devoid of interest in respect of the uniform and accurate application of Union law in the field of public procurement procedure and the right to effective judicial protection, precludes a national rule that deprives a tenderer in a public procurement procedure of the possibility of seeking, individually, compensation for the loss suffered as a result of a decision adopted by an authority, other than the contracting authority, involved in that procedure in line with the applicable national rules, which is such as to influence the result of that procedure.[20]

In *Nachrichtenagentur* the CJEU provided the definitions of the terms *awarded* and *awarding* in order to determine under which conditions an amendment brought to a contract may imply that a new award is granted. A transfer of services between the initial service provider and a limited liability company fully owned and controlled by the named service provider is not covered by the definition of an award. A modification of the initial contract in order to accommodate external changes is not an award. The use of a supplementary agreement during the period of validity of a contract concluded for an indefinite period, through which the contracting authority agrees with the contractor, to renew for a period of three years a waiver of the right to terminate the contract by notice and agrees to lay down higher rebates than those initially provided for with respect to certain volume-related prices within a specified area of supply are not covered by the definition of award.[21] In conclusion there are many rules of substantive nature that can determine the content and the scope of a decision for judicial review.

II. TWO LEVELS OF ENFORCEMENT

According to Article 17 TEU the Commission is the guardian of the Treaties. The supranational level of enforcement relates to the competencies retained by the Commission to supervise the compliance of the Member States with their obligations

---

[17] *Stadt Halle*, cited supra footnote 6.

[18] Case C-448/01, *EVN AG* [2003] ECR I-14527.

[19] *HI*, cited supra footnote 11.

[20] Joined Cases C-145/08 and C-149/08, *Club Hotel Loutraki* [2010] ECR I-4165 para 80; The Greek Council for Radio and TV ('ESR') was the authority in question.

[21] Case C-454/06, *pressetext Nachrichtenagentur* [2008] ECR I-4401.

under EU law. It follows from Article 258 TFEU that the Commission can bring a Member State before the Court, if it considers that it has failed to fulfil an obligation under the Treaty including compliance with specific provisions of secondary law. A tenderer who submits a complaint to the Commission will not be party to the proceedings brought by the latter under Article 258 TFEU.[22]

In practice there are three distinct situations in which an infringement takes place: non-communication of measures transposing directives, non-conformity of national measures, that is, incorrect transposition and thirdly, an inaccurate application of EU law meaning that the specific application of certain secondary provisions is not compliant. In the third situation, the parallel application of both national and supra-national rules on public procurement is possible.

The Commission recommends the prior use of such national means of redress, whether administrative, judicial or other, before lodging a complaint with the Commission, because of the advantages they may offer for complainants. By using national remedies complainants may assert their rights more directly and more personally than by using the infringement procedure, which usually also takes more time. In contrast with the case of national proceedings, any person has *locus standi* to lodge a complaint under Article 258 TFEU concerning a specific breach of Union law by a Member State and may enjoy the benefit of anonymity. It is not necessary to demonstrate a formal interest in bringing proceedings. Neither do complainants have to prove that they are principally and directly concerned by the infringement. Anonymity is an advantage for a complainant who needs to entertain excellent business relations with the contracting authority in question.

In fact, before referring a case to the CJEU, the Commission shall hold a series of contacts with the Member State concerned to try to terminate the infringement. Moreover, any finding of an infringement by the CJEU has no impact on the rights of the complainant, since it does not serve to resolve individual cases. It merely obliges the Member State to comply with Union law and in particular, any individual claims for damages would have to be brought by complainants before the national courts.[23]

Iceland, Liechtenstein and Norway, have notified as well the full implementation of the Remedies Directive.[24] EFTA's Surveillance Authority (ESA), according to Article 23 of Surveillance and Court Agreement (SCA), is responsible for the supervision of compliance with the obligations concerning public procurement assumed under the EEA Agreement.[25] Under Article 31 SCA, the ESA is competent to bring actions before the EFTA-Court against an EEA-member for failing to fulfil an obligation under the EEA Agreement.[26] Switzerland, founding member of the EFTA, rejected the

---

[22] Article 258 TFEU corresponds to Article 31 of the SCA.

[23] Commission Communication to the Council and Parliament updating the handling of relations with the complainant in respect of the application of Union law, COM/2012/0154 final.

[24] Compliance date for the obligation to incorporate the Remedies Directive stipulated by the Decision of the Joint Committee No. 83/2011 was 1 November 2012. See annex XVI, 5, 5a of the EEA Agreement.

[25] The Surveillance and Court Agreement, [1994] OJ L344/3; and EFTA States' official gazettes, article 5(1)(a); Article 23 SCA corresponds in substance with Articles 3 and 8 of Directive 2007/66/EC entitled 'Corrective mechanisms'.

[26] The Surveillance and Court Agreement, cited supra footnote 25, Article 31(2).

adherence to the EEA Agreement via a referendum in 1992, thus the Government Procurement Agreement of the WTO represents the cornerstone of the Swiss international procurement legislation.

In *Aleris Ungplan*, a subsidiary of a Swedish company, contested under Article 36 SCA[27] the decision of ESA not to initiate procedures under Article 31 SCA,[28] as regards an award of youth care services and the exclusion of commercial operators according to Norwegian law. The relevant substantive law for the contested ESA decisions relied on the freedom of establishment, the principle of non-discrimination and Articles 31 EEA, 65 EEA and 109 EEA, and Article 2 of Directive 2004/18/EC with specific reference to the regime of non-priority services. The ESA decided that there were no grounds to further pursue the cases under Article 31 SCA[29] and the EFTA Court maintained this decision, since the application submitted by the plaintiff under Article 36 SCA was manifestly inadmissible.[30] The findings under Article 31 SCA resulting from the contested examination performed by ESA are not binding on national courts, though they constitute a factual element, which a national court seized to rule on the dispute may certainly take into account.[31] There is a connection between the national and the supranational procedures, even if the character of an ESA decision, exactly as in the case of a corresponding Commission decision under Article 258 TFEU, is not compulsory law.

Article 260 TFEU allows the Commission to bring an action against a Member State, who failed to comply with a prior ruling of the Court. If the Court finds that the Member State has indeed failed to comply with its judgment, it may impose a lump sum or a periodic penalty payment. In case of a serious and persistent failure to comply with Union law a Member State may be ordered to pay both a periodic penalty and a lump sum. According to the third paragraph of Article 260 TFEU, an action under Article 258 TFEU on the grounds that a Member State has failed to notify measures transposing a directive adopted under legislative procedure can incur a payment obligation for the Member State in question. Necessary interim measures may be prescribed in all cases pursuant to the provisions of Article 279 TFEU.

An order for interim measures can be obtained providing that a *prima facie* case is presented in the application and by this means the imminent character of serious and irreparable damage of an irreversible nature may be anticipated. According to the case-law, a *prima facie* case is present where at least one of the applicant's pleas appears at first sight to be too weighty to be discounted, or cannot be discounted without a detailed examination, which is reserved for the decision on the merits.[32] Moreover, according to consistent case-law, the risks of each of the possible solutions

---

[27] Article 36(2) SCA corresponds to Article 263(4) TFEU.

[28] Article 31 SCA corresponds to Article 258 TFEU.

[29] College Decision 248-10-COL to close a case against Norway for failure to comply with the EEA procurement rules.

[30] Case C-29/92, *Asia Motor France* [1992] ECR I-3935 paras 19 to 21, and the case-law cited, and Case T-29/93, *Calvo Alonso-Cortès* [1993] ECR II-1389 para 55, and Case T-58/09, *Schemaventotto* [2010] ECR II-03863 paras 125 and 126.

[31] Case E-13/10, *Aleris Ungplan* [2011] EFTA Ct. Rep, p. 3 para 28.

[32] Order of the President of the Court of Justice, Case C-149/95 P(R), *Commission v Atlantic Container Line and Others* [1995] ECR I-2165 paras 26–27.

must be balanced against each other in interim relief proceedings. It must particularly be examined whether the interest of the applicant to suspend the effect of the contested decision weighs more heavily than the interest in the immediate implementation of that decision.[33]

Preliminary ruling proceedings conducted under Article 267 TFEU are based on a clear separation of functions between the national courts and the CJEU. It is the national court alone, before which the dispute has been brought, and which must assume responsibility for the judicial decision to be made, to determine in the light of the particular circumstances of the case both the need for a preliminary ruling in order to enable it to deliver judgment and the relevance of the questions which it refers to the Court. Where the questions submitted by the national court concern the interpretation of Union law, the CJEU is bound to give a ruling.[34]

A preliminary ruling does not create or alter the law, but is purely declaratory, with the consequence that in principle it takes effect from the date on which the rule interpreted entered into force.[35] In EFTA law we can find a weaker device stipulated by Article 34 SCA that only gives to the national courts a right to request advisory opinions on the interpretation of the EEA Agreement. Three categories of situations subject to preliminary or advisory rulings can be distinguished depending on whether the contract has been concluded before or after the time limit for transposition and whether the directive has been implemented in time.

A. If the implementation is carried on within the prescribed transposition period, then the national implementing provisions become applicable on the public contracts according to the transitional provisions of the implementing act, but no later than 20 December 2009 for the EU Member States and 1 November 2012 for the other EEA members.
B. If the implementation is delayed,[36] then certain provisions of the directive, which are unconditional and sufficiently clear and precise, incur direct vertical effect and individuals can rely on them before the national courts.[37] The public procurement directives are undeniably intended to confer rights on individuals.
C. If the implementation is incongruous with the provisions of the directive, the national court must do its best to interpret the domestic law in agreement with Union law, if it is not possible to deliver such an interpretation, it must disapply the incongruous provisions of national law and finally if it is not possible to disapply them, an action for damages for state liability remains the only available means of redress.

---

33 *Commission v Atlantic Container Line and Others*, cited supra footnote 32, para 50.

34 See, in particular, Case C-379/98, *PreussenElektra,* [2001] ECR I-2099 para 38; Case C-341/05, *Laval un Partneri* [2007] ECR I-11767 para 45; and Case C-450/06, *Varec* [2008] ECR I-00581 para 23.

35 Case C-2/06, *Kempter* [2008] ECR I-411 para 35.

36 See to that effect Case 148/78, *Ratti* [1979] ECR I-1629.

37 See to that effect, Case 41-74, *Van Duyn* [1974] ECR I-1337.

The principle whereby a State must be liable for loss and damage caused to individuals as a result of breaches of EU law for which the State can be held responsible is inherent in the legal system established by the Treaties. However we can observe that most commonly a case of incorrect implementation of a directive is dealt with under the procedures stipulated by article 258 TFEU and not brought before the national courts relying on the *Francovich* doctrine.

The State may nevertheless be held responsible for damage caused to individuals by infringements of EU law, where the rule which has been infringed is intended to confer rights on them, the breach of that rule is sufficiently serious, and there is a direct causal link between the breach and the loss or damage sustained by the individuals.

> ... it is for the internal legal order of each Member State, once those conditions have been complied with, to determine the criteria on the basis of which the damage arising from an infringement of EU law on the award of public contracts must be determined and estimated, provided the principles of equivalence and effectiveness are complied with.[38]

Whatever the case may be an infringement of EU law will be sufficiently serious, where the decision concerned was made in manifest breach of the case-law of the CJEU on the subject matter.[39] Other factors for determining the serious character of an infringement comprise above all the degree of clarity and precision of the rule infringed, whether the infringement was intentional, whether the error of law was excusable or inexcusable, the position taken, where applicable, by a Union institution and non-compliance by the court in question with its obligation to make a reference for a preliminary ruling under Article 267(3) TFEU.[40]

In the author's view the provisions of a directive that are sufficiently clear and precise and confer individual rights must be enforceable before the national court after the expiry of the transposition period and must be given full effect in any event. If the application of these provisions is rendered impossible under national law, as it is the case of *contra legem* interpretation, the degree of erroneousness of the implementation must be deemed as being sufficiently serious, because in this case the requisite solution must be legislative, that is, the adoption of new legislation and the repeal of the manifestly unlawful provisions.

Additionally, it must be reminded that the implementation in accordance with a directive's provisions by the authority vested with the power to adopt regulations, cannot in itself achieve the clarity and precision needed to meet the requirement of legal certainty.[41] The named requirement ensures that individuals should have the

---

38 Case C-568/08, *Combinatie Spijker* [2010] ECR I-12655 para 92.

39 See, *inter alia*, to that effect Joined Cases C-46/93 and C-48/93, *Brasserie du Pêcheur and Factortame* [1996] ECR I-1029 para 57; Case C-118/00, *Larsy* [2001] ECR I-5063 para 44; and Case C-224/01, *Köbler* [2003] ECR I-10239 para 56.

40 *Köbler*, cited supra footnote 39, para 55.

41 See, to this effect, Case C-236/95, *Commission v Greece* [1996] ECR I-4459, paras 12 and 13, and Case C-144/99, *Commission* v *Netherlands* [2001] ECR I-3541, para 21.

benefit of a clear and precise legal situation enabling them to ascertain the full extent of their rights and, where appropriate, to rely on them before the national courts.[42]

A reference for a preliminary ruling cannot determine the outcome of the case, the decision in the main proceedings being taken by the referring court, the interpretation and application of the relevant rules of domestic law is limited by general principles of law and it cannot serve as the basis for an interpretation of national law *contra legem*. The appreciation of the gravity of the infringement has been left to the national courts ignoring thus the fact that the rights of individuals deriving from Union law will most probably be rendered ineffective, if the viability of the ultimate prescribed solution of an action for damages relying on the *Francovich* ruling is not assumable in any sense.

III. NATIONAL ENFORCEMENT OF UNION PROCUREMENT RULES

The effectiveness of Union law shall also be preserved by the national courts through the available mechanism for preliminary rulings. The main rule is that the principles of national procedural autonomy and of the uniform application of Union law are applicable, if the national courts deal with a case comprised within the spectrum of Union law rights and obligations.[43] The exercise of national procedural autonomy must respect the principles of equivalence and effectiveness. Article 1(3) of the Remedies Directive imposed an obligation on the Member States to ensure, under their own detailed rules, that review procedures are accessible at least to any person having or having had an interest in obtaining a particular contract and who has been or risks being harmed by an alleged infringement.[44]

The Member States are not obliged to make those review procedures available to any person wishing to obtain a public contract, but they may require that the person concerned has been or risks being harmed by the infringement he alleges.[45] A potential claimant for damages is also a person who has *locus standi* to lodge a complaint against an award decision before the review body or the national court.

> ... in the absence of [Union] rules governing the matter, it is for the domestic legal system of each Member State to designate the courts and tribunals having jurisdiction and to lay down the detailed procedural rules governing actions for safeguarding rights which individuals derive directly from [Union] law, provided that such rules are not less favourable than those governing similar domestic actions (principle of equivalence) and that they do not render practically impossible or excessively difficult the exercise of rights conferred by [Union] law (principle of effectiveness).[46]

---

42 See to this effect, in particular, Case C-236/95, *Commission v Greece* [1996] ECR I-4459, para 13, and Case C-177/04, *Commission v France* [2006] ECR I-2461 para 48.

43 Directive 2007/66/EC, [2007] OJ L335/31–46, recital (34).

44 See also Directive 2007/66/EC, cited supra footnote 43, recital (17).

45 Case C-249/01, *Hackermüller* [2003] ECR I-6319 para 18.

46 Case C-453/99, *Courage & Crehan* [2001] ECR I-6297 para 29; see also Case C-91/08, *Wall AG* [2010] ECR I-2815 para 65.

From the beginning it is important to distinguish between two situations. The *Teleaustria* type of situation, where coordinated rules on remedies were not applicable and the legal protection of individual rights derived directly from provisions of primary law and the *Stadt Graz* type of situation, where the applicable remedies are harmonised meaning that the right to be awarded civil damages for infringements of public procurement law is specifically stipulated, thus not left to the discretion of the Member States.[47]

> ... a declaration that an application for damages, brought by the unsuccessful tenderer following the annulment of that decision by an administrative court, is well founded cannot – contrary to the wording, context and objective of the provisions of Directive 89/665 which establish the right to such damages – depend, for its part, on a finding that the contracting authority involved is at fault.[48]

The aim of the Remedies Directive is to guarantee judicial remedies, which are as rapid as possible and effective against decisions taken by contracting authorities in violation of the law on public contracts and the principle of effectiveness underlies the objectives pursued by that directive. In theory, the national provisions implementing a directive come under the procedural autonomy of the Member States, limited by the principles of equivalence and effectiveness, however it is also necessary to examine whether the implementation is correct.

In addition, when hearing a case between individuals, a national court, which is required, when applying the provisions of domestic law adopted for the purpose of transposing obligations laid down by a directive, to consider the whole body of rules of national law and to interpret them, so far as possible, in the light of the wording and purpose of the directive in order to achieve an outcome consistent with the objectives pursued by it.[49] If certain remedies are explicitly required, the scope of the procedural autonomy is accordingly reduced.

Member States shall not apply their procedural rules in such a manner as to undermine Union interests such as the effectiveness of anti-infringement policies in the area of public procurement, unless such restriction is based on overriding reasons, necessary and proportional in relation to the contemplated aim.[50] The rationale of the Remedies Directive is to achieve full effectiveness of Union law and, above all, to ensure the *effet utile* of the prohibitions stipulated by the directives. Unless the prescribed remedies are actually made available and enforceable before the national courts, the rationale of the Remedies Directive would be thwarted.

---

47 Case C-314/09, *Stadt Graz v Strabag AG* [2010] ECR I-8769; See also *Hackermüller* cited supra footnote 45, and Case C-213/07, *Michaniki* [2008] ECR I-09999 concerning the rule that the grounds for exclusion must be open to review and *Universale-Bau,* cited supra footnote 4 and Case C-241/06, *Lämmerzahl* [2007] ECR I-8415 concerning the compulsory content of a contract notice or of the tender documents. C-314/01, *Siemens AG Österreich* [2004] ECR I-2549 requires that clauses of a tender invitation must be open to review.

48 *Stadt Graz,* cited supra footnote 47.

49 Joined Cases C-397/01 to C-403/01, *Pfeiffer* [2004] ECR I-8835 para 119.

50 Directive 2007/66/EC, cited supra footnote 43, recitals 22–24 and Article 2d3.

The scope of the national procedural autonomy has been considerably reduced, by the very adoption of specific harmonised remedies. The following remedies are generally made available not only in the EEA area, but also worldwide:

- Setting aside a decision of award partially or fully or amending it.
- Setting aside any other decision for public procurement.
- Interim measures against the procurement procedure, an automatic interim bar is available in some countries, but in most countries the suspension is not automatic but a proportionality test is required.
- Annulment of a concluded contract.
- Damages are granted if the following standard criteria are met: loss suffered by the claimant, a breach of the law by the contracting authority or entity, causality. The negative contract interest is redressed in all the EEA states, in contrast damages for lost profits are seldom available since it is difficult to provide the evidence required for the positive contract interest.[51]
- Pecuniary penalties and periodic penalty payments form part of the public procurement remedy systems.

A directive does not offer a complete cover of the subject matter and therefore what has been left outside the scope of the coordinated rules must be regulated by the Member States in the spirit of sincere cooperation and effectiveness. Matters like the actual determination of limitation periods, access to file, effect of the national decisions, quantification of harm and rules on evidence and burden of proof have been left to the discretion of the Member States with the amendment that the national choices must be equivalent and effective.

A. Independent Review Bodies

Certain features are generally adopted by the domestic laws that regulate the activity of the national review bodies in all member states: the existence of a legal prescription, the type of outcome of the proceedings, the legal standing of claimants and the imposition of fees and deposits.

The scope of review is nevertheless different, in 15 Member States[52] the same system applies to all public contracts. In Germany, Ireland and the UK the system is applicable only to contracts over the thresholds, while the other nine Member States[53] have two distinct systems. Moreover some countries have different rules for contracting entities. The amount of fees to be paid is in some countries only symbolic and in other countries very onerous such as in Germany and in Czech Republic.

According to settled case-law, in order to determine whether a body making a reference is a court or tribunal for the purposes of Article 267 TFEU, which is a

---

[51] See for that effect, Case T 2883-04, *Ishavet v Municipal Council of Gothenburg*, Judgment of Supreme Court of Sweden, 31 May 2007.

[52] Austria, Belgium, Czech Republic, Denmark, Estonia, Finland, France, Hungary, Italy, Lithuania, Portugal, Poland, Romania Slovak Republic, and Sweden.

[53] Bulgaria, Cyprus, Greece, Latvia, Luxembourg, Malta, Netherlands, Slovakia, Slovenia.

question governed by EU law alone, the Court takes account of a number of factors, such as whether the body is established by law, whether it is permanent, whether its jurisdiction is compulsory, whether its procedure is *inter partes*, whether it applies rules of law and whether it is independent.[54]

When a body of first instance, independent of the contracting authority reviews a contract award decision, Member States shall ensure that the contracting authority cannot conclude the contract before the review body has made a decision on the application either for interim measures or for review.[55] Members of such an independent body shall be hired and removed from office under the same conditions as members of the judiciary as to the authority in charge with their appointment, their period of office, and their dismissal. In any case the President of an independent review body shall have the same legal and professional qualifications as members of the judiciary. The independent body shall take its decisions following a procedure in which both sides are heard, and these decisions shall, by means determined by each Member State, be legally binding.[56]

In Denmark, not only tenderers and candidates have standing rights before the review body, but also the Competition Authority and the Ministry of the Economy, Finances and Industry as well as the corresponding authorities from any EU or EFTA state. The Danish review body has the authority to suspend, annul or modify the award decisions, to impose economic sanctions and to award compensation for damages suffered by the complainant. A decision of the review body can be contested within eight weeks from the notification of the parties.[57] The Danish review body is composed by a board of seven judges, a vice-president and a president. Moreover a number of legal experts are hired as auxiliary staff.[58] Denmark has a unique system allowing the choice between bringing the case before an ordinary court and submitting it to the attention of the specialised body. Moreover, the Competition Authority may provide advisory support concerning the interpretation and the application of the rules on public procurement and it deals with the control and review on public procurement procedures.[59]

In Romania the specialised review body, the National Council for Solving Complaints, has 36 members, among which at least half must hold an academic degree in law. The judges are public clerks with special status, assigned to their positions by the decision of the prime minister at the proposal of the Council president as a result of a

---

[54] Case C-118/09, *Koller* [2010] para 22; see, *inter alia*, Case C-54/96, *Dorsch Consult* [1997] ECR I-4961, para 23; Case C-53/03, Syfait and Others [2005] ECR I-4609, para 29; Case C-246/05, *Häupl* [2007] ECR I-4673, paragraph 16; and order in Case C-109/07 *Pilato* [2008] ECR I-3503, para 22.

[55] Directive 2007/66/EC, cited supra footnote 43, Article 2(3).

[56] Directive 2007/66/EC, cited supra footnote 43, Article 2(9).

[57] On 1 June 2013 a new Danish Act No 511 of 27 May 2013 came into force giving the review body the power to reject fully or partially a complaint for reasons of lacking jurisdiction on the subject matter, not paying the fee or where the complaint is manifestly unfounded or with no actual prospect of success.

[58] Specialised review body: Klagenævnet for Udbud; Relevant law: Act 492 of 12 May 2010 entered into force on 1 July 2010 (Lov om håndhævelse af udbudsreglerne).

[59] Danish Competition Authority: Konkurrencestyrelsen; See also The Comparative Survey on the national procurement systems across the PPN, Roma December 2010, p. XX.

pre-employment exam. A complaint is always examined by a panel of three judges. The auxiliary personnel allocated to each panel are represented by a legal adviser, an engineer, an economist and a public procurement expert. The competence of the Council comprises the review of legality of both *ex-ante* and *ex-post* award decisions in relation to the date of concluding the contract.[60]

In Iceland the specialised review panel is composed of three members, one judge president, an engineer and an attorney.[61] In the event that a plaintiff, a defendant or another party with a legitimate interest deserving protection is dissatisfied with a ruling of the Icelandic review body, such party may initiate an action for annulment before a court of law. Such proceedings shall be initiated within six months from the date that the party obtained, or could obtain, knowledge of the ruling in question.

In Norway the review body was established in 2002 by Royal Decree and consists of ten highly qualified lawyers appointed by the King for a period of four years. Three members of the body partake in the examination of each complaint. According to the Norwegian Act of public procurement the role of the national body is only advisory. Although the decisions of the body are not legally binding, due to the high quality of the recommendations, the body's opinions are followed by the parties in nearly all cases. If a complaint is submitted within the standstill period, the review body asks the contracting authority to defer the signing of the contract until the conclusion of the case. The principle of transparency is respected by allowing interested parties access to the complaint file. The body shall give priority to complaints, where the contracts have not yet been signed.[62]

In the UK, all actions concerning public procurement must be brought before the High Court.[63] Proceedings in a high-level court may be costly, time-consuming, and detached from the region of the procurement contract. On the contrary, proceedings in a low-level, first-instance court may be less expensive, faster, and closer to the region of the procurement contract, though these bodies may lack experience and expertise.

In France an application for judicial review can be requested also by a public prosecutor in cases where the European Commission notified reasons for which it considered that a breach of obligations related to the publication of a contract notice or a call for competition has been committed.[64] France, exactly like the UK and Sweden

---

[60] Specialised review body: Consiliului Național de Soluționare a Contestațiilor; Relevant law: G.E.O. 34/2006 of 19 April 2006 approved by Law 337/2006 of 17 July 2006 as amended by G.E.O. 72/2009 of 17 June 2009 entered into force on 26 June 2009; See also the amendments brought by Law no. 279/2011 published on 12 December 2011.

[61] Specialised review body: Kærunefnd útboðsmála; Relevant law: Act 84/2007 amended by Act 58/2013 of 11 April 2013 (Ný lög um breytingar á lögum um opinber innkaup).

[62] Specialised review body: Klagenemnda for offentlige anskaffelser; Relevant law: Act 2006-06-30-41 amended by Act (2012-05-11-25) entered into force 1 July 2012; See also The Comparative Survey on the national procurement systems across the PPN, Roma December 2010, p. XXI.

[63] Relevant law: Public Contracts Regulations 2009 No 2992 applicable on contract award procedures commenced from 20 December 2009 onwards. Article 47C(2).

[64] Art. 1441-2.-III/ Code de procédure civile (Part III, Title IV, Chapter VI: Litigation related to the award of public contracts); Décret n° 2009-1456 du 27 novembre 2009 relatif aux procédures de recours applicables aux contrats de la commande publique; Ordonnance no

has not established any specialised review body, the litigation taking place before the administrative tribunals according to the code of civil procedure.

Effective redress systems for challenging procurement decisions should provide well-timed access, autonomous review, efficient and judicious resolution of complaints and adequate remedies. The system of specialised review bodies provides in addition also a more professionally informed decision-making and increases the level of competence on public procurement matters in general through publishing the opinions and clarifying the interpretation of the rules and principles. The statistics show that in member states where a specialised review body has been instituted by law, the number of litigations is higher than in countries where review of the irregularities is a matter for the ordinary or administrative courts. The availability of the review is lower in the latter case, if the long period of trial and the higher cost of litigation are to be considered.[65]

B. Temporal Restrictions

B.1 Interim protection

The most important function of interim measures relates to the possibility to suspend an award procedure, especially prior to the conclusion of the contract. Member States shall guarantee that the measures concerning the review procedures include provision for powers to take, at the first opportunity and by way of interlocutory procedures, interim measures in the pursuit of correcting the alleged violation or preventing further damage to the interests concerned, including measures to suspend or to ensure the suspension of the procedure for the award of a public contract or the implementation of any decision taken by the contracting authority.

Member States may provide that the body responsible for review procedures may consider the plausible result of interim measures for all interests likely to be injured, as well as the public interest, and may decide not to grant such measures, when their negative outcome could exceed their benefits.[66] An order for interim protection does not form part of the judicial process that leads to a final decision. The CJEU has admitted some actions for failure to fulfil obligations brought by the Commission in relation to national proceedings for interim measures of merely ancillary character instead of an actually autonomous procedure separated from the main proceedings.[67]

The preparatory nature of the act against which the action is brought is one of the grounds of inadmissibility of an action for annulment, and a ground which a court may examine of its own motion.[68] However, acts or decisions adopted in the course of the preparatory proceedings, which in their turn are the culmination of a special procedure

---

2009-515 du 7 mai 2009 relative aux procédures de recours applicables aux contrats de la commande publique, art. 9.

[65] Commission Staff Working Paper, Evaluation Report Impact and Effectiveness of EU Public Procurement Legislation, SEC(2011) 853 final, Brussels, 27 June 2011.

[66] Directive 2007/66/EC, cited supra footnote 43, Article 2(3)–(4).

[67] For example, in Case C-236/95, *Commission v Greece* [1996] ECR I-4459, para 11, and Case C-214/00, *Commission v Spain* [2003] ECR I-4667, para 98, from which it is clear that it must be possible to take interim measures, independently of any prior action.

[68] Case 346/87, *Bossi v Commission* [1989] ECR 303.

being distinct from those intended to empower the institution to take a decision on the substance of the case, must be open to challenge.[69]

The national court in *Combinatie Spijker* carried out an erroneous interpretation of the relevant substantive directive in order to adopt an order on interim measures. The ruling of the CJEU underlined that it is inherent in the review system that the court hearing the substance may adopt an interpretation of EU law, which is different from that of the court hearing an application for interim measures. Such a divergence in assessment does not entail that a court system such as that at issue in the main proceedings does not comply with the requirements of the procedural directives.[70]

B.2 Time limits to enact review proceedings

Member States are entitled in the light of the objective of swiftness pursued by the procedural directives to combine the legal remedies enabling the annulment of a decision of a contracting authority with reasonable limitation periods for bringing proceedings, in an attempt to prevent the candidates and tenderers from being able, at any moment, to invoke infringements of that legislation, thus obliging the contracting authority to restart the entire procedure in order to correct such infringements.[71]

An interested person should have a reasonable minimum period within which to refer to the competent review body before the conclusion of the contract, in the event that that person would wish to challenge the reply or lack of reply from the contracting authority or contracting entity. As the duration of the standstill period varies from one Member State to another, it is also important that the tenderers and candidates concerned should be informed of the effective period available to them to bring review proceedings. An independent minimum standstill period is required that should not end before the review body has taken a decision on the application.[72]

Four cases are important in the field of time limits: *Universale-Bau*, *Santex*, *Lämmerzahl* and *Uniplex*. In *Universale-Bau* the CJEU stated that the setting of reasonable limitation periods for bringing proceedings must be regarded as generally satisfying the requirement of effectiveness, since it is an application of the fundamental principle of legal certainty. In *Santex* the conduct of the contracting authority misled the harmed tenderer and rendered excessively difficult the exercise of the rights conferred on him by Union law. Since the matter of reasonable limitation periods belongs to the area of national procedural autonomy, the CJEU stated that the following steps must be followed in order to ensure observance of the principle of effectiveness:

(i) The national court must first apply domestic law, while interpreting it in a way which accords with the requirements of Union law.[73]

---

[69] Joined Cases 8/66 to 11/66, *Cimenteries CBR* [1967] ECR 75, 92, and Case 60/81 *IBM v Commission* [1981] ECR 2639 para 11.

[70] *Combinatie Spijker*, cited supra footnote 38, para 79.

[71] *Stadt Graz*, cited supra footnote 47, para 37.

[72] Directive 2007/66/EC, cited supra footnote 43, recitals (11)–(12).

[73] Case C-165/91, *Van Munster* [1994] ECR I-4661 para 34, and Case C-262/97, *Engelbrecht* [2000] I-7321 para 39.

(ii) If a congruent application is not possible, the national court must set aside any provision in so far as its application would, in the circumstances of the case, lead to a result contrary to Union law.[74]

(iii) If disapplying the incongruent provisions of domestic law is not possible, then the rules on state liability provide the only possible remedy.[75]

In *Lämmerzahl* the failure of the contracting authority to inform the tenderer concerning total quantity or scope of the contract implied that the limitation period was not triggered in relation to a decision on the choice of procedure for awarding a public contract or on the estimated value of that contract. In any case the limitation period does not concern the review of decisions of the contracting authority, including those occurring in stages of an award procedure after the end of that limitation period.

In *Uniplex* the CJEU established that the period for bringing proceedings seeking to obtain a declaration on the existence of an infringement of the public procurement rules or to obtain damages for the infringement of those rules should start to run from the date on which the claimant knew, or ought to have known, of that infringement. The national court is obliged to extend the limitation period in such a manner as to ensure that the claimant has a period equivalent to that which it would have had if the period provided for by the applicable national legislation had run from the date on which the claimant knew, or ought to have known, of the infringement.[76]

Where the duration of a limitation period is placed at the discretion of the competent court, the predictability of its effects cannot be apposite. Consequently, the British regulation 47D(2) did not ensure an effective transposition of the relevant EU directives and as a result, it had to be amended in August 2011.[77] The previous version of the Public Procurement Regulations provided that 'such proceedings must be started promptly and in any event within 3 months beginning with the date when rounds for starting the proceedings first arose' and after the amendment that came into force on 1 October 2011 the wording has become the following:

> ... such proceedings must be started within 3 months beginning with the date when the economic operator first knew or ought to have known that grounds for starting the proceedings had arisen.[78]

In *CS Communications* the CJEU decided that the effectiveness of the rights conferred by the procedural directives and, in particular, of the right to effective and rapid remedies is not undermined by a national provision stating that the body responsible for review is bound or, as the case may be, authorised to take account of the prospects of

---

[74] Case C-347/96, *Solred* [1998] ECR I-937 para 30, and *Engelbrecht*, cited supra footnote 73, para 40.

[75] *Combinatie Spijker*, cited supra footnote 38, para 92.

[76] Case C-406/08, *Uniplex* [2010] ECR I-817 para 50.

[77] The Public Procurement (Miscellaneous Amendments) Regulations 2011; See to this effect *Uniplex*, cited supra footnote 76, paras 42–43.

[78] Regulation 47D(2) of Public Contracts Regulations Act 2009, SI 2009/2992 as amended by SI 2011/2053; see also Regulation 47(7)(b) of the Public Contracts Regulations 2006 ('the 2006 Regulations'), adopted in order to implement Directive 89/665 into domestic law.

success of an application for a decision of a contracting authority to be set aside on the ground of illegality.[79]

Regarding remedies other than compensation for damages, the time limits serve to attain a balance between the private interests of tenderers on the one hand and the public interest in legal certainty and the need to commence the execution of the contract as soon as possible. The national court shall interpret the domestic provisions establishing a limitation period to the extent that it is possible in trying to attain harmony with the objectives pursued by the Remedies Directive.[80]

B.3 Standstill provisions

A contract may not be concluded subsequent to a decision to award a contract falling within the scope of the substantive directives before the expiry of a period of at least ten calendar days with effect from the day following the date on which the contract award decision is sent to the tenderers and candidates concerned if electronic means are used or, if other means of communication are used, before the expiry of a period of either at least 15 calendar days with effect from the day following the date on which the contract award decision is sent to the tenderers and candidates concerned or at least 10 calendar days with effect from the day following the date of the receipt of the contract award decision.[81]

Derogations from the standstill period apply where prior publication of a notice in the Official Journal is not required; in the case of specific contracts based on a framework agreement as provided for in Article 32 of Directive 2004/18/EC or on a dynamic purchasing system as provided for in Article 15 of Directive 2004/17/EC or Article 33 of Directive 2004/18/EC; or if the only tenderer concerned is the one who is awarded the contract and there are no candidates concerned. In the latter case there is no other person remaining in the tendering procedure with an interest in receiving the notification and in benefiting from a standstill period to allow for effective review.[82]

Seeking review shortly before the end of the minimum standstill period should not result in depriving the body responsible for review procedures of the minimum time needed to act, but the standstill period should be accordingly extended. An independent minimum standstill period is necessary that should not end before the review body has taken a decision on the application. This should not prevent the review body from making a prior assessment of whether the review as such is admissible.

Member States may provide that this period shall end, either when the review body has taken a decision on the application for interim measures, including on a further suspension of the conclusion of the contract, or when the review body has taken a decision on the merits of the case, in particular on the application for the setting aside of a unlawful decision.[83] The recital (4) has established that it is necessary to provide for a minimum standstill period during which the conclusion of the contract in question

---

79 Case C-424/01, *CS Communications* [2003] ECR I-3249 para 32.
80 *Santex,* cited supra footnote 13, para 63.
81 Directive 2007/66/EC, cited supra footnote 43, Article 2a2.
82 Directive 2007/66/EC, cited supra footnote 43, recital 8, Article 2b.
83 Directive 2007/66/EC, cited supra footnote 43, recital (12).

is suspended, irrespective of whether the conclusion occurs at the time of signature of the contract.

The suspension of the execution of the awarded contract shall end no earlier than the expiry of the standstill period referred to in Article 2a(2) and Article 2d(4) and (5).[84] It followed from the old procedural directives that a reasonable time must elapse between the time when the award decision is notified to the unsuccessful tenderers and the conclusion of the contract as to enable them to submit an application for suspending the execution of the contract. The possibility of applying for interim protection is not sufficiently guaranteed by the existence of a judicial verification in the main proceedings. Indeed, if the contract had already been entered into, the review of an unlawful decision of the contracting authority could no longer rectify the infringement in question by setting aside the award decision and according to the rule in *Alcatel* the only possibility was to apply for damages.[85] The Remedies Directive filled the gap by introducing the possibility to apply for a declaration of ineffectiveness.

C. Ineffectiveness

Recital 13 of the Remedies Directive informs that ineffectiveness entails in essence that 'the rights and obligations of the parties under the contract should cease to be enforced and performed'. The ineffectiveness should not be automatic, but should be determined by or should be the result of a decision of an independent review body. A review body autonomous of the contracting authority or contracting entity should analyse all relevant aspects in order to ascertain whether overriding reasons relating to a general interest require that the effects of the contract should be maintained.[86]

Member States may provide that application for review with a view on obtaining a declaration of ineffectiveness must be made before 30 calendar days after the publication of a contract award notice, known under the abbreviation C.A.N., provided that this notice includes justification of the decision of the contracting authority to award the contract without prior publication of a contract notice in the Official Journal or in any case, before expiry of a period of at least six months after the conclusion of the contract.[87]

There are three grounds for ineffectiveness: (a) if the contracting authority has awarded a contract without prior publication of a contract notice in the Official Journal without this being permissible in accordance with the provisions of the substantive directives; (b) in case of an infringement of the standstill provisions,[88] if this infringement has deprived the tenderer applying for review of the possibility to pursue pre-contractual remedies where such an infringement is combined with an infringement of the substantive directives, if that infringement has affected the chances of the tenderer applying for a review to obtain the contract; and (c) in the cases referred to in the second subparagraph of Article 2b(c) of Remedies Directive, if Member States have

---

[84] Directive 2007/66/EC, cited supra footnote 43, Article 2(1)a and 2(3).

[85] C-327/08, *Commission v France* [2009] ECR I-102 paras 56, 58.

[86] Directive 2007/66/EC, cited supra footnote 43, recital (13).

[87] Directive 2007/66/EC, cited supra footnote 43, article 2f1.

[88] Article 1(5), Article 2(3) or Article 2a(2).

invoked the derogation from the standstill period for contracts based on a framework agreement and a dynamic purchasing system.

According to the proposal for a regulation on international public procurement, contracts concluded with an economic operator in violation of a Commission decision on intended exclusions notified by contracting authorities or in violation of measures limiting access of non-covered goods and services should be declared ineffective within the meaning of Article 2d of the Remedies Directive.[89] The proposal supported by Commissioners De Gucht and Barnier maintains the use of the corrective mechanism that can be applied by the Commission as provided by the old procedural directives for the case of misapplication by contracting authorities/entities of exceptions to measures limiting access of non-covered goods and services.[90]

It is improbable that a contracting authority would simply fail to publish a contract notice in relation to a tender that fell within the scope of the public procurement laws and an exception to the strict obligation to publish a contract notice may apply only where there is some reasonable element of doubt as to whether the procurement rules apply, for example: the inappropriate use of the negotiated procedure without a prior contract notice; the inaccurate classification as a non-priority service falling within the ambit of annex II B; or an amendment of an existing contract that is sufficiently material as to lead to a new procurement. An illegal direct award[91] cannot be defined as an award procedure or a decision to award a public contract in the meaning of Union procurement law. Where the conditions for exceptional or special arrangements are met under the substantive provisions,[92] a direct award is not precluded by Union law.[93]

Contracting authorities which have awarded a public contract or concluded a framework agreement shall send a notice of the results of the award procedure no later than 48 days after the award of the contract or the conclusion of the framework agreement. The same applies for the award of contracts based on a dynamic purchasing system, though the contracting authorities may group such notices on a quarterly basis and send them within 48 days of the end of each quarter. The application for a declaration of ineffectiveness must be made before the expiry of at least 30 calendar days with effect from the day following the date on which the C.A.N. was published.

---

89 Proposal, cited supra footnote 10, Article 16(2).

90 Proposal cited supra footnote 10, Article 16(1) that refers to Article 13 of Directive 89/665/EEC, Article 8 of Directive 92/13/EEC, respectively Articles 3 and 8 of Directive 2007/66/EC. Recital (28) states that the corrective mechanism should be refocused on serious infringements of Union law on public procurement.

91 Direct awards within the meaning of Directive 2007/66/EC should include all contract awards made without prior publication of a contract notice in the Official Journal of the European Union within the meaning of Directive 2004/18/EC ([2004] OJ L134/114–240). This corresponds to a procedure without prior call for competition within the meaning of Directive 2004/17/EC ([2004] OJ L134/1–113).

92 Article 5(2), Articles 18 to 26, Articles 29 and 30 or Article 62 of Directive 2004/17/EC ([2004] OJ L134/1–113) in conjunction with Article 40(3) of Directive 2004/17/EC ([2004] OJ L134/1–113) or in the case of an award of a service contract in accordance with Article 32 of Directive 2004/17/EC ([2004] OJ L134/1–113).

93 Directive 2007/66/EC, cited supra footnote 43, recitals 15–16.

In cases in which the contracting authority considers that a direct award is permissible and publishes a notice concerning its intention to conclude a contract as provided by Article 3a and does not conclude it before the expiry of at least ten calendar days with effect from the day following the date of the publication of the notice, the sanction of ineffectiveness may be avoided. The voluntary publication of a notice in the Official Journal expressing the intention to conclude a contract, which triggers a standstill period allowing for effective remedies, does not imply any extension of obligations deriving from the substantive directives.[94] This form of notification is known as V.E.A.T., a voluntary *ex-ante* transparency notice. It should contain the following information in accordance with Article 3a of the Remedies Directive:

(i) the name and contact details of the contracting authority;
(ii) a description of the object of the contract;
(iii) a justification of the decision of the contracting authority to award the contract without prior publication of a contract notice in the Official Journal;
(iv) the name and contact details of the economic operator in favour of whom a contract award decision has been taken; and
(v) where appropriate, any other information deemed useful by the contracting authority.

V.E.A.T. provides means to avoid a declaration of ineffectiveness in cases where no manifest error of assessment in applying the substantive rules has been committed and no contract has been concluded by the contracting authority before the expiry of a period of at least 10 calendar days with effect from the day following the date of the publication of this notice.[95]

The interpretation of Article 2d(4) of the Remedies Directive allowing that a contract is not rendered ineffective was required by a reference lodged on 15 January 2013 by the Consiglio di Stato in case C-19/13, *Ministero dell'Interno v Fastweb*, still pending for a preliminary ruling before the Court.[96] The application refers to the assessment of compatibility of V.E.A.T. exception rule with the principles of equality of the parties, of non-discrimination and protection of competition, and the right to an effective remedy enshrined in Article 47 of the Charter.

Article 2d(1) induces a duty to consider the contract ineffective and Article 2e(1) gives the possibility to replace the ineffectiveness with alternative sanctions in specific situations. The ineffectiveness may be circumvented, if overriding reasons relating to the general interest require that the effects of the contract should be maintained. The economic reasons directly linked to the contract concerned, such as the costs resulting from the delay in the execution of the contract, the costs resulting from the launching of a new procurement procedure, the costs resulting from the change of the economic operator performing the contract and the costs of legal obligations resulting from the ineffectiveness cannot be used as appropriate justifications.

---

94 Directive 2007/66/EC, cited supra footnote 43, recital 26 and Article 3a.

95 Directive 2007/66/EC, cited supra footnote 43, Article 2d4.

96 Case C-19/13, *Fastweb*, application: [2013] OJ C86/11.

D. Damages

Anyone who has suffered harm caused by an infringement of Union procurement law shall be able to claim full compensation for that harm. Full compensation shall place anyone who has suffered harm in the position in which that person would have been, had the infringement not been committed. It shall consequently take account of compensation for actual loss and for loss of profit, and payment of interest from the time the harm occurred until the compensation in respect of that harm has in fact been paid. The Member States shall ensure that an injured tenderer can in effect exercise the right to be awarded damages.[97]

Member States may provide that where damages are claimed on the grounds that a decision was taken illegally, the contested decision must first be set aside by a body having the necessary powers. Excepting the cases where a decision must be set aside prior to the award of damages, a Member State may provide that, after the conclusion of a contract in accordance with Article 1(5)(3) or Articles 2a–2f, the powers of the body responsible for review procedures shall be limited to awarding damages to any person harmed by an infringement.[98]

Article 2(1)(c) of the Remedies Directive stipulates that the Member States shall ensure that the measures taken concerning the review procedures include provisions granting powers to award damages to persons harmed by an infringement. Moreover, Article 2e states that the award of damages does not constitute an appropriate penalty for the purposes of replacing ineffectiveness with an alternative sanction.

The Remedies Directive must be interpreted as precluding national legislation, which makes the right to damages for an infringement of public procurement law conditional on the culpable character, including where the application of that legislation rests on a presumption that the contracting authority is at fault and on the fact that the latter cannot rely on a lack of individual abilities, hence on the defence that it cannot be held liable for the alleged infringement.[99]

A court responsible for hearing review procedures connected with an action for damages is not precluded from raising of its own motion the unlawfulness of a decision of the contracting authority other than the one contested by the complainant. In this case the court may dismiss the application for damages, because the award procedure was in any event unlawful and the harm, which the tenderer may have suffered, would have been caused even in the absence of the unlawfulness alleged by the tenderer.[100]

It is unclear from the wording of the Remedies Directives, whether damages are available for all violations of the Union public procurement rules or only for certain serious violations that entail the ineffectiveness of the contract. In *Alcatel* it has been established that the Member States are not allowed to restrict the powers of the review bodies to merely awarding damages, but decisions taken by the contracting authority during the public award procedure that occur before the conclusion of the contract must

---

[97] See to that effect Case C-271/91, *Marshall* [1993] ECR I-4367 paras 24–32 and Case C-568/08, *Combinatie Spijker*, Opinion of AG Villalón, [2010] ECR I-12655 points 109–111.

[98] Directive 2007/66/EC, cited supra footnote 43, Article 2(6).

[99] Case C 314/09, *Strabag and Others* [2010] ECR I-0000 para 45.

[100] *GAT*, cited supra footnote 13, para 56.

be open to review and if necessary, the contract must be set aside regardless of the possibility of obtaining damages.[101]

Furthermore, the principle of effectiveness requires that the time limits with regard to an application for a declaration of illegality having the effect of dissolving the contract made in preparation for bringing an action for damages should not start to run before the plaintiff was aware or ought to have been aware of the injury.[102] Moreover, where no alternative methods of achieving knowledge about the occurrence of an injury and subsequently of producing the supporting evidence are available to a potential claimant for damages, a refusal to grant him access to the procurement documents renders nugatory the right to compensation, which they derive from Union law.[103]

D.1 Access to tender documents and confidentiality duties

According to the provisions of the substantive directives, the contracting authority shall not disclose information forwarded to it by economic operators, which they have designated as confidential; such information includes, in particular, technical or trade secrets and the confidential aspects of tenders.[104] The right to the protection of confidential information is substantial in nature and the protection of business secrets is a general principle of law, while the maintenance of fair competition in the context of contract award procedures is an important public interest, the protection of which is acknowledged in the case-law.[105]

> … the adversarial principle does not mean that the parties are entitled to unlimited and absolute access to all of the information relating to the award procedure concerned which has been filed with the body responsible for the review. On the contrary, that right of access must be balanced against the right of other economic operators to the protection of their confidential information and their business secrets.[106]

The body responsible for the review must necessarily be able to have at its disposal the information required in order to decide in full knowledge of the facts, including confidential information and business secrets.[107] It is for that body to decide to what extent and how to safeguard the confidentiality and secrecy of that information, having regard to the requirements of effective legal protection and the rights of defence of the parties to the dispute and, in the case of judicial review or a review by another body which is a court or tribunal within the meaning of Article 267 TFEU, so as to ensure that the proceedings overall concur with the right enshrined in Article 47 of the Charter.

Any request for access to documents contained in the file of national review body must be assessed on a case-by-case basis, taking into account all the relevant factors in

---

101 *Alcatel Austria*, cited supra footnote 12, para 43.

102 Case C-454/06, Opinion of Advocate General Kokott delivered on 13 March 2008, *APA Austria Presse* [2008] ECR I-04401 point 167.

103 By analogy, Case C-536/11, *Donau Chemie* [2013] ECR I-0000, para 32.

104 See Directive 2004/18/EC, [2004] OJ L134/114–240, Article 6, Directive 2004/17/EC, [2004] OJ L134/1–113, Article 13.

105 *Varec*, cited supra footnote 34, paras 47, 50.

106 *Varec*, cited supra footnote 34, para 51.

107 See, by analogy, Case C-438/04, *Mobistar* [2006] ECR I-6675 para 40.

the specific case. It is for the national courts to weigh up, first, the interest of the requesting party in obtaining access to those documents in order to prepare its action for damages, especially in the light of other possibilities it may have. Secondly, the national courts must consider the actual harmful consequences ensuing from such access with reference to the public interests or the legitimate interests of other private parties.[108]

Having regard to the adversarial principle that forms part of the rights of the defence, enshrined in Article 47 of the Charter, the parties to a case must have the right to scrutinise all the documents or observations submitted to the court for the purpose of influencing its decision, and to comment on them.[109] A rule of general access under which any document relating to the review proceedings must be disclosed to a claimant requesting it on the sole ground that that party is intending to bring an action for damages is not indispensable in order to ensure effective protection of the right to compensation, as it is highly implausible that the action for damages must be anchored in all of the evidence in the related file. In addition, that rule could entail the violation of other rights conferred by Union law, *inter alia*, on the successful supplier, such as the right to protection of professional secrecy or of business secrecy and the protection of legitimate expectations, or on the individuals concerned, such as the right to protection of personal data.[110]

In all communication, exchange and storage of information, contracting authorities and contracting entities shall ensure that the integrity of data and the confidentiality of tenders and applications are preserved. They shall examine the content of tenders and applications only after the time limit set for submitting them has expired. Without prejudice to the obligations relating to the advertising of awarded contracts and to the information of candidates and tenderers set out in the substantive directives, the contracting authority shall not disclose information forwarded to it by economic operators, which they have designated as confidential, including, but not limited to, technical or trade secrets and the confidential aspects of tenders.[111]

After *Donau Chemie* and *Varec,* it has become clear that the review bodies and national courts must carry out a proportionality test between the means and the goals involved in each and every particular case, where the full effectiveness of the individual rights derived from Union law and the protection of private or public interest may collide. The contracting authorities should mention on the transmitted documents whether or not they contain business secrets or other confidential material, while the review bodies and courts must verify the secretive or confidential character of those documents.

D.2 Disclosure of evidence and burden of proof

Requirements of equivalence and effectiveness illustrate the general obligation of the Member States to ensure judicial protection of an individual's rights under Union law

---

[108] See, by analogy, *Donau Chemie*, cited supra footnote 103, paras 43–45.

[109] *Varec*, cited supra footnote 34, para 45; Case C-300/11, *ZZ v Secretary of State* [2013] ECR I-0000 para 55.

[110] See by analogy, *Donau Chemie*, cited above footnote 103.

[111] COM/2011/0897 final – 2011/0437 (COD).

and apply both with regard to the appointment of the courts and tribunals having jurisdiction to hear and determine actions founded on Union law and regarding the definition of comprehensive procedural rules.[112] Member States should provide that the court be granted the power to assess the amount of harm and ensure that the limitation period shall not begin to run before an injured party knows, or can reasonably be expected to have knowledge of the conduct constituting the infringement, for instance a form of undue preferential treatment and the qualification of such conduct as an infringement of Union procurement law and the fact that the infringement caused injury to him.[113]

Injured parties should be able to seek compensation not only for the actual loss suffered, *damnum emergens*, but also for the gain of which they have been deprived, *lucrum cessans*, plus interest. The actual loss is easy to calculate in the case of public procurement law, because it refers to the tender preparation and related costs, while the loss of profit requires being able to prove that the tenderer would have won the contract, if the contracting authority had not failed to follow the law.[114]

However, in the case of a single tender award, that is, an illegal form of direct award, a supplier can neither attest any costs for preparation nor can claim that it would have won the contract, because it could not know about the lost opportunity. In most cases exactly because no form of financial effort has been made by the potential tenderers, they are less prone to react and bring an action against this form of illegality.

The finding that a Member State has failed to fulfil its obligations does not depend on a finding as to the damage flowing from that failure.[115] Moreover, an action for failure to fulfil obligations makes possible not only an examination of the compatibility of a Member State's laws, regulations and administrative provisions with Union law, but also a determination that there has been an infringement of Union law by the national bodies in a specific individual case.[116]

In this sense there is a connection between the infringement procedure conducted under Article 258 TFEU against the Member State and a potential action for damages brought before a national court against the national bodies in question. As long as the validity of a public contract is maintained despite the fact that it has been awarded in breach of EU law, the named breach is not cured. However, the CJEU is responsible for determining whether or not the alleged breach of obligations exists, even if the State concerned no longer denies the breach and recognises that any individuals who have suffered damage because of it have a right to compensation.[117]

---

112 Joined Cases C-317/08, C-318/08, C-319/08 and C-320/08, *Alassini* [2010] ECR I-2213.

113 See to that effect, *Uniplex*, cited supra footnote 76, para 47; See also, by analogy Article 10 of 2013/0185 (COD).

114 Case C-568/08, *Combinatie Spijker*, Opinion of AG Cruz Villalón, point 109; See Chapter 11 in Bovis, *EC Public Procurement: Case Law and Regulation* (Oxford: Oxford University Press, 2006).

115 Case C-263/96, *Commission v Belgium* [1997] ECR I-7453 para 30, and Joined Cases C-20/01 and C-28/01, *Commission v Germany* [2003] ECR I-3609 para 42.

116 See, concerning the award of public contracts, *Commission v Germany*, cited supra footnote 115, para 30, and Case C-275/08, *Commission v Germany* [2009] ECR I-168 para 27.

117 Case C-243/89, *Commission v Denmark* [1993] ECR I-3353 para 30.

D.3 Locus standi

According to *Hackermüller* a tenderer shall be able to contest the ground of exclusion on the basis of which the review body intends to conclude that he neither has been nor risks being harmed by the decision he alleges to be unlawful.[118] In a recent preliminary ruling, *Fastweb*, the situation was that both bids, the successful and the unsuccessful one, did not meet the technical requirements and the public award should have been recommenced. The contracting authority awarded a public contract relating to voice and data telephony to Telecom Italia and PathNet in disregard of the tender specifications.

However the Italian procedural law gave temporal priority to the counterclaim challenging the *locus standi* of the unsuccessful tenderer, who brought an action for review on the grounds that the defendant, Telecom Italia, had been unlawfully admitted to the award procedure. The initial examination made by the Italian court showed that neither Fastweb nor Telecom Italia would have won the contract, if the tender specifications had been respected. The preliminary ruling confirmed that both tenderers had a legitimate interest in the exclusion of the bid submitted by the other, which may have led to a finding that the contracting authority was unable to select a lawful bid.[119] Member States have the right to provide, in addition to the explicit grounds for exclusion, for other grounds designed to ensure observance of the principles of equal treatment and transparency.[120]

According to *Michaniki* these additional grounds of exclusion must be proportionate and open to review. A systematic rule of exclusion, which also involves an absolute obligation on the contracting authorities to exclude a tenderer runs counter to the Union's interest in ensuring the widest possible participation by tenderers in a call for tenders, and goes beyond what is necessary to attain the objective pursued by the principles of equal treatment and transparency.[121]

Also in *CoNISMa* a tenderer was excluded from the award of public service contracts with a value greater than the threshold for the application of the relevant directives, because it did not have a particular legal form, even if under the law of the Member State of establishment it had the right to provide the services in question. Entities, such as universities and research institutes being primarily non-profit-making were precluded from taking part in a procedure for the award of a public contract on grounds related to the observance of the principles of equal treatment and transparency. By narrowing the concept of 'economic operator', the notion of 'public contract' was consequently restricted, since contracts between contracting authorities and such non-profit entities could be awarded by mutual agreement. The grounds of exclusion were deemed inconsistent with the rules of equal treatment and transparency.[122]

Article 1(8) of Directive 2004/18/EC defines the status of 'economic operator' not only to any natural or legal person, but also, specifically, to any 'public entity' or group

---

118 *Hackermüller*, cited supra footnote 45, para 29.

119 Case C-100/12, *Fastweb* [2013] ECR I-00000 para 33.

120 See, to that effect, Case C-213/07 *Michaniki* [2008] ECR I-9999 paras 43, 44 and 47, and Case C-538/07 *Assitur* [2009] ECR I-4219 paras 20 and 21.

121 Case C-376/08, *Serrantoni* [2009] ECR I-12169 para 40.

122 Case C-305/08, *CoNISMa* [2009] ECR I-12129 para 43.

consisting of such entities offering services on the market. The concept of 'public entity' includes bodies, which are not primarily profit-making, are not structured as an undertaking and do not have a continuous presence on the market[123] and other contracting authorities.[124]

The detailed rules on disclosure, burden and level of proof, *locus standi*, access to file and choice of competent courts are all matters comprised within the area of national procedural autonomy. Member States shall ensure that the burden and the level of proof and of fact pleading required for the quantification of harm does not render the exercise of the injured tenderer's right to damages nearly impossible or excessively difficult.[125]

In conclusion any type of absolute hindrance or automatic ground for denying access to justice in any shape or form results in an infringement of the proportionality principle and brings about the incompatibility of the national procedural rules with Union law. Union law imposes hence an obligation on Member States to disapply rules that hinder the exercise of an examination of both sides of the balance and empowers the national courts and review bodies to perform a proportionality test and consider always the necessity, suitability and proportionality of a measure that impedes the access to justice of a tenderer.

E. Case Law on Public Procurement

On 7 July 2013 the only application pending for preliminary ruling that requested the interpretation of the Remedies Directive was Case C-19/13, *Ministero dell'Interno v Fastweb Spa*. No more than two preliminary rulings on the interpretation of the named directive have been published in the register: Case C-348/10, *Norma-A SIA* and Case C-100/12, *Fastweb SpA v Azienda Sanitaria Locale di Alessandria*. Seven cases of preliminary ruling and three Commission actions have been handled by the CJEU and published in the ECR since the expiry of the transposition period prescribed by the Remedies Directive. According to *Norma-A SIA* the new remedies directive applies on contracts concluded after the date of 20 December 2009, but the adoption of a new directive must have had an anticipatory influence on all awards handled during the period of transposition.

E.1 Before adoption

Competition promotes economy, efficiency and effectiveness in public expenditure and also contributes to the competitiveness of contractors. The objectives of the directives on procurement awards are the opening-up of public contracts to competition within the European Union under conditions of transparency and non-discrimination. Since these directives do not contain specific provisions allowing their effective application to be

---

123 *CoNISMa*, cited supra footnote 122, para 30.

124 Case C-159/11, *Azienda Sanitaria Locale di Lecce* [2012] ECR I-0000 para 26.

125 See, in particular, Case 33/76, *Rewe-Zentralfinanz and Rewe-Zentral* [1976] ECR 1989 para 5; Case C-432/05, *Unibet* [2007] ECR I-2271 para 43; Case C-268/06, *Impact* [2008] ECR I-2483 para 46; and Case C-246/09, *Bulicke* [2010] ECR I-7003 para 25; *Combinatie Spijker*, cited supra footnote 38, para 91.

guaranteed, the Remedies Directive fulfils that role by requiring the Member States to establish effective and rapid review procedures.

The rationale of the Remedies Directive is to allow, by the establishment of appropriate review procedures, the effective application of the substantive provisions of European Union law on public contracts, which seek to ensure, for traders established in the Member States, the opening-up to competition which is undistorted and as wide as possible.[126]

E.2 The anticipatory effect before expiry

By definition, legal rules arising from the treaties are intended from their adoption to alter the legal orders of the Member States, a fact which justifies the removal of obstacles to such integration. However, as regards directives, the difficulty stems from the fact that the obstacle is constituted by a failure on the part of Member States, when the very nature of that category of measures implies that their effectiveness depends on the adoption of a measure of domestic law. Before the period for transposition of a directive has expired, Member States cannot be reproached for not having yet adopted measures implementing it in national law.[127]

It follows from the second paragraph of Article 4(3) TEU in conjunction with the third paragraph of Article 288 TFEU and the directive in question itself that, during the period prescribed for transposition of a directive, the Member States to which it is addressed must refrain from taking any measures liable seriously to compromise the attainment of the result prescribed by it.[128]

Given that all the authorities of the Member States are subject to the obligation to ensure that provisions of Union law take full effect,[129] the obligation to refrain from taking measures applies also to national courts. It follows that, from the date upon which a directive has entered into force, the courts of the Member States must refrain as far as possible from interpreting domestic law in a manner which might seriously compromise, after the period for transposition has expired, attainment of the objective pursued by that directive.[130]

It is clear from settled case-law that, under the principle of cooperation in good faith laid down in Article 4(3) TEU, Member States are required to nullify the unlawful consequences of a breach of Union law.[131] Such an obligation is owed, within the sphere of its competence, by every public body of the Member State concerned.[132]

---

[126] See mutatis mutandis, Case C-337/06, *Bayerischer Rundfunk and Others* [2007] ECR I-11173 paras 38 and 39 ; See also Case C-348/10, *Norma-A SIA*, [2011] ECR I-0000 para 31.

[127] See Case C-129/96, *Inter-Environnement Wallonie* [1997] ECR I-7411 para 43.

[128] *Inter-Environnement Wallonie*, cited supra footnote 127, para 45; Case C-14/02 *ATRAL* [2003] ECR I-4431, para 58; and Case C-144/04, *Mangold* [2005] ECR I-09981 para 67.

[129] Joined Cases C 6/90 and C-9/90, *Francovich and Others* [1991] ECR I-5357 para 32; Case C-453/00 *Kühne & Heitz* [2004] ECR I-837 para 20; and *Pfeiffer*, cited supra footnote 49, para 111.

[130] Case C-212/04, *Adeneler* [2006] ECR I-6057 para 123.

[131] See, *inter alia*, Case 6/60 *Humblet v Belgian State* [1960] ECR 559, p. 569, and *Francovich and Others*, cited supra footnote 129, para 36.

[132] Case C-8/88 *Germany v Commission* [1990] ECR I-2321 para 13, and Case C-201/02, *Wells* [2004] ECR I-723 para 64 and the case-law cited.

However, the obligations incurred by the Member States before the expiry of the transposition period make reference to the anticipated effect of the directive, not to the specific means of achieving it.

E.3 Delayed transposition

Where a directive is transposed belatedly, the general obligation owed by national courts to interpret domestic law in conformity with the directive exists only once the period for its transposition has expired. An interesting aspect of the public procurement law is the fact that the obligations owed to economic actors are incumbent on public authorities, that is, on the state itself and it has already been established that in relation to the state any directive incurs direct effect that is to say, that individuals have the right to invoke before the courts the effect of a unconditional and sufficiently precise, but not yet transposed directive in relation to the Member State.

A Member State which has not adopted the implementing measures required by the directive during the prescribed period, may not rely, as against individuals, on its own failure to perform the obligations which the directive entails.[133] The obligation to interpret national law in conformity with Union law concerns all provisions of national law, whether adopted before or after the directive in question.[134] The effectiveness of Union law required at the very least that, taking account of the limits imposed by the nature of directives and by the content of the relevant provisions of the directive in question, parties who considered they had suffered injury as a result of failure to transpose a directive that conferred rights on them whilst leaving Member States a certain margin of discretion should be granted the ability to plead consistent interpretation.[135]

Case C-76/97, *Tögel* clarifies the situation of delayed transposition and makes the distinction between provisions with direct effect and other provisions of secondary law. It must be obvious from an individual examination of the wording of the provisions in question that they are unconditional and sufficiently clear and precise in order for an individual to be able to rely on them before the national court during the period of delay. A contracting authority is not obliged to intervene in existing legal situations concluded for an indefinite or long term previously to the end of the transposition period of a substantive law directive. The opposite is true in the case of awards made after expiry of the transposition period provided for by that directive.

The provisions of substantive directives have direct effect although the CJEU also commented that there may be some exceptions. The conditions for direct effect imposed on the provisions of a directive are to be unconditional, sufficiently clear and precise in order to create rights for individuals which may be relied on before a court. Some EU rules on public procurement might not have direct effect, because they do not

---

[133] *Ratti* cited supra footnote 36, para 22. Conversely, the right of individuals to rely on a directive against a defaulting Member State before the courts is, in the view of the Court of Justice, a minimum guaranty resulting from the binding nature of directives (Case 102/79, *Commission v Belgium* [1980] ECR I-1473 para 12).

[134] Case C-106/89, *Marleasing* [1990] ECR I-4135 para 8, and *Pfeiffer*, cited supra footnote 49, para 115.

[135] Case C-287/98, *Grand Duchy of Luxembourg v Berthe Linster* [2000] ECR I-6917 point 61.

meet the condition that they are intended to create rights for individuals.[136] On the other hand, certain obligations do not have direct effect, as they require a choice by Member States over how their obligations are to be given effect. CJEU has considered that the rules requiring Member States to make statistical reports to the European Commission might not be considered to create rights for individuals, even though they impose legally binding obligations on Member States.[137]

Some of the obligations in the procedural directives do meet the conditions for direct effect, for example a requirement concerning the duration of the minimum time-limits for challenge in conjunction with the requirement of effectiveness. In *Santex* the CJEU stated that the Italian courts were required to disapply a time limit in national legislation for bringing proceedings in public procurement, which the CJEU considered was too short to comply with EU law requirements to provide reasonable time limits for aggrieved firms to bring proceedings.[138]

The fact that a directive has direct effect does not relieve states of the obligation to implement those rules by means that give third parties enforcement rights within the domestic legal system.[139] Furthermore, the fact that legislation that does not appear to confer the required rights is given a creative interpretation by national courts in order to secure those rights does not mean that the Member State has complied with its obligation to implement the coordinated rules; rights conferred in this way are not sufficiently clear.[140] And last it should be noted that, where certain conditions are met, an individual who suffers loss from the failure of a Member State, may obtain damages from the Member State concerned.[141] This avenue is available under certain conditions:

(i) the directive was intended to confer rights on individuals;
(ii) the breach of EU law in not implementing the directive was 'sufficiently serious' based on:
   (a) whether the breach was intentional, and
   (b) whether the relevant legal rule as interpreted in the case-law was clear and precise; and
(iii) a causal link exists between the breach and the loss with the detailed rules on causation, for example, the nature of proof required and the probability with which loss must be proven, being left to the legal systems of Member States.

It is for the national court to interpret domestic law, so far as possible, in the light of the wording and the purpose of the relevant directive with a view to achieving the results sought by the latter, favouring the interpretation of the national rules which is the most consistent with that purpose and thus aiming to achieve an outcome

136 Case C-76/97, *Walter Tögel* [1998] ECR I-5357 paras 41–47.

137 *Tögel*, cited supra footnote 136, paras 21–28.

138 *Santex*, cited supra footnote 131, para 64.

139 Case C-433/93, *Commission v Germany* [1995] ECR I-2303 para 24; Case 102/79, *Commission v Belgium* [1980] ECR I-1473 para 12.

140 Case C-236/95, *Commission v Greece* [1996] ECR I-4459 paras 12–13.

141 *Francovich*, cited supra footnote 129.

compatible with the provisions of the directive, setting aside, if necessary, any contrary provision of national law.[142]

E.4 After full transposition

The Remedies Directive respects fundamental rights and observes the principles recognised in particular by the Charter of Fundamental Rights of the European Union. In particular, this Directive seeks to ensure full respect for the right to an effective remedy and to a fair hearing, in accordance with the first and second subparagraphs of Article 47 of the Charter.[143] The provisions of directives must be implemented with undeniable binding force, and specificity, precision and clarity are necessary to satisfy the requirements of legal certainty.[144]

The incompatibility of national legislation with Union provisions can be remedied for good only by means of binding national provisions having the same legal force as those which must be amended.[145] Administrative practices, which by their nature are modifiable at will by the authorities and are not given the appropriate publicity, cannot be regarded as constituting fulfilment of the obligations owed by the Member States in the context of transposition of a directive.[146]

The Member States are required, within the bounds of the freedom left to them by the third paragraph of Article 288 TFEU, to choose the most appropriate forms and methods to ensure the effectiveness of directives, in the light of their objective.[147] This provision relates to matters such as the choice between retroactive or proactive ineffectiveness and the possibility of applying specific procedural rules on public procurement proceedings.

The requirement for national law to be interpreted in conformity with Union law is inherent in the system of the Treaties, since it permits national courts, for the matters within their jurisdiction, to ensure the full effectiveness of Union law, when they determine the disputes before them.[148] The obligation on a national court to refer to the content of a directive when interpreting and applying the relevant rules of domestic law is nevertheless limited by general principles of law, particularly those of legal certainty and non-retroactivity, and that obligation cannot serve as the basis for an interpretation of national law *contra legem*.[149]

Under its second subparagraph of Article 19(1) TEU, it falls to the Member States to 'provide remedies sufficient to ensure effective legal protection in the fields covered by Union law'. This provision gives momentum, direction and sense to the tasks of the Member States flowing from the Treaties. Since private individuals do not have direct access to a supranational court, excepting the case of an action for annulment of a

---

142 Case C-414/07, *Magoora* [2008] ECR I-0000 para 44.

143 Directive 2007/66/EC, cited supra footnote 43, recital (36).

144 See, particularly, Case C-225/97, *Commission v France* [1999] ECR I-3011 para 37.

145 See, particularly, Case C-160/99, *Commission v France* [2000] ECR I-6137 para 23.

146 See, particularly, Case C-508/04 *Commission v Austria* [2007] ECR I-3787 para 80.

147 Case 48/75, *Royer* [1976] ECR 497 para 75, and Joined Cases C-58/95, C-75/95, C-112/95, C-119/95, C-123/95, C-135/95, C-140/95, C-141/95, C-154/95 and C-157/95, *Gallotti and Others* [1996] ECR I-4345 para 14.

148 *Pfeiffer and Others*, cited supra footnote 47, para 114.

149 See, by analogy, Case C-105/03, *Pupino* [2005] ECR I-5285 paras 44 and 47.

Union act as stipulated by Article 263(4) TFEU, the right to an effective judicial protection is preserved via a mechanism of indirect access as provided by the preliminary ruling procedure.

Considering the matter of judicial proceedings and especially the adversarial principle that forms part of the rights enshrined in Article 47 of the Charter, the parties to a case must have the right to examine all the documents or observations submitted to the court for the purpose of influencing its decision, and to comment on them.[150] Since the right to an effective remedy before a tribunal is not absolute, it must be considered in relation to its function. Restrictions may be imposed, provided that they meet objectives of general interest and do not constitute a disproportionate and intolerable interference impairing the very substance of the rights.[151]

IV. TRANSPARENCY AND EFFECTIVENESS

The obligation of transparency imposed on the contracting authority consists in ensuring, for the benefit of any potential tenderer, a degree of advertising sufficient to enable the services market to be opened up to competition and the impartiality of procurement procedures to be reviewed.[152] It derives directly from the Union law, in particular Articles 49 TFEU and 56 TFEU[153] and it is essentially intended to preclude any risk of favouritism or arbitrariness on the part of the contracting authority.[154] Transparency is both a corollary of equality principle and a guarantor of access to justice.

> the fundamental rules and the general principles of the FEU Treaty, in particular the principles of equal treatment and of non-discrimination on grounds of nationality and the consequent obligation of transparency apply, provided that the contract concerned has a certain cross-border interest in the light, inter alia, of its value and the place where it is carried out.[155]

Article 47 of the Charter is mentioned in the preamble of the Remedies Directive stating that the directive respects fundamental rights and observes the principles recognised in particular by the Charter and seeks to ensure full respect for the right to an effective remedy and to a fair hearing.[156] Article 47 of the Charter gives expression to the principle of effective judicial protection and provides means of interpretation for

---

[150] *Varec*, cited supra footnote 34, para 45; Case C-89/08 P *Commission v Ireland and Others* [2009] ECR I-11245 para 52; and Case C-472/11 *Banif Plus Bank* [2013] ECR I-0000 para 30.

[151] Case C-450/06, *Varec*, Opinion of AG Sharpston, [2008] ECR I-581 point 49.

[152] Case C-324/98, *Telaustria* [2000] I-10745 para 62.

[153] *Wall AG*, cited supra footnote 46, para 68.

[154] See, to that effect, Case C-496/99 P *Commission v CAS Succhi di Frutta* [2004] ECR I-3801 para 111.

[155] Joined Cases C-147/06 and C-148/06 *SECAP and Santorso* [2008] ECR I-3565 paras 20, 21 and 31.

[156] Directive 2007/66/EC, cited supra footnote 43, Recital (36).

rights and obligations resulting from the implementation of EU law as established by a constant jurisprudence.

> [I]t must be observed that, under Article 51(1) of the Charter, its provisions are addressed to the Member States only when they are implementing Union law. Under Article 51(2), the Charter does not extend the field of application of Union law beyond the powers of the Union, or establish any new power or task for the Union or modify powers and tasks as defined in the Treaties. Accordingly, the Court is called upon to interpret, in the light of the Charter, the law of the European Union within the limits of the powers conferred on it.[157]

Decentralisation in the enforcement and application of public procurement law aimed to provide for more litigation before the competent national courts and ensure an acceptable degree of compliance of Member States and contracting authorities. Moreover, an increased transparency and more accountability in the award of public contracts were meant to improve the justiciability of public contracts redress.[158] In the working document preceding the proposal for a new directive on public procurement remedies, the Commission has put forward an analogy between the regime of civil damages for antitrust infringements as established by *Courage* doctrine and the right to claim damages for loss caused by serious violations of the public procurement rules.[159]

> ... the existence of such a right strengthens the working of the [Union] competition rules and discourages agreements or practices, which are frequently covert, which are liable to restrict or distort competition. From that point of view, actions for damages before the national courts can make a significant contribution to the maintenance of effective competition in the [Union].[160]

An increased level of justiciability could also lead in part to speculative litigation and consequently to delayed procurement processes, reluctance in engaging with the private sector from the side of contracting authorities and finally, to increased procurement costs as a result of the latent risks involved by the newly implemented remedies.[161] The lack of effectiveness of an illegally awarded public contract was designed by the EU law-makers as an exceptional consequence applicable merely to serious violations of law.

The regulatory guarantees established by the procedural directives may constitute a necessary, but not a sufficient condition to break down the barriers to cross-border participation in public procurement markets. In its study from 2011, the Commission concluded that direct cross-border procurement has not increased as far as was

---

157 Case C-370/12, *Pringle v Government of Ireland* [2012] I-0000 para 179.

158 C. Bovis, *Legal Redress in Public Procurement Contracts* (Cheltenham, UK and Northampton, MA, USA: Edward Elgar, 2012), p. 21.

159 Commission staff working document – Annex to the Proposal for a Directive of the European Parliament and of the Council amending Council Directives 89/665/EEC and 92/13/EEC with regard to improving the effectiveness of review procedures concerning the award of public contracts (COM(2006) 195) – Impact assessment report – Remedies in the field of public procurement, Brussels, 4 May 2006.

160 *Courage & Crehan*, cited supra footnote 46, para 27.

161 Bovis, idem supra footnote 158.

expected, although it is usual in smaller Member States. Many economic operators still appear to be deterred from competing for tenders in other Member States by a mix of competitive, structural and legal or administrative factors.

The Commission evaluation suggested that there might be circumstances where the costs of running regulated procedures were disproportionate in relation to the anticipated benefits, but in general the positive cost-benefit analysis was favourable. A degree of unfairness is incumbent to any regulated systems and it can be mitigated only by having clear rules, effective policies and efficient enforcement. The adverse effects of such unenforceability should be nevertheless mitigated, if necessary and appropriate by substituting restitution in kind with restitution in value. In addition, the unenforceability of a contract could still be avoided, if the review body or the national court considered that overriding reasons based on the general interest justified an exception.[162]

The right of access to file under national law is also interrelated in substance with the general legal principles of transparency and good administration. Since the objective of the substantive directives is the opening-up of public contracts to competition within the Union under conditions of transparency and non-discrimination, and those directives do not contain specific provisions allowing their effective application to be guaranteed, the Remedies Directive fulfils that role by requiring the Member States to establish effective and rapid review procedures.

It is for the domestic legal system to regulate the legal procedures for safeguarding the rights which individuals derive from that obligation of transparency in such a way that those procedures are no less favourable than similar domestic procedures and do not make the exercise of those rights practically impossible or excessively difficult. The national court shall interpret and apply the national law, where possible, in agreement with the requirements of Union law and foremost by observing the obligation of transparency.[163]

No matter if we talk about time limits, alternative resolutions, access to files, burden of proof, interim provisions or quantification of harm, the same type of reasoning applies when the full effectiveness of a right derived from Union law is balanced against a public or a private interest legitimately protected by national law. Neither the right, nor the interest may enjoy absolute protection, but the Court is first required to ensure that the exercise of the EU right is not rendered ineffective and secondly that a proportionality test is performed and any restriction that is unnecessary or disproportionate shall be precluded.

As was mentioned at the beginning of the chapter, the decentralised approach leads to increased litigation and enhanced effectiveness of rights enjoyed by individuals under EU public procurement law, while maintaining a degree of swiftness and allowing the contracting authorities and the successful tenderer to be able to benefit from the protection of their legitimate expectations. Transparency has two aspects, a primordial one substantive in nature related to the right to be informed and the corresponding obligations of the contracting authorities under EU law such as the duty of prior publication, correct notification, clarity of the grounds of exclusion and the exactness and completeness of tender specifications, but also a national procedural

---

[162] Commission staff working document, cited supra footnote 65.

[163] *Santex,* cited supra footnote 13, para 63.

aspect, namely the disclosure rules, the right of access to documents, the right to intervene in a procedure and all the measures connected to the relevant rules enshrined in the national legal order.

Certain areas in which the lack of clarity is incumbent can be identified such as diffused boundaries between works and supply/services contracts; the application of the 'aggregation rules', both regarding the level at which products or services should be aggregated and the treatment of discrete operating units within the same entity; the use of 'framework agreements' in the public sector; the more relaxed criteria for short listing in the public sector; the extent to which renewals, extensions or amendments to existing contractual agreements constitute new contracts; the extent to which modifications of a bid are permitted in open and restricted procedures; the rules on criteria and evidence for assessing qualification in the utilities sector. A concrete example of lack of clarity in the case of national procedural provisions is offered by the *Uniplex* rule stating that 'proceedings are brought promptly' without specifying what was meant by 'promptly'.

Transparency is a matter of quality and availability of the information provided by the contracting authorities and the availability in its turn has both a temporal and a spatial dimension. The spatial dimension has to do with the media used to disseminate the information, while the temporal dimension refers to the time interval during which the information is made available. The date on which the claimant knew, or ought to have known, of the infringement of the public procurement rule marks the beginning of the period during which an action for setting aside an award decision, declaration of ineffectiveness of a public contract or an action for damages may be brought before a court. Transparency is a measure of equality of opportunity, but also a measure of the possibility of obtaining legal redress in case a violation of the equality principle has been committed.

Swiftness on the other hand has a dual nature and in the case, when the transparency duty was disregarded by a contracting authority, the limitation of the time interval during which a tenderer may react against an infringement does not serve the pursuit of effectiveness. Just the opposite, once an infringement has been revealed, a swift and operative review procedure enhances the effectiveness of the EU directives on public procurement. Direct awards within the meaning of the Remedies Directive should include all contract awards made without prior publication of a contract notice in the Official Journal within the meaning of Directive 2004/18/EC. This corresponds to a procedure without prior call for competition within the meaning of Directive 2004/17/EC.

With the intention of counterbalancing the legal uncertainty, which may result from ineffectiveness, Member States should provide for an exemption from any finding of ineffectiveness in cases, where the contracting authority or contracting entity deems that the direct award of any contract without prior publication of a contract notice in the Official Journal is allowed in accordance with the substantive directives and has applied a minimum standstill period allowing for effective remedies.

V. CONCLUSIONS

The key principles enshrined in the proposal preceding the Remedies Directive were more clarity, transparency and legal certainty throughout the selection process. The tenet of transparency provides economic operators with the assurance that all tender applications will be treated equally and elevates the principles of equal treatment and non-discrimination on grounds of nationality. Another well-settled dimension of transparency is its value of corollary of democratic governance and good administration. A third dimension of transparency has been less explored, that is, transparency as a guarantor of an effective judicial protection, allowing the impartiality of procurement procedures to be reviewed.

Ubi jus ibi remedium is a Roman law dictum that affirms that a right without a remedy is a vain thing. Article 47 of the Charter states that everyone whose rights and freedoms under Union law are violated has a right to an effective remedy before a tribunal. The substantive directives governing the coordinated rules on award of public contracts define the rights of tenderers and candidates and the corresponding obligations of the contracting authorities.

Moreover the procedural directives have introduced also a procedural type of protection in the form of standstill and suspension rules and their importance is emphasised by the consequences related to the breach of a standstill provision. However the applicability of these consequences depends on the established violation of certain substantive provisions that may produce an injury to the right holder. The remedy of ineffectiveness is applicable, only if the breach of a standstill provision occurs in conjunction with a breach of a substantive rule affecting the chances of the tenderer applying for a review to obtain the contract.

Strengthening the effectiveness of national review procedures should persuade those concerned to employ predominantly the possibilities for review by way of interlocutory procedure before the conclusion of a contract. The rationale of interlocutory procedures is to prevent serious and irreparable harm from being caused to the unsuccessful tenderer during the pendency of a lawsuit and to enhance judicial economy.

Member States shall take the measures required to ensure that award decisions concerning contracts falling within the scope of the substantive directives may be reviewed effectively and, in particular, as rapidly as possible in accordance with the conditions set out in Articles 2-2f of the Remedies Directive, on the grounds that such decisions have infringed Union law in the field of public procurement or national rules transposing that law. The rapidity of the review and the ability to rely on the precontractual remedies or interlocutory procedures depend on the actual possibility of being informed in good time about the named breach that might affect one's chances to apply for a review to obtain the contract.

In order to safeguard the efficient exercise of the rights conferred on individuals by Union law, the Remedies Directive has introduced provisions meant to ensure that the opportunity to submit a tender benefits from a sufficient level of advertising and that the lack of clarity and the incomplete character of specifications or of the necessary justifications are sanctionable by not triggering the relevant time limits. The interest of the contractual partners in being able to rely on the protection of legal certainty and legitimate expectations has been considered by allowing the possibility to resort, where appropriate, to alternative forms of publicity, such as the V.E.A.T. and by providing for an allowance in money for cases of ineffective contracts, where restitution in kind is not possible. The public interest can, in exceptional circumstances, afford protection by maintaining the validity of a public contract obtained as a result of an unlawful award procedure.

13. The role of the European Court of Justice in public procurement

Kristian Pedersen and Erik Olsson

INTRODUCTION

The importance of the European Court of Justice, hereinafter the Court, for public procurement law cannot be exaggerated. Although the procurement directives lay down a general framework, public procurement law is in its essence judge-made. This is not only true for the large portions of law falling outside the scope of the directives, i.e. procurement below the thresholds, procurement of service concessions and procurement of Annex B services, but also for the application of the procurement directives as such.

As of the present time, the Court has delivered some 240 judgments on public procurement, covering everything from the duty to publish a notice to the right of access to efficient remedies. As is the nature of public procurement, most of the judgments deal somehow with the question of the scope of the public procurement directives. Most questions put before the Court concern public authorities that for some reason have chosen not to use the procedures laid down in the public procurement directives. As the Court's case-law has developed, the Court has, however, made clear that there is a certain standard of transparency and equal treatment to be observed also outside the scope of the directives, having as its legal basis the direct application of the Treaty articles on free movement, that is, Article 34 TFEU (free movement of goods), Article 45 TFEU (free movement of persons), Article 49 TFEU (freedom of establishment) and Article 56 TFEU (free movement of services). The application of the Treaty on public procurement outside the scope of the directives is however always dependent on the contract in question having a certain level of cross border interest.[1]

In this chapter we will examine the role of the Court in public procurement law by examining some areas where the Court's jurisprudence has been of particular importance for the development of public procurement law, namely concessions, the exemptions for in-house cooperation, environmental considerations, the *Lianakis* case-law and the effectiveness of remedies. Although illustrative of the importance of the Court to

[1] See for instance Case C-507/03, *Commission of the European Communities v Ireland*, p. 29; Case C-274/09, *Privater Rettungsdienst und Krankentransport Stadler v Zweckverband für Rettungsdienst und Feuerwehralarmierung Passau*, p. 49 and Case T-258/06, *Federal Republic of Germany v European Commission*, p. 80. For a comprehensive study of the rules applicable to public procurements falling outside the scope of the directives see Sundstrand, Public Procurement – Primary Law Regulation of Public Contracts (Swedish: Offentlig upphandling – primärrättens reglering av offentliga kontrakt), Jure förlag, 2012.

the development of public procurement law these are mere examples and there is hardly any question of public procurement law where the Court has not played a central role.

Before further describing these examples of Court-developed law, it might, however, be helpful to briefly recall the role and composition of the Court and its relationship with the national courts.

THE ROLE AND COMPOSITION OF THE COURT

The jurisdiction of the Court is defined in a number of articles of the TFEU but is perhaps best summarized in Article 19 of the Treaty on European Union.

> The Court of Justice of the European Union shall include the Court of Justice, the General Court and specialised courts. It shall ensure that in the interpretation and application of the Treaties the law is observed.

In this sense the primary, and arguably the only, task of the Court is, and always will be, a task common to all justified courts, namely the protection and assurance of the rule of law. The Court has from time to time been criticized for going beyond its jurisdiction, encroaching on the exclusive (or perhaps retained) competences of the Member States, pushing a free-movement agenda by some perceived to be political rather than an expression of the judicial function. It is, however, important to understand that when the multifaceted nature of the Treaties has brought the Court to examine organizations, measures or fields of national law which are not expressly under its jurisdiction, this has, at least in the Court's view, been done as an exercise of the rule of law. If this meant pushing a free movement agenda it is because the Court perceived this agenda to be the law of the Treaties. If the Court has encroached on the competences of the Member States this was done because it was deemed necessary for the effectiveness of the law as expressed in the Treaties, that is, the law of the Union.

From a public procurement perspective, the Court has exercised its function mainly in cases brought by the Commission against Member States for infringement of the public procurement rules, Article 263 TFEU, or within the framework of a preliminary ruling from a national court, Article 267 TFEU. The Court, or more specifically the Tribunal, is also confronted with public procurement cases regarding public procurements by the European Union institutions.

The Court is composed of 27 judges, one from each Member State, and eight Advocates General. Normally the Court convenes in chambers of three or five judges. However, when a Member State or an institution of the EU so requests, or where the case is particularly difficult or important, a case can be assigned to a grand chamber, composed of 13 judges. In cases of exceptional importance the Court may decide to refer the case to the full Court, composed of all 27 judges.[2] This is extremely rare and has never happened in a public procurement case.

---

2 See Article 60 of the Rules of procedure of the court of justice, L265/1.

To date nine public procurement cases have been decided in grand chamber.[3] The role of the Advocates General is to deliver to the Court an impartial reasoned opinion. An opinion of an Advocate General contains the legal considerations of the Advocate General and a suggested ruling on the case. Although the opinion of the Advocate General is not legally binding it is often well-reasoned and informed and can offer valuable guidance on the proper understanding of EU law, not least where the Court ultimately reaches a conclusion which is in accordance with the opinion. Where a case does not raise a question of new law the Court, after hearing the Advocate General, can decide to give a judgment without the opinion of the Advocate General. This is becoming increasingly common and it is, at least in public procurement cases, not always entirely apparent that this practice is reserved for cases of lesser importance.[4]

THE RELATIONSHIP BETWEEN THE EUROPEAN COURT OF JUSTICE AND NATIONAL COURTS

Is there any subject dearer to the study of European law than the relationship between the Court and the national courts? The primacy of EU law requires national courts to give EU law precedence over national law, even rules of the national constitution. At the same time, the Court cannot be said to be hierarchically superior to any national court; it cannot annul the decision of any national court, nor can an individual appeal the decisions of a national court to the Court. Even where the Court is asked to answer questions of EU law, within the framework of a preliminary ruling, the key word is *preliminary* and the final decision on the merits of the case remains with the national court. Even if the Court could, by way of an infringement proceeding brought by the Commission, impose financial sanctions on a national court for infringing EU law, this possibility seems mostly theoretical. Indeed, the Court is very much dependent on national courts not only for supplying the Court with cases through the preliminary ruling procedure but also, and far more importantly, for applying the case-law of the Court in all the cases that every day pass through the national court systems and that contain aspects of EU law. This relationship requires respect rather than coercion,

---

[3] See Case C-231/03, *Consorzio Aziende Metano (Coname) v Comune di Cingia de' Botti*; Case C-507/03, *Commission v Ireland*; Case C-532/03, *Commission v Ireland*; Case C-337/05, *Commission v Italian Republic*; Case C-213/07 *Michaniki AE v Ethniko Symvoulio Radiotileorasis and Ypourgos Epikrateias*; Case C-480/06, *Commission v Federal Republic of Germany*; Case C-91/08, *Wall AG v La ville de Francfort-sur-le-Main and Frankfurter Entsorgungs- und Service (FES) GmbH*; Case C-271/08, *Commission v Federal Republic of Germany*; Case C-159/11, *Azienda Sanitaria Locale di Lecce and Università del Salento v Ordine degli Ingegneri della Provincia di Lecce and Others.*

[4] See for instance, Case C-599/10, *SAG Slovensko*; Case C-95/10 *Strong Segurança*; Case C-215/09 *Mehiläinen*, Case C-314/09 *Stadt Graz*; Case C-376/08 *Serrantoni*; Case C-138/08 *Hochtief*; *Case* C-206/08 *Eurawasser*; Case C-573/07 *Sea*; Case C-157/06 *Commission v Italian Republic*; Case C-444/06, *Commission v Kingdom of Spain*; Case C-532/06 *Lianakis*; Case C-357/06 *Frigerio Luigim*; Case C-382/05 *Commission v Republic of Italy*; Case C-234/03 *Contse*; Joined Cases C-462/03 and C-463/03 *Strabag*; Case C-84/03 *Commission v Kingdom of Spain.*

collegiality rather than supremacy, which is why the Court would most likely be hesitant to impose any sanction on a national court for a decision made in the performance of its judicial function.

Aware of the risk of being accused of having a procurement-centric world view, we would still argue that the delicate relationship between the Court and the national courts is nowhere better illustrated than in public procurement law. Nowhere is it more apparent that national courts are indeed *Union courts* applying directly not only the implemented provisions of directives but the fundamental principles of procurement law as derived from the Treaty itself. While the Court has tried some 240 public procurement cases since the conception of European procurement law, the Swedish court system alone hits this number by mid-February every year. Each one of these cases contains a very real application and often also *interpretation* of EU law. The duty to refer, as laid down by the tests of *acte clair* and *acte éclaré*, is for the most part an illusion.[5] In the absolute majority of all cases national courts do not deal with questions of EU law, regardless of complexity or novelty, by referring them to the Court for a preliminary ruling. They deal with them by ruling on them – by interpreting and applying EU law in the national context.

There is good reason to be critical towards some national courts unwillingness to refer cases to the Court. If the courts of a Member State try some 3,500 public procurement cases every year it is an anomaly that none of these cases has ever been referred to the Court.[6] At the same time the bar for referral, as set by the tests of *acte clair* and *acte éclaré*, is incompatible with the reality of public procurement as it faces the national court. The requirements of expedience set by the often urgent need for completing a procurement in order to perform services of public interest, makes the prospect of a two year stay of proceedings in order to make a referral to the Court unattractive, to say the least. Indeed, the urgency of the public procurement process and its principle-based nature has left national courts with the task of solving questions of highly complex EU law and often in a quite short amount of time. It is submitted that for the most part national courts rise to the occasion and that some of the finer samples of EU law are not necessarily found in the pages of the Court reports but in day-to-day judgments of national courts of first instance.

At the core of understanding the relationship between the Court and national courts in public procurement, and thereby understanding the practical implications of the primacy of EU law in this field, lies the reality of the requirement of speedy

---

5 As has been made clear by the judgments of *Da Costa*, Case 28-30/62 and *CILFIT*, Case 283/81 national courts have no obligation to refer a case for a preliminary ruling when the question raised is materially identical with a question which has already been the subject of a preliminary ruling in a similar case (*acte éclaré*) or where the national court has established that the correct application of community law is so obvious as to leave no scope for any reasonable doubt (*acte clair*).

6 See Bernitz, 'Preliminary Rulings by the EU Court of Justice – The Attitude and Practice of the Swedish Courts', SIEPS Reports [2010:2] and Bernitz, 'Preliminary References and Swedish Courts: What Explains the Continuing Restrictive Attitude?' in P. Cardonnel, A. Rosas and N. Wahl (eds), *Constitutionalising the EU Judicial System – Essays in Honour of Pernilla Lindh* (Oxford: Hart Publishing, 2012), pp. 177 ff.

proceedings.[7] The national courts do in general respect the primacy of EU law as long as the content and meaning of EU law is readily and clearly available. Where a court will ignore arguments of EU law and resort to solve what are in essence EU law questions on the basis of national law principles, is where the content of EU law seems obscure, complex or incomplete. This has to some extent led to a practice which could best be described as the *primacy of the one-liners*. Where a paragraph of a judgment of the Court easily lends itself to quotation it will fairly quickly spread throughout the national court systems and its primacy will be broadly accepted. However, principles that are more complex in nature, being explained in several paragraphs of a judgment or indeed in several consecutive judgments will have a harder time reaching broad application. In this way the primacy of EU law is, as any other judge-made law, more than anything dependent on the conciseness and quality of the Court's jurisprudence. For some reason this key element of the relationship between the Court and the national courts is often overlooked in doctrinal debate.

In the following we will discuss some specific areas of public procurement law where the jurisprudence of the Court has not only had far-reaching implications for the understanding of EU public procurement law but where this understanding has also been allowed to spread to national procurement law. In our opinion, it must be understood that these are two entirely different things.

THE ROLE OF THE COURT IN DEFINING SERVICE CONCESSIONS

Service concessions are defined in the procurement directives as contracts of the same type as a public service contract except for the fact that the consideration for the provision of services consists either solely of the right to exploit the service or of this right together with payment.[8] As is stated in Article 17 of the Classic Directive and article 18 of the Utilities Directive, the procurement directives do not apply to service concessions.

---

[7] The requirement of speedy proceedings should be viewed in the context of the obligation laid down in Article 2(1) of the Remedies Directive 89/665, requiring member States to ensure review procedures which include the power for a reviewing body to take at the earliest opportunity and by way of interlocutory procedures, interim measures with the aim of correcting the alleged infringement or preventing further damage to the interests concerned, including measures to suspend or to ensure the suspension of the procedure for the award of a public contract or the implementation of any decision taken by the contracting authority. This requirement for interim measures mean that public procurement cases must be dealt with post-haste ensuring that the procurement procedure is not halted for longer than what is absolutely necessary for ensuring access to court for the claimant.

[8] See Article 1(4) of Directive 2004/18/EC of the European Parliament and of the Council of 31 March 2004 on the coordination of procedures for the award of public works contracts, public supply contracts and public service contracts (the Classical Directive) and Article 1(3b) of Directive 2004/17/EC of the European Parliament and of the Council of 31 March 2004 coordinating the procurement procedures of entities operating in the water, energy, transport and postal services sectors (the Utilities Directive).

With regard to service concessions the Court has played two key roles in the development of procurement law. First, the case-law of the Court has been integral in defining the concept of service concessions and in drawing the border between *service concessions*, exempt from the directives, and *service contracts*, covered by the procurement directives. Secondly, the Court has defined the rules to be applied outside the scope of the directives, that is to say the requirements of transparency and equal treatment to be applied on the award of service concessions on the basis of the Treaty itself. In this regard the Court's case-law on other services which fall outside the scope of the directives, such as Annex B-services and contracts which are of a certain cross-border interest but have a value below the thresholds for application of the Procurement Directives, is of importance by analogy.

The Definition of a Service Concession

In the case-law of the Court, as in the directives, service concessions are largely defined by contrast to traditional service contracts. As the case-law of the Court has developed there are two main characteristics of a service concession. First, it is of importance how the supplier is remunerated for the services in question and, secondly, it is required that the risks involved in the operation of the service is transferred to the supplier. Even though there is a point in separating these two criteria they are intimately linked since the model for remuneration is often the source of the risk run by the supplier.

As to the question of remuneration, it appears that it is often enough for a contract to be considered a service concession if all payment for the services in fact comes from the individuals using the service. This was the case in *Parking Brixen* (the operation of a parking facility), *Coditel Brabant* (the operation of a municipal cable television network) and in *ANAV* (the operation of a local public transport service) where the Court considered the contracts in question to be service concession contracts on the grounds of the supplier being solely remunerated through the right to charge the users of the service for the services rendered.[9]

It might seem that all services that are exclusively paid for by the persons using the services would qualify as service concessions. However, as is made clear by the definition of a service concession, this does not necessarily mean that all payment must come from the users in order for a contract to constitute a service concession. What is important is instead that the service provider assumes the risk connected with operating the services in question. Where all reimbursement is provided by the persons using the service there seems to be an assumption that the service provider is running the required risk. It is in this regard important to note that this does not necessarily mean that the financial risk taken by the supplier has to be substantial or equal to the

[9] Case C-458/03, *Parking Brixen GmbH v Gemeinde Brixen and Stadtwerke Brixen AG*; Case C-324/07, *Coditel Brabant SA v Commune d'Uccle and Région de Bruxelles-Capitale*; Case C-410/04, *Associazione Nazionale Autotrasporto Viaggiatori (ANAV) v Comune di Bari and AMTAB Servizio SpA.*

financial risk usually run on an open market.[10] It is not unusual that certain sectors, in particular sectors involving public service utilities, are subject to rules which may have the effect of limiting the financial risks entailed. As stated in *Eurawasser* it must remain open to the contracting authorities, acting in all good faith, to ensure the supply of services by way of a concession, if they consider that to be the best method of ensuring the public service in question, even if the risk linked to such an operation is limited. Moreover, it would not be reasonable to expect a public authority granting a concession to create conditions which were more competitive and involved greater financial risk than those which already exist in that sector. In such circumstances, as the contracting authority has no influence on the detailed rules of public law governing the service, it is impossible for it to introduce and, therefore, to transfer risk factors which are excluded by those rules. However, even if the risk run by the contracting authority is very limited, it is necessary that the contracting authority transfers to the concessionaire all, or at least a significant share, of the operating risk which it faces, in order for a service concession to be found to exist.

As the Court has pointed out, the risk linked to the provision of a service must be understood as the risk of exposure to the vagaries of the market, which may, in particular, consist of the risk of competition from other operators, the risk that supply of the services will not match demand, the risk that those liable will be unable to pay for the services provided, the risk that the costs of operating the services will not be met by revenue and also the risk of liability for harm or damage resulting from an inadequacy of the service.[11] By contrast, risks such as those linked to bad management or errors of judgment by the economic operator are not relevant for the purposes of classification as a public service contract or a service concession, since those risks are inherent in every contract, whether it is a public service contract or a service concession.

It is generally not allowed for the public authority to compensate for losses related to the provision of the service or to offer some sort of guarantee if the service was to turn out not to be profitable. Such measures are generally considered to decrease the risk run by the service provider thereby making the service concession into a service contract.

One aspect of service concessions that is often overlooked is that the service provided must be of such a nature that there are actual risks/benefits that *can be transferred*, regardless of how limited these risks are. If the service is not associated with any risk/benefit when provided by the contracting authority then no risk/benefit can be transferred and the service would instead be considered to be a service contract. In Sweden, for instance, it has become popular to award contracts concerning health services to several service providers and then allow the patient to choose freely between these different providers, thereby exposing the providers to an element of risk. The compensation to be paid to each service provider is connected to the number of patients served but paid in full by the contracting authority. In our view such an

---

10 Case C-206/08 *Wasser- und Abwasserzweckverband Gotha und Landkreisgemeinden (WAZV Gotha) v Eurawasser Aufbereitungs- und Entsorgungsgesellschaft mbH*. p. 65.

11 Case C-348/10 *Norma-A SIA and Dekom SIA v Latgales plānošanas reģions* p. 48 para 49.

arrangement cannot be considered to be a service concession for mainly two reasons. First, the service providers are not entitled to collect payment from third parties.[12] The remuneration is indeed connected to the number of patients treated but this is normally true for any framework agreement regarding health services and should not matter when the payment is indeed paid in full by the contracting authority.[13] Secondly, there is no transferrable risk. The concept of concessions rests on the prospect of a contracting authority transferring a service which has, at least the *potential* of being a source of income, as well as loss, for the contracting authority. Such is the case with any service where the contracting authority provides for some form of payment from the user of the service. However, services which are in total financed by the contracting authority, that is, which are financed through *taxation* rather than *fees*, can never be a source of income or loss in the sense of concessions. The more people who use the service the greater the cost for the Treasury will be. Regardless of how efficiently the service is provided, it will never be profitable for the authority. Such a service can, in our view, never be considered to be a service concession, since there is no risk/benefit to be transferred. Even after the transfer of the responsibility of the service, every new customer will be an increased cost for the contracting authority rather than a source of income. Although *Hans Oymanns* lends some support to our view in this regard, it should be noted that there are no case-law from the Court dealing with this situation.[14] The Court's clarification on this point would therefore be most welcome.

The Requirements of Transparency and Equal Treatment to be Applied on the Award of Service Concessions

As stated above the procurement directives contain no rules on the award of service concessions. The only rule on service concessions, aside from the definition, is Article 3 in the Classic Sector Directive which states that where a contracting authority grants special or exclusive rights to carry out a public service activity to an entity other than such a contracting authority, the act by which that right is granted shall provide that, in respect of the supply contracts which it awards to third parties as part of its activities, the entity concerned must comply with the principle of non-discrimination on the basis of nationality.

However, early on the Court made clear that even if service concessions are not included in the scope of the directives the contracting entities concluding them are, nonetheless, bound to comply with the fundamental rules of the Treaty, in general, and the principle of non-discrimination on the ground of nationality, in particular.[15] The question is of course what these obligations entail in terms of the procedure for the award of a service concession.

---

[12] See Case C-348/10 *Norma-A SIA and Dekom SIA v Latgales plānošanas reģions* p. 42.

[13] See in this respect Case C-300/07, *Hans & Christophorus Oymanns GbR, Orthopädie Schuhtechnik v AOK*, p. 73–74 Rheinland/Hamburg.

[14] Case C-300/07, *Hans & Christophorus Oymanns GbR, Orthopädie Schuhtechnik v AOK*, see also the well-argued opinion of Advocate General Mazák in the same case.

[15] Case C-324/98, *Telaustria Verlags GmbH and Telefonadress GmbH v Telekom Austria AG*, joined party: Herold Business Data AG.

First of all the Court made clear that there is an obligation of transparency meaning that the contracting authority should ensure, for the benefit of any potential tenderer, a degree of publicity sufficient to enable the service market to be opened up to competition and the impartiality of procurement procedures to be reviewed. Part of this obligation is to observe equal treatment of tenderers in order to afford equality of opportunity to all tenderers when formulating their tenders, regardless of their nationality.[16] Contracting authorities should in other words make sure that service providers in territories outside of the Member State can access appropriate information regarding the concession before it is awarded, so that, if they so wish, they can express their interest in obtaining the concession.[17] The principles of equal treatment, non-discrimination and transparency also imply a degree of advertising that would allow for the impartiality of the procurement procedures to be reviewed.[18]

In the absence of legislation in the field the Commission has issued several interpretative documents to outline the obligations of equal-treatment and transparency set out by the Court's interpretation of the Treaty. Already in 2000 the Commission issued an interpretative communication on concessions under Community law, outlining some obligations for the award of concessions.[19] In short the Commission held that the principle of equal treatment implies that all potential concessionaires should know the rules of the tender in advance and that the rules should apply to everybody in the same way. In order to permit an objective comparison between tenders, the tenders should all conform to the tender specifications and an awarding authority is not allowed to take account of changes to a specific tender after the tenders are opened. Furthermore, according to the principle of proportionality, any measure chosen should be both necessary and appropriate in the light of the objectives sought. A Member State may not impose technical, professional or financial conditions that are excessive or disproportionate when selecting candidates. Nor should the duration of the concession be set in such a way that it limits open competition beyond what is required to ensure that the investment is paid off and there is a reasonable return on invested capital, whilst maintaining a risk inherent in exploitation by the concessionaire.

In addition to the interpretative communication on concessions the Commission has published an interpretative communication on the Community law applicable to contract awards not or not fully subject to the provisions of the public procurement directives.[20] Although the interpretative communication only covers contracts below the thresholds for application of the directives and Annex B-services, the legal basis for the regulation of these procurements is the same Treaty articles and principles that govern

---

[16] Case C-458/03, *Parking Brixen GmbH v Gemeinde Brixen and Stadtwerke Brixen AG*, p. 48.

[17] Case C-231/03, *Consorzio Aziende Metano (Coname) v Comune di Cingia de' Botti*, pp. 16–19.

[18] Case C-324/07, *Coditel Brabant SA v Commune d'Uccle and Région de Bruxelles-Capitale*, p. 25.

[19] Commission Interpretative Communication on concessions under community law, [2000] OJ C121/02.

[20] Commission Interpretative Communication on the Community law applicable to contract awards not or not fully subject to the provisions of the Public Procurement Directives.

the award of service concessions. The case-law invoked in the interpretive communication can therefore easily be applied to the understanding of the requirements of transparency and equal treatment on the award of service concessions. As made clear by the case-law invoked in the interpretative communications the following obligations apply to the award of service concessions:

- an obligation to ensure adequate publicity (advertising) of some form of an invitation to tender, such as for instance National Official Journals, local newspapers (where adequate) or the Official Journal of the European Union;[21]
- a requirement that the invitation contains the essential details of the contract to be awarded and the award method to be used;[22]
- an obligation to conduct the award procedure in a way that is in line with the general principles of procurement, that is, by not referring to a certain trade mark and so on in the technical specifications, allowing equal access regardless of the nationality of the tenderer, observing mutual recognition of diplomas and certificates and observing appropriate time-limits for the expression of interest and submission of tenders;[23]
- an obligation to award the contract in accordance with what has been stated in the tender documents and observing equal treatment in the award of the contract; and
- making sure that there are effective remedies against any infringement of the procurement principles equivalent to those awarded for infringements of national law.[24]

As the case-law of the Court has developed it has become increasingly clear that the rules for the award of concessions should be codified. In December 2011, the Commission published a proposal for a new directive for the award of concessions outlining these obligations. According to the proposal, concessions will be covered by the Remedies Directives so that service providers will have the opportunity of appeal award decisions and other decisions taken by the contracting authority in connection with concessions. As of now, it is still not clear if and when such legislation will come into force. In few fields of law has the Court been as important in the creation of a

---

21 See Case C-324/98, *Telaustria Verlags GmbH and Telefonadress GmbH v Telekom Austria AG*, joined party: Herold Business Data AG., p. 62; Case C-231/93, *Consorzio Aziende Metano (Coname) v Comune di Cingia de' Botti* p. 4 as interpreted in the Interpretative communication, page 5–6.

22 See Case C-231/93 *Consorzio Aziende Metano (Coname) v Comune di Cingia de' Botti* p. 21.

23 See Case C-470/99 *Universale-Bau AG, Bietergemeinschaft: 1) Hinteregger & Söhne Bauges.m.b.H. Salzburg, 2) ÖSTÜ-STETTIN Hoch- und Tiefbau GmbH v Entsorgungsbetriebe Simmering GmbH.* p. 93 as interpreted in the interpretative communication, pp. 7–8.

24 Case C-50/00 *Unión de Pequeños Agricultores v Council of the European Union* p. 39 and Case 222/86 *Union nationale des entraîneurs et cadres techniques professionnels du football (Unectef) v Georges Heylens and others* p. 14. See also general case-law in Case C-46/93 and C-48/93 *Brasserie du Pêcheur SA v Bundesrepublik Deutschland and The Queen v Secretary of State for Transport, ex parte: Factortame Ltd and others* p. 83 and Case C-327/00 *Santex SpA v Unità Socio Sanitaria Locale n. 42 di Pavia, and Sca Mölnlycke SpA, Artsana SpA and Fater SpA*. p. 55.

regulatory framework as is the case with service concessions. The Court has not only helped define the concept of service concessions as such, but also to a large extent created the regulatory framework in itself by defining what requirements need to be met when awarding a concession. To some extent this burden will be lifted from the shoulders of the Court once a new possible concession directive is adopted. One should not, however, make the mistake of thinking that there will be no need for further case-law on the matter. The wording of the directive will surely still have the same ambiguous definition of a service concession and we will need several more cases before it is fully brought to light what in fact constitutes a concession.

THE ROLE OF THE COURT IN DEFINING IN-HOUSE AWARDS

According to the procurement directives, the previous as well as the current ones, public contracts are contracts for pecuniary interest concluded in writing between economic operators (suppliers, service providers or contractors) and contracting authorities.[25] Such economic operators may very well themselves be contracting authorities, that is, as a general rule, public contracts awarded by an authority to another fall within the scope of the directives.[26]

However, according to the case-law of the Court, first developed in the *Teckal* line of case-law and then in the *Hamburg* line of case-law, a contracting authority has the possibility of performing the tasks conferred on it in the public interest by using its own administrative, technical and other resources, without being obliged to call on outside entities, that is to say entities not forming part of its own organization. In such a case, no contract for pecuniary interest is concluded with an entity considered to be legally distinct from the contracting authority, and there is therefore no need to apply the provisions of the directive.[27]

Through its case-law the Court has developed two tests for assessing whether a purchase is to be considered to be internal, even though it is made between two separate legal entities. It is these two tests, which in large measure have helped shape the view of what in fact constitutes a procurement contract, which we will examine in this section.

Institutional Cooperation as Developed by the *Teckal* Case-Law

The first line of case-law, often called the *Teckal* case-law after the case that started it all, is concerned with institutionalised cooperation between contracting authorities, that is, where the cooperation takes place between entities that are connected to one another

---

[25] Previously Directive 92/50/EEC [1992] OJ L209/1–24 (services) Article1(a); Directive 93/36/EEC [1993] OJ L199/1–53 (supply) Article1(a); Directive 93/37/EEC [1993] OJ L199/54–83 (works) Article 1(a) and Directive 93/38/EEC [1993] OJ L199/84–138 (utilities) Article 1.4 now Directive 2004/18 [2004] OJ L134/114–240 (classic sector) Article 1.2(a) and Directive 2004/17 [2004] OJ L134/1–113 (utilities sector) Article 1.2.(a).

[26] Case C-84/03 *Commission v Kingdom of Spain.*

[27] Case C-26/03, *Stadt Halle, RPL Recyclingpark Lochau GmbH v Arbeitsgemeinschaft Thermische Restabfall- und Energieverwertungsanlage TREA Leuna.*

through ownership.[28] The standard *Teckal* situation is where a contract is awarded to an entity owned by the contracting authority. The Court has made clear that the award of contracts between such entities falls outside the scope of the public procurement rules where the authority awarding the contract exercises control over the entity awarded the contract similar to that which the authority exercises over its own departments, and where the entity carries out most of its activity with the authority or authorities which own it. As the *Teckal* doctrine has developed in some 20 cases it has been clarified that the participation, even as a minority, of a private undertaking in the capital of a company in which the contracting authority in question is also a participant excludes the possibility of that contracting authority exercising over the company a control similar to that which it exercises over its own departments.[29] Furthermore, in *Coditel Brabant*, the Court found that the delegation by a municipality of a public service to an inter-municipal cooperative, the object of which was exclusively to provide services to the affiliated municipalities, could legally take place without a call for tenders. The Court considered that the affiliated municipalities had to be regarded as though they together were exercising control over the cooperative.[30]

The *Teckal* exemption quickly drove municipalities and other local authorities to organise their cooperation in institutionalised form, that is to say through subsidiaries fully owned by the participating municipalities. At least in Sweden, contractual cooperation became unusual and for many years it was thought that, save for the narrow scope of the *Teckal* exemption, cooperation between independent contracting authorities was as a general rule covered by the procurement rules. This assumption was however proven wrong by the Court in the so called *Hamburg* judgment.

---

[28] The Court has developed the *Teckal doctrine* in a number of cases. Case C-107/98, *Teckal Srl v Comune di Viano*; Case C-94/99, *ARGE Gewässerschutz v Bundesministerium für Land- und Forstwirtschaft*; Case C-349/97, *Kingdom of Spain v Commission*; Case C-26/03, *Stadt Halle, RPL Recyclingpark Lochau GmbH v Arbeitsgemeinschaft Thermische Restabfall- und Energieverwertungsanlage TREA Leuna*; Case C-84/03, *Commission v Kingdom of Spain* ; Case C-231/03, *Consorzio Aziende Metano (Coname) v Comune di Cingia de' Botti*; Case C-458/03, *Parking Brixen GmbH v Gemeinde Brixen, Stadtwerke Brixen AG* ; Case C-29/04, *Commission v Republic of Austria. (Mödling)*; Case C-410/04, *Associazione Nazionale Autotransporto Viaggiatori (ANAV) v Comune di Bari, AMTAB Servizio SpA*; Case C-340/04, *Carbotermo SpA and Consorzio Alisei v Comune di Busto Arsizio and AGESP SpA.*; Case C-220/05, *Jean Auroux and others v Commune de Roanne*; Case C-337/05, *Commission v Italian Republic (Augusta Bell Helicopters)*; Case C- 220/06, *Asociación Profesional de Empresas de Reparto y Manipulado de Correspondencia v Administración General del Estado*; Case C-295/05 *Asociación Nacional de Empresas Forestales (Asemfo) v Transformación Agraria SA (Tragsa) and Administración del Estado*; Case C-324/07, *Coditel Brabant SA v Commune d'Uccle and Région de Bruxelles-Capitale*; Case C-337/05, *Commission v Italian Republic*, Case C-573/07, *Sea Srl v Comune di Ponte Nossa (Sea)*; Case C-196/08, *Acoset SpA v Conferenza Sindaci e Presidenza Prov. Reg. ATO Idrico Ragusa and others (Acoset)*; Case C-215/09, *Mehiläninen Oy and Terveystalo Healthcare Oy v Uleåborgs stad*; Joined Cases C-182/11 and C-183/11, *Econord v Comune di Cagno and others*.

[29] Case C-26/03, *Stadt Halle, RPL Recyclingpark Lochau GmbH v Arbeitsgemeinschaft Thermische Restabfall- und Energieverwertungsanlage TREA Leuna*.

[30] Case C-324/07, *Coditel Brabant SA v Commune d'Uccle and Région de Bruxelles-Capitale*.

NON-INSTITUTIONAL COOPERATION AS DEVELOPED BY THE *HAMBURG* CASE-LAW

In the *Commission v Germany* judgement, often referred to as the *Hamburg* judgment after the authority being awarded the contract in question, the Court made clear that there were additional, non-institutionalised, situations of cooperation that might fall outside the scope of the procurement directive.[31] In the case four administrative districts '*Landkreise*' had concluded a contract with the City of Hamburg relating to the disposal of waste in a new incineration facility. In the contract, the City of Hamburg agreed to make the facility available to the *Landkreise* for an annual fee to be paid to the City of Hamburg. Since the Landkreise did not exercise control over the City of Hamburg, or any other separate legal entity, the *Teckal* exemption was quite obviously not applicable. The Commission brought proceedings against Germany and the Court was faced with the question of whether the contract was covered by the procurement directives. The Court observed that the contract established cooperation between local authorities with the aim of ensuring performance of a public task which they all had to perform, namely waste disposal.

After having reviewed the factual circumstances surrounding the contract the Court concluded that the contract in question formed both the basis and the legal framework for the future construction and operation of a facility intended to perform a public service, namely thermal incineration of waste. The contract was concluded solely by public authorities, without the participation of any private party, and did not, according to the Court, provide for or prejudice the award of any contracts that might be necessary in respect of the construction and operation of the waste treatment facility. Referring to its decision in *Coditel Brabant* the Court reiterated that a public authority has the possibility of performing the public interest tasks conferred on it by using its own resources, without being obliged to call on outside entities not forming part of its own departments, and that it may do so in cooperation with other public authorities.[32] The Court lastly stated that EU law does not require public authorities to use any particular legal form in order to carry out jointly their public service tasks. Such cooperation does not undermine the free movement of services and the opening-up of undistorted competition in all the Member States, where implementation of that cooperation is governed solely by considerations and requirements relating to the pursuit of objectives in the public interest and the principle of equal treatment of the persons concerned, is respected, so that no private undertaking is placed in a position of advantage vis-à-vis competitors. In light of these circumstances and since there was, according to the Court, nothing to indicate that the local authorities at issue were contriving to circumvent the rules on public procurement, the Court dismissed the Commission's action.

---

[31] Case C-480/06, *Commission v Federal Republic of Germany.*

[32] Case C-324/07, *Coditel Brabant SA v Commune d'Uccle and Région de Bruxelles-Capitale.*

In the *Azienda*-case the Court followed up on its judgment in *Commission v Germany* and clarified the criteria to be satisfied in order for the *Hamburg*-exemption to be applicable.[33] These criteria can be summarized as follows:

- a contract establishing cooperation between public entities with the aim of ensuring that a public task that they all have to perform is carried out;
- concluded exclusively by public entities, without the participation of any private party;
- where no private provider of services is placed in a position of advantage vis-à-vis its competitors; and
- where the implementation of that cooperation is governed solely by considerations and requirements relating to the pursuit of objectives in the public interest.

What separates the *Hamburg* exemption from the *Teckal* exemption is that the *Hamburg*-exemption is applicable to situations of purely contractual cooperation, whereas the *Teckal* exemption is only applicable to institutionalised cooperation where the cooperation is exercised within the framework of an entity fully or partially owned by the awarding authority or authorities.

The Potential for Legislation on In-house Awards

From its conception the exemptions for institutionalised and non-institutionalised cooperation has caught the attention of the Union legislator. As early as 2002 the Commission had drafted a proposal for a *Teckal* exemption to be written into the EU directives on services and works.[34] As the current directives on public procurement and utilities procurement were adopted they did not, however, include any provision on in-house awards.

When the *Hamburg* judgement was handed down, the European Parliament was fast to act, adopting a resolution acknowledging the new exemption and interpreting the judgment so that the public procurement directives should not apply where the purpose of a partnership established by a contract is the provision of a public-service task conferred on all the local authorities concerned and where the task is carried out without the involvement of private individuals or undertakings, and the activity involved is essentially performed on behalf of the public authorities concerned.[35]

---

[33] Case C-159/11, *Azienda Sanitaria Locale di Lecce, Università del Salento v Ordine degli Ingegneri della Provincia di Lecce and others.*

[34] Amended proposal for a European Parliament and Council Directive concerning the coordination of procedures for the award of public supply contracts, public service contracts and public works contracts (presented by the Commission pursuant to Article 250(2) of the EC Treaty)/*COM/2002/0236 final – COD 2000/0115*.

[35] European Parliament resolution of 18 May 2010 on new developments in public procurement (2009/2175(INI)).

Shortly thereafter, in October 2011, the Commission issued a staff working paper giving its interpretation on the view of the new exemption.[36] As the Commission understood the exemption it contained at least the following criteria:

- the arrangement involves only contracting authorities, and there is no participation of private capital;
- the character of the agreement is that of real co-operation aimed at the joint performance of a common task, as opposed to a normal public contract; and
- the cooperation is governed only by considerations relating to the public interest.

Only two months later the Commission also published its proposal for new public procurement directives, where an express exemption for purely contractual cooperation was included.[37]

The European Parliament and the Council has since published compromise amendments to the text proposed by the Commission and the final version of the new directives is expected to be adopted by the Council in December 2013.[38] It is very clear from the Court's case-law on in-house awards that the Court is pragmatic and functional rather than formalistic in its approach to public procurement law. In the same way that it is not possible to circumvent the procurement rules simply by labelling a contract as a lease of land if it is indeed a public works contract, the application of procurement law should not be dependent on the chosen form of organization. As stated by the Court, EU law does not require public authorities to use any particular legal form in order to carry out jointly their public service tasks.[39]

The case-law of *Teckal*, and perhaps even more clearly, the case-law of *Hamburg* also illustrate the increasing respect given by Union law to the autonomy of local government. As is now stated in Article 4 of the Treaty of the European Union, the Union shall respect national identities of the member states, inherent in their fundamental structures, political and constitutional, inclusive of regional and local self-government.

The concept of local government autonomy or even the broader concept of *institutional autonomy* is not new but it is our impression that the inclusion of this concept in the Lisbon Treaty has done much to bring this concept to the top of the

36 Commission staff working paper concerning the application of EU public procurement law to relations between contracting authorities ('public-public cooperation') Brussels, 4 October 2011 SEC(2011) 1169 final.

37 Proposal for a directive of the European Parliament and of the Council on public procurement COM(2011) 896 final.

38 European Parliament Compromise Amendments 1–92, Clusters 1, 2, 4, 5, 6, 7, 8, 9 and 10. Draft report Marc Tarabella (PE489.699v01) on the proposal for a directive of the European Parliament and of the Council on public procurement (COM(2011)0896 – C7-0006/2012 – 2011/0438(COD).

39 Case C-480/06, *Commission v Federal Republic of Germany*.

Courts' mind.[40] The interest of leaving local government room for institutional autonomy has clearly been raised to the status of being in itself something akin to a principle of Union law. It is clear to us that the Court realizes that local government autonomy, or at least a wide margin of local government *competence* is necessary for the effective and proper implementation of other Union interest. Always ahead of the curve, perhaps Advocate General Trstenjak put it best in her openly *obiter dictum* statements on inter-municipal cooperation in her opinion to *Coditel Brabant*.[41]

> To tackle the many traditional and new tasks of municipalities – and local authorities in general – is, particularly in times of restricted budgets, not always easy, especially for smaller authorities. In addition, many tasks, in particular in the areas of environment and transport are not confined to the municipality. Conversely, inter-municipal cooperation without calling on private capital is owing to its synergistic effects a method used in many Member States for performing public functions in an efficient and cost-effective manner.

It is interesting to note that the *Azienda* judgment was given in the middle of the legislative process and that it is quite apparent that the wording of the operative parts of the judgment is such that it can quite easily be adopted into a provision of law. This is especially apparent if one compares the wording of the *Azienda* judgment with the lengthy and *in-casu* style of the *Hamburg* judgment or even the reasoning opinion of Advocate General Trstenjak in the *Azienda* case. It is seems as if the Court is trying to remain influential over what is essentially a court-made exemption, so that the exemption is not over interpreted as it is codified in new directives.

THE DEVELOPMENT OF EU POLICY ON ENVIRONMENTAL CONSIDERATIONS IN PUBLIC PROCUREMENT

Environmental Considerations in Public Procurement

Another field of public procurement law in which the Court has not only interpreted, but also developed, the legal framework is what is often referred to as 'green procurement' (environmentally friendly procurement). Contracting authorities often, besides procuring supplies, services and works in order to fulfil their public service tasks, pursue other objectives than the purely economic ones, objectives commonly referred to as 'secondary' or 'horizontal' policies.[42] Among these policies the historically most prominent has been the various environmental considerations implemented by

---

[40] The concept of institutional autonomy, i.e. the right for Member States to determine how they fulfil their Union obligations, which organs will be made responsible for the implementation and application of Union law and what procedures will be followed, is extensively discussed by Jans et al. in *Europeanisation of Public Law* (Groningen: Europa Law Publishing, 2007).

[41] See Case C-324/07, *Coditel Brabant SA v Commune d'Uccle and Région de Bruxelles-Capitale Opinion of Advocate General Trstenjak.*

[42] Arrowsmith and Kunzlik, *Social and Environmental Policies in EU Procurement Law* (Cambridge: Cambridge University Press 2009), p. 13.

Member States as well as individual contracting authorities, although social and ethical considerations have also been gaining ground during the last couple of years.

The following section of the chapter will deal with the EU policy on environmental considerations in public procurement, and the role of the Court in contributing to the development of law, rather than just interpreting it. Ethical and social considerations will also be also dealt with.

The Early Days of Environmental Considerations

For a long time, the Commission advocated the view that the object of public procurement was essentially an economic one and that, for this reason, all considerations, whether environmental or other, had to confer a *direct economic advantage* upon the contracting authority. This view was expressed, *inter alia*, in the Commission's 1998 Communication on public procurement.

> The directives allow the inclusion of the objective of protection of the environment in the criteria of selection of candidates in so far as these criteria are aimed at testing their economic, financial and technical capacity.
>
> As regards the award of contracts, environmental elements can serve to identify 'the most economically advantageous offer', in cases where these elements imply an economic advantage for the purchasing entity, attributable to the product or service which is the object of the procurement. In evaluating tenders, a purchasing organization can, for example, take account of costs for maintenance, treatment of waste or re-cycling.[43]

According to the Commission's view, environmental considerations of a broader more general nature, going beyond identifying suitable candidates or the economically most advantageous offer, were incompatible with EU public procurement law. However, case-law from the Court was soon to prove otherwise.

Beentjes and *Nord Pas de Calais*

Although neither the *Beentjes* case,[44] nor the *Nord Pas de Calais* case,[45] specifically concerned environmental considerations, both these cases are considered to have had a major impact on the development of horizontal policies in EU public procurement, also affecting the inclusion of environmental considerations in public procurement.

In *Beentjes* the Court found a condition relating to the employment of long-term unemployed persons to be compatible with the relevant directive, provided that it had no direct or indirect discriminatory effect on tenderers from other Member States (which was a matter for the national court to decide). In *Nord Pas de Calais* the Court, with reference to *Beentjes*, stated that the directives did not preclude the possibility for contracting authorities to use as a criterion a condition linked to a campaign against

[43] Commission communication of 11 March 1988, Public Procurement in the European Union (COM(1998) 143 final), p. 27.

[44] Case 31/87, *Gebroeders Beentjes BV v State of the Netherlands*.

[45] Case C-225/98, *Commission v French Republic*.

unemployment, provided that that condition was consistent with all the fundamental principles of Union law, in particular the principle of non-discrimination.

Hence, both these rulings from the Court supported the view that there was in fact room for horizontal policies in public procurement, provided that certain conditions were met, thereby paving the way for a new approach on, *inter alia*, environmental considerations.

Concordia Bus

In *Concordia Bus* the purchasing unit of the city of Helsinki had called for tenders for operating the urban bus network within the city of Helsinki.[46] The contract was to be awarded to the undertaking whose tender was most economically advantageous overall to the city, assessed by reference to three categories of criteria; the overall price of operation, the quality of the bus fleet, and the operator's quality and environment management. As regards the quality of the vehicle fleet, a tenderer could receive a maximum of 10 additional points on the basis of a number of criteria. Points were awarded, *inter alia*, for the use of buses with nitrogen oxide emissions and external noise emissions below certain levels.

In its reference for a preliminary ruling, the Finnish Supreme Administrative Court asked, *inter alia*, if the relevant provisions of the directive were to be interpreted as meaning that, when organizing a tender procedure concerning the operation of bus transport within the city, the contracting entity may, among the criteria for awarding the contract on the basis of the economically most advantageous tender, take into account environmental considerations so that if the nitrogen oxide emissions or noise level of the individual buses are below a certain level, extra points for the fleet may be given in the evaluation of tenders. *Concordia* contended, in the case, that in a public tender procedure the criteria for the decision must, in accordance with the wording of the relevant provisions of Union law, always be of an economic nature. The other parties to the proceedings, the Member States which had submitted observations and the Commission, submitted that it was permissible to include ecological criteria in the criteria for the award of a public contract. In addition, however, the Commission contended that the criteria for the award of public contracts had to be of direct economic advantage to the contracting authority.

In its ruling, the Court stated that the relevant provision of the directive could not be interpreted as meaning that each of the award criteria used by the contracting authority to identify the economically most advantageous tender must necessarily be of a purely economic nature. According to the Court, it could not be excluded that factors which are not purely economic may influence the value of a tender from the point of view of the contracting authority. That conclusion was, according to the Court, also supported by the wording of the provision, which expressly referred to the criterion of the aesthetic characteristics of a tender.

However, having said that, the Court went on to clarify that this did not mean that any criterion relating to the preservation of the environment may be taken into

---

[46] Case C-513/99, *Concordia Bus Finland Oy Ab, formerly Stagecoach Finland Oy Ab v Helsingin kaupunki and HKL-Bussiliikenne.*

consideration by the contracting authority. On the contrary, to be allowed, such a criterion had to be linked to the subject-matter of the contract, not confer an unrestricted freedom of choice on the authority, be expressly mentioned in the contract documents or the tender notice, and comply with all the fundamental principles of EU Union law, in particular the principle of non-discrimination.

EVN and Wienstrom

In *EVN and Wienstrom*, an Austrian contracting authority had made a call for tenders for the award of a public contract for the supply of electricity.[47] The contract to be awarded consisted of a framework contract followed by individual contracts for the supply of electricity to all the Federal Republic's administrative offices in the Land of Kärnten. The invitation to tender included the following provision under the heading Award criteria; the economically most advantageous tender according to the following criteria: impact of the services on the environment in accordance with the contract documents. According to the contract documents, the electricity supplier had to undertake to supply the Federal offices with electricity produced from renewable energy sources. The supplier was not, however, required to submit proof of his electricity sources.

In addition, it was specified that tenders would be eliminated if they did not contain any proof that in the past two years and/or in the next two years the tenderer had produced or purchased, and/or would produce or purchase, and had supplied and/or would supply to final consumers, a certain amount of electricity from renewable energy sources. The award criteria laid down were net price per kWh, with a weighting of 55 per cent, and energy produced from renewable energy sources, with a weighting of 45 per cent. In its reference for a preliminary ruling, the Austrian Federal Procurement Office, *inter alia*, asked whether the relevant provision of the directive prohibited a contracting authority from using an award criterion in relation to the supply of electricity which required a tenderer to state how much electricity he could supply from renewable energy sources, where the maximum number of points was given to whichever tenderer stated the highest amount and the supply volume is taken into account only to the extent that it exceeded the volume of consumption to be expected in the context of the contract. In its ruling, the Court stated that the relevant provisions did not preclude a contracting authority from applying, in the context of the assessment of the most economically advantageous tender for a contract for the supply of electricity, a criterion requiring that the electricity supplied be produced from renewable energy sources, provided that that criterion was linked to the subject-matter of the contract, did not confer an unrestricted freedom of choice on the authority, was expressly mentioned in the contract documents or the contract notice, and complied with all the fundamental principles of Community law, in particular the principle of non-discrimination.

The Court also went on to state that where a contracting authority applies an award criterion indicating that it neither intends, nor is able, to verify the accuracy of the information supplied by the tenderers, it infringes the principle of equal treatment,

---

[47] Case C-448/01, *EVN AG and Wienstrom GmbH v Republik Österreich.*

because such a criterion does not ensure the transparency and objectivity of the tender procedure.

In addition, the Court also clarified that an award criterion cannot be regarded as incompatible with EU law simply because it does not necessarily serve to achieve the objective pursued.

However, according to the Court, where an award criterion takes into account only the supply volume of renewable energy to the extent that it exceeds the volume of consumption expected in the context of the procurement, the award criterion is not compatible with EU legislation on public procurement.

Through its general statements on horizontal policies in *Beentjes* and *Nord Pas de Calais*, and the more specific statements in *Concordia Bus* and *EVN and Wienstrom*, the Court broadened the scope for environmental considerations in EU procurement law at a time when many stakeholders, including the Commission, believed the room for non-economic award criteria to be very limited. In doing so, the Court added an new dimension to EU public procurement policy, making it possible for contracting authorities not only to use procurement to acquire supplies, services and works, but also to pursue other policy objectives, of a non-economic nature, provided that these are compatible with the general principles of EU law.

Indeed, if the 1990s was a time of free movement, the trend today within EU policy, and law, seems to be an increasing focus on using public procurement for other purposes, including the pursuit of horizontal policies. Perhaps this is best described as an example of the emerging social dimension of EU law, but it may also be perceived as a parallel to the increasing focus on corporate social responsibility emerging in many sectors of private business.

However, without denying the potential which lies in using public procurement as a tool for horizontal policies, it is submitted that this use must be analyzed from an efficiency perspective. It is, for instance, not obvious that the content and level of environmental considerations is something which is to be decided by individual contracting authorities or entities rather than by the national legislators or even the EU legislator. Not least for the sake of ensuring that tenderers do not have to adapt to different kinds of requirements in different procurements, we would welcome sector specific legislative initiatives on the sort and level of environmental requirements to be applied in public procurements.

LIANAKIS AND THE IMPORTANCE OF KEEPING DIFFERENT STAGES IN PROCUREMENT SEPARATED

The procurement directives may be characterized as 'procedural', in the sense that they define and regulate the procedures that contracting authorities and entities must apply when deciding which economic operators to award contracts. Hence, the procurement rules are all about getting from 'point A', being the choice of procedure, to 'point B', being the conclusion of the contract after the standstill period following the award decision. The most important is, however, what takes place in between, that is, the actual procurement. A procurement may, for the purpose of analysis, roughly be divided into the following phases; choice of procedure, publication of a contract notice, submission of tenders, qualitative selection (including application of the grounds for exclusion and qualification criteria regarding economic and financial standing as well as technical and professional ability), evaluation of tenders, award decision and conclusion of the contract. Although all these phases are equally important, in the sense that they all are necessary for conducting a procurement according to the directives, two of the phases are of particular practical importance, not least from a commercial perspective. These are the qualitative selection of tenderers and the evaluation of tenders.

At first glance, the difference between the two phases seems almost obvious and, hence, keeping them separate, that is, not confusing them or making them overlapping, seems unproblematic. However, when analyzing the matter more closely, and particularly when doing so from a practical rather than a theoretical perspective, one often finds it more difficult than expected to keep them apart. This is the case not least for procurement of services, since the technical and professional ability of the service provider indeed can be perceived to be of paramount importance for the quality of the services performed.

In addition, the Court has taken a strict view on the importance of separating the qualitative selection of tenderers from the evaluation of tenders, interpreting the relevant rules of the directives in a way which differs from the interpretation generally made in many of the Member States.

This section of the chapter will deal with the Court's readiness to prevent Member State's practices from deviating too far from the rules of the directives, using the Court's case law in *Lianakis*[48] and subsequent case-law as an example.

Qualitative Selection of Tenderers and Evaluation of Tenders – Some Introductory Remarks

The purpose of qualitative selection is to analyze the tenderers' suitability and ability to deliver the goods, provide the services or perform the works which are the subject matter of the contract. The qualitative selection does not entail any relative assessment of the tenderers, or to what extent they fulfil the selection criteria. Hence, a qualitative selection is 'absolute' (all or nothing), in the sense that either a tenderer is deemed to fulfil the selection criteria or it is deemed not to fulfil the selection criteria. In the former case the tenderer moves on to the next phase, the evaluation of tenders; in the latter the tender is rejected.

It should be noted that a qualitative selection phase is not mandatory, that is, contracting authorities and entities are not obliged to assess the suitability and ability of tenderers.[49] However, from a commercial perspective most contracting authorities and entities will want to make sure that the tenderers at least fulfil some basic requirements, in order to avoid having to award the contract to a tenderer which in fact is likely not to be able to perform the contract (or not likely to perform it well). In practice, the vast

[48] Case C-532/06, *Emm. G. Lianakis AE, Sima Anonymi Techniki Etaireia Meleton kai Epivlepseon and Nikolaos Vlachopoulos v Dimos Alexandroupolis and Others.*

[49] With the exception of application of the mandatory grounds for exclusion, where applicable.

majority of contracting authorities and entities indeed do include a qualitative selection phase in their procurements.

The tender evaluation phase is the part of a procurement during which the contracting authority or entity assesses which of the submitted tenders that best meet the needs of the authority or entity, as specified in the tender documents. There are two grounds for awarding contracts in public procurements; the most economically advantageous tender or lowest price.

A prerequisite for accepting the tender with the lowest price is that the tender meets all the mandatory requirements in the tender documents. By setting high mandatory quality requirements, the contracting authority or entity can ensure that the offered goods, services or works are of high quality, although only the price will be subject to evaluation.

When 'the most economically advantageous tender' is used as the ground for evaluation the tender which fulfils all the mandatory requirements and is the most economically advantageous, on the basis of the award criteria in the tender documents, is to be accepted. The award criteria may, for example, relate to quality, price, technical merit, aesthetic and functional characteristics, environmental characteristics, running costs, cost-effectiveness, after-sales service and technical assistance, delivery date and delivery period or period of completion. The list is, however, not exhaustive but merely illustrative.

Case-law before *Lianakis*

The fact that qualitative selection and tender evaluation are two separate processes, which must not be confused, had already been established in the Court's judgments in *Beentjes* and *GAT*.[50] In those cases, the Court found that even though contracting authorities themselves are allowed to choose the evaluation criteria they wish to apply, there is a limitation on the freedom of choice, in that the criteria selected must be criteria aimed at determining which tender is the most economically advantageous tender.

Thus, it has long been clear that it is not permitted to confuse the qualitative selection of tenderers with the evaluation of tenders. However, the general interpretation of case-law still was that it was permitted to take a tenderer's ability, capacity, and so on into account during evaluation, as long as this was done in order to identify the most economically advantageous tender, rather than, as during the qualitative selection, in order to assess whether a tenderer at all has the ability to perform the contract. In other words, it was considered possible during qualitative selection to assess *whether* tenderers could fulfil the contract in question (quantitative assessment of ability, capacity, and so on) and then during evaluation of tenders to assess *how well* they could be expected to perform the contract (qualitative assessment of ability, capacity, and so on). However, it would soon become apparent that the Court interpreted the relevant provisions of the procurement directives differently.

[50] Case 31/87, *Gebroeders Beentjes BV v State of the Netherlands* and Case C-315/01, *Gesellschaft für Abfallentsorgungs-Technik GmbH (GAT) v Österreichische Autobahnen und Schnellstraßen AG (ÖSAG)*.

Lianakis and Subsequent Case-law

In *Lianakis*, the Municipal Council of the Greek city of Alexandroupolis issued a call for tenders for a contract to carry out a project in respect of the cadastre, town plan and implementing measure for the Palagia area, a part of Alexandroupolis. The contract notice referred to the award criteria in order of priority: (1) the proven experience of the expert on projects carried out over the last three years; (2) the firm's manpower and equipment; and (3) the ability to complete the project by the anticipated deadline, together with the firm's commitments and its professional potential. During the evaluation procedure, in order to evaluate the tenderers' bids, the project award committee of the Municipality of Alexandroupolis ('the Project Award Committee') defined the weighting factors and sub-criteria in respect of the award criteria referred to in the contract notice. The Lianakis consortium was allocated the third place in the tender evaluation.

The consortium challenged the decision taken by the Municipal Council of Alexandroupolis, initially before the Council itself and subsequently before the Greek Council of State on the basis, in particular, of allegations of infringement of Article 36(2) Directive 92/50. The Council of State decided to stay the proceedings and to refer the following question to the Court for a preliminary ruling:

> If the contract notice for the award of a contract for services makes provision only for the order of priority of the award criteria, without stipulating the weighting factors for each criterion, does Article 36 of Directive 92/50 allow criteria to be weighted by the evaluation committee at a later date and, if so, under what conditions?

However, before answering the question referred to it, the Court decided to analyze another question, namely whether, in a tendering procedure, the directive precluded the contracting authority from taking into account as 'award criteria', rather than as 'qualitative selection criteria', the tenderers' experience, manpower and equipment, or their ability to perform the contract by the anticipated deadline. In other words, the Court found it necessary to, first of all, establish the lawfulness of the criteria chosen as 'award criteria', before considering whether it was possible for the weighting factors and sub-criteria in respect of the award criteria to be set at a later date. Since this was a question which would not necessarily have had to be answered in order for the Court to give guidance to the referring national court, it is submitted that the Court in fact took the opportunity to address the matter on a more general level, as a response to Member States' practice which was perceived to deviate from the provisions of the directives. Referring to its previous case-law, the Court stated that the concept of 'award criteria' does not include criteria that are not aimed at identifying the tender which is economically the most advantageous, but is instead essentially linked to the evaluation of the tenderers' ability to perform the contract in question.

According to the Court, the criteria selected as 'award criteria' by the contracting authority in the case related principally to the experience, qualifications and means of ensuring proper performance of the contract in question. Thus, those were criteria concerned with the tenderers' suitability to perform the contract which did not have the status of 'award criteria' pursuant to Article 36(1) Directive 92/50, that is, were not allowed. *Lianakis* concerned procurement in the classic sector. However, in the subsequent case *Commission v Greece*, which concerned a procurement in the utilities sectors, the Court re-iterated its statements from *Lianakis*, making it clear that the conclusions in *Lianakis* were equally relevant for the utilities sectors.[51]

As is apparent from the case-law accounted for above, the Court has placed great emphasis on the need to limit the concept of 'award criteria', that is, criteria for evaluation of tenders and award of contracts, to only such contracts that are specifically aimed at identifying the most economically advantageous tender, thereby excluding criteria which merely aim at evaluating the tenderers' ability to perform the contract in question.

This interpretation of the procurement directives may admittedly seem strict, possibly even overly strict, and impractical for the everyday procurements of contracting authorities and entities. Particularly in procurements of services, the interpretation may cause difficulties.

Although this has never been mentioned explicitly in the Court's case-law, it is submitted that the principle of proportionality forms the basis of the Court's analysis. One of the main reasons for not allowing criteria linked to the tenderers' suitability and ability to be used as award criteria, instead of criteria for qualitative selection, is that this would risk resulting in disproportionate evaluation. If criteria linked to the tenderers' suitability and ability are to be used as award criteria this can lead to favouring of tenderers that for instance have longer experience, or more manpower and equipment, than what is actually needed for performance of the contract in question, simply because the longer the experience, or the more manpower or equipment, the higher the score awarded will be. This effect would not as easily appear if the same criteria were to be applied as criteria for qualitative selection, since the contracting authority or entity would then be forced to set a definite level for the criteria, which all tenderers would have to meet to be considered 'good enough', that is, to move on to the evaluation of tenders.

Hence, the relative nature of the evaluation of tenders, that is, that it entails a comparison between tenders, means that evaluating 'organizational aspects' of the tenderers rather than the actual tenders risks resulting in disproportionate evaluation, while as the 'absolute' nature of qualitative selection does not entail such a risk, at least not where the criteria in themselves are fixed at a reasonable level (which is a matter that may be analyzed in accordance with the principle of proportionality). In other words, the rule, according to the Court, should be that a contracting authority or entity should award the contract to a qualified tender having submitted the most advantageous tender, not to the most qualified tenderer. This view also brings with it a certain SME-perspective since over time it will lead to a lowering of the barriers of entry to the markets for the supply of goods, services and works to the public sector.

Hence, while there, on the one hand, are good arguments in favour of the position taken by the Court there is also, on the other hand, room for advocating a more flexible approach on the matter. The latter has been acknowledged by the Commission in its proposal for a new procurement directive for the classic sector, in which the organization, qualification and experience of the staff assigned to performing the

---

[51] Case C-199/07 *Commission v Hellenic Republic.*

contract in question may be taken into account in the evaluation in procurements of service contracts and contracts involving the design of works.[52]

However, should Member States' practice develop in such a way that the boundary between qualitative selection and tender evaluation would become blurred, it is submitted that the Court would be likely to once more intervene.

REMEDIES IN PUBLIC PROCUREMENT

Introduction

Yet another aspect of public procurement law which the Court has truly developed in its case-law is remedies, that is, the legal recourses available to economic operators (and supervisory authorities, such as the Commission) in cases where contracting authorities do not fulfil their obligations under EU procurement law.

Remedies, it is submitted, are a vital part of any legislation aimed at inducing a certain behaviour among the entities covered, especially when this behaviour is sometimes perceived as a burden, and a limitation, rather than something positive.

This section of the chapter will deal with the matter of remedies and the role of the Court in developing the law, rather than just interpreting the law, illustrated by two examples; standstill, and termination of contracts.

The Remedies Directives

Already from the outset the remedies directives[53] stipulated that Member States must make available rapid and effective remedies to any economic operator, having or having had an interest in obtaining a particular contract and who has been or risks being harmed by an alleged infringement. However, before the 2007 amendments the Remedies Directives did not provide for any particular period under which review procedures were to be available before the contracting authority could enter into a contract with the chosen tenderer. In addition, once the contract had been signed the only remedy which Member States had to make available was damages. In practice, since the contract was often signed shortly, if not immediately, after the award decision this meant that there was no real access for an aggrieved economic operator to any other remedy than damages.[54] Furthermore, once a contract had been signed, the

---

[52] Proposal for a directive of the European Parliament and of the Council on public procurement COM(2011) 896 final.

[53] Council directive of 21 December 1989 on the coordination of the laws, regulations and administrative provisions relating to the application of review procedures to the award of public supply and public works contracts (89/665/EEC) and Council directive 92/13/EEC of 25 February 1992 coordinating the laws, regulations and administrative provisions relating to the application of Community rules on the procurement procedures of entities operating in the water, energy, transport and telecommunications sectors.

[54] This is often described as 'the race to signature', cf. Commission Impact Assessment Report SEC(2006) 557.

directives did not provide for any measures for a third party, neither an aggrieved economic operator nor the Commission, to have the contract terminated (rescinded).

Standstill

In *Alcatel*[55] the Austrian Federal Ministry of Science and Transport had published an invitation to tender for the supply, installation and demonstration of hardware and software components of an electronic system for automatic data transmission to be installed on Austrian motorways. The contract in question was awarded to Kapsch AG and was signed on the same day as the award decision. The other tenderers, who learned of the contract through the press, applied to the Federal Procurement Office for review.

The Federal Procurement Office, however, dismissed the applications for interim measures to suspend performance of the contract on the ground that, pursuant to Austrian public procurement law, once an award was made it no longer had the power to make interim orders. A complaint was lodged against that decision with the Austrian Constitutional Court, which set aside the decision. The Federal Procurement Office then reopened the procedure and made an order provisionally prohibiting the contracting authority from further performance of the contract. The Republic of Austria lodged a complaint against that order before the Constitutional Court, which gave suspensive effect to the complaint, with the result that the interim measure adopted by the Federal Procurement Office was provisionally inoperative.

In these circumstances the Federal Procurement Office decided to stay the proceedings and make a reference for a preliminary ruling to the Court. In its judgment the Court stated that it was clear from the first and second recitals in the preamble to Directive 89/665 (the Remedies Directive), that the directive reinforced existing arrangements at both national and Union level for ensuring effective application of the procurement directives, in particular at the stage where infringements could still be rectified. The Court also found it to be clear from the wording of the remedies directive that the limitation of review procedures applied only after the conclusion of the contract following the awarding decision, and that the Remedies Directive thus drew a distinction between the stage *prior to the conclusion of the contract*, and the stage *subsequent to its conclusion*, in respect of which a Member State may provide that the powers of the body responsible for the review procedures were to be limited to awarding damages to any person harmed by an infringement.

In the case, the Austrian Government contended that if the Remedies Directive was to be interpreted as drawing a distinction between the decision awarding a contract and the conclusion of that contract, the directive failed to specify in any way what time should elapse between the two stages. However, the Court found the argument based on the lack of an intervening period between the decision awarding a contract and the conclusion of the contract to be irrelevant. The fact that there was no express provision in that connection could not justify interpreting the Remedies Directive in such a way

---

[55] Case C-81/98 *Alcatel Austria AG and Others, Siemens AG Österreich and Sag-Schrack Anlagentechnik AG v Bundesministerium für Wissenschaft und Verkehr.*

as to remove decisions awarding public contracts systematically from the purview of the measures provided for in the directive.

The Court then went on to conclude that the Remedies Directive was to be interpreted as meaning that the Member States were required to ensure that the contracting authority's decision prior to the conclusion of the contract in all cases was open to review in a procedure whereby an applicant may have that decision set aside if the relevant conditions were met, notwithstanding the possibility, once the contract had been concluded, of obtaining an award of damages. Thus, according to the Court, the Member States were obliged to allow for a possibility for applying for review of an award decision prior to the conclusion of the contract.

Even though the Remedies Directive did not contain any express provisions to that effect, the Member States were obliged to allow for a standstill period between the award decision and the conclusion of the contract, in order to give full effect to the directive.

Termination of Contracts

In joined Cases C-20/01 and C-28/01 *Commission v Germany*[56] the Court found that since the Municipality of Bockhorn had entered into a contract for collection of waste water and the City of Braunschweig had entered into a contract for waste disposal, both without having invited tenders, the Federal Republic of Germany had failed to fulfil its obligations under the relevant procurement directive (Directive 92/50 EEC).

This, one might have thought, would have been the end of the matter, since the general view among Member States was, at the time, that the Remedies Directives did not impose any obligation on Member States to provide for termination of illegally awarded contracts. However, the Commission decided to follow up on the judgment, by requesting the German Government to notify it of the measures taken to comply with the judgment and, when not finding the answer satisfactory, decided to bring an action before the Court.

In the case, C-503/04 *Commission v Germany*,[57] the Commission requested the Court to declare that, by failing to adopt all the necessary measures to comply with the judgment in the joined cases C-20/01 and C-28/01, the Federal Republic of Germany had failed to fulfill its obligations under Article 228(1) EC (now Article 260 TFEU), and to order that member state to pay to the Commission a penalty payment of €31,680 for each day of delay in implementing the measures necessary to comply with that judgment in respect of the contract relating to the municipality of Bockhorn and of €126,720 for each day of delay in implementing the measures necessary to comply with judgment in respect of the contract relating to the City of Brunswick, in each case from the date of delivery of that judgment until the measures were implemented. However, since the German Government declared that the contract concluded by the municipality of Bockhorn was to be annulled, the Commission decided to pursue its action only in relation to the contract relating the City of Brunswick.

[56] Joined Cases C-20/01 and C-28/01, *Commission v Federal Republic of Germany*.
[57] Case C-503/04, *Commission Federal Republic of Germany*.

In the case, the Commission took the view that the Federal Republic of Germany had not adopted measures sufficient to comply with the previous judgment, since that Member State did not, before the date of expiry of the period laid down in the reasoned opinion, rescind the contract concluded by the City of Brunswick. The Federal Republic of Germany, on the other hand, took the position that rescission of the contract was not required. In addition, the Federal Republic of Germany, supported by the French Republic, the Kingdom of the Netherlands and the Republic of Finland, submitted that the second subparagraph of Article 2(6) of Directive 89/665, which allowed Member States to provide in their legislation that, after the conclusion of a contract following the award of a public contract, the bringing of an action could give rise only to an award of damages and, thus, to exclude any possibility of rescission of that contract, precluded a finding of failure to fulfil obligations within the meaning of Article 226 EC (now Article 258 TFEU), with regard to such a contract entailing the obligation to rescind it. According to those Member States, the principles of legal certainty and of the protection of legitimate expectations, the principle *pacta sunt servanda*, the fundamental right to property, Article 295 EC (now Article 345 TFEU) and the case-law of the Court regarding the limitation in time of the effects of a judgment also precluded such a result.

However, the Court found, on four grounds, that these arguments could not be upheld.

First, the Court clarified that although the remedies directives permitted the Member States to preserve the effects of contracts concluded in breach of the procurement directives, thus protecting the legitimate expectations of the parties of such a contract, its effect cannot be, unless the scope of the Treaty provisions establishing the internal market was to be reduced, that the contracting authority's conduct vis-à-vis third parties was to be regarded as in conformity with Union law following the conclusion of such contracts.

Secondly, according to the Court, even if it were to be accepted that the principles of legal certainty and of the protection of legitimate expectations, the principle *pacta sunt servanda* and the right to property could be used against the contracting authority by the other party to the contract in the event of rescission, Member States could not rely on these to justify the non-implementation of a judgment establishing a failure to fulfil obligations under Article 226 EC and thereby evade their own liability under Union law.

Thirdly, with regard to Article 295 EC, according to which 'this Treaty shall in no way prejudice the rules in Member States governing the system of property ownership', the Court stated that that article did not have the effect of exempting the Member States' systems of property ownership from the fundamental rules of the Treaty and that the particular features of the system of property ownership in a Member State could therefore not justify the continuation of a failure to fulfill obligations which consists of an obstacle to the freedom to provide services in disregard of the provisions of Directive 92/50.

Fourthly, with regard to the case-law, invoked by the Member States, on the limitation in time of the effects of a judgment, the Court went on to state that, in any event, that case-law did not justify the non-implementation of a judgment establishing a failure to fulfil obligations under Article 226 EC.

Accordingly, the Court found that, by having failed to adopt all the necessary measures to comply with the judgment in the joined Cases C-20/01 and C-28/01 regarding the conclusion of the contract for waste disposal by the City of Brunswick, the Federal Republic of Germany had failed to fulfil its obligations under Article 228 EC.

Thus, although the Federal Republic of Germany had complied with the provisions of the remedies directives, it was still found to be in breach of its Treaty obligations, that is, its general obligations under Union law, since it had not done what was required in order to bring the Treaty violations established in the first judgment to an end. The Court's judgment in C-503/04, *Commission v Germany* thereby establishes that a Member State may have to go further in relation to its obligations under primary EU law, than what is required in relation to economic operators under the secondary EU law of the procurement directives.

ANALYSIS

No piece of legislation, nor any legal system, can be complete in the sense that it covers all possible situations that may arise in the course of business. This is often particularly true for legislative acts of EU law, such as directives, since these by their very nature are compromises between the sometimes conflicting interests of different stakeholders. Public procurement law serves as a good example of this, since the EU legislator's aim of ensuring cross border trade also for public contracts sometimes runs contrary to some Member States' policy objectives. In turn, this kind of law making by compromise may lead to inefficiencies in the application of directives, both at the national level and the EU level.

The case-law accounted for above provides illustrative examples of such inefficiencies, the first one being an inefficiency in the application of the directives at the national level, and the second one being an inefficiency at the EU level, that is, between the Member States and the Union.

As is clear from this case-law the Court plays a vital role in this context, as a guardian of the coherence and efficiency of EU law, making sure that the underlying objectives sought by the legislator, manifested not only in directives but also in the Treaties, are attained despite the sometimes imperfect nature of individual pieces of legislation, such as the procurement directives. In other words, once the Member States, in their capacity of participants in the legislative process, have set a course the Court has the role of making sure that the journey ends approximately where the legislator originally intended.

CONCLUDING REMARKS

In our opinion, the examples described above serve to illustrate the roles that the Court has, and has taken, within the field of public procurement law. These may be summarized as follows:

- Creator of a regulatory framework
- Participant in the legislative process
- Catalyst of policy development
- Harmonizer of Member State application, responsible for 'filling in the gaps' in the provisions of the directives.

In the role of *creator of regulatory framework* as in the case of service concessions, the Court has developed procedural rules, although of a rather rudimentary nature, where no secondary law rules previously existed. In doing so, the Court has, however, been careful always to emphasize that these procedural rules are only a manifestation of the basic principles of the Treaty. However, by 'giving life' to the principles of the Treaty by way of interpreting them in the public procurement context the Court has in fact developed secondary legislation in a field where the EU legislator has not yet developed, or perhaps has failed to develop, legislation although such legislation is needed for the advancement of the Treaties. Although this may be perceived as the Court encroaching on the competences of the legislator and the Member States, one could also analyze the situation from another perspective. It is submitted that what the Court has actually done is to clarify that the provisions of the Treaty themselves, as formulated by the legislator, entail obligations of a very real nature for the authorities of Member States, also in the field of public procurement, obligations which Member States cannot avoid simply by not exercising their powers as a part of the legislative machinery. In essence, the message the Court is sending to Member States is that as long as the Treaty remains unchanged there will, in the interest of free movement or other Union interests, be rules for the award of public contracts of cross border interest regardless of whether or not they are covered by secondary legislation.

In the role of *participant in the legislative process* the Court has shown its readiness to actively take part in the legislative process, at least in matters where the legislator intends to codify the case-law of the Court. It is our opinion that the Court, in its ruling in *Azienda*, took great care to formulate the *Hamburg* exemption in a manner more suited for implementation in new directives than was the case with the wording of the judgment in *Commission v Germany*. However controversial, it is difficult to interpret this in any other way than that the Court, possibly surprised that the Member States so quickly included a *Hamburg* exemption in the ongoing legislative process for new directives, decided to clarify its standpoint in the matter as means of influencing the legislative process. Since a prerequisite for new provisions in the procurement directives aimed at implementing case-law is usually that the provisions do not go beyond codifying the underlying case, since the Commission and many other stakeholders otherwise tend to object, it is submitted that the Court's *modus operandi* in this case is likely to be successful.

As a *catalyst of policy development* it is obvious that the Court in *Concordia Bus* and *EVN and Wienstrom* went further than both the position of the Commission and the analysis made by many commentators. In doing so the Court seems to have been more 'tuned in' to the opinion of the general public in environmental matters than indeed many decision makers. By its rulings in *Concordia Bus* and *EVN and Wienstrom* the Court significantly broadened the scope for secondary policies in public procurement, not only in terms of environmental considerations but also for social and ethical considerations. It is submitted that this development, *inter alia*, manifested in *Concordia Bus* and *EVN and Wienstrom*, is logical considering the general increase in focus in EU law, from a purely economic free movement perspective, towards what is often referred to as the *social dimension* of EU law.

As with all directives, the procurement directives leave a wide margin of competence to the Member State when it comes to how the directive should be implemented and applied. Indeed the procurement directives could not stand alone as regulations and are in all aspects dependent on a national context for their effective application. Furthermore, the nature of procurement requires that individual authorities make commercial decisions which are sound and suitable for the needs of the authority and the market situation for the relevant service or supply. There is no rule of the directive that will give an authority guidance on how to make a good deal. It is required that authorities think for themselves and construct their own purchase-models. However, this margin of appreciation cannot go so far as to erode the core principles of the directives or lead to such divergence in member state behaviour that the directives lose their harmonizing effect. Here the Court plays an important role in reining in the behaviours of different Member States, allowing them enough room for modern and ever-changing business models while hindering behaviour that risks obscuring the full force and effect of the directives. We consider *Lianakis* to be an expression of this role of the Court as harmonizer of Member State application.

Last but not least, the Court has also assumed *responsibility for 'filling in the gaps' in the provisions of the directives*, in order to ensure the efficiency and coherence of public procurement law. This may, admittedly, be perceived as a role closely linked to the role of *creator of a regulatory framework*. However, it is submitted that there is an important difference between the roles, in the sense that while creating new law in fields not covered by secondary law entails a process of 'expansion' of the legal framework, possibly in conflict with the legislator, filling in the gaps is instead aimed at ensuring that secondary legislation adopted by the legislator becomes efficient, as intended by the legislator, and applied in a coherent manner throughout the entire union. The latter is for example manifested in the teleological interpretations of the provisions of the remedies directives, as in *Alcatel* and *Commission v Germany*, where the facts of both cases prompted the Court to fill in the gaps by analyzing the underlying intentions of the legislator and the purpose of the relevant provisions rather than their scope according to the actual wording.

PART 4

PUBLIC PROCUREMENT AND COMPETITION

14. Public procurement and competition: some challenges arising from recent developments in EU public procurement law

Albert Sanchez Graells

1. INTRODUCTION

This chapter explores the recent OECD push for more competition in public procurement and its role as an influential factor in the 2014 reform of EU public procurement rules. It goes on to critically assess three of the main challenges to keeping public procurement procompetitive: (i) the difficult balance in terms of procurement transparency created by the clash between competition and corruption concerns; (ii) the magnification of the undesired (potential) anticompetitive effects of public procurement that centralized procurement may generate, as well as its increasing use as an improper tool of market regulation; and (iii) the possible competitive distortions and the potential advantages resulting from the generalization of eProcurement. The conclusions extract some common patterns derived from the previous analysis and suggest some policy recommendations mainly oriented at boosting oversight and professionalization of procurement.

The relationship between public procurement and competition has been receiving an increasing amount of attention, both in academic[1] and policy-making circles.[2] It has

[1] R.D. Anderson, W.E. Kovacic and A.C. Muller, 'Ensuring Integrity and Competition in Public Procurement Markets: A Dual Challenge for Good Governance' in S. Arrowsmith and R.D. Anderson (eds), *The WTO Regime on Government Procurement: Challenge and Reform* (Cambridge: Cambridge University Press, 2011) 681–718; D. Malhotra, 'Study on Government Procurement. Study for Evidence Based Competition Advocacy' (*CUTS Institute for Regulation and Competition*, January 2012) available 1 February 2016 at http://www.circ.in/pdf/Government_Procurement.pdf; A. Sanchez Graells, *Public Procurement and the EU Competition Rules*, 2nd edn. (Oxford: Hart Publishing, 2015); O. Dekel, 'The Legal Theory of Competitive Bidding for Government Contracts' (2008) 37(2) *Public Contract Law Journal* 237–68; C. Munro, 'Competition Law and Public Procurement: Two Sides of the Same Coin?' (2006) 15(6) *Public Procurement Law Review* 352–61. For a different and critical view, opposing the fundamental normative considerations that derive from this approach, see S. Arrowsmith, 'The Purpose of the EU Procurement Directives: Ends, Means and the Implications for National Regulatory Space for Commercial and Horizontal Procurement Policies' (2011–2012) 14 *Cambridge Yearbook of European Legal Studies* 1; and P. Kunzlik, 'Neoliberalism and the European Public Procurement Regime' (2012–2013) 15 *Cambridge Yearbook of European Legal Studies* 283.

[2] See the summary in OECD, 'Competition and Procurement: Key Findings' (OECD Policy Roundtables, 2011), available 1 February 2016 at http://www.oecd.org/regreform/liberalisationdcompetitioninterventioninregulatedsectors/48315205.pdf. See also OFT/●econ, 'Assessing the

been clearly stressed that the 'starting point for achieving best value for money in government procurement is a regulatory framework that is based on the principle of competition and that submits public spending to the adherence to competitive procurement methods'.[3] In that regard, it is becoming common ground that public procurement holds a complex and bidirectional relationship with market competition and that, consequently, a tighter link between public procurement and competition law enforcement needs to be established.[4] Indeed, the effectiveness of public procurement and its ability to contribute to the proper and most efficient carrying on of public interest obligations is conditional upon the existence of competition in two respects or separate dimensions.[5]

One of them has been expressly recognized for a long time by public procurement regulations, which have tried to foster *competition within the specific tender*. Public procurement rules protect and promote competition in this narrow sense as a means to achieve value for money and to ensure the legitimacy of purchasing decisions. From this perspective, competition is seen as a means to allow the public purchaser to obtain the benefits of competitive pressure among (participating) bidders,[6] as well as a key instrument to deter favouritism and other corrupt practices and deviations of power.[7]

However, a subtler and stronger dependence of public procurement on *competition in the market* exists, but it is implicit and has generally been overlooked by most public procurement studies.[8] In order to attain value for money and to work as a proper tool

---

Impact of Public Sector Procurement on Competition' (September 2004), available 1 February 2016 at http://webarchive.nationalarchives.gov.uk/20140402142426/http://www.oft.gov.uk/shared_oft/reports/comp_policy/oft742b.pdf.

[3] UNCTAD, Intergovernmental Group of Experts on Competition Law and Policy, *Competition policy and public procurement* (2012), available 1 February 2016 at http://unctad.org/meetings/en/SessionalDocuments/ciclpd14_en.pdf.

[4] A. Heimler, 'Cartels in Public Procurement' (2012) 8(3) *Journal of Competition Law & Economics* 1. See also A. Sanchez Graells, 'Prevention and Deterrence of Bid Rigging: A Look from the New EU Directive on Public Procurement', in G. Racca and C. Yukins (eds), *Integrity and Efficiency in Sustainable Public Contracts* (Brussels: Bruylant, 2014) 171–98.

[5] On the relationship between general interest and competition considerations in public procurement, see F. Gartner, '*Des rapports entre contrats administratifs et intêret général*' (2006) 22 *Révue française de droit administratif* 19, 21.

[6] In very clear terms, the Court of Justice of the EU recently stressed that the main goal of the procurement exercise is to create competition so that the contracting authority obtains the works, goods or services it requires in the best possible (market) conditions and that market agents can exploit any existing competitive advantages in the setting of the internal market; see Case C-549/13, *Bundesdruckerei* EU:C:2014:2235, para 34.

[7] P.A. Trepte, 'Transparency and Accountability as Tools for Promoting Integrity and Preventing Corruption in Procurement: Possibilities and Limitations' (2006) 5/10 *OECD Papers* 1.

[8] Exceptionally, the relevance of competition in the market (as protected by competition law) for the proper functioning is stressed by P.A. Trepte, *Regulating Procurement. Understanding the Ends and Means of Public Procurement Regulation* (Oxford: Oxford University Press, 2004) 57, 61 and 122. It has been held that the notion of competition in the sphere of public procurement rules is different than the broader notion of competition that constitutes a fundamental principle of EU law, although close links between them must be acknowledged; see J.F. Brisson, *Les fondements juridiques du droit des marchés publics* (Paris: Imprimerie

for the public sector, public procurement activities need to take place in competitive markets.[9] Public procurement rules assume that markets are generally competitive – in the broad sense – or, more simply, take as a given their economic structure and competitive dynamics.[10] Indeed, the existence of competitive intensity in the market is usually taken for granted, or simply disregarded, in public procurement studies. In general terms, this approach is correct in that public procurement is not designed to prevent distortions of competition between undertakings. However, *issues regarding competition in the market are not alien to public procurement*,[11] and need to receive a stronger emphasis.[12] This is becoming commonplace, although this second dimension of the interplay between market competition and effective public procurement is still not universally recognized and has not yet generated strong regulatory changes.[13]

Similarly, the sources of competition-related concerns in the field of public procurement are twofold. On the one hand, procuring entities are becoming fully aware of the threats and negative consequences derived from tenderers' collusion or bid rigging in public tenders – particularly in view of their knock-on impact on the effective attainment of the public policy objectives they set out to fulfil, and ultimately to the detriment of taxpayers. On the other hand, there is a growing awareness of the negative effects that public procurement rules and practice can generate on market structures and

---

Nationale, 2004) 25; and O. Black, *Conceptual Foundations of Antitrust* (Cambridge: Cambridge University Press, 2005) 9. However, both concepts of competition are present in public procurement rules and competition in the broader sense is also one of the fundamental principles of EU public procurement law. Therefore, the impact of public procurement on competition in the market should always be stressed.

[9] See S.L. Schooner, 'Pondering the Decline of Federal Government Contract Litigation in the United States' (1999) 8 *Public Procurement Law Review* 242, 248. Indeed, the case has been made convincingly by R.D. Anderson and W.E. Kovacic, 'Competition Policy and International Trade Liberalisation: Essential Complements to Ensure Good Performance in Public Procurement Markets' (2009) 18 *Public Procurement Law Review* 67, 70–72. Similarly, stressing the importance to shield public procurement from anticompetitive market practices, see D.E. Brunk, 'Governmental Procurement: "FAR" from a Competitive Process' in G. Piga and K.V. Thai (eds) *Advancing Public Procurement: Practices, Innovation and Knowledge-Sharing* (Boca Raton: PrAcademics Press, 2006) 156.

[10] See G. Piga and K.V. Thai, 'The Economics of Public Procurement: Preface' (2006) *Rivista di Politica Economica* 3, 5; also, K.V. Thai, 'Public Procurement Re-examined' (2001) 1 *Journal of Public Procurement* 9, 34.

[11] W. Sauter and H. Schepel, *State and Market in European Union Law. The Public and Private Spheres of the Internal Market before the EU Courts* (Cambridge: Cambridge University Press, 2009) 49.

[12] The idea is not new; see C.W. Sherrer, 'Achieving a Higher and More Competitive State-of-the-Art in DOD Procurement Procedures' (1982) 15 *National Contract Management Journal* 71, 76.

[13] This may be bound to change on the basis of the consolidation of the principle of competition in Article 18(1) of Directive 2014/24, as discussed below. For related commentary, see A. Sanchez Graells, 'Public procurement: An overview of EU and national case law', 16 July 2015, *e-Competitions*, Art. N° 73813; and ibid, 'Truly Competitive Public Procurement as a Europe 2020 Lever: What Role for the Principle of Competition in Moderating Horizontal Policies?' (2016) 22(2) *European Public Law* 377–394.

competitive dynamics, particularly as a result of new techniques for centralized or strategic procurement – although those effects are not always taken into due consideration, and sometimes seem to be exploited in a potentially counterproductive manner.[14]

Indeed, public procurement rules can themselves generate significant distortions of competitive market dynamics[15] – and, in so doing, can be largely self-defeating, as they can restrict the effective chances for the public buyer to obtain best value.[16] Public procurement regulations tend to establish a market-like mechanism that, in most instances, ends up isolating parts of the market – that is, creating 'public (sub-)markets' – which become highly regulated (by public procurement rules themselves) in various aspects and that, in the end, can result in restrictions or distortions of competition that limit the ability of the public buyer to obtain value for money. Hence, in order to promote the efficiency of the procurement activities and value for money, public procurement rules need to be procompetitive and guarantee that they do not distort competition in the market.[17]

All in all, from a competition perspective, public procurement is starting to be seen as both a particularly well-suited scenario where collusion often takes place (which is a source of growing concern and reaction by competition authorities), and as a source of publicly created distortions of competition – or, at least, as a relatively new instrument of (undercover) market regulation that deserves some detailed analysis. Possibly, these changing views will prompt regulatory reform to better accommodate competition concerns in the public procurement setting. Such regulatory changes could be facilitated by the renewed OECD efforts to further competition in this important area of public policy, as they are picked up and followed by domestic legislators and governments. However, these are not straightforward changes due to the complexity of the issues arising from simultaneous developments in public procurement practice and the ensuing regulatory adjustments – especially in areas such as the fight against corruption or the modernization and virtualization of public procurement procedures (that is, eProcurement). In the end, public procurement reform is subject to competing and conflicting goals and, to that extent, competition considerations deserve particular attention if the system is to promote efficiency and, ultimately, to maximize the returns

[14] For discussion, see A. Sanchez Graells and I. Herrera-Anchustegui, 'Impact of Public Procurement Aggregation on Competition: Risks, Rationale and Justification for the Rules in Directive 2014/24', in R. Fernández Acevedo and P. Valcárcel Fernández (eds), *Centralización de compras públicas* (Madrid: Civitas, forthcoming), available 1 February 2016 at http://ssrn.com/abstract=2534496.

[15] A fact that was clearly stressed by D.F. Kettl, *Sharing Power. Public Governance and Private Markets* (Washington: Brookings Institution, 1993) 31. See also Anderson and Kovacic, 'Competition Policy and International Trade Liberalisation', above n 9, 89–91; and G. Amato, 'Practical Economic Guidelines for Reforming Regulation to Eliminate its Anticompetitive Effects' in G. Amato and L.L. Laudati (eds), *The Anticompetitive Impact of Regulation* (Cheltenham, UK and Northampton, MA, USA: Edward Elgar, 2001) 459.

[16] Indeed, the need to have 'good legislation' to foster the proper and competitive functioning of procurement markets has been stressed; see L. Fiorentino, 'Public Procurement and Competition' in K.V. Thai et al (eds) *International Public Procurement Conference Proceedings* (2006) 847.

[17] Similarly, J.J. Snider Smith, 'Competition and Transparency: What Works for Public Procurement Reform' (2008) 38 *Public Contract Law Journal* 85, 110–11.

for public expenditure without distorting the structures and dynamics of the markets where the public buyer is particularly active or relevant in terms of aggregated demand.

With these preliminary considerations in mind, this chapter aims to critically assess some recent developments in EU public procurement law from a competition perspective, and to focus on the underlying trends that they illustrate, as well as on the challenges that they raise for the promotion of highly competitive markets where the public buyer has a strong demand position or where public procurement regulations impose (or facilitate) anticompetitive solutions. The main objective of the chapter, then, is to highlight some areas where the need for public procurement reform is dire, and to suggest policy directions that would favour a more procompetitive framework.

Following this introduction, this chapter will explore the recent OECD push for more competition in public procurement as an influential factor in the 2014 reform of EU public procurement rules (Section 2). Afterwards, it will critically assess three of the main challenges to keeping public procurement procompetitive. First, the focus will be on the difficult balance in terms of procurement transparency created by the clash between competition and corruption concerns (Section 3). Secondly, attention will be paid to the magnification of the undesired anticompetitive effects of public procurement that centralized or strategic procurement may generate, as well as their increasing use as an improper tool of market regulation (Section 4). Finally, the analysis will move to the possible competitive distortions and the potential advantages resulting from the generalization of eProcurement, which is ranking ever higher in procurement reform agendas (although, in the current scenario of economic crisis, governments may not be able to easily put their money where their mouths are, at least in the short term) (Section 5). The conclusions will try to extract some common patterns derived from the previous analysis and to suggest some policy recommendations (Section 6).

2. A NEW OECD PUSH AND ITS FORESEEABLE IMPACT ON THE REVISION OF EU PUBLIC PROCUREMENT LAW

On 17 July 2012, the OECD Council adopted a *Recommendation on Fighting Bid Rigging in Public Procurement*[18] that is intended to bring procompetitive public procurement design and practice to the spotlight and to prompt legislators and governments to give high priority to the adoption of anti-collusion measures. In its very clear terms, the OECD:

> [r]ecommends that Members assess the various features of their public procurement laws and practices and their impact on the likelihood of collusion between bidders. Members should strive for public procurement tenders at all levels of government that are *designed to promote more effective competition and to reduce the risk of bid rigging* while ensuring overall value for money. (emphasis added)

[18] OECD, *Recommendation on Fighting Bid Rigging in Public Procurement* [C(2012)115, 17 July 2012], available 1 February 2016 at http://acts.oecd.org/Instruments/ShowInstrumentView.aspx?InstrumentID=284&InstrumentPID=299&Lang=en&Book=False.

The OECD has complemented this general recommendation with a set of more specific *Guidelines for Fighting Bid Rigging in Public Procurement*,[19] aimed to help procurement officials implement a more procompetitive and anti-collusion public procurement practice. At the same time, the *Recommendation* and *Guidelines* on fighting bid rigging need to be complemented with the additional best practices to ensure *competitive neutrality*[20] and to avoid distortions where (former) state-owned enterprises participate in public tenders. Taken together, the OECD's 2012 *Recommendation* and *Guidelines* are a comprehensive body of economically sound normative proposals that offer a useful blueprint for a procompetitive revision of public procurement rules in the EU, and elsewhere.

In this regard, it is interesting to see how, despite the time lag between the start of the revision of the EU public procurement Directives in December 2011[21] and the adoption of the 2012 OECD's Recommendation, the EU's efforts to reform the pre-existing 2004 public procurement rules already included to some extent procompetitive and anti-collusion solutions that are in line with the revision recommended by the OECD in July 2012. However, some of the initial procompetitive drive of the 2011 Proposal was lost during political negotiations leading to the adoption of Directive 2014/24,[22] and it remains to be seen how (incrementally) procompetitive the new EU public procurement rules become after Member States transpose them and the Court of Justice of the European Union (CJEU) starts interpreting them. In any case, some of the clearest links between competition and public tenders concerned with bid rigging have been stressed in the new EU public procurement rules, thereby allowing contracting authorities to effectively reduce the risk of bid rigging and, in case they detect any instance of tenderers' collusion, react effectively.[23]

The European Commission has shown that it is aware of the fact that, given that public procurement strongly relies on competitive markets, there is a clear need to ensure that the design of public procurement rules and administrative practices are fit

---

19 OECD, *Guidelines for Fighting Bid Rigging in Public Procurement* [DAF/COMP(2009)1/FINAL, 2009], available 1 February 2016 at http://www.oecd.org/daf/competition/cartelsandanticompetitiveagreements/42851044.pdf.

20 OECD, *Competitive Neutrality: Maintaining a Level Playing Field between Public and Private Business* 97-104 (30 August 2012), available 1 February 2016 at http://dx.doi.org/10.1787/9789264178953-en. For discussion, see A. Sanchez Graells, 'Competitive Neutrality in Public Procurement and Competition Policy: An Ongoing Challenge Analysed in View of the Proposed New Directive' (2012), submitted to the 5th International Public Procurement Conference, August 2012, at http://ssrn.com/abstract=1991302 accessed 4 August 2015.

21 Proposal for a Directive of the European Parliament and of the Council on public procurement (hereinafter the 2011 Proposal) [COM(2011)896 final, 20 December 2011], available 1 February 2016 at http://eur-lex.europa.eu/legal-content/EN/ALL/?uri=CELEX:52011PC0896.

22 Directive 2014/24/EU of the European Parliament and of the Council of 26 February 2014 on public procurement and repealing Directive 2004/18/EC [2014] OJ L94/65.

23 See the recent case, Case C-470/13, *Generali-Providencia Biztosító* EU:C:2014:2469. For discussion, see A. Sanchez Graells, 'CJEU supports interaction between competition and public procurement rules (C-470/13)', *howtocrackanut*, 19 December 2014, available 1 February 2016 http://howtocrackanut.com/blog/2014/12/cjeu-supports-interaction-between.html.

and appropriate to promote competition and, particularly, to avoid instances of bid rigging. This was emphasized (although in still relatively obscure terms) in the framework of the revision of the EU public procurement rules – where the Commission stressed, for instance, that '[w]hilst greater use of repetitive purchasing techniques should have overall positive benefits for [contracting authorities], there are some concerns about market closure and the longer-term access of firms to such tools. This would have to be addressed to ensure transparency and non-discrimination and prevent a restriction of competition'.[24] Indeed:

> [t]he first objective [of this revision process was] to increase the efficiency of public spending. This includes on the one hand, the search for best possible procurement outcomes (best value for money). To reach this aim, *it is vital to generate the strongest possible competition for public contracts awarded in the internal market. Bidders must be given the opportunity to compete on a level-playing field and distortions of competition must be avoided.* At the same time, it is crucial to increase the efficiency of procurement procedures as such. (emphasis added)[25]

Even if only in relation with centralized procurement, the recitals of the 2011 Proposal expressly mentioned the risk of collusion, in the following terms: '… the aggregation and centralisation of purchases should be carefully monitored *in order to avoid excessive concentration of purchasing power and collusion*, and to preserve transparency and competition, as well as market access opportunities for small and medium-sized enterprises' [recital (20); emphasis added].

Indeed, all this seems to be significantly in line with the OECD's 2012 Recommendation, and indicates a general trend underlying the revision of the EU procurement Directives to try to make them more procompetitive (together with modernization and procedural simplification).

It is worth stressing that Article 15 of the 2011 Proposal, entitled 'Principles of procurement', consolidated the relevance of undistorted competition (or competitive neutrality) by clearly emphasizing that: 'The design of the procurement shall not be made *with the objective* … of *artificially narrowing competition*' (emphasis added). In the author's view, this provision agglutinated the pro-competitive orientation present in the EU procurement Directives from their initial design in the 1970s and brought to light the underlying principle of competition embedded in their 2004 version[26] – which could be defined or phrased in these terms: 'Public procurement rules have to be interpreted and applied in a procompetitive way, so that they do not hinder, limit, or

---

24 European Commission, *Executive Summary of the Impact Assessment Accompanying the Proposal for a Directive on Public Procurement* [SEC(2011)1586 final, 20 December 2011], available 1 February 2016 at http://ec.europa.eu/transparency/regdoc/?fuseaction=list&coteId=2&year=2011&number=1586&language=EN.

25 European Commission, *Green Paper on the Modernization of EU Public Procurement Policy – Towards a More Efficient European Procurement Market* [COM(2011)15 final, 27 January 2011], available 1 February 2016 at http://ec.europa.eu/internal_market/consultations/docs/2011/public_procurement/synthesis_document_en.pdf.

26 A. Sanchez Graells, 'The Principle of Competition Embedded in EC Public Procurement Directives' (Working Paper, University of Nottingham, 2009), available 1 February 2016 at http://ssrn.com/abstract=1928724.

distort competition. Contracting entities must refrain from implementing any procurement practices that prevent, restrict or distort competition'.

Therefore, it seems clear that the initial revision of the current EU public procurement rules had a clear orientation towards safeguarding (or, at least, promoting) competitive neutrality as a booster for enhanced competition and, in the end, increased value for money through better procurement efficiency. As I have said elsewhere,[27] with the inclusion of Article 15 in the 2011 Proposal, it seemed to be getting clearer and clearer that market integration in procurement must go hand in hand with promoting and protecting effective competition for public contracts, and the drafting of Article 15 of the 2011 Proposal for a new Directive finally seemed to overcome some difficulties in the development of EU procurement rules – which still suffer the problem of being excessively focused on preventing discrimination based on nationality (which has overshadowed other discrimination problems, protectionist policies and competition restrictions and distortions in European public procurement)[28] – although a broader objective of fostering competition on the basis of fair and open access to procurement (not only for bidders from different Member States) can be identified in Directive 2004/18[29] and is further reinforced in the new procurement Directive.

Now, due to political pressures and the mechanics of EU legislative processes, such a clear-cut movement towards a clearly pro-competitive orientation in the EU procurement rules got distorted and deformed with the October 2012 Compromise Text, which gave a new drafting to Article 15, were competition concerns were harder to identify and the underlying principle of competition remained unnecessarily obscure. Indeed, in that version, Article 15 of the proposed new Directive would read: 'The design of the procurement shall not be made with the *intention of … unduly favouring or disadvantaging certain economic operators or certain works, supplies or services*' (emphasis added). Even if the prevention of undue advantages or disadvantages is clearly connected with the keeping of an undistorted competitive environment, it was not so clear that it imposed a positive mandate not to restrict (or to maximize) competition – not least because it also had potential links with anti-corruption mechanisms oriented towards preventing favouritism, and this ambivalence could have ended up diminishing the effectiveness of the principle altogether.[30]

---

[27] A. Sanchez Graells, 'Are the Procurement Rules a Barrier for Cross-Border Trade within the European Market? A View on Proposals to Lower that Barrier and Spur Growth' in C. Tvarnø, G.S. Ølykke and C. Risvig Hansen, *EU Public Procurement: Modernisation, Growth and Innovation* (Copenhagen: DJØF, 2012) 107–33.

[28] A. Sanchez Graells, *Public Procurement and the EU Competition Rules*, above n 1, 108–10 and 212–19.

[29] Directive 2004/18/EC of the European Parliament and of the Council of 31 March 2004 on the coordination of procedures for the award of public works contracts, public supply contracts and public service contracts (Directive 2004/18) [2004] OJ L134/114.

[30] Indeed, anticorruption goals had also been decaffeinated in the October 2012 version, which suppressed the mention contained in the version of Article 15 in the July 2012 Compromise Text that 'Contracting authorities … shall act in a transparent and proportionate manner that *avoids or remedies conflicts of interest and prevents corrupt practices*' (emphasis added).

This would have been a potential step back in the modernization of the EU procurement system and a failure to provide a clear consolidation of the principle of competition in the text of the Directives, which is a general principle of EU Law already explicitly recognized in the field of public procurement,[31] and that provides a fantastic analytical framework on which to develop welfare-enhancing public procurement rules and practice. Therefore, the further amendment of the provision should be welcome in restricting the scope for (apparently) non-discriminatory restrictions of competition in public procurement that would only result in losses of economic welfare for EU citizens.[32] In that regard, the fact that Article 18(1) of Directive 2014/24 finally consolidated the principle of competition in the EU public procurement system should be stressed and conceptualized as the clear normative and legal guideline for the interpretation of the rest of the 2014 procurement rules.

According to Article 18(1) of Directive 2014/24, '[t]he design of the procurement shall not be made *with the intention … of artificially narrowing competition*'.[33] There are significant issues derived from the interpretation of this provision, particularly regarding the intentional element (as opposed to the objective analysis that would have resulted from the original drafting of Art 15 of the 2011 Proposal). Nonetheless, in the author's view, the proper interpretation is still that, as a result of this general principle and in order to give it effectiveness, the public procurement rules have to be interpreted and applied in a procompetitive way, so that they do not hinder, limit, or distort competition. Contracting entities must refrain from implementing any procurement practices that prevent, restrict or distort competition. This should lead the analysis of the procurement rules more closely directed to competition considerations, such as the ones discussed below.

2.1 General Measures: 'Collusion-conscious' (and Procompetitive) Tender Design

In general, as can be extracted from the OECD *Recommendation* and *Guidelines*, there is a number of measures that contracting authorities can adopt to try to minimize pro-collusive features of their tender procedures, such as: (1) defining their requirements clearly and avoiding predictability in procurement; (2) designing the tender process to effectively reduce communication among bidders; (3) carefully choosing evaluation and award criteria; or (4) raising staff awareness about the risks of bid rigging in procurement.[34]

Even if it is true that the EU Directives do not contain specific requirements in any of these areas, the rules of the Directives allow for contracting authorities to exercise

---

[31] Joined Cases C-285/99 and C-286/99, *Lombardini and Mantovani* [2001] ECR I-9233 para 76; Joined Cases C-147/06 and C-148/06, *SECAP* [2008] ECR I-3565 para 29.

[32] A. Sanchez Graells, 'Distortions of Competition Generated by the Public (Power) Buyer: A Perceived Gap in EC Competition Law and Proposals to Bridge It' [Oxford CCLP (L) 23, August 2009], available 1 February 2016 at http://ssrn.com/abstract=1458949.

[33] Some of the interpretative difficulties and challenges that the principle creates are not relevant for the purposes of this chapter and, consequently, will not be discussed in detail. For discussion of this reform and an initial attempt to interpret the principle, see Sanchez Graells (n 1) 207–14.

[34] OECD, *Guidelines for Fighting Bid Rigging in Public Procurement.*

discretion in regard to all those factors – and, consequently, it is safe to assume that the legal framework is well aligned for the design of 'collusion-conscious' tender procedures – particularly as regards the division of procurement requirements into lots and the effective use of evaluation rules and award restrictions to prevent bid rigging by means of the artificial splitting of lots amongst colluders.[35]

In this regard, the consolidation of the new general principle of competition in Article 18(1) of Directive 2014/24 should raise the awareness of contracting authorities about the competition implications of procurement rules and tender documents and decisions, and should spur the development of a more competition-oriented public procurement practice. This is particularly true in connection with the possibility to exclude competition law infringers from ongoing tender procedures.

2.2 Exclusion of Competition Law Infringers and Outline of a Proposal for a Fuller Suspension and Debarment System to be Created at EU Level

A specific and important instrument in the prevention and deterrence of bid rigging in public procurement can be found in the rules controlling the disqualification of competition law offenders (in particular, members of a previously discovered cartel or participants in a cartel caught with a smoking gun in a given tender procedure). If contracting authorities could exclude potential tenderers that have breached competition law in previous occasions – either in a particular instance or, more permanently, by suspending or debarring them from future participation – the (financial) interests at stake for any undertaking to participate in bid rigging would rise significantly. Where an effective exclusion, suspension and debarment system is in place, cartelists know that they risk not only competition law prosecution, but also losing all chances to secure public contracts for a significant period of time, or even permanently. That risk of being excluded from a significant tranche of the market (particularly in sectors where public buyers accumulate a significant volume of purchases) seems a powerful tool that has, so far, been used only in a limited manner in EU law. If so, the extent of the potential (economic) losses should significantly increase the incentive to tenderers to refrain from colluding.[36]

In this regard, it is interesting to see that, as a complement to other measures oriented at reducing red tape and fostering participation by SMEs[37] – in order to strengthen competition (that is, to make the competitive tension between bidders more intense) – the new Directive also includes a specific provision that tries to clarify the rules on disqualification of competition law infringers and, consequently, aims to prevent, deter and punish instances of collusion on public procurement.

To be sure, the 2004 EU procurement rules already contained provisions that would allow contracting authorities or entities to disqualify infringers of competition law, given that breaches of competition law should always be considered instances of grave

---

35 For further details, see Sanchez Graells (n 4) *in totum.*

36 Implicitly, identifying similar risks of economic loss that would generate anti-collusion incentives (in that case, entry) see R.P. McAfee and J. McMillan, *Incentives in Government Contracting*, (Toronto: University of Toronto Press, 1988), 21, 111 and 150.

37 On those measures, see Sanchez Graells (n 27) 107.

professional misbehaviour (in particular, under Article 45(2)(c) and (d) of Directive 2004/18).[38] This seems clearly established in Recital 101 of the new Directive, whereby: 'Contracting authorities should further be given the possibility to exclude economic operators which have proven unreliable, for instance because of violations of environmental or social obligations, including rules on accessibility for disabled persons or other forms of grave professional misconduct, such as violations of competition rules or of intellectual property rights.' However, some further clarification and a streamlining of the disqualification procedure would be welcome.

As indicated in the explanatory memorandum of the 2011 Proposal for a new EU Directive, it 'contain[ed] a specific provision against illicit behaviour by candidates and tenderers, such as ... entering into agreements with other participants to manipulate the outcome of the procedure [which] have to be excluded from the procedure. Such illicit activities violate basic principles of European Union and can result in serious distortions of competition'. More specifically, Article 22 of the 2011 Proposal for a new EU Directive required that, at the beginning of the procedure, tenderers 'provide a declaration on honour that they have not undertaken and will not undertake to: ... (b) enter into agreements with other candidates and tenderers aimed at distorting competition'. Further, in accordance with Article 68 of the 2011 Proposal, regulating impediments to award, '[c]ontracting authorities shall not award the contract to the tenderer submitting the best tender where ... (b) the declaration provided by the tenderer pursuant to Article 22 is false'. Therefore, if the contracting authority became aware of any illicit, anticompetitive behaviour on the part of tenderers, it was required to disqualify them by applying the impediment to award in Article 68(b) of the 2011 Proposal. However, I found that solution partial and that it required further thought.

The final text of Directive 2014/24 has suppressed Articles 22 and 68 of the 2011 Proposal and derived the issue to the new drafting of the grounds for the exclusion of tenderers in Article 57. In that regard, it is worth stressing that, according to Article 57(4)(d): 'Contracting authorities may exclude or may be required by Member States to exclude from participation in a procurement procedure any economic operator in any of the following situations: ... (d) where the contracting authority has sufficiently plausible indications to conclude that the economic operator has entered into agreements with other economic operators aimed at distorting competition'. Moreover, it must be highlighted that, according to Article 57(5), 'At any time during the procedure, contracting authorities may exclude or may be required by Member States to exclude an economic operator where it turns out that the economic operator is, in view of acts committed or omitted either before or during the procedure, in one of the situations referred to in paragraph 4'. Interestingly, Article 57(6) of the new Directive also generates room for self-cleaning actions: 'Any economic operator that is in one of the situations referred to in paragraphs 1 and 4 may provide evidence to the effect that measures taken by the economic operator are sufficient to demonstrate its reliability despite the existence of a relevant ground for exclusion. If such evidence is considered

[38] See Sanchez Graells, *Public Procurement and the EU Competition Rules* (n 1), 253–55; *contra*, C. Bovis, *EC Public Procurement: Case Law and Regulation* (Oxford: Oxford University Press, 2006) 16.

as sufficient, the economic operator concerned shall not be excluded from the procurement procedure'.

Some of the relevant aspects of the disqualification regime will still need to be designed at national level, though, since Article 55(7) foresees that: 'By law, regulation or administrative provision and having regard to Union law, Member States shall specify the implementing conditions for this Article. They shall, in particular, determine the maximum period of exclusion if no measures as specified in paragraph 6 are taken by the economic operator to demonstrate its reliability. Where the period of exclusion has not been set by final judgment, that period shall not exceed five years from the date of the conviction by final judgment in the cases referred to in paragraph 1 and three years from the date of the relevant event in the cases referred to in paragraph 4'. Overall, the new text overcomes some of the difficulties in the initial disqualification system foreseen in Articles 22 and 68 of the 2011 Proposal.

Indeed, the disqualification system envisaged in Articles 22 and 68 of the 2011 Directive fell short of ensuring that infringers of competition law do not participate in public procurement – mainly, due to two considerations. On the one hand, it only allowed for disqualification prior to award of the contract. However, it can be foreseen that most instances of bid rigging will only be discovered later and, maybe even after the execution of the contract is complete (when the remedy of the impediment to award will be absolutely ineffective) (this is remedied by Article 57(4) of the new version). On the other hand, it could generate some doubts as to the possibility to apply Article 45(2)(c) and (d) (renumbered as Article 55(3)(c) and (d) of the 2011 Proposal) in relation with violations of competition that are not connected with the tender at hand (which is now expressly excluded by the wording of Article 57(4)(d), in what is in the author's opinion a criticizable restriction of the disqualification mechanism). Even if the new Directive increases legal certainty in some cases, there is still a need for a further developed suspension and debarment system in EU public procurement rules.[39]

Given the optional terms in which Article 57 of the new rules is drafted, such open regulation at EU level can give rise to different regimes across different Member States and, consequently, might facilitate strategic behaviour by infringing undertakings – thereby reducing deterrence. A stricter and uniform system of suspension and debarment of competition law infringers would contribute to strengthening the pro-competitive orientation of the public procurement system and to limiting privately-created distortions of competition.[40]

From a comparative perspective, it seems important to highlight that the United States' Federal Acquisitions Regulation (US FAR) establishes a clearer regime of suspension and debarment of competition infringers. At the very least, it is remarkable that a 'violation of Federal or State antitrust statutes relating to the submission of offers' constitutes both a cause for suspension (US FAR 9.407-2(a)(2)) and for debarment (US FAR 9.406-2(a)(2)) of the offending contractor. Thus, the infringer can be suspended for a temporary period pending the completion of investigation and any

---

39 Sanchez Graells, *Public Procurement and the EU Competition Rules* (n 1), 382–5.

40 Which, however, would not be without cost; see G.L. Albano et al, 'Preventing Collusion in Public Procurement', in N. Dimitri et al (eds), *Handbook of Procurement* (Cambridge, Cambridge University Press, 2006) 347–80.

ensuing legal proceedings (US FAR 9.407-4(a)) and, eventually, debarred (that is, prevented from participating in all public tenders) for a period commensurate with the seriousness of the cause, and generally of up to three years (US FAR 9.406-4(a)(1)). The decisions on suspension and debarment are not taken by the contracting authority itself, but by a previously designated suspension and debarment official (US FAR 9.406-3(a) and US FAR 9.407-3(a)). Generally, debarment will exclude the contractor from all public tenders conducted during its extension, unless it is restricted to certain types of contracts or certain contracting authorities (US FAR 9.406-3(e)(1)(iv) with US FAR 9.406-1(c)). It is worth noting that suspension and debarment decisions are not meant to punish contractors, but to protect the public interest in the proper functioning of the procurement system (US FAR 9.402(b)).

In a nutshell, the general features of the regime established in the US FAR make it seem superior to the current EU public procurement rules in that the decision on the exclusion of the affected tenderer is not discretionary for the specific contracting authority (which might have a conflict of interest, particularly if the competition infringer is a well-known or an incumbent contractor), but adopted by a previously designated authority within the same agency.

Therefore, in light of the US regime, it is my opinion that it is desirable to strengthen the rules contained in the new Directive by adopting a rule whereby competition infringers could be suspended and/or debarred by an authority different from the contracting authority – and, subject to Member States' internal organization, the best alternative seems to be the competition authority or, eventually, the courts. Suspension and debarment should be triggered particularly by mandatory reporting of competition law breaches, but should also be available as a self-standing sanction in case the investigation is initiated by any other means – particularly, competition authorities should be empowered to adopt debarment decisions as a complement of any other competition sanctions and remedies (such as criminal sentences, fines and damages awards).

Such a regime should apply to all breaches of substantive competition law rules (not only collusion in public procurement processes), unless it can be proven that they are irrelevant in the public procurement setting (which seems unlikely): that is, they should not be automatically limited to cases of bid rigging, and the (high) burden of proving the irrelevance of the anticompetitive practices in the public procurement setting should rest with the infringers. However, in the case of violations of competition law other than collusion in public procurement contracts, the duration and scope of the debarment could be more limited than in the case of the former, and clearly aimed at protecting the public interest in the proper functioning of procurement procedures – that is, not as an additional or substitutive competition sanction.

An exception to the suspension and debarment regime could be created to avoid reducing disproportionately or completely eliminating competition in highly concentrated markets (US FAR 9.405)[41] – where the exclusion of a potential contractor would

---

[41] R.E. Kramer, 'Awarding Contracts to Suspended and Debarred Firms: Are Stricter Rules Necessary?' (2004) *Public Contract Law Journal* 539; and J.S. Zucker, 'The Boeing Suspension: Has Increased Consolidation Tied the United States Department of Defense's Hands?' (2004) *Public Procurement Law Review* 260.

render the procurement procedure largely ineffective. However, in these highly exceptional cases, a waiver of suspension or debarment should only be granted at the request of the affected contracting authorities (which should advance sufficient reasons in the public interest associated to the participation of the suspended or debarred tenderer) and, in any case, it should be substituted with an alternative sanction, such as the imposition of substitute fines or a deferral or extension of the debarment period after market conditions allow for the development of competition (if this is plausible).

Moreover, the provisions related to 'self-cleaning' included in Article 57(6) of the new EU Directive on procurement could help mitigate the effects of suspension or debarment when tenderers actually adopted effective measures to prevent further violations of competition law. In this regard, it should be noted that, under the latter provision, any candidate or tenderer that is in one situation that could trigger exclusion may provide the contracting authority with evidence demonstrating its reliability despite the existence of the relevant ground for exclusion. For this purpose, the candidate or tenderer shall prove that it has compensated any damage caused by the criminal offence or misconduct, clarified the facts and circumstances in a comprehensive manner by actively collaborating with the investigating authorities and taken concrete technical, organizational and personal measures that are appropriate to prevent further criminal offences or misconduct. In such cases, contracting authorities shall evaluate the measures taken by the candidates and tenderers taking into account the gravity and particular circumstances of the criminal offence or misconduct; and, where the contracting authority considers the measures to be insufficient, it shall state the reasons for its decision. Therefore, this is an area where the development of effective competition compliance manuals can gain significant relevance in the future.[42]

To sum up, even if the new Directive does improve upon the rules on the exclusion of tenderers for violations of competition law currently included in the EU public procurement directives, the new system can still be smartened up because it grants full discretion to contracting authorities (which may be in a conflict of interest). After briefly considering the system applicable in the US, it seems desirable to prompt Member States to implement the new EU rules by granting the competence to suspend and debar infringers to an authority other than the contracting authority (and, preferably, to the competition authority), and to make suspension and debarment decisions mandatorily enforceable by contracting authorities. Suspension and debarment should not only be triggered by mandatory reports of suspected competition violations, but should also be configured as self-standing competition remedies aimed at protecting the public interest in the proper functioning of the procurement system. Limited waivers of the suspension and debarment regime could be introduced to avoid situations in which competition for public contracts might be excessively restricted – subject to adequate substitutive measures.

---

[42] In general, on competition compliance and the adoption of an effective policy (including self-cleaning measures), see the guidance offered by the Commission, in ec.europa.eu/competition/antitrust/compliance/index_en.html (available 1 February 2016), and the Competition and Markets authority, in https://www.gov.uk/government/collections/cma-ca98-and-cartels-guidance (available 1 February 2016).

3. STRENGTHENING OF TENDERERS' RIGHTS, TRANSPARENCY AND COLLUSION: AN IMPOSSIBLE BALANCE?

In parallel to the formal revision of the EU rules contained in the current public procurement Directives, some traits of the procurement system have been the object of recent significant developments in the case law of the CJEU and the General Court (GC) of the European Union. One of such areas relates to the level of transparency that must be given to key decisions and documents in public tenders and, more specifically, to the degree of disclosure of (potentially) confidential information that is necessary to uphold the procedural rights granted to tenderers, particularly in view of their ability to effectively challenge award decisions.[43]

This is an issue that generates significant competition law concerns[44] that, in the author's opinion, have not been taken into proper consideration by the EU Courts[45] – and which the revision of the current rules is not aimed at correcting. Such concerns derive from the close implications that transparency has in terms of the likelihood of collusion and bid rigging. So far, the EU Courts have addressed the issue of transparency exclusively in the light of the need to prevent discriminatory practices and favouritism (or corruption, in a broad sense) and to effectively equip tenderers to raise successful challenges against procurement decisions where warranted; but the Courts have overlooked the need to balance such considerations with the prevention of collusion in public procurement procedures. As clearly indicated by the OECD:

> Strategies to address collusion and corruption in public procurement must address a fundamental tension: while transparency of the process is considered to be indispensible to corruption prevention, *excessive and unnecessary transparency in fact facilitates the formation and successful implementation of bid rigging cartels*. The extent to which transparency is a desirable aspect of a procurement process therefore depends on the circumstances, and may require trade-offs between best practice approaches to avoidance of collusion and corruption. (emphasis added)[46]

---

[43] See A. Sanchez Graells, 'The Difficult Balance between Transparency and Competition in Public Procurement: Some Recent Trends in the Case Law of the European Courts and a Look at the New Directives' (2013) *University of Leicester School of Law Research Paper No. 13-11*, available 1 February 2016 at http://ssrn.com/abstract=2353005.

[44] For discussion on the interrelation between transparency, competition, collusion and corruption from an economic perspective, see E.A. Podkolzina et al, 'Information Transparency in Public Procurement: How it Works in Russian Regions' (Higher School of Economics Research Paper No. WP BRP 01/EC/2011, 12 October 2011), available 1 February 2016 at http://ssrn.com/abstract=1998069.

[45] See Cases T-9/10, *Evropaïki Dynamiki v Commission (Microsoft SharePoint)* EU:T:2013:88; C-629/11 P, *Evropaïki Dynamiki v Commission (ESP-ISEP)* EU:C:2012:617; T-183/10, *Sviluppo Globale GEIE v Commission* EU:T:2012:534; T-667/11, *Veloss and Attimedia v Parliament* EU:T:2015:5; and the commentary in, e.g. A. Sanchez Graells, 'GC gets it totally wrong and pushes once more for excessive price transparency in public procurement (T-667/11)' *howtocrackanut*, 29 January 2015, available 1 February 2016 at http://howtocrackanut.com/blog/2015/01/gc-gets-it-totally-wrong-and-pushes.html.

[46] OECD, 'Competition and Procurement: Key Findings', above n 2, 19.

Despite this clear clash of goals between anti-corruption (or, more generally effective oversight) and anti-collusion measures, and probably inadvertently, the case-law of the EU Courts has created a set of rules on transparency that trigger competition concerns.[47] The legal basis for such transparency obligations ultimately rests in Article 41(2)(c) of Directive 2004/18 (and, from transposition, in Article 55(2)(c) of Directive 2014/24, which is identical) – and its twin provision in Article 100(2) of the Financial Regulation[48] – which require contracting authorities to inform any tenderer who has made an admissible tender, upon their request and as quickly as possible, of the characteristics and relative advantages of the tender selected as well as the name of the successful tenderer(s). Indeed, in their recent decisions interpreting this duty to disclose evaluation documentation to disappointed bidders in order to allow them to effectively challenge award decisions, the CJEU and the GC have reinforced very strict debriefing standards that require contracting authorities to provide substantial information concerning other tenderers' offers (notably, at least, the winning tenderer's) to all participating tenderers.

The EU Courts[49] have considered that this obligation is sufficiently discharged only when the contracting authority provides very detailed information about the tender evaluation process and, in particular, gives information that enables the disappointed tenderer to perform a relative comparison of its offer vis-à-vis the tender of the winning bidder – with the only limits that the contracting authority is not obliged to provide a full copy of the evaluation report,[50] nor a detailed comparative analysis of the successful tender and of the unsuccessful tender[51] (but, in principle, could do either of those things if the authority so wished). In particular, the CJEU has considered appropriate that the contracting authority (in that case, the European Commission) provided the disappointed tenderer with extracts of the evaluation report that 'contained tables relating, in particular, to the technical evaluation of the tenders … and indicating, for each award criterion, the number of points obtained by [the disappointed tenderer] in comparison with the successful tenderer, broken down each time into sub-criteria, as well as the maximum number of points attainable per sub-criterion and the weighting of each of those sub-criteria in the overall evaluation'.[52]

---

[47] The situation is comparable to that of most other OECD jurisdictions, since all of them have implemented very strict transparency requirements in their public procurement systems, most likely as an anticorruption device; OECD, *Transparency in public procurement* (Government at a Glance, 2011), available 1 February 2016 at http://dx.doi.org/10.1787/gov_glance-2011-47-en.

[48] Council Regulation (EC, Euratom) 1605/2002 of 25 June 2002 on the Financial Regulation applicable to the general budget of the European Communities (Financial Regulation) [2002] OJ L248/1.

[49] Case C-629/11, P *Evropaïki Dynamiki v European Commission (ESP-ISEP)* [2012] nyr; Case T-183/10 *Sviluppo Globale GEIE v Commission* [2012] nyr.

[50] Case C-561/10 P, *Evropaïki Dynamiki v European Commission (SEI-BUD/AMD/CR)* [2011] nyr para 25.

[51] Case C-235/11 P, *Evropaïki Dynamiki v European Commission (CITL/CR)* [2011] nyr paras. 50 and 51.

[52] Case C-629/11 P, *Evropaïki Dynamiki v European Commission (ESP-ISEP)* [2012] nyr para 26.

From the judgment, it is not only clear that the current practice is to debrief disappointed tenderers in full, but also that the current rules require the disclosure of certain information (of most relevance, the name of the winning bidder) that may create excessive transparency – as any tenderer is in a position to fully understand the content of the winning bid and, consequently, can take that (otherwise) confidential information into consideration in future tenders.

Moreover, contracting authorities are put under significant pressure to fully discharge their debriefing obligations, in view of the preponderance that they have been given in terms of due process rights:

> It is noteworthy in this regard that the right to good administration under Article 41 of the Charter of Fundamental Rights of the European Union (OJ 2007 C 303, p. 1) sets an obligation on the administration to justify its decisions and that this motivation is not only in general, the expression of the transparency of administrative action, but it must also allow the individual to decide, with full knowledge of the facts, if it is useful for her to apply to a court. There is therefore a close relationship between the obligation to state reasons and the fundamental right to effective judicial protection and the right to an effective remedy under Article 47 of the Charter of Fundamental Rights.[53]

In this situation, it is not difficult to see that contracting authorities will have a dangerous incentive to disclose very detailed and precise information 'of the characteristics and relative advantages of the tender selected as well as the name of the successful tenderer(s)'. And, consequently, there is a significant risk of strategic use of tender protest mechanisms in order to try to obtain confidential information or business secrets from competitors. Moreover, this generates *per se* a degree of transparency that makes collusion and bid rigging extremely easy to sustain and to keep concealed thanks to the use of the contracting authority itself as a communication mechanism between colluding tenderers.[54]

To be sure, Article 41(3) of Directive 2004/18[55] (from transposition, Article 55(3) of Directive 2014/24) and Article 100(2) of the Financial Regulation include an exception

---

[53] Case T-183/10, *Sviluppo Globale GEIE v Commission* [2012] nyr para 40 (own translation from French).

[54] See OECD, 'Procurement Markets' (1999) 1 *OECD Journal of Competition Law and Policy* 83, 85–7 and 92–5; B.D. Bernheim and M.D. Whinston, 'Multimarket Contact and Collusive Behavior' (1990) 21 *RAND Journal of Economics* 1; A. Skrzypacz and H. Hopenhayn, 'Tacit Collusion in Repeated Auctions' (2004) 114 *Journal of Economic Theory* 153; Albano et al, 'Preventing Collusion in Procurement' (n 40) 352–3; W.E. Kovacic et al, 'Bidding Rings and the Design of Anti–Collusive Measures for Auctions and Procurements' in N Dimitri et al (eds), *Handbook of Procurement* (Cambridge: Cambridge University Press, 2006) 381, 402; R.A. Miller, 'Economy, Efficiency and Effectiveness in Government Procurement' (1975–1976) 42 *Brooklyn Law Review* 208, 215–33; and J.M. Kuhlman, 'Price Fixing, Non-Price Competition and "Focal Point" Pricing: A Rose by Any Other Name?' (1978) 10 *Antitrust Law and Economics Review* 75.

[55] To be more precise, the applicability of Article 41(3) to Article 41(2) of Directive 2004/18 is controversial, as the literal tenor of the provision only mentions paragraph 1. However a systematic interpretation together with Article 6 of Directive 2004/18 on confidentiality would, in the author's opinion, support the possibility to withhold information also in the case of Article 41(2) of Directive 2004/18. In any case, in order to overcome these difficulties, Article 53(3) of

whereby contracting authorities can decide to withhold certain information where 'disclosure would hinder application of the law, would be contrary to the public interest or *would harm the legitimate business interests of public or private undertakings or could distort fair competition between those undertakings*' (emphasis added). This should be connected to the more general provision on the treatment of confidential information contained in Article 6 of Directive 2004/18 (and now in Article 21 of Directive 2014/24), which determines that 'in accordance with the national law to which the contracting authority is subject, the contracting authority shall not disclose information forwarded to it by economic operators which they have designated as confidential; such information includes, in particular, technical or trade secrets and the confidential aspects of tenders'.

As pointed out elsewhere, contracting authorities and review courts should be particularly careful in not imposing excessive disclosure when there are actual risks of strategic use of challenge procedures or the market structure is such that the increased degree of transparency could (inadvertently) facilitate or reinforce collusion.[56] In the author's view, therefore, in the exercise of such discretion and as a mandate of the principle of competition, contracting authorities are bound to restrict the disclosure of information given to tenderers to prevent instances of subsequent unfair competition or collusion – and, in order to do that properly, must identify and properly justify the negative effects which the withholding of the information seeks to avoid.

Along the same lines, and although there is no equivalent provision in Directive 89/665 and Directive 92/13 (both as amended by Directive 2007/66[57]), the same restrictions to the disclosure of information should apply in bid protests and review procedures, so that contracting authorities (in the case of mandatory reviews prior to challenges, or otherwise), independent review bodies and domestic courts are bound to prevent disclosures of information that could result in restrictions or distortions of competition. In such cases, limiting the access of information to the minimum extent required to ensure the effective protection of the rights of the applicants in review procedures will require a balancing of interests by the competent authority – which, in the author's view, should take into due consideration the potential impact on competition of the disclosure of certain information. Such an obligation can be stressed or reinforced by general rules on the treatment of business secrets and other commercially sensitive information of general application according to Member State domestic legislation, as clearly emphasized by Article 6 of Directive 2004/18 – which is due to

---

the October 2012 Compromise Text expressly extends the exception of paragraph 3 to paragraphs 1 and 2 of what currently is Article 41 of Directive 2004/18. This should be particularly welcome in view that Article 53(2) extends disclosure obligations and requires contracting authorities to inform 'any tenderer that has made an admissible tender of the conduct and progress of negotiations and dialogue with tenderers'. The application of Article 53(3) should leave without effect this extension of disclosure obligations in most of the cases since, on the contrary, the level of transparency would clearly be excessive in most instances and the protection of confidential information and business secrets would be severely diminished.

[56] Sanchez Graells, *Public Procurement and the EU Competition Rules* (n 1), 358–9.

[57] Directive 2007/66/EC of the European Parliament and of the Council of 11 December 2007 amending Council Directives 89/665/EEC and 92/13/EEC with regard to improving the effectiveness of review procedures concerning the award of public contracts [2007] OJ L335/31.

become slightly more complicated in view of the introduction of references to domestic legislation concerning access to information in Article 21 of Directive 2014/24.

In brief summary, this is an area where the strengthening of the rights of information (generally) and the mandatory disclosure of very detailed aspects of the winning tenders (including the name of the awardee of the public contract) needs to be counterbalanced by a careful exercise of administrative discretion by contracting authorities in order to avoid an excessive degree of transparency. In this regard, it would be desirable that both contracting authorities and review bodies and domestic courts bore in mind the anticompetitive consequences that excessive disclosure and transparency can create. Otherwise, the effectiveness of any other measures to prevent bid rigging in public procurement may remain substantially ineffective.

4. CENTRALIZATION AND THE CHANGING ROLE OF PUBLIC PROCUREMENT: A SLIPPERY SLOPE TOWARDS MARKET REGULATION

Moving on to the second area of concern in the evolution and revision of the EU public procurement system, it is worth stressing that, as the effects of the ongoing economic crisis continue to hit governments around the world and with particular intensity in Europe, strategic procurement in the form of centralized purchasing is receiving particular attention as a tool to mitigate the effects of budgetary reductions, especially at local authority level.[58] The potential benefits and drawbacks of centralized procurement are well known. On the positive side, the main arguments for centralized procurement are that it has the potential to offer better value for money (both in terms of price and quality) of procured supplies, services and works through increased purchasing power of the centralized agency, including through reduced government overheads; that it allows for an increased concentration of procurement expertise, better delivery of training and more focused performance management of procurement staff; and that it fosters greater standardization of technical requirements, procurement contracts and transactions, management controls and reporting to support greater transparency of government operations.[59] On the flip side, the main arguments for decentralized procurement are that it can reduce the scope for large scale corruption and mistakes through affecting large volume purchases that result in overspending (although it leaves room for petty corruption and common mistakes that are hard to monitor due to their dispersion, so the net effect remains unknown); that it allows for a closer matching of supplies, services and works delivered to the requirements of

[58] For a description of current trends of centralized procurement in the EU, see Commission Staff Working Document, *Annual Public Procurement Implementation Review 2012*, 25–26 [SWD(2012)342 final, 9 October 2012], available 1 February 2016 at http://ec.europa.eu/internal_market/publicprocurement/docs/implementation/20121011-staff-working-document_en.pdf.

[59] OECD, *Centralised and Decentralised Public Procurement* [CCNM/SIGMA/PUMA (2000)108, 25 October 2000], available 1 February 2016 at <http://unpan1.un.org/intradoc/groups/public/documents/NISPAcee/UNPAN006806.pdf.

end-users (both government agencies and citizens); and that it provides greater possibility for small and medium enterprises to successfully compete for government tenders.[60] However, this qualitative account of the standard arguments for and against centralization does not take into consideration the competition implications of centralized procurement strategies (and, remarkably, of the creation of centralized procurement bodies).

From a competition perspective, it is important to stress that centralized procurement strategies act as a magnifying glass and increase the potential distortions of market competition that are inherent to all public procurement systems.[61] This is due both to the fact that central purchasing bodies act as market makers rather than being 'pure' buyers (which adds a new dimension of 'market regulation' to the standard public procurement setting); and to the accumulation of buying power that derives from the centralization of demand.

4.1 Central Purchasing Bodies as Market Makers and Market Regulators

Indeed, a relatively new role of public buyers can be identified in the creation of central purchasing bodies.[62] These bodies or agencies are set-up as public sector intermediaries, since they are created with the main purpose of assuming tender functions on behalf of a relatively large number of public buyers – and, sometimes, are also assigned regulatory functions concerning the procurement of certain goods and services such as the drafting of general procurement policies.[63] Central purchasing bodies aggregate demand and tender (framework) contracts for certain types of goods and services (works are generally excluded) that will be later assigned or transferred to 'final' public buyers. In a way, central purchasing bodies could be considered as market-makers, since they create a *market platform* or *two-sided market* for the provision of goods and services to final public buyers.[64] The existence of such a platform can be legally reinforced by making acquisitions from the central body

---

[60] Ibid. For an economic assessment of the arguments for and against centralization, see N. Dimitri et al, 'When Should Procurement be Centralized?' in Dimitri *et al* (eds), *Handbook of Procurement* (n 40) 47.

[61] Sanchez Graells, *Public Procurement and the EU Competition Rules* (n 1), 54–5 and 292–9.

[62] Central agencies have existed for a relatively long time in the US and some EU Member States. However, their regulation as a matter of EU law is relatively recent; see P.A. Trepte, *Public Procurement in the EU: A Practitioner's Guide*, 2nd edn (Oxford: Oxford University Press, 2007) 127–9. The current situation as regards the existence of central purchasing bodies in the EU Member States has been described in OECD, *Centralised Purchasing Systems in the European Union* (Sigma Papers, No. 47, 29 April 2011), available 1 February 2016 at http://dx.doi.org/10.1787/5kgkgqv703xw-en.

[63] G.L. Albano et al, 'Regulating Joint Bidding in Procurement' (2009) 5 *Journal of Competition Law and Economics* 335, 350.

[64] In general, on the economics of two-sided markets and their competition implications, see M. Armstrong, 'Two-Sided Markets: Economic Theory and Policy Implications' in J.P. Choi (ed.), *Recent Developments in Antitrust. Theory and Evidence*, CESifo Seminar Series (Cambridge, MA: MIT Press, 2007) 39; J.C. Rochet and J. Tirole, 'Competition Policy in Two-Sided Markets, with a Special Emphasis on Payment Cards' in P. Buccirossi (ed.), *Handbook of*

mandatory for final public buyers – who would be prevented from acquiring those goods or services from the market, either in all circumstances, or when the conditions offered by undertakings in separate tenders are not more favourable than those offered by the central purchasing body.[65]

For analytical purposes, the market activities of these central purchasing agencies can be split into two. As regards *demand* of goods and services, their market behaviour does not depart significantly from the behaviour of final public buyers independently considered (that is, from the role of the public buyer as an agent); with the relevant exception that they accumulate buying power and, consequently, can generate and accumulate competitive effects of a larger magnitude. As was clearly indicated,

> There are a variety of ways in which public procurement could contribute to a restriction of competition between suppliers. For example, contracts may be aggregated to an extent where only a subset of competitors in the market can fulfil the requirements ... The main features of a situation in which there are possible restrictions on competition are: [a)] the public sector accounts for a significant proportion of demand within a sector; [b)] procurement is centralised/co-ordinated and buyer power is being exercised ...[66]

As far as the *offer* of those goods and services to final public buyers is concerned, the potential competitive effects will depend substantially on whether there is room for competition between the central agency and undertakings for the supply to final public buyers, or not. If competition is excluded and intermediation by the central body is legally mandated, there seems to be no or very limited scope for competitive analysis.[67] On the contrary, if competition is possible (for the supply of final public buyers or, even further, for the supply of any customers) 'standard' competition law mechanisms should apply to the central purchasing body as an undertaking – given that the development of a clearly economic 'downstream' activity consisting in the 'resale' of goods and services would exclude the difficulties for the direct application of competition law to this type of public buyers.[68] Moreover, in these cases, ensuring competitive neutrality and equality of opportunity for independent suppliers and the

---

Antitrust Economics (Cambridge, MA:MIT Press, 2008) 543; and D.S. Evans and R. Schmalensee, 'Markets with Two-Sided Platforms' in ABA, *Issues in Competition Law and Policy* (ABA Section of Antitrust Law, 2008) 667.

65 See L. Carpineti, 'Shall Public Entities Be Obliged or Free to Buy Through a Central Procurement Agency? Some Insights' in G. Piga and K.V. Thai (eds) *International Public Procurement Conference Proceedings – Enhancing Best Practices in Public Procurement* (2008) 77.

66 OFT/●econ, 'Assessing the Impact of Public Sector Procurement on Competition', above n 2, 25.

67 A different issue would be the analysis of the decision to reserve to the central purchasing agency the supply of those goods and services, which could be (i) considered a case of *in-house* provision and, hence, subject to the specific rules of the EU Directives and case-law on public to public provision; or, otherwise, (ii) considered the granting of an exclusive right, to be appraised under Article 106 TFEU and other State aid related provisions.

68 In this regard, Sanchez Graells, 'Distortions of Competition Generated by the Public (Power) Buyer: A Perceived Gap in EC Competition Law and Proposals to Bridge It' (n 32).

centralized purchasing body to win contracts tendered by any (decentralized) contracting authority will be of the utmost importance.

Furthermore, other concerns arise when these central purchasing bodies adopt market regulation functions, such as the standardization of technical specifications, the setting of 'catalogue or list' prices, the setting of 'standard' contractual or delivery conditions, or when they explicitly implement procurement strategies aimed at spreading work amongst contractors or otherwise diversify the supplier base.[69] In these cases, the role of the central purchasing agency changes from being a 'pure' public buyer (with significant demand power) towards becoming a planner or a market regulator, similar to those in the utilities sector.

Such a change of role generates significant competition issues, particularly in markets where the centralized procurement body accumulates a significant part of demand and, consequently, can change the competitive dynamics in the whole market (and not 'simply' in the public tranche of the market). This will be particularly problematic from a dynamic perspective if the central purchasing body's policies result in market exit by some suppliers (remarkably, those that cannot meet its requirements or that have otherwise been excluded from contracts and framework agreements concluded by the centralized agency; which are likely to be SMEs) or in an increase in production costs across the industry (such as those derived from complying with unnecessarily high standards, for instance, in terms of environmental or social protection, which are secondary policies generally favoured by centralized purchasing bodies). In these cases, the waterbed effects derived from the (quasi) regulatory activities of the centralized purchasing body can generate significant welfare losses.[70] And this is not irrelevant, particularly in view of the questionable legitimacy of centralized purchasing agencies to deploy market regulation functions (as well as the open question whether they have the actual legal empowerment and required expertise to do so).

4.2 Increased Leeway for the Aggregation of Buying Power through Centralization in Directive 2014/24

Despite the competition concerns that derive from the aggregation of market power and the assumption of a (quasi) regulatory role by some centralized procurement bodies, Directive 2014/24 is enthusiastic about the development of these and other centralized procurement strategies by the EU Member States and aims to provide a flexible framework. The underlying assumption from a competition perspective is that centralized procurement can promote competition: 'In view of the large volumes purchased, such techniques may help increase competition and should help to professionalise public purchasing' (Recital (69)). How exactly would demand aggregation result in

---

[69] C. Kennedy-Loest, 'Spreading Contract Work to Ensure Security of Supply and Maintain Competition: Issues under the EC Directives' (2007) 16 *Public Procurement Law Review* 116.

[70] For an account of waterbed effects and other sources of welfare losses derived from the exercise of (aggregated) buying power, see OECD, *Monopsony and Buyer Power* [DAF/COMP(2008)38, 17 December 2009], available 1 February 2016 at http://www.oecd.org/daf/competition/44445750.pdf.

increased competition is not explained and, in any case, remains an empirical question.[71] Indeed, as recently stressed, there is:

> significant savings potential attainable through purchasing centralisation [... but] centralization and all other developments associated with it may lead to the exclusion of SMEs from public supply chains, which can have wider supply market and thus e.g. pricing impacts. Specifically, if the market of suppliers capable of entering and winning public purchasing contracts becomes very concentrated as SMEs are left out, this can affect the pricing behaviour of the remaining suppliers competing for the products [sic]; i.e. they may not offer as big discounts as before if they are aware of the reduced competition. This may reduce the savings available in centralized contracts; public sector organisations thus need to account for the impact their actions may have on the supply market.[72]

Therefore, it seems clear to me that the benefits of procurement centralization should not be overstated and that these mechanisms and strategies should be subjected to particularly close monitoring in order to try to prevent competitive distortions and foreclosure effects. This is recognized in the preamble of Directive 2014/24: 'the aggregation and centralisation of purchases should be carefully monitored in order to avoid excessive concentration of purchasing power and collusion, and to preserve transparency and competition, as well as market access opportunities for small and medium-sized enterprises' (Recital (59)). However, the rules of the proposed new Directive remain silent on monitoring of centralized procurement (due to the deletion of Article 84 of the 2011 Proposal, which expressly set up public oversight devices) and is restricted to the much more general and likely less effective means of enforcement supervision foreseen in Article 83. The rules in Directive 2014/24 are clearly insufficient to regulate centralized purchasing activities and central purchasing bodies, since they are limited to enabling Member States to develop these procurement strategies as they see fit – and are solely concerned with the allocation of responsibility (and, arguable, liability) for compliance with EU public procurement rules.

This is an unsatisfactory situation, since the Directives may have (should have) provided some further guidance to Member States on the limits and balances necessary to ensure that centralized procurement – with its likelihood of waterbed or knock-on effects and its trend towards the development of (quasi) regulatory functions – does not create distortions of competition. At least, the standard caveat that Member States shall refrain from using centralized procurement strategies when they can restrict or distort competition should be introduced.

Moreover, Directive 2014/24 requires that all centralized procurement is conducted electronically (Article 37(3)). Indeed, as stressed in Recital (72):

---

[71] For a critical assessment, see Sanchez Graells and Herrera Anchustegui (n 14) *in totum*. See also I. Herrera Anchustegui, 'Centralizing public procurement and competitiveness in Directive 2014/24' (2015) *European Law Reporter*, forthcoming.

[72] K. Karjalainen, 'Challenges of Purchasing Centralisation – Empirical Evidence from Public Procurement' 46 (PhD Dissertation, Helsinki School of Economics, Acta Universitatis Oeconomicae Helsingiensis, 2009), available 1 February 2016 at http://epub.lib.aalto.fi/pdf/diss/a344.pdf; see also K. Serpytis et al, 'Evaluation of Financial Effects of Procurement Centralisation' (2011) 90(3) *Ekonomika* 104.

> Electronic means of communication are particularly well suited to supporting centralised purchasing practices and tools because of the possibility they offer to re-use and automatically process data and to minimise information and transaction costs. The use of such electronic means of communication should therefore, as a first step, be rendered compulsory for central purchasing bodies, while also facilitating converging practices across the Union. This should be followed by a general obligation to use electronic means of communication in all procurement procedures after a transition period of 30 months.

This links some of the potential advantages and problems derived from centralized procurement to those arising from the current push for the generalization of eProcurement, which is explored in the following section. Moreover, the use of centralized procurement as a 'pilot' experience towards the extension of eProcurement across the EU may prove inaccurate, given the specificities of centralized procurement and the higher incentives for all parties involved.

5. THE CHALLENGES OF ePROCUREMENT: A VIABLE CURE FOR ALL DISEASES?

Given its expected advantages in the reduction of administrative costs, the promotion of generalized use of eProcurement has ranked highly on procurement reform agendas in the EU since the previous revision of the EU Directives almost ten years ago. Currently, the push for eProcurement is seen as a main lever to achieve increased efficiency of the procurement system[73] and to promote enhanced access to procurement by SMEs, as well as a device to promote competition[74] and to allow for a better monitoring of potential competition restrictions and, particularly, of bid rigging. Indeed, this is one of the key specific OECD recommendations to fight bid rigging in public procurement:

> Strengthen efforts to fight collusion and enhance competition in public tenders by encouraging procurement agencies to use electronic bidding systems, which may be accessible to a broader group of bidders and less expensive, and to store information about public procurement opportunities in order to allow appropriate analysis of bidding behaviour and of bid data.[75]

---

[73] The *Digital Agenda for Europe* [COM(2010)245] and the *eGovernment Action Plan 2011–2015* [COM(2010) 743] highlight the importance of connecting eProcurement capacities across the Single Market. Moreover, eProcurement actions have been included in the Single Market Act I [COM(2011)206 final, which only focuses on procurement simplification] and the Single Market Act II [COM(2012) 573 final, 3 October 2012, which aims to make electronic invoicing the standard invoicing mode for public procurement].

[74] B.K.O. Tas and A. Genis-Gruber, 'E-Procurement Savings and the Competition Effect: Analysis of Cultural Differences Through a Unified Model' (TOBB University, Dept. of Economics, Working Paper 08-15, November 2008), available 1 February 2016 at https://ideas.repec.org/a/igg/jeco00/v9y2011i3p20-38.html.

[75] OECD, *Recommendation on Fighting Bid Rigging in Public Procurement* (n 18), I.2.5.

Directive 2014/24 contains several provisions oriented towards an enhanced (and mandatory in the near future) use of electronic means of communication (Article 22) and other eProcurement tools, such as electronic auctions (Article 35) and the use of electronic catalogues (Article 36). Indeed, the objective was to make eProcurement mandatory by mid-2016 at the latest,[76] but this has now been delayed until mid-2018 (that is, after a transition period of 30 months from approval of the Directive; Article 90). However, the feasibility of this objective can be doubted, given that it basically implies a full transformation of the way public procurement is currently conducted in the EU. As indicated very recently, 'Use of e-procurement has increased to some extent since publication of the 2004 Action Plan. Nevertheless, in aggregate terms, e-procurement is still used in only 5 to 10% of procurement procedures carried out across the EU and the ambitious political targets set out in the Manchester Ministerial Declaration in 2005 have not yet been achieved'.[77]

Therefore, for most Member States (and particularly at levels other than central government), the exclusive conduct of eProcurement requires a complete reform of their procedures and, most likely, a very heavy level of investment in equipment and training. Such a drastic movement towards full eProcurement in the near future raises some competition concerns at different levels. At a systemic level, and taking into consideration that the ICT sector is one of those that are generating more complicated competition issues (not least, due to the complexities of coordination of IP law and competition law, the peculiarities of standardization and technological pooling, the effects of network and two-sided industries, and so on), the creation of the required eProcurement infrastructure appears as potentially problematic. On the one hand, only a limited number of players can develop and implement solutions that would support a State-wide 'electronic reform' of the public procurement system – probably as a result of a competitive dialogue or some other form of innovative procurement for the development of the ICT tools and the supply of the massive amounts of equipment that may be required. This in itself should raise warning flags against the conduct of aggregated projects for the move towards eProcurement of the whole of the public administration of any given Member State at once – given that they can result in a limited amount of effective competition, winner's curse problems and lock in threats. On the other hand, if a fragmented approach is undertaken, there may be significant issues of interoperability and compatibility of the system and of lack of uniformity that, in the end, fails to reduce (electronic) administrative costs as expected. Moreover, the required investment to have a fully-functioning eProcurement system in less than three years may be an unbearable financial burden for some Member States which are facing significant financial pressures and the need to reduce public expenditures. In that regard, prioritizing investments on the infrastructure and expertise required to conduct eProcurement may prove difficult if it comes at the cost of further cuts in social

---

[76] Communication from the Commission, *A strategy for e-procurement* [COM(2012)179 final, 20 April 2012], available 1 February 2016 at http://eur-lex.europa.eu/legal-content/EN/ALL/?uri=CELEX:52012DC0179.

[77] Commission Working Document, *Annual Public Procurement Implementation Review 2012* (n 58), 22.

policies more directly felt by the citizens. Lack of political commitment (or feasibility) may, consequently, be an important hurdle in the road towards full eProcurement.

In the view of the Commission:

> [the] proposals [in the 2012 eProcurement Strategy and the 2011 Proposal for a new Directive on public procurement] encourage inter-operability between e-procurement systems and contain provisions designed to ensure that suppliers encounter no technical barriers when bidding on different systems. To this end, [the Commission is] empower[ed] to adopt delegated acts in a number of specific areas to render mandatory the use of specific technical standards. These could draw on work carried out in the relevant standardisation bodies and on recommendations issued by the e-Tendering Expert Group.[78]

However, it remains to be seen to what extent the Commission is able to dispel the foreseeable difficulties and competition restrictions from a major migration towards eProcurement in a relatively limited timeframe. It seems advisable to involve the Directorate General for Competition in the process, so that the competitive effects of any 'technical' decisions are properly assessed (particularly in terms of standardization and mandatory use of devices).

At a different, more operational level, and regarding the routine conduct of eProcurement, it is important to stress that from a competition perspective one of the main advantages of eProcurement to fight collusion does not rest on the mechanics of the system, but on the use of the data that eProcurement can easily produce. In that regard, monitoring of procurement activities under the very general and vague mechanisms foreseen in Article 83(2) of Directive 2014/24 may be insufficient, despite the requirement that 'Member States shall ensure that the application of public procurement rules is monitored'. More guidance is needed and, more specifically, it seems desirable to involve the national competition authorities in the oversight of public procurement activities, to screen and monitor both potential instances of bid rigging and potential sources of public restrictions of competition in tender procedures. In this regard, a more ambitious proposal to link the public oversight of public procurement to competition law enforcement would be preferable.

Indeed, as already submitted elsewhere, the granting of certain oversight powers to competition authorities would be highly desirable;[79] which would reinforce the institutional framework for a more competition-oriented public procurement system.[80] This development is not foreign to the systems of some Member States and their experiences seem to offer solid grounds for the extension of this institutional arrangement to other Member States. In this regard, it is important to stress that some Member States have integrated their competition authorities and central public procurement authorities entrusted with oversight responsibilities, or (almost identically) have granted

[78] Commission, *A strategy for e-procurement* (n 76), 6.

[79] Sanchez Graells, *Public Procurement and the EU Competition Rules* (n 1), 388–9.

[80] Along these lines, it has been proposed that such bid protest functions be attributed to competition authorities as independent agencies; see J. Berasategi, 'La integración de la contratación pública en la defensa de la competencia' (2007) 247 *Gaceta jurídica de la UE y de la competencia* 35, 39–40; 'El control administrativo independiente de la contratación pública' (2007) 6650 *Diario La Ley* 1. These proposals were discussed in the recent reform of Spanish public procurement law, but were not adopted.

oversight competences in public procurement matters to their national competition authorities – which become public procurement tribunals or bid protest bodies. This is currently the case, at least, in Germany, Sweden, Denmark, and the Czech Republic[81] – and it used to be the case in Finland until 2002 (when a Market Court took over the handling of public procurement issues).[82]

However, a full integration of competition and public procurement (oversight) authorities in all cases would not be desirable in those instances in which competition elements are not relevant to the substance of the case – which can be based on issues of pure administrative law or in due process considerations. In this regard, the assignment of competences for the review of all public procurement cases by the competition authority could result in submitting some cases to the consideration of an authority that might lack the required expertise (at least, in the initial phases), and could drain significant resources that the competition authority could use more efficiently in the development of other tasks. Therefore, an intermediate model seems preferable, where competition authorities should file guidance opinions (preferably, of a binding character) in bid protest procedures to be decided by specialized public procurement oversight authorities or by the courts (that is, an *amicus curiae*-like device). Alternatively, a system of case assignment between both bodies (competition and general public procurement oversight authorities, or the courts) could be implemented, so that competition authorities were competent only in cases where competition-related issues were preponderant. Be it as it may, this issue seems to remain fully within Member States' competences and the adoption of a uniform solution at EU level seems problematic. Nonetheless, the suggested developments seem worth considering, particularly in view of the opportunity created by the need to transpose the new EU Directive on public procurement.

6. CONCLUSIONS: A CLEAR NEED TO BOOST OVERSIGHT AND PROFESSIONALIZATION

This chapter has discussed certain competition implications in the main areas of recent development and reform of EU public procurement rules. Some of them are clearly oriented towards the promotion of competition by means of a reduction of the likelihood of anticompetitive practices – namely, the introduction of tools to effectively address instances of bid rigging by means of disqualification of the offending tenderers, as well as the increased flexibility conferred upon contracting authorities, which can be used to follow the OECD's 2012 Recommendation on fighting bid rigging in public

---

[81] Commission Working Document, *Annual Public Procurement Implementation Review 2012* (n 58), 20.

[82] Each national system presents its peculiarities, but they share basic institutional arrangements in that the competition authority is entrusted with the general oversight of public procurement activities and decides bid protest procedures. For additional details, see Public Procurement Network, *The Comparative Survey of the National Public Procurement Systems Across the PPN* (2010), available 1 February 2016 at http://www.ppneurope.org/docs/Italian Presidency/Comparative%20survey%20on%20PP%20systems%20across%20PPN.pdf.

procurement. As has been discussed, the measures introduced in Directive 2014/24 for the reform of the previous EU public procurement Directives are a step in the right direction, but may fall short of fully achieving their final goals unless some additional devices are created – particularly, a full-fledged suspension and debarment system administered by or with the active engagement of national competition authorities.

Other developments may, however, inadvertently run against the objective of promoting undistorted competition in the public procurement setting (particularly, the ever increasing degree of transparency and disclosure of information imposed as a consequence of the strengthening of the procedural rights of disappointed tenderers and of general legislation on access to information); or may create significant risks of anticompetitive distortions derived from public procurement rules and the ensuing administrative practices, as is particularly the case of centralized public procurement (which is becoming a common tool of aggregation of buying power and, increasingly, an instrument of disguised or indirect market regulation) and the foreseen generalization of eProcurement within a short time framework. In all these instances, it may seem that the EU legislator and the EU Courts are not fully aware of the potentially negative implications of certain rules and requirements embedded in the EU public procurement system or that, when they are aware of them, fail to propose the required oversight mechanisms – and, consequently, some further reforms may be necessary to make the system truly procompetitive.

Most of the shortcomings of the system derive from an insufficiency of the current devices for the monitoring and oversight of public procurement activities. This sometimes results in (or complements a pre-existing) excessive degree of transparency and an insufficient involvement of competition authorities. Given the strong interrelation between competition and procurement, such a gap in the institutional architecture for the enforcement of public procurement (and competition) law is highly relevant. And it will become even more acute in the future, in view of the increasing use of public procurement as a tool of economic and market regulation, as well as the immediate challenges raised by the extension of both centralized procurement and eProcurement. Failure to develop a more effective system of joint enforcement of public procurement and competition rules can result in a significant reduction of social welfare, both as a failure to effectively tackle the pervasive problem of bid rigging and as a result of the further losses that an abuse of public buying power can generate (coupled with the exponential complications derived from the migration towards a fully virtual scenario of eProcurement). These observations are not intended to cast a gloomy shadow on the development of public procurement, but simply to prompt an effective regulatory response to the challenges that need to be overcome in order to keep competitive markets where public procurement activities take place.

The best approach to do so is to fully integrate public procurement within the sphere of activities of competition authorities. First, to ensure a more expedient and consistent enforcement against bid riggers and to benefit from the expertise these authorities already have on the fight against cartels in this and other areas of economic activity. Secondly, in order to promote a system of effective oversight of the activities of contracting authorities in this important field of the economy. Such submission of contracting authorities to the oversight of competition authorities may add a significant check on their activities (together with any pre-existing audit or other type of budgetary or legal compliance control of public procurement) and could allow for a significant redesign of bid protest mechanisms – allowing, for instance, for a major reduction of the information disclosed publicly and the creation of (semi)opaque review mechanisms whereby disappointed tenderers could prompt the intervention of the competition authority without, however, having direct access to the information in the public procurement file. In turn, this could be subjected to new forms of judicial review before specialized courts – in a setting where, still, disclosure of information remained significantly restricted in order to minimize transparency in these markets. Finally, the involvement of competition authorities in terms of advocacy could also prove significant and beneficial, particularly if competition authorities developed useful guidance concerning both centralized procurement and eProcurement.

Obviously, the reform of the oversight and bid protest system and the involvement of competition authorities would be no panacea to all sources of competition distortions in public procurement. There would still be need for training and professionalization of officials entrusted with public procurement responsibilities, who would remain the principal agents in the implementations of the OECD's and other sets of recommendations to keep public procurement procompetitive and who would be in charge of exercising sound administrative discretion on a daily basis. Therefore, additional efforts in terms of professionalization and training should be undertaken. The same applies to judges involved in the review of public procurement cases, particularly in intermediate review courts, which would benefit from training and sensitization regarding the competition implications of public procurement activities.

Therefore, the most significant area where reforms are needed concerns the enforcement structure of public procurement (and competition) law, both at the administrative and judicial level. If those changes are implemented, they will have an immediate positive effect on the improvement of day-to-day decisions due to a better informed and guided exercise of administrative discretion. Then, it will be easier to correct any specific rigidities or competition distortive rules in the public procurement Directives or in national legislations. Nonetheless, most sources of competition distortions derive from the interpretation and application of a set of rules that, as such, are not necessarily distortive (with the evident exception of rules imposing very demanding minimum levels of transparency). Consequently, changes in the enforcement devices and better competition related training for all those involved in public procurement would already make a significant contribution to the development of a more competition-oriented public procurement system.

15. Public procurement and State aid

Mihalis Kekelekis and Kine Neslein[*]

1. INTRODUCTION AND PURPOSE OF PUBLIC PROCUREMENT RULES AND STATE AID RULES

Public procurement, as well as State aid, constitutes instruments, which are traditionally used by Member States to define or direct their economic policies. Article 3 of the Treaty of the European Union stresses the need for the European Union (EU) to establish an internal market. In order for the internal market to function, Articles 3 and 4 of the Treaty of the Functioning of the European Union (TFEU) provides the EU and the Member States with competence to establish the necessary rules.

The public procurement rules aim to prevent the foreclosure of the internal market. If left unregulated, Member States are likely to favour national undertakings. Hence, the award of public contracts by public authorities in the Member States is subject to the principles of equal treatment, non-discrimination, transparency and proportionality. The public procurement rules open the market for public contracts to competition and ensure compliance with basic EU law principles.

The State aid rules on the other hand aim to prevent trade between Member States from being affected by advantages granted by public authorities. The purpose of State aid regulation is therefore to avoid distortions of the competition on the market by States granting subsidies and other financial advantages to undertakings. Such State measures can distort intra-EU competition both by excluding foreign competitors, as well as by attracting foreign competitors to a particular market or region. State aid can also have the effect of creating subsidy races between Member States.

Whereas a purpose of the public procurement rules, in addition to the maintenance of the internal market, is ensuring public purchases of the best quality and value for money, State aid rules make sure that the granting of unnecessary aid is avoided. At the core of this correlation we find the 'market economy investor principle', according to which a private operator would not pay a price above current or foreseeable rates in the market.

The fundamental principles of the public procurement rules are secured by the obligation on public contracting authorities, to use specified procedures when carrying out their procurements. Public procurement legislation is also aimed at stimulation,

* Mihalis Kekelekis is a Senior Officer at the Competition & State Aid Directorate of the EFTA Surveillance Authority. Kine Neslein is a Senior Associate at Wikborg Rein Advokatfirma DA in Oslo. The views expressed in this chapter are strictly personal and do not whatsoever reflect the official position of the Authority or Wikborg Rein Advokatfirma. We are grateful to comments received in earlier drafts by Per-Andreas Bjørgan, Phedon Nicolaides and Christian Jordal.

innovation and sustainable development, as well as playing the role of an anti-corruption tool.

The State aid rules, on the other hand, lay down the obligation of Member States to abstain from granting aid. In some circumstances, however, government interventions are seen as necessary for a well-functioning and equitable economy. The TFEU, complemented by a series of legislative acts, therefore provides for a number of exemptions. These rules are monitored by the European Commission, *inter alia*, through the obligation of Member States to notify planned State aid and obtain the Commission's prior permission to grant it.

The European Commission's ('Commission') Green Paper on the modernisation of EU public procurement policy makes it clear that 'the review may present certain opportunities to increase convergence between the application of the EU public procurement and State aid rules'.[1] In view of this anticipated convergence, this chapter presents an overview of both the public procurements and State aid rules, and discusses their interplay.

2. OVERVIEW OF PUBLIC PROCUREMENT LEGISLATION IN THE EU

2.1 The Public Sector and the Utilities Directives

The term 'public procurement' is not defined in the TFEU. The term, however, covers the purchasing of goods and services, and the ordering of works on behalf of a public authority or their dependent bodies. The legal basis in primary EU law are the principles of the TFEU, namely the free movement of goods[2] and capital,[3] the freedom to provide services[4] and the freedom of establishment.[5] Further, public procurement is subject to the fundamental principles deriving from the provisions of the TFEU, such as the principles of equal treatment, non-discrimination, mutual recognition, proportionality and transparency.

In secondary EU law, public procurement is regulated by the procurement directives: the 'classic' or 'public sector' directive (Directive 2014/24/EU on the coordination of procedures for the award of public works contracts, public supply contracts and public service contracts[6] and amendments) and the utilities directive (Directive 2014/25/EU coordinating the procurement procedures of entities operating in the water, energy,

---

[1] European Commission's Green Paper on the modernisation of EU public procurement policy – Towards a more efficient European Procurement Market, COM (2011) 15 final, p. 5.

[2] Article 28 et seq.

[3] Article 63 et seq.

[4] Article 56 et seq.

[5] Article 49 et seq.

[6] Directive 2014/24/EU of the European Parliament and of the Council of 26 February 2014 on public procurement and repealing Directive 2004/18/EC, [2014] OJ 94/65.

transport and postal services sectors,[7] and amendments).[8] The latter entities are not necessarily public authorities, some may be private companies. However, it was felt to be necessary to include them in the procurement regime of the EU in order to open up the European markets and prevent the favouring of national industry.[9]

The procurement directives apply to contracts 'for pecuniary interest concluded in writing … having as their object the execution of works, the supply of products or the provision of services',[10] which are not explicitly excluded in accordance with exceptions provided for in the procurement directives,[11] and which exceed certain financial thresholds. The thresholds are laid down in yearly amendment directives.[12]

In any case, the European Court of Justice ('the Court') has confirmed in its case-law that the internal market rules of the Treaty apply also to contracts outside the scope of the procurement directives, as long as the contract is of interest to economic operators located in other Member States.[13]

2.2 Short Overview of Rules Applicable to Public Contracts under the Procurement Directives

When awarding contracts comprised by the Public Sector or Utilities Directives, contracting authorities must use as award criteria the lowest price or the most economically advantageous tender and life cycle costing. In the latter case various additional criteria linked to the subject matter of the contract in question can be used, such as quality, price, technical merit, aesthetic and functional characteristics, environmental characteristics, and so on. The contracting authority shall specify the relative weighting of these criteria.

The characteristics of the goods, services or works are further defined by the technical specifications which ensure that they fulfil their intended use. The qualification criteria, on the other hand, are conditions that may be required for the participation in a public procurement. These intend to ensure the suitability of bidders by requiring,

[7] Directive 2014/25/EU of the European Parliament and of the Council of 26 February 2014 on procurement by entities operating in the water, energy, transport and postal services sectors and repealing Directive 2004/17/EC, [2014] OJ 94/243.

[8] Throughout the text the term 'procurement directives' will be used, save as otherwise provided herein.

[9] S. Arrowsmith, *The Law of Public and Utilities Procurement*, 2nd edn. (London: Sweet & Maxwell, 2005), p. 1.

[10] Article 1(2)(a) of the Public Sector Directive and of the Utilities Directive.

[11] Chapter II, section 3 to the Public Sector Directive, and Title II, Chapter II, Section 2 of the Utilities Directive.

[12] For 2015 see Commission Delegated Regulations (EU) 2015/2170 and 2015/2171 of 24 November 2015 in respect of the application thresholds for the procedures for the award of contracts.

[13] See for example Cases C-324/98, *Telaustria* [2000] ECR I-10745 para 60; C-231/03, *Coname* [2005] ECR I-07287 para 16, and C-458/03, *Parking Brixen* [2005] ECR I-8585 para 46. See also the Commission Interpretative Communication on the Community law applicable to contract awards not or not fully subject to the provisions of the Public Procurement Directives, [2006] OJ C179/2.

inter alia, a certain economic and financial capacity and certain technical abilities.

When carrying out a procurement process of contracts subject to the procurement directives, contracting authorities are also obliged to follow rules on information and transparency. They must, with some exceptions, publish information notices drawn up in accordance with standard Commission forms, and shall provide information on decisions taken concerning the award of a contract.

Furthermore, the contracting authority must use one of the prescribed procurement procedures:

- the open procedure – any interested economic operator may submit a tender;
- the restricted procedure – any economic operator may ask to participate in the procedure but only invited bidders may submit a tender;
- the competitive procedure with negotiation – economic operators are chosen and contacted by the contracting authority, and the terms of the contract are then negotiated between the parties; or
- the competitive dialogue, which is only available for contracts comprised by the Public Sector Directive – can be used for complex contracts if the contracting authority is unable to define the technical solutions to satisfy its needs, or is not able to specify the legal and/or financial make-up of a project.
- the innovation partnership.

Specific procedures apply to service design contests and works concessions (the latter is only covered by the Public Service Directive).

The directives impose timelines for the different stages of the procurement process (receipt of request to participate, receipt of bids, invitations to negotiate and so on) that are specific to each type of procedure.

In certain exceptional cases, and under conditions prescribed by the procurement directives, contracting authorities may award a contract without prior call for competition.[14]

2.3 The Remedies Directive

In addition, the remedies directives[15] coordinate the systems of national review procedures that businesses can use when they consider that a public authority has

[14] See Summaries of EU legislation:

Public works contracts, public supply contracts and public service contracts, available 2 February 2016 at http://europa.eu/legislation_summaries/internal_market/businesses/public_procurement/l22009_en.htm. Public procurement in the water, energy, transport and postal services sector, available 2 February 2016 at http://europa.eu/legislation_summaries/internal_market/businesses/public_procurement/l22010_en.htm.

[15] Council Directive 89/665/EEC of 21 December 1989 on the coordination of the laws, regulations and administrative provisions relating to the application of review procedures to the award of public supply and public works contracts, [1989] OJ L395/33 and Council Directive 92/13/EEC of 25 February 1992 coordinating the laws, regulations and administrative provisions relating to the application of Community rules on the procurement procedures of entities operating in the water, energy, transport and telecommunications sectors [1992] OJ L76/14.

awarded a contract unfairly.[16] The remedies directives were substantially amended by Directive 2007/66/EC.[17] The amendment directive was published at the end of 2007, and had to be implemented into national laws by the end of 2009. The amendment directive introduced new features to improve the means of redress available to bidders. The main features being:

- a 'standstill period' obliging contracting authorities to wait for at least ten days after the award of the contract before it can be signed.[18] This gives bidders time for effective review of the contract award decision and decide whether to initiate a review procedure. If this is done within the standstill period, the procurement process is 'automatically suspended' until the review body takes a decision on the compatibility of the procedure;[19]
- stricter rules against illegal direct awards of public contracts. The national review body is able to consider contracts ineffective in case of breach of the above mentioned rules or if they have been illegally awarded without transparency and prior competitive tendering.[20]

2.4 Reform Process

A revision of the procurement directives was announced in December 2011.[21] The Commission has issued proposals for revised directives with the aim of modernising European rules on public tendering, through the following main objectives:

- to simplify and provide more flexible rules, in particular through the increased use of negotiations and electronic communications, as well as to decrease administrative burden;
- to encourage access to public procurement for SMEs, *inter alia*, by reducing the evidentiary requirements for bidding;

---

16 See the Commission information page on the Remedies Directives, available 2 February 2016 at http://ec.europa.eu/growth/single-market/public-procurement/rules-implementation/remedies-directives/index_en.htm.

17 Directive 2007/66/EC of the European Parliament and of the Council of 11 December 2007 amending Council Directives 89/665/EEC and 92/13/EEC with regard to improving the effectiveness of review procedures concerning the award of public contracts, [2007] OJ L335/31.

18 Article 2a(2) of Directives 89/665 and 92/13.

19 Article 1(5) and 2(3) of Directives 89/665 and 92/13.

20 Article 2d of Directives 89/665 and 92/13.

21 Proposal for a Directive of The European Parliament and of the Council on public procurement COM(2011) 896 final and Proposal for a Directive of The European Parliament and of the Council on procurement by entities operating in the water, energy, transport and postal services sectors, COM(2011) 895 final. See also the Commission Staff Working Paper, Impact Assessment Accompanying the document Proposal for a Directive of the European Parliament and of the Council on Public Procurement and the Proposal for a Directive of the European Parliament and of the Council on procurement by entities operating in the water, energy, transport and postal sectors, SEC(2011) 1585 final. See also the Commission press release on the reform procedure, available 2 February 2016 at http://europa.eu/rapid/press-release_IP-11-1580_en.htm?locale=en.

- to improve the quality of public procurement by way of increased room for considering social and environmental criteria, and, through this, to contribute to the achievement of the EU 2020 Strategy.
- to improve the prevention of corruption by creating a culture of integrity and fair play.

The reform process also comprises a new directive on service concessions.[22] Service concessions were before the reform exempted from the scope of the public sector directive, and have therefore, until now, only partially been regulated by EU law. The proposed directive covers partnership agreements between a body that is generally public, and a business, that is often private. The latter takes on the operative risk linked to maintenance and development of infrastructure or the supply of services of general economic interest (SGEI). For example, the payment for the provision of services may lie entirely in the ticket fares charged to users of public transportation, without any payment from the public body itself. The scope of the remedies directive has also been extended to apply to service concessions.

The European Parliament's Committee on Internal Market and Consumer Protection (IMCO) voted on the proposals for all three Directives in December 2012 and January 2013. In February 2013 a decision was taken to start first reading negotiations with the Council. The plenary vote in the European Parliament for the whole revision package is currently foreseen for the autumn of 2013.

2.5 General Context of Public Procurement Rules

2.5.1 Performance of tasks directly by a public authority

The public procurement rules do not apply if a public authority decides to provide services itself.

As the Court states in *Stadt Halle*:

> A public authority which is a contracting authority has the possibility of performing the tasks conferred on it in the public interest by using its own administrative, technical and other resources, without being obliged to call on outside entities not forming part of its own departments. In such a case, there can be no question of a contract for pecuniary interest concluded with an entity legally distinct from the contracting authority. There is therefore no need to apply the Community rules in the field of public procurement.[23]

2.5.2 Performance of tasks by an in-house operator

The award of a contract directly to an in-house operator constitutes as well a derogation from the application of the public procurement rules.

---

22 Directive 2014/23/EC. See also the Commission Staff Working Document, Impact Assessment of an initiative on concessions. Accompanying the document Proposal for a Directive of the European Parliament and of the Council on the award of concession contracts, SEC(2011) 1588 final.

23 Case C-26/03, *Stadt Halle and RPL Recyclingpark Lochau GmbH v Arbeitsgemeinschaft Thermische Restabfall- und Energieverwertungsanlage TREA Leuna* [2005] ECR I-1, para 48.

The notion of 'in-house operator' was defined in the *Teckal* case,[24] where the Court was asked to rule on the applicability of EU procurement law to a direct award of a contract for the management of heating services to several municipality buildings of a consortium of 45 municipalities, including the contracting authority itself. The Court defined the 'in-house operator' as a distinct entity (thus having a distinct legal personality) over which the person concerned is exercising a control similar to that which is exercised over its own departments. In addition, the person must carry out the essential part of its activities with the controlling local authority or authorities.

As regards the 'control', in *Stadt Halle* the Court stated that a semi-public company does not fulfil the *Teckal* criteria because first:

> … any private capital investment in an undertaking, on the other hand, follows considerations proper to private interests and pursues objectives of a different kind (than public entities).[25]

It followed:

> Second, the award of a public contract to a semi-public company without calling for tenders would interfere with the objective of free and undistorted competition and the principle of equal treatment of the persons concerned, referred to in Directive 92/50, in particular in that such a procedure would offer a private undertaking with a capital presence in that undertaking an advantage over its competitors.[26]

The *Coname* case brought further elements as regards the notion of shared control by more public authorities over an entity. The Court was asked to decide on the direct award of a concession to a company whose share capital is predominantly public (held by the province and almost all the municipalities in that province) and in which the awarding authority only holds a 0.97 per cent share in the capital. The Court pointed out that a share of 0.97 per cent is too small to permit any control.[27]

---

[24] Case C-107/98, *Teckal Srl v Comune di Viano and Azienda Gas-Acqua Consorziale (AGAC)* [1999] ECR I-8121.

[25] Paragraph 50. See also Case C-573/07, *Sea Srl v Comune di Ponte Nossa* [2009] ECR I-8127, where the Court confirmed that private participation excludes public control and added that the mere fact that shares in the contractor could be sold to private investors is not in itself important unless, at the time of contract award, there exists a real prospect in the short term of such a sale.

[26] Paragraph 51.

[27] Case C-231/03, *Consorzio Aziende Metano (Corame) v Comune di Cingia de' Botti* [2005] ECR I-7287. See the recently adopted judgement in Joined Cases C-182/11 and 183/11, *Econord SpA v Comune di Cagno, Comune di Varese and Comune di Solbiate* (not yet reported), where the Court held that the requirement for joint control by the participating authorities over an entity is fulfilled, where each of those authorities not only holds capital in the entity, but also plays a role in its managing bodies. See also Case C-324/07 *Coditel Brabant* [2008] ECR I-8457 and C-295/05 *Asemfo v Tragsa* [2007] ECR I-2999, on the notion of joint control. The *Hamburg* case (C-480/06) also establishes that certain other co-operative arrangements that do not involve an entity subject to the control, or joint control of the contracting authority, can be concluded outside the scope of the directives. This is referred to as so-called "horizontal co-operation".

In *Carbotermo*[28] the Court further considered the meaning of the notion of 'essential part of the activities with the controlling authority' under the Directive 93/38 (now Directive 2014/25/EU) and the application of the 80 per cent rule and whether this notion can be derived by analogy there from,[29] as some legal scholars have suggested.[30] The answer to this question was negative. The Court stated that, as the EU legislator did not choose to incorporate an analogous exception in the public sector directive, there is no legal basis for extending the definition to this field.[31]

Furthermore, the Court had to decide if the meaning of 'essential part of its activities with the controlling authority' only refers to an undertaking carrying out the essential part of its activities in the territory of that authority. The Court regarded the issue of which territory the services are provided as irrelevant for the second *Teckal* criterion. The fact that the undertaking in question might be paid by the controlling authority or third party users of the services was also considered irrelevant for establishing the degree of essential part of activities. The Court held that:

> ... [T]he undertaking in question can be viewed as carrying out the essential part of its activities with the controlling authority within the meaning of *Teckal* only if that undertaking's activities are devoted principally to that authority and any other activities are only of marginal significance.[32]

2.5.3 Performance of task by third parties

The public procurement rules apply only in cases where the public authorities decide to externalise the public services to third parties.

In this case the services are performed either through the conclusion of a 'public contract' or a 'service concession'.

As stipulated in the public sector directive 'public contracts are contracts for pecuniary interest concluded in writing between one or more economic operators and one or more contracting authorities and having as their object the execution of works,

---

28 Case C-340/04, *Carbotermo SpA v Comune di Busto Arsizio* [2006] ECR I-4137.

29 According to Article 13 of Directive 93/38 (now Article 29 of Directive 2014/25/EC) 'This Directive shall not apply to service contracts which: (a) a contracting entity awards to an affiliated undertaking; (b) are awarded by a joint venture formed by a number of contracting entities for the purpose of carrying out a relevant activity within the meaning of Article 2 (2) to one of those contracting entities or to an undertaking which is affiliated with one of these contracting entities, provided that at least 80% of the average turnover of that undertaking with respect to services arising within the Community for the preceding three years derives from the provision of such services to undertakings with which it is affiliated. Where more than one undertaking affiliated with the contracting entity provides the same service or similar services, the total turnover deriving from the provision of services by those undertakings shall be taken into account.'

30 R. Noch, *Vergaberecht kompakt* (Dusseldorf: Werner 2008), p. 83 et seq.

31 Paragraph 54.

32 Paragraphs 63–68. See also Case C-295/05, *Asemfo v Tragsa* [2007] ECR I-2999, where the 'essential part' condition was met with the entity concerned carrying out 90% of its activities with the contracting authorities (55% with its minority owner and 35% with its majority owner).

the supply of products or the provision of services within the meaning of this Directive'.[33]

According to Section 3 of Chapter I of Title I of the directive, certain contracts are subject to lighter procurement regimes, such as contracts for social, health and educational services.[34]

Nevertheless, the public authorities must also comply with the basic principles of EU law, such as transparency and non-discrimination, as long as the services in question are of interests to economic operators situated in different Member States. In this respect, the Court has held the following:

> It follows that the advertising arrangement, introduced by the Community legislature for contracts relating to services coming within the ambit of Annex I B, cannot be interpreted as precluding application of the principles resulting from Articles 43 EC and 49 EC, in the event that such contracts nevertheless are of certain cross-border interest. Also, in so far as a contract relating to services falling under Annex I B is of such interest, the award, in the absence of any transparency, of that contract to an undertaking located in the same Member State as the contracting authority amounts to a difference in treatment to the detriment of undertakings which might be interested in that contract but which are located in other Member States. Unless it is justified by objective circumstances, such a difference in treatment, which, by excluding all undertakings located in another Member State, operates mainly to the detriment of the latter undertakings, amounts to indirect discrimination on the basis of nationality, prohibited under Articles 43 EC and 49 EC.[35]

In cases of mixed contracts including services that are fully covered by the public procurement rules (for example, research or advertising service) and services that are not fully covered (for example, as mentioned above, heavy rail and metro services, or social services), Article 22 of the public sector directive stresses that the directive will apply to a limited extent (that is, only Article 23 and 35(4)), if the value of the, for example, social services, is greater than the value of the other services.[36]

If the value of the public contract is below the thresholds the public authorities must in any case comply with the basic principles of EU law, as mentioned above, such as transparency and non-discrimination, as long as the services in question are of interest to economic operators situated in different Member States.[37]

---

[33] Article 1.

[34] Article 74 of the Public Sector Directive, cf. Annex XIV listing the services subject to a lighter regime.

[35] Case C-507/03, *Commission v Italy* [2007] ECR I-9777, paras 29–31.

[36] See Case C-76/97, *Toegel* [1998] ECR I-5357, paras 29–40.

[37] Service concessions (and public contracts) that have no-cross border interest are not bound by the principles of EU law. For instance, in cases involving contracts for legal services worth an average of around €5,000 or town planning services worth between €6,000 and €26,500, the Commission has considered that, in view of their low value (around 10% or less of the threshold for application of the Directive) and the individual circumstances of the cases, the contracts in question were not relevant to the internal market. (See Commission Staff Working Document – Guide to the application of the European Union rules on state aid, public procurement and the internal market to services of general economic interest, and in particular to social services of general interest, 15.2.2013, SWD(2013) 53 final, point 201).

The public sector directive also defines 'service concessions' as 'contract[s] of the same type as a public service contract except for the fact that the consideration for the provision of services consists either solely in the right to exploit the service or in this right together with payment'.[38]

The Member States provide the private party with exclusive rights to operate or maintain an investment for a given period of time. In return, the private party that carries the risk is responsible for all investments and pays back to the Member State either a fixed sum, a percentage of the revenue obtained through the operation of the investment or a combination of both. On the positive side, concession contracts intensify competition inducing private players to minimise costs, as well as allow public assets to be maintained and operated efficiently. On the negative side, however, concession contracts require complex design and monitoring systems.

The 2004 public procurement rules do not apply to service concessions, given the wide divergence of national practices as regards the delegation of the management of public services and modes of delegation, which could create a situation of very great imbalance in the opening-up of public concession contracts.[39] The above, however, does not preclude the application of the basic principles of the Treaty, particularly the freedom to provide services, and the general principles of EU law, as derived from case-law, notably non-discrimination, equality of treatment, transparency and mutual recognition.[40] The 2014 reform package includes a new Concessions Directive (Directive 2014/23/EU) which covers both service concessions and works concessions.

3. OVERVIEW OF STATE AID LEGISLATION IN THE EU[41]

3.1 The Concept of State Aid and Recipients of Aid

The basic objective of State aid policy in the EU is laid down in Article 107(1) TFEU, which provides that:

---

[38] Article 1.

[39] Document No 4444/92 ADD 1 of 25 February 1992, Statement of reasons of the Council, point 6, which resulted in the adoption of Directive 92/50 on public service contracts, [1992] OJ L209; Document No 5250/90 ADD 1 of 22 March 1990, Statement of reasons of the Council, point 10, which resulted in the adoption of Directive 90/531 on public utilities contracts as amended by Directive 93/38, [1993] OJ L199. Both the Directives above have been amended by Directives 2004/17 and 2004/18 respectively.

[40] Recital 18, public sector directive, and Commission Interpretative Communication on Concessions under Community Law, [2000] OJ C121/2. See also Case C-324/98, *Telaustria* [2000] ECR I-10745, where the Court stressed the importance of compliance with the fundamental rules of the Treaty, when concluding public service contracts or concessions. In particular, the obligation of transparency shall include a degree of advertising of the public procurement procedures.

[41] This section consists of extracts from the book of P. Nicolaides, M. Kekelekis and M. Kleis, State Aid Policy in the European Community – Principles and Practice (Alphen aan den Rijn: Kluwer Law International, 2008).

> Save as otherwise in the Treaties, any aid granted by a Member State or through state resources in any form whatsoever which distorts or threatens to distort competition by favouring certain undertakings or the production of certain goods shall, in so far as it affects trade between Member States, be incompatible with the internal market.

This wording indicates that State aid is in principle prohibited within the internal market. Article 107(1) TFEU does not present a concrete definition of the concept of State aid by reference to its cause, objective or intention of the granting authority but rather defines it by reference to its effect.[42] The meaning of aid is derived from the interpretation of Article 107 TFEU in the rulings of the EU courts and the decisions of the Commission. Thus, a measure of public support is classified as State aid only if the conditions defined in that paragraph are all satisfied. Alternatively, not all measures of public support, even those that may involve public subsidies, are necessarily classified as State aid.

The five conditions that must all hold are the following:

(a) *Aid must be granted by the State or through State resources.* 'Member States' includes central governments and their ministries or departments, regional and local governments or councils and municipalities. 'State resources', on the other hand, refers to public or private bodies established or designated by the State and which use resources which belong to the State or are controlled by the State.[43] Article 107(1) TFEU thus applies to all State aid and covers all transfers of resources without being necessary to make a distinction whether the aid is granted by the agents of the State or enterprises controlled by the State or by the State itself.[44]
(b) *This aid must confer an advantage to the recipients.* State aid has been interpreted by the Commission and the Union Courts to include any transfer of State resources that favours one or more undertakings, resulting in a competitive advantage that could not have been obtained under normal market conditions, whereas the recipient(s) of the aid do not have to provide anything in return. Aid itself is any relief from the expenses, which are normally borne by undertakings in their daily operations. The concept of aid is very wide and includes any advantage of monetary nature conferred by the State or State resources, which would not have otherwise been enjoyed by the recipient. Such advantages encompass not only grants, subsidies, loans or guarantees actually given by the State, but also anything owed to the State, which the latter fails to collect or receive, such as taxes, social security payments, interest on loans and dividends on invested public capital, as well as anything that the State gives up without objective reason such as products and services it sells at excessively low prices and anything the State gives away without objective reason such as products and services it purchases at excessively high prices.

---

[42] Case 30/59, *Steenkolenmijnen v High Authority* [1961] ECR 1, at p. 19.

[43] Case C-72-73/91, *Sloman Neptun Schiffahrts AG v Seebetriebsrat Bodo Ziesemer* [1993] ECR I-887 para 19.

[44] Case C-290/83, *Commission v France* [1985] ECR 439 para 14.

(c) *The advantage must favour certain undertakings or economic activities.* This has been interpreted over the years to mean that aid must be 'selective' or 'specific' rather than general. 'General' measures of economic policy are not aid. No concrete definition of 'general measures' either in the Commission's practice or the Union Courts' jurisprudence has been given. Some guidance, however, has been given on a case-by-case basis. For instance, measures designed to reduce the taxation of labour for all firms have a relatively greater effect on labour-intensive industries than on capital-intensive industries, without necessarily constituting State aid.

(d) *Aid must affect trade between Member States.* There is no definition or quantitative measure of when aid is capable of affecting trade. It is settled case-law however, that aid may affect intra-Union trade even if it is of relatively small amount.[45] The Commission is not required to define in detail markets or analyse rigorously their structures and the ensuing competitive relationships in order to establish a real effect on trade between Member States, which would anyway be impossible if aid is not yet implemented.

(e) *Aid must distort competition in the internal market.* Competition is distorted, if the aid in question strengthens the competitive position of the recipient, say by reducing its operating or investment costs, in relation to its rivals.[46] Always the relevant question is what would be the competitive position of the recipient in the absence of aid? If this would be worse in relation to its rivals, then aid distorts competition.

The recipients of aid must be undertakings, which are natural or legal persons engaging in economic activities. The concept of an undertaking is not defined anywhere in the Treaty. It refers broadly to any natural or legal person, regardless of legal status and means by which it is financed, who carries out economic activities of certain regularity and duration and which could be done for remuneration.

According to settled case-law, an economic activity is 'any activity consisting in offering goods and services on a given market'.[47] An economic activity presupposes the assumption of risk for the purpose for remuneration. Remuneration constitutes consideration normally agreed upon between the provider and the recipient. This suggests that an economic activity is the voluntary offer of goods and services under conditions that generate profit or return or at least cover the costs of the goods and services in question.[48]

---

45 Case C-280/00, *Altmark* [2003] ECR I-7747 paras 77–81.

46 Case 234/84, *Belgium v Commission* [1986] ECR 2263 para 22. See also, Case C-148/04, *Unicredito Italiano* [2005] ECR I-11137 and C-71/04, *Xunta de Galicia* [2005] ECR I-7419.

47 Case C-35/96, *Commission v Italy* [1998] ECR I-3851 para 36. See also, Cases C-180/98 to C-184/98, *Pavel Pavlov and Others* [2000] ECR I-6451 para 75.

48 Joined Cases C-159/91 and C-160/91, *Christian Poucet v Assurances Générales de France and Caisse Mutuelle Regionale du Languedoc – Roussillon* [1993] ECR I-637.

3.2 Compatibility of State Aid

Article 107(1) TFEU provides that State aid is considered incompatible with the internal market and thus prohibited, 'save as otherwise provided in this Treaty'. In this context, Article 107(2) TFEU lays down that certain aid is automatically compatible with the internal market.[49] Secondly, Article 107(3) TFEU enables the Commission to consider the compatibility of certain aid with the internal market on the basis of a number of objectives to be attained.[50]

It is important to state in this context that State aid is in principle considered incompatible with the internal market as long as the Member States are not able to give nor has the Commission found any grounds establishing that the aid concerned meets the conditions for exception laid down in Article 107(3) TFEU.[51]

The Commission has the exclusive competence to assess the compatibility of State aid measures with the internal market. For the implementation of the compatibility exceptions, it has adopted numerous guidelines and frameworks, where the Commission sets its decision-making practice and indicates in detail all the criteria and conditions on the basis of which the compatibility assessment is carried out.[52]

---

[49] Article 107(2) TFEU reads: 'The following shall be compatible with the internal market:

(a) aid having a social character, granted to individual consumers, provided that such aid is granted without discrimination related to the origin of the products concerned;
(b) aid to make good the damage caused by natural disasters or exceptional occurrences;
(c) aid granted to the economy of certain areas of the Federal Republic of Germany affected by the division of Germany, in so far as such aid is required in order to compensate for the economic disadvantages caused by that division. Five years after the entry into force of the Treaty of Lisbon, the Council, acting on a proposal from the Commission, may adopt a decision repealing this point.'

[50] Article 107(3) TFEU reads: 'The following may be considered to be compatible with the internal market:

(a) aid to promote the economic development of areas where the standard of living is abnormally low or where there is serious underemployment, and of the regions referred to in Article 349, in view of their structural, economic and social situation;
(b) aid to promote the execution of an important project of common European interest or to remedy a serious disturbance in the economy of a Member State;
(c) aid to facilitate the development of certain economic activities or of certain economic areas, where such aid does not adversely affect trading conditions to an extent contrary to the common interest;
(d) aid to promote culture and heritage conservation where such aid does not affect trading conditions and competition in the Union to an extent that is contrary to the common interest;
(e) such other categories of aid as may be specified by decision of the Council on a proposal from the Commission.'

[51] Case 730/79, *Philip Morris v Commission* [1980] ECR 2671.

[52] See http//ec.europa.eu/competition/state_aid/legislation/legislation.html (available 2 February 2016).

3.3 State Aid Procedures

The rules on State aid procedures are laid down in Article 108 TFEU, according to which the Commission has the sole responsibility to supervise the plans of Member States to grant or alter aid and to keep under constant review all systems of aid existing in those Member States. In order to increase transparency and legal certainty, Council Regulation 2015/1589 of 13 July 2015 was adopted, which lays down detailed rules for the application of Article 108 TFEU.[53]

The Community's system of control of State aid requires Member States to notify their aid schemes to the Commission and obtain its authorisation before they implement them. Article 108 EC is clear in this respect. Member States must wait for the final decision of the Commission before they implement a new scheme or even modify an existing one.

The Commission's discretion and power is considerable. Although the Treaty provides for the possibility of Member States to petition the Council on the basis of Article 108(2) TFEU and ask it to decide on national State aid schemes on the basis of unanimity, this is an option which is used rarely and mostly in relation to agricultural products. In practice such decisions are the sole responsibility of the Commission. Not only is the Commission entrusted with the vetting of aid schemes, it may also order suspension of aid given without authorisation, even if it would have been authorised, had it been notified. Moreover, the Commission may order the suspension of legally provided aid until illegal aid is recovered in cases where aid would be cumulated and exceed allowable ceilings.

Also, for aid that has been implemented without the Commission's prior approval (unlawful aid), the Commission, acting *ex officio* or following a complaint, may reach the conclusion that the unlawful aid is not compatible with the internal market. In such case, it must order recovery of the unlawfully paid aid.

4. INTERPLAY BETWEEN PUBLIC PROCUREMENT AND STATE AID

Both the public procurement and State aid rules seek to secure a level playing field for competitors, ensuring a market where competitive companies succeed. The sections below examine in more detail this interplay.

4.1 Complying with Public Procurement Rules in State Aid Procedures

4.1.1 In the context of assessing the existence of aid

The European Courts have confirmed the parallel application of State aid and public procurement rules.[54] Adherence to the public procurement procedure is in most

---

[53] [2015] OJ L248/99. This Regulation replaces Council Regulation No 659/1999 of 22 March 1999 laying down detailed rules for the application of Article 108 TFEU, [1999] OJ L83/1.

[54] See for example Case C-280/00 *Altmark* [2003] ECR I-07747.

instances sufficient to eliminate an economic advantage, within the meaning of Article 107(1) TFEU, to the contractor. As stated in the Commission's Communication on compensation for services of general economic interest 'an open, transparent and non-discriminatory public procurement procedure is an appropriate method to compare different potential offers and set the compensation so as to exclude the presence of aid'.[55]

Therefore, the key issue to consider is whether a public procurement procedure favours certain undertakings by providing them an economic advantage. Given that, on the basis of the wording of Article 107(1) TFEU, public purchases are not automatically excluded from State aid control ('aid ... in any form whatsoever'), under certain circumstances, public procurement activities may also have to be scrutinised in State aid procedures. The sections below provide details on the relevance of public procurement rules in State aid decision-making.[56]

i. Infrastructure funding Where the construction or management of infrastructure is carried out by a company, the Commission has decided in the past that this operation constitutes an economic activity that may give rise to State aid issues.[57]

However, even in case the management of infrastructure is awarded to one company, the application of Article 107(1) TFEU can be excluded if the infrastructure is rented out on market conditions and the operator pays adequate fees at the market price level. In this case, the use of open competition through tendering procedure would remove any doubts that the rent reflects market conditions. In general, public tenders are useful means of public funding of these kinds of projects. Even though there is an element of State aid involved, the Commission would more easily authorise the aid because the competitive tendering process would minimise the amount of aid granted. Given that in most of the infrastructure projects there is long duration envisaged for implementation and investment returns, the management is carried out on the basis of concessions. The State provides the private party with exclusive rights to operate or maintain an investment for a given period of time. In return, the private party that carries the risk is responsible for all investments and pays back to the State either a fixed sum, a percentage of the revenue obtained through the operation of the investment or a combination of both.[58]

---

55 Communication from the Commission on the application of the European Union State aid rules to compensation granted for the provision of services of general economic interest, [2012] OJ C8/2, at para 64.

56 For more case examples and a detailed analysis of the relationship between public procurement and advantage, see P. Nicolaides and I. Ruse, 'Competitive Selection of Undertakings and State Aid: Why and When Does it Not Eliminate Advantage?', (2012) 1 EPPPL 5.

57 Commission Decision of 2 August 2002 on various measures and the State aid invested by Spain in Terra Mitica SA, [2003] OJ L91/23.

58 In a recent opening of investigation on a case concerning public financing of infrastructure and equipment at the Port of Piraeus (State aid C 21/09 (ex N 105/08, ex N 168/08 and ex N 169/08, OJ 2009 C 245/21), which among others involved the State financing of equipment put at the disposal of a concession holder, the Commission considered that there is no State aid at the level of the concessionaire since it is paying the market price for its use on the basis of an open public tender.

In the London Underground Public-Private Partnership case, the Commission concluded that 'when these types of infrastructure arrangements are concluded after the observance of an open, transparent and non-discriminatory procedure, it is, in principle, presumed that the level of any market sector support can be regarded as representing the market price for the execution of the project. This conclusion should lead to the assumption that, in principle, no State aid is involved'.[59]

ii. Sale of land The Commission Communication on the sale of land indicates that a sale of land following a 'sufficiently well-publicized, open and unconditional bidding procedure' excludes the presence of State aid.[60]

The Communication defines a sufficiently well-publicized offer as:

> an offer [that] ... is repeatedly advertised over a reasonably long period (two months or more) in the national press, estate gazettes or other appropriate publications and through real-estate agents addressing a broad range of potential buyers, so that it can come to the notice of all potential buyers. The intended sale of land and buildings, which in view of their high value or other features may attract investors operating on a Europe-wide or international scale, should be announced in publications which have a regular international circulation. Such offers should also be made known through agents addressing clients on a Europe-wide or international scale.

The Commission has held that the use of only one of these two means of advertising a sale of land is not sufficient, and that a combination of the two is required if all potential buyers are to be informed of the tender.[61]

Further, according to the Communication, an unconditional offer is:

> (b) an offer ... when any buyer, irrespective of whether or not he runs a business or of the nature of his business, is generally free to acquire the land and buildings and to use it for his own purposes. Restrictions may be imposed for the prevention of public nuisance, for reasons of environmental protection or to avoid purely speculative bids. Urban and regional planning restrictions imposed on the owner pursuant to domestic law on the use of the land and buildings do not affect the unconditional nature of an offer. (c) If it is a condition of the sale that the future owner is to assume special obligations – other than those arising from general domestic law or decision of the planning authorities or those relating to the general protection and conservation of the environment and to public health – for the benefit of the public authorities or in the general public interest, the offer is to be regarded as 'unconditional' within the meaning of the above definition only if all potential buyers would have to, and be able to, meet that obligation, irrespective of whether or not they run a business or of the nature of their business.

---

[59] Case N 264/2002, London Underground Public Private Partnership, at para 79.

[60] Commission Communication on State aid elements in sales of land and buildings by public authorities, [1997] OJ C209/3, at para 1.

[61] Commission Decision of 12 July 2000 on the State aid granted by France to Scott Paper SA Kimberly-Clark, [2002] OJ L12/1, at para 140. The same conclusion was also reached by the EFTA Surveillance Authority in its decision (470/09/COL) of 25 November 2009 on the sale of 'Slaktehustomten' [property 168/321] in Bergen municipality, [2010] OJ C67/11. The decision can be found on the website of the Authority: http://www.eftasurv.int/state-aid/state-aid-register/ (available 2 February 2016).

Arguably, by imposing certain conditions to the buyer (that go beyond the general obligations, which would apply to any buyer), the State potentially lowers the sales pricc and thus forgoes additional revenues.

In the *Slaktehustomten* case, the EFTA Surveillance Authority ('the Authority') dealt with a complaint arguing that that alterations to the conditions of the sales agreement and applicable zoning regulations involved State aid, as these changes entailed that the value of Slaktehustomten had increased without the municipality being compensated accordingly. The Authority found that no such changes had been made and that any potential changes would be covered by a compensation clause in the contract.[62]

In the *Craiova* case, the tender procedure organised was geared primarily to achieving a given level of production and amount of employment in the region. For the Commission, these conditions constituted strong indicators that the sales price was lowered and certain potential investors had been deterred from showing a concrete interest in the company.[63]

As regards the requirement for an open procedure, this is not defined in the Communication. Nevertheless, according to Article 27 of the public sector directive, an open procedure is defined as a procedure in which any interested party may submit a tender, and there are no access restrictions (for example, to information)[64] or qualifications that must be met in order to participate. It is to be understood that this criterion of openness is supplemented by the requirement of transparency, which ensures a non-discrimination selection procedure.[65]

iii. Broadband funding According to the recently adopted new Commission Broadband guidelines, in discussing advantage:

> [t]he aid is usually granted directly to investors of the network, which in most cases are chosen by means of a competitive tender process. When the State's contribution is not provided on normal market terms and consequently qualifies as State aid under the market economy investor principle, the use of a competitive selection process ensures that any aid is limited to the minimum amount necessary for the particular project. However, it does not eliminate the aid, as the public authority will still provide a subsidy to the winning bidder (for instance, in terms of 'gap funding' or in-kind contribution) and the purpose of such procedure is precisely the selection of the aid beneficiary. The financial support received will enable the successful bidder to conduct this commercial activity on conditions which would not otherwise be available on the market. Besides the direct beneficiary of the aid, third-party operators receiving wholesale access to the subsidised infrastructure may be indirect beneficiaries.[66]

---

[62] Ibid p. 7–8.

[63] Commission Decision of 27 February 2008 on State aid C 46/07 (ex NN 59/07) implemented by Romania for Automobile Craiova (formerly Daewoo Romania), [2008] OJ L239/12, paras 55 et seq.

[64] Ibid paras 67 et seq.

[65] Von Donat, 'State Aid and Public Procurement Law', in Heidenhain, *European State Aid Law Handbook* (Oxford: Hart Publishing, 2009).

[66] [2013] OJ C25/1, at para 12.

In the Welsh Public Sector Network Scheme,[67] the Commission assessed State aid and advantage at two levels: first, at the level of the service provider, and secondly, at the level of the users of the network and third parties. At the former level, the Commission concluded that the award of a service contract for the provision of network services was made in line with the EU procurement directives, using a competitive procedure with prior publication at EU level in which open access was guaranteed. Also, the contract was awarded to the most economically advantageous tender, using criteria which corresponded to the objective of achieving best value for money, and without giving rise to any extra advantages beyond the scope of the contract (for example, commercial exploitation of spare capacity).

As to the users of the network, these were held not to constitute undertakings as they were all part of the public administration exercising public functions, and not economic activities. Similarly, concerning third parties, the Commission found no advantage, given that the need for significant new infrastructure was unlikely and wholesale access was not envisaged beyond potentially existing regulatory requirements. However, had the users been economic operators and had there been a possibility for wholesale access for commercial use on preferential terms, State aid could have been present.[68]

iv. Services of General Economic Interest (SGEI) and the Altmark ruling The *Altmark* ruling laid down four cumulative conditions in order for compensation for public service obligations not to constitute State aid and thus be exempt from the notification requirement of Article 108(3) TFEU.[69] These conditions apply in order to examine the existence of State aid and eliminate the advantage. If any of these conditions is not met then aid is considered present:

> First, the recipient undertaking must actually have public service obligations to discharge, and the obligations must be clearly defined.
>
> Second, the parameters on the basis of which the compensation is calculated must be established in advance in an objective and transparent manner.
>
> Third, the compensation cannot exceed what is necessary to cover all or part of the costs incurred in the discharge of public service obligations, taking into account the relevant receipts and a reasonable profit for discharging those obligations.
>
> Fourth, where the undertaking which is to discharge public service obligations is not chosen pursuant to a public procurement procedure which would allow for the selection of the tenderer capable of providing those services at the least cost to the community, the level of compensation needed must be determined on the basis of an analysis of the costs which a typical undertaking, well run and adequately provided with means of transport so as to be able to meet the necessary public service requirements, would have incurred in discharging those obligations, taking into account the relevant receipts and a reasonable profit for discharging the obligations.[70]

---

67 Case N 46/2007.

68 N. Tosics and N. Gaal, 'Public Procurement and State Aid Control – The Issue of Economic Advantage', *Competition Policy Newsletter*, Winter 2007.

69 Case C-280/00, [2003] ECR I-7747, paras 88–93.

70 Ibid, paras 88–93.

The first leg of the fourth condition refers to 'a public procurement procedure which would allow for the selection of the tenderer capable of providing those services at the least cost to the community'. In *Concordia* the Court stated that:

> ... where, in the context of a public contract for the provision of urban bus transport service, the contracting authority decides to award a contract to the tenderer who submits the economically most advantageous tender, it may take into consideration ecological criteria [that] comply with all the fundamental principles of Community law, in particular the principle of non-discrimination.[71]

Likewise, the public procurement rules refer to the application of one award criterion only: 'the most economically advantageous tender' comprising price or cost and may include the best price-quality ratio.[72] As explicitly indicated in the public sector directive.

In view of the above, it does not suffice to have a public procurement procedure that is open, non-discriminatory, objective and competitive, if criteria other than the price play a major role (for example, compensation on the basis of an increase of the number of passengers). The reference to the 'least cost to the community', thus, does not necessarily imply the 'lowest cost'. In a case concerning natural conservation areas the Commission implied that criteria other than price play a role when stating that 'the conservation organisations are selected in an open and transparent public procedure. However, the bidding process is not based on the lowest price of the services, or *on the most economically advantageous offer*,[73] but rather on the qualifications of the organizations and – only for the nature conservation projects – on the environmental merits of the projects' (emphasis added).[74]

The reference to the 'least cost to the community' must thus be connected to '... a material analysis that goes beyond *the mere respect of the applicable procurement rules*' (emphasis added).[75] This implies the choice of the bidder offering the best value for money. Although jurisprudence has not dealt with the difference between the 'least cost to the community' of Altmark and the 'the most economically advantageous tender' of the procurement directives, we would argue that the State aid practice of the Commission reveals none. For State aid purposes, what is important is that the selected bidder represents the best value for money, as it is indeed required by the public procurement rules.[76]

In the transport sector, it is not always the best practice to choose the lowest price alone. In a number of cases the Commission has accepted public procurement

---

71 Case C-513/99, [2002] ECR I-7213, points 1 and 3.

72 Article 67 of the public sector directive and Article 82 of the utilities directive.

73 This notion is wider than that of the lowest price and also takes into account qualitative factors.

74 Case NN 8/2009. See also Action on annulment T-347/2009, *Germany v Commission*, [2009] OJ C267.

75 Case N 475/2003 – Public Service Obligation (PSO) Notification.

76 S. Santamoto, 'Advantage in the context of services of general economic interest under *Altmark*', in *EU Competition Law, Volume IV, State Aid* (Deventer: Claeys & Casteels, 2008) p. 379 et seq.

procedures that offer the best service for lowest cost.[77] In the case concerning public transport services in the District of Wittenberg for example, the tender documents set the price set on the basis of 20 quality criteria. The objective of each of these criteria is described in detail and performance points are provided. The Commission accepted this as an effective bidding process where the bid that offers the best price (not necessarily the lowest) for a fixed service wins.[78]

But, an objective procurement process is not followed when by definition it has as its aim to exclude certain operators. In the Southern Moravia Bus Companies case the regional authorities distributed the invitation to tender only to known carriers of Southern Moravia excluding operators from other Member States, regions or districts.[79]

4.1.2 In the context of assessing the compatibility of aid

i. State aid guidelines and the common assessment principles The 2012, State aid modernization initiative (SAM), sets out the main principles for state aid assessment. These principles consist of seven cumulative compatibility criteria:

(1) The aid measure must be aimed at a well-defined objective of common interest;
(2) It must be targeted towards a situation where aid can bring about a material improvement that the market cannot deliver itself, for example by remedying a market failure or addressing an equity or cohesion concern;
(3) It must be an appropriate policy instrument;
(4) The aid must produce an incentive effect, by changing the behaviour of firms;
(5) The aid amount must be limited to the minimum needed;
(6) The distortions of competition and effect on trade are limited, so that the overall balance is positive;
(7) The relevant acts and pertinent information about aid awards must be transparent and the public must have open access.

The public procurement rules have been used to implement these criteria and corroborate the existence of compatibility. For example, in the Broadband Guidelines it is stated, in reference to the competitive selection process, that:

> [w]henever the granting authorities select a third-party operator to deploy and operate the subsidised infrastructure, the selection process shall be conducted in line with spirit and the the principles of the EU Public Procurement Directives. It ensures that there is transparency for all investors wishing to bid for the implementation and/or management of the subsidised project. Equal and non-discriminatory treatment of all bidders and objective evaluation criteria are indispensable conditions. The competitive tender is a method to reduce budgetary costs, to minimise the potential State aid involved and at the same time reduces the selective

[77] Cases N 604/2005 – State aid to bus enterprises in the region of Wittenberg, N 207/2009 – Financing of the public transport services in the region of Wittenberg, and N 206/2009 – Financing of the public transport service in district of Anhalt – Bitterfeld.

[78] N 207/2009 – Financing of the public transport services in the region of Wittenberg.

[79] Commission Decision of 26 November 2008 on State aid C 3/08 (ex NN 102/05), Czech Republic, [2009] OJ L97/14.

> nature of the measure insofar as the choice of the beneficiary is not known in advance. Member States shall ensure a transparent process and a competitive outcome and shall use a dedicated central website at the national level to publish all on-going tender procedures on broadband State aid measures.[80]

In the *Høg-Jæren wind park* case, the Authority assessed the use of a tender procedure in order to conclude on the necessity, as well as the proportionality of aid. In particular, the Authority stated, as regards the necessity, that the fact that Høg-Jæren was chosen in a public tender shows that the investment in that wind park increased environmental protection to a higher degree than investments in other wind power projects. In relation to proportionality, the Authority stated that the use of a public tender ensured both that costs were kept to a minimum and that the overall aid amount was limited to cover unprofitability.[81]

ii. The SGEI Framework Pursuant to Article 106 TFEU, Member States are allowed to take into account legitimate national interests and exempt, under certain conditions, national measures pertaining to SGEI, from the Treaty-based prohibitions of distortion of competition and State aid.

In 2005 the Commission published additional rules (the *Altmark* package) to guide itself and the Member States on what is needed for authorising State aid for SGEI. The package contained three documents dealing with measures that constituted State aid and did not have to be notified (the Decision)[82] and measures which constituted aid and had to be notified (the Framework).[83] The third document of the package was the amended Transparency Directive.[84]

In 2012, the Commission revised the SGEI rules and new documents were adopted. In addition to a Decision and a Framework on public service compensation for SGEI, the package contains a Regulation on SGEI *de minimis* and a Communication explaining different concepts of State aid which are relevant for SGEI.[85]

---

80 EU Guidelines for the application of State aid rules in relation to the rapid deployment of broadband networks, [2013] OJ C25/l, Paragraph 78(c). See also Commission cases in N 508/2008 – Remote broadband services in Northern Ireland and N 475/2007 – National Broadband Scheme Ireland.

81 EFTA Surveillance Authority decision (488/10/COL) of 15 December 2010 on aid to Jæren Energi AS for Høg- Jæren wind park, [2011] OJ C156/8. The decision can be found on the website of the Authority: http://www.eftasurv.int/state-aid/state-aid-register/ (available 2 February 2016).

82 Commission Decision 2005/842/EC on the application of Article 86(2) of the EC Treaty to State aid in the form of public service compensation granted to certain undertakings entrusted with the operation of services of general economic interest, [2005] OJ L312/67.

83 Community framework for State aid in the form of public service compensation, [2005] OJ C297/4.

84 Commission Directive 2006/111/EC on the transparency of financial relations between Member States and public undertakings as well as on financial transparency within certain undertakings, [2006] OJ L318/17.

85 Communication from the Commission on the application of the European Union State aid rules to compensation granted for the provision of services of general economic interest, [2012] OJ C8/4; Commission Decision of 20 December on the application of Article 106(2) of

The Framework contains a number of conditions that all need to be satisfied for compatibility purposes. Compliance with the Transparency Directive and the public procurement rules constitute one of the compatibility conditions.[86] This will also be checked *ex officio* by the Commission in the State aid assessment. A non-observance of these rules will be considered to be contrary to the development of trade contrary to the interest of the Union and will make the aid incompatible. The assessment of the public procurement rules will include the general principles of transparency, equal treatment and non-discrimination resulting directly from the Treaty.

This represents a departure from the established practice in this field, according to which these sets of rules were independent and only had to be assessed together in case of a close and indissoluble link between the State aid and the selection procedure. In all other cases a flaw of the selection procedure was not relevant for the assessment of the compatibility of aid.

In the Post Office limited (POL) case, the Commission accepted the negotiated procedure without prior consultation as complying with the Framework, given that POL was the only operator whose network could provide the SGEI. In addition, the UK authorities committed to ensure, in the future, the compliance of all POL's public contracts with the EU public procurement rules.[87]

Further, the Framework contains provisions for efficiency incentives. As stated, '[i]n devising the method of compensation, Member States must introduce incentives for the efficient provision of SGEI of a high standard, unless they can duly justify that it is not feasible or appropriate to do so'.[88] The question is whether a public procurement process can automatically ensure the efficiency incentives. The reply could arguably be affirmative if bidders do not have any prior information about each other. On the other hand, if the most efficient bidder is known in advance, the public procurement process becomes less transparent, the efficient bidder will be able to bid just below the minimum cost of the second lowest bidder and, as a result, the bid will not necessarily be the lowest the process can achieve, with future efficiencies.

The Framework states that:

> [e]fficiency incentives can be designed in different ways to best suit the specificity of each case or sector. For instance, Member States can define upfront a fixed compensation level which anticipates and incorporates the efficiency gains that the undertaking can be expected to make over the lifetime of the entrustment act. Alternatively, Member States can define

---

the Treaty on the Functioning of the European Union to State aid in the form of public service compensation granted to certain undertakings entrusted with the operation of services of general economic interest, [2012] OJ L7/3; Communication from the Commission, European Union framework for State aid in the form of public service compensation (2011), [2012] OJ C8/15; Commission Regulation on the application of Articles 107 and 108 of the Treaty on the Functioning of the European Union to *de minimis* aid granted to undertakings providing services of general economic interest, [2012] OJ L114/8.

[86] Framework, paras 18–19.

[87] Case SA.33054 (2012/N) – United Kingdom, Post Office Limited (POL): Compensation for net costs incurred to keep a non-commercially viable network for the period 2012–15 and the continuation of a working capital facility, paras 67–69.

[88] Paragraph 39 et seq.

> productive efficiency targets in the entrustment act whereby the level of compensation is made dependent upon the extent to which the targets have been met ...[89]

It is to be understood that an open tender can be sufficient, whereas in a negotiated procedure, the efficiency incentives should be included in the entrustment act. In the POL case, the company was required, on the basis of the entrustment act, and in conjunction with the business plan, to achieve yearly efficiency milestones (for example, the introduction of new network models over the previous year or the development of replacement agency contracts). Failure to do so would result in the UK not being obliged any longer to provide the subsidy. In addition, given that in this case POL would receive a fixed upfront compensation that was below the expected net cost of the SGEI, POL was likely to be incentivised to increase its efficiency. This would allow it to keep the efficiency gains as long as overcompensation was avoided.[90]

iii. Regulation 1370/2007 The original legislation laying down common principles for public service transport dated back to 1969.[91] The Commission launched a first proposal for a new Regulation in July 2000.[92] As Member States were not able to agree on the initial draft, a revised proposal[93] took into account these objections, as well as the views expressed by the Council and the European Parliament. After seven years and following several amendments, Regulation 1370/2007 on public passenger transport services by rail and by road and repealing Council Regulations 1191/69 and 1107/70 ('the PSO Regulation') was adopted in 2007. This has been in force since 3 December 2009.[94]

Under this PSO Regulation, public authorities compensating public transport operators for PSOs are free to choose whether to award a contract to an external provider by means of competitive tendering or to entrust this operation to an internal operator. The former contract has to be awarded on the basis of an open, competitive tendering procedure, in which the principles of procurement law,[95] that is, transparency and equal treatment, must be complied with. The latter option, as analysed above, implies the provision of the service by the authority itself or by an internal operator which it controls and this can be made by a direct award without a tendering process.

The public authorities have the obligation to conclude public service contracts when granting exclusive rights and/or compensation for the provision of public transport

[89] Paragraphs 40–41.

[90] Case SA.33054 (2012/N) – United Kingdom, Post Office Limited (POL): Compensation for net costs incurred to keep a non-commercially viable network for the period 2012–15 and the continuation of a working capital facility, paras 95 et seq.

[91] Regulation 1191/69 of the Council of 26 June 1969 on action by Member States concerning the obligations inherent in the concept of a public service in transport by rail, road and inland waterway, [1969] OJ L156/1–10; Regulation 1107/70 of the Council of 4 June 1970 on the granting of aids for transport by rail, road and inland waterway, [1970] OJ L130/1.

[92] COM/2000/0007 final – COD 2000/0212.

[93] Proposal for a Regulation of the European Parliament and Council on public passenger transport services by rail and by road, COM(2005) 319, 20 July 2005.

[94] Regulation 1370/2007 on public passenger transport services by rail and by road and repealing Council Regulations 1191/69 and 1107/70, [2007] OJ L315/1.

[95] Directives 2004/17/EC and Directive 2004/18/EC.

services.[96] The PSO Regulation establishes the mandatory content of public service contracts: clear definition of PSO, compensation established in advance in an objective and transparent manner in a way to prevent overcompensation and exact arrangements of the allocation of costs.[97]

The first three conditions established by the PSO Regulation are almost identical with the first three conditions established in the *Altmark* ruling.[98] The fourth *Altmark* condition referring to the costs of an efficient company is not included among the prerequisites for the mandatory content of a contract which has to be concluded under the PSO Regulation. Consequently, a compensation covering the actual costs regardless of the level of efficiency of the undertaking is allowed. As regards the contracts awarded directly or connected with the general rule, the rules applicable to compensation contained in the Annex to the PSO Regulation will apply. These include the obligation to keep separate accounts when the operator not only operates services subject to public transports service obligations but also engages in other activities.[99]

As under the previous legal regime,[100] Member States are exempted from the notification obligation under Article 108 TFEU. They must only produce, once a year, a report on the compensation details for the bus and rail transport sector.[101]

4.1.3 In the context of favourable contract terms or changes to contract terms

i. Favourable contract terms An open, transparent and non-discriminatory public procurement procedure is comparable to a normal commercial transaction and thus entails no State aid. However, when the terms of the public contract are excessive and provide benefits beyond what is obtainable under normal market conditions, then State aid rules come into play, with the aid being the difference between the value of the contract concluded and the value of the contract that could have been obtained under normal market conditions.

In the UK case on regional broadband support in Wales, the Commission found advantage at the level of the service provider. It particularly stated that:

> [a] tender tends to minimise potential advantages to the service provider in terms of excessive returns. However, even if a service provider would not receive an excessive return on its overall investment, it receives financial support which provides the possibility of entering the market and establishing its business on conditions not otherwise available on the market. In addition, the subsidy will allow the service provider to offer the services at lower prices than it would have been able to offer had it had to bear all the costs itself and, as a consequence, such a service provider will be able to attract more customers than under normal conditions. As a result of the State contribution, the selected providers are likely to build or upgrade new or additional infrastructure and communications equipment necessary to offer the services. The providers will be in a position to exploit this infrastructure and equipment as well as

96 Article 3(1), PSO Regulation.
97 Article 4(1), PSO Regulation.
98 Case C-280/00, [2003] ECR I-7747.
99 Annex of PSO Regulation, at para 5.
100 Article 17(2), Regulation 1191/69.
101 Article 7(1), PSO Regulation.

customer relationships partly acquired with State funds even after the lifetime of the project. Hence, it may benefit from continuing residual advantages from the project.[102]

Further, the exercise of large discretion by the contracting authorities – especially in cases of negotiation procedures – may constitute an element that encompasses State aid. In the Antwerp International Airport case the Commission considered that the fact that the public procurement directives were complied with did not exclude the possibility of State aid, given that the contracting authority reserved a substantial discretion as regards the final choice, particularly because the award criteria were not determined in advance.[103]

ii. Changes to contract terms Aid may also arise from changes in the contracts following their award to the successful bidders. As a result, they may no longer be in compliance to normal market conditions.

In the *BAI v Commission* case concerning the purchase of travel vouchers to be used for a ferry service between England and Spain, BAI had complained to the Commission that the price paid by the Spanish authorities for the contract concerned was much higher than the normal commercial price, given that travel vouchers had to be paid even for journeys that were not carried out. As a result, the Spanish authorities would carry out losses from these services. The Commission had concluded that the terms of the contract were excessively favourable and State aid was, hence, involved. The Spanish authorities were required to amend the contractual terms and buy double the number of vouchers in order to become comparable to normal market conditions.

The Court of First Instance (now General Court), however, concluded that additional vouchers were not actually needed.

> On the contrary, it appears from the file that, in order to maintain the payment under that agreement at a level equivalent to that of the payment provided for by the original agreement, it was necessary, in view of the reduction in the reference unit price, to increase considerably the total number of travel vouchers to be purchased by the authorities.[104]

The above judgment has been confirmed by the Court in *P&O European Ferries* case, where the Court stated that although a public procurement procedure was followed:

> the mere fact that a Member State purchases goods and services on market conditions is not sufficient for that transaction to constitute a commercial transaction concluded under conditions, which a private investor would have accepted, or in other words a normal commercial transaction, if it turns out that the State did not have an actual need for those goods and services.[105]

---

102 Case N 57/2005 – UK regional broadband support in Wales, paras 23–24.

103 Case N 355/2004 – PPP Antwerp International Airport. See also Case N 149/2006 – Irish Roads, where the Commission did not exclude the possibility that an element of State aid still remained as a result of negotiation procedures for the construction of roads.

104 Case T-14/96, [1999] ECR II-139, at para 79.

105 Joined Cases T-116/01 and T-118/01, *P&O European Ferries v Commission* [2003] ECR II-2957 para 117.

The issue of changes to contract terms has also been dealt with by the EFTA Court in its recent *Hurtigruten* judgement in the context of compensation for SGEI. The EFTA Court upheld the Authority's decision that a renegotiation clause to an initial public contract without laying down any parameters for the calculation of any supplementary compensation should the compensation awarded through the initial contract be deemed insufficient, could not be considered an objective an transparent method to assess the compensation in the sense of second and fourth *Altmark* criteria.[106]

More recently, the Commission, in the Polish case concerning aid for the construction and operation of the A2 Motorway, stated that the use of open procedure was not sufficient to eliminate advantage.[107] The measure concerned public-private partnership arrangements[108] with AWSA II for the construction and management of the road. AWSA II was selected following an open public procurement process and a concession agreement was signed between AWSA II and the national authorities. Initially, AWSA II was bearing most of the responsibility and risk (especially traffic and revenue risks) for the construction and operation of motorway. The systems was characterised by the almost exclusive reliance on tolls. Later in the process, the State stepped in to ensure the smooth construction and supported preparatory works, as well as provided a guarantee on loans. The role of the State kept growing assuming thus more risk within the public-private partnership. That led to re-negotiations of the financial terms of the concession agreement. As a result, the Commission concluded that State resources in the final arrangement were higher than what initially foreseen in the launch of the tender and that could not exclude an economic advantage to AWSA II.

4.2 Complying with State Aid Rules in Public Procurement Procedures

4.2.1 Abnormally low offers

Low price offers are generally advantageous to the contracting authority. However, too low prices may be warnings that the undertaking in question has problems related to insolvency, might deliver products of lower quality than expected, or is the recipient of State aid. If State aid has been unlawfully granted, the bidder risks recovery, which again could threaten its financial or economic security. The question is what options the contracting authority and competing bidders have in these situations.

The judgment in *ARGE,*[109] concerned a tender for analysing water samples from various lakes and rivers in Austria over two two-year periods. The Court stated that 'it is not excluded that, in certain specific circumstances, Directive 92/50 [replaced by

---

106 Joined Cases E-10/11 and E-11/11, *Hurtigruten v EFTA Surveillance Authority* (not yet reported).

107 Case N 462/*09* – Poland – Aid for the construction and operation of the A2 Motorway, Świecko – Nowy Tomyśl section. See also Case N 264/2002 – London Underground, where the Commission held that the changes made to the contract after the award were not substantial enough to attract more or different applicants to bid, given that there were objectively determined and there were also envisaged in the tender documents.

108 For consideration of State aid and public private partnerships see C. Bovis, 'State Aid and Public Private Partnerships – Containing the Treat to Free Markets and Competition' (2010) 3 EPPPL 125.

109 Case C-94/99, *ARGE* [2000] ECR I-11037.

Directive 2004/18/EC] requires, or at the very least allows, the contracting authorities to take into account the existence of subsidies, and in particular of aid incompatible with the Treaty, in order, where appropriate, to exclude tenderers in receipt of such aid'.[110]

Furthermore, the Court took into account that the obligation to repay incompatible State aid may threaten the financial security of the bidder. The Court found that 'a tenderer may be excluded from a selection procedure where the contracting authority considers that it has received aid incompatible with the Treaty and that the obligation to repay illegal aid would threaten its financial well-being, so that that tenderer may be regarded as unable to offer the necessary financial or economic security'.[111]

State aid issues are normally dealt with under the State aid rules. However, Article 69 of the public sector directive[112] requires the contracting authority to clarify State aid matters. Article 69(1) and (2)(f) reads:

1. Contracting authorities shall require economic operators to explain the price or costs proposed in the tender where tenders appear to be abnormally low in relation to the works, supplies or services.
2. The explanations referred to in paragraph 1 may in particular relate to:

   (f) the possibility of the tenderer obtaining State aid.

The provision sets out a duty for the contracting authority to seek clarification from the bidder and to make inquiries into whether State aid has been awarded. The use of specified procedures for determining whether the bid is acceptable or not is mandatory.

The word 'alone' indicates that incompatible State aid is a sufficient reason to reject the offer. It is not necessary to uncover other grounds, for example the risk of non-performance.[113]

However, the provision requires a causal link between State aid and the low bid. It is only incompatible aid that can justify deselecting a bid. If the aid is compatible the bid cannot be rejected on the basis of Article 69. Furthermore, it follows from the wording of Article 69 that aid must have been either granted to the specific project involved in the procurement procedure or, in case of aid granted to other projects, it must be proven to have been used for pricing the bid towards this project.

Article 69 is a provision that protects the interest of the contracting authority. While it seems that the burden of proving that the provider has received State aid is on the contracting authority, the burden of proof as to its compatibility is on the bidder.[114] If the bidder is unable to prove that the aid is compatible the authority can evade the difficulties that follow from choosing a bidder that might have received incompatible State aid. It also seems that for the procuring entity to characterise a tender as being 'abnormally low', with the result that it may be rejected, it is not necessary that the bid

110 Paragraph 29.

111 Paragraph 30.

112 See Case C-599/10, SAG ELV Slovensko a.s. and Others v Úrad pre verejné obstarévanie, [2012], (not yet reported).

113 Arrowsmith, *The Law of Public and Utilities Procurement*, above, fn 9, p. 538.

114 Ibid p. 538.

appears low in comparison with the market price, it is sufficient that it appears to be a low bid for that particular undertaking.[115]

4.2.2 The principle of equality

As mentioned above in the introductory section, it is an aim of both the public procurement and State aid rules to ensure a level playing field amongst competitors on the internal market. The principle of equal treatment of bidders in public procurement procedures stems from this aim. In this context, it can be argued that it would not ensure a level playing field between bidders to allow undertakings that have received State aid, even if the aid is lawful, to participate in public bids.

Article 55 gives contracting authorities the option to reject tenders on the basis of unlawful State aid. But, can lawful State aid be hindrance for the participation in a tender? Can an undertaking participate in a tender even though its bid is considerably lower due to the presence of State aid, or does the principle of equality stand in the way of this?

In the above mentioned *ARGE* case certain of the tenders were submitted by service providers from the public sector. ARGE, an association of undertakings and civil engineers, challenged the participation of those companies in the procedure for the award of the public procurement contracts concerned, claiming that, as semi-public tenderers, they received substantial State subsidies.

The Court concluded that 'the mere fact that the contracting authority allows bodies receiving subsidies of any kind, whether from that contracting authority or from other authorities, which enable them to submit tenders at prices appreciably lower than those of the other, unsubsidised, tenderers to take part in a procedure for the award of a public service contract does not amount to a breach of the principle of equal treatment.'[116]

The exemptions from the prohibition of State aid laid down in the Treaty and complementing legislative acts, are seen as necessary for a well-functioning and equitable economy, and are subject to monitoring by the Commission. It can thus be argued that the unconditional exclusion of all State aid beneficiaries in public tenders would undermine the purpose of these exemptions.

4.2.3 The use of secondary criteria

Primary criteria are factors that are directly related to the subject matter of the contract, that is, price or cost, using a cost effectiveness approach, or the best price-quality ratio. Secondary criteria are, on the other hand, factors that are desirable but not directly related to the subject matter of the contract. Examples can be the combating of unemployment in certain regions, or environmental protection.[117]

As mentioned, one of the main objectives of the public procurement reform procedure is the improvement of the quality of public procurement by way of increased room for considering social and environmental criteria. The Commission's Green Paper

---

115 Ibid p. 539.

116 Paragraphs 25 and 32.

117 See section 2.2 of this Chapter.

on the modernisation of EU public procurement policy[118] focuses on the contribution that public authorities can give in achieving the Europe 2020 strategic goals, by using their purchasing power to procure goods and services with higher 'societal' value, for example in terms of fostering innovation, fighting climate change, reducing energy consumption, and improving inclusion of disadvantaged groups and so on.

The question is whether increasing the purchase price to take account of secondary criteria leads to the existence of State aid? The answer is 'no' *per se*. There is no State aid where additional payment for social or environmental benefit merely represents a commercial price for securing that benefit. In such cases there is no advantage to the contractor, and thus no State aid is involved. However, State aid arises if the price paid for the secondary element is above market price and thereby confers an advantage on the contracting party.

That was one of the consideration of the *BAI v Commission* judgement, which, as mentioned above, concerned favourable terms offered by the Spanish authorities to a ferry company for 'social and cultural' reasons of establishing a ferry service between England and Spain. Article 107(1), as the judgment reiterated, makes no distinction according to the causes or aims of the aid in question, but defines it in relation to its effects.[119]

Secondary objectives are best pursued as tender requirements. Tenderers will submit their own solutions (and prices) for dealing with social requirements. The procurement procedure will therefore result in the contracting authority paying a commercial price. Hence, there is a presumption that no State aid is involved.

In order to ensure effective competition between economic operators and avoid arbitrary decisions by public authorities, the current EU public procurement rules require that award criteria must be linked to the subject-matter of the contract, and may not confer an unrestricted freedom of choice on the contracting authority.[120] However, the 2014 directives increase the room for considering social and environmental criteria.

The Commission's Communication on compensation for SGEIs demands that all 'award criteria, including environmental or social ones, [must be] closely related to the subject-matter of the service provided and allow for the most economically advantageous offer to match the value of the market.'[121]

As underlined by the Green Paper itself, the link with the subject-matter of the contract ensures that the purchase itself remains central to the process in which taxpayers' money is being spent. This is an important guarantee to make sure that the contracting authorities obtain the best possible offer with efficient use of public money. The guarantee also ensures a measure of consistency between the EU public procurement policy and the rules in the field of State aid, as it makes sure that no undue economic advantage is conferred on economic operators through the award of public

---

[118] Green Paper on the modernisation of EU public procurement policy, Towards a more efficient European Procurement Market, 27 January 2011 COM(2011) 15 final, p. 33.

[119] Case T-14/96, [1999] ECR II-139.

[120] Article 67(2) and (4) of the public sector directive and Article 82(2) and (4) of the utilities directive.

[121] Communication from the Commission on the application of the European Union State aid rules to compensation granted for the provision of services of general economic interest, at para 67.

contracts. Loosening the link with the subject-matter of the contract might therefore entail a risk of distancing the application of EU public procurement rules from that of the State aid rules, and may eventually run counter to the objective of more convergence between those two sets of rules.[122]

[122] Green Paper on the modernisation of EU public procurement policy, p. 39.

16. EU public procurement and probity

Tünde Tátrai

'The people who can best describe corruption are those themselves engaged in corruption.'[1]

This chapter deals with the connection between public procurement and probity; it examines the legal background – including the previous Public Procurement Directives and the current new Directives – to the prevention of corruption and fraud in procurement procedures. Our assumption is that the use of traditional instruments may be inadequate in the struggle for ethical public procurement. Prevention and access to relevant, procurement-related information on the part of the legislator are as much part of the subject matter as the independent audit activity of the contracting authorities and the focus on the real meaning and content of probity.

Public procurement is not the cause of corruption but a consequence of social and economic problems. A high level of corruption depends not only on the attitudes of the public procurement market, but also on that of society in general. The legal background can help prevent the misuse of public procurement but cannot change the habits of the market players. That is why it is necessary to use the Public Procurement Directives also to create a culture, to call attention to the fact that not only the conflict of interest rules or mandatory exclusion may lead to success in our endeavours for more ethical procurement. If sufficient, relevant and comparable statistical data and information on the public procurement market are not available, or the protocols enabling contracting authorities to audit their own activities, only superficial treatment will be implemented, at the level of legislation. When the issue is examined from the viewpoint of probity – as this chapter aims to do – prevention, monitoring and genuine transparency based on widely studied literature will therefore gain a new meaning.

1. NEED FOR DATA, NEED FOR DEFINITION, NEED FOR CHANGE

Public expenditure on works, goods and services accounts for roughly 17.7 per cent of EU GDP (2011). Almost a fifth of this expenditure falls within the scope of the EU Directives on public procurement (that is, approximately €425 billion, or 3.4 per cent of EU GDP[2]), that is, public procurement above the EU public procurement threshold.

Figure 16.1 shows how diverse the value of public procurement is relative to GDP in the individual Member States. Accurate data are available on procurements exceeding

[1] Hillman (2004) p. 2.

[2] Figures available 3 February 2016 at http://ec.europa.eu/internal_market/public procurement/docs/modernising_rules/public-procurement-indicators.

the EU threshold; that is, only a moderate quantity of comparable data are available on the total public procurement market. Accordingly, we do not have comparable information on the interpretation and evaluation of conflict of interest by the Member States, or the violations of procurement rules characteristic of individual Member States, which would have a bearing on our subject matter. Useful information was obtained in the course of developing the new European Directives; also, the area is subject to genuine research activity; all this, however, cannot be regarded as more than meagre foundations to be discussed later.

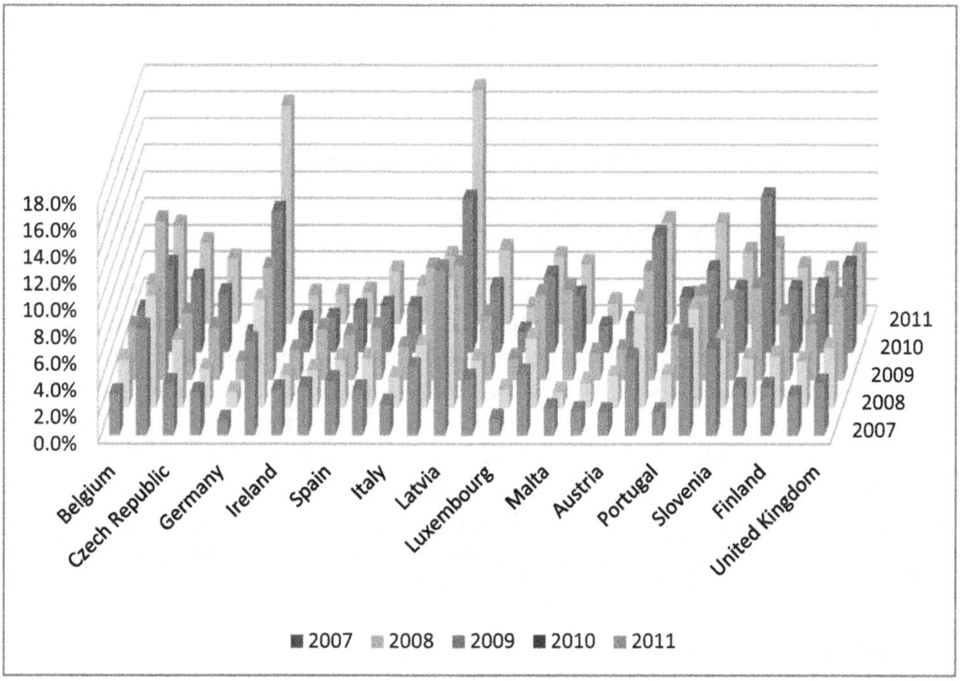

Source: http://ec.europa.eu/internal_market/publicprocurement/docs/modernising_rules/public-procurement-indicators-2011_en.pdf, p. 7

Figure 16.1 The estimated value of tenders published in TED in percentage of GDP

The legal background was transformed in Europe; a direct consequence of this was that the public procurement market has come to expect more from the new legal provisions. The previous EU Directives on public procurement[3] did not include specific provisions on prevention and conflicts of interest and comprised only a few specific rules on sanctioning favouritism and corruption.

[3] Directive 2004/18/EC on the coordination of procedures for the award of public works contracts, public supply contracts and public service contracts ([2004] OJ L134/114) and Directive 2004/17/EC coordinating the procurement procedures of entities operating in the water, energy, transport and postal services sectors ([2004] OJ L134/1).

In the course of the preparation of the new Directives the Commission announced in the Single Market Act that it would, on the basis of wide consultations, put forward legislative proposals for a revised and modernised public procurement legislative framework by the end of 2011. The consultation[4] was opened by the publication of the Green Paper on 27 January 2011. In total, 623 responses were received. The replies came from a wide variety of stakeholder groups including central Member State authorities, local and regional public purchasers and their associations, undertakings, industry associations, academics, civil society organisations and individual citizens. This survey can be regarded as a milestone as it was not at general but expert level, and some expressly useful research questions were posed.

Below we summarise the conclusions of the responses to the questions of the Green Paper relevant to our subject matter. The answers of the experts addressed the issues of corruption, conflict of interest, exclusion criteria and unfair advantages as relevant to our subject matter and will help in understanding the new legal environment.

1.1 Corruption/Conflict of Interest[5]

By the synthesis of replies,[6] all stakeholders agreed on the fact that procurement markets are exposed to risks of favouritism and corruption. Most stakeholders (except for academia/legal experts), however, consider that European instruments are not needed to mitigate these risks, but that this issue should rather be addressed through national legislation, for reasons of subsidiarity and in order to take into account the very different administrative and business cultures in the Member States.

However, a majority of business, civil society and legal experts see a necessity for a common European definition of 'conflict of interest'. Contracting authorities and Member States are mostly against the introduction of European rules on conflict of interest, as they consider the national rules sufficient.

1.2 Exclusion Grounds

There was consensus amongst all stakeholder groups that Article 45 of Directive 2004/18/EC is a useful instrument to sanction unsound business behaviours.

---

[4] Green Paper on the modernisation of EU public procurement policy. Towards a more efficient European Public Procurement Market, COM(2011) 15 final.

[5] '98: Would you be in favour of introducing an EU definition of conflict of interest in public procurement? What activities/situations harbouring a potential risk should be covered (personal relationships, business interests such as shareholdings, incompatibilities with external activities/ etc.)?

99: Do you think that there is a need for safeguards to prevent, identify and resolve conflict-of-interest situations effectively at EU level? If so, which kind of safeguards would you consider useful?

108: Do you think that in light of the Lisbon Treaty, minimum standards for criminal sanctions should be developed at EU level, in particular circumstances, such as corruption or undeclared conflicts of interest?'

[6] Green Paper on the modernisation of EU public procurement policy Towards a more efficient European Procurement Market.

Nevertheless, certain clarifications are considered useful by many respondents, notably with regard to generic notions such as 'professional misconduct', as well as rules on a maximum duration of debarment. Businesses and Member States also advocated that Article 45 should also address the issue of self-cleaning, to create legal certainty and overcome the fragmentation of practices in the EU.

Contracting authorities are mostly opposed to the introduction of EU rules on self-cleaning.

1.3 Avoiding Unfair Advantages

The consultation did not show clear tendencies on whether EU rules should explicitly address the issue of advantages of certain tenderers because of their prior association with the tender design. Several respondents propose, as a possible remedy to unfair advantages, an obligation for the contracting authority to make available certain information to all interested candidates where this is necessary to ensure a fair bidding process.

In the preparation of a modernised EU public procurement legislation, the Commission promised to carefully consider these issues. Later we shall see with what success, as embedded in the new Directives.[7]

There seemed to be a demand to expand the scope of the previous regulation. To describe the circumstances of the previous situation in the EU and the legal background, we define the most important terms concerning public procurement and probity, such as ethical procurement, corruption and self-cleaning. It will help us understand the need for relatively new directions in the EU.

2. PUBLIC PROCUREMENT SPECIFIC DEFINITIONS

Probity means the quality of having strong moral principles; honesty and decency. What does this mean in the world of public procurement; what is required by the demand for irreproachable public procurement? Ethical behaviour that is free of corruption and based on trust necessitates a more accurate demarcation of its interpretation environment.

As we take stock of the most important expressions related to the issue of probity, our approach may be considered novel. We approach the subject matter not only from the viewpoint of corruption, but also from that of the positive, improving intent. Below we shed light on how the topic of corruption can be part of the struggle for ethical public procurement. Further, under the definitions we present a novelty less frequently referred to: self-cleaning which is a solution based on trust and sincerity. The purpose of the definitions is to point out the diversity in interpreting the phrases used in

[7] Communication from the Commission to the European Parliament, the Council and the European Economic and Social Committee Fighting Corruption in the EU, available 3 February 2016 at http://ec.europa.eu/home-affairs/news/intro/docs/110606/308/1_EN_ACT_part1_v12%5B1%5D.pdf.

connection with probity, owing to which the term probity itself should be used in as broad a sense as possible.

First, ethical public procurement, as a term related to probity, will be addressed, this being one of the most important definitions.

2.1 Ethical Procurement

As the National Institute of Government Purchasing (NIGP) Code of Ethics says:

> Ethical procurement prohibits breach of the public's trust by discouraging a public employee from attempting to realise personal gain through conduct inconsistent with the proper discharge of the employee's duties. Ethics are the principles which define behaviour as right, good and appropriate. Employees in public service should uphold certain values. Any attempt to realise personal gain by conduct inconsistent with the proper discharge of the employee's duties is a breach of the public trust. The value of the transactions in the procurement process along with pressures to lower costs could result in bribery, corruption and other practices which could be deemed unethical. In the public sector where goods and services are funded by public expenditure, it is imperative that procurement operates ethically, with impartiality, transparency, and professionalism. Ethical procurement best practice starts with the employees in procurement following an ethical code which dictates their behaviour and actions while conducting business. Ethical procurement practices should be extended to all stakeholders, contracting authorities, tenderers, controlling bodies etc. in the procurement cycle.[8]

That is to say, morality must permeate the entire process of public procurement.

In the following we intend to explore the content of ethical procurement and assess the most widely voiced problem of public procurement: the connection between conflict of interest and corruption.

Harland et al (2007) developed a seven-stage model for public procurement on the basis of their international research on public procurement.[9] With the model, they tried to define the national priorities of public procurement in the stages of development (see Table 16.1).

Amending their seven-stage model, the researchers found that most public procurement priorities relate to stages 2–5, and the priorities that relate to policy objectives are considered lower ranking. This shows that while it was beneficial to be able to demonstrate a broader policy role, in practice, all measures and drivers steered public procurement practitioners towards a more compliant, efficiency-focused role. The higher ranking priorities, accountability, transparency and probity, are practical enough for experts to fit them into their thinking; nevertheless, policy-oriented ethical procurement provides a wider platform for sustaining a better public image and conduct of procurement.

Dealing with procurement ethics, researchers focus more on what an agency can do for ethical behaviour. As Hunsaker says:[10] 'Public procurement professionals must keep

---

[8] Code of Ethics – NIGP, available 3 February 2016 at http://www.nigp.org/eweb/StartPage.aspx?Site=NIGP&webcode=abt-codeofethics.

[9] Knight et al (2007) p. 353

[10] Hunsaker (2009) p. 411.

Table 16.1 The seven stages of development and national priorities of public procurement – focusing on ethics, transparency, accountability

Original seven stages of development	Lower ranking priorities	Higher ranking priorities
1. Sourcing and delivering goods and services		
2. Compliance with legislation/regulation		
3. Efficient use of public funds		
4. Accountability	Ethics	Accountability, transparency, probity
5. Value for money		
6. Supporter of broader government policy objectives		
7. Deliverer of broader government policy objectives		

abreast of not only the laws that govern their practice, but be aware of the need for transparency in the way they conduct their transactions.' And she focuses on 'what an agency can do to thwart potential ethics violations'. The aim is to prevent unethical practice before it occurs and to create a more positive public image. In line with this, NIGP tried to limit the main elements of ethical procurement.

According to NIGP's point of view, '1. conflict of interest', '2. conduct with suppliers' and '3. corruption' are the main elements of ethical procurement, for each of which it defines certain rules of conduct, as follows:

1. Conflict of Interest

Public Procurement professionals shall:

- Avoid any private or professional activity that would create a conflict of interest or the appearance of impropriety;
- Avoid engaging in personal business with any supplier representative or similar person;
- Avoid lending money to or borrowing money from any supplier;
- Avoid any and all potential for nepotism;
- Avoid any overlap of duties in the procurement process;
- Safeguard the procurement process from political or outside influence.

2. Conduct with Suppliers

Business dealings with suppliers must be fair and transparent. Procurement shall:

- Refrain from showing favouritism or being influenced by suppliers through the acceptance of gifts, gratuities, loans or favours;
- Safeguard supplier confidentiality;
- Refrain from requiring suppliers to pay to be included on an approved or preferred supplier list;
- Refrain from requesting donations of goods or services to the public entity;
- Select suppliers on the basis of meeting appropriate and fair criteria;
- Discourage the arbitrary or unfair use of purchasing leverage or influence when dealing with suppliers;
- Avoid the exertion of undue influence or abuses of power;
- Treat all suppliers fair and equal.

> 3. Corruption
>
> Public procurement professionals who become aware of any corrupt activity have a duty to the profession and to their employing organisations to alert their management and/or elected officials. Public procurement shall not tolerate bribery or corruption in any form.[11,12]

With this approach of NIGP, transparent and fair business dealing with suppliers and independent public employees and processes come to be on the same level as fighting corruption activities. This way of thinking tells us more about fair and equal competition and prevention.

Arrowsmith (2011) calls attention to the importance of 'conduct' from the point of view of the Agreement on Government Procurement (GPA), and points out concerning the Revised GPA[13] that it is the most radical innovation in the new provision relating to corruption and conflict of interest. Indeed, the revised text incorporates the 'conduct of procurement' as an important new substantive provision.

The provision in Article V.4 reads as follows:

> Conduct of Procurement
>
> 1. A procuring entity shall conduct covered procurement in a transparent and impartial manner that:
>
>   ...
>
>   (b) avoids conflicts of interest; and
>   (c) prevents corrupt practices'

According to the GPA logic, Article V.4. limits the meaning of 'conduct' and focuses on conflicts of interest and corruption.

> Further the fact that such rules are included in the GPA can have an impact in preventing corruption, and the fact that GPA accession can help states implement such rules against domestic vested interests and lock them into their systems means that in practice the GPA can assist states in addressing the problem of corruption.[14]

As Arrowsmith indicates, the revised GPA can assist states in the implementation of anti-corruption rules and address the problem of corruption.

The GPA implementation processes and the EU Directives concerned are not far from each other. The symbolic and general rules, the clear approaches help the Member States implement the Directives in their own contexts. But in terms of defining ethical procurement, conflict of interest or corruption, the European regulation shows a narrower interpretation of the subject matter introduced above.

As Arnáiz (2006) points out, with the Directives concerned:

> the sphere of action of the Member States has been significantly demarcated. As has been seen, the current regulatory framework binds the national legislator with respect to the

---

11 The NIGP definitions and content were simplified and shortened.

12 Code of Ethics – NIGP, available 3 February 2016 at http://www.nigp.org/eweb/StartPage.aspx?Site=NIGP&webcode=abt-codeofethics

13 Arrowsmith (2011) pp. 334–6.

14 Arrowsmith (2011). p. 289.

> mandatory inclusion of crimes of corruption as the cause of exclusion from contracts. This is in clear contrast to the previous situation in which the general rule allowed each Member State to consider such conduct as liable to lead to exclusion. Legal security is strengthened in this way, with more guarantees not only due to the legislative harmonisation that the Directive entails, but also because it is an efficient instrument in the fight against corruption. Nevertheless, and despite all the very best intentions behind the measure, its impact will depend on the strength of implementation by the Member States.[15]

One of the most frequently discussed issues of ethical procurement is corruption, as defined below.

2.2 Corruption

Corruption in public procurement has a massive ethical impact. As Greenwood and Klotz (2009) point out: 'When people observe that corrupt behaviour is not being sanctioned, they easily reduce their own integrity standards. This applies also to suppliers of goods and services in such environments, which realise that offering a competitive price and quality is insufficient to obtain contracts'.[16]

The definitions in Table 16.2 uniformly divide the types of corruption into two basic types, active and passive corruption. The consequences are the same with respect to the regulations, independently of the classification of the economic operators' activity.

There are several classifications of the forms of corruption in public procurement. This chapter, however, takes an approach that is expressly not that of criminal law.

According to the NIGP approach, the typical forms of corruption are bribery, extortion, trading in influence, laundering the proceeds of corrupt practices, and nepotism.

- **Bribery** is the offering, promising, giving, authorizing or accepting of any undue financial or other advantage to, by or for any persons associated with the procurement process, or for anyone else in order to obtain or retain a business or other improper advantage. Bribery often includes (i) kicking back a portion of a contract payment to government or party officials or to employees of the other contracting party, their close relatives, friends or business partners or (ii) using intermediaries such as agents, subcontractors, consultants or other third parties, to channel payments to government or party officials, or to employees of the contracting parties, their relatives, friends or business partners.
- **Extortion or Solicitation** is the demanding of a bribe, whether or not coupled with a threat, if the demand is refused. Procurement professionals will oppose any attempt of extortion or solicitation and are encouraged to report such attempts through available formal or informal reporting mechanisms.
- **Trading in Influence** is the offering or solicitation of an undue advantage in order to exert an improper, real, or supposed influence.
- **Laundering the proceeds of the corrupt practices mentioned above** is the concealing or disguising the illegitimate origin, source, location, disposition, movement or ownership of property and/or money, knowing that such is the proceeds of crime.

---

15 Arnáiz (2006) p. 345.

16 Greenwood and Klotz (2009) p. 58.

- **Nepotism** is the use of authority or influence to show favouritism to relatives or friends without merit.[17]

The above definitions are of interest because they define the individual activities and forms of behaviour not from the viewpoint of criminal law, but instead, attempt to build a particular interpretation around procurement-specific activities expected from a procurement-oriented organisation.

Table 16.2 The definition of corruption is similar in the previous Directive 2004/18 and the new Directives

	Council Act of 26 May 1997[1]	98/742/JHA[2]	2003/568/JHA[3]
Passive corruption	The deliberate action of an official, who, directly or through an intermediary, requests or receives advantages of any kind whatsoever, for himself or for a third party, or accepts a promise of such an advantage, to act or refrain from acting in accordance with his duty or in the exercise of his functions in breach of his official duties	The deliberate action of a person who, in the course of his business activities, directly or through an intermediary, requests or receives an undue advantage of any kind whatsoever, or accepts the promise of such an advantage, for himself or for a third party, for him to perform or refrain from performing an act, in breach of his duties	Directly or through an intermediary, requesting or receiving an undue advantage of any kind, or accepting the promise of such an advantage, for oneself or for a third party, while in any capacity directing or working for a private-sector entity, in order to perform or refrain from performing any act, in breach of one's duties
Active corruption	The deliberate action of whosoever promises or gives, directly or through an intermediary, an advantage of any kind whatsoever to an official for himself or for a third party for him to act or refrain from acting in accordance with his duty or in the exercise of his functions in breach of his official duties	The deliberate action of whosoever promises, offers or gives, directly or through an intermediary, an undue advantage of any kind whatsoever to a person, for himself or for a third party, in the course of the business activities of that person in order that the person should perform or refrain from performing an act, in breach of his duties	Promising, offering or giving, directly or through an intermediary, to a person who in any capacity directs or works for a private-sector entity an undue advantage of any kind, for that person or for a third party, in order that that person should perform or refrain from performing any act, in breach of that person's duties

Notes:
1. Article 3 of the Council Act of 26 May 1997 – referred to by the present and planned directives.
2. Joint Action of 22 December 1998 adopted by the Council on the basis of Article K.3 of the Treaty on European Union, on corruption in the private sector (Article 2, 3) – referred to by the previous directives.
3. Article 2(1) of Council Framework Decision 2003/568/JHA – referred to by the present directives.

[17] Available 3 February 2016 at http://www.nigp.org/docs/default-source/New-Site/global-best-practices/ethical.pdf?sfvrsn=2

Recently, a study on corruption in EU public procurement ordered by the European Anti-fraud Office (OLAF)[18] distinguished four types of corruption: bid rigging, kickbacks, conflict of interest and others including deliberate mismanagement or ignorance. The technical basis of this categorisation is, for the time being, unclear; it is worth noting, however, that breaking with the traditional listing of corrupt practices, the list of types mixes active acts of corruption and the relationship of situations and causes of corruption.[19]

It can be established, however, that novelties and different interpretations keep appearing expressly with respect to the public procurement market of the EU, too.

To identify the primary forms of corruption in public procurement, various studies broke down the process of procurement into phases, indicating a better grounded structure. Greenwood and Klotz (2009) addressed the pre-bidding, bidding and post-bidding phases.

- The pre-bidding phase 'includes a needs assessment by the public authority along with preparation of the bid design. In the needs assessment stage, the government entity is required to determine what goods or services it is seeking to purchase and how much it is willing to spend'.
- The bidding phase 'occurs when a government entity invites bids and determines which bidder will be awarded the contract'.
- Post-bidding phase 'belongs to the performance and implementation phase of the contract'.[20]

Dorn et al (2008) divide the procurement process as follows: preparation of specifications, selection of tenderers and execution of contracts, attributing specific risks to each (red flags).[21]

In each of the phases mentioned above, market players have the opportunity of using unacceptable means and resources. Corruption practices use all the processes of procurement including the phases of preparation and implementation. The wide spectrum of corrupt practices embraces the case when corrupt officials prepare reports to justify false departmental needs, or when the selection criteria used to determine the winning bidder or when the contractor compensates officers for poor-quality performance. There is no way to find a single solution to reduce corruption risk in public procurement procedures, but we can find best practices if we understand the meaning of corruption.

According to Greenwood and Klotz (2009),[22] the key principles of best anti-corruption practices in public procurement are as follows:

---

[18] Available 3 February 2016 at http://ec.europa.eu/anti_fraud/documents/anti-fraud-policy/research-and-studies/pwc_olaf_study_en.pdf.

[19] Later in the chapter some of the data of this study will be referred to.

[20] Greenwood and Klotz (2009) pp. 61–2.

[21] Dorn et al. (2008).

[22] Greenwood and Klotz (2009).

- transparency,
- good management and the prevention of misconduct,
- monitoring compliance, accountability and enforcement.

Prevention, monitoring and transparency form a triangle, which can encompass not only the post-bidding, but also the bidding and the pre-bidding phases. The European regulation focuses on transparency in general and mainly on the personal situation of the tenderer.[23] Of these, transparency is an objective in itself. As Trepte said:

> It is a term for describing various mechanisms used to achieve a number of specific goals. These goals depend on the identity of the intended beneficiaries of transparent mechanisms ... The regulation of procurement applies overlapping transparency conditions for the benefit of all the three main parties involved in public procurement: the public authority (contracting authority), the procurement agent and the tenderer ... The purpose of transparency conditions can be summarised according to the relationship of the parties.[24]

Following the interpretation of the above, frequently used terms, it is worth exploring a new concept, which is based on a relationship of trust between the parties – which is often missed. There is a need for an innovation that can help refresh the European way of thinking concerning corruption and transparency such as the self-cleaning method.

2.3 Self-cleaning[25]

The EC Directives[26] require Member States to exclude an economic operator from public contracts if the operator has been the subject of a conviction by final judgement for corruption or fraud, money laundering or participation in a criminal organisation. Within these rules the concept of self-cleaning might be raised as an argument to avoid exclusion. The general idea would be that an economic operator can regain the possibility of participating in public contracts by demonstrating that it has taken effective measures to ensure that wrongful acts will not recur in the future.

In some Member States the concept of self-cleaning has been established (Germany and Austria). The essence of the method is that 'the firm that might be excluded from public procurement procedure because of some kind of wrongdoing should be admitted to the self-cleaning process, on the basis that it has taken measures to ensure that the wrongdoing of the past will not occur again in the future'.[27]

The measures to be taken include:

---

23 Bovis (2007).

24 Trepte (2004) pp. 392–4.

25 Pünder, Priess and Arrowsmith (2009).

26 Directive 2004/08/EC of the European Parliament and of the Council of 31 March 2004 on the coordination of procedures for the award of public works contracts, public supply contracts and public service contracts; Directive 2004/17/EC of the European Parliament and of the Council of 31 March 2004 coordinating the procurement procedures of entities operating in the water, energy, transport and postal services sectors.

27 Arrowsmith, Priess and Friton (2009) pp. 4–7. in Pünder, Priess and Arrowsmith (2009).

- Clarification of the relevant facts and circumstances: the company has to assist in order to clarify the facts and the responsibility of all persons involved in a comprehensive manner.
- Reparation of the damage caused: it is required to repair the financial damage caused.
- Personnel measures: the company has to ensure that all persons who have been strongly involved in the wrongdoing are dismissed.
- Structural and organisational measures: the company has to verify organisational preventive measures, reviews, guidelines and take care of the future.

The recognition of self-cleaning measures can particularly help EU legislators to eliminate legal uncertainty and to set down explicit rules for the acknowledgement of self-cleaning measures in new directives.

How then do we interpret the term probity in public procurement? By our approach, probity as the main principle requires ethical ways of thinking, ethical attitudes, the avoidance of corrupt forms of behaviour as well as the creation of trust among market agents, who themselves are able to clean the market and to create a more advanced procurement environment. Probity therefore may characterise a regulatory environment model, a way of thinking on the part of both contracting authorities and bidders as well as the building up of a public procurement structure. Probity should permeate procurement not only in the common sense of the term, but it should also determine its stakeholders, institutional structure and the conditions of its environment.

Having defined the most important terms concerning public procurement and probity, we now summarise the existing European anti-corruption policy in public procurement in order to explore what can be expected from policy makers.

3. EU POLICY CONCERNING CORRUPTION IN PUBLIC PROCUREMENT

EU public procurement law and policy address corruption in relation to awarding public contracts. Corruption, particularly its organised form, has long constituted a significant problem for the European Union and its Member States as it has negative effects, *inter alia*, on public trust in government, fair competition, efficient resource allocation, and integrity in providing public services. Nevertheless, the issue rose to the top of the European agenda with the accession of the Central and Eastern European countries, particularly Romania and Bulgaria.[28] This interest is further fuelled by the perception that corruption is on the rise on the continent[29] and by the accumulated evidence on the negative consequences of various forms of corruption, for example, on economic growth.[30] The comparable experience with corruption in most of the recent candidate countries such as Turkey ensures that public and political interest remains high.

---

28 Vachudova (2009) p. 43.
29 Bull and Newell (2003).
30 Kaufmann (2005).

The objectives of EU procurement legislation remain well-understood and widely supported by EU citizens. The Eurobarometer (2011) survey shows a large understanding/support for the role of procurement in the fight against favouritism and corruption. It also demonstrates widespread understanding of the importance of opening procurement markets to competition (see Figures 16.2 and 16.3).[31]

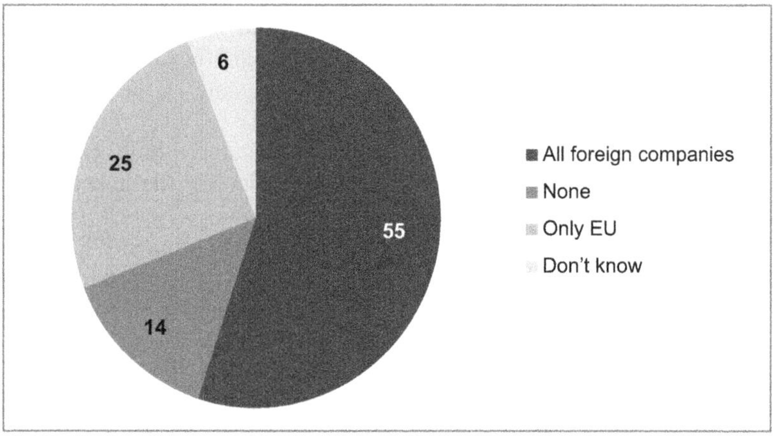

Source: EU public procurement legislation: delivering results – Summary of evaluation report.

Figure 16.2 Public perceptions of EU procurement policy (2011): do you think that foreign companies should be able to compete for public contracts in your country?

However, there is no uniform methodology to measure corruption in public procurement in the EU and its Member States, which makes it difficult to take effective action against it. By understanding the need for tackling political, organised and other forms of corruption and being entitled to do so by the Article 29 of the Treaty of the European Union and Article 85 of the Treaty of Lisbon, the EU has taken a great number of initiatives in this direction. The most recent milestones of European action show an increased effort in tackling corruption both at the EU and Member State levels.

The Commission's Communication on Fighting Corruption in the EU[32] demonstrated the political will to fight corruption at EU level and to support Member States in their own efforts. It has established an EU Anti-corruption Report[33] to be completed biannually from 2013 onwards, which is expected to provide additional impetus to Member State efforts in the fight against corruption. Crucially, the EU recognises that

[31] EU public procurement legislation: delivering results – Summary of evaluation report. European Commission Internal Market and Services http://ec.europa.eu/internal_market/publicprocurement/docs/modernising_rules/executive-summary_en.pdf.

[32] Communication from the Commission to the European Parliament, the Council and the European Economic and Social Committee on Fighting Corruption in the EU (COM(2011) 308 final), adopted on 6 June 2011.

[33] Commission Decision of 6.6.2011 on Establishing an EU Anti-corruption reporting mechanism for periodic assessment ('EU Anti-corruption Report'), C(2011) 3673 final.

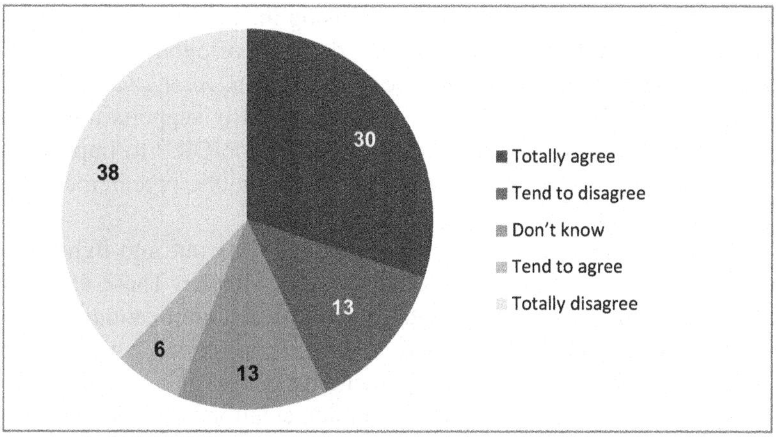

Source: EU public procurement legislation: delivering results – Summary of evaluation report.

Figure 16.3 Public perceptions of EU procurement policy (2011): to what extent do you agree or disagree with the fact that common EU-wide rules for public authorities on how they have to award contracts help to combat favouritism and corruption?

the legal frameworks are well-developed and plentiful in most Member States, but rigorous implementation is lacking in many cases, hence more efforts need to be put into policy implementation and enforcement. It would be crucial, however, for policy implementation and enforcement to have recourse to reliable data on actual practice rather than to legal concepts or perceptions.

A stronger focus on corruption in EU internal policies is also set out in the Commission's Communication on Fighting Corruption in the EU,[34] which implies a more effective legal framework and monitoring regarding public procurement both at EU and Member State levels. The Commission has also taken measures for improving its Anti-Fraud Strategy,[35] the functioning of OLAF,[36] the EU public procurement regulatory framework[37] and the protection of the financial interests of the EU in general.[38]

---

[34] Communication from the Commission to the European Parliament, the Council and the European Economic and Social Committee on Fighting Corruption in the EU (COM)2011) 308 final), adopted on 6 June 2011.

[35] Communication from the Commission on the Commission Anti-Fraud Strategy. COM(2011) 376 final.

[36] Amended Proposal for a Regulation of the European Parliament and of the Council amending Regulation (EC) No 1073/1999 concerning investigations conducted by the European Anti-fraud Office (OLAF) and repealing Regulation (EURATOM) No 1074/1999.

[37] Available 3 February 2016 at http://ec.europa.eu/growth/single-market/public-procurement/index_en.htm.

[38] Communication from the Commission on the protection of the financial interests of the European Union by criminal law and by administrative investigations. COM(2011) 293 final.

The EU is taking a series of steps for modernising the public procurement systems in Europe,[39] and it has established its own online database of public procurement tenders: TED (Tenders Electronic Daily)[40] publishes information, *inter alia*, on the details of award decisions and calls for tenders. In addition, the EU supports initiatives such as PEPPOL (Pan-European Procurement Online)[41] and e-PRIOR[42] to improve connectivity and increase interoperability across EU institutions' public procurement systems and Member States' systems.

The wealth of these measures in itself shows the efforts put into fighting corruption in general and corruption in public procurement in particular. These efforts, nevertheless, would require sufficient quality data enabling the identification of gaps and the ways forward. These reports recognised the need for going beyond measurement exercises removed from actual practice of spending public money and to provide data which would effectively support policy implementation and the enforcement of regulations.

4. MEASURING CORRUPTION IN PUBLIC PROCUREMENT IN THE EU[43]

Ensuring the transparency, openness, predictability and impartiality of public institutions is a central element of anti-corruption efforts.[44] Another important element of anti-corruption policies is the permanent evaluation and monitoring of the activities of public institutions with respect to corruption risks.[45]

The public procurement markets of OECD and EU countries are of significant size compared to their GDP (see Figure 16.4): less than 20 per cent of EU GDP was spent on public procurement in 2011. This fact in itself warrants the analysis of public procurement procedures and corruption.

The problem with the OECD statistics from a public procurement point of view is that the levels of general government procurement and state-owned utilities procurement are not equivalent to public procurement spending. The obligation for contracting entities to purchase via public procurement above their national threshold, and non-state-owned utilities' procurement spending have an influence on the public procurement statistics. Comparable detailed statistics concerning public procurement spending in the European Union do not exist. The data given by the EU Member States are based on different, mostly unknown methodologies, and are simply incomparable.

39 Available 3 February 2016 at http://ec.europa.eu/growth/public-consultations/index_en.htm?tpa=1038.

40 Available 3 February 2016 at http://ted.europa.eu/TED/main/HomePage.do.

41 Available 3 February 2016 at http://www.peppol.eu/about_peppol.

42 Available 3 February 2016 at http://www.epractice.eu/cases/ePRIOR.

43 Based on a tender document of the Corruption Research Centre of Hungary, Corvinus University of Budapest and Transparency International 2012.

44 Lambsdorff (2007); Rose-Ackerman (2006).

45 Kreutner (2009); Olken (2007).

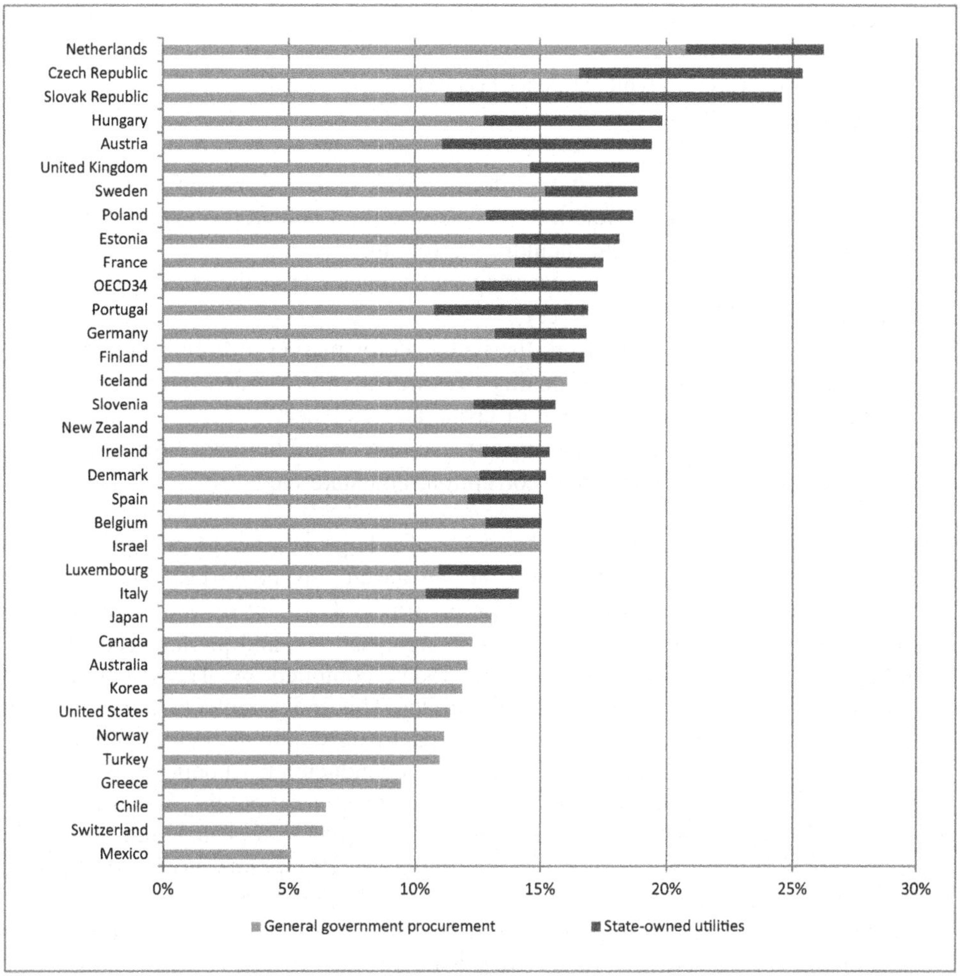

Source: OECD, 2011, p. 149 (available 3 February 2016 at http://www.oecd-ilibrary.org/sites/gov_glance-2011-en/09/01/index.html?contentType=/ns/StatisticalPublication,/ns/Chapter&itemId=/content/chapter/gov_glance-2011-46-en&containerItemId=/content/serial/22214399&accessItemIds=&mimeType=text/html).

Figure 16.4 Public procurement of government and state-owned enterprises compared to GDP, %, 2011

Concerning public procurement, two widely known indexes are described in the following: the Worldwide Governance Indicators and the Corruption Perception Index.

According to Kaufmann (2005),[46] the quality of governance and corruption cannot be measured. The World Bank developed the aggregate Worldwide Governance Indicators (WGI), which cover more than 215 countries, based on more than 350 variables, obtained from dozens of institutions worldwide over the period 1996–2011. The

[46] Kaufmann (2005).

Governance Indicators capture six key dimensions of institutional quality or governance, and measure, through two indicators each, the political, economic, and institutional dimensions of governance described above.

The following six dimensions are measured:

(1) *Voice and accountability* – measuring political, civil and human rights;
(2) *Political instability and violence* – measuring the likelihood of violent threats to, or changes in, government, including terrorism;
(3) *Government effectiveness* – measuring the competence of the bureaucracy and the quality of public service delivery;
(4) *Regulatory quality* – measuring the incidence of market-unfriendly policies;
(5) *Rule of law* – measuring the quality of contract enforcement, the police, and the courts, as well as the likelihood of crime and violence;
(6) *Control of corruption* – measuring the exercise of public power for private gain, including both petty and grand corruption, and state capture.

These aggregate indicators combine the views of a large number of enterprise, citizen and expert survey respondents in industrial and developing countries. They are based on 30 individual data sources produced by a variety of survey institutes, think tanks, non-governmental organisations, international organisations, and private sector firms.[47]

Since 1995, the Corruption Perceptions Index compiled by Transparency International is a solid measurement tool to that effect. This index ranks countries in terms of the degree to which corruption is perceived to exist among public officials and politicians and is drawn up on the basis of surveys conducted by independent entities in each country among business people, analysts and the general public. According to this Index, in 2013, 7 out of the 28 States that make up the European Union received a score that was below 50, out of the maximum of 100 points given to the most transparent countries and 0 to the most corrupt (see Figure 16.5).[48]

The annual CPI makes an important contribution to raising awareness of the issue of corruption and is a powerful advocacy tool that creates an incentive for governments to act to fight corruption.

The new, updated Corruption Perceptions Index 2012 was calculated using an updated methodology. The Corruption Perceptions Index uses an approach that provides greater clarity on how the index is constructed, making it easier to trace how the data from the sources are rescaled for inclusion in the Index.[49]

Previously, CPI was based on perceptions of corruption in each country/territory, relative to the other countries scored and ranked on this index. This was because the Index captured the rank position of each country in each data source, so that country scores were highly dependent on the changes in scores of the countries around it in the index. From 2012, TI uses the raw scores from each of the data sources, which

[47] Available 3 February 2016 at http://info.worldbank.org/governance/wgi/index.aspx#home.

[48] Arnáiz (2006) – modified on the basis of new TI data.

[49] The CPI 2012 is presented on a 0–100 scale, and demonstrates clearly that scores from the CPI 2011 and previous editions should not be compared with scores from 2012. Under the previously used methodology, CPI scores were not comparable over time.

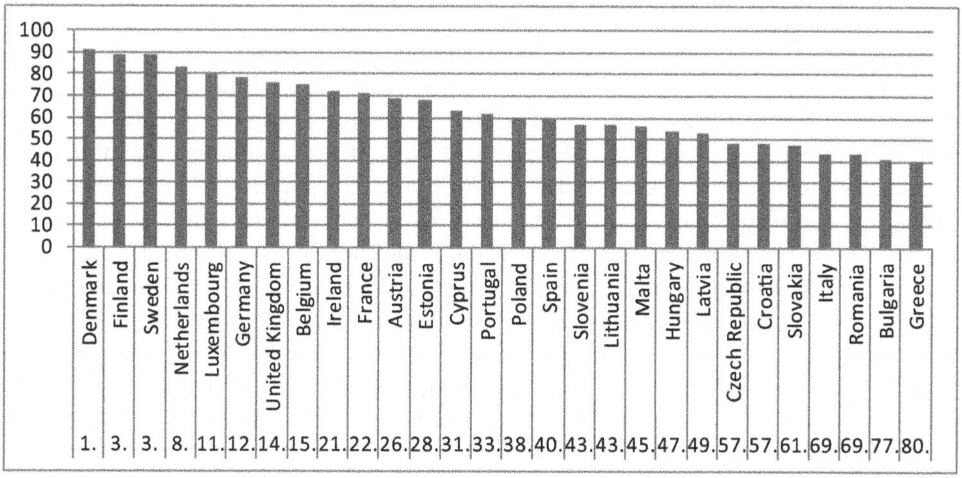

Note: The Corruption Perceptions Index ranks countries and territories based on how corrupt their public sector is perceived to be. A country or territory's score indicates the perceived level of public sector corruption on a scale of 0–100, where 0 means that a country is perceived as highly corrupt and 100 means it is perceived as very clean. This table reveals the global transparency rank position of EU Member States.

Source: http://cpi.transparency.org/cpi2013/results/

Figure 16.5 Corruption Perception Index of Transparency International (2013)

provides greater transparency as to how the CPI scores have been constructed and better enables capturing changes over time.[50]

The CPI focuses on the corruption of the government sector and defines corruption as taking advantage of public functions for the sake of personal advantage and profit. The research on improvement of CPI put questions connected with corrupt practices of abusing executive government power for personal gain (like bribing public servants, greasing in public procurement processes, fraudulent misuse of public funds) and examined the strength of anti-corruption policies including public administration and political corruption.

The general level of corruption in different states is hard to measure on the basis of exact empirical facts, the number of acts of bribery, or the number of accusations, judicial cases. In the latter case, comparable data do not reflect the actual level of corruption but the quality of work by prosecutors, courts and the media in the investigation of corruption. The best way of creating a new database covering more countries is to rely on the experience and findings of those who directly face corruption in any country.[51]

---

[50] Previous editions of the CPI drew on more than one year's data from the business surveys, where more than one year of data fell within the data period of the CPI. From 2012, TI will only use the most recent year's data from each source for each country. This will better show changes from one year to the next.

[51] Transparency International, available 3 February 2016 at http://www.transparency.org/.

The creation of a database containing elementary data on public procurement procedures in a systematic structure among many other indicators enables mathematical-statistical analysis of the inputs, throughputs and outputs of public procurement. Hence, a corruption risk and costs analysis is made possible based on hard facts rather than perceptions, which could fundamentally diminish the information asymmetry mentioned above, and thus narrow down the space for corrupt transactions. Perception-based indicators can only be used for this purpose to a limited extent.

The Public Procurement Transparency Index developed by the Hungarian TI and their experts has been a worthy attempt. Through this, it was established that 40 per cent of Hungarian municipalities are not at all compliant with the incidentally fairly strict transparency rules (they got a score of 0 in the index, while the fully compliant ones received a score of 10). This very simple index examined two aspects, the uploaded contents and their accessibility, compliance with formal requirements. The purpose of this attempt was to raise awareness, as it is very difficult to call someone to account for violations of public procurement transparency rules or to sanction these; in this case, measuring transparency and communicating the results held out the promise of better results in achieving a cleaner procurement environment. This index, however, focused on one phenomenon only.

Currently, there is no comprehensive, standardised, unified and publicly available database in the European Union containing data on public procurement procedures in several countries and enabling the analysis of corruption costs, the comparative analysis of public procurement practices in individual Member States and the identification of best practices.

There are also attempts at identifying the costs of corruption. In 2012, OLAF started to develop an evaluation mechanism of corruption focusing on public procurement involving EU funding. The subject of the invitation to tender was 'Development of an EU Evaluation Mechanism in the area of Anti-Corruption with a particular focus on identifying and reducing the costs of corruption in Public Procurement involving EU Funds'.[52]

The main output of the project was the study 'A Public Procurement: costs we pay for corruption – Identifying and Reducing Corruption in Public Procurement in the EU'[53] which specifies them in concrete terms: 'The direct public loss encountered in corrupt and grey cases (cases with weaker indication of being corrupt) analysed amounts to 18% of the overall project budgets concerned, of which 13% can be attributed to corruption.'

OLAF continued this project,[54] with a view to Identifying and Reducing Corruption in Public Procurement in the EU Development of a methodology to estimate the direct costs of corruption and other elements for an EU-evaluation mechanism in the area of anti-corruption (30 June 2013). The study is very wide-ranging, based largely on interviews and case studies.

---

[52] TED 2011/S 186-303435.

[53] The study distinguishes four types of corruption in EU public procurement: bid rigging, kickbacks, conflict of interest and other, including deliberate mismanagement or ignorance based on 96 corrupt/grey cases.

[54] See http://ec.europa.eu/anti_fraud/documents/anti-fraud-policy/research-and-studies/identifying_reducing_corruption_in_public_procurement_en.pdf (available 3 February 2016).

> The comprehensive methodology is built on several assumptions that can be derived from the literature: the value of indicators and the importance of costs.
>
> At the most fundamental level, all those involved in corruption seek to hide their behaviour. All efforts to estimate the extent or the costs of corruption are based on one specific assumption, namely that some aspects of corruption can be detected, even though the full picture of corruption is unknown. The comprehensive methodology builds on this assumption, namely that differences in characteristics – measurable appearances or representations – will emerge between corrupt cases and 'clean' cases. These characteristics can be measured using indicators of corruption – the so called 'red flags'. An indicator provides specific information on the state or condition, in this case of the procurement process. In the context of this study, a red flag provides information on the chance of corruption being present. More red flags indicate a higher chance of corruption.[55]

The methodology is not particularly sophisticated. In terms of its content, perhaps it gives the most added value in the context of the selected sectoral characteristics. The methodology provides a good basis for improvement, even though the literature used is not really public procurement specific. Its statement – with which we fully agree – that the available data are limited is also important in analysing the text of the Directives. The preparation of the study was a good occasion to draw up the first comparative analyses of the practical problems encountered by eight Member States in public procurement, giving an overview of differences and specificities.

Let us now turn to a discussion of corruption in the previous and the new Directives.

5. THE 'MODERNISATION OF THE EU DIRECTIVES'

Below we present the modernisation of the EU legal framework by comparing the old and the new rules. The conclusions to be drawn will qualify the modernisation of the public procurement rules from the viewpoint of probity.

5.1 The Previous Directives

The previous regulation of public procurement procedures in the European Union is implemented through two EU Directives:

- Directive 2004/17/EC of the European Parliament and of the Council of 31 March 2004 coordinating the procurement procedures of entities operating in the water, energy, transport and postal services sectors; and
- Directive 2004/18/EC of the European Parliament and of the Council of 31 March 2004 on the coordination of procedures for the award of public works contracts, public supply contracts and public service contracts.

The Directives contributed to the European Union's general policy to fight corruption, but did not focus on ethical questions concerning public procurement procedures.

---

[55] Ibid p. 21.

The Directives directly or indirectly concerned with corruption touch on four main areas. Among them, mandatory exclusion was subject to most criticism by experts. The real move forward was the acceleration of communication between stakeholders and the improvement of the IT support of procurement procedures. We will now describe the corruption-related rules in the Directives in force.

(1) transparency and publication;
(2) general consideration in the awarding phase of the procedure;
(3) communication between participants of the procedure;
(4) statistical obligations and monitoring.

Below we summarise the content of the rules of the previous and the new directives.

5.1.1 Transparency and publication

Transparency is often suggested as a tool for reducing the potential for corruption. Directive 2004/18 regards transparency, together with freedom of movement of goods or non-discrimination and competition, as a fundamental principle. According to Arrowsmith (2004), the Directives, each acting within its own scope, are intended to ensure the conditions of real competition among firms in the award of contracts put out to tender by the contracting authorities. To that end, they incorporate in their articles selection procedures for the contractor based on participation and governed by the prior publication of the contracts, although it is true that the principles of advertising and participation may be attenuated under the particular circumstances that were fixed by the Directives. In order to avoid the risk of favouritism on the part of the contracting authorities, these Directives established a number of criteria for commonly held standards in the award of contracts for all Member States seeking to guarantee respect for the principles of equal treatment and non-discrimination on the grounds of nationality.[56]

The Directives use various aspects of transparency.

1. Opening-up For public contracts above a certain value, Directive 2004/18 calls for the Community coordination of national procedures for the award of such contracts which were based on these principles so as to ensure their effects and to guarantee the opening-up of public procurement to competition. These coordinating provisions should therefore be interpreted in accordance with both the aforementioned rules and principles and other rules of the Treaty.

2. Selection process Verification of the suitability of tenderers or candidates in public procurement procedures and selection should be carried out in transparent conditions. In the same spirit of transparency, the contracting authority should be required to indicate the selection criteria it will use and the level of specific competence it may or may not demand of the economic operators before admitting them to the procurement procedure.

3. Evaluation criteria Contracts should be awarded on the basis of objective criteria, which ensure compliance with the principles of transparency, non-discrimination and

---

56 Arrowsmith (2004).

equal treatment, and which guarantee that tenders are assessed under the conditions of effective competition. To ensure compliance with the principle of equal treatment in the award of contracts, it is appropriate to lay down an obligation to ensure the necessary transparency to enable all tenderers to be reasonably informed of the criteria and arrangements, which will be applied to identify the most economically advantageous tender.

4. Use of e-purchasing techniques and ICT Contracting authorities may make use of electronic purchasing techniques, providing such use complies with the rules drawn up under this Directive and the principles of equal treatment, non-discrimination and transparency.

Since the use of the technique of electronic auctions is likely to increase, such auctions should be given a Community definition and governed by specific rules in order to ensure that they operate fully in accordance with the principles of equal treatment, non-discrimination and transparency. In order to guarantee compliance with the principle of transparency, only the elements suitable for automatic evaluation by electronic means, without any intervention and/or appreciation by the contracting authority, may be the object of electronic auctions, that is, only the elements which are quantifiable so that they can be expressed in figures or percentages.

In view of new developments in information and communications technology, and the simplifications these can bring in terms of publicising contracts and the efficiency and transparency of procurement processes, electronic means should be put on a par with traditional means of communication and information exchange.

Transparency rules and the publication of notices are strongly connected. The Articles concerning advertising and publication are detailed and focus on the main element of ensuring transparency. Articles 35–37 (Chapter VI) deal with publication of notices and mandatory or non-mandatory publications.

Among the rules on advertising and transparency, Article 35 details the prior publication of information. Article 36 specifies the form and manner of publication of notices. The direct aim of the Article is to define the content of the notices and to ensure that contracting authorities publish more relevant information in the notices to help tenderers in their decision to apply for the notice or not.

5.1.2 Awarding phase of the procedure

The Directives have traditionally focused on achieving the best result in the fight against corruption in the awarding phase of the procedure. One of the main elements of this was to define the mandatory exclusions applied in the evaluation process.

Public contracts are not to be awarded to economic operators who participated in a criminal organisation or who were found guilty of corruption or fraud to the detriment of the financial interests of the European Communities or money laundering. Where appropriate, the contracting authorities must ask candidates or tenderers to supply relevant documents and – where they have doubts concerning the personal situation of a candidate or tenderer – they may seek the cooperation of the competent authorities of the Member State concerned. The exclusion of such economic operators should take place as soon as the contracting authority learns of a judgment concerning such offences rendered in accordance with national law that has the force of *res judicata*. If national law contains provisions to this effect, non-compliance with environmental legislation or legislation on unlawful agreements in public contracts which has been the subject of a final judgment or a decision having equivalent effect may be considered an offence concerning the professional conduct of the economic operator concerned or grave misconduct.

Non-observance of national provisions implementing Council Directives 2000/78/EC (1) and 76/207/EEC (2) concerning equal treatment of workers, which have been the subject of a final judgment or a decision having equivalent effect may be considered an offence concerning the professional conduct of the economic operator concerned or grave misconduct.[57]

The adoption of these measures is nothing new in public procurement directives, nor is it exclusive to contractual regulation.

> Article 23 of Directive 71/305/EEC of 26 July 1971 concerning the coordination of procedures for the award of public works contracts, had already made provision for the possibility of excluding any tenderers or candidates from public contracts, who failed to provide sufficient guarantees of their ability to execute the contract, or who would have been in breach of the legislation in force at that time'.[58]

Article 45 focuses on the personal situation of the candidate or tenderer.

Article 45(1) of Directive 2004/18/EC provides, in certain circumstances, for the mandatory exclusion of any candidate or tenderer from participation in a public contract who has been the subject of a conviction by final judgment for participation in a criminal organisation, corruption, fraud to the detriment of the financial interests of the Communities or money laundering:

> Any candidate or tenderer who has been the subject of a conviction by final judgment of which the contracting authority is aware for one or more of the reasons listed below shall be excluded from participation in a public contract:
>
> (a) participation in a criminal organisation, as defined in Article 2(1) of Council Joint Action 98/733/JHA.
> (b) corruption, as defined in Article 3 of the Council Act of 26 May 1997 and Article 3 of Council Joint Action 98/742/JHA, respectively;
> (c) fraud within the meaning of Article 1 of the Convention relating to the protection of the financial interests of the European Communities.
> (d) money laundering, as defined in Article 1 of Council Directive 91/308/EEC of 10 June 1991 on prevention of the use of the financial system for the purpose of money laundering.

In relation to this same approach, Article 54(4) of Directive 2004/17/EC (the 'Utilities Directive') also meets the requirement of stipulating the criteria for mandatory exclusion contained in Article 45(1) of Directive 2004/18/EC, but the obligation to apply such exclusions is restricted to certain subjects. It is only mandatory for the contracting entities that are public contracting authorities, since the fight against corruption involves all public authorities regardless of the sector in which they are active.

---

57 EU Directive 18/2004/EC Recital (43).

58 Arnáiz (2006) p. 338.

> The criteria set out in paragraphs 1 and 2 may include the exclusion criteria listed in Article 45 of Directive 2004/18/EC on the terms and conditions set out therein. Where the contracting entity is a contracting authority within the meaning of Article 2(1)(a), the criteria and rules referred to in paragraphs 1 and 2 of this Article shall include the exclusion criteria listed in Article 45(1) of Directive 2004/18/EC.[59]

The reason for this restriction is to be found in the area in which this Directive is applied. Directive 2004/17/EC applies to contracting authorities as well as to public undertakings and private firms that operate in the water, energy, transport and postal services sectors on the basis of special or exclusive rights. These contracting entities are not obliged to apply the criteria for exclusion, given that such an obligation would necessarily presuppose that such entities would have access to information held on judicial records, which would pose serious problems concerning data protection. Furthermore, it is necessary to bear in mind that such information might refer to companies competing in the same sector, who would see their data disclosed and perhaps, unduly used.

> Nevertheless, beyond this common denominator, the reasons for denial of access to tender procedures are manifold, given that it is not possible to cite one single legal basis for all the causes in Article 45. Exclusion deriving from a criminal conviction, as in the case of exclusion arising from acts of corruption, is a disqualification that restricts an individual or a legal person from exercising certain activities. This disqualification therefore acts as an additional sanction to encourage compliance with the legislation.[60]

As Arnáiz (2006) puts it: 'As has been seen, the current regulatory framework binds the national legislator with respect to the mandatory inclusion of crimes of corruption as the cause of exclusion from contracts. This is in clear contrast to the previous situation in which the general rule allowed each Member State to consider such conduct as liable to lead to exclusion'. Arnáiz mentions that legal security is strengthened in this way by more guarantees, not only due to those of legislative harmonisation the Directive entails. Nevertheless, and despite all the very best intentions behind the measure, its impact will depend on the strength of implementation by the Member States.

Williams (2006) provides a critical assessment of these provisions.

(1) The problem with the provisions requiring contracting authorities to exclude from contracts firms convicted of corruption is that it is not clear how effective they are likely to be in addressing corruption.
(2) Their application can lead to significant costs and delays in procurement – for example, because of difficulties in establishing whether persons associated with the firm (such as subsidiaries or directors) have any relevant criminal convictions.

[59] EU Directive 17/2004/EC.
[60] Arnáiz (2006) p. 345.

These concerns have led to the final version of the provisions being considerably watered down from that originally proposed by the Commission.

(3) It is questionable whether it is appropriate to use procurement to impose such sanctions and whether sufficient procedural safeguards are provided for affected firms.

> In view of the practical difficulties of operating such provisions, Member States implementing them may have to choose between making the provisions effective, with attendant procedural and financial burdens or leaving the measures as largely symbolic.[61]

5.1.3 Communication between the participants of the procedure

There was a need to ensure confirmative communication between market players and to define the time limits, documents, information on procurement procedures and the applicable rules of communication.

(1) Time limits (Articles 38–39).
(2) Information content and means of transmission (Articles 40–41).
(3) Rules applicable for communication (Article 42).
(4) Content of the reports (Article 43).

The content of the rules of communication will now be summarised:

Articles 38–39 detail the time limits for the receipt of the requests to participate and for receipt of tenders, specifications, supplementary documents and additional documents, information.

Articles 40–41 detail the conditions of invitations to submit a tender, participate in the dialogue or negotiate and informing candidates and tenderers of the decision.

The applicable rules for communication under Article 42 try to meet the different needs regarding the way of communication. The general rule was that the means of communication chosen must be generally available and thus not restrict economic operators' access to the tendering procedure. The tools to be used for communicating by electronic means, as well as their technical characteristics, must be non-discriminatory, generally available and interoperable with the information and communication technology products in general use. From the viewpoint of non-discrimination, interoperability has become a principle of communication. The Directives do not look at interoperability and access to information together as part of the transparency problem. The Directives separate the two sets of rules and treat them as two different parts of the regulation scheme.

Literature has little addressed the effects of the difference between the several and parallel forms of communication used. It can be said that the conversion to fully electronic communication is conducive to abuse, because the demonstrability of data flow and the lack of interoperability can be a major set-back, when the market players, who are the most vulnerable from an IT point of view, do not get sufficient information.

---

61 Williams (2006) p. 1.

Article 43 regulates the written report to be drawn up on every contract, and so on. For all these obligations to document the progress of award procedures conducted electronically, contracting authorities' reporting has not yet been a success story.

5.1.4 Statistical obligation and monitoring

Title V on Statistical obligations, executory powers and final provisions has an impact on our topic. In order to permit assessment of the results of applying the Directives, these rules complete the existing ones with two further obligations: that of statistical reporting and that of monitoring and control.

(1) Article 75 – Statistical obligations.
(2) Article 76 – Content of statistical report.
(3) Article 81 – Monitoring mechanisms.

The statistical obligations (Articles 75 and 76) and the content of statistical reports do not reflect the need to establish a comparable and accessible EU-wide database. The rules of drawing up reports separately addressing public supply, services and works contracts awarded by contracting authorities during the preceding year do not control the quality of the given information. Under Article 81, the monitoring mechanism is meant to ensure the implementation of the Directives by effective, available and transparent mechanisms. For this purpose they may, among others, appoint or establish an independent body. The rules do not reflect each other, and the monitoring body's responsibilities do not affect the content of the statistics and the quality of the annual report.

5.2 The New Directives

Earlier on this chapter presented the demands formulated by European experts in the course of the modernisation of the Directives. Below we present how the objectives formulated were incorporated in the draft and how some of them were omitted. The summary therefore shows how the approach was streamlined until the final adoption of the text.

The proposals for the new Directives originally prioritised the fight against corruption and ensuring the clarity and integrity of public procurement procedures.

Among the new elements in the current directives, we have to emphasise for example the detailed regulation of conflict of interest. On the basis of the arguments for and the draft of the Directive, the new ways and procedures of public procurement regulation in the European Union are discernible. The original purposes of 'sound procedures' touched on the following three main areas:

> Conflict of interest: The original proposal of the directive contained a specific provision on conflict of interest covering actual, potential or perceived conflict of interest situations affecting staff members of the contracting authority or of procurement service providers intervening in the procedure and members of the contracting authority's management who may influence the outcome of an award procedure even if they are not formally involved in it.
>
> Illicit conduct: The proposal made it clear that candidates or tenderers engaging in illicit behaviour – such as attempts to improperly influence the decision-making process or entering

> into agreements with other participants to manipulate the outcome of the procedure – have to be excluded from the procedure. Such illicit activities violate the basic principles of the European Union and can result in serious distortion of competition.
>
> Unfair advantages: Market consultations are a useful instrument for contracting authorities to obtain information on the structure, capability and capacity of a market while at the same time informing market actors on public purchasers' procurement projects and requirements. However, preliminary contacts with market participants must not result in unfair advantages and distortion of competition. The proposal contains therefore a specific provision on safeguards against undue preference to participants who have advised the contracting authority or been involved in the preparation of the procedure.

From among these main objectives, 'illicit conduct'[62] failed to find its way through the debates into European legislation, while 'Conflict of Interest' and a new 'Preliminary market consultation' became parts of the new system. In the following, we will observe, on the basis of the logic of present Directives, the novelties, step-backs or advances of the public procurement regulatory process.

5.2.1 Transparency and publication

The Article on 'Electronic availability of procurement documents' is a novelty in the planned Directives, where the regulator helps market players to reorganise their public procurement into electronic public procurement systems. As a result, contracting authorities will have to spend certain resources on keeping copies of all contracts and granting access to these documents at least for the duration of the contracts; however, access to specific documents or items of information may be denied to the extent and under the conditions provided for in the applicable EU or national rules on access to documents and data protection. Otherwise the new Directives do not contain major novelties.

5.2.2 Conflict of interest

It seems to be a step forward that conflict of interest is among the main principles of the new Directives. Furthermore, the prevention of corruption is also mentioned.

The previous Directives did not define conflict of interest. The internal regulation of EU Member States shows a diverse picture: there are Member States where conflict of interest is regulated circumstantially, and Member States where the internal regulation is silent on the issue.

The European Court of Law expressly declared that there is a need for the regulation of conflict of interest deduced from the principle of equal treatment. In its judgment in the *Fabricom*[63] and *Michaniki AE*[64] cases, the Court confirmed that tenderers who participated in the preparation of procurement procedures have a more advantageous position and obtain more information than other competitors. Regulators should ensure that no informational asymmetry arises.

---

62 Proposals for the new Directives.

63 Joined Cases *C-21/03 and C-34/03. Fabricom SA. v. État belge* Judgment of 3 March 2005. 2005, I-1559. o.

64 C-213/07 *Michaniki AE v Ethniko Symvoulio Radiotileorasis and Ypourgos Epikrateias*, judgment of 16 December 2008.

According to the definition, the concept of conflict of interest means any situation where staff members of a contracting authority or of a procurement service provider who, acting on its behalf, are involved in the procurement procedure or may influence its outcome have a direct or indirect financial, economic or other personal interest which might be perceived to compromise their impartiality and independence in the context of the procurement procedure.

The exclusion of interested persons could be a tool, but not the only solution for contracting authorities. The exclusion should fulfil the function of the final legal tool and not an automatic reaction. Member States are obliged to work out their internal regulation to enable interested people and economic operators to prove that they can perform their tasks in an objective and impartial way. The new definition is shorter and has less meaning than the originally intended version, but even so the existence of a definition means an important step forward in the new Directives.[65]

5.2.3 General consideration in the awarding phase of the procedure

The new Directives continue to apply sanctions with the gravest consequence in the evaluation phase of the procedure: exclusion of the economic operator.[66] The range of cases which may be excluded was expanded, yet the nature of the solution did not change. Consequently, we still cannot expect a uniform approach from the Member States, that is, national regulations allowing for ideas for reasons of exclusions and national specificities will be retained, giving even less possibility to foreign bidders to verify that they are not subject to the reasons for exclusion.

From this point of view there is only one novelty, self-cleaning, which does constitute progress compared to the previous Directives.

Public contracts are not to be awarded to economic operators that have participated in a criminal organisation or have been found guilty of corruption, fraud to the detriment of the Union's financial interests, terrorist offences, money laundering or terrorist financing.

The Directives provide also the possibility of 'self-cleaning' without using this term. Contracting authorities may accept candidates or tenderers in spite of the existence of an exclusion ground if the measures taken by the economic operator 'are sufficient to demonstrate its reliability despite the existence of a relevant ground for exclusion'.[67] If the contracting authority considers the evidence as sufficient, it shall not exclude the economic operator concerned. Contracting authorities shall evaluate the measures taken by the economic operators taking into account the gravity and particular circumstances of the criminal offence or misconduct. Where the contracting authority considers the measures to be insufficient, it shall state the reasons for its decision.

---

[65] 2014/24/EK Article 24. 'The concept of conflicts of interest shall at least cover any situation where staff members of the contracting authority or of a procurement service provider acting on behalf of the contracting authority who are involved in the conduct of the procurement procedure or may influence the outcome of that procedure have, directly or indirectly, a financial, economic or other personal interest which might be perceived to compromise their impartiality and independence in the context of the procurement procedure'.

[66] 2014/24/EK Article 57.

[67] 2014/24/EK Article 57.6.

5.2.4 Communication between participants

There are two new elements concerning the communication between participants: focusing on e-communication and the introduction of preliminary market consultation, and prior involvement of candidates and tenderers.

Electronic means of information and communication can greatly simplify the publication of contracts and increase the efficiency and transparency of procurement processes. They should become the standard means of communication and information exchange in procurement procedures, as they greatly enhance the possibilities of economic operators to participate in procurement procedures across the internal market. For that purpose, transmission of notices in electronic form, electronic availability of the procurement documents and – after a 30 months long transition period – fully electronic communication, meaning communication by electronic means at all stages of the procedure, including the transmission of requests for participation and, in particular, the transmission of the tenders (e-submission) should be made mandatory. Furthermore, pursuant to this Directive, no elements of the public procurement process after the award of the contract should be covered by the obligation to use electronic means of communication.[68] From this point of view, the new Directives narrow down the definition if e-procurement and focus only on the tendering phase. The Pan European On-Line Project (PEPPOL) and several national e-procurement solutions have already made further steps in this direction. Mandatory e-communication should be the first step, but not the only one, we hope. It is true that the use of electronic means of information and communication, in particular full electronic availability of procurement documents and electronic transmission of communication does lead to increased transparency and time saving. But online public procurement does not build up transparency itself. If the only obligation is to publish and communicate via the internet, without control, than the only change will be the increased risks of a lack of evidence concerning the dataflow.

Under preliminary market consultations the existing and general communication between economic operators and contracting authorities will not be hidden any more. Before launching a procurement procedure, contracting authorities may conduct market consultations with a view to the preparation of the procurement and to inform economic operators of their procurement plans and requirements. 'For this purpose, contracting authorities may for example seek or accept advice from independent experts or authorities or from market participants, which may be used in the planning and conducting of procurement procedures, provided that such advice does not have the effect of distorting competition and does not result in a violation of the principles of non-discrimination and transparency'.[69]

---

[68] 2014/24/EK. Recital (52) 'It should also be clarified that mandatory use of electronic means of communications pursuant to this Directive should not, however, oblige contracting authorities to carry out electronic processing of tenders, nor should it mandate electronic evaluation or automatic processing. Furthermore, pursuant to this Directive, no elements of the public procurement process after the award of the contract should be covered by the obligation to use electronic means of communication, nor should internal communication within the contracting authority'.

[69] 2014/24/EK Article 40.

Such consultations between participants would be fruitful, if the contracting authority's purpose is to widen the scope and increase competition between participants. Otherwise, preliminary consultations will remain the same, hidden communication. Furthermore, consultation must defend market players from the accusation of conflict of interest, but the line of demarcation is slippery.

5.2.5 Statistics and monitoring

The issue of statistics and monitoring has been gradually downplayed in the course of discussions. Locked up in 'Enforcement', the literature refers only to general monitoring activity and the control of data submitted, while the role and employment of independent data-provider institutions are barely mentioned.

Member States must obviously ensure that the application of public procurement rules is monitored. This monitoring must be used to prevent, detect and adequately report cases of procurement fraud, corruption, conflict of interest and other serious irregularities. But this requires not scanty regulation, but a detailed, reliable, traceable regulation of dataflow and the competent institutions.

Concerning statistical information, the Directives address the problem of missing statistics, but they fail to establish the comparability of data supplied by the Member States. This approach implies a one-sided supply of data. The professed aim of the proposal, to create global reports and exchange data between systems, is not fulfilled.

> The electronic systems for publication of contract award notices, managed by the Commission, should also be improved with a view of facilitating the entry of data while making it easier to extract global reports and exchange data between systems.[70]

The incorporation of national reporting and administrative cooperation as new elements verify that reporting deficiencies can be dealt with not simply by formulating demands for more sophisticated data; ultimately, the aim should be comparability and enhanced cooperation.

5.2.6 Further shortcomings

The aforesaid elements of the proposal contain several novelties, which mitigate our dissatisfaction due to its shortcomings. Sadly, however, in the course of the debates, the crucial 'illicit conduct' was left out of the new proposals.

Originally, 'illicit conduct' made it possible for contracting authorities to exclude candidates or tenderers from a procedure at any moment if it was established that, in the ongoing award procedure, they have:

- attempted to unduly influence the decision-making process of the contracting authority or obtain confidential information which may confer upon them undue advantages in the award procedure;
- entered into agreements with other candidates and tenderers aiming at distorting competition or have attempted to enter into such agreements;

---

[70] 2014/24/EK. Recital (126).

- deliberately provided misleading information that may have a material influence on decisions concerning exclusion, selection or award.

In this case, it is not the details of the exclusion, but the fact itself that would count, calling the attention of the candidates and tenderers to the direct consequences of their illicit conduct. The example shows, the definition of 'conflict of interest' is acceptable in a simplified form, but 'illicit conduct' is not in the European Directives. Based on the above, the way to proceed lies in the interpretation of conflict of interest, in bringing the rules concerning the transparency of contracts but first and foremost in the theoretical renewal of reporting. Each example depends, to a large extent, on how seriously Member States take this matter, in what way transparency and particularly access to data of adequate content, format and standard can be ensured and monitored. That is to say, progress can only be regarded as moderate. Below we present examples, benchmarks and patterns, which may give food for thought on the issue of probity and may also be suitable for inclusion in regulation.

6. WORST AND BEST PRACTICES

In the light of the new Directives, we have cherry-picked the approaches, worst and best practices, which may facilitate the enforcement of probity as main principle.

The transparent and competitive public procurement systems created by this legal framework do not only serve the objectives of the internal market. 'EU wide publication and competitive procedures facilitate maximum participation, competition, and ultimately value for money. Modern purchasing techniques and other measures and practices facilitate efficiency. Effective remedies through independent review bodies ensure fairness and create trust in the system. Finally, these remedies and the generally transparent nature of the public procurement systems envisaged by the EC Treaty and the EC Public Procurement Directives also favour probity'.[71] public procurement regulation is not the best tool against corruption and will remain ineffective without other measures, for example in the areas of criminal law and training. The EC Public Procurement Directives have been criticised as being too strict and lagging behind modern purchasing techniques employed in the private sector.[72]

In this part, we seek to draw attention, with the help of literature, to issues and results that can serve as a model for exploring the missing or incomplete approaches of the proposal for the new Directives.

We know little about the effects of the defects of measuring corruption, its direct or indirect influence. The solution cannot be to merely ensure transparency, competition and to introduce electronic procurement techniques under current or forthcoming Directives.

It is clear that publishing tender documents improves the knowledge of the needs of the purchaser, fosters participation and raises accountability for the procurer, making corruption a more difficult and therefore less likely outcome.

---

[71] Trybus (2005) p. 11.

[72] Trybus (2005).

According to the hypothesis of Coppier and Piga (2007), 'countries that adopt more "transparent procurement", as calculated by the share of tenders advertised publicly, are also the ones where corruption is considered more pervasive'.[73] Piga et al. suggest alternative ways to reduce corruption in procurement. They describe an 'economy where in equilibrium countries more prone to corruption find it optimal to increase transparency more to curb corruption itself. As transparency is costly to implement, this will not be enough to bring corruption levels to those of inherently less corrupt societies'.[74]

> The results are reassuring in that they find that the stylized fact mentioned above may have nothing to do with transparency playing a role in enhancing corruption opportunities. Each country has its own culture and institutions and that transparency might not be enough to eradicate corruption at a cost which is compatible with society's agreement to eradicate it.[75]

As L. Picci (2007) suggests, using IT technologies to publish the results of similar tenders across the country on user-friendly platforms so as to allow public procurement stakeholders to monitor contract characteristics across administrations. Picci proposes a governance model of public works that relies on an internet-based 'reputation system'. 'It allows for the routine production of statistics that are useful for monitoring purposes and it provides a coherent framework to limit rent-seeking and corruption'.[76] But we have to address the more general problem of the difficulty to collect suitable quantitative information.

Simplifying the question and forcing procurement techniques through are not going to be truly helpful either.

Chong et al. (2011) tested a proposition in the case of one feature of public contracting which is particularly sensitive to probity: the choice of the award procedure in public procurement. They wanted to assess whether the massive use of auction in public procurement is dictated by economic efficiency or political considerations. The choice of an auction procedure to award public procurement contracts, which is seen as a way to avoid suspicion of favouritism, may be justified by the high risk of political opportunism more than by economic efficiency.

The empirical results show that 'political considerations have an impact on procurement decisions, introducing bias in the choice of auction procedure. When political scrutiny is low, public buyers feel less pressure to be suspected of favouritism and have more room for manoeuvre in the choice of the award procedure'.[77]

Similarly, competition itself does not eliminate corruption, just as corruption does not necessarily result in inefficiency.

The research by Burguet et al. (2004) explicitly studied competitive procurement administered by a corrupt agent willing to manipulate the evaluation of contract proposals in exchange for bribes. 'With complete information and no corruption, the efficient firm will win the contract for sure. If the agent is corrupt and has large

73 Coppier and Piga (2007) pp. 183–4.
74 Coppier and Piga (2007) pp. 183–4.
75 Coppier and Piga (2007) p. 198.
76 Picci (2007) p. 159.
77 Chong et al. (2011) p. 2744.

manipulation power, however, bribery makes it costly for the efficient firm to secure a sure win, so in equilibrium the efficient firm loses the contract with positive probability. The optimal scoring rule for the buyer deemphasises quality relative to price and does not fully handicap, and may even favour, the efficient firm'. The article focuses on competitive procurement with corruption.[78]

Other effects of corruption on competition are known as well.

Celentani and Ganuza (2000) considered a procurement problem in which the procurement agent is supposed to allocate the realisation of a project according to a competitive mechanism that values bids in terms of the proposed price and quality. They computed the equilibrium level of corruption, and they studied the impact on corruption of the competitiveness of the environment, and in particular of:

- an increase in the number of potential suppliers of the goods or services to be procured,
- competitive (rather than collusive) behaviour of procurement agents, and
- an increase of competition in the market for procurement agents.

They identified the effects that 'influence the equilibrium level of corruption and showed that, contrary to conventional wisdom, corruption may well be increasing in competition'.[79]

It is a fact that the prevailing situation does not make it possible to provide solutions acceptable for all EU Member States.

The well-known researcher Kelman (1990) emphasises the power of existing political and legal culture, and explores and explains the 'procurement culture' to which he often refers.[80]

As research results demonstrate, overcoming corruption is even more difficult in economic distress. According to the research by Büchner et al. (2006), a procurement contract is granted by a bureaucrat (the auctioneer) who is interested in a low price and a bribe from the provider. In the experiment, bribes are negatively framed so to capture that society is better off if bribes are rare or low. 'Although bids are lower than predicted, behaviour is qualitatively in line with the linear equilibrium prediction. When bribes generate a negative externality, there is a significant increase in the variability of the data.'[81]

It is a false approach that, if corruption is endemic, public attention and improvement action will be focused on eradicating it as a priority. 'The role of public procurement is changing and becoming more strategically important to governments through increased recognition of its role in supporting and delivering broader government objectives, and in newer, more complex arrangements such as public-private partnerships'.[82]

The solutions offer new approaches from an ethical and monitoring point of view. These are not meant to be the only solutions. McCue is justified in writing that

78 Burque (2004) p. 50.
79 Celentani and Ganuza (2000) p. 1273.
80 Kelman (1990).
81 Büchner et al (2006) p. 1.
82 Harland et al (2007) p. 355.

'purchasing professionals in the public sector continue to have to balance the inherent tensions between maintaining control of the purchasing function and loosening the bonds of bureaucracy.'[83]

Roberts (2010) suggests the introduction of mandatory contractor codes of ethics. Without government contractors requiring their employees to comply with a uniform Code of Ethics and Conduct, public trust in government procurement processes cannot be restored, even though this is much more symbolic than substantive. 'The heavy focus on compliance with criminal and civil prohibitions tends to obscure the fact that non-criminal or non-civil ethics violations have the ability to severely damage public trust in the integrity[84] of the procurement process'.[85]

Shead (2001)[86] writes about how to keep the bureaucrats honest. In his opinion, 'the use of probity audits has flourished in the public sector in recent years'. This growth has been accompanied by the development of probity guidelines by a number of central agencies and infrastructure providers across Australia. 'These guidelines tend to focus on competitive procurement processes and ignore broader factors applying to other processes in which probity audits are also used. Further, as there are no professional standards governing a probity audit, it is important that agencies have a clear understanding of their benefits and limitations and of the skills and experience required of a probity auditor before they commission one'.

An interesting example is the probity checklist below by Beth (2006) dividing the probity auditing work into two phases, the probity planning and the relevant procurement process.[87]

PROBITY PLANNING

Determine whether a probity auditor and/or adviser is needed
Obtain conflict of interest declarations from team members
Obtain confidentiality agreements from external participants
Finalise the probity plan, if one is being used
Consider confidentiality requirements
Set up physical security procedures, such as the document register or data room
Ensure team members are familiar with all relevant policies and documents
Set up procedures so all potential suppliers have access to the same information

[83] McCue et al (2007) p. 261.

[84] For this purpose Transparency International developed the Integrity Pact during the 1990s to prevent corruption in public contracting. The pact is essentially an agreement between a government or government department (at the national, sub-national or local level) and all bidders for a public contract. It stipulates rights and obligations to the effect that neither side will: pay, offer, demand or accept bribes; collude with competitors to obtain the contract; or engage in such abuses while executing the contract. See more at http://archive.transparency.org/global_priorities/public_contracting/integrity_pacts#sthash.SFnSXeMV.dpuf (available 3 February 2016).

[85] Roberts (2010) p. 247.

[86] Shead (2001) p. 66.

[87] Beth (2006) slide 10.

PROCUREMENT PROCESS

Review probity at the end of the bid preparation process
Set up a process for receiving, recording and acknowledging submissions
Set up a procedure for opening the bid box
Document any changes that occur, and notify all potential suppliers
Ensure evaluation of submissions is fair, consistent and competitive
Review probity at the end of the evaluation process
Notify the successful bidder as soon as possible
Notify the unsuccessful bidders as soon as possible
Debrief unsuccessful bidders
Ensure all actions are documented, and the documents are stored appropriately
Review probity at the end of the process

But circumstances have to be taken into account because the solutions mentioned are not applicable unconditionally. Kells (2011) highlights the contradiction between different audit mechanisms. 'If, in the context of an "audit explosion", public sector projects are subject to multiple and uncoordinated forms of independent scrutiny, then the different scrutinisers could reach contradictory conclusions, adopt incompatible methods, and ultimately provide less effective oversight'. The aim is not to introduce a brand new administrative and controlling mechanism. In the Australian state of Victoria, three independent scrutiny mechanisms operated concurrently on transport megaprojects. The three mechanisms – performance auditing, probity auditing and gateway reviews – are not coordinated and yet have overlapping goals relating to integrity and value for money. 'The paper describes the three scrutiny mechanisms, before presenting evidence that the mechanisms can generate contradictory conclusions that remain unreconciled, and that the mechanisms conflict in ways that affect the viability of at least one of the mechanisms'.[88]

McCrudden (2006)[89] considers the 'new' use of public procurement in the pursuit of CSR in general, but considers in particular the relationship between CSR, public procurement, and the law. Historically, there are 'consistent attempts to link public procurement with the government policy of the day, in areas as diverse as national industrial policy, reducing unemployment, improving employment conditions, support for small businesses, local development, employment of disabled workers, and equal pay for men and women, to mention only a few. With the increasing popularity of "corporate social responsibility," it is hardly surprising then, that CSR has become linked to the use of public procurement'. The definition of CSR is contested and so, for the moment, Moon's definition will suffice: 'In essence CSR refers to business responsiveness to social agendas in its behaviour and to the performance of these responsibilities'.[90]

There are some who dispute the multi-vectoral public procurement aspect and draw attention to the dangers of using public procurement for many purposes.

88 Kells (2011) p. 61.
89 McCrudden (2006) p. 2.
90 McCrudden (2006) p. 2.

This may widen the scope of procurement, but it also makes regulators focus on several priorities. Public procurement is thus increasingly seen as a problem-solving tool. Tátrai and Nyikos (2012)[91] in their article point out that different purposes can smother each other and the contradictory purposes can have contradictory consequences depending on national regulations. They weaken the fight against corruption, and erode focus. If there is no balance between purposes, no determinable and explicit purpose and a stable institutional background, then in the course of the implementation of the new directives the public procurement regulatory system is going to fall into further disarray.

Efficiency in spending public money is often forgotten in public procurement priorities favouring SMEs, reducing unemployment or solving the fiscal crisis by cutting back on public procurement. Their research and paper point out that public procurement should be better oriented and should focus on primary issues, such as efficiency and transparency.

What is missing or omitted from the proposal? In summary: ethical procurement and its theoretical background are missing. What is lacking is the demand for genuine transparency, the clear specification of providing statistical data and monitoring, the determination of the new direction of introducing self-cleaning, requiring public procurement market players to examine their own public procurement practice form the point of view of probity. Fighting corruption and transparency are among the several purposes ticked off by the regulator. The researches mentioned clearly highlight the insufficiency of ensuring transparency and the need for a public procurement-management and competition-oriented approach in the EU. Though success is far from being complete, there are some hopeful signs.

7. PROBITY AS A PRINCIPLE OF PUBLIC PROCUREMENT REGULATION

In the course of the analyses of public procurement and probity, we have come to realise that there is not enough knowledge about the European public procurement market and even less about its corrupt characteristics and practices. The approach of the new Directives is out-of-date, focusing on the awarding phase of the procedure despite the fact that corrupt activities take place also in the preparation and the performance phases of public procurement. The proposals for the new Directives follow former policy with rather restrained renewal. A genuine step forward requires a new approach. Summarising the main results of research, the following suggestions can be formulated in order to step beyond the corruption scare and find rational solutions.

7.1 Recommendations

(1) There is a need to develop an independent monitoring system capable of collecting and comparing data with a unified methodology and logic, and of

---

[91] Tátrai and Nyikos (2012) p. 29.

giving a real picture of the size of the public procurement market. The existing and emerging corruption indices help map the market, that is why we need to know both the underlying and the ostensible methodology indices use, so that we can understand why published public procurement data about EU Member States are as they are. A more proactive professional attitude is needed than what we have occasion to know.

(2) Real transparency serves prevention. It is not enough to make electronic public procurement obligatory when monitoring systems are not capable of providing all the documents of a procedure to controlling bodies automatically, and of tracking the main data of concluded contracts in a comparable and controllable way from year to year. The aimless supplying or uploading of data on to different websites is virtual transparency only, and does not serve the interest of public procurement.

(3) Knowing best practices and incorporating them into regulations are not only playing with words. 'Probity' as a principle of public procurement applies to the preparation phase, communication between parties, the evaluation process, the performance control and the amendment of contracts. The purpose is not to hinder corruption by administrative obstacles but to prevent it. Beside traditional regulatory content (mandatory exclusion of economic operators), it is necessary to make 'probity auditing' part of the regulatory background. If the importance of sustainability, green procurement, social considerations, increases in public procurement, the fight against corruption can also be included in public procurement CSR. For this, however, the incorporation of a definition of 'conflict of interest' will not suffice.

It is also time to note that using public procurement for different purposes tends to divest the efficient spending of public money of its import. This proves the fundamental lack of controlled and comparable data about the EU public procurement market. Probity analyses, illicit conduct and prevention are not merely symbolic terms, but point to substance as soon as they become parts of regulation. By these techniques, the regulator demonstrates that not only does he want to achieve results through mandatory exclusion or the sanctioning of conflict of interest, but also to establish and inculcate a European public procurement culture through providing for self-cleaning, independent monitoring bodies and scrutiny mechanisms.

REFERENCES

Arnáiz, T.M (2006). Ground for Exclusion in Public Procurement: Measures in the Fight Against Corruption in European Union. International Public Procurement Conference Proceedings 21--23 September 2006. Available 3 February 2016 at http://www.ippa.org/IPPC2/PROCEEDINGS/Article_12_Amaiz.pdf.

Arrowsmith, S. (2004). 'An Assessment of the New Legislative Package on Public Procurement' 41(5) *Common Market Law Review* 1277–325.

Arrowsmith, S. (2011). 'The Revised Agreement on Government Procurement: Changes to the Procedural Rules and Other Transparency Provisions' in S. Arrowsmith and R.D. Anderson (eds), *The WTO Regime on Government Procurement: Challenge and Reform*. Cambridge: Cambridge University Press, pp. 285–335.

Beth, E. (2006). Integrity in public procurement: Mapping out good practices. Detailed outline of the report OECD Symposium, Paris, 30 November 2006.

Bovis, C. (2007). *EU Public Procurement Law*. Cheltenham, UK and Northampton, MA, USA: Edward Elgar.

Bull, M.J. and J.L. Newell (2003). 'Conclusions: Political Corruption in Contemporary Democracies' in M.J. Bull and J.L. Newell (eds), *Corruption in Contemporary Politics*. London: Palgrave Macmillan.

Burguet, R. and Y.-K. Che (2004). 'Competitive Procurement with Corruption' 35(1) *RAND Journal of Economics* 50–68.

Büchner, S., A. Freytag, L.G. Gonzales and Werner Güth (2006). Bribery and Public Procurement – An Experimental Study. Jena Univ., Wirtschaftswissenschaftliche Fakultät January 2006.

Celentani, M. and J.J. Ganuza (2000). 'Corruption and Competition in Procurement' 46(7) *European Economic Review* 1273–303.

Chong, E., C. Staropoli and A. Yvrance-Billon (2011). 'The Auction Versus Negotiation Tradeoff in Public Procurement under Political Scrutiny'. Available 3 February 2016 at http://www.ippa.org/IPPC5/Proceedings/Part11/PAPER11-6.pdf, pp. 2744–69.

Coppier, R. and G. Piga (2007): Why do Transparent Public Procurement and Corruption go Hand in Hand?' in G. Piga and V.T. Khi (2007), *The Economics of Public Procurement*. Basingstoke: Palgrave Macmillan, pp. 183–99.

Dorn, N., M. Levi and S. White (2008). 'Do European Procurement Rules Generate or Prevent Crime?' 15(3) *Journal of Financial Crime* 243–60.

Greenwood, M. and J.M. Klotz (2009). 'The Fight against Corruption in Public Procurement: An Introduction to Best Practices' in R.H. García (ed.), *International Public Procurement*. London: Globe Business Publishing, pp. 57–74.

Harland, K., J. Telgen, L. Knight, G. Callender, K.V. Thai (2007). 'Challenges Facing Public Procurement' in L. Knight, C. Harland, J. Telgen, K.V. Thai, G. Callender and K. McKen (eds), *Public Procurement – International Cases and Commentary*. London: Routledge, pp. 351–7.

Hillman, A.L. (2004). 'Corruption and Public Finance: An IMF Perspective' 20(4) *European Journal of Political Economy* 1067–77.

Hunsaker, K. (2009). 'Ethics in Public Procurement: Buying Public Trust' 9(3&4) *Journal of Public Procurement* 411–19.

Kaufmann, D. (2005). *Myths and Realities of Governance and Corruption*. Washington: The Brookings Institution, Chapter 2.1. Available 3 February 2016 at http://mpra.ub.uni-muenchen.de/8089/1/Myths_Realities_Gov_Corruption.pdf.

Kells, S. (2011). 'Conflict between Independent Scrutinisers of Transport Megaprojects: Evidence from Australia' EJTIR 11(1) 61–79.

Kelman, S. (1990) *Procurement and Public Management: The Fear of Discretion and the Quality of Government Performance*. Washington, D.C.: The AEI Press.

Kreutner, M. (ed.) (2009). *Practice Meets Science Contemporary Anti-Corruption Dialogue*. Vienna: IACSS.

Lambsdorff, J.G. (2007). *The Institutional Economics of Corruption and Reform Theory, Evidence and Policy*. Cambridge: Cambridge University Press.

McCue, C.P., K.W. Buffington, A.D. Howell. (2007) 'The Fraud/Red Tape Dilemma in Public Procurement', in L. Knight, C. Harland, J. Telgen, K.V. Thai, G. Callender and K. McKen (eds), *Public Procurement – International Cases and Commentary*. London: Routledge, pp. 247–63.

McCrudden, C. (2006). 'Corporate Social Responsibility and Public Procurement'. University of Oxford Faculty of Law Legal Studies Research Paper Series Working Paper No 9/2006. Available 3 February 2016 at http://unpan1.un.org/intradoc/groups/public/documents/apcity/unpan047103.pdf.

Olken, B.A. (2007). 'Monitoring Corruption: Evidence from a Field Experiment in Indonesia' 115(2) *Journal of Political Economy* 200–49.

Picci, L. (2007). 'Reputation-based Governance of Public Works' in G. Piga and V.T. Khi. (2007), *The Economics of Public Procurement*. Basingstoke: Palgrave Macmillan, pp. 159–82.

Pünder H., H.J. Priess and S. Arrowsmith (2009). *Self-Cleaning in Public Procurement Law*. Cologne: Carl Heymanns Verlag. Schriften der Buserius Law School, pp. 2–33.

Roberts, R.N. (2010). 'Mandatory Contractor Codes of Ethics and Defense Procurement Integrity' 10(2) *Journal of Public Procurement* 247–74.

Shead, B. (2001). 'Probity Auditing: Keeping the Bureaucrats Honest?' 60(2) *Australian Journal of Public Administration* 66–70.

Tátrai, T. and Gy. Nyikos (2012). 'The Uses and Abuses of Public Procurement in Hungary' in G.L. Albano, K.F. Snider and K.V. Thai (eds), *Charting a Course in Public Procurement Innovation and Knowledge Sharing*. Boca Raton: PrAcademics Press, 29–53.

Trepte, P. (2004). *Regulating Procurement, Understanding the Ends and Means of Public Procurement Regulation*. Oxford: Oxford University Press.
Trybus, M. (2005). 'Improving the Efficiency of Public Procurement Systems in the Context of the European Union Enlargement Process' 35(3) Pub. Cont. L.J. 409–24.
Vachudova, M.A. (2009). 'Corruption and Compliance in the EU's Post-Communist Members and Candidates' 47(4) *Journal of Common Market Studies* 43–62.
Williams S. (2006). 'The Mandatory Exclusions for Corruption in the new EC Procurement Directives' 31(5) *European Law Review* 711–34. Available 3 February 2016 at http://www.nottinghamuniversity.com/pprg/documentsarchive/fulltextarticles/sope_exclusions_in_proc.pdf.

PART 5

PUBLIC PROCUREMENT AND PUBLIC SERVICES

17. The new EU defence procurement regime*

Martin Trybus

1. INTRODUCTION

There have been EU procurement Directives since the 1970s, but only in 2009, after years of preparation and discussion, a Defence and Security Procurement Directive 2009/81/EC[1] (hereinafter 'Defence Procurement Directive') entered into force. Part of a wider EU 'defence package',[2] it regulates the procurement of armaments and other sensitive supplies, services and works not only by the defence ministries but also other relevant contracting authorities and entities of the Member States. As in the other procurement Directives discussed in this volume, this covers, *inter alia*, the precise definition of the goods and services, their publication in the Official Journal of the EU (OJ), procurement procedures, the qualification and rejection of bidders, and award criteria. It also covers a review and remedies regime for aggrieved bidders in its Title IV, which for the public sector and utilities is regulated in separate Directives. The Defence Procurement Directive is largely based on the old Public Sector Procurement Directive 2004/18/EC. However, the latter was adapted to take the specific characteristics of defence and security procurement, its complexity and in particular security of supply and security of information, into account. This was necessary to limit the use of the national security and secrecy and public security derogations in the TFEU, namely

* This chapter was especially written for this collection but is based to a large extent on the monograph, M. Trybus, *Buying Defence and Security in Europe: The EU Defence and Security Procurement Directive in Context* (Cambridge: Cambridge University Press 2014); and especially the articles: M. Trybus, 'The Hidden Remedies Directive: Review and Remedies under the EU Defence and Security Remedies Directive' (2013) 22 *Public Procurement Law Review* 135–55 and M. Trybus, 'The Tailor-made EU Defence and Security Procurement Directive: Limitation, Flexibility, Description, and Substitution', (2013) 39 *European Law Review* 3–29; the latter also published as M. Trybus, 'Defence Procurement' in M. Trybus, R. Caranta, and G. Edelstam (eds), *EU Law of Public Contracts: Public Procurement and Beyond* (Brussels: Bruylant 2014), 249–83; and the book chapter, M. Trybus, 'Der Einfluss der EU-Richtlinie zur Beschaffung im Verteidigungs-und Sicherheitsbereich', in M. Essig and A. Glas (eds), *Performance Based Logistics*, (Berlin: Springer Gabler 2014).

[1] Directive 2009/81/EC of the European Parliament and of the Council of 13 July 2009 on the coordination of procedures for the award of certain works contracts, supply contracts and service contracts by contracting authorities or entities in the fields of defence and security, and amending Directives 2004/17/EC and 2004/18/EC, [2009] OJ L216/76.

[2] The EU Defence Package also consists of Directive 2009/43/EC simplifying terms and conditions of transfers of defence-related products within the Community [2009] OJ L146/1 and the Commission Communication, *A Strategy for a Stronger and More Competitive European Defence Industry*, COM (2007) 764 final. On the initial drafts: P. Koutrakos (2008), 'The Commission's "defence package"' 33 *European Law Review* 1–2.

Articles 36, 52(1), and especially 346 TFEU, thereby keeping the majority of contracts 'inside' the regime of the Defence Procurement Directive and the Treaty. Many of the innovations of the new Public Sector Procurement Directive 2014/24/EU will probably make their way into a revised Defence Procurement Directive in 2016. However, a discussion of these innovations in this context would require an entire chapter in itself.

Many legal, political, economic, and historical reasons have been cited for the absence of specific defence procurement Directive before 2009: national security, sovereignty in the core area of defence, and industrial considerations. Thus while goods and services are subject to the internal market and had been covered by the old Public Sector Procurement Directive and its predecessors, in practice the extensive use of a number of derogations, most notably what is now Article 346 TFEU, took most armaments and related services outside the EU's trade, competition, and procurement rules. This resulted in 28 separate defence markets characterised by protectionism, inefficiencies, and sometimes corruption, resulting in reduced levels of innovation and competitiveness, high prices, and a lack of transparency. Overall, a widespread incomprehension or defiance of the then existing legal framework of defence procurement could be observed. For example, few of the relevant contracts were published in the OJ. This does not necessarily mean that defence contracts were not subject to procurement regulation. Contracts were often published but in national or other media, not in the OJ. Contracts were awarded on the basis of prescribed procedures, but not on the basis of the EU procurement Directives.[3] Most importantly, these procedures only rarely resulted in the award of a contract to a bidder from another EU Member State. This situation represented an extensive exclusion from the public procurement regime of the internal market in practice because the importance of the defence market to the European economy is considerable. According to 2012 figures of the European Defence Agency (EDA), the EU Member States spent €194 billion on defence in 2010. Their total procurement budget for armaments, civil goods, services and works, including operations and maintenance, was estimated at €86 billion[4] and the European defence industries have an annual turnover of €55 billion employing 300,000 people.[5]

The extensive interpretation of Article 346 TFEU further discussed in the next paragraph below also led to initiatives concerning defence procurement outside the internal market. These include the activities of the EDA inside the intergovernmental Common Foreign and Security Policy (CFSP) and Common Security and Defence Policy (CSDP) but *outside* the internal market, in which all Member States except

[3] On the procedures in France, Germany and the United Kingdom see the respective chapters in M. Trybus (1999), *European Defence Procurement Law: International and National Procurement Systems as Models for a Liberalised Defence Procurement Market in Europe* (The Hague: Kluwer Law International 1999).

[4] Based on the 26 Member States then participating in the European Defence Agency. The figure is the overall €86 billion figure for procurement and research and development, including €9 billion for the latter, and including 22–23% of the overall €194 spent on operations and maintenance, see: http://www.eda.europa.eu/News/12-01-25/EU_and_US_government_Defence_spending (accessed 4 November 2013 – no longer available in February 2015).

[5] 2007 figures of COM (2007) 764 final, 2; the Communication also points out that 20 years ago these figures were almost twice as high.

Denmark participate,[6] the separate intergovernmental Organisation for Joint Armaments Procurement (OCCAR) in which Belgium, France, Germany, Italy, Spain, and the United Kingdom participate,[7] the equally separate and intergovernmental Letter of Intent organisation which includes France, Germany, Italy, Spain, Sweden, and the United Kingdom,[8] or the bilateral Anglo-French Defence Treaty of 2010.[9] An analysis of the contributions of these approaches would go beyond the aim of this chapter. However, the EDA had created most importantly a non-binding Code of Conduct on Defence Procurement[10] which had brought a considerable part of the relevant contracts within a relatively open, competitive and transparent defence procurement regime.[11] This EDA regime with the Code of Conduct on Defence Procurement at its core has not been abolished in response to the introduction of the Defence Procurement Directive and its – at least formally – comprehensive transposition into the national laws of the 28 Member States.

The Defence Procurement Directive became possible because of the clarification of the interpretation by the ECJ of the special derogation in Article 346(1)(b) TFEU which allows any Member State 'to take such measures as it considers necessary for the protection of the essential interests of its security which are connected with the production or trade in arms, munitions and war material ...'.[12] This derogation applies to the Treaty as a whole. In 1958 the Council drew a list of products to which Article 346(1)(b) TFEU applies[13] according to Article 346(2) TFEU. In *Spanish Weapons* the ECJ clarified that Article 346(1)(b) TFEU does not represent an automatic or

---

6 http://www.eda.europa.eu/ (accessed 3 February 2016).

7 http://www.occar.int/ (accessed 3 February 2016).

8 http://www.mod.uk/DefenceInternet/AboutDefence/WhatWeDo/Legal/LetterofIntent (accessed 3 February 2016). On all these approaches see: A. Georgopoulos, 'The European Armaments Policy: A *conditio sine qua non* for the European Defence and Security Policy' in M. Trybus and N.D. White (eds), *European Security Law* (Oxford: Oxford University Press 2005) 198–222; A. Georgopoulos, 'Defence procurement and EU law' (2005) 30 *European Law Review* 559–72.

9 Cm (2010) 7976.

10 See M. Trybus, 'The New European Defence Agency: A Contribution to a Common European Security and Defence Policy or a Challenge to the Community *acquis*?', (2006) 43 *Common Market Law Review* 667–703; A. Georgopoulos, 'The European Defence Agency's Code of Conduct for Armaments Acquisitions: A Case of Paramnesia?' (2006) 15 *Public Procurement Law Review* 51–61; and B. Heuninckx, 'Towards a coherent European defence procurement regime? European Defence Agency and European Commission Initiatives' (2008) 17 *Public Procurement Law Review* 1–20.

11 See B. Heuninckx, 'The European Defence Agency Electronic Bulletin Board: a survey after two years' (2009) 18 *Public Procurement Law Review* 43–66.

12 On Article 346 TFEU in detail, see Trybus, *Buying Defence and Security in Europe*, title note, at 87–128; M. Trybus, *European Union Law and Defence Integration* (Oxford: Hart Publishing 2005), chapter 5 and M. Trybus, 'The EC Treaty as an Instrument of European Defence Integration: Judicial Scrutiny of Defence and Security Exceptions' (2002) 39 *Common Market Law Review* 1347–72.

13 Council-Decision 298/58 of 15 April 1958 (not published). However, see the Council response to Written Question E-1324/01 by Bart Staes (Verts/ALE) to the Council, [2002] OJ C364E, 85–6.

categorical exclusion of armaments from the application of the TFEU.[14] As a derogation it needs to be interpreted narrowly,[15] Member States need to specifically invoke and substantiate the exemption and prove that a situation justifying its use actually exists, on a case-by-case basis, and the Court will apply a proportionality test. This narrow interpretation of Article 346(1)(b) TFEU was reiterated in a 2006 Interpretative Communication of the Commission.[16] It means that the application of the Treaty is the rule, that Member States can only derogate from the TFEU in exceptional circumstances and that derogation is subject to controls, requirements, and constraints. *Spanish Weapons* was later confirmed and refined in the *Agusta* judgments,[17] the *Military Exports* judgments,[18] and in *Finnish Turntables*.[19] Before this case-law many Member States had interpreted Article 346 TFEU as a categorical exemption of armaments from the scope of the Treaty and, as described above, acted accordingly when awarding defence contracts.

The EU Defence Procurement Directive represents a Public Sector Procurement Directive (2004/18/EC) adapted to the special needs of defence and security procurement.[20] The purpose of the adaptations is to avoid Member States derogating from the Directive and Treaty on the basis of Article 346 TFEU,[21] but also Articles 36 and 53 TFEU.[22] Most national security needs of the Member States are accommodated to keep most procurement activities inside the Directive and Treaty. Four techniques of adaptation: limitation, flexibility, description, and substitution were used. The provisions are those on personal and especially material scope including thresholds and in particular exceptions (2.), procurement procedures and the situations in which they can be used (3.), contract performance conditions, the qualification of bidders to ensure their reliability, award criteria determining the eventual contractor (4.), offsets and subcontracting (5.) and finally on review and remedies (6.).

---

[14] Case C-414/97, *Commission v Spain* [1999] ECR I-5585, [2000] 2 CMLR 4.

[15] Case 222/84, *Johnston* [1986] ECR 1651, [1986] 3 CMLR 240, para 26. See also Case 13/98 *Salgoil* [1968] ECR 453, 463, [1969] CMLR 181, 192 and Case 7/68, *Commission v Italy* [1968] ECR 633, 644.

[16] COM (2006)779 final.

[17] Case C-337/05, *Commission v Italy* [2008] ECR I-2173 and Case C-157/06, *Commission v Italy* [2008] ECR I-7313.

[18] Case C-284/05, *Commission v Finland* [2009] ECR I-11705; Case C-294/05, *Commission v Sweden* [2009] ECR I-11777; Case C-387/05, *Commission v Italy* [2009] ECR I-11831; Case C-409/05, *Commission v Greece* [2009] ECR I-11859; Case C-461/05, *Commission v Denmark* [2009] ECR I-11887; Case C-38/06, *Commission v Portugal* [2010] ECR I-1569; Case C-239/06, *Commission v Italy* [2009] ECR I-11913.

[19] Case C-615/10, *Insinööritoimisto InsTiimi Oy*, ECLI:EU:C:2012:324.

[20] The Commission Guidance Note *Field of Application*, available 3 February 2016 at http://ec.europa.eu/internal_market/publicprocurement/docs/defence/guide-scope_en.pdf at 2.

[21] See Recitals 4, 5, 9, and 12 Defence Directive.

[22] N. Pourbaix, 'The Future Scope of Application of Article 346 TFEU' (2011) 20 *Public Procurement Law Review* 1–8.

2. THE LIMITATION OF THE SCOPE OF THE DEFENCE PROCUREMENT DIRECTIVE

A crucial issue to be considered at the beginning of any analysis of procurement law is its scope or field of application, its coverage. This concerns the questions of which contracting entities and which of their contracts are covered by the relevant legislation. The latter aspect looks at the contract type, its value, and exceptions (material scope). The earlier looks at the legal nature of the contracting entity (the personal scope). The personal scope of the Defence Procurement Directive is not limited to ministries of defence but extends to all the contracting authorities and entities also covered by the Public Sector and Utilities Procurement Directives discussed in the other chapters of this book. The legislator had alternatives with a larger or smaller personal scope and in particular the Defence Procurement Directive could have been limited to contracting entities in the field of defence. However, this would have only made sense with a material scope limited to armaments, which was not the approach taken, as will be discussed below. Furthermore, the differences between defence and security are becoming increasingly blurred, with many entities other than the armed forces carrying relevant responsibilities. Therefore it is submitted that the creation of a security-specific instrument for all contracting authorities covered by the other procurement Directives makes sense.

According to Article 2 Defence Procurement Directive it applies only to military equipment, sensitive equipment, works, supplies, and services directly related to military and sensitive equipment[23] and finally works and services for specifically military purposes. Thus the material scope of the Defence Procurement Directive covers some but not all purchases of these entities previously covered by the old Public Sector Procurement Directive. Ministries of defence, for example, have to follow national law transposing either the Defence Procurement Directive or the old and new Public Sector Procurement Directive, depending on the type of good, service, or work they wish to procure,[24] unless they need to invoke a security exemption.[25]

Article 2 Defence Procurement Directive already contains a crucial exclusion limiting the scope of the Directive as it is subject to Articles 36, 51, 52, 62, and 346 TFEU. The case-law providing the authoritative interpretation of especially Article 346

---

[23] See: Commission Guidance Note *Field of Application*, *supra* note 20.

[24] B. Heunickx, 'The EU Defence and Security Procurement Directive: Trick or Treat? (2011) 20 *Public Procurement Law Review* 9, at 11: 'When the Defence and Security Directive applies, the Public Sector Directive does not apply'; see also T. Briggs, 'The New Defence Procurement Directive' (2009) 18 *Public Procurement Law Review* NA129, NA130.

[25] In Britain, for example, before the implementation of the Defence Directive about 12% of the contracts were subject to the Public Contracts Regulations 2006 (based on the Public Sector Directive), 12% to Article 346 TFEU and other exemptions, and 76% below the value thresholds of the Public Sector Directive. After the transposition, 2% will be subject to the Public Contracts Regulations 2006, 4% exempt, 15% will be subject to the Defence and Security Contracts Regulations 2011, and 79% below the threshold values of Public Sector Directive and Defence Directive. See D. Kiltie (UK Ministry of Defence), 'Implementing and applying Directive 2009/81/EC in the UK', from the seminar *European Defence and Security Procurement*, Maastricht, EIPA, 20 January 2012.

TFEU was discussed in the introduction above. Although this should be the exception from the rule and the entire Defence Procurement Directive is drafted to avoid it, Member States can still derogate from the instrument for reasons of national and public security.[26] The Directive cannot change the Treaty and it merely expressly integrates the Treaty exclusions into the Directive.[27] These exclusions would have applied anyway. However, the difference from the previous situation is that the Defence Procurement Directive is designed to take the public and national security concerns of the Member States into account.

2.1 Thresholds

Similar to the other procurement Directives, the Defence Procurement Directive is only applicable *above* certain contract value thresholds. Article 8 Defence Procurement Directive as amended[28] provides for thresholds of €414,000 for supply and service contracts and €5,186,000 for works contracts.[29] Thresholds represent a limitation of scope, because they clarify that the Directive does *not* apply to contracts with a value *below* the thresholds.

The threshold for works contracts equals that in the Public Sector Procurement Directive. In contrast, the value thresholds for supplies and services are considerably higher with respect to central government (€134,000) and other contracting entities (€207,000).[30] The thresholds in the Defence Procurement Directive actually equal those of the Utilities Procurement Directive.[31] The values of many of the most visible contracts, such as fighter planes or battleships, are well above these thresholds. However, many of the relevant contracts will cover the re-supply of parts, repairs, training, accessories, smaller weapon systems, or ammunition, and are frequently below these thresholds.[32] Therefore the difference in thresholds matters: a relevant ministry of defence purchase with a contract value between €134,000 and €414,000 is now outside the scope of both the Defence Procurement Directive and the Public Sector Procurement Directive, whereas in the past it would have been covered by the latter. Thus a number of contracts which used to be covered by secondary internal market legislation

---

[26] In contrast the former EDA Code of Conduct on Defence Procurement only applied when Article 346 TFEU applied.

[27] See the Commission Guidance Note *Field of Application*, *supra* note 20, 1.

[28] Article 3 Commission Regulation No 1336/2013/EU of 13 December 2013 amending Directives 2004/17/EC, 2004/18/EC and 2009/81/EC of the European Parliament and of the Council in respect of the application thresholds for the procedures for the awards of contract [2013] OJ L335/17. See Article 68 Defence Directive.

[29] Value thresholds are not only set by the Directive itself but revised and adapted on a biannual basis. The current figures are valid from 1 January 2014 until 31 December 2016. See Article 4 Regulation 1336/2013/EU.

[30] See also Briggs, *supra* note 24, NA132.

[31] Article 16 Utilities Procurement Directive 2004/17/EC as amended by Article 1(1) Commission Regulation 1336/2013/EU.

[32] I have benefited from discussions with Baudouin Heunickx on this point of the type of contracts to be covered by the Defence Directive. See also the figures in the next footnote below.

are now outside such regulation altogether.[33] The higher thresholds in comparison to the Public Sector Procurement Directive represent an adaptation by limitation as the scope is reduced, even though the principles of the Treaty would still apply to these contracts.[34]

2.2 Exceptions

All procurement Directives feature exceptions, but in its Article 13(a) to (d) and (f) the Defence Procurement Directive features specific exceptions in addition to those also contained in the Public Sector Procurement Directive. An additional exception represents an adaptation through limitation in comparison to the Public Sector Procurement Directive.

2.2.1 Secrecy

The exclusion in Article 13(a) on 'contracts for which the application of the rules of this Directive would oblige a Member State to supply information the disclosure of which it considers contrary to the essential interests of its security' is a reflection of the Treaty exemption in Article 346(1)(a) TFEU.[35] This covers situations in which security and secrecy considerations would be compromised by advertising contracts or by complying with other transparency requirements. A similar exemption is contained in the Public Sector Procurement Directive[36] but the exclusion in letter (a) accommodates many of the relevant secrecy considerations in the substantive rules of the Defence Procurement Directive and thereby reduces the necessity to use Article 346 TFEU. Nevertheless, the exception is also needed in the Defence Procurement Directive for extreme cases in which even the Directive does not sufficiently accommodate security of information requirements.[37]

---

[33] So Kiltie, *supra* note 25, expects a slightly higher percentage of United Kingdom Ministry of Defence contracts to be below the thresholds: 79% rather than 76%. Considering that with France the United Kingdom has one of the largest procurement budgets in the EU, it can be assumed that in many Member States this percentage is similar or even higher.

[34] See M. Trybus, 'Public Procurement in European Union Internal Market Law', in R. Nogouellou and U. Stelkens (eds), *Comparative Law on Public Contracts Treatise* (Brussels: Bruylant 2010), 81–121.

[35] Article 346(1)(a) TFEU reads: '1. The provisions of the Treaties shall not preclude the application of the following rules: (a) no Member State shall be obliged to supply information the disclosure of which it considers contrary to the essential interests of its security ...'.

[36] Article 14 Public Sector Procurement Directive 2004/18/EC on secret contracts and contracts requiring special security measures. See Trybus, *European Union Law and Defence Integration*, *supra* note 12, 213–21 (214–16).

[37] The Commission's B. Schmitt and N. Spiegel (the drafters of the Defence Directive) reported in their presentation 'The specificities of the European Defence and Security Procurement Directive' at the seminar *European Defence Procurement and Other Defence Market Initiatives*, at the EIPA, Maastricht, 15 November 2010 (notes of the author, on file), that the inclusion of the provision is also a 'gesture' to the Member States and to the 'security community'. Moreover, it could be argued that there is a slight difference between the provisions in that Article 13(a) Defence Directive specifically refers to 'contracts' whereas Article 346(1)(b) TFEU does not.

2.2.2 Intelligence services

The exclusion in Article 13(b) on 'contracts for the purposes of intelligence activities' is connected to the exclusion in letter (a). However, the secret nature of intelligence activities[38] made it necessary, in the opinion of the legislator, to exclude them from the new Directive.[39] Article 13(b) excludes 'activities' not entire intelligence agencies.[40]

2.2.3 Cooperative programmes

The exclusion in Article 13(c) covers 'contracts awarded in the framework of a cooperative programme based on research and development, conducted jointly by at least two Member States for the development of a new product and, where applicable, the later phases of all or part of the life-cycle of this product'. This refers to the large collaborative programmes, such as the Eurofighter/Typhoon aircraft between two or more Member States which are a regular occurrence for the development of new equipment.[41] The programme has to include at least two Member States, involve the development of a new product, and may include later phases of its life cycle.[42]

This provision also regulates the delimitation of activities between the EU internal market and the activities of the intergovernmental EDA and OCCAR mentioned above. In particular the activities of the latter are mainly situated in the collaborative projects covered by this exemption. The exemption leaves these projects to frameworks outside the EU internal market[43] and is significant since it relates to the financially, strategically, militarily, industrially, and politically most important large projects of crucial new high-technology equipment. Thus, an important part of defence procurement is outside the Defence Procurement Directive. Research and development is also the subject of a situation that according to Article 28(2)(a) Defence Procurement Directive allows the use of the negotiated procedure without publication, as will be discussed in the context of procurement procedures below. It was initially not intended as an exemption but Member States were 'quite insistent' on also including an exclusion.[44] Even the now-

---

[38] Schmitt and Spiegel, ibid say that there is a risk of vagueness to speak of 'services' rather than of 'activities'.

[39] See on this issue (in the USA) the contribution of S. Chesterman, 'The Privatization of Intelligence' in the blog *EJIL Talk!* (2009) available 3 February 2016 at http://www.ejiltalk.org/privatization_of_intel/ with further references.

[40] K. Vierlich-Jürcke, "Specificities of the Defence Procurement Directive" at the seminar *European Defence and Security Procurement* at the EIPA, Maastricht, 19 January 2012, (slide 15, on file).

[41] Either through OCCAR, EDA, or NATO logistics organisations (NAMSA) and NATO production logistics organisations such as the Tornado Development Production and Logistics Management Agency (NETMA/NEFMO and NAMMO), or by using the so called 'lead national concept'. See the presentation by B. Heuninckx, 'Collaborative Defence Procurement', at the seminar *European Defence and Security Procurement*, EIPA, Maastricht, 19 January 2012 (slide 12, on file).

[42] Schmitt and Spiegel, *supra* note 37 (slide 12 on file); N. Spiegel, 'Directive 2009/81/EC: Defence specificities', at the seminar *The European Defence and Security Procurement Directive and the Challenges for its Implementation*, European Institute of Public Administration (EIPA), Maastricht, 21 June 2010 (slide 11, on file).

[43] See also Recital 28 Defence Directive.

[44] Schmitt and Spiegel, *supra* note 37.

abolished EDA Code of Conduct on Defence Procurement excluded 'collaborative procurements'. Hence their *in*clusion would have been difficult and politically sensitive.[45] Therefore, *ex*clusion (limitation) represents a pragmatic approach, since *in*clusion would have required addressing a multitude of problems, such as the applicability of EU law to international organisations,[46] including the applicability of the TFEU to Member States acting within EDA or OCCAR. This might have met opposition from at least some Member States and have derailed or delayed the Defence Procurement Directive as a whole.[47]

2.2.4 Deployed forces

The exclusion in Article 13(d) covers 'contracts awarded in a third country, including for civil purchases, carried out when forces are deployed outside the territory of the Union where operational needs require them to be concluded with economic operators located in the area of operations … .' This reflects the peacekeeping dimension of defence policy, on a national basis, as part of the relatively new CSDP, or other frameworks such as NATO or the UN,[48] which is clearly outside the scope of the EU internal market. There are also political, practical, and military reasons allowing troops on peacekeeping missions to procure some of their needs in the country of their deployment. Exclusion (d) accommodates these reasons and is intended for basic commodities such as water and food, normally below the thresholds anyway.[49]

2.2.5 Government to government

The exclusion in Article 13(f) deals with 'contracts awarded by a government to another government relating to: (i) the supply of military equipment or sensitive equipment, (ii) works and services directly linked to such equipment, or (iii) works and services specifically for military purposes, or sensitive works and sensitive services … .'[50] This exclusion privileges a common practice of 'procuring' military supplies, works, and services from another government.[51] The exemption was originally intended for surplus equipment but in its current wording includes new items.[52] The latter implies a danger of abuse when the selling government is purchasing from the private sector with the

[45] See on this topic B. Heunickx, 'A Primer on Collaborative Defence Procurement in Europe: Troubles Achievements and Prospects' (2008) 17 *Public Procurement Law Review* 123–45 and in great detail his 2011 doctoral thesis at the University of Nottingham.

[46] See the Ph.D. thesis of Heuninckx in great detail on these problems.

[47] Thanks to Baudouin Heuninckx for bringing this point to my attention.

[48] Schmitt and Spiegel, *supra* note 37: 'it is tailor-made for crisis operations'.

[49] Ibid. Moreover, if above the threshold, they would be subject to the Public Sector Directive.

[50] See in great detail A. Estrup Ippolito, 'Government to Government contracts in EU defence procurement' (2014) 23 *Public Procurement Law Review* 249–65.

[51] The Public Sector Directive does generally apply to contracts awarded by one contracting authority to another contracting authority, unless the latter is controlled by the earlier and the contract is therefore in-house, see especially Case C-108/98, *Teckal* [1999] ECR I-8121.

[52] Schmitt and Spiegel, *supra* note 37.

intention of selling to another government.[53] This situation would not be covered. In relation to new equipment the exemption will only apply to supplies purchased by one government for its own purposes which later prove to be excess to requirements or no longer suitable for the purposes of the armed forces so that they can be sold.

The EU legislator has limited the Defence Procurement Directive also through the exceptions. Exclusions and thresholds exempt a significant part of the European armaments market from the scope of the Directive[54] and the share of defence contracts actually covered by the Directive might be only around 10 per cent.[55] The more important impact of the new instrument might be felt in non-military security markets rather than in the armaments sector.[56] This might have been the price to overcome reservations against the Defence Procurement Directive, but the exclusions and especially the cooperative programmes exception, will have to be discussed in the context of the revision of the Directive.

3. DEFENCE PROCUREMENT PROCEDURES

The procurement procedures of the Defence Procurement Directive are not specifically adapted to national security, but increased flexibility regarding the choice of the procedures that can be used, in favour of negotiated procedures, is intended to adapt to the special requirements of defence and security. This increased flexibility is intended to allow contracts to be procured on the basis of the Defence Procurement Directive rather than making a lack of flexibility the reason to invoke Article 346 TFEU.

First, in contrast to Public Sector and Utilities Procurement Directives, the Defence Procurement Directive does not provide the open procedure at all,[57] although this is not an aspect of more flexibility as such, as fewer options cannot increase flexibility. The lack of the open procedure is not entirely convincing. There are contracts, in a market of mostly anyway limited industrial capacities, where the limitation of competition through shortlisting in a restricted procedure is simply unnecessary. For example, for the acquisition of ammunition, for which technical specifications are standardised and

---

[53] As Vierlich-Jürcke, *supra* note 40, emphasised: "[it] cannot be used to circumvent the directive" (slide 16 on file). See also Article 11 Defence Procurement Directive.

[54] Heuninckx, 'Trick or Treat?', *supra* note 24, at 13: '[...] the exemptions from applicability of the Directive are many ...'; B. Heuninckx, 'Lurking at the Boundaries: Applicability of EU law to Defence and Security Procurement' (2010) 19 *Public Procurement Law Review* 91–118 at 110: 'The Defence and Security Directive also lists a fairly large number of specific exemptions.' See also Briggs, *supra* note 24, NA132–133.

[55] Based on the figures in *supra* note 9, this would still be contracts worth €8–9 billion per year.

[56] See the figures of Kiltie, *supra* note 25, (slide 34, on file) for Britain. The police, border agencies, or utilities such as airports will be able to take advantage of the thresholds but not of many of the exclusions, which might make the Directive more important to them than to the ministries of defence.

[57] Article 25 Defence Directive 'choice of procedures' does not mention the open procedure, nor is it mentioned anywhere else in the provisions of the Directive or its preamble. See also Heuninckx, 'Trick or Treat?', *supra* note 24, 14 and C. Kennedy-Loest and N. Pourbaix, 'The new Defence Procurement Directive' (2010) 11 *ERA Forum* 399, 403.

the number of suppliers is limited, the open procedure is currently routinely used.[58] Moreover, it is the most competitive procedure. It is submitted that the legislator should have given the open procedure a chance and seen whether this option is used in practice.[59]

Second, the restricted procedure[60] does not have the importance it has in the other Directives as, in contrast to the Public Sector Procurement Directive but similar to the Utilities Procurement Directive, the Defence Procurement Directive allows the free use of the negotiated procedure with prior publication of a contract notice, without the need to justify this choice on the basis of legally prescribed situations.[61] Thus the negotiated procedure *with* prior publication of a contract notice is not *de jure* but *de facto* the default procedure of the Defence Procurement Directive.[62] In other words, this is the procedure the legislator considers to be most suitable for defence and security procurement.[63]

Only the negotiated procedure *without* prior publication of a contract notice is limited to regulated situations. As a third aspect of flexibility, the list of these situations is longer than that in the other procurement Directives. It contains a number of military and security specific situations.[64] Article 28 Defence Procurement Directive contains the situations of the Public Sector Procurement Directive and a number of additional defence-specific situations, namely on research and development[65] and for forces deployed or to be deployed abroad.[66] Moreover, one of the grounds is more flexible than in the Public Sector Procurement Directive.[67] This procedure and the situations in which it can be used, is crucial since it is very close to procuring outside the Directive, with only limited procedural rules.[68] The approach of adding a limited number of

---

58 Thanks Baudouin Heuninckx for pointing this out to me.

59 Vierlich-Jürcke, *supra* note 40, said that she was having "second thoughts" about not including the open procedure. Schmitt and Spiegel, *supra* note 37, made a similar statement. In contrast, Kiltie, *supra* note 25, said he was happy about the open procedure not being included because otherwise he might be required to use it.

60 There is a difference between the restricted procedures as according to Article 44(3) Public Sector Procurement Directive the number of economic operators to be shortlisted for full tenders is five whereas according to Article 38(3) Defence Procurement Directive the number is three. The lower number increases flexibility for the contracting authority.

61 Article 25(2) Defence Procurement Directive.

62 Heuninckx, 'Trick or Treat?', *supra* note 24, 14: "the 'standard' procedure". The differentiation of *de facto* and *de jure* is also an expression of Baudouin Heuninckx.

63 See Recital 47 Defence Procurement Directive.

64 Article 28(1)(c) Defence Procurement Directive 'urgency resulting from a crisis', (2)(a) 'research and development services', and especially (5) 'armed forces deployed abroad'. See also Recital 58. The accelerated versions of the restricted procedure and the negotiated procedure with publication are also limited to a situation of 'urgency', see Article 33(7) Defence Procurement Directive.

65 Article 28(2)(a) Defence Procurement Directive.

66 Article 28(5) Defence Procurement Directive.

67 The 'additional deliveries' ground in Article 28(3)(a) Defence Procurement Directive, the increased flexibility being due to the long in-service life of military equipment, but open to abuse if not applied strictly, see Heuninckx, 'Trick or Treat?', *supra* note 24, 17.

68 In 2006 Wilson, Scott and Pyman found (based on data for the world market rather than specifically for the EU) that governments award about half or more of their defence procurement

military specific situations and nuances to the Public Sector Procurement Directive situations is appropriate.[69] A larger number of more flexible grounds allowing but not requiring the use of this uncompetitive procedure resulted in more flexibility.

The preference for the negotiated procedures is intended to accommodate the specific needs of defence and security procurement,[70] also in response to the requests of stakeholders expressed during the consultation mentioned above,[71] following the example of the Utilities Procurement Directive.[72] However, this 'adaptation' of the rules of the Public Sector Procurement Directive is not entirely convincing.[73] With good will and professionalism of the relevant procurement personnel, non-discriminatory, fair, and transparent competition is perfectly possible in the context of negotiated procedures *with* prior publication of a contract notice.[74] However, due to the dangers of their abuse and genuinely incorrect application,[75] this flexibility has to be really necessary. This cannot simply be assumed for all defence and security contracts and will depend on the context and circumstances of each individual case. It could be argued that a longer list of circumstances justifying the negotiated procedure with prior publication of a contract notice would have been an alternative approach to achieve more flexibility than in the Public Sector Procurement Directive.

Finally, the relationship of competitive dialogue and negotiated procedure with competition is questionable.[76] The former is limited to 'particularly complex

---

requirements to a single supplier. This figure reflects the close relationship and unique position of some companies in the market and opens the process to possible misconduct: R. Wilson, D. Scott and M. Pyman, 'The extent of single sourcing and attendant corruption risk in defence procurement: a first look', presented at the conference *Public Procurement: Global Revolution III*, Nottingham, 19–20 June 2006. The Defence Directive limits its negotiated procedure without competition, which still remains subject to transparency requirements and judicial review.

[69] Kiltie, *supra* note 25, considers this to be 'well done' in the Directive, the situations are 'clear and all welcome' – 'very, very welcome'.

[70] See Recital 47 Defence Procurement Directive. See also Recital 48 and on the negotiated procedure without competition Recital 50.

[71] COM (2005) 626 final, 5, 7.

[72] See Article 40 Utilities Procurement Directive 204/17/EC.

[73] And this is also an opinion expressed by some stakeholders, see COM (2005) 626 final, 8. However, this was a minority view.

[74] Transparency is ensured, *inter alia*, by the publication of the contract notice and the requirements to be set in that notice (Article 26(1) Defence Procurement Directive). Equal treatment and non-discrimination are expressly required, *inter alia*, in Article 26(2) Defence Procurement Directive. Article 26(3) Defence Procurement Directive contains one of the references to the award criteria which have to be applied in negotiated procedures with competition.

[75] Due to these dangers negotiated procedures are more risky for tenderers but also more susceptible to legal challenges (founded or not).

[76] Heuninckx, 'Trick or Treat?' , *supra* note 24, at 17–18; Kennedy-Loest and Pourbaix, *supra* note 57, at 403. M. Burnett, 'Use of Negotiated Procedures and Competitive Dialogue in the Defence and Security Sectors', at the seminar *The European Defence and Security Procurement Directive and Challenges for its Implementation*, EIPA, Maastricht, 21 June 2010, puts the "key question – why use competitive dialogue when there is unrestricted choice of the negotiated procedure with prior publication?" (slide 32, on file).

contracts'[77] whereas, as mentioned above, the latter is freely available. The competitive dialogue is conducted with selected operators to define the best way to meet the needs of the procuring entity followed by full bids.[78] It is slightly more formalised,[79] with rules on the protection of the confidentiality of the information provided by participants, a formal end of the dialogue, and best and final offers (tenders).[80] It is 'less flexible, and often lengthier and more costly'.[81] The negotiated procedure is less formalised and thus more open to abuse.[82] If then the competitive dialogue accommodates the need for negotiation while at the same time being more resistant to abuse, the legislator should have regulated the relationship between the two procedures the other way round: allowing the free use of the competitive dialogue and limiting the use of the negotiated procedure with competition to exceptional situations.[83] The need for the coexistence of both procedures in the Defence Procurement Directive is also doubtful. The competitive dialogue was not included in the Utilities Procurement Directive, where the use of the negotiated procedure with competition is also free. The restricted use of the former and the free use of the latter might make the competitive dialogue redundant in practice.[84] However, it should also be pointed out that, beyond France and Britain, the competitive dialogue is only used to a very limited extent,[85] showing unease with this complex procedure.

There is considerably more flexibility in the Defence Procurement Directive with regards to procedures and the legislator could not have provided more flexibility, other than allowing the free use of the negotiated procedure without prior publication of a contract notice, which eliminates competition and reduces procedural requirements to a minimum thereby coming close to procurement outside a Directive. This would have created a situation very similar to the previous one without a specific Directive. In other words, the Defence Procurement Directive would have been useless.

---

77 Article 27(1) Defence Procurement Directive.

78 Article 27(3) Defence Procurement Directive.

79 When comparing Articles 26 and 27 Defence Procurement Directive, there is not much more formalisation in the competitive dialogue, however, with the notable exception of the formal closure of the dialogue and best and final offer stage. Thanks to B. Heuninckx for pointing this out to the author.

80 Article 27(3) Defence Procurement Directive.

81 Kennedy-Loest and Pourbaix, *supra* note 57, at 403.

82 Heuninckx, 'Trick or Treat', *supra* note 24, at 15.

83 Ibid at 16.

84 Kennedy-Loest and Pourbaix, *supra* note 57, at 403; Heuninckx, 'Trick or Treat?', *supra* note 24, at 16. Burnett, *supra* note 76, reports that 80% of competitive dialogues were conducted in France and Britain, with only few in Denmark and Sweden and for example none in Greece. See in detail: S. Arrowsmith and S. Treumer (eds), *Competitive Dialogue in EU Procurement* (Cambridge: Cambridge University Press 2012).

85 Vierlich-Jürcke, *supra* note 40.

4. SPECIFICATIONS, CONTRACT CONDITIONS, QUALIFICATION, AND AWARD CRITERIA

In order to limit the necessity to invoke Article 346 TFEU, the Defence Procurement Directive also includes a number of defence-specific and expressly described requirements and conditions which are also legally possible but not expressly spelled out in the other procurement Directives. Security of supply and security of information are the main requirements thus accommodated. Security of supply is a national security concern about procured products not being delivered. Delivery can be affected, for example, by transfer licenses, which are a feature of the European defence and security market different from the internal market for other goods. Security of information is a national security concern about the confidentiality of sensitive information not being sufficiently safeguarded. The most important rules on different stages of the procurement procedure adapted to address these concerns are contained in the provisions on technical specifications, contract performance conditions, qualification, and award criteria.

4.1 Technical Specifications and Contract Performance Conditions

Rules on technical specifications regulate the definition of a product on the basis of which economic operators prepare their tenders in the context of open and restricted procedures. Tenders not compliant with these specifications have to be rejected. The rules are intended to prevent these 'product definitions' from being abused to discriminate against tenderers because of their nationality.[86] In contrast to the Public Sector Procurement Directive, Article 18 Defence Procurement Directive on technical specifications expressly refers to 'defence standards[87] ... and defence material specifications similar to those standards', which is appropriate. However, this is not a substantive adaptation but merely descriptive, as these standards can also be used under the old and new Public Sector Procurement Directives.

There is a close connection between these rules on technical specifications and contract performance conditions which will only be in operation after the conclusion or making of the contract. While the old Public Sector Procurement Directive only requires these conditions to be compatible with EU law,[88] the Defence Procurement Directive provides many specific contract performance conditions. These especially concern security of information and security of supply and have to be communicated at the beginning of the procurement procedure,[89] partly explaining their close connection to specifications. Regarding security of information, Article 7 Defence Procurement Directive provides for a general power of contracting entities to impose requirements

[86] On the rules of Utilities and Public Sector Directives: C. Bovis, *EC Public Procurement: Case Law and Regulation* (Oxford: Oxford University Press 2006), 220–3 and 397–9.

[87] Defence standards are defined in Point 3 Annex III Defence Procurement Directive.

[88] Article 26 Public Sector Procurement Directive 2004/18/EC. Equally short is Article 38 Utilities Procurement Directive.

[89] In the contract documentation (contract notices, contract documents, descriptive documents or supporting documents), see Articles 20, 22, and 23 Defence Procurement Directive.

aimed at protecting classified information[90] throughout the tendering and contracting phases.[91] Moreover, Article 22 Defence Procurement Directive allows contract conditions to secure the protection of classified information on the required security level.[92] Regarding security of supply, Article 23 Defence Procurement Directive allows several contract conditions to ensure the delivery of supplies: concerning the transfer, export, and transit of products, regarding security of supply in crisis situations,[93] when there are additional needs, for spare parts, and information obligations regarding possible changes of the production site or in the supply chain. Every possible disruption appears to be covered. Such requirements are also allowed and customary within the scope of the other procurement Directives. The added value of expressly stipulating them is that there is no doubt about them being in compliance with EU law. This reduces litigation risks and encourages the use of these requirements by contracting officers.

4.2 Qualification of Bidders

In the defence procurement context, the reliability of bidders is particularly important, especially if bidders from other Member States, with which the contracting authorities might not have any previous experience, are to have a realistic chance. The qualification rules of the other procurement Directives are also contained in the Defence Procurement Directive.[94] According to its Article 39 bidders with a relevant 'negative' history can be excluded. Violations against security of information, security of supply, and other national security requirements are expressly stipulated.[95] Moreover, the technical capacity to be proved according to Article 42 Defence Procurement Directive includes defence and security specific requirements.[96] However, these requirements are also possible on the basis of the corresponding rules of the other procurement Directives. Again, the added value of expressly stipulating them in the Defence Procurement Directive is that there is no doubt about them being in compliance with EU law, thus reducing litigation risks and encouraging their use.

In the defence sector economic operators need security clearances certifying their ability to handle confidential information to do business with the government. There is

---

[90] See the definition of classified information in Article 1(8) Defence Procurement Directive. See also Recital 20 Defence Procurement Directive.

[91] See Briggs, *supra* note 24, NA133.

[92] In principle these requirements are also applicable to subcontractors. See Article 22(b)–(d) Defence Procurement Directive.

[93] The definition of a crisis for the purposes of the Defence Procurement Directive is contained in its Article 1(1). According to Spiegel, *supra* note 42, the definition was included on the initiative of the Rapporteur in the European Parliament Alexander, Count Lambsdorff.

[94] On the rules of the Public Sector Procurement Directive see P. Trepte, *Public Procurement in the EU: A Practitioner's Guide* 2nd edn. (Oxford: Oxford University Press 2007) 335–53.

[95] Article 39(2)(d) and (e) Defence Procurement Directive. See also Article 39(1)(d) Defence Procurement Directive regarding "terrorist offences or offences linked to terrorist activities' and "money laundering and terrorist financing" respectively.

[96] Article 42(1)(h) and (j) Defence Procurement Directive.

no EU-wide regime on security clearances. Therefore bidders have to comply with national rules on security clearances, based on a 'basic principle' of mutual recognition,[97] but with the final decision and power to make additional investigations left to the Member States.[98] Member States have bilateral agreements and some but not all include mutual recognition.[99] There were efforts to achieve more general mutual recognition but nothing could be achieved due to national sovereignty concerns.[100] While this might lead to problems, if for example national security clearances are not equivalent, the fact that Member States cannot always ask for their own national security clearance is already a step in the right direction. After all, *inter alia*, time delays in obtaining national security clearances have potential for discrimination and therefore litigation. It is submitted that there would be obvious practical advantages of an EU-wide security clearance, to avoid such discrimination.[101] However, this would require a high degree of trust between Member States, which probably does not exist (yet).

Overall, the specific requirements of the defence sector have also been accommodated in the rules on qualification. According to Article 39(1) Defence Procurement Directive, the qualification criteria in Articles 41–46 Defence Procurement Directive are also the selection criteria[102] for candidates to be invited to tender in the restricted procedure, the negotiated procedure with prior call for tender, and the competitive dialogue. There are no significant differences to the similar rules of the other procurement Directives, apart from expressly described qualification criteria and the fact that in restricted procedures the number of economic operators selected to tender may be limited to three.[103]

4.3 Award Criteria

Similar to the respective provisions in the other procurement Directives before the 2014 reform, Article 47 Defence Procurement Directive provides for the lowest price and the economically most advantageous tender as award criteria. The criterion of lowest price is only suitable for simple 'off the shelf' acquisitions and normally only used in open and restricted procedures. Due to the complexity of many armaments contracts and the

---

97 Heuninckx, 'Trick or Treat?' *supra* note 24, 21. See Article 42(j) Defence Procurement Directive. Additional time may be given to bidders to obtain security clearances which they do not have. The national security authority of the Member State of the bidder may be asked to check their premises.

98 See last paragraph of Article 22 Defence Procurement Directive and the last part of Recital 68 Defence Procurement Directive.

99 See Recital 68 Defence Procurement Directive and Schmitt and Spiegel, *supra* note 37.

100 Ibid.

101 However, Member States are currently not prepared to introduce such a regime: Vierlich-Jürcke, *supra* note 40.

102 'Selection could also be called 'pre-selection' to distinguish it from the actual award of the contract discussed under the next heading. It could also be called 'shortlisting', although this is a slightly colloquial term not used in the Directives.

103 Five according to Article 44(3) 3rd sentence Public Sector Procurement Directive 2004/18/EC.

absence of the open procedure this criterion will be of less importance under the Defence Procurement Directive. The other criterion of the economically most advantageous tender allows taking account of a multitude of economic (sub-) criteria which are connected to the subject matter of the contract, such as quality, delivery date, after-sales service, and so on.[104] Security of supply and 'interoperability and operational characteristics' can expressly be taken into account as sub-criteria. Security of information is not expressly mentioned as a sub-criterion in the text of the Defence Procurement Directive or the Commission's Guidance Note *Security of Information*.[105] It has been argued that it may be considered when determining the economically most advantageous offer, for example when the measures of the bidder for the protection of sensitive information in the context of the execution of the contract are assessed.[106]

Again, the added value of stipulating and thus describing defence and security specific standards, contract performance conditions, qualification criteria, and award sub-criteria in the Defence Procurement Directive is that it raises awareness amongst contracting officers to use them and offers possibilities to accommodate security of supply and information inside the Directive. Moreover, it is clear that these requirements are in compliance with the Directive. Together with the limitation and flexibility described above, description raises the threshold for the use of especially Article 346 TFEU. Furthermore, questions will be asked, by the Commission or the ECJ, when a Member State invokes one of the security exemptions in the Treaty without having made use of the conditions and criteria offered in the Defence Procurement Directive. The requirements do not add substance but are merely descriptive and many other requirements can be added in practice, as long as they are in compliance with EU law. Therefore a longer list of descriptive requirements in the Directive, which could have been an alternative, is not necessary.

5. OFFSETS AND SUBCONTRACTS

In sharp contrast to 'civilian' contracts, offsets[107] are a regular occurrence in defence procurement when contracts are awarded to economic operators from a country other than that of the contracting entity and as part of such contracts, 'compensation' for the funds of the awarding country is required from the government of the economic operator. This can amount to more than 100 per cent of the value of the original

---

[104] Alternatively the 'notion' of the most economically advantageous tender could be described as a concept encompassing various economic criteria. In that understanding the considerations described as 'sub-criteria' in this section of the article wold be the actual 'criteria' which determine the economically most advantageous tender. I benefitted from discussing this issue with B. Heuninckx.

[105] http://ec.europa.eu/internal_market/publicprocurement/docs/defence/guide-soi_en.pdf (accessed 3 February 2016).

[106] Kennedy-Loest and Pourbaix, *supra* note 57, 405.

[107] Related terms describing offsets are: industrial compensation, industrial cooperation, industrial and regional benefits, balances, *juste retour* (English: fair returns), or equilibrium.

contract.[108] Offsets can take various forms, as direct offsets to the defence industries of the awarding country, for example through the establishment of (job-creating) production sites in the awarding country, or indirect offsets to the civilian industries.[109] Practices vary considerably between Member States; some do not require offsets at all, in others they are a legal requirement, for example as an award criterion.[110] This can mean that the offset agreement has no connection with the subject matter of the original defence contract and that qualification or quality become less important.

Offsets cannot be reconciled with the Defence Procurement Directive and are difficult to justify on the basis of Article 346 TFEU,[111] as they normally meet economic and financial requirements rather than national security considerations.[112] They undermine the internal market and procurement regime, since they make an open, transparent and competitive procurement procedure without discrimination very difficult or entirely impossible. Neither the TFEU[113] nor the Defence Procurement Directive mention offsets at all,[114] but the Commission issued a Guidance Note on *Offsets* clearly setting out: '... the Directive cannot allow, tolerate or regulate [offsets]'.[115]

---

108 According to the 2007 figures of a 2008 EDA Study: E. Anders Erikson, M. Axelson, K. Hartley, M. Mason, A.-S.Stenérius and M. Trybus, *Study on the Effects of Offsets on the Development of a European Defence Industry and Market* (SCS Henley on Thames, UK and FOI Stockholm, Sweden for the EDA: Brussels, 2007), available 3 February 2016 at http://www.eda.europa.eu/docs/documents/eda_06-dim-022_study_on_the_effects_of_offsets_on_the_development_of_a_european_defence_industry_and_market_1, 4, the underlying contract volume for offsets in the then 24 participating Member States was €4.2 billion. At an average offset percentage of 135% (!), this made an offset volume of €5.6 billion.

109 The overall distribution according to type was direct offsets 40%, indirect military offsets 35%, and civil indirect offsets 25%. See: EDA *Study on the Effects of Offsets*, ibid.

110 France and Germany do not accept offsets as a matter of policy. Britain, Italy, Sweden, and the Netherlands (net EU exporters with transatlantic imports) use indirect military offsets. Finland, Poland, Portugal, Greece and Spain (big importers some with some exports) use different kinds of offsets, mainly direct. The Member States without defence industries use indirect civil offsets. See the EDA *Study on the Effects of Offsets*, *supra* note 108, 4.

111 Ibid, 27.

112 Economic and financial considerations will not always be at the centre of an offsets agreement. Requiring licensed production facilities in an offset agreement, for example, could be considered necessary to create a local maintenance capability that could be relied on to repair the military equipment in case the supply chain is disrupted by conflict. Offsets that clearly aim at ensuring national security and meet the test of Article 346 TFEU discussed above could still be justified, just liked any other Member State measure. Thanks to B. Heuninckx for pointing this out to me. However, the requirements of Article 346 TFEU will be difficult to meet for an offset arrangement.

113 Neither did the EEC or EC Treaties in their Rome, Maastricht, Amsterdam, or Nice versions.

114 Offsets were discussed during the legislative process: B. Schmitt, 'Directive on Defence and Security Procurement', *European Defence Procurement Seminar*, EIPA, Maastricht, 11 May 2009 as cited by Heuninckx, 'Trick or Treat?', *supra* note 24, 19.

115 http://ec.europa.eu/internal_market/publicprocurement/docs/defence/guide-offsets_en.pdf (accessed 3 February 2016), 1.

The other procurement Directive mostly left the supply chain of subcontractors to be organised by the prime contractor.[116] In contrast, under the Defence Procurement Directive contracting authorities may require parts of a prime contract being awarded as subcontracts to third parties, a move intended to drive competition into the supply chain and to open opportunities to SMEs. Article 21 Defence Procurement Directive provides four options for subcontracting requirements explained further in Title III[117] and the Commission's Guidance Note entitled *Subcontracting*:[118]

- 'Option A' only prohibits discrimination on grounds of nationality and leaves the prime contractor free to choose subcontractors.[119]
- In 'Option B' the prime contractor decides what share and which parts of the contract are subcontracted but has to indicate that share, the subject matter of the subcontract, and the identity of the subcontractor in the tender.[120]
- In Option C the contracting authority requires the prime contractor to award all or parts of the subcontracts on the basis of a competitive procedure.[121]
- In Option D the contracting authority can require a minimum share of the prime contract of up to 30 per cent to be subcontracted, ask for the relevant parts to be identified in the tender, and to be awarded on the basis of a competitive procedure.[122]

Options A and B are also possible under the other procurement Directives but Options C and D are innovations of the Defence Procurement Directive.

These subcontracting rules are the result of a compromise between the six Member States with developed defence industries[123] and the rest who have very limited or no

[116] See Article 25 Public Sector Procurement Directive 2004/18/EC.

[117] Articles 50–54 Defence Procurement Directive.

[118] http://ec.europa.eu/internal_market/publicprocurement/docs/defence/guide-subcontracting_en.pdf (accessed 3 February 2016).

[119] Article 21(1) Defence Procurement Directive: since all Member States have to transpose this paragraph it is strictly speaking not an option for the Member States. It is of course an option for the contracting authorities. See Guidance Note *Subcontracting*, ibid, 3.

[120] Article 21(2) Defence Procurement Directive. Again, as all Member States have to transpose this paragraph it is strictly speaking not an option for the Member States. See Guidance Note *Subcontracting*, *supra* note 118, 4.

[121] Article 21(3) Defence Procurement Directive. The rules on these competitive procedures are contained in Title III (Articles 50–54) Defence Directive. See Guidance Note *Subcontracting*, ibid. On the transposition of this Option C in the Member States see the following footnote.

[122] Article 21(4) Defence Procurement Directive. See Guidance Note *Subcontracting*, *supra* note 118, 5. Option D is a true option since Member States do not have to transpose it. See Guidance Note *Subcontracting*, ibid. Out of the 15 Member States which had notified their formally completed transposition to the Commission in January 2012 most had implemented this Option C and the following Option D, but not as an obligation: the contracting entities can choose between Options A–D, Vierlich-Jürcke, *supra* note 40. So far only Britain did not implement Options C and Kiltie, *supra* note 37. The 30% can be exceeded, see Article 21(4) Defence Procurement Directive.

[123] France, Germany, Italy, Spain, Sweden, and Britain.

capabilities.[124] The latter want opportunities for their industries at least as subcontractors.[125] The rules not only reduce the share of the prime contractor but also impose a considerable burden on them when subcontracting,[126] though only in the context of Options C and D, which might be the reason why so far no Member State has transposed them as obligations.[127]

Subcontracts and offsets are closely connected, not least because they are both about industrial participation and the Defence Procurement Directive facilitates the former and implicitly (almost) prohibits the latter.[128] Other than winning the prime contract, without violations of the Defence Procurement Directive and the TFEU the industries of the contracting Member State can only participate through subcontracts; and only if they represent the economically most advantageous tender.

The subcontracting regime is intended as a substitute for the 'now' (almost) prohibited offsets.[129] Rather than only banning offsets, the legislator offered something instead – taking the different industrial capacities of the Member States into account and the question is what alternative the legislator had. The exclusion of large cooperative programmes and their fair returns practices in Article 13(c) Defence Procurement Directive discussed above is also related to the (near) prohibition of offsets. This 'limitation' also eases the 'prohibition' in addition to 'substitution'.

6. REVIEW AND REMEDIES

Contrary to the public and utilities sectors where public procurement review and remedies are regulated in a separate Remedies Directives,[130] the public procurement review and remedies system of the Defence Procurement Directive is covered in its Title IV. Thus what could have been a separate 'Defence and Security Procurement Remedies Directive' is an integral part of Directive 2009/81/EC. Title IV of the Defence Procurement Directive is based on the Public Sector Remedies Directive, with certain defence specific adaptations.

---

124 Kennedy-Loest and Pourbaix, *supra* note 57, 409. See also: Guidance Note *Subcontracting*, *supra* note 118, 1.

125 B. Schmitt (2009), as cited by Heuninckx, 'Trick or Treat?', *supra* note 24, 19.

126 Kennedy-Loest and Pourbaix, *supra* note 57, 409; Heuninckx, 'Trick or Treat?', *supra* note 24, 20 also points out the possible burden for prime contractors, but also suggest that these obligations 'embody good commercial practice'.

127 See Vierlich-Jürcke (January 2012), *supra* note 40. According to B. Heuninckx Belgium did implement Options C and D (but not as obligations). However, the Belgian Ministry of Defence decided that they would *not* require Options C and D from tenderers, even though those options are allowed by the relevant Royal Decree.

128 See Guidance Note *Offsets*, *supra* note 115, 1.

129 Ibid.

130 Public Sector Procurement Remedies Directive 89/665/EEC [1989] OJ L395/33 as amended especially by Directive 2007/66/EC [2007] OJ L335/31 and Utilities Procurement Remedies Directive 92/13/EEC [1992] OJ L76/14 as amended especially by Directive 2007/66/EC, ibid.

According to Article 56(10) Defence Procurement Directive the relevant review bodies of the Member States have to take the defence interests of the Member States in general and security of information in particular into account. This addresses directly the defence and security concerns in the relevant derogations of the Treaty, especially Article 346 TFEU and Member States can even opt for the establishment of special defence and security procurement review bodies when transposing the Defence Procurement Directive, as provided in its Article 56(10) subparagraph 2. This would involve the establishment of new and separate national defence and security procurement courts, tribunals, or review chambers, in addition to those hearing cases under the public sector and utilities regimes. The alternative is to simply extend the jurisdiction of the existing procurement review bodies to the scope of the Defence Procurement Directive, with certain adjustments to safeguard confidentiality and national security. However, specialised defence and security procurement review bodies did not exist in any Member State prior to the Defence Procurement Directive and would have had to be newly established. This would obviously have had financial, organisational, legal and even constitutional implications. It is perhaps not surprising that the Member States did not take advantage of this option.

As existing procurement review bodies are charged with deciding cases under the Defence Procurement Directive, various measures to adapt to the often sensitive character of the cases can be provided and the last subparagraph of Article 56(10) Defence Procurement Directive provides:

> Member States shall determine how review bodies are to reconcile the confidentiality of classified information with respect for the rights of the defence, and, in the case of a judicial review [...], shall do so in such a way that the procedure complies, as a whole, with the right to a fair trial.

It is possible to reconcile the protection of the confidentiality of classified information in defence and procurement review proceedings with the right to a fair trial and to a defence without violating the Charter of Fundamental Rights, ECHR, or constitutions of the Member States since this adaptation is only minor and proportionate.

In the context of interlocutory proceedings, the Defence Procurement Directive contains an adaptation in expressly stipulating that the review body has to take the defence and security interests of the Member State into account when balancing interests in Article 56(5) Defence Directive. There is no definition of the relevant 'defence and security interests' and the Commission could have added a 'Guidance Note on Review and Remedies' to its catalogue of guidance notes[131] to clarify at least these important notions. A document published by the British Ministry of Defence,[132]

---

[131] Scope, exceptions, research and development, security of supply, security of information, subcontracting, offsets: http://ec.europa.eu/growth/single-market/public-procurement/rules-implementation/defence/index_en.htm (accessed 3 February 2016).

[132] Ministry of Defence/Finance, The Defence and Security Public Contract Regulations Chapter 17 – Legal Review, Remedies and Ineffectiveness, Version 2.0 dated 23/02/2012, paras 37–40, https://www.gov.uk/government/uploads/system/uploads/attachment_data/file/27668/dspcr_chapter17_legal_review_rem.pdf (accessed 3 February 2016).

however, lists relevant defence[133] and security interests;[134] guidance covering both interlocutory proceedings and situations in which a review body might refrain from declaring a contract ineffective as discussed below. However, defence and security interests are only special aspects of the public interest which can be considered in decisions on applications for interim measures under the Public Sector Remedies Directive. Therefore expressly stipulating defence and security interests in the rules on interlocutory proceedings is merely descriptive. It does not add to the substance of the provision when compared to Article 2(5) Public Sector Remedies Directive.

As there is now a clear procurement legal framework in the form of the Defence Procurement Directive, illegally avoiding the instrument carries the risk of ineffectiveness.[135] Article 60(3) Defence Procurement Directive was adapted, allowing review bodies *not* to annul the contract if:

> … reasons relating to a general interest, *first and foremost* in connection with defence and/or security interests, require that the effects of the contract should be maintained … (emphasis added)

The criticism on the lack of a definition of 'defence and/or security interests' expressed in the context of interlocutory proceedings above applies equally to this provision: a Commission Guidance Note would have been useful. Similar to the Public Sector Remedies Directive, Article 60(3) Defence Procurement Directive limits the economic interests to be taken into account in this context. However, in addition:

> *In any event*, a contract may not be considered ineffective if the consequences of this ineffectiveness would *seriously* endanger the very existence of a *wider* defence or security programme which is essential for a Member State's security interests. (emphasis added)

This accommodates the strategic importance of large defence industrial programmes. The opening words 'in any event' suggests that in this particular situation the limitations to economic interests being taken into account, such as that they may not be directly linked to the contract concerned, do not apply. This is mitigated by limiting expressions: the danger must be serious and the relevant programme must be 'wider'. Thus the review bodies will have to take degrees of danger and the size of the programme into account. Again, a Commission Guidance Note on remedies could have been useful here.[136] Article 60(3) Defence Procurement Directive allows flexibility because of the consequences of the annulment of a concluded contract: the procurement procedure would have to be repeated, the deployment of the respective equipment

---

[133] Ibid: '(1) effective conduct of military operations; (2) safety of members of our Armed Forces or our Allies; (3) operational sovereignty of our Armed Forces; or (4) key defence industrial or technical capabilities regarded as essential for national security reasons'.

[134] *Supra* note 132: '(1) effective conduct of security or police operations; (2) safety of members of our security agencies and police forces; (3) ability of our security agencies and police forces to conduct future operations as required by the Government; or (4) key security industrial or technical capabilities regarded as essential for national security reasons'.

[135] The remedy has been adapted, see below.

[136] The UK MoD guidance mentioned above, *supra* note 132 at para 39, is not helpful on this issue either.

could be delayed, with implications for the mission of the relevant forces. The remedy of ineffectiveness is, however, only available in two or three cases of radical violations of the procurement rules. It would be a rather odd situation if a strategically important contract would be directly and illegally awarded and would then escape annulment because of its defence implications. Although 'alternative penalties' would have to be imposed in such a case,[137] these would only be very mild sanctions against a relatively drastic violation of the procurement rules.

Similar to the treatment of defence interests in the context of interlocutory proceedings, there is no reason to assume that these interests cannot be taken into account as part of the wider notion of 'reasons relating to a general interest' in Article 2d (3) Public Sector Remedies Directive.[138] However, the use of the words 'first and foremost' might make the review bodies more willing to maintain the contract where the general interest considerations are specifically related to defence or security. 'Civilian' scenarios leading to the contract being maintained are not expressly mentioned in either Directive and the review bodies might be less likely to declare a contract ineffective in those scenarios than in a situation where this would affect defence interests. Therefore the defence and security references in Article 60(3) Defence Procurement Directive are descriptive but nevertheless meet their objectives. They do not only alert the review bodies of the possibility to not declare the contract ineffective for defence and security reasons but also give these considerations a 'privileged' status as 'first among equals'. The 'privileging' description of these interests in Article 60(3) is also a message to the Member States as it might contribute to reducing cases in which they invoke security exemptions such as Article 346 TFEU to avoid ineffectiveness. Defence and security interests are accommodated *inside* the rules on ineffectiveness. An extreme case is thinkable in which a review body declares a contract ineffective disagreeing with the contracting authority about the existence of an Article 60(3) Defence Procurement Directive situation. In this case the Member State could still invoke a security exemption such as Article 346 TFEU to avoid ineffectiveness. This could lead to enforcement action in the ECJ where the assessment of the review body might have an impact.

---

[137] Last subparagraph of Article 60(3) Defence Procurement Directive. Alternative penalties according to Article 60(2) Defence Procurement Directive are fines and shortening of the duration of the contract.

[138] The example provided by the then United Kingdom Office of Government Commerce for a relevant scenario in the context of the implementation of Directive 2007/66/EC was also from the military context: 'For example, the ineffectiveness of a contract for essential medical supplies to troops in a war-zone could have disastrous consequences for any injured troops, which would not be in the general interest.' *Implementation of the Remedies Directive: OGC Guidance on the 2009 amending regulations Part 3: The new remedies rules* para 60 p. 15, available 3 February 2016 at http://webarchive.nationalarchives.gov.uk/20110601212617/http:/www.ogc.gov.uk/documents/Remedies_Guidance_Part_3_Remedies_Rules(1).pdf.

7. CONCLUSIONS

With the new Defence Procurement Directive 2009/81/EC, the EU legislator has produced a 'tailor-made' instrument for the procurement of armaments and other security sensitive goods and services. The 'cloth' of the old Public Sector Procurement Directive 2004/18/EC was used as raw material and tailored to adapt it to the special requirements of defence and security. The objective is to make the use of Article 346 TFEU and other security exemptions unnecessary in defence and security procurement by providing a Directive adapted to security concerns. Overall, the EU legislator has made every effort to provide a suitable instrument and, while the new Directive could be improved and goes too far in some of the adaptations to the characteristics of the defence sector, it does represent an adequate instrument for defence procurement inside the internal market.

Although not always meeting the August 2011 transposition deadline,[139] as of April 2013 all EU Member States had transposed the Defence Procurement Directive and between 2011 and 2014 about 900 contracts had been awarded under the transposed Defence Procurement Directive representing a total of €1.8 billion.[140] Within the limits of the Defence Procurement Directive set by its scope discussed above, the governments of the EU Member States are now regulating the practice of their contracting entities through EU internal market law rather than on a national basis or through the EDA regime mentioned in the introduction above, unless they invoked Article 346 TFEU. The Commission initiated the Directive and thus opted for legislation not instead of but in addition to the use of enforcement action against Member States.[141] It can be assumed that the Commission will regularly question why the new regime tailored for defence and security was not used, more than under the previous regime. However, it is hoped that it will become less necessary over time as the new rules get increasingly accepted and used in practice. The Commission had carefully considered, compared, and finally dismissed alternative options to a separate Defence Procurement Directive, including the continuation of the status quo, regulation through the EDA, further clarifying Interpretative Communications, and an amended Public Sector Procurement Directive.[142] All options considered, only a separate Defence Procurement

---

139 Many Member States did not transpose the Defence Directive on time, see R. Williams, 'Commission Takes Action on Implementation of Defence Procurement Rules', (2012) 21 *Public Procurement Law Review* NA223–224.

140 See http://export.gov/europeanunion/defenseprocurement/ (accessed 3 February 2016). In July 2012 only 23 Member State had transposed: *Report from the Commission to the European Parliament and the Council on transposition of Directive 2009/81/EC on Defence and Security Procurement*, COM (2012) 565 final, http://eur-lex.europa.eu/legal-content/EN/TXT/PDF/?uri=CELEX:52012DC0565&from=EN (accessed 3 February 2016), at 2.

141 The Commission can litigate in the ECJ against Member States violating EU law on the basis of Article 258 TFEU and for violations of Articles 346 and 347 TFEU also on the basis of Article 348 TFEU. The intention to use these mechanisms more frequently once the transposition deadline for the new Directive has elapsed was expressed by Vierlich-Jürcke, *supra* note 40.

142 Commission Staff Working Document – Impact Assessment SEC (2007) 1593, http://ec.europa.eu/smart-regulation/impact/ia_carried_out/docs/ia_2007/sec_2007_1593_en.pdf (accessed 3 February 2016), at 32–44.

Directive would offer the user-friendly, legally binding, and visible instrument to change from the current separation of the EU into 28 separate national markets to an EU internal defence and security procurement market, ensuring value for money for the taxpayer, the best possible equipment and services for the armed forces, and competitive European defence industries.

The Directive will not suffice on its own. Other barriers to trade in arms will have to be addressed, *inter alia*, the lack of an EU-wide security of information framework and State ownership of and aids to the defence industries. Furthermore, the relevant trade relations with third countries, especially the USA, require attention.[143] The Commission is already preparing the next steps[144] and a revision of the Defence Procurement Directive is envisaged for 2016.

---

[143] Most of them are currently also addressed or at least investigated in the context of the Commission.

[144] Communication from the Commission to the European Parliament, the Council, the European Economic and Social Committee and the Committee of the Regions, *Towards a more competitive and efficient defence and security sector*, COM (2013) 542 final, http://eur-lex.europa.eu/legal-content/EN/TXT/HTML/?uri=CELEX:52013DC0542&from=EN (accessed 3 February 2016) and Report from the Commission to the European Parliament, the Council, the European Economic and Social Committee and the Committee of the Regions, *A New Deal for European Defence: Implementation Roadmap for Communication COM (2013) 542*, COM (2014) 387 final, http://eur-lex.europa.eu/legal-content/EN/TXT/PDF/?uri=CELEX:52014DC0387&from=EN (accessed 3 February 2016).

18. Public service partnerships

Christopher Bovis

I. INTRODUCTION

European States are changing their role and their responsibilities in the process of delivering public services. Recent developments have shown that public services require state intervention for their provision, organization and delivery. Public services often emerge and interface in a *sui generis* marketplace that does not correspond to private markets. This axiom implies the relative inability of anti-trust law and policy to regulate this marketplace, alongside an overwhelming need for safeguarding the principles of transparency and accountability. The aforementioned principles underpin modern EU public sector governance. The notion of partnerships in delivering public services has been gaining intellectual credibility and has been attracting regulatory momentum over the last decade. This chapter focuses on the conceptual insights of instruments such as public-private partnerships, concessions and public forms of cooperation in the format of public-public partnerships and in-house arrangements. The objective is to elaborate on a new era in public sector management in the EU that links the concept of public service with current and future principles of public sector management.

Diachronically and traditionally the role of the state has been as the conduit for providing public services.[1] The term *public services*, which often refers to services that are offered to the general public, highlights that a service has been assigned a specific role in the public interest, or refers to the ownership or status of the entity providing the service. In the latter situation, public service fuses with the concept of *public sector*, which covers the state and its organs, bodies governed by public law and undertakings controlled by public authorities.

Two models for the treatment and regulation of public services have been developed based on different theoretical and conceptual values. One model theorizes that public services capture the general needs of the public and are delivered through market based mechanisms, whereby the public sector interfaces or competes with private sector undertakings; by contrast, other models describe public services as being essential

[1] See C.H. Bovis, 'The State, Competition and Public Services' in P. Birkinshaw and M. Varney (eds), *The European Union Legal Order after Lisbon* (Alphen aan den Rijn: Kluwer 2010), 137; L. Flynn, 'Competition Policy and Public Services in EC Law after the Maastricht and Amsterdam Treaties' in D. O'Keeffe and P. Tworney (eds)., *Legal Issues of the Amsterdam Treaty* (Oxford: Hart Publishing 1999) 196–7; J.L. Buendia Sierra, *Exclusive Rights and State Monopolies under EC Law* (Oxford: Oxford University Press 1999) 330; A. Moriceau, 'Services d'intérêt économique general et valeurs communes' (2008) 519 Revue du Marché Commun et de l'Union Europénne 358; M. Ross, 'Article 16 E.C. and Services of General Interest: From Derogation to Obligation?' (2000) 1 European Law Review 22–38.

facilities (for example defense, policing) which should be sheltered from competition in order to ensure the integrity of their delivery.[2]

Externalization and Public Procurement

The public interest task conferred on a contracting authority might ultimately be carried out by resources external to the contracting authority. This can be the case where the competence for the given public task is transferred, as such, to another public authority. The performance of a given task may also be entrusted to another entity altogether. This may be done (i) without establishing contractual links; (ii) by calling on another contracting authority, which enjoys an exclusive right; or (iii) through joint procurement with other contracting authorities or through central purchasing bodies. Legal competence for a public task could be understood as the exclusive obligation and right to fulfil the task by an entity's own administrative, technical or other means, or even by calling upon external entities. The term 'competence' for a given public task includes the official authority necessary to establish the regulatory framework for fulfilling the task at the level of the authority concerned.

The organization of national administration as such does not fall within the competence of the European Union (EU). Consequently, it is up to each Member State to reorganize its administration and, as part of such re-organization, to allow for the transfer of competences for given public tasks from one public authority to another.

The objective of public procurement rules is to regulate situations where a contracting authority procures goods, services or works (that is, purchases the output of certain economic activities in order to satisfy its own needs or those of its citizens). A contracting authority transferring all competences for a given public task does not purchase any service for its own purposes. Instead, it hands over the responsibility for a certain task to another entity.

The transfer of competence for a given public task from one contracting authority to another is not governed by normal public procurement rules, which are based in part on Article 56 TFEU (ex Article 49 TEC), that is, the freedom to provide services.[3] Transferring competence for a given public task from one public body to another involves transferring both the official authority and any associated economic activities. In the area of waste management, for example, the transfer of all competences means transferring the right to set tariffs, to fix rules for collecting, sorting, storing and treating waste, as well as the right to manage and ultimately to carry out the task according to these rules. All these rights constitute official authority. Part of these rights

---

[2] See T. Prosser, *The Limits of Competition Law* (Oxford: Oxford University Press 2005); see also C. Graham, 'Essential Facilities and Services of General Interest' in *Diretto e Politiche dell'Unione Europea* (2007) 29; W. Sauter, 'Services of general economic interest and universal service in EU Law' (2008) 33(2) *European Law Review* 172.

[3] Article 56 TFEU (ex Article 49 TEC) stipulates: 'Within the framework of the provisions set out below, restrictions on freedom to provide services within the Union shall be prohibited in respect of nationals of Member States who are established in a Member State other than that of the person for whom the services are intended. The European Parliament and the Council, acting in accordance with the ordinary legislative procedure, may extend the provisions of the Chapter to nationals of a third country who provide services and who are established within the Union'.

is the right to determine how the actual economic activities that need to be performed in order to fulfil the public task are to be performed: either by the public body itself or by a third party mandated by it.

Although situations where competence is transferred occur in Member States, neither EU legislation nor the case-law of the European Court of Justice explicitly recognize such situations. The Court has referred to the transfer of official authority when a Member State invoked the transfer of competences from a public body to a third person.[4] According to this case-law, a transfer of competences has not taken place if, (i) the public entity that is originally competent remains primarily responsible for a project because it has a legal obligation not to withdraw from its task; (ii) the new entity may only take legally relevant actions after the public entity that is originally competent has given its approval; and (iii) the new entity is financed by the public entity that is originally competent to fulfil its tasks, with the result that it has no room for manoeuvre.[5] On this basis, the distinctive feature of transferring competences from one public body to another as part of the reorganization of public administration is the comprehensive nature of the transfer. The body transferring competence does not retain any responsibility. The beneficiary of the transfer must exercise the competence independently and based entirely upon its own responsibility. In particular, the transferring body does not retain the right to determine the performance of economic activities undertaken in the context of the respective public task. Such economic tasks are performed under the authority of the beneficiary of the transfer. However, this does not exclude the possibility that the transferring body might have some influence on the practical organization of the performance of the public task in question. In fact, officials of the transferring public body could be members of the executive or management bodies of the authority to which competence for the public task in question was transferred. The transferring authority may also retain the right to receive certain information.

The EU Public Procurement Directives presuppose the existence of a contract, which necessitates at least two, legally distinct entities that are independent of each other in regard to decision-making. A contract is essentially a meeting of wills, whereby the parties to it are able to decide whether they wish to initiate or to terminate the contractual link.[6] Other indications of the existence of a contract are the ability of the parties to negotiate on the actual contents of the services to be rendered and the tariffs of those services. A contract implies a transactional relationship. If there is no contract, the EU Public Procurement Directives do not apply. The Court's case-law finds that if an entity carries out an activity on account of its obligations resulting from national legislation, rather than on a contractual basis, it is not covered by the EU Public Procurement Directives. More specifically, in the *Tragsa* case the Court found

---

[4] Case C-264/03, *Commission v France* [2005] ECR I-8831, para 54. See also Opinion of Advocate General Maduro of 24 November 2004, paras 39–41.

[5] Case C-264/03, *Commssion v France, supra.*

[6] Case C-295/05, *Asociación Nacional de Empresas Forestales (Asemfo) v Transformación Agraria SA (Tragsa) and Administración del Estado* [2007] ECR I-2999, para 54 and Case C-220/06, *Asociación Profesional de Empresas de Reparto y Manipulado de Correspondencia v Administración General del Estado* [2007] ECR I-12175, para 55.

that, on the basis of the relevant national law, Tragsa – a public undertaking – had no choice as to the acceptance of an assignment, or the tariff for its services, but was obliged by law to execute the demands of the contracting authority, in so far as it was an instrument and technical service of that authority. The Court held that Tragsa's relations with the contracting authorities using its services were not contractual, but internal, dependent and subordinate in every respect. Consequently, the EU Public Procurement Directive did not apply to this relationship. However, it should be noted that the application of the TFEU does not depend on the existence of a contract. The Treaty applies whenever a contracting authority, 'entrusts the supply of economic activities to a third party'.[7] By contrast, the Court also recognized the in-house exception in the context of the Treaty.

Public Procurement Rules and Exclusive Rights in the Delivery of Public Services

The term 'exclusive rights' could refer to quite different phenomena, ranging from reserving a whole economic sector to public authorities to the exclusive assignment of one specific task to one specific undertaking. However, not every exclusive right justifies the exemption of the award of a public service contract. Article 18 stipulates that the respective exclusive right needs to be granted by a law, regulation or administrative provision, which is published and compatible with the Treaty.[8] Furthermore, Article 18 only concerns rights granted to particular public sector bodies to provide certain services, on an exclusive basis, to the public sector. The limitation of this exception to contracts awarded to entities which are themselves contracting authorities ensures competitive procurement on downstream markets, since the contracting authority enjoying the exclusive right has to comply with the EU Public Procurement Directives for its own purchases. The published law, regulation or administrative provision must be compatible with the relevant rules of the Treaty, in particular Articles 49 (ex Article 43 TEC) and 56 (ex Article 49 TEC) of the TFEU and the rules and principles that flow from these articles.[9] These rules and principles include non-discrimination, transparency, proportionality, mutual recognition and the

---

[7] See Bovis, 'The State, Competition and Public Services', supra note 1.

[8] Article 18 of Directive 2004/18/EC of the European Parliament and of the Council of 31 March 2004 on the coordination of procedures for the award of public works contracts, public supply contracts and public service contracts provides for service contracts awarded on the basis of an exclusive right and in particular stipulates: 'This Directive shall not apply to public service contracts awarded by a contracting authority to another contracting authority or to an association of contracting authorities on the basis of an exclusive right which they enjoy pursuant to a published law, regulation or administrative provision which is compatible with the Treaty'.

[9] Article 49 TFEU (ex Article 43 TEC) stipulates: 'Within the framework of the provisions set out below, restrictions on the freedom of establishment of nationals of a Member State in the territory of another Member State shall be prohibited. Such prohibition shall also apply to restrictions on the setting-up of agencies, branches or subsidiaries by nationals of any Member State established in the territory of any Member State'.

Article 56 TFEU (ex Article 49 TEC) stipulates: 'Within the framework of the provisions set out below, restrictions on freedom to provide services within the Union shall be prohibited in respect of nationals of Member States who are established in a Member State other than that of the person for whom the services are intended. The European Parliament and the Council, acting

protection of the rights of individuals. If a contracting authority enjoys an exclusive right in terms of Article 18 of Directive 2004/18/EC, other contracting authorities can only award the respective services contacts to this entity.[10] The key reason for introducing this provision was to avoid competitive award procedures in cases where – due to the existence of an exclusive right – only one entity could ultimately be awarded the contract in question.

An exclusive right, which by definition restricts the freedom of other entities to provide services, is justified only under certain conditions.[11] Thus, the exclusive right must be justified either by a derogation expressly provided for by the Treaty (for example, exercise of official authority (Article 51 TFEU (ex Article 45 TEC)), grounds of public policy, public security, or public health (Article 52 TFEU (ex Article 46 TEC))[12] or, in accordance with the case-law of the Court which has established imperative requirements thought to be in the general interest, which must be appropriate for achieving the objective that they pursue, not go beyond what is necessary in order to attain it, and must in any event be applied without discrimination.[13]

---

in accordance with the ordinary legislative procedure, may extend the provisions of the Chapter to nationals of a third country who provide services and who are established within the Union'.

[10] Directive 2004/18/EC, [2004] OJ L134/114.

[11] Case 203/08, *The Sporting Exchange Ltd, Trading as Betfair v Minister van Justitie* [2010] not yet published, paras 23–25; C-124/97, *Markku Juhani Läärä, Cotswold Microsystems Ltd and Oy Transatlantic Software Ltd v Kihlakunnansyyttäjä (Jyväskylä) and Suomen valtio (Finnish State)*, [1999] ECR I-6067, paras 29–31; C-42/07, *Liga Portuguesa de Futebol Profissional and Bwin International Ltd v Departamento de Jogos da Santa Casa da Misericórdia de Lisboa* [2009] ECR I-7633, paras 52–55.

[12] Article 51 TFEU (ex Article 45 TEC) stipulates: 'the provisions of this Chapter shall not apply, so far as any given Member State is concerned, to activities which in that State are connected, even occasionally, with the exercise of official authority. The European Parliament and the Council, acting in accordance with the ordinary legislative procedure, may rule that the provisions of this Chapter shall not apply to certain activities'.

Article 52 TFEU ex Article 45 TEC) stipulates: 'the provisions of this Chapter and measures taken in pursuance thereof shall not prejudice the applicability of provisions laid down by law, regulation or administrative action providing for special treatment for foreign nationals on grounds of public policy, public security or public health. The European Parliament and the Council shall, acting in accordance with the ordinary legislative procedure, issue directives for the coordination of the abovementioned provisions'.

[13] Case C-243/01, *Gambelli* [2003] ECR I-13031, para 65; C-288/89, *Stichting Collectieve Antennevoorziening Gouda and others v Commissariaat voor de Media* [1991] ECR I-4007. Furthermore, decisions to award exclusive rights to undertakings can amount to an infringement of the Treaty where the public service requirements to be fulfilled by the service provider are not properly specified. See Case C-66/86, *Silver Line Reisebüro* [1989] ECR I-803. Alternatively, where the service provider is manifestly unable to meet the demand awarding exclusive rights to undertakings can also constitute an infringement of the Treaty. See Case C-41/90, *Höfner* [1991] ECR I-1979. Finally, where there is an alternative way of fulfilling the requirements that would have a less detrimental effect on competition, the award can be viewed as a Treaty violation. See Case T-266/97, *Vlaamse Televisie Maatschappij* [1999] ECR II-2329. Also, the condition that the granting of the exclusive right is compatible with the Treaty is not fulfilled if the measure by which it is awarded in incompatible with secondary EU legislation. See Case C-220/06, *Correos*, paras 64–66.

Article 18 of Directive 2004/18 EC concerns rights granted to particular public sector bodies to provide certain services, on an exclusive basis, to the public sector. If the justification for the restriction of the freedom to provide services is an imperative requirement in the general interest, one of the conditions to be met is that the measure in question must be non-discriminatory. This means that, in general, no private entity should be placed in a more advantageous position than its competitors. Therefore, if an exclusive right were to be awarded to a contracting authority involving private capital (which may arise in the case of a body governed by public law), it is difficult to see how this principle could be complied with in the absence of a transparent procedure that ensures equal treatment. On the other hand, in view of the history and purpose of Article 18, as well as recent case-law on comparable situations, this might not be necessary if the beneficiary of the exclusive right is a state body, such as a contracting authority without private capital.

Joint procurement may take many different forms, ranging from organizing one specific common call for tenders, to systematic recourse, to specialization (for example, one contracting authority being responsible for certain types of procurements to be used by all entities concerned, another carrying out a different type of procurement and so on) to setting up a specific structure for joint procurement. The relationships between the various participants themselves may or may not be subject to EU rules on public procurement, depending on the method chosen. In the case of simple administrative cooperation in drawing up common specifications that does not necessitate any contracts for pecuniary interests between the parties, that is, when public authorities limit themselves to organizing a common call for tenders, they are applying the public procurement rules together, but their cooperation is not subject to these rules. Article 1(9) of Directive 2004/18/EC defines contracting authorities, *inter alia*, as 'associations formed by one or several such authorities, meaning one or several regional or local authorities or bodies governed by public law'.[14] This provision might be of interest in the context of public-public cooperation.

Furthermore, certain centralized purchasing techniques have been developed in the Member States. Central purchasing bodies are contracting authorities responsible for making acquisitions or for awarding public contracts/framework agreements intended for other contracting authorities. Article 11 of Directive 2004/18/EC explicitly provides that contracting authorities may purchase works, supplies and/or services from or through a central purchasing body. A central purchasing body may operate either as a

---

[14] Article 1(9) of Directive 2004/18EC stipulates the following: '"Contracting authorities" means the State, regional or local authorities, bodies governed by public law, associations formed by one or several of such authorities or one or several of such bodies governed by public law. A "body governed by public law" means any body:

(a) established for the specific purpose of meeting needs in the general interest, not having an industrial or commercial character;
(b) having legal personality; and
(c) financed, for the most part, by the State, regional or local authorities, or other bodies governed by public law; or subject to management supervision by those bodies; or having an administrative, managerial or supervisory board, more than half of whose members are appointed by the State, regional or local authorities, or by other bodies governed by public law'.

wholesaler (it purchases so that other authorities may purchase *from* it), or it may act as an intermediary which handles the award procedures and the administration of contracts so that other authorities may purchase *through* it.[15] In neither case does a procurement procedure need to be organized in respect of the relationship between the central purchasing body and the authorities having recourse to it, as long as the central purchasing authority has itself awarded its contracts in accordance with the relevant EU Public Procurement Directives.

II. THE EVOLUTION OF PUBLIC–PRIVATE PARTNERSHIPS

Public-private partnerships denote a sophisticated interface between public authorities and private sector undertakings, which aims at delivering infrastructure projects, as well as public services.[16] According to the EU institutions, the term public-private partnership refers to 'forms of cooperation between public authorities and the world of business which aim to ensure the funding, construction, renovation, management or maintenance of an infrastructure or the provision of a service'.[17] At the European level, as part of the Initiative for Growth, the Council has approved a series of measures designed to increase investment in the infrastructure of the trans-European transport networks and also in the areas of research, innovation and development,[18] as well as the delivery of services of general interest.[19]

The United Nations (UN) followed suit and embraced the concept, defining public private partnerships as:

---

[15] Article 11 of Directive 2004/18EC covers public contracts and framework agreements awarded by central purchasing bodies and stipulates: 'Member States may stipulate that contracting authorities may purchase works, supplies and/or services from or through a central purchasing body. Contracting authorities which purchase works, supplies and/or services from or through a central purchasing body shall be deemed to have complied with this Directive insofar as the central purchasing body has complied with it'.

[16] See European Commission, Report to the Laeken European Council: Services of General Interest, COM (2001) 598; European Commission, Communication from the Commission to the Council, the European Parliament, the Economic and Social Committee and the Committee of the Regions on the Status of Work on the Examination of a Proposal for a Framework Directive on Services of General Interest, COM (2002) 689; European Commission, Green Paper on Services of General Interest, COM (2003) 270; European Commission, Communication from the Commission to the European Parliament, the Council, the European Economic and Social Committee and the Committee of the Regions: White Paper on Services of General Interest, COM (2004) 374.

[17] See European Commission, Green Paper on Public-Private Partnerships and Community Law on Public Contracts and Concessions, COM (2004) 327.

[18] See Conclusions of the Presidency, Brussels European Council, 12 December 2003, Council of the European Union, Brussels, 5 February 2004, 5381/04. See Communication from the Commission to the Council and to the Parliament 'Public finances in EMU 2003', published in European Economy No 3/2003 (COM (2003) 283 final).

[19] See COM (2003) 270.

> Innovative methods used by the public sector to contract with the private sector, who bring their capital and their ability to deliver projects on time and to budget, while the public sector retains the responsibility to provide these services to the public in a way that benefits the public and delivers economic development and an improvement in the quality of life.[20]

The UN devised a blueprint to close the gap between the poorest countries and industrialized nations in the UN Millennium Declaration, committing its members to a new global partnership and emphasizing the potential of public-private partnerships in achieving the realization of the United Nations Millennium Development Goals.[21]

The principal benefit from involving the private sector in the delivery of public services has been attributed to the fact that the public sector does not have to commit its own capital resources in funding the delivery of public services, whereas other benefits include quality improvement, innovation, management efficiency and effectiveness, elements that are often underlying private sector entrepreneurship.[22] Consequently, the public sector receives value-for-money in the delivery of public services, while it can also be maintained that through this process the state manages in a better, more strategic way the public finances. Value for money denotes a concept which is associated with the economy, the effectiveness and the efficiency of a public service, product or process, that is, a comparison of the input costs against the value of the outputs and a qualitative and quantitative judgment of the manner in which the resources involved have been utilized and managed.[23]

The erosion of confidence in the role of the public sector as organizer and asset holder in the sphere of public services has led to attempts to moderate the widespread dissatisfaction from traditional public procurement methods in delivering public services and infrastructure projects.[24] The outcome revealed that the nexus of contractual relations between public authorities and the private sector were not providing genuine value-for-money outcomes.[25] The criticism has been primarily directed towards: (i) adversarial contractual relations as a result of competitive tendering; (ii) inappropriate risk allocation; and (iii) poor contractual performances resulting in delayed and over-budget completions.[26]

---

20 See United Nations Economic Commission for Europe, *Guidebook on promoting Good Governance in Public Private Partnerships*, ECE/CECI/4, United Nations, 2008.

21 Citation needed for UN Millennium Declaration.

22 See P. Grout, 'The Economics of the Private Finance Initiative' in (1997) 13 *Oxford Review of Economic Policy* 53–66.

23 See J. Kay, 'Efficiency and Private Capital in the Provision of Infrastructure' in *Infrastructure Policies for the 1990s* (Paris: OECD 1993).

24 See C.H. Bovis, 'Public-private Partnerships in the 21st Century', (2010) 11(3) *ERA Forum* 379.

25 In its policy statement, *Public Sector Comparators and Value for Money,* February 1998, the HM Treasury Taskforce in the United Kingdom set out the role of comparators in public procurement, stressing the importance of the value-for-money principle. The comparators are indices that help to distinguish between the lowest cost and the best value for money for public authorities and also their uses as an exercise of financial management and a means of demonstrating savings to public authorities.

26 See C.H. Bovis, *Public Procurement: Case Law and Regulation* (Oxford: Oxford University Press 2006), Chapter 11, 594.

Competitive tendering in public procurement has been reproached for creating a confrontational environment, where the antagonizing relations, which emanate from the tendering processes, are often adversely reflected in the performance stage of the contract. In addition, competitive tendering has been dissociated with innovation and quality. Also, as a result of inefficiently written specifications upon which the tenders have been constructed, the deliverables or the outcomes often differ dramatically from contractual expectations and stipulations.[27]

On the other hand, risk allocation is probably the most crucial element in contractual relations between public and private sectors that affects pricing as well as the overall contractual framework. Risk represents the level of financial exposure of a party prior to, after the conclusion of, or during its performance of a contract. In a traditional public contract, risk is apportioned in accordance with the expected modalities, features, or perceptions of the public and private sectors; contractual elements of risk, which are associated with the design or construction of a project, maintenance and operational matters, are usually passed to the private sector. On the other hand, risks related to the required investment, financing and currency transactions, planning issues, residualization, obsolescence, political and legal aspects, industrial relations and usage volumes remain with the public sector.

In traditional public procurement, the risk allocation tends to favour the supply side (the private sector), which mainly assumes the risks related to the tendering process, and includes project risks. During the performance stage of the contract and up to its completion, the public sector would, usually, place an amount of risk to the private sector by requiring performance bonds or other means of financial guarantees. Risk allocation is the result of negotiations between the parties and is normally expected to reflect the pricing element of contractual arrangements between them. Thus, risk allocation and overall pricing for a traditional public contract operate in an analogous relation within a contract. The more risk a party assumes, the higher the price to be paid by the other party, and *vice versa*.

It is difficult to ascertain what represents an acceptable transfer of risk in a contract between the public and private sectors. Risk allocation primarily reflects the parties' perception of a transaction with reference to their own criteria. These criteria are often influenced by a range of parameters such as speculation, fear and certainty, as well as by a number of qualitative attributes of the parties, such as forecast and planning, as well as market intelligence. In traditional public contracts the public sector inevitably accepts excessive risks as a result of its procurement practices. Where the award of publicly funded contracts is predominately based upon *the lowest price*, which constitutes one of the two permissible award criteria under the procurement rules (the other being the criterion of *the most economically advantageous tender*), this would normally reflect the amount of risk the relevant public sector contracting authorities are prepared to accept.[28]

---

27 See generally J.J. Laffont and J. Tirole, *A Theory of Incentives in Procurement and Regulation* (Cambridge, MA: MIT Press 1993).

28 Two criteria laid down in the public procurement Directives provide the conditions under which contracting authorities award public contracts: the lowest price or the most economically advantageous offer. See Directive 2004/18 [2004] OJ L134, Article 26 (on the coordination of

Finally, traditional procurement methods have often revealed a picture of poor contracts management as a result of inefficient control systems operated by public authorities. Poor contracts management systems have often resulted in out-of-control contractual performances with all the adverse financial consequences attributed to the delayed completions of the projects. The traditional public procurement process often suffers from unnecessarily repetitive functions, which do not offer long-term savings and value-for-money-considerations – particularly the advertisement, selection and qualification processes – and could pose a considerable financial burden on the public sector.

One of the most advanced Public-Private Partnerships (PPP) programs has been developed in the United Kingdom.[29] The PPPs, including Public Finance Initiatives (PFI) schemes, are currently responsible for about 24 per cent of public investment, with projects in most of the key infrastructure areas.[30] Many European Union states, including Ireland, Sweden, Finland, Germany, Greece, Italy, the Netherlands, Portugal and Spain, have developed legal and policy frameworks to deliver PPP projects, although their share in total public investment is between 5 and 15 per cent. Reflecting a need for infrastructure investment on a large scale, and weak fiscal positions, a number of countries in Central and Eastern Europe, including the Czech Republic, Hungary and Poland, have embarked on PPPs.[31]

Other countries in the world with significant PPP programs include Canada, Japan and Australia, in particular the state of Victoria.[32] PPPs in most of the above countries focus on road infrastructure projects, while the United States has considerable experience with leasing programs in the delivery of public services.[33] Mexico and Chile have pioneered the use of PPPs to promote private sector participation in public investment projects in South America. In Mexico, PPPs were first used in the 1980s to finance highways and, since the mid-1990s, a growing number of public investment projects in the energy sector. There are plans to extend the use of PPPs to the provision of other public services. Chile has a well-established PPP program that has been used

---

procedures for the award of public works contracts, public supply contracts, and public service contracts); see also Directive 2004/17 [2004] OJ L134, Article 30, (coordinating the procurement procedures of entities operating in the water, energy, transport and postal services sectors). The first criterion indicates that, subject to the qualitative criteria and financial and economic standing, contracting authorities do not rely on any other factor than the price quoted to complete the contract. The most economically advantageous offer includes a series of factors chosen by the contracting authority, including price, delivery or completion date, running costs, cost-effectiveness, profitability, technical merit, product or work quality, aesthetic and functional characteristics, after-sales service and technical assistance, commitments with regard to spare parts and components and maintenance costs, and security of supplies.

[29] See HM Treasury, *Public Private Partnerships: The Government's Approach* (2000). See also, HM Treasury, *PFI: Meeting the Investment Challenge* (2003).

[30] See L. De Pierris, 'Improving the Infrastructure' (2003) 40 *PFI Journal* 44–45.

[31] See M. Spackman, 'Public-Private Partnerships: Lessons from the British Approach', (2002) 26 Economic Systems 283–301.

[32] See Department of Treasury and Finance, *Partnerships* (Melbourne Victoria 2000). See also, Department of Treasury and Finance, *Practitioners' Guide-Guidance Material* (2001).

[33] See, Office of Management and Budget, *Preparation, Submission, and Execution of the Budget*, OMB Circular No. A-11 (2002).

for the development of transport, airports, prisons and irrigation. Brazil is planning significant use of PPPs and there is also a regional approach to infrastructure development across the countries in South America. PPPs have also emerged in Asia, especially in India, Korea and Singapore, and there is strong interest in PPPs in South Africa.[34]

The Characteristics of Public–Private Partnerships

Public-private partnerships have been utilized as a credible solution to bridge the infrastructure deficit of many states in both the developed and developing world. PPPs can provide a number of specific benefits to the public sector. In particular, they can offer value for money solutions, where the PPP can attain lower costs, higher levels of service through innovation, and reduced risk for the public sector. One of the most significant attributes of PPPs is the increased certainty of outcomes both in terms of on-time delivery of projects (the private partner is strongly motivated to complete the project as early as possible to control its costs and so that the payment stream can commence) and in terms of within-budget delivery of projects (the payment scheduled is fixed before construction commences, protecting the public from exposure to cost overruns).

Public-private partnerships possess some distinctive characteristics, when compared with traditional public-private contractual formats. These characteristics reveal a different ethos in public sector management. The pivotal characteristic is that the private sector partner is expected to play a strategic role in financing and delivering the infrastructure project or the public service by providing its input into the various phases such as the design, implementation, construction, completion, operation and maintenance stages of the project. As a result, the duration of the relations between public and private sectors must reflect the need for longevity, in order to allow affordability for repayment on the part of the public sector and also the ability of the private sector to recoup its investment profitably. Another characteristic that complements both the strategic role of the private sector and its long-term engagement in delivering infrastructure and public services is reflected in the distribution of risks between the public and private sectors, and in the expectation that the private sector will assume substantial risks. Risk assessment in PPPs is a totally different exercise than the assessment of risk in traditional public contracts.[35]

A range of different risks features in PPPs: construction or project risk, which is related to design problems, building cost overruns and project delays; financial risk, which is related to variability in interest rates, exchange rates and other factors affecting financing costs; performance risk, which is related to the availability of an asset and the continuity and quality of the relevant service provision; demand risk, which is related to the ongoing need for the relevant public services; and residual value

[34] See D. Grimsey and M. Lewis, *Public Private Partnerships: The Worldwide Revolution in Infrastructure Provision and Project Finance* (Cheltenham, UK and Northampton, MA, USA 2007).

[35] See D. Moss, *When All Else Fails: Government as the Ultimate Risk Manager* (Cambridge, MA: Harvard University Press 2002).

risk, which is related to the future market price of an asset.[36] Finally, political risks cover a general term used to describe risks arising from external or internal factors that are determined or influenced by governments. External political risks, such as currency convertibility, war, sanctions and political instability may be avoided, mitigated, hedged or insured against and could be significantly mitigated by actions of the state within which the PPP is structured. On the other hand, internal political risks, such as taxation, terrorism, inflation and industrial unrest are usually uninsurable and could affect the risk allocation within PPPs. Their respective mitigation would potentially reflect on the perceptions of the parties to manage such risks.

Another essential dynamic of PPPs is that the private sector provides the financing. PPP financing is specialized financing which is different from both public finance and corporate finance. The PPP debt financing is regarded as off-balance-sheet borrowing, which means that the borrowing does not affect the state's public sector borrowing requirements and any measurements or calculations of measures of its indebtedness. PPPs allow the public sector to access alternative sources of capital.

PPPs seek to transfer risk from the public sector to the private sector. Whilst the provision of private capital and the strategic involvement of the private sector partner in managing the delivery of public services could prove beneficial, significant risk transfer from the public to the private sector is necessary to derive a genuine value-for-money partnership. The impact of risk transfer on financing costs and the pricing of risk to ensure efficient risk transfer are crucial in understanding how risk is treated within public-private partnerships.

The cost of capital needed to finance a public-private partnership depends only on the characteristics of project related risks and not on the source of finance. However, the source of financing can influence project risk depending on the maturity and sophistication of the risk bearing markets. On the one hand, within advanced risk bearing markets, it is irrelevant whether project risk is borne by the public sector or the private sector. On the other hand, when risk-bearing markets are less developed, project risk depends on how widely that risk is spread. Since the public sector can spread risk across taxpayers in general, the usual argument is that this gives the public sector an advantage over the private sector in terms of managing risk. Nevertheless, the private sector can spread risk across financial markets. The outcome is likely to be that project risk is lower in the private sector. The public sector's ability to forcibly spread risk across taxpayers, while financial markets have to be provided with an incentive to accept risk, may put the private sector at more of a disadvantage as far as large and risky projects are concerned. The scope for the private sector to spread risk will also be somewhat limited in countries with less developed financial markets.

This outcome might contravene the assumption that private sector borrowing generally costs more than government borrowing. However, this mainly reflects differences in default risk. The public sector's power to tax reduces the likelihood that it will default on its debt, and the private sector is therefore prepared to lend to the public sector at close to the risk-free interest rate to finance risky projects. The crucial

---

[36] See H. Polackova-Brixi, and A. Schick (eds), *Government at Risk: Contingent Liabilities and Fiscal Risk* (Washington, DC: World Bank 2002).

issue is whether PPPs result in efficiency gains that offset higher private sector borrowing costs.[37]

Risk transfer from the public sector to the private sector has a significant influence on whether a PPP is a more efficient and cost-effective alternative to public investment and publicly funded provision of services. The public sector and the private sector typically adopt different approaches to pricing market risk. The public sector tends to use the social time preference rate (STPR) or some other risk-free rate to discount future cash flows when appraising projects.[38] The private sector in a PPP project will include a risk premium in the discount rate it applies to future project earnings. Under the widely used capital asset pricing model (CAPM), the expected rate of return on an asset is defined as the risk-free rate of return plus a risk premium, the latter being the product of the market risk premium and a coefficient that measures the variance between the returns on that asset and market returns.[39]

The Legal Formats of Public–Private Partnerships

Three major legal types of public private partnerships exist: the concession, the contractual public-private partnership and finally, the institutional public-private partnership, often described as the 'joint-venture model'.[40]

The notion of public concessions

A concession is a public contract where the consideration of the private sector for the provision of services consists either solely in the right to exploit the service or in this right together with some form of payment by the public sector. The notion of a concession is based on the fact that no contractual payment remuneration is paid by the granting public entity to the concessionaire. The latter must therefore simply be given the right to economically exploit the concession, although this right may be accompanied by a requirement to pay some consideration to the grantor, depending on elements of risk allocation agreed between the parties.

There are three main distinctive features in public concessions. First, the beneficiaries of the service provided must be third parties (usually the public or end users of a public service) rather than the awarding public entity itself. Secondly, the subject of the service upon which the concession is based must concern a matter that is in the public interest. Finally, the concessionaire must assume the economic risk related to the performance of the relevant service.[41] A public concession is a revenue generating PPP which involves an infrastructure or a service, the use of which necessitates the payment

---

[37] See K. Arrow and R. Lind, 'Uncertainty and the Evaluation of Public Investment Decisions' (1970) 60 American Economic Review 364–78.

[38] See C.H. Bovis, *Future Directions in Public Private Partnerships,* in Muller, Zouridis, Frishman and Kistemaker, (eds), *The Law of the Future and the Future of the Law* (Oslo: Torkel Opsahl 2012) 782.

[39] Ibid.

[40] See International Monetary Fund Dep't of Fiscal Affairs, *Public-Private Partnerships* (2004).

[41] See Case C-324/98, *Telaustria Verlags GmbH and Telefonadress GmbH v Post & Telekom Austria AG* [2000] ECR I-10745.

of fees borne directly by end users, and any operation or function emanating from the sale, rent, or exploitation of public land or buildings.[42]

It is maintained that the absence of consideration passing from the granting entity to the concessionaire constitutes the essence of a public concession.[43] The above characteristic represents a fundamental feature of a concession whose importance is not limited to projects that are concerned with infrastructure or the delivery of public works projects, but also extends to projects concerning the delivery of public services. This feature finds justification in the fact that the concessionaire itself must bear the principal, or at least the substantive, economic risk attaching to the performance of the service involved. If the argument is satisfied that the economic burden or risk has effectively been passed to the concessionaire by the grantor of the concession, then there must be a very strong presumption that the arrangement concluded between them amounts to a concession rather than a contract.

The single most important indication of whether economic risk is to be borne by the concessionaire will emerge from examining the nature of the exploitation in which the supposed concession requires it to engage.[44] Thus, where, for example, the public authorities effectively guarantee to indemnify the concessionaire against future losses, or where there is no effective exploitation by the concessionaire of the service whose performance is ceded, the arrangement at issue could not amount to a concession.[45]

There is no overriding legal definition of a public services concession under EU Law or international law.[46] It is, therefore, necessary in each case to look at a number of factors that will indicate whether in reality the arrangement amounts to a written contract for a pecuniary interest with respect to the provision of public services. In the

---

42 See Bovis, 'Future Directions in Public Private Partnerships', supra note 38, 782.

43 See C.H. Bovis, 'Public Procurement and Public Services in the EU' in Lianos and Odudu (eds), *Regulating Trade in Services in the EU and the WTO: Trust, Distrust And Economic Integration* (Cambridge: Cambridge University Press 2012) 287.

44 See Case C-360/96, *Arnhem and Rheden* [1998] ECR I-6821 para 25. *Arnhem and Rheden* provides a strong indication that the European Court views the requirement to exploit the right ceded in order to obtain remuneration as the core of what constitutes a genuine concession. The Court maintained that an important feature of service concessions in the Community context is that the concessionaire automatically assumes the economic risk associated with the provision and management of the services that are the subject of the concession.

45 See European Commission Interpretative Communication of Community Law on Public Procurement Concessions [2000] OJ C21 2 fn.10.

46 A concession is a public contract where the consideration of the private sector for the provision of services consists either solely in the right to exploit the service or in this right together with some form of payment by the public sector. The notion of a concession is based on the fact that no contractual payment remuneration is paid by the granting public entity to the concessionaire. The latter must therefore simply be given the right to economically exploit the concession, although this right may be accompanied by a requirement to pay some consideration to the grantor, depending on elements of risk allocation agreed between the parties. There are three main distinctive features in public concessions. First, the beneficiary of the service provided must be third parties (usually the public or end-users of a public service) rather than the awarding public entity itself. Secondly, the subject of the service upon which the concession is based must concern a matter which is in the public interest. Finally, the concessionaire must assume the economic risk related to the performance of the relevant service. See C.H. Bovis, *Public Private Partnerships* 452 (London: Routledge 2012) 452.

case of a concession, the beneficiary of the service must be a third party unconnected with the contractual relationship and the concessionaire effectively must obtain at least a significant proportion of its remuneration, not from the granting entity, but from the exploitation of the service. Therefore, a case-by-case approach should be adopted to answer the question of whether a contract amounts to a concession or a service contract. Such a fact-specific inquiry necessarily takes account of all indicative factors, the most important of which is whether the supposed concession amounts to a conferral of a right to exploit a particular service as well as the simultaneous transfer of a significant proportion of the risk associated with that transfer to the concessionaire. The likelihood that the concessionaire will be able beneficially to exploit the concession would not suffice to ascertain that there is no economic risk. Such assessment would need to satisfy the probability of economic loss on the part of the concessionaire.[47]

The significance of concessions for the internal market

Concession contracts are different from public contracts, which are traditionally used by public authorities to procure supplies, works or services. In the case of public contracts, an economic operator is awarded a fixed payment for completing the required work or service. Concessions, on the other hand, are contractual arrangements between a public authority and an economic operator (the concession holder) where the latter receives substantial remuneration by being permitted to exploit the work or service. Hence, concessions involving private partners are a particular form of PPP. Although PPPs have never been defined in EU Public Procurement legislation, they are usually referred to as relationships of cooperation between a public authority and a private partner, where the latter bears risks that are traditionally borne by the public sector and often contribute to financing the project.[48] Some PPPs are structured as public contracts, but the majority of PPPs take the form of concessions.

The award of public contracts and work concessions is subject to EU rules.[49] The same rules do not apply to different categories of concessions and public contracts. Unlike public contracts, which are exhaustively regulated in secondary legislation, and works concessions, which are partially covered by secondary rules, the award of service concessions is only subject to the general principles of the Treaty. This has resulted in

---

[47] See S. Van Grasse, *De Concessie in het raam van de publiek-private samenwerking* (Brugge: Die Keure 2007). See also, A. Alexis, 'Services Publics et Aides d'Etat' (2002) 1 Revue du droit 'Union Europḗene 63–107; J. Arnould, *Les Contrats de Concession de Privatisation et des Services 'in-house' au Regard des Règles Communautaires* (2000) 2 –23.

[48] See Bovis, *Public Private Partnerships*, supra note 46, 452.

[49] Directive 2004/18 EC has adopted a special, mitigated regime for the award of concession contracts in its Article 1(3). The provisions of the Directive only apply to concession contracts when the value is at least €6,242,000 million. There are no rules given as to the way in which the contract value must be calculated. For the award of concession contracts, contracting authorities must apply similar rules on advertising as the advertising rules concerning open and restricted procedures for the award of every works contract. Also, the provisions on technical standards and on criteria for qualitative selection of candidates and tenderers do apply to the award of concession contracts. The Directive does not prescribe the use of specific award procedures for concession contracts.

irregularities and economic inefficiencies, and has a negative impact on the achievement of value for public money. In order to apply the Treaty principles more effectively and efficiently, secondary legislation was developed containing specific rules on award procedures.[50]

The European legislature decided to differentiate between *public contracts*, conceived of as the procurement of works, goods, or services against payment and *concession contracts*, where works or services are provided to contracting authorities or to users in consideration for the right to exploit a facility.[51] With regard to the latter, it should be pointed out that the award of *works concessions* under the Classic Directive is currently subject to a limited number of provisions only.[52] In particular, it is compulsory to publish a concession notice in the Official Journal and to respect a minimal period for the submission of applications. Moreover, there are rules on the obligations of concession holders. Bidders also enjoy judicial protection and review procedures provided by the Remedies Directive 2007/66.[53] Their award is supplemented by the general Treaty principles. On the other hand, the award of works concessions under the Utilities Directive is only subject to the general principles of the TFEU.[54] Similarly, *service concessions* are currently subject only to the general principles of the TFEU.

In practice, the distinction between works concessions and service concessions may prove to be difficult to determine. Concession contracts underpin an important share of economic activity in the EU. They are particularly significant in economic sectors that are of great importance to both citizens and economic operators, such as network industries and services of general economic interest. They are important vehicles in the long-term structural development of infrastructures and strategic services, as they help to harness private sector expertise, achieve efficiency and deliver innovation. Moreover,

---

50 Article 59 Directive 2004/18 EC stipulates that the Directive does not provide for a specific award procedure envisaged for public works concession. Contracting authorities are free to select the standard procedures specified for the award of public contracts. However, contracting authorities must allow a time limit not less than 52 days from the date of dispatch of the notice for the presentation of applications for the concession.

51 According to Article 1(2)(b) of Directive 2004/18 EC, public works contracts are public contracts which have as their object either the execution or both the design and execution, of works, or the completion, by whatever means, of a work corresponding to the requirements specified by the contracting authority. A work means the outcome of building or civil engineering works taken as a whole which is sufficient of itself to fulfil an economic or technical function. According to Article 1(3) of Directive 2004/18 EC, public works concession is a contract of the same type as a public works contract except for the fact that the consideration for the works to be carried out consists either solely in the right to exploit the work or in this right together with payment. According to Article 1(4) of Directive 2004/18 EC, service concession is a contract of the same type as a public service contract except for the fact that the consideration for the provision of services consists either solely in the right to exploit the service or in this right together with payment.

52 Directive 2004/18, [2004] OJ L134 on the coordination of procedures for the award of public works contracts, public supply contracts and public service contracts.

53 See Directive 2007/66/EC of 11 December 2007, [2007] OJ L335/31.

54 Directive 2004/17, [2004] OJ L134 coordinating the procurement procedures of entities operating in the water, energy, transport and postal services sectors.

their role is also likely to become more prominent in years to come in the face of increasing constraints on public finances. Indeed, by transferring the main operating risks to a private partner and alleviating the public authorities of this burden, concessions make it possible, in certain cases, to carry out much needed public works and services while keeping the corresponding commitments out of the government balance sheet. There is further potential for increased take-up of concessions in many projects supported by the European funds, where the use of PPPs in co-funded projects is currently low.

A decision by Member States and contracting authorities to resort to a concession should be assessed on a case-by-case basis and its costs and benefits should always carefully and comprehensively be compared with those of alternative solutions. The fact that Member States use different definitions for concessions and the current lack of transparency on their award makes systematic and precise measurement of their economic and social importance difficult. Comparable data across the internal market are generally lacking or remain inconsistent, particularly in Member States where concessions are not sufficiently regulated.[55]

With regard to PPPs and concessions in several Member States where concessions are subject to specific rules, concessions are mostly used in water distribution and treatment, road and rail transport, ports and airports services, motorway maintenance and management, waste management, energy or heating services, leisure facilities and car parks. Concessions in these sectors imply significant amounts of capital investment.[56]

Concessions in the utilities sectors

The Utilities Directive covers important sectors such as water, ports, airports, energy and heating. These sectors are characterized by a significant number of concessions, but even works concessions are at present excluded from the scope of application of

---

[55] In the Commission's 2006 report on the evaluation of the performance of Network industries providing services of general economic interest, network industries were estimated to account for 7% of the €15 total value added. In the new Member States this share was calculated to be much higher, ranging from 9.8% in Hungary to 14.3% in the Slovak Republic. In 2005, slightly more than 10.5 million people were employed in €25 network industries corresponding to 5.4% of the total workforce. For public services in the EU, the Commission estimates the number of persons employed by Services of General Interest to be over 64 million. The number of enterprises providing SGI is estimated to be more than 500,000. SGI providers of electricity, gas, water, transport, post and telecommunications and research contribute to 6.4% of the total investment in the EU which, for the year 2006 was over €150bn. See European Commission, Public Services in the European Union and in the 27 Member States, Mapping of the Public Services, CEEP Managed Project, May 2010.

[56] According to the European Investment Bank, in more than 1,300 PPP contracts were signed in the EU from 1990 to 2009, representing a capital value of more than €250 billion. The EIB itself, which is Europe's foremost funder of PPP projects, has a portfolio of 120 projects representing an investment of around €25 billion. Funding of new projects was in excess of €3.5 billion in 2008 and in 2009 was worth €2 billion despite difficult economic conditions. See European Commission, Assessment of an Initiative on Concessions, Brussels, 20 December 2011, SEC(2011) 1588fin.

this Directive.[57] This situation appears unjustified. Both the contracting authorities and other contracting authorities in the Utilities sectors are bound to apply Treaty principles with regard to concessions. Consequently, when dealing with concessions in these sectors, they encounter the above-mentioned problems relating to the imperfect application of the Treaty, lack of legal certainty and barriers to entry. If works and service concessions were to be covered by the classic Directive, but utilities remained outside its scope, this would add yet another level of legal uncertainty regarding which set of rules apply.

Concessions in priority and non-priority services

Non-priority services (for example, port services, catering, health, education and social services) are at present only partially covered by the Public Procurement Directives. The intention of the legislator was that certain specific service contracts, which were considered not to have much potential for cross-border trade, should be excluded from the full application of the rules of the Directives, for a transitional period.[58] Nevertheless, services such as social, health and education continue to have a limited cross-border dimension, due to the strong impact of different national cultural traditions. Furthermore, concessions are less prevalent in the above sectors. It must also

---

[57] Directive 2004/17, [2004] OJ L134 coordinating the procurement procedures of entities operating in the water, energy, transport and postal services sectors.

[58] The predecessor to 2004/18 EC Directive, Directive 92/50, [1992] OJ L209 had adopted a two-tier approach in classifying services procured by contracting authorities. This classification is based on a 'priority' and a 'non-priority' list of services, according to the relative value of such services in intra-community trade. *Priority services* include: Maintenance and repair services; Land transport services (except for rail transport services), including armoured car services and courier services, except transport of mail; Air transport services of passengers and freight, except transport of mail; Transport of mail by land and by air; Telecommunications services (except voice telephony, telex, radiotelephony, paging and satellite services); Financial services including (a) Insurance services, (b) Banking and investment services (except contracts for financial services in connection with the issue, sale, purchase or transfer of securities or other financial instruments, and central bank services); Computer and related services; Research and development services; Accounting, auditing and book-keeping services; Market research and public opinion polling services; Management consultant services (except arbitration and conciliation services) and related services; Architectural services; engineering services and integrated engineering services; urban planning and landscape architectural services; related scientific and technical consulting services; technical testing and analysis services; Advertising services; Building-cleaning services on a fee or contract basis; Publishing and printing services on a fee or contract basis; Sewage and refuse disposal services; Sanitation and similar services. *Non-Priority services* include: Hotel and restaurant services; Rail transport services; Water transport services; Supporting and auxiliary transport services; Legal services; Personnel placement and supply services; Investigation and security services; Education and vocational education services; Health and social services; Recreational, cultural and sporting services. The division was not permanent and the European Commission had the situation under constant review, by assessing the performance of 'non-priority' services sectors. The two-tier approach, in practical terms, means that the award of priority services contracts are subject to the rigorous regime of the public procurement Directives (advertisement, selection of tenderers, award procedures, award criteria), whereas the award of non-priority services contracts must follow the basic rules of non-discrimination and publicity of the results of the award.

be said that the full coverage of these services by the complete framework is politically very sensitive. It is therefore appropriate to establish a specific regime for the award of these services. This regime should include the obligation to publish by contracting authorities at the beginning of the budgetary year, a prior information notice. Such a notice would ensure adequate transparency, without prejudice to national systems of purchase of this kind of services. Such a legal framework should also encompass a requirement to publish a concession award notice.

Concessions in Public Passenger Transport

At the time when the Transport Regulation 1370/2007 was adopted, service concessions in this field were governed by the Treaty principles.[59] Nevertheless, this sector was considered sufficiently distinctive to be subject to a more precise and specific set of rules (including the possibility of awarding contracts to 'internal operators').[60] For this reason, and in order not to interfere with the objectives of EU transport policy, and to maintain the stability of the legal framework, service concessions currently subject to the Transport Regulation should be excluded from the scope of the future EU legislation on concessions. Moreover, as the current rules applicable in this sector already provide for transparency and a fair degree of legal certainty, changing the legal framework applicable to these concessions is not considered a priority.

Concessions in air transport

Pursuant to Regulation 1008/2008, a Member State may impose a public service obligation (PSO) with respect to scheduled air services between two airports in the Union, in particular when one of them serves an outlying or developing region.[61] To this end, the Regulation lays out a very detailed procedure for setting up these PSOs and for compulsory tendering.

Concessions awarded to entities enjoying exclusive rights

In the utilities sector, the grant of exclusive rights for the operation of a network is part of specific legislative measures aimed at liberalizing such sectors. An exclusive right granted in compliance with EU law makes it unnecessary and redundant to follow a competitive procedure for the award of a concession of network management services to the holder of an exclusive right since no other competitor would be in a position to apply for such contract. Moreover, the transparency resulting from a mandatory publication of the act granting the exclusive right should permit all interested parties to fully evaluate the compliance of such right with Treaty or Union sectoral legislation.

---

[59] Regulation (EC) No 1370/2007 of the European Parliament and of the Council of 23 October 2007 on public passenger transport services by rail and by road and repealing Council Regulations (EEC) Nos 1191/69 and 1107/70, [2007] OJ L315.

[60] See M. Kekelekis and I.E. Rusu, 'The Award of Public Contracts and the notion of "Internal Operator" Under Regulation 1370/2007 on Public Passenger Transport Services by Rail and by Road', (2010) 6 *Public Procurement Law Review* 198–216.

[61] See Regulation 1008/2008 of the European Parliament and of the Council of 24 September 2008 on common rules for the operation of air services in the Community (Recast), [2008] OJ L293.

Concessions of sub-dimensional value

Currently, secondary legislation on Public Procurement applies only to public contracts and works concessions of a value equal to or superior to a certain threshold, above which they are subject to a presumption of cross-border interest. Similarly, national provisions on concessions usually apply only to contracts above a certain value. Thresholds currently applicable to public contracts and works concessions indicate not only their economic importance, but also reflect a political consensus on their cross-border interest. The appropriate threshold for service concessions should therefore reflect the extent to which economic operators located in other Member States are interested in such concessions. However, such interest depends not only on the value of the concession but also on its geographic location, the sector concerned, differences in economic wealth, the rate at which concessions are used, and costs (including labour costs). To assess the cross-border interest would mean gathering data on the actual participation of non-domestic companies in bidding procedures for concessions of different values. Accessing such information is extremely difficult if not impossible, given the existing lack of transparency.

Furthermore, reference to existing national thresholds is largely irrelevant, not only because they differ widely in those Member States which have regulated concessions, but also because national thresholds reflect interests of national policy rather than the cross-border interest of the contracts. It does not appear appropriate to take the existing thresholds for service contracts and automatically extend them to service concessions, since concession contracts have a higher value and are more complex and longer-term. The same applies to the method used for calculating the value of public service contracts. Indeed, given that in concession contracts the investments and revenues are often spread over many years, it seems inadequate to calculate the contract value on the basis of a fixed and limited initial time span (as is the case with public contracts). Consequently, the threshold value applicable to a service concession should be calculated on the basis of the total value of services provided during the whole duration of the concession. Against this background, it does not seem appropriate to establish a threshold for service concessions that is equal to or slightly greater than the one applicable to public service contracts but calculated on the basis of the total value of services stipulated. The risk is that this threshold would cover concessions that have no clear cross-border interest and would impose unreasonable costs and administrative burdens both on contracting authorities and companies.

Direct awards and concessions

In many Member States concession markets remain predominantly national, with a limited presence of companies originating in other EU Member States. Entry barriers stem from divergent national legal regimes for the award of concessions, as well as from inappropriate or even unlawful practices of the national awarding authorities. Identified divergence of legal regimes in Member States reveals several potential problems, including issues with the definition of concession, whereby economic operators have to contend with a complex pattern of setups considered to be concessions in different Member States (for example, administrative authorizations or licenses) and contracts qualifying as concessions under EU law but not considered as such by national legislators. In addition, divergent publication standards where, as a result of different national frameworks, concessions of the same type and importance are being published at different levels in different Member States and even within the same Member State (for example, in a local or trade newspaper, on the contracting entity's website, in the official journal, or even in the Official Journal of the European Union) frustrate an EU-wide concession market from developing.[62]

Barriers emanating from a divergence of national regimes are made worse by the often unlawful practices of contracting authorities, which stem from the lack of clarity of EU rules. One of the fundamental problems in this regard is the direct award of a concession contract with a cross-border interest. Direct awards originate from inadequate application of the principle of transparency, either by national lawmakers or by contracting authorities.[63] This concerns, in particular, Member States that do not regulate the award of concessions, but it also often concerns Member States where the award is governed by national rules.

Direct awards have particularly negative consequences for the proper functioning of the internal market. This applies to concession contracts, which are often extended or renewed without any competition or transparency. Another unlawful practice concerns the award of public contracts in accordance with lenient rules applicable to concessions, thus undermining the effectiveness of Public Procurement rules. In other instances, concessions are granted as licenses or authorizations (usually encompassing exclusive rights) in breach of the Treaty principles. This means that a concession contract is wrongly qualified as a unilateral act and may be granted without a competitive procedure. Despite this, the Court has made it clear that granting a license encompassing an exclusive right must comply with the principles of equal treatment and transparency.[64] It also acknowledged the existence of a wide derogation from these principles, excluding from this transparency obligation licenses granted to either public operators subject to direct State supervision or private operators subject to strict control by the public authorities.

Finally, the lack of clear rules also leads to the unlawful use of non-objective selection and award criteria.[65] This is the case when objectives unrelated to the subject

[62] This is the case of a German notion of '*Konzession*.' Licences or authorizations are acts whereby a public authority authorizes the exercise of an economic activity. While certain conditions for carrying out the activity usually need to be met by the licensee, or he might have been assigned certain public service obligations linked to the licensed activity, the authorization does not principally aim at assigning a given public task to the licensee. See European Commission, Assessment of an Initiative on Concessions, Brussels, 20 December 2011, SEC(2011) 1588fin.

[63] See European Commission, *Green Paper on Public-Private Partnerships and Community Law on Public Contracts and Concessions*, COM (2004) 327 fin.

[64] See Case C-203/08, *Sporting Exchange Ltd Betfair v Minister van Justitie*, Judgment of the Court (Second Chamber) of 3 June 2010.

[65] Under the Directive, qualification criteria need to relate to technical, economic and financial capacity, whereas award criteria relate to price or the economically most advantageous tender. These requirements do not concern either work or service concessions. For example in France, until recently the award was to a large extent dependent on the '*intuitu personae*' or the relation of personal trust between the contracting authority and the concessionaire. In Lithuania, the 'effect of the tender on the social and economic development of the country or an appropriate region' may be used as an award criterion which may give rise, in view of its wide

matter of the contract are included in the evaluation of the best offer. For instance, contracting authorities may want to take into account tenderers' social commitments not related to the subject matter of the contract or relations of trust with one of the bidders. Non-objective and discriminatory criteria undermine the fairness of the award. The same can be said about discretion in setting selection criteria, which may lead to certain companies being disadvantaged. This problem concerns Small and Medium Enterprises (SMEs) in particular, which appear to be reduced largely to the role of subcontractors.[66]

The above problems primarily concern service concessions and works concessions in the Utilities sector, as the existing provisions on works concessions in the Classic Directive cover the issues of publication. By contrast, the problems related to the misapplication of the Treaty principles at later stages of the award procedure may also concern works concessions, although to a lesser extent.

Pursuant to Article 47 of the Charter of Fundamental Rights of the EU, anyone whose rights and freedoms guaranteed by the law of the Union are violated has the right to an effective remedy.[67] However, this right is not fully ensured to tenderers participating in procedures for the award of concessions. The Remedies Directive does not cover concessions falling outside the scope of the Classic Directive.[68] Hence, tenderers do not benefit from an adequate system guaranteeing effective enforcement of EU Treaty principles. Although some Member States (such as France, Portugal and Romania) extended the application of the Remedies Directive to service concessions, a number of others (Germany, UK, Sweden and the Netherlands, for instance) have not done so.[69] It is maintained that some important guarantees provided for by the Remedies Directive (such as the obligation to refrain from concluding a contract before the expiry of the standstill period or the conditions for ineffectiveness of concessions awarded directly) are not available in many Member States. As a result, the aggrieved economic operators cannot adequately tackle potential violation of the EU Treaty principles. Moreover, any arbitrariness of contracting authorities enjoying wide discretion throughout the tendering process escapes effective scrutiny. Taking into account the number of concessions reported to be either awarded directly or tendered according to inadequate standards, this may effectively lead to a continuous failure to redress national situations of deficiency or non-compliance with the application of the Treaty principles.

Legal certainty is essential to any economic activity and is particularly important in the context of long-term, high-value contracts such as most concessions. However, the grant of concessions is currently impaired, on the one hand by the lack of a clear and adequate definition of these contracts in EU law and, on the other hand, by the imprecise character of the obligations arising from the Treaty principles. These

---

scope, to possible discrimination. European Commission, Assessment of an Initiative on Concessions, Brussels, 20 December 2011, SEC (2011) 1588fin.

[66] See Report on the Public Consultation on the Green Paper on PPP and Community Law on Public Contracts and Concessions 11, SEC (2005) 629.

[67] Article 47 of the Charter of Fundamental Rights in the EU, [2000] OJ C364/1.

[68] See Directive 2007/66/EC of 11 December 2007, [2007] OJ L335/31.

[69] See European Commission, Assessment of an Initiative on Concessions, Brussels, 20 December 2011, SEC(2011) 1588fin.

problems are often not resolved by national regimes for awarding concessions. Uncertainty with regard to the definition of concession appears already at the stage of qualification of a given arrangement as falling within the scope of the rules on public purchases. The distinction between public contracts and concessions on the one hand and other types of agreements or unilateral acts (such as licenses and authorization schemes) on the other hand, is unclear and stakeholders (for example, in the ports sector) reported that it is often difficult to know which legal regime applies to a given scheme.[70] Furthermore, the lack of clarity stretches to certain activities carried out in the form of public-public cooperation.

The current definition of concessions makes it difficult to distinguish between concessions and public contracts. The Commission provided some clarity in this respect in its Interpretative Communication, explaining that the risk inherent in the exploitation of the work or service that the concessionaire has to bear is the essential feature of a concession.[71] Although the case-law of the Court shed some light on this definition, fundamental elements, such as the level and types of risk, still remain unclear.[72] There is also some uncertainty regarding the distinction between works concessions and service concessions. Indeed, most works concessions also involve, to a certain extent, the provision of services. And, as it is not always easy to ascertain what the main purpose of the contract is, certain works concessions might be awarded as service concessions, thus unduly avoiding the application of the secondary rules.[73]

Moreover, Member States' definitions of concession do not remove the aforementioned uncertainty at EU level. Some of them are as unclear as the current definition in the Directive. Moreover, it is unclear whether those national definitions that provide additional clarification do in fact comply with EU law.

The legal uncertainty regarding the definition of concessions is compounded by doubts regarding the content and application of the obligations of transparency and non-discrimination arising under the Treaty, which guide the award of concessions. Although the Court confirmed in *Telaustria* that contracting authorities that award concessions are bound to comply with the fundamental rules of the Treaty, it did not

---

70 See Bovis, 'Public Procurement and Public Services in the EU', *supra* note 43, 287.

71 See Commission Interpretative Communication on Concessions under Community Law [2000] OJ C121/2–13.

72 Case-law is still not sufficiently clear, in particular regarding the level of operating risk to be transferred to the economic operator so that a contract can qualify as a concession. It appears that Case C-437/07, *Commission v Italy* [2008] ECR I-153 and Cases C-300/07, C-300/07, *Hans & Christophorus Oymanns GbR, Orthopädie Schuhtechnik v AOK Rheinland/Hamburg* [2009] ECR I-4779 are difficult to interpret along with Case C-206/08, *WAZV.Gotha v Eurawasser Aufbereitungs* [2009] ECR I-8377. The uncertainty is increased by lingering doubts on the categories of risk that can be transferred to the concessionaire. While demand risk for services seems to be widely accepted as relevant for the definition of a concession, there is uncertainty as to what other categories of risk (availability, construction, legal, and political) should also qualify. See Eurawasser [2009] ECR I-08377, at para 79 (where the court ruled that 'general risk resulting from amendments to the rules made in the course of performance of the contract cannot be taken into account').

73 See Case C-331/92, *Gestion Hotelera Internacional* [1994] ECR I-1329; see also Case C-220/05, *Jean Auroux and Others v Commune de Roanne* [2007] ECR I-385, paras 36–37.

sufficiently explain the content of those rules.[74] Thus it remains difficult to judge the adequacy of measures aimed at ensuring compliance with the principles of equal treatment, non-discrimination and transparency. A problem of uncertainty as to the applicable rules has also been identified in case of a contract modification. Many stakeholders have identified this issue as an important one. Although the case-law of the Court applicable to modifications of public contracts also applies to concessions, the level of certainty provided by these judgments does not seem to be adequate.

As concession award regimes in Member States are often unclear, or in the case of services concessions, non-existent, the burden of ensuring, in each specific case, the compliance with the procedures to be followed under the Treaty principles falls on contracting authorities. Contracting authorities are faced with a situation where they apply national rules or ad hoc award procedures that do not necessarily meet EU Treaty standards. Similarly, economic operators remain uncertain about the legality of the procedures followed.

The current situation of uncertainty at several levels is causing significant economic inefficiencies and is prejudicial to contracting authorities, economic operators and users of the services provided. For contracting authorities, the lack of legal certainty increases the risks and costs of cancellation or early termination of illegally awarded contracts, and ultimately prevents them from using concessions where this type of contract might be a good solution. This may have the effect of reducing the uptake of PPPs, resulting in missed opportunities for engaging private investments and know-how. This is particularly the case in new Member States, where uncertainty is compounded by a lack of experience. Indeed, contracting authorities may often prefer to remain within the framework of the direct provision of services, rather than confer these activities to a private operator on the basis of a concession.

The contractual PPP

The contractual model of public private partnerships reflects on a relation between public and private sectors, which is based solely on contractual links. It is unlikely that there would be any element of exclusive asset exploitation or end user payments levied by the private sector partner. However, mechanisms of profit sharing, efficiency gain sharing, as well as risk allocation between the public and private partners distinguish contractual PPPs from traditional public contracts for works or services. The contractual model of PPPs assumes that the private sector partner will provide the financing for completing the project and the public sector partner will pay back by way of 'service or unitary charges' which reflect payments based on usage volumes or demand (that is, payments in lieu of fees or tolls for public lighting, hospitals, schools, or roads with shadow tolls). A variety of types of contractual PPPs have been developed in many jurisdictions including the EU, US, Canada, Australia and Malaysia.

The institutional PPP

The institutional model of public private partnerships involves the establishment of a separate legal entity held jointly by the public partner and the private partner. The joint entity has the task of ensuring the raising of finance and the delivery of a public

[74] See Case C-324/98, *Telaustria and Telefonadress* [2000] ECR I-10745.

service or an infrastructure project for the benefit of the public. The direct interface between the public partner and the private partner in a forum with a distinctive legal personality allows the public partner, through its presence in the body of shareholders and in the decision-making bodies of the joint entity, to retain a relatively high degree of control over the development and delivery of the project. The joint entity could also allow the public partner to develop its own experience of running and improving the public service in question, while having recourse to the support of a private partner. An institutional public private partnership can be established either by creating an entity controlled by the public and private sector partners, or by the private sector taking control of an existing public undertaking or by the participation of a private partner in an existing publicly owned company which has obtained public contracts or concessions.[75]

III. THE OPERATIONAL TYPES OF PUBLIC–PRIVATE PARTNERSHIPS

Three major operational types of public private partnerships exist:

First, the private sector designs, builds, owns, develops, operates and manages an asset with no obligation to transfer ownership to the public sector. PPPs with such modalities include formats such as:

- Design-Build-Finance-Operate (DBFO), where the private sector partner designs, builds, finances and operates a public asset covering all aspects of management and maintenance with an option to sell at the end of the contractual period.[76]
- Build-own-operate (BOO), where the private sector partner finances, builds, owns and operates a facility or service for a stipulated period. Public sector control is exercised through the original contract or through a regulatory authority. After a specified period, there could be the possibility that ownership is transferred back to the public sector.[77]
- Build-develop-operate (BDO), where the private sector finances, builds, develops commercially and operates for a stipulated period an asset or a facility.[78]
- Design-construct-manage-finance (DCMF), where the private sector finances the design and construction of a facility or infrastructure and subsequently manages it for a stipulated period.[79]

---

[75] Bovis, 'Future Directions in Public Private Partnerships', *supra* note 38, 782.

[76] Design-Build-Finance-Operate (DBFO) Public Private Partnerships include the delivery of hospitals where ownership of the facility stock is retained by the private sector.

[77] Build-own-operate (BOO) Public Private Partnerships include the delivery of prisons, where regulatory regimes regarding standards operate alongside the retention of ownership of the assets by the private sector.

[78] Build-develop-operate (BDO) Public Private Partnerships include the delivery of commercial developments such as exhibition centers and recreational facilities where ownership of the facility stock is retained by the private sector.

[79] Design-construct-manage-finance (DCMF) Public Private Partnerships include the finance and delivery of schools and university accommodation projects.

Secondly, the private sector buys or leases an existing asset from the public sector, renovates, modernizes and/or expands it, and then operates the asset, again with no obligation to transfer ownership back to the public sector. PPPs with such modalities include formats such as:

- Buy-build-operate (BBO), where the public sector transfers a public asset to the private or quasi-public sector partner to operate and maintain for a specified period of time. Public sector control is exercised at the time of transfer.[80]
- Lease-develop-operate (LDO), where the public sector leases a public asset to the private or quasi-public sector partner to operate and maintain for a specified period of time. Public sector control is exercised at the initiation of lease.[81]
- Operate under License (OL): The private sector partner receives a license or rights to operate a public service, usually for a specified term. This is often used in IT projects. The options available for delivery of public services range from direct provision by a ministry or government department to outright privatization, where the public sector transfers all responsibilities, risks and rewards for service delivery to the private sector. Within this spectrum, public-private partnerships can be categorized based on the extent of public and private sector involvement and the degree of risk allocation.[82]

Thirdly, the private sector designs and builds an asset, operates it, and then transfers it to the public sector when the operating contract ends, or at some other specified time. The private partner may subsequently rent or lease the asset from the public sector. PPPs with such modalities include formats such as:

- Build-operate-transfer (BOT), where the private sector designs, finances and constructs a new facility under a long-term contract, and operates the facility during the term of the contract after which ownership is transferred back to the public sector if not already transferred upon completion of the facility.[83]
- Build-own-operate-transfer (BOOT), where a private entity receives a franchise or a concession to finance, design, build and operate a facility (and to charge user

[80] Buy-build-operate (BBO) Public Private Partnerships include housing and regeneration development contracts between local and municipal authorities and the private sector.

[81] Lease-develop-operate (LDO) Public Private Partnerships include housing and regeneration development projects and the delivery of commercial developments such as exhibition centres and recreational facilities where the lease-holding of the facility stock is retained by the private sector.

[82] Operate under License (OL) Public Private Partnerships include the delivery of IT related projects in the health, transport and defence sectors, where the private sector engages through licenses with the public sector to deliver a project.

[83] Build-operate-transfer (BOT) Public Private Partnerships include the delivery of infrastructure projects in transport such as motorways and bridges.

fees) for a specified period, after which ownership is transferred back to the public sector.[84]

- Build-lease-operate-transfer (BLOT), where a private entity receives a franchise to finance, design, build and operate a leased facility (and to charge user fees) for the lease period, against payment of a rent.[85]

IV. THE FINANCING OF PUBLIC–PRIVATE PARTNERSHIPS

A public-private partnership financing can take one of the following forms: (i) *a stand-alone project*, where the funding raised is for only one specific project; (ii) *a Special Purpose Vehicle* as the borrower, where an independent legal vehicle (SPV) is created to raise the funds required for the project; (iii) a high ratio of debt to equity through either gearing or leverage, where the newly created project company usually has the minimum equity required to issue debt for a reasonable cost, with equity generally averaging between 10 to 30 per cent of the total capital required for infrastructure projects; (iv) *private lending* based on project specific cash flow and not a corporate balance sheet, where the project company borrows funds from lenders. The lenders look to the projected future revenue stream generated by the project and the project company's assets to repay all loans; and (v) *various financial guarantees*, where the guarantees are provided by the private sector partners, often limited to their equity contributions.[86] The state usually does not provide financial guarantees to lenders. As a result of the private sector guarantees, the lender receives its payment from the income generated from the project or directly from the public sector.

The private sector can raise funds for investment in public-private partnerships through a variety of ways. First, where services are destined for the public as end-users, the private sector can access private financing in the money markets using the projected income stream from the public paying for the public services (that is, toll revenue) as collateral. However, where the public sector is the main recipient or purchaser of the relevant services from the PPP, payments related to the demand for services or service payments by the public sector under operating contracts, which are based on continuity of service supply, can be used (that is, shadow tolls paid by the public sector). The public sector may also make a direct contribution to project costs. This can take the form of equity (where there is profit sharing), a loan, or a subsidy (where social returns exceed private returns). The public sector can also guarantee private sector borrowing.

Secondly, public-private partnership financing can be provided via special purpose vehicles (SPVs) comprising consortia of banks and other financial institutions, which are set up to combine and coordinate the use of their capital and expertise, as well as

[84] Build-own-operate-transfer (BOOT) Public Private Partnerships include the delivery of government buildings and accommodation project, with the option or obligation to transfer ownership of an asset at the end of the Partnership's life span.

[85] Build-lease-operate-transfer (BLOT) Public Private Partnerships include the delivery of transport infrastructure projects such as airports and ports.

[86] See T. Irwin, Government Guarantees: Allocating and Valuing Risk in Privately Financed Infrastructure Projects (Washington, DC: World Bank 2007).

share any relevant risks. Accountancy treatment of the SPV's consolidated accounts is aligned with the party that controls the SPV.[87] If the private sector partner controls the SPV, its debt is recorded off-balance sheet for public sector borrowing considerations. If an SPV is controlled by the public sector, it should be consolidated with public sector borrowing, and its operations should be reflected in the fiscal accounts. A private partner controlled SPV could be used to move debt from the public sector balance sheet through the direct involvement of public financial institutions, an explicit government guarantee of borrowing by an SPV, or a presumption that the public sector stands behind it. However, if risk stays with the public sector, even if the SPV is controlled by the private sector partner, the SPV consolidation should be recorded in the public sector accounts.[88]

Thirdly, a public-private partnership can be financed by securitization of claims on future project revenues. In a typical PPP securitization operation, the public sector would sell a financial asset – its claim on future project revenue – to an SPV. The SPV would then sell securities backed by this asset to private investors and use the proceeds to pay the public sector, which in turn would use them to finance the PPP. Interest and amortization would be paid by the SPV to investors from the public sector's share of project revenue. Since investors' claim is against the SPV, government involvement in the PPP appears limited. However, the public sector is in effect financing the PPP, although recording sale proceeds received from the SPV as revenue masks this fact. Securitization operations have often raised questions as to their appropriate accounting treatment. If assets or real estate are sold to an SPV below market price for the latter to use as collateral in issuing bonds on its own account to pay the public sector, the bonds should be treated as debt and the sale of the real estate should be recorded on budget because the risks and rewards related to ownership have not been transferred to the SPV.

V. RISK AND PUBLIC–PRIVATE PARTNERSHIPS

Assessing Risk Transfer in Public–private Partnerships

Some criteria have been devised to assess the degree of risk transfer involved in PPPs. Where PPP contracts do not provide a basis on which to distinguish between the risks associated with ownership and operation, the extent of risk transfer can be assessed by reference to the overall risk characteristics of a PPP, where the specific aim for separable contracts (a distinction between asset ownership and delivery of public

[87] The International Financial Reporting Interpretations Committee (IFRIC) of the International Accounting Standards Board (IASB) identifies four criteria for consolidation: (i) SPV operations are decided by the originator; (ii) the originator controls the SPV; (iii) the originator benefits most from the SPV; and (iv) the originator assumes SPV risk. See International Public Sector Accounting Standards (IPSASs) and Statistical Bases of Financial Reporting: An Analysis of Differences and Recommendations for Governance Of PPPs, January 2005.

[88] See International Monetary Fund, *Limits on External Debt or Borrowing in Fund Arrangements-Proposed Change in Coverage of Debt Limits*, EBS/00/128 (2000).

service elements) and non-separable contracts, is to determine whether the public sector or the private operator has an asset in a PPP.[89]

For non-separable contracts, the baseline for the assessment rests on the balance of demand risk and residual value risk borne by the public sector and the private operator. Demand risk, which is an operating risk, and is the dominant consideration, is borne by the public sector if service payments to a private operator are independent of future need for the service. Residual value risk, which is an ownership risk, is borne by the public sector if a PPP asset is transferred to the public sector for less than its true residual value. Residual value risk is borne by the public sector because the private operator reflects the difference between the expected residual value of the asset and the price at which the asset will be transferred to the public sector in the price it charges the public sector for services, or the revenue the public sector receives from a project. If the asset ends up being worth more or less than the amount reflected in the service payment or government revenue, any resulting gain benefits the public sector and any loss is borne by the public sector. Reference can also be made to various qualitative indicators, including government guarantees of private sector liabilities, and the extent of government influence over asset design and operation. The final conclusion is a judgment based on all relevant factors.

The European Union has provided guidance on the classification of PPP assets based on risk transfer. Eurostat has issued a Decision which holds that a private partner will be assumed to bear the balance of PPP risk if it bears most of the construction risk, and either most of the availability risk (which is also referred to as performance risk) or most of the demand risk.[90] The Eurostat Decision covers long-term contracts in areas where the private partner builds an asset and delivers services mainly to the public sector. Eurostat recommends that assets involved in public-private partnerships should be classified as non-government assets, and therefore recorded off balance sheet for government if: (i) the private partner bears the construction risk, and (ii) the private partner bears one of either availability or demand risk.

Construction risk covers events such as late delivery, low standards, additional costs, technical deficiency and external negative effects. If the public sector makes payments to the private partner irrespective of the state of the asset, this indicates that the public sector bears most of the construction risk. Availability risk relates to the ability of the private partner to deliver the agreed volume and quality of service. Public sector payments to the private partners that are independent of service delivery indicate that the public sector bears most of the delivery risk. Demand risk covers the impact of the business cycle, market trends, competition and technological progress on the continued need for the service. Public sector payments to the private partner that are independent of demand indicate that the public sector bears most of the demand risk. Changes in demand due to changes in government policy are excluded.

89 See International Financial Reporting Interpretations Committee [IFRIC], *Consolidation: Special Purpose Entities*, Standing Interpretation Committee (SIC) 12 (1999).

90 See Eurostat decision on *Deficit and Debt Treatment of Public Private Partnerships*, STAT/04/18, 11 February 2004.

VI. THE PROCUREMENT OF PUBLIC–PRIVATE PARTNERSHIPS

Considerable emphasis has been placed on observing the principles of transparency and accountability, competitiveness and value for money during the procurement process of public-private partnerships.[91] When a transaction creating a mixed-capital entity is accompanied by the award of tasks through an act that can be designated as a public contract, or even a concession, it is important that there be compliance with the principles of transparency and accountability, as well as the principle of non-discrimination. The principles of transparency and accountability depict the skeleton of public procurement regulation. They have direct influence on two fronts: (a) the behavioural patterns of the state, public bodies and contracting authorities and (b) the emergence and structure of a *sui generis* market place. The regulation of public procurement, through the principles of transparency and accountability provides for a pedestal of the legal, economic and policy interface between public and private sectors. Changes have been signalled by European Institutions towards a rethink of the role of the private sector in delivering public services. The conceptual themes of public private partnerships (PPPs) and services of general economic interest are classic examples. The principles of transparency and accountability emanating from public procurement regulation also have a transferable nature within public administrations of Member States. Although generic at first sight, their application unfolds desirable effects in the spheres of law and policy, effects which have long lasting influences.

The selection of a private partner called on to undertake such tasks while functioning as part of a mixed entity can therefore not be based exclusively on the quality of its capital contribution or its experience, but should also take account of the characteristics of its offer in terms of the specific services to be provided. The conditions governing the creation of the entity must be clearly laid down when issuing the call for competition for the tasks that one wishes to entrust to the private partner. Also, these conditions must not discriminate against or constitute an unjustified barrier to the freedom to provide services or to the freedom of establishment, or be disproportionate to the desired objective.

In this context, the transaction involving the creation of such an entity does not generally present a problem in terms of the applicable Community law when it constitutes a means of executing the task entrusted under a contract to a private partner. However, the conditions governing the creation of the entity must be clearly laid down when issuing the call for competition for those tasks that one wishes to entrust to the private partner. Also, these conditions must not discriminate against or constitute an unjustified barrier to the freedom to provide services or the freedom of establishment, or be disproportionate to the desired objective.

In many jurisdictions, legislation allows the mixed entities, in which the participation by the public sector involves the contracting body, to participate in a procedure for the award of a public contract or concession even when these entities are only in the course

---

[91] See C.H. Bovis, 'The Effects of the Principles of Transparency and Accountability on Public Procurement Regulation' in H. Hoffman and A. Türk (eds), *Legal Challenges in EU Administrative Law* (Cheltenham, UK and Northampton, MA, USA: Edward Elgar 2009) 288–321.

of being incorporated.[92] In this scenario, the entity will be definitively incorporated only after the contract has actually been awarded to it. In many states a practice has developed that tends to confuse the phase of incorporating the entity and the phase of allocating the tasks.[93] Thus the purpose of the procedure launched by the contracting authority is to create a mixed entity to which certain tasks are entrusted.

Such a solution is not satisfactory. In the first case, there is a risk that the effective competition will be distorted by the privileged position enjoyed by the company being incorporated and, consequently, by the private partner participating in this company. In the second case, the specific procedure for selecting the private partner also poses many problems. The contracting authorities encounter certain difficulties in defining the subject matter of the contract or concession in a sufficiently clear and precise manner, as they are obliged to do. This in turn raises problems not only with regard to the principles of transparency and equality of treatment, but even risks prejudicing the general interest objectives that the public authority wishes to attain. It is also evident that the lifetime of the created entity does not generally coincide with the duration of the contract or concession awarded, and this appears to encourage the extension of the task entrusted to this entity without true competition at the time of this renewal. In addition, it should be noted that the joint creation of such entities must respect the principle of non-discrimination with respect to nationality in general, and the free circulation of capital in particular. Thus, for example, the public authorities cannot normally make their position as shareholder in such an entity contingent on excessive privileges that do not derive from a normal application of company law.[94]

On the other hand, the creation of an institutional public private partnership may also lead to a change in the body of shareholders of a public entity. When public authorities grant an economic operator a definite influence in a business under a transaction involving a capital transfer, and when this transaction has the effect of entrusting to this operator tasks falling within the scope of the law on public contracts which had been previously exercised, directly or indirectly, by the public authorities, the provisions on freedom of establishment require compliance with the principles of transparency and equality of treatment in order to ensure that every potential operator has equal access to performing those activities that had been reserved.

---

[92] For example, national legislation in Spain, Italy, France, Portugal and Germany allows the participation of a mixed-capital entity in public procurement for the award of a service or works contract during their incorporation stages. See Bovis, 'Future Directions in Public Private Partnerships', *supra* note 38, 782.

[93] In the UK, Sweden, the Netherlands, Austria and Belgium, national legislation allows for the fusion of award of a partnership or a concession contract and the incorporation of the entity which will perform the public service or task allocated as a result of the conclusion of the Public-Private Partnership. See Bovis, 'Future Directions in Public Private Partnerships', *supra* note 38, 782.

[94] See Case C-367/98, *Commission v Portugal* [2002] ECR I-4731; Case C-483/99, *Commission v France* [2002] ECR I-4781. See also Case C-463/00, *Commission v Spain* [2003] ECR I-4581; Case C-98/01, *Commission v United Kingdom* [2003] ECR I-4641. On the possible justifications in this framework, see Case C-503/99, *Commission v Belgium* [2002] ECR I-4809.

VII. PUBLIC-PUBLIC COOPERATION IN DELIVERING PUBLIC SERVICES

The In-House Arrangements

EU law does not restrict the freedom of a contracting authority to perform the public interest tasks conferred on it by using its own administrative, technical and other resources. As such, contracting authorities need not call upon outside entities, which are not a part of their own structures.[95] If a contracting authority performs a public task by using its own resources in such a way that no contract for pecuniary interest is concluded, EU public procurement law does not apply. Moreover, the possibility to perform public tasks using its own resources may also be exercised in cooperation with other contracting authorities. Several contracting authorities may mutually assist each other. If this does not involve remuneration or any exchange of reciprocal rights and obligations, there is no contractual interface within the meaning of EU public procurement law, and thus, EU public procurement legislation does not apply.

Article 6 of the Services Directive provides for the inapplicability of the public procurement Directives to service contracts that are awarded to an entity – that is itself a contracting authority within the meaning of the Directive – on the basis of an exclusive right that is granted to the contracting authority by a law, regulation, or administrative provision of the Member State.[96] Article 13 of the Utilities Directive provides for the exclusion of certain contracts between contracting authorities and affiliated undertakings.[97] An affiliated undertaking, for the purposes of Article 1(3) of the Utilities Directive, is one the annual accounts that are consolidated with those of the contracting entity in accordance with the requirements of the Seventh Company Law Directive.[98] There are service contracts awarded to a service provider affiliated with the contracting entity, and there are service contracts awarded to a service provider affiliated with a contracting entity participating in a joint venture, formed for the purpose of carrying out an activity covered by the Directive. The explanatory memorandum accompanying the text amending the Utilities Directive states that this provision relates, in particular, to three types of service provisions within groups.[99]

---

[95] See Case C-26/03, *Stadt Halle and RPL Recyclingpark Lochau GmbH v. Arbeitsgemeinschaft Thermische Restabfall- und Energieverwertungsanlage TREA Leuna* [2005] ECR I-1, para 48.

[96] This practice resembles the market testing process often employed in the United Kingdom between a contracting authority and an in-house team. See I. Harden, 'Defining the range of application of the public sector procurement Directives in the United Kingdom' (1992) 1 *Public Procurement Law Review* 362.

[97] See Article 13 of Directive 2004/17, [2004] OJ L134 coordinating the procurement procedures of entities operating in the water, energy, transport and postal services sectors.

[98] See Directive 83/349/EEC as regards the valuation rules for the annual and consolidated accounts of certain types of companies as well as of banks and other financial institutions as amended by Directive 2001/65/EC of the European Parliament, [2001] OJ L283.

[99] See Directive 90/531, [1990] OJ L297 on the procurement procedures of entities operating in the water, energy, transport and telecommunications sectors.(COM (91) 347-SYN 36 1).

These categories, which may or may not be distinct, are: (i) the provision of common services such as accounting, recruitment and management; (ii) the provision of specialized services embodying the know-how of the group; and (iii) the provision of a specialized service to a joint venture.[100]

The exclusion from the provisions of the Directive is subject, however, to two conditions: first, the service provider must be an undertaking affiliated with the contracting authority and, second, at least 80 per cent of its average turnover arising within the European Community for the preceding three years must be derived from the provision of the same or similar services to undertakings with which it is affiliated.[101] The Commission is empowered to monitor the application of this Article and require the notification of the names of the undertakings concerned and the nature and value of the service contracts involved.

Dependency, in terms of overall control of an entity by the state or another contracting authority presupposes a control similar to that which the state of another contracting authority exercises over its own departments. The 'similarity' of control denotes lack of independence with regard to decision-making. The Court in *Teckal,* concluded that a contract between a contracting authority and an entity, over which the former exercises control similar to the control that it exercises over its own departments, and at the same time that entity carries out the essential part of its activities with the contracting authority, is not a public contract, irrespective of that entity being a contracting authority or not.[102] The similarity of control as a reflection of dependency reveals another facet of the thrust of contracting authorities: the non-applicability of the public procurement rules for in-house relationships.

Similarity of Control

Teckal provided flexibility in determining the concept of 'contracting authorities' and established the non-applicability of the procurement rules to in-house relations.[103] The first criterion of *Teckal* is present when 'control similar to that which the contracting entity exercises over one of its own departments' is evident.[104] The notion of control

---

[100] Ibid.

[101] Ibid.

[102] See Case C-107/98, *Teckal Slr v Comune di Viano* [1999] ECR I-8121.

[103] Ibid.

[104] The *Teckal* first criterion is present when *control similar to that which the contracting entity exercises over one of its own departments* is evident. The notion of control and the *similarity* requirement merit a comprehensive approach, and not one solely based on company law features or one which is based on the level of the contracting authority's shareholding (or, conversely, that of the minority shareholder). Normally, corporate control indicates decisive influence over management, operational and strategic decisions, in a similar fashion to the concept of majority shareholder control found in various company laws of the Member States. Nevertheless, any appraisal of the legal position of a majority shareholder in order to assert control must be taken in conjunction with the statutes governing the relevant entity over which the control is exercised and not by sole reference to national company law provisions, as often minority shareholdings give rights of decisive influence, such as specific oversight and blocking rights. See C.H. Bovis, 'Public Procurement in the EU: Jurisprudence and Conceptual Directions' (2012) 49 *Common Market Law Review* 1–44.

and the *similarity* requirement merit a comprehensive approach, which should not be based solely on either company law features or on the level of the contracting authority's shareholding. Normally, corporate control indicates decisive influence over management actions, operational and strategic decisions in a similar manner to the concept of majority shareholder control found in company laws of Member States. Nevertheless, any appraisal of the legal position of a majority shareholder in order to assert control must be taken in conjunction with the statutes governing the relevant entity over which the control is exercised and not by sole reference to national company law provisions, as often minority shareholdings provide for rights of decisive influence, such as specific oversight and blocking rights.

The notion of control for the purposes of in-house contracts, as developed by the Court, entails much more than the ingredients of 'dominant influence' as a company law notion, or as a public procurement notion, which defines certain bodies as contracting authorities. In particular, control is extended beyond the 'dominant influence' notion found in the Utilities Directive.[105] For the purposes of in-house relations, the object of such control should not be confined to strategic market decisions or procurement decisions, but should embrace individual management and operational decisions as well. Corporate control is exercised by conclusive influence on both strategic objectives and significant decisions.

In *Parking Brixen*, the Court stated that the important point in relation to the control criterion is that there should be 'a potential power of decisive influence over both strategic objectives and significant decisions'.[106] With respect to the means of control, the ability to possess rights to give instructions and rights to make appointments, as well as evidence of supervisory powers, reflect upon a guiding principle which is *de facto* conclusive of the power to influence corporate behaviour and is not emanating from legislative provisions alone.

In *Carbotermo* it was maintained that joint-stock public companies exhibit similarity of control where a contracting authority holds, alone or together with other public authorities, all of the share capital in an entity.[107] However, if the board of management of that entity is vested with the broadest possible powers, and in the absence of any control or specific voting powers for restricting the board's freedom of action, the similarity of control is not present. If control exercised by a contracting authority over an entity could be viewed as consisting essentially of the majority shareholders' rights

---

[105] See Utilities Directive 2004/17, [2004] OJ L134 coordinating the procurement procedures of entities operating in the water, energy, transport and postal services sectors and in particular Article 2(1)(b) (in relation to public undertakings). A public undertaking is any undertaking over which the contracting authorities may exercise directly or indirectly a dominant influence by virtue of their ownership of it, their financial participation therein, or the rules that govern it. Contracting authorities exercise dominant influence over public undertakings when, directly or indirectly, in relation to an undertaking, they hold the majority of the undertaking's subscribed capital, control the majority of the votes attaching to shares issued by the undertaking, or can appoint more than half of the undertaking's administrative, management, or supervisory body.

[106] See Case C-458/03, *Parking Brixen GmbH v Gemeinde Brixen and Stadtwerke Brixen AG* [2005] ECR I-8612, para 65.

[107] See Case C-340/04, *Carbotermo SpA, Consorzio Alisei v Comune di Busto Arsizio, AGESP SpA* [2006] ECR I 4137.

conferred by company law, such control cannot be deemed as similar to that exercised upon the contracting authority's own departments. Moreover, if control is exercised through an intermediary, such as a holding company, the intervention of such an intermediary may render the similarity of control requirement irrelevant, or it may weaken any control exercised by the contracting authority over a joint-stock company merely because it holds shares in that company. Nevertheless, if an entity is jointly controlled by several contracting authorities, the control criterion is satisfied provided that all of the contracting authorities exhibit control over the relevant entity that is similar to that over their own departments.[108] In such situations, as in the case of inter-municipal cooperative societies, whose members are contracting authorities themselves, if joint control is exercised by the majority of controlling contracting authorities, the similarity of control criterion is met.[109]

Therefore, the concept of control must be understood in functional, not formal terms. There is nothing to prevent it from being applied to the relationship between a contracting authority and legal persons governed by private law, such as a limited liability company. The use of the term 'departments' derives from the original reason for setting up autonomous bodies, which was to entrust particular departments with a function or the delivery of a specific public service.[110] The control exercised over an entity or an undertaking by a public authority must be similar to that which the authority exercises over its own departments, but not identical in every respect and must be effective. But, it is not essential that it be exercised individually.[111]

However, the existence of private capital, participating in an entity which has corporate links with a contracting authority, negates the similarity of control requirement. *Stadt Halle* held that private sector participation cannot emulate the pursuit of public interest objectives entrusted to public sector entities.[112] The relationship between a public authority, which is a contracting authority, and its own departments is governed by considerations and requirements proper to the pursuit of objectives in the public interest. Any private capital investment in an undertaking follows considerations appropriate for private interests and pursues objectives of a different kind.[113] The participation, even as a minority, of a private undertaking in the capital of a company in which the awarding public authority is also a participant excludes the possibility that the public authority will exercise control that is similar to that which it exercises over its own departments over such a company.[114]

---

[108] See ibid at para 37; see also Case C-295/05, *Asociación Nacional de Empresas Forestales (Asemfo) v. Transformación Agraria SA (Tragsa) and Administración del Estado* [2007] ECR I-2999, para 57.

[109] See Case C-324/07, *Coditel Brabant SA v Commune d'Uccle, Région de Bruxelles-Capitale* [2009] 1 *Common Market Law Review* 29.

[110] See Bovis, 'Public Procurement and Public Services in the EU', *supra* note 43.

[111] See Case C-458/03, *Parking Brixen GmbH v Gemeinde Brixen and Stadtwerke Brixen AG* [2005] ECR I-8612, para 62.

[112] See Case C-26/03, *Stadt Halle, RPL Recyclingpark Lochau GmbH v Arbeitsgemeinschaft Thermische Restabfall und Energieverwertungsanlage TREA Leuna*[2005] ECR I-1.

[113] See ibid para 50.

[114] See ibid para 49.

The category of semi-public entities or undertakings, which in their own rights are regarded as contracting authorities, could not be viewed as entities upon which a contracting authority can exercise similar control to that over its own departments. In *Mödling*, the Court followed the *Stadt Halle* reasoning and interestingly held that if the award of an in-house public contract took place in accordance with the *Teckal* criteria, and within a very short period the controlling contracting authority transferred shares in the controlled entity to a private undertaking, then this is considered a device designed to conceal the award of public service contracts to semi-public companies. As a result, such a device would prejudice the effectiveness and the principles of the public procurement Directives.[115]

Parking Brixen prevents similarity of control in situations where there is visibility of imminent participation of private capital in a wholly owned public undertaking or entity. Interestingly, although *ANAV* extends the *Teckal* criteria to companies limited by shares, it appears to link prospective privatizations as grounds for not meeting the *Teckal* exception.[116] The Court held that if, for the duration of a contract, the capital of the controlled entity, which has been awarded the contract based on the *Teckal* in-house criteria, is open to private shareholders, then this would constitute an award of a public contract to a semi-public company without any call for competition. This, in turn, would interfere with the objectives pursued by the Procurement Directives and the principles of Community law.[117]

The combination of inferences found in *Parking Brixen* and *ANAV* should be viewed as defense mechanisms in order to prevent abuse of the *Teckal* exception, even when, at the time of the award of an in-house public contract, there is no private sector participation in the capital of the controlled entity. One could question this logic, as the Court reflected on situations where it invited national courts to pay consideration to future privatization exercises or to open up wholly owned public undertakings' capital to private investors, dictated by either law or regulation or selected as policy choices by the contracting authority.[118] Emphasis was drawn upon the concept of institutional public-private partnerships, where contracting authorities entrust the delivery of public services. Additionally, prospective privatizations could cause problems with the actual contractual arrangements, if *ANAV* is to apply to in-house relations once a contract is well into its delivery.

Sea appears to correct the potential problems stemming from *AVAV*. As a general rule, the existence of a private holding in the capital of the company to which a public contract is awarded must be determined at the time of that award.[119] Account should be taken in cases when national applicable legislation provides for the compulsory opening of that company whose entire capital it holds, in the short term, to other

---

[115] See Case C-29/04, *Commission v Austria* [2005] ECR I-563.

[116] See Case C-410/04, *Associazione Nazionale Autotrasporto Viaggiatori (ANAV) v Comune di Bari, AMTAB Servizio SpA* [2006] ECR I-3303.

[117] See ibid, para 48.

[118] See Case C-573/07, *Sea Srl. v Comune di Ponte Nossa* [2009] ECR I-8127, para 24.

[119] See Case C-573/07, *Sea Srl. v Comune di Ponte Nossa* [2009] ECR I-08127; see also Case C-26/03, *Stadt Halle, RPL Recyclingpark Lochau GmbH v Arbeitsgemeinschaft Thermische Restabfall und Energieverwertungsanlage TREA Leuna* [2005] ECR I-1, paras 15, 52.

capital.[120] However, when shares in the contracting entity, which were previously wholly owned by the contracting authority, are transferred to a private undertaking shortly after the award of a contract to that undertaking, the in-house exemption is not possible because the transfer is viewed as an artificial device to circumvent public procurement rules.[121] Nevertheless, shares in a public company could be sold at any time to third parties. It would be inconsistent with the principle of legal certainty not to apply the in-house exemption on the mere possibility that the capital structure of a publicly controlled company might change in the future.

The Capital Holding of an In-house Entity

According to the case-law, a contracting authority cannot exercise in-house control over an entity when one or more private undertakings also participate in the ownership of that entity.[122] That is the case even if the contracting authority is able to independently make all decisions regarding that entity, regardless of the private holding. The Court reasoned that the relationship between a contracting authority and its own departments is governed by considerations and requirements proper to the pursuit of objectives in the public interest.

By contrast, any private capital investment in an undertaking follows considerations proper to private interests and pursues objectives of a different kind. This is also relevant for pure capital injections by a private company into the in-house entity (for example, the buying of shares, not the provision of standard loans), even if this does not involve any operational contribution. As a general rule, the determination of the existence of a private holding in the capital of the company to which the public contract at issue is awarded must be undertaken at the time of the award.[123] Exceptionally, special circumstances may require events occurring after the date on which the contract was awarded to be taken into consideration. Such is the case, in particular, when shares in the contracting company, previously wholly owned by the contracting authority, are transferred to a private undertaking shortly after the contract at issue has been awarded to that company by means of an artificial device designed to circumvent the relevant EU rules.[124] The future opening of the company's capital is taken into account only if there is a real prospect of such opening in the short term at the time of the award of a contract to the company.[125]

---

120 See Case C-458/03, *Parking Brixen* [2005] ECR I-8612, paras 67, 72.

121 See Case C-29/04, *Commission v Austria* [2005] ECR I-9705, paras 38–41.

122 'By contrast, the participation, even as a minority, of a private undertaking in the capital of a company in which the contracting authority in question is also a participant excludes in any event the possibility that the contracting authority exercising over that company a control similar to that which it exercises over its own departments. See *Stadt Halle, RPL Recyclingpark Lochau GmbH v Arbeitsgemeinschaft Thermische Restabfall und Energieverwertungsanlage TREA Leuna* [2005] ECR I-1 para 49.

123 See Case C-29/04, *Commission v Austria* [2005] ECR I-9705, paras 24–26.

124 See Case C-29/04, *Commission v Austria* [2005] ECR I-9705, paras 38–41.

125 This position has meanwhile been confirmed by the ECJ in Case C-371/05, *Commission v Italy*, [2008] ECR I-110, para 29.

The mere theoretical possibility of a private party participating in the capital of an in-house entity does not in itself undermine the in-house relationship between the contracting authority and its company. However, if a contract were to be awarded to the company without being put out to competitive tender on the basis of the in-house exception, the subsequent acquisition of a stake in the company by private investors at any time during the period of validity of the contract would constitute an alteration of a fundamental condition of the award of the contract. Under these circumstances, the contract has to be put out to competitive tender. Conversely, the sole ownership by contracting authorities should be regarded as an indication of the existence of the control required for the in-house exception, but not as a factor that is decisive *per se.*[126] This indication is rebutted where contracting authorities establish a profit-making company that is fully independent of them. This is also illustrated by the *Parking Brixen* case, in which the entity was, at the time of the award, owned by one contracting authority but enjoyed a degree of independence, which led the Court to deny the in-house status.[127]

If a company's capital is wholly owned by the contracting authority, alone or together with other public authorities, when the contract in question is awarded to that company, the potential opening of the company's capital to private investors may not be taken into consideration unless there exists a real prospect in the short term of such an opening. Therefore, when the capital of the contracting company is wholly public and in which there is no actual sign of any impending opening of that company's capital to private shareholders, the mere fact that private undertakings, at some point in time, may hold capital in the company does not support the conclusion that the condition relating to the control by the public authority over that company is not present. That conclusion is not contradictory to *Coname*, which indicated that the fact that a company is open to private capital prevents it from being regarded as a structure for the 'in-house' management of a public service on behalf of the municipalities that form part of it.[128] In this case, a public service was awarded to a company in which not all, but most, of the capital was public at the time of that award. *Sea* clarifies that when a contract is awarded to a public capital company, without subjection to competitive tender, the fact that subsequent to the award but during the contract's period of validity, private shareholders were permitted to hold capital in the company constitutes an alteration of a fundamental condition of the contract. This scenario does not regard the contract as an in-house arrangement. It therefore requires the full applicability of the Public Procurement Directives.

---

[126] See Case C-340/04, *Carbotermo SpA and Consorzio Alisei v Comune di Busto Arsizio and AGESP SpA*. [2006] ECR I-04137, para 37, (the fact that the contracting authority holds, alone or together with other public authorities, all of the share capital in a successful tenderer tends to indicate, without being decisive, that that contracting authority exercises over that company a control similar to that which it exercises over its own departments'.

[127] See Case C-458/03, *Parking Brixen GmbH v. Gemeinde Brixen and Stadtwerke Brixen AG* [2005] ECR I-8585, para 70.

[128] See Case C-231/03, *Coname* [2005] ECR I-7287, paras 5, 28.

Operational Dependency

The second *Teckal* criterion specifies that an essential part of the controlled entity's activities must be carried out for the benefit of the controlling contracting authority or authorities.[129] *Sea* held that the control exercised over that company by the shareholder authorities may be regarded as similar to that which they exercise over their own departments when the company's activity is limited to the territory of those authorities and is carried on essentially for its benefit.[130] The Court maintained, in *Parking Brixen*, that the essential part of the controlled entities actives cannot be carried out for the benefit of the controlling public authority if the geographical area has been extended to the entire country and abroad.[131]

The 'essential part' criterion relates to a certain minimum proportion of the total activities performed by the controlled body.[132] However, not only quantitative elements must be taken into account in determining the term 'essential'. While it could be convenient to define the essential part criterion in line with a provision governing awards to undertakings affiliated with the contracting authority, namely the 80 per cent criterion, the Court has rejected such an approach on the grounds that a transposition of an exceptional provision from the Utilities Directive to the Public Sector Directive is of questionable *vires*.[133] *Carbotermo* revealed interesting insights on operational dependency.[134] The Court declared that the 80 per cent rule of affiliated operational dependency cannot be imported into the public sector procurement because such provision is regarded as being a restrictively interpreted exception applicable only to supply contracts covering affiliated undertakings. Supply contracts covering affiliated undertakings are distinctively different from public sector procurement entities because they are subject to a procedural notification regime, which cannot be implemented in public sector procurement Directives. Finally, supply contracts covering affiliated undertakings were explicitly ignored by the Community legislature during the 2004 reform of the Public Procurement Directives from incorporation into the public sector Directive 2004/18.[135]

---

[129] See Case C-107/98, *Teckal Slr v Comune di Viano* [1999] ECR I-8121.

[130] See Case C-573/07, *Sea Srl. v Comune di Ponte Nossa* [2009] ECR I-8127.

[131] See Case C-458/03, *Parking Brixen GmbH v Gemeinde Brixen and Stadtwerke Brixen AG* [2005] ECR I-8612, para 65.

[132] See C.H. Bovis, 'Public Procurement in the EU: Jurisprudence and Conceptual Directions' (2012) 49 *Common Market Law Review* 1–44.

[133] See Directive 2004/18, [2004] OJ L134 on the coordination of procedures for the award of public works contracts, public supply contracts and public service contracts. Also, see Directive 2004/17, [2004] OJ L134 coordinating the procurement procedures of entities operating in the water, energy, transport and postal services sectors.

[134] See Case C-340/04, *Carbotermo Spa v Comune di Busto Arsizio* [2006] ECR I-4137.

[135] See the proposal from the European Commission [2001] OJ C29E/11 and [2002] OJ C203E/210; the opinion of the Economic and Social Committee [2001] OJ C193/7; the opinion of the Committee of the Regions [2001] OJ C144/23; the opinion of the European Parliament of 17 January 2002 [2002] OJ C271E/176), Council Common Position of 20 March 2003 [2003] OJ C147/1) and Position of the European Parliament of 2 July 2003. See also the Legislative Resolution of the European Parliament of 29 January 2004 and Decision of the Council of 2 February 2004.

So, although an 'essential part' indicates a quantitative measure in relation to turnover or financial quantum of the volume of activities performed by the controlled entity, qualitative factors such as strategic services, organizational planning, market analysis, the profitability of the entity in pursuit of the activities for the controlling authority, and also the market dynamics under which the controlled entity operates should be taken into account. *Carbotermo* also ruled that to determine whether an undertaking carries out the essential part of its activities with the controlling authority account must be taken of all the activities that the undertaking carries out on the basis of an award made by the contracting authority, regardless of who pays for those activities.[136] The Court reiterated that the territory where the activities are carried out is highly relevant for determining the essential feature of the *Teckal* exception.

If the public authority that receives an essential part of an entity's activities controls that entity through another company, the control criterion is still present, provided that control is demonstrable at all levels of the contracting authority's corporate interface.

Public–Public Partnerships

A public authority may perform public interest tasks conferred to it by using its own administrative, technical and other resources, without being obliged to call on outside entities that are not a part of its own departments.[137] The possibility for public authorities to use their own resources to perform the public interest tasks conferred on them may also be exercised in cooperation with other public authorities.[138]

Commission v Germany provided a superb demonstration of flexibility in the hands of contracting authorities in relation to their freedom to organize and deliver public services.[139] Co-operation between independent contracting authorities in the form of establishing an entity upon which no similar control is exercised to that over their own departments, resulting in the entrustment of a contract on behalf of the participant contracting authorities, can be deemed to meet the criteria for an in-house exception. Such a classification is warranted provided a variety of conditions are satisfied: (i) the remit of such public cooperation exists in relation to a public task or service specified under Community law, (ii) there is no intention to circumvent public procurement rules, and (iii) the contractual relation is based on neither a pecuniary interest consideration nor payments between the entity and the participant contracting authorities. The Court used an analogy with *Coditel Brabant* where contractual relations between inter-municipal cooperative societies whose members are contracting authorities and a jointly controlled entity can be deemed in-house.[140]

---

[136] See Case C-340/04, *Carbotermo SpA, Consorzio Alisei v Comune di Busto Arsizio, AGESP SpA* [2006] ECR I-4137.

[137] See Case C-26/03, *Stadt Halle and RPL Lochau* [2005] ECR I-1, para 48.

[138] See Case 295/05, *Asociación Nacional de Empresas Forestales (Asemfo) v. Transformación Agraria SA (Tragsa) and Administración del Estado* [2007] ECR I-2999, para 65.

[139] See Case C-480/06, *Commission v Germany* [2009] ECR I-4747.

[140] See Case C-324/07, *Coditel Brabant SA v Commune d'Uccle, Région de Bruxelles-Capitale* [2009] 1 CMLR 29.

The Court also accepted public-public cooperation outside the concept of jointly controlled in-house entities. The Court stressed that EU law does not require contracting authorities to use any particular legal form in order to jointly carry out their public service tasks. For the purposes of this document, this type of cooperation is qualified as 'non-institutional' or 'horizontal', involving different contracting authorities. Until now this has been the only judgment of the Court on public-public cooperation that has not involved jointly controlled in-house entities. The Court appears to have relied on many individual circumstances that were relevant to this particular case in order to arrive at its conclusion.[141] Nevertheless, considering the aspects of the judgment that could be of general relevance, it appears reasonable to conclude that contracting authorities may establish horizontal cooperation among themselves (without creating a jointly controlled 'in-house' entity). In order to do so, they must conclude agreements not covered by EU public procurement law. Such a conclusion is reasonable only if, at a minimum, the following conditions are met: (i) the arrangement involves only contracting authorities, and there is no participation of private capital; (ii) the character of the agreement is that of real cooperation aimed at the joint performance of a common task, as opposed to a normal public contract; and (iii) their cooperation is governed only by considerations relating to the public interest.[142]

The aim of public-public cooperation is to jointly ensure the execution of a public task that all of the cooperating partners have to perform. Such joint execution is characterized by the participation and mutual obligations of the contractual partners, which lead to mutual synergy effects. This does not necessarily mean that each of the cooperating partners participates equally in the actual performance of the task – the cooperation may be based on a division of tasks or on a certain specialization. Nevertheless, the contract needs to address a common aim, namely the joint performance of the same task. Case-law also suggests that the character of the agreement needs to be that of real cooperation, as opposed to a normal public contract where one party is performing a certain task against remuneration.[143] Such a unilateral assignment of a task by one contracting authority to another cannot be considered as cooperation.

Cooperation is governed by considerations relating to the pursuit of objectives in the public interest. Thus, while it may involve mutual rights and obligations, it must not involve financial transfers between the public cooperating partners, other than those corresponding to the reimbursement of actual costs of the works/services/supplies: service provision against remuneration is a characteristic of public contracts subject to the EU public procurement rules.

---

[141] The Court concluded that public-public cooperation does itself reflect no similarity of control, rather the remit of such relation to deliver a public task or service specified under Community law; the ultimate tests are no intention to circumvent public procurement rules and not pecuniary contractual relation. See Case C-480/06, *Commission v Germany* [2009] ECR I-4747; the Court also inferred to inter-municipal cooperative societies whose members are contracting authorities and a jointly controlled entity as a benchmark feature of specific criteria of public-public cooperation. See Case C-324/07, *Coditel Brabant SA v Commune d'Uccle, Région de Bruxelles-Capitale* [2009] 1 CMLR 29.

[142] See Case C-480/06, *Commission v Germany* [2009] ECR I-4747.

[143] See Case C-324/07, *Coditel Brabant SA v Commune d'Uccle, Région de Bruxelles-Capitale* [2009] 1 CMLR 29.

Restrictions on Public–Public Cooperation

The Court stated that the cooperation should only be governed by public interest considerations. Thus, it would not be exempt if it were guided, that is, principally determined, by other considerations, especially commercial ones. Therefore, in principle, the cooperating partners should not perform activities on the market as part of the cooperation. In other words, the cooperation agreement should not include activities to be offered on the open market. It can be established that normal public contracts between contracting authorities continue to be subject to the procurement obligations (for example, the purchase of certain services from another contracting authority). However, contracting authorities can establish structures to cooperate with each other, whether they are institutional or not. It has been argued that the entry into force of the Lisbon Treaty puts this case-law of the Court into a different light.[144] It is true that the Lisbon Treaty caused major changes to the EU legal system as a whole, which should be taken into account also when interpreting secondary EU legislation.

One of the relevant modifications introduced by the Lisbon Treaty is the acknowledgement of local and regional self-governance.[145] Furthermore, Article 1 of Protocol (No. 26) on Services of General Interest of the Lisbon Treaty on the Functioning of the EU acknowledges the essential role, and wide discretion, of national, regional and local authorities in providing, commissioning and organizing services of general economic interest as closely as possible to the needs of the users.[146] These provisions confirm authorities' right to decide how to execute the services that they are obliged to provide to the public. On the other hand, while the existence of this right was not disputed, even in the past, it is clear that it needs to be exercised in accordance with other provisions of EU law. Accordingly, certain choices made by contracting authorities might imply the need to comply with EU public procurement law. EU law does not force contracting authorities to externalize, but to ensure that if contracting authorities decide to involve a separate entity – public or private – on a commercial basis, this is done in a transparent and non-discriminatory manner. In view of the Commission services, the two forms of vertical and horizontal public-public cooperation are two equally available means for contracting authorities to organize the performance of their public tasks outside the scope of application of EU public procurement law. The Court clearly confirmed that EU law does not require contracting authorities to use any particular legal form in order to carry out jointly their public service tasks. While there are structurally two different types of public–public cooperation outside EU public procurement law, they share some common characteristics.

---

[144] Drijber and Stergiou, 'Public Procurement Law and Internal Market Law' (2009) 46 *Common Market Law Review* 805–46; See Bovis, 'Public Procurement and Public Services in the EU', *supra* note 43.

[145] See Article 4(2) TFEU.

[146] See Article 1 of Protocol (No. 26) on Services of General Interest. This Protocol provides that services of general economic interest are subject to the rules of the internal market while noting users' preferences may differ, taking into consideration different geographical, social or cultural situations. Non-economic services are not covered by the rules of the single market and competition, and are not subject to specific EU legislation.

A contracting authority may perform the public interest tasks with its own resources, without recourse to entities outside its own departments, and it may do so in cooperation with other contracting authorities, either in an institutional cooperation through a jointly controlled in-house entity or without establishing such an institutional form. Secondly, it seems clear from the case-law of the Court that in order to be exempted from the application of the EU public procurement rules, any public-public cooperation must remain purely public.[147] The participation of private capital in one of the cooperating entities will thus prevent the cooperation from being exempted from public procurement rules.

If the cooperating entities are market oriented, they are in direct competition with private operators having the same or similar commercial objectives and instruments. Cooperation which is exempt from the procurement rules and aimed at fulfilling a public task should only involve entities which are principally not active on the market with a commercial purpose. This results primarily from the fact that the cooperation partners must be contracting authorities. The status of public authorities entails limits to their activities, while bodies governed by public law have to be 'established for the specific purpose of meeting needs in the general interest, not having an industrial or commercial character'.[148] Furthermore, in vertical cooperation, the in-house entity has to perform the essential part of its activities for the contracting authorities that control it. Any activity performed on the market has to remain incidental to these core activities, because a possible market orientation would weaken the joint control required in vertical cooperation.

In relation to horizontal cooperation, the Court stated that, where cooperation between public authorities is governed solely by considerations and requirements relating to the pursuit of objectives in the public interest, it does not undermine the principal objective of the EU rules on public procurement, namely the free movement of services and the opening-up of undistorted competition in all the Member States This is the case if the cooperation does not involve any commercial considerations. The Court stressed that EU law does not require contracting authorities to use any particular legal form in order to carry out jointly their public service tasks. Although there is no such requirement, looking at the two forms of vertical and horizontal public-public cooperation it should be noted that the type of connection between the cooperating entities is different and needs to be addressed.

In an institutional cooperation, it is the presence of a (joint) in-house control that could lead even an agreement to being exempted from the scope of the procurement regime that would normally be covered by it. In other words, the in-house exception relates to an otherwise covered public procurement contract for the performance of a task against remuneration. By contrast, in the case of non-institutional cooperation, in

---

147 See Cases C-26/03, *Stadt Halle and RPL Lochau* [2005] ECR I-1, para 48; C-295/05, *Asociación Nacional de Empresas Forestales (Asemfo) v Transformación Agraria SA (Tragsa) and Administración del Estado* [2007] ECR I-2999, para 65; C-480/06, *Commission v Germany* [2009] ECR I-4747; C-324/07, *Coditel Brabant SA v Commune d'Uccle, Région de Bruxelles-Capitale* [2009] 1 CMLR 29.

148 See C.H. Bovis, 'Developing Public Procurement Regulation: Jurisprudence and its Influence on Law Making', (2006) 43 Common Market Law Review 461–95.

order to distinguish it from a normal public contract, it seems to be important that the character of the former is that of cooperation involving mutual rights and obligations going beyond 'performance of a task against remuneration' and that the aim of the cooperation is not of a commercial nature.[149]

CONCLUSIONS

The phenomenon of public-private partnerships and the recent developments in public-public cooperation represent a genuine attempt to revolutionize the delivery of public services by introducing the private sector as a strategic investor and financier of public services.[150] First, the private sector assumes a direct responsibility in serving the public interest, as part of its contractual obligations *vis-à-vis* the public sector. The motive and the intention behind such an approach focuses on the benefits that would follow as a result of the private sector's involvement in the delivery of public services. Efficiency gains, qualitative improvement, innovation, value-for-money and flexibility appear as the most important ones, whereas an overall better allocation of public capital resources sums up the advantages of engaging with the private sector in delivery of public services. Public-private partnerships as a concept of public sector management have changed the methodology of assessing delivery of public services both in qualitative and quantitative terms.

The case for PPPs rests on the relative efficiency of the private sector. However, this efficiency must demonstrate itself in a dynamic mode, reflecting the need for competition in the provision of the relevant services through the PPP. In traditional corporatism, public procurement through tendering secured the repeated competition for a market that is inherently monopolistic, yet still contestable, by new entries or offerings. However, the scope for competition in the activities undertaken by PPPs is more limited, because they tend to be less contestable for reasons involving the longevity of the engagement between public and private sectors, and the fact that social infrastructure is undervalued, and economic infrastructure involves large sunk costs.[151]

For PPPs to operate in a competitive environment globally, safeguard the principles of transparency and accountability in public sector management, incentive-based regulation is paramount. Where a private sector operator can sell public services to the public, but there is little scope for competition, the public sector must regulate prices. However, the challenge is to design well-functioning regulation that increases output towards the social optimum, stabilizes prices in a sustainable manner, and limits monopoly profit, while preserving the incentive for private sector to be more efficient and reduce costs. The Commission announced its intention to introduce a legislative

---

[149] Ibid.

[150] See C.H. Bovis, 'The Conceptual Links between State Aid and Public Procurement in the Financing of Services of General Economic Interest', in M. Krajewski, U.B. Neergaard and J.W. van de Gronden (eds), *The Changing Legal Framework for Services of General Interest in Europe, Between Competition and Solidarity* (The Hague: Asser Press 2009) 149–71.

[151] See M. Bult-Spiering and G. Dewulf, *Strategic Issues in Public-Private Partnerships: An International Perspective* (Oxford: Blackwell Publishing 2007).

framework on concessions.[152] The Europe 2020 strategy highlights the importance of PPPs for accelerating growth and boosting innovation.[153] In addition, the Single Market Act announced the adoption of a legislative initiative on concessions in 2011 in order to promote PPPs and to help deliver better value for money for users of services and for contracting authorities, while improving market access for EU undertakings by ensuring transparency, equal treatment and a level playing field across the EU.[154] The Commission considers a legislative proposal in the field of concessions as one of the key measures that will facilitate the setting up of PPPs and as such, considers it a means of stimulating economic recovery in the context of the current economic downturn. PPPs are also important for accomplishing structural reforms and could play an increasing role in accompanying EU policies in the context of the multiannual financial framework.

The main reasons for the adoption of a set of rules on concessions, which are separate from the framework of the substantive Public Procurement Directives, is to reflect the differences of the objectives pursued, as well as the very nature of the envisaged rules on concessions. The purpose of the new directive on concessions envisages a comprehensive, clear and unambiguous set of provisions in an economic area of the Member States, which so far has been characterized by a continuous uncertainty and erroneous interpretation, often leaving room for unlawful practices. Further, concession contracts display a number of distinct characteristics as compared to public contracts. These include the exposure of the contractor to the economic risk of providing the services, much longer contractual duration in comparison to traditional public contracts, greater structural complexity and higher contract value. The most distinctive feature of service concessions reveals a plethora of national rules determining the status of concessions in Member States. The proposal provides for an extension of the scope of the Remedies Directives to all concession contracts above the threshold in order to guarantee effective channels for challenging the award decision in court and provide minimal judicial standards that must be observed by contracting authorities or entities.[155]

[152] See Commission Communication, *The Single Market Act Twelve levers to boost growth and strengthen confidence* of 13 April 2011, COM/2011/0206 fin.

[153] See Commission Communication, Europe 2020, A strategy for smart, sustainable and inclusive growth, COM (2010)2020 final.

[154] See Commission, *Guide to the application of the European Union rules on State aid, public procurement and the internal market to services of general economic interest, and in particular to social services of general interest*, SEC(2010)1545 final. See Commission, *Buying Social: A Guide to Taking Account of Social Considerations in Public Procurement*, SEC(2010)1258, fin.

[155] See Directive 2007/66/EC of 11 December 2007, [2007] OJ L335/31.

19. Concessions and public procurement

Steven van Garsse

INTRODUCTION

Concessions have been given a lot of attention over the past years as instruments for the implementation of public-private partnerships.[1] The European Parliament, the Council and the European Commission have recently studied concessions in the context of a new specific Directive which envisages the organisation of increased transparency.[2] Taking into consideration the fact that concessions were quasi unregulated, the result would be negative effects for the implementation of the internal market and a negative impact on the achievement of best value for public money.[3]

Concessions from an EU Perspective

However, the use of concessions or concession contracts is nothing new. A concession was used at the time that the Eiffel Tower was constructed in France. In 1887 a concession agreement was signed between the Minister of Trade and Industry, the city of Paris and Gustave Eiffel, a French engineer.[4] The agreement provided among other things that Mr Eiffel had to finance the largest part of the construction, but would also acquire the right to exploit the tower (including the possibility to establish cafés and

---

[1] S. Arrowsmith, *The Law of Public and Utilities Procurement* 2nd edn. (London: Sweet & Maxwell 2005) 31; C. Bovis, *EC Public Procurement: Case Law and Regulation* (Oxford: Oxford University Press 2006) 463; F. Moises, J.-F. Jaminet and A. Vandeburie, *Promotion immobilière publique. Partenariats public-privé en Region walonne et en Communauté française* (Paris: Larcier 2009) 164; C. Guettier, *Droits des contrats administratifs* (Paris: PUF 2004) 8; P. Flamme, M.-A. Flamme and C. Dardenne, *Les marchés publics Européens et Belges* 2nd edn (Paris: Larcier 2009) 253; S. Van Garsse, 'De concessieve techniek: oud en nieuw instrument van PPS' in D. D'Hooghe and F. Vandendriessche (eds), *Publiek-private samenwerking* (Brugge: die Keure 2004) 27; F. Lichère, *Public-Private Partnerships: Reports of the XVIII Congress of the International Academy of Comparative Law* (Brussels: Bruylant 2011) xiii.

[2] See, *inter alia*, Proposal for a directive of the European Parliament and of the Council on the award of concession contracts, SEC(2011) 1588 final, SEC(2011) 1589 final, Brussels, 20 December 2011 COM(2011) 897 final 2011/0437 (COD); Press release, Procurement package: MEPs close deal with Council on concession contracts, IMCO, 26 June 2013.

[3] Commission Staff Working Document Impact Assessment of an Initiative on Concessions. Accompanying the document Proposal for a directive of the European Parliament and of the Council on the award of concession contracts COM(2011) 897 final, SEC(2011) 1589 final, Brussels, 20 December 2011 SEC(2011) 1588 final.

[4] X, Bezançon, *2000 ans d'histoire du partenariat public-privé pour la réalisation des équipements et services collectifs* (Paris: Presses de l'école nationale des Ponts et chaussées 2004) 225.

restaurants there) during the World Exhibition of 1889 as well as for a period of 20 years following this. In Belgium a large part of the railway network was historically constructed by private concessionaires.[5] Use was made thereby of very specific legislation as a result of which private concessionaires acquired the right, after competing, to construct a specified rail track connection at their own cost and thereupon to operate this long-term, also at their personal risk and expense.

However, to simply retrace the concessions concept to instruments of public-private partnership and/or unregulated forms of public procurement would be incorrect. The term concession is much wider. There are many different types of concession. The concept is also not used in all countries in the same way, and it is even used in different ways within one single country and within one branch of the law.[6] This contribution will therefore first of all discuss the concept of concession. Thereupon it will discuss the forms which are given the most attention in procurement law: the concessions for (public) works and (public) services. Attention must thereby be paid to the gradual anchoring of the concessions in procurement law and to the demarcation of the concepts, as well as to the legal regime as this has been shaped, among other things, through case-law. Thereupon the new Directive concerning concessions will be discussed. Not only will the demarcation of the area of application of the new Directive be discussed, but also the legal regime which must be taken into consideration under this Directive.

The Concession Concept from a Comparative Law Perspective

From an etymological point of view the word concession originates from the Latin 'concedere', which mean among other things 'to give', 'to licence' or 'to grant'. This meaning has also often returned to concessions today. The word concession is used for example for a grant of a tract of land made by a government in return for stipulated services or a promise that the land will be used for a specific purpose, but also more generally for an exclusive right to approve being allowed somewhere to organise a specified economic activity and/or service of general interest.[7]

In some cases the concession is given a contractual character (a 'concession agreement').[8] In other cases the concession is considered to be a unilateral

---

[5] For example in 1870 the majority of the lines was in the hands of concessionaires: H. Van der Wee, 'Twee eeuwen spoorwegen en economische ontwikkeling' in B. Van Der Herten, M. Van Meerten and G. Verbeurgt (eds), *Sporen in België. 15 jaar spoorwegen. 5 jaar NMBS* (Leuven: Leuven University Press 2001) 78.

[6] *Infra.*

[7] G. Loyrette Nouel, *Concession Assessment Project, Cover Analysis Report* (EBRD 2004) 16: 'Concessions are often defined as 'the right to use' (sometimes qualified as exclusive) certain objects ... and perform certain activities ... . Concessions are also defined in certain laws by reference to a lease ... sometimes restricted to certain sectors.'

[8] See for example Article 1(4) Directive 2004/18/EC of the European Parliament and of the Council of 31 March 2004 on the coordination of procedures for the award of public works contracts, public supply contracts and public service contracts, [2004] OJ L134: 'Service concession is a contract of the same type as a public service contract except for the fact that the

act.[9] Sometimes concessions are considered to be legal concepts with a partly contractual character and partly unilateral character.[10] In certain countries concessions, or more precisely certain types of concessions, are anchored through a statutory context. In other countries there is no (specific) statutory context whatsoever available.[11] The legal status of the concessions is also not unambiguous. Sometimes concessions are located in private law (private law concession agreements), sometimes concessions are located in public law (public law concession agreement and public law concession decision).[12]

When we look into the use of the term concession from an administrative law perspective in a continental European context, one or more of the following types of concessions can be traced:[13]

- The domain concession: an (administrative)[14] contract for the exclusive use of government property which forms part of the public domain (this is a category of

---

consideration for the provision of services consists either solely in the right to exploit the service or in this right together with payment.'

[9] Cf J. W Salacuse, *The Three Laws of International Investment. National, Contractual and International Frameworks for Foreign Capital* (Oxford: Oxford University Press 2013) 228.

[10] Cf Belgium: port/domain concessions and public service concessions are frequently considered as mixed. See C.E. Knesselare, 85.875, 14 March 2000; E. Van Hooydonk, *Beginselen van Havenbestuursrecht* (Brugge: die Keure 1996) 279 at 121; M. Pâques, *De l'acte unilatéral au contrat dans l'action administrative* (Brussels: Story-Scientia 1991) 203–4. Cf in France for public service concession: L. Richer, *Droit des contrats administratifs* (Paris: LGDJ 2004) 62–4 and more recently the interpretation whereby the mixed character is ascribed to the fact that specific clauses of the concession would have a regulatory effect or character. Ibid.

[11] G. Loyrette Nouel, *Concession Assessment Project, Cover Analysis Report* (EBRD 2004) and Analytical Overview of the Framework of EU Member States regarding the Awarding of Concession Contracts. Briefing note (2012) 7, available 4 February 2016 at http://www.europarl.europa.eu/document/activities/cont/201206/20120619ATT47200/20120619ATT47200EN.pdf.

[12] For example M. Davids, *De weg naar zelfstandigheid: de voorgeschiedenis van de verzelfstandiging van de PTT in 1989* (Hilversum: Uitgeverij Verloren 1999) 183; DLMT Dankers-Hagenaars, *Op het spoor van de concessie. Een onderzoek naar het rechtskarakter van de concessie in Nederland en in Frankrijk* (The Hague: Boom Juridische Uitgevers 2000) 227–8; M.B. Nijhof, *De concessie in Europeesrechtelijk perspectief* (Deventer: Kluwer 2000) 229–300.

[13] Compare Phd research: A. Blondeau, *La concession de service public. Etude d'histoire du droit administratif* (Grenoble: Imprimerie Allier Père et Fils 1929) 6; C. Bettinger, *La concession de service public et de travaux publics* (Paris : Berger-Levrault 1978) 2; DLMT Dankers-Hagenaars, *Op het spoor van de concessie. Een onderzoek naar het rechtskarakter van de concessie in Nederland en in Frankrijk* (The Hague: Boom Juridische Uitgevers 2000) 13 and 31; S. Van Garsse, *De concessie in het raam van de publiek-private samenwerking. Een analyse van het openbaar en het privaat domein, van de domeinconcessies, de concessies van openbare werken, de concessies van diensten en hun aanbesteding* (Antwerp: die Keure 2007) 47.

[14] With the term 'administrative' one often intends to indicate that not the same rules apply, or not automatically, as to other 'normal' contracts, or that also specific rules of administrative law. In Civil Law countries the rules which date back to the Code Napoleon (Code Civil, etc.) apply to normal contracts. Cf. L. Marcus, *L'Unité des contrats publics* (Paris: Dalloz 2010) and R. Noguellou and U. Stelkens (eds), *Droit Comparé des Contrats Publics –Comparative Law on Public Contracts* (Brussels: Bruylant 2010); A.Q.C. Tak, *De overheid in het burgerlijk recht* ('s-Gravenhage: VUGA 1997) 272.

property with a public designation which is subject to a special legal regime). A typical example of this is the concessions in port areas. Private concessionaires acquire an exclusive right of use to use a part of the port area for operating their port-related activities (transfer, storage and so on).

- The concession for public services:[15] an (administrative) contract whereby the government grants the right to operate a public service at the risk of the concessionaire. A typical example is a service concession to operate a transport service such as a tramway.
- The concession for public works: an (administrative) contract whereby the assignment is given to construct a specified work at the risk of the concessionaire and the latter acquires the right to operate this work. A typical example is a toll road concession.
- The concession for the operation of natural resources: the contract or the legal act whereby the beneficiary acquires the right to exploit natural resources in a specified area. A typical example is mining concessions with which one acquires the rights so that mining can be carried out underground.

It can be ascertained in a more international context that the term is mainly used for the construction of large infrastructure works and/or public services, often in the context of public-private partnerships. The term is sometimes referred to as a technique for assignment or a form of organisation whether or not with specific characteristics *vis-à-vis* other techniques, and other times as one of the most important agreements necessary for the construction of the project.[16]

It is clear from the above that the concept of concession can have various meanings. It was noted elsewhere therefore that the term concession in itself has little significance. From a legal point of view the term only has meaning if the type of concession concerned is additionally stated. To prevent a confusion of ideas it is therefore necessary to always identify and/or clarify which type of concession is concerned.

---

[15] See for example in France: 'Le contrat qui charge un particulier ou une société d'exécuter un ouvrage public ou d'assurer un service public à ses frais, avec ou sans subvention, avec ou sans garantie d'intérët et qui les rémunère en lui confidant l'exploitation de l'ouvrage ou de l'exploitation du service public avec le droit de percevoir des redevances sur les usagers de l'ouvrage ou sur ceux qui bénéficient du service public'. (CE 30 march 1916, Cie d'éclairage de Bordeaux (1916)RDP *213*, concl. M Chardenet). See in Belgium: 'un contrat administratif par lequel les autorités publiques chargent temporairement un particulier de gérer un service public à ses frais, risques et périls, sous leur contröle et selon les modalities qu'ells determinant, moyennant une remuneration u'il doit en principe percevour à charge des usagers'. P. Orianne, *La Loi et le contrat dans les concessions de service public* (Paris : Larcier 1961) 84.

[16] Cf. Eurostat: concessions are defined as projects where most of the revenue is generated by third party users. (Commission Staff Working Document Impact Assessment of an Initiative on Concessions. Accompanying the document Proposal for a directive of the European Parliament and of the Council on the award of concession contracts COM(2011) 897 final, SEC(2011) 1589 final, Brussels, 20 December 2011 SEC(2011) 1588 final, 1). Cf. *EBRD Core Principles for a Modern Concession Law – selection and justification of principles* Prepared by the EBRD Legal Team (sd) 7p; OECD, *Basic Elements of a law on Concessions Agreements*, 1999–2000. See also infra III.3.

In the following the emphasis is on concessions for (public) services and for (public) works. Those concessions are the ones which are given the most attention today at a European and international level. Those are the concessions which are the closest related to public procurement. Although it cannot be excluded that a number of the principles which are considered below (can be) are, as more general principles of EU law, relevant to other types of concessions, the utmost care must be taken to avoid confusion. Seeing that the other types of concessions have an entirely different objective (for example port concessions apply to the giving into use of a part of the port domain in which the concessionaire will develop private activities). The other objective and the often entirely different characteristics of those concessions imply that the principles of procurement law, as will also be explained below for services and works concessions, and the case-law which clarifies those principles cannot simply be applied as a blanket rule.

I. THE CONCESSIONS OF WORKS AND SERVICES IN EUROPEAN PROCUREMENT LAW

1. The Gradual Anchoring[17]

A. The immediate interest in the concessions

Taking into consideration the great importance of the concessions as a form of management and as a method of implementation for large construction projects in many Member States, the European institutions have paid the necessary attention to concessions from their commencement. The concession thus appeared as a point for attention in the General Programme for the Abolition of Restrictions on Freedom to Provide Services.[18]

Nonetheless, as will become evident, one was originally reticent with regard to concessions. Especially via the detour of procurement law, slowly but surely a more or less demarcated legal regime was outlined. We shall outline the development hereinafter.

B. The first Directives concerning public procurement (1970–1980)

Already during (the preparation of) the first Directives concerning public procurement, concessions were not entirely neglected.[19] This became evident first from the origins of the Liberalisation Directive of 26 July 1971 concerning the abolition of restrictions on

---

[17] S. Van Garsse, De concessie in het raam van de publiek-private samenwerking. Een analyse van het openbaar en het privaat domein, van de domeinconcessies, de concessies van openbare werken, de concessies van diensten en hun aanbesteding (Antwerp: die Keure 2007) 618–29.

[18] [1962] OJ 15 January, 33.

[19] M.-A. Flamme, 'La libération de la concurrence dans le marchés publics au sein de la C.E.E.' (1965) RMC 280 and 284; J. La Violette-Vanderpoorten, 'Les directives européennes relatives aux marchés publics de travaux' (1972) RMC 484–93; O. Raymundie, *Gestion déléguée des services publics en France et en Europe* (Paris: Le Moniteur 2006) 165–6.

freedom to provide services in respect of public works contracts and on the award of public works contracts to contractors acting through agencies or branches.[20] Therefore at first in the preamble of a proposal for a Liberalisation Directive it was determined that the Directive would also have to concern concessions for works.[21] This is because if this was not to be the case a considerable part of the works would escape the objectives of the Directive.[22] To achieve that objective the concept of public procurement was, *inter alia*, extended to concessions with private law entities and agreements between a concession holder and a contractor.[23] After comments from the Economic and Social Committee this also included concessions with public law legal entities.[24] The text proposals were ultimately not followed in the Liberalisation Directive. In the final Directive the only express reference to concessions that can be traced is in a recital.[25]

This is evident secondly from the Coordination Directive for the procedures for the awarding of public works contracts, also of 26 July 1971, and the coming into effect from that date.[26] There would also have been considerable prolonged discussion concerning the issue of whether or not it was advisable to regulate the concessions for works in the Coordination Directive.[27]

The concept of regulating concessions (for works) would be confronted with serious criticism from France and Italy.[28] Ultimately a compromise was reached within the Council. The concessions for public works were on the one hand expressly kept outside

---

[20] Council Directive 71/304/EEG of 26 July 1971, [1971] OJ L185/1.

[21] 'Voorstel voor een eerste richtlijn betreffende de deelneming van aannemers aan de gunning en de uitvoering van werken voor rekening van de staat, van zijn territoriale lichamen en andere publiekrechtelijke rechtspersonen, OJ 29 January 1965, 150; Resolution of the European Parliament' [1965] OJ 12 April, 885.

[22] 'Raadpleging van het Economisch en Sociaal Comité inzake een voorstel voor een eerste richtlijn betreffende de deelneming van aannemers aan de gunning en de uitvoering van werken voor rekening van de staat, van zijn territoriale lichamen en andere publiekrechtelijke rechtspersonen en een voorstel van wijzigingen in de Algemene Programma's inzake recht van vestiging en diensten' [1965] OJ 29 January, 150.

[23] Cf Article 4 'Voorstel voor een eerste richtlijn betreffende de deelneming van aannemers aan de gunning en de uitvoering van werken voor rekening van de staat, van zijn territoriale lichamen en andere publiekrechtelijke rechtspersonen' [1965] OJ 29 January, 152.

[24] 'Advies van het Economisch en Sociaal Comité' [1965] OJ 29 January, 160. Parallel in the proposal for amendment of the General Programmes concerning the right of establishment and services it was suggested to add that the rules concerning the award of public contracts for the implementation of works should also apply to the awarding of concessions for the implementation of public works. Cf 'Voorstel van wijzigingen in de algemene programma's inzake recht van vestiging en diensten' [1965] OJ 156/65.

[25] See nonetheless implicitly: Article 3(a) of Council Directive 71/304/EEG of 26 July 1971, [1971] OJ L185/1.

[26] Council Directive 71/305/EEC of 26 July 1971 concerning the coordination of procedures for the award of publics works contracts, [1971] OJ L185/5.

[27] J. La Violette-Vanderpoorten, 'Les directives européennes relatives aux marchés publics de travaux' (1972) RMC 484 ff.

[28] J. La Violette-Vanderpoorten, 'Les directives européennes relatives aux marchés publics de travaux' (1972) RMC 485.

the area of application of the Coordination Directive.[29] But on the other hand in Article 3(2) of the Directive it is determined that when the works concession holder is itself a contracting authority, the concession holder will (of course) be obliged to comply with the (national) procedures concerning public procurement for the works which the concession holder subcontracts to third parties. Also, in Article 3(3) of the Directive it is determined that if the concession grantor provides a works concession to a concession holder other than a contracting authority, the concession grantor must impose an obligation on the concession holder in the instrument of concession to comply with the principle of non-discrimination on the basis of nationality during the awarding of subcontracts to third parties. Furthermore a morally binding joint declaration of the representatives of the Member States was adopted concerning the procedures which must be followed with regard to concessions for the implementation of works.[30] This mainly contained notification requirements and regulations concerning the subcontracting of work by private concession holders. There soon followed a Directive concerning the details of publication of notices of public works contracts and concessions in the Official Journal of the European Union.[31]

C. The partial integration of concessions in the public procurement Directives (1980–1993)

When the result hoped for was not achieved with this approach concerning concessions, new attempts were made at a European level to integrate concessions into the new Directive(s). This time the integration of concessions in the public procurement Directives was met with more success.

On the one hand in the preamble of Directive 89/440/EEC for amendment of the Directive 71/305/EEC concerning works it was included that, due to the increasing importance of concessions in the field of public works and their specific nature, it was required that the rules concerning advertising should be brought within Directive

---

[29] Article 3(1) states: 'if the contracting authority conclude an agreement similar to that as referred to in article 1, under a), with the exception of the fact that the consideration for the works comprises of either exclusively the right to operate the work, or this right together with a payment, this Directive does not apply to this so-called "concession" agreement'. Hereby the proposal was in line with the original proposal of the European Commission (proposal for a first Directive of the Council concerning the coordination of the procedures for the award of public contracts for works, 23 July 1964, COM(64), 233 def. Article 1(1)(d). The Commission then explained this by referring to the fact that it concerned a legal concept which differed completely from the procurement of public contracts. The coordination of the various types of awarding a concession for the implementation of works would safeguard the principle of non-discrimination best, but one would still encounter great difficulties. Seeing that it would not be possible to choose the concessionaire on the basis of rules which were more or less coordinated with competition. Cf P. Heijnsbroeck, *Grond voor gelijkheid Gelijke kansen op werken bij gronduitgifte door de overheid* (The Hague: IBR 2013) 225–6 and footnote 11.

[30] 'Déclaration des représentants des gouvernements des États membres, réunis au sein du Conseil, sur les procédures à suivre en matière de concessions de travaux' [1971] OJ C82/13.

[31] Council Directive 72/277/EEC of 26 July 1972, [1972] OJ L176/12.

71/305/EEC.[32] On the other hand various provisions on this matter were included in the Directive itself. However, the amendments were not really revolutionary. In fact basically the joint declaration of the representatives of the Member States of 1971 referred to earlier was integrated.[33]

Of more interest were the attempts, a few years later during the elaboration of a *Services Directive*, to integrate the concession for a public service. According to the Commission it was necessary for the safeguarding of the coherence of the procurement procedures that the (services) Directive also applied to the concessions for services.[34] [35]

The European Commission described the concession agreement for services as 'a contract other than a public works concession within the meaning of article 1, under d), of Directive 71/305/EEC concluded between an authority and another entity of its choice whereby the former transfers the execution of a service to the public lying within its responsibility to the latter and the latter agrees to provide the activity in return for the right together with payment'.[36]

The ideas were not welcomed by some Member States.[37] In particular, France was obstructive. It was noted that not all Member States made use of concessions which created a problem with reciprocity.[38] Member States such as Germany, where usually public services are arranged by internal or external independent public law legal entities, would remain inaccessible, whilst companies of those Member States could indeed compete for concessions on the French market.[39] Furthermore, it would have played a role that in some Member States concessions are mostly granted by unilateral acts which would therefore have fallen outside the Commission's proposed definition which was based on concessions granted by a (consensual) contract.[40] Questions were also raised regarding the bringing into line of public procurement and concessions for

---

32 [1989] OJ L210/1. This directive and later amendments were codified by Council Directive 93/37/EEC of 14 June 1993 concerning the co-ordination for the award of public works contracts [1993] OJ L199/54.

33 See also M.-A. Flamme and P. Flamme, 'Vers l'Europe des marchés publics? A propos de la directive 'fournitures' du 22 mars 1988' (1988) RMC 467 at 39.

34 [1991] OJ C23/1.

35 Proposal of 28 August 1991, [1991] OJ C250/7.

36 Ibid, Article 3(h).

37 Cf [1992] OJ L209. See also Conclusions of AG Fennelly of 18 May 2000 (Case C-324/98 *Telaustria Verlags GmbH and Telefonadress GmbH v Post & Telekom Austria AG*) para 21 and footnote 15.

38 Cf J.-B. Auby 'Perspectives d'évolution de la concession de service public' in C. Brechnon-Moulènes (ed.), *La concession de service public face au droit communautaire* (Paris: Sirey 1992) 94; O. Raymundie, *Gestion déléguée des services pubics en France et en Europe* (Paris: Le Moniteur 2006) 132; J.-F. Auby and O. Raymundie, *Le service public* (Paris: Le Moniteur 2003) 458 at 230.

39 O. Raymundie, *Gestion déléguée des services pubics en France et en Europe* (Paris: Le Moniteur 2006) 132. See also M.-A. Flamme, P. Mathei, P. Flamme and A. Delvaux in C. Dardenne, *Praktische Commentaar bij de reglementering van de overheidsopdrachten. Deel* 1 (Brussels: NCB 1996–1997)134–5.

40 C. Bovis, *EC Public Procurement: Case Law and Regulation* (Oxford: Oxford University Press 2006) 337 footnote 13.

services.[41] Ultimately during the legislative process, the Council eliminated all references to public service concessions, in particular because of the differences between the Member States as regards the delegation of the management of public services and modes of delegation, which could create a situation of very great imbalance in the opening-up of the public concession contracts.[42]

Also, during the elaboration of the special sectors Directive, express attention was paid to concessions. It was determined on the one hand originally in the proposal for the Directive that the Directive, *inter alia*, applied to[43] public or private undertakings holding public service concessions or to whom the State or regional or local authorities have granted special or exclusive rights. Ultimately the references to concessions are also left out here.[44]

On the other hand the Commission in a later proposal included, *inter alia*, the following definition of concessions:[45] 'A "concession" is a contract concluded in writing between a contracting entity which is a public authority within the meaning of point 2 and a contracting entity which is not a public contracting entity within the meaning of point 1 whereby the latter accepts the responsibility for constructing, supplying or managing a network falling within the scope of Article 2 (3)(a)(i) at its own expense and risk, in return for a remuneration'.

This provision was also not included in the definitive text.[46] The Council would also after internal disagreement not wish to follow the proposal of the Commission, this time on the ground that such concessions existed in only one Member State and that it was inappropriate to proceed with their regulation in the absence of a detailed study of the various forms of public service concessions granted in the Member States in those sectors.[47]

---

41 J.-F. Auby and O. Raymundie, *Le service public* (Paris: Le Moniteur 2003) 458 at 230.

42 Common position of the Council of 25 februari 1992, doc. Nr. 4444-92-ADD-1; Cf G. Guisolphe, 'Les concessions de service public et les directives communautaires sur les marchés publics' in C. Brechnon-Moulènes (ed.), *La concession de service public face au droit communautaire* (Paris: Sirey 1992) 88; Case C-324/98 *Telaustria Verlags GmbH and Telefonadress GmbH v Post & Telekom Austria AG*, para 48.

43 COM(86) 679. C. Brechnon-Moulènes, 'Rapport Introductif' in C. Brechnon-Moulènes (ed), *La concession de service public face au droit communautaire* (Paris: Sirey 1992) 7 and [1988] OJ C167/65; Opinion on the proposal for a Council Directive amending Directive 71/305/EEC concerning the coordination of procedures for the award of public works contracts [1987] OJ C319/58 no 3.2.1. et seq.

44 Council Directive 90/531/EEG of 17 September 1990, [1990] OJ L297 replaced by Council Directive 93/38/EEC of 14 June 1993 co-ordinating the procurement procedures of entities operating in the water, energy, transport and telecommunications sector, [1993] OJ L199/84.

45 Proposal for a Council Directive on the procurement procedures of entities providing water, energy, and transport services, COM(88) 377 final, 31 [1998] OJ C319. See Article 1(6). See also Article 2(7).

46 Common position of 22 March 1990, doc no 5250/90 ADD 1.

47 Case C-324/98 *Telaustria Verlags GmbH and Telefonadress GmbH v Post & Telekom Austria AG*, 50.

D. The period (1996–2004) and the Directives for public procurement 2004/17 and 2004/18

In the Green Paper *Public Procurement in the European Union, Exploring the Way Forward* attention was once again focused on the problem of concession agreements or similar contracts which did not fall within the scope of the Directives.[48] The Commission pointed out, *inter alia*, that the contracting authorities seem to incorrectly assume that Community Law does not apply to this type of contract. In many cases these did not take the measures necessary to guarantee transparency and openness for competition. The Commission emphasised that one still had to comply with the Treaty in case of such agreements.[49] In particular, the rules concerning the free movement of goods and services, as well as the fundamental principles of non-discrimination, equal treatment, transparency and reciprocity must be adhered to. The Commission continued to state that in the future, for the purpose of a further opening up for competition, it will consider determining rules which allow competition to play a role when exclusive rights for the execution of public services are assigned through concession agreements.[50]

In the communication Public Procurement in the European Union which announced the preparation of the new Directive, specific plans of the Commission to deal with concession agreements once and for all were revealed:[51]

> In the interests of simplification and clarification, the Commission envisages the following action to establish uniform principles for all types of concession:
>
> In the first stage the Commission will draw up an interpretative document explaining and spelling out the rules and principles that it considers, on the basis of the cases it has to deal with, should apply to concessions …
>
> In a second stage, the Commission envisages proposing amendments to the Directives in order to cover all forms of concessions, that are not yet subject to regulation …

The first phase of the plans was realised with the interpretative communication on Concessions under community law.[52] The second phase, as one could expect, would be realised following the formulation of the proposals for new Directives in the classic and special sectors. However, it could not be further from the truth. In the first proposals for a Directive no special attention was ultimately paid to concession agreements. Criticism consequently followed. For example the Economic and Social Committee argued for more clarity with regard to concessions.[53] Furthermore, various amendments were

---

48 European Commission, Green Paper, Public Procurement in the European Union, Exploring the Way Forward (1996) COM 583 (final).

49 Ibid 14.

50 Ibid 15.

51 European Commission, Communication, Public Procurement in the European Union, COM (98)143, 9–10.

52 European Commission, Interpretative communication on Concessions under community law, [2000] OJ C121/2.

53 Opinion of the Economic and Social Committee on the 'Proposal for a Directive of the European Parliament and of the Council on the coordination of procedures for the award of public supply contracts, public service contracts and public works contracts, [2001] OJ C193/7.

proposed to provide more clarity concerning this type of agreement.[54] Ultimately the proposals for the Directive remained virtually unchanged on this point.

The public procurement Directives 2004/17 and 2004/18 therefore added very little that was new. However, it is interesting that the earlier exclusion of various concessions can currently expressly be traced to the Directive.[55] It is furthermore interesting to note that a definition of concession agreements for services is included. The definition nevertheless does not seem to have the intention of describing the concession for services in detail, but of clarifying what is not regulated by the Directives. Still, the importance of the description should not be underestimated. Seeing that the definition ultimately also determines whether an agreement is a public contract for services or a concession for services.

2. The Demarcation and Definition of the Concept of Concession for Works and Services

A. The distinctive characteristics

In Directive 2004/17 and Directive 2004/18 a concession for works/services is defined as a contract of the same type as a public works/service contract except for the fact that the consideration for the works/services to be carried out/provided consists either solely in the right to exploit the work/service or in this right together with payment. Public

---

[54] During the first reading of the Directives an amendment was submitted to the European Parliament to include a recital in the preamble in which the European Commission was asked to examine the possibility of adopting a proposal for a Directive to regulate systematically the concessions sector and so-called 'project financing' (Amendment no 17, Report S. Zappala of 29 October 2001, A5-0378/2001 def., 17.) In the explanatory notes it is stated that for public authorities, the possibility of using private capital to finance public works in exchange for the right to manage the works in question until the capital invested has been completely repaid is undoubtedly an additional means of enabling them to carry out the tasks entrusted to them. Where this approach ('project financing') has been tried, it is yielding good results. The introduction of this new formula calls for new and more systematic rules to govern the concessions sector. This amendment was originally, at first reading, adopted by the European Parliament (Position of the European Parliament adopted on 17 January 2002 with a view to the adoption of European Parliament and Council Directive .../.../EC on the coordination of procedures for the award of public supply contracts, public service contracts and public works contracts, [2002] OJ C271E/182, Recital (48)), and since then also by the Commission (although with a slight amendment). See Amended proposal for a European Parliament and Council Directive concerning the coordination of procedures for the award of public supply contracts, public service contracts and public works contracts, Com(2002) 236 final, 2000/0115(COD), [2002] OJ C203E/211: 'The Commission is asked to examine the possibility of reinforcing legal certainty in the concessions sector and in public/private partnerships, and to adopt a legislative proposal if it feels this is necessary'). However, the proposal was rejected in the Council because it deemed it not suitable to include such as declaration in the text (Common position (EC) no. 33/2003 of 20 March 2003, adopted by the Council, in accordance with the procedure of article 251 of the Treaty establishing the European Community, for the purpose of the adoption of a Directive of the European Parliament and the Council on the coordination of procedures for the award of public supply contracts, public service contracts and public works contracts [2003] OJ C147E).

[55] Article 18 Directive 2004/17; Article 17 Directive 2004/18.

contracts are defined as contracts for pecuniary interest concluded in writing between one or more economic operators and one or more contracting authorities and having as their object the execution of works, the supply of products or the provision of services.

A number of characteristics immediately appear from the descriptions which must distinguish concessions for works and services from other legal concepts such as classic permits, but also public procurement. The European Commission as well as the European Court of Justice have clarified those characteristics over the past years. Hereinafter we will consider further the contract element, works and/or services, right to exploit and the operating risk.

B. Contract

From the case-law of the European Court of Justice and the interpretative communication on concession contracts it follows that the concept contract must be interpreted from a European perspective, regardless of the legal classification in national law. In the interpretative communication it is stated that it relates to every act to be attributed to the State with which a government institution contracts out all or part of the management of services, which usually form part of its responsibilities, to a third party, either by means of a contract, or by means of a unilateral legal act to which this third party has agreed.[56] Also unilateral legal acts in national law can therefore fall under the scope of the community concept 'concession contract'. However, the consensual character is important. Furthermore, it is of course of importance that the implementation of the goods or services is striven for. This point will be returned to later.

The public procurement case-law of the European Court of Justice has meanwhile confirmed that the concept of contract must be interpreted broadly. The circumstance that a contract falls under public law and is concluded in the context of the exercising of governmental authority does not object to the existence of a contractual element.[57] In the *Asemfo* ruling the Court of Justice did hold that the relations inasmuch as that company is an instrument and a technical service of those bodies, are not contractual, but in every respect internal, dependent and subordinate. In this case the company did not have any freedom regarding whether or not to execute an assignment given by the competent authorities or to determine the rate to be applied to its services.[58] The Court of Justice refined its judgment in the *Correos* ruling.[59] This case concerned an exclusive right for the delivery of postal services. The Spanish government argued that the Cooperation Agreement could not be subject to the rules governing the award of public service contracts because of its nature, which is instrumental rather than contractual. Correos was unable to refuse to enter into a cooperation agreement, but was under an obligation to accept it. According to the Court of Justice the relationship could definitely be classified as contractual. This would only be otherwise if the

---

[56] European Commission, Interpretative communication on Concessions under community law, [2000] OJ C121/5.

[57] Case C-399/98, *Ordine degli Architetti and Others*, para 73.

[58] Case C-295/05, *Asociación Nacional de Empresas Forestales (Asemfo) v Transformación Agraria SA (Tragsa) and Administración del Estado*, paras 50 and 51.

[59] Case C-220/06, *Asociación Profesional de Empresas de Reparto y Manipulado de Correspondencia v Administración General del Estado*, paras 84 and 85.

Cooperation Agreement is in actual fact a unilateral administrative measure creating obligations solely for Correos and departing significantly from the normal conditions of a commercial offer made by that company.

C. Works and/or provision of services

Concessions, as stated in the description, are related to services and/or works. If the concession contract is principally concerned with the realisation of a work, then it should be considered to be a works concession. In contrast, a concession contract in which the construction work is incidental or which only involves operating an existing work, is regarded as a service concession.[60]

The valuable consideration of the contract means that the contracting authority which has concluded a public works/service concession receives a service pursuant to that contract in return for the right to exploit (cf. *infra*). That service consists in the realisation of works or the provision of services. The importance of the legally binding character is also an element to which the Court of Justice has already paid attention.[61]

In quite a similar way, a concession can be distinguished from a (classic) permit by the obligation of performance which is vested in the concessionaire. In fact, as the Court points out, what is important is that it obliges the transferee to pursue the activity transferred.[62] The element is also implicitly on the agenda in the interpretative communication about concession contracts.[63] The communication does not concern acts whereby a public authority (merely) 'authorises' the exercise of an economic activity. Examples: taxi concessions, authorisations to use the public highway (newspaper kiosks, café terraces), or acts relating to pharmacies and filling stations. Classic permits or admissions where there is no obligation for the construction or works or provision of services, as also already stated earlier, are indeed not concessions for works or services.

A question which sometimes arises is whether the works or services must have a special character. Although some language versions of the Directives talk about 'public' works/travaux 'public' it does not appear that special importance must be attached to this, since other language versions do not contain such terminology from which one could deduce that a special type of works is referred to.[64] And although the services often will relate to public services or services of general (economic) interest this also

---

[60] European Commission, Interpretative communication on Concessions under community law, [2000] OJ C121/5.

[61] Cf Case C-451/08, *Helmutt Müller v Bundesanstalt fur Immobilienaufgaben*, para 62: 'the concept of "public works contracts", within the meaning of Article 1(2)(b) of Directive 2004/18, requires that the contractor assume a direct or indirect obligation to carry out the works which are the subject of the contract and that that obligation be legally enforceable in accordance with the procedural rules laid down by national law'.

[62] Case C-221/12, *Belgacom NV v Interkommunale voor Teledistributie van het Gewest Antwerpen (INTEGAN) and Others*, paras 27 and 33.

[63] European Commission, Interpretative communication on Concessions under community law, [2000] OJ C121/5 footnote 25.

[64] P. Heijnsbroeck, *Grond voor gelijkheid Gelijke kansen op werken bij gronduitgifte door de overheid* (The Hague: IBR 2013) 238–9.

does not seem to be any requirement.[65] Actually, the current definitions do not contain any reference to the concept of 'public services' or 'services of general economic interest'. However, it will of course in principle always concern services or works for which the concession granting authorities are responsible. Furthermore the contracting authority must be in a position to transfer (to some extent) the responsibility. The *Müller* ruling is interesting in that respect, where the Court of Justice established that the economic operator already personally had the possession of property rights to the grounds involved. The Court of Justice held that in order for a contracting authority to be able to transfer to the other contracting party the right to exploit a work within the terms of that provision, that contracting authority must be in a position to exploit that work. That will normally not be the case where the only basis for the right of exploitation is the right of ownership of the economic operator concerned. The owner of land has the right to exploit that land in compliance with the applicable statutory rules. As long as an economic operator enjoys the right to exploit the land which he owns, it is in principle impossible for a public authority to grant a concession relating to that exploitation.[66]

D. Consideration: right to exploit

One of the most important distinctive characteristics, certainly with regard to public procurement is the consideration. Seeing that the largest difference between a public contract and a concession for works and services is situated in the direct remuneration for a service, respectively, the providing of a right to exploit the service.

The European Commission's Guide to Community rules on public works contracts (based on the old Directive) explained the difference in remuneration.[67]

> For the purposes of the Directive, a public works concession is the same as a public works contract, except that the consideration is usually in the form of the right to exploit the works but is sometimes pecuniary as well. The key element in determining whether a public works contract or concession is involved is the form that the consideration takes. For the works to be classed as a concession, consideration must consist, at least in part, of the right

[65] P. Delvolvé, 'La concession de service public et le droit communautaire, Rapport de synthese' in C. Brechnon-Moulènes (ed), *La concession de service public face au droit communautaire* (Paris: Sirey 1992) 113 at 20 'En droit communautaire, le service public est indifférent à l'identification de la concession'. Cf. also S. Van Garsse , *De concessie in het raam van de publiek-private samenwerking. Een analyse van het openbaar en het privaat domein, van de domeinconcessies, de concessies van openbare werken, de concessies van diensten en hun aanbesteding* (Antwerp: die Keure 2007) 413; A. Mattera, 'La communication interprétative de la Commission sur les concessions de service d'utilité publique: instrument de transparence et de liberalization' (RDUE 2000) 272; Opinion of AG Fenelly conclusion of 19 May 2000 (Case C-324/98 *Telaustria Verlags GmbH and Telefonadress GmbH v Post & Telekom Austria AG*) paras 34–37; C. Bovis, 'The Notion of Public Service Concession as a Component of Public-Private Partnerships' (2007) 1 EPPPL 15; contra M.B. Nijhof, *De concessie in Europeesrechtelijk perspectief* (Deventer: Kluwer 2000) 49; Opinion of AG La Pergola of 19 February 1998 (Case C-360/96, *Gemeente Arnhem and Gemeente Rheden v BFI Holding BV*).

[66] Case C-451/08, *Helmutt Müller v Bundesanstalt fïr Immobilienaufgaben*, paras 72–74

[67] *Public Procurement in the European Union, Guide to the Community rules on Public Works Contracts,* 61.

> to exploit the works, i.e. of the profit which the concessionaire, depending on his ability to manage the project, will gain from that right. It is of little importance whether the revenue from that management is handled physically by the awarding authority or by the concessionaire; what matters is that all or part of such revenue is paid to the latter in consideration for the works ...'[68]

The case-law confirms meanwhile that it follows, from the comparison of the definitions of public contract for services and a concession contract for services, that the difference between a public contract for services and a concession contract is situated in the consideration for the provision of the service.[69] A public contract for services includes consideration which, also if this is not the only consideration, is paid directly by the contracting authority to the service provider. In case of a concession contract for services the consideration for the provision of service comprises of the right to operate the service, whether or not together with a payment. However, that the concession holder has acquired the right to exploit and operate appears to be a necessary, but not a sufficient, condition.

E. Operating risk

A concession for works and/or services was, as has been seen to be, described as a contract of the same type as a public works/service contract, with the exception of the fact that the consideration for the works/services to be carried out/provided consists either solely in the right to operate the work/service or in this right together with payment. A literal reading of this definition could lead to the assumption that a contract that transfers a right to operate would be a concession, even if the remuneration (payments) would cover almost all the cost.[70] However, this reading was never accepted as has already been considered above.

In reality the definition allows the Member States to make a payment in return for work carried out, provided that this does not eliminate a significant element of the risk inherent in exploitation.[71] What is needed is therefore a shift of responsibility and a

---

68 Ibid: 'Depending on the management terms prescribed by the awarding authority, the latter may guarantee the concessionaire a minimum income. However, were the authority to remunerate the concessionaire with fixed – e.g. monthly or annual – sums in consideration for the works and for the management activity, without such remuneration being in any way proportional to the management revenue, the contract would not be a concession but a public works contract, the scope of which included, in addition to the execution of the works, provision of the requisite services for managing the project. In such a case, the 'right to exploit the works' would no longer be meaningful since the risks and benefits associated with exploitation would in reality be retained by the contracting authority'.

69 Case C-274/09, *Privater Rettungsdienst und Krankentransport Stadler v Zweckverband für Rettungsdienst und Feuerwehralarmierung Passau*, para 24.

70 Concessions Note, 3, available 4 February 2016 at http://www.europarl.europa.eu/RegData/etudes/note/join/2010/429994/IPOL-IMCO_NT(2010)429994_EN.pdf.

71 The exact degree to which the consideration can be paid by the contracting authority for the contract still to fall within the definition of a concession is unclear. By specifying that there may be payment in addition to the right to exploit the work, the Community legislator assumes that the operation of the structure must be the main source of the concessionaire's revenue. Therefore the determining factor in concessions continues to be the existence of the exploitation

shift of risks. This idea already appeared very early on in the case-law of the Court of Justice. As the Court of Justice held in 1994 that there could not be a concession and therefore transfer of operating rights if there was not an actual transfer of responsibility.[72] In the *Arnhem* case the Court of Justice held in 1998 that there was not a concession because the remuneration for the goods or services was not related to the operation, but in reality concerned a price so that all operating risk was removed.[73]

Therefore, in case of awarding a concession there must be transfer of the, or an, operating risk, as risk is inherent in the economic operation of the service.[74] The question arises of what is exactly meant with the operating risk. How much risk and which risk must be transferred? Over the past years the case-law has provided more clarity about on the one hand the nature of the risk and on the other hand the degree of risks to which one must be exposed.

In *Parking Brixen* the Court of Justice established that the remuneration of the service provider was not made by the authority awarding the concession, but indeed by third party users.[75] The method of remuneration means, as stated by the Court of Justice, that the provider takes the risk of operating the service and this is thus a characteristic of a service concession. With this ruling the Court of Justice stated for the first time very clearly that in case of concessions there must be an 'operating risk'.[76] If the remuneration takes place through payments from third parties, then the requirement is fulfilled,[77] or at least in principle.[78] The circumstance that the service provider is remunerated by payments from third parties (users), is one means of exercising the right, granted to the provider, to exploit the service as the Court of Justice stated in another ruling.[79] However, it also becomes clear from this ruling that there are other forms of remuneration. For example direct remuneration by the government. The existence of direct remuneration of the service provider by the government agency involved does not in fact imply necessarily the existence of a public

risk in connection with the investment made or the capital invested. The Commission's Communication clarifies this aspect in its interpretative Communication on concessions. Cf. European Commission, Interpretative communication on Concessions under community law, [2000] OJ C121/2.

72 Case C-272/91, *Commission of the European Communities v Italian Republic*, para 32.

73 Case C-360/96, *Gemeente Arnhem and Gemeente Rheden v BFI Holding BV*, para 25.

74 Case C-206/08, *Wasser- und Abwasserzweckverband Gotha und Landkreisgemeinden (WAZV Gotha) v Eurawasser Aufbereitungs- und Entsorgungsgesellschaft mbH*, para 66.

75 Case C-458/03, *Parking Brixen GmbH v Gemeinde Brixen and Stadtwerke Brixen AG*, para 40.

76 Ibid.

77 Ibid 43 and 40; Cf. Opinion of AG Mazak of 9 September 2010 (Case C-274/09, *Privater Rettungsdienst und Krankentransport Stadler v Zweckverband für Rettungsdienst und Feuerwehralarmierung Passau*), para 27 seems to agree that the issue of risk is irrelevant where there is to direct remuneration from the contracting authority.

78 Case C-274/09, *Privater Rettungsdienst und Krankentransport Stadler v Zweckverband für Rettungsdienst und Feuerwehralarmierung Passau*, paras 25–26.

79 Case C-206/08, *Wasser- und Abwasserzweckverband Gotha und Landkreisgemeinden (WAZV Gotha) v Eurawasser Aufbereitungs- und Entsorgungsgesellschaft mbH*, para 53.

contract for services. It suffices to refer to an opinion of Advocate General Mazak at the Court of Justice:[80]

> the existence of direct remuneration of the service provider by the public authority concerned does not necessarily imply that there is a public service contract. It follows from the finding of the Court that indirect remuneration is 'one means of' exercising the right, granted to the provider, to exploit the service, that there are also other means of exercising that right. That explains why, in *Contse and Others, Commission v Italy and Hans & Christophorus Oymanns*, the Court examined whether the contracts at issue could constitute service concessions, even though the service providers had been remunerated directly by the public authorities concerned.

His finding is also supported in the legal literature and the interpretive communication of the European Commission.[81] A typical example is a concession for motorways with shadow toll.

The case-law meanwhile also made it repeatedly clear that there must be an actual economic risk on the part of the concessionaire. The concession holder may not be assured of an integral cover of the costs which are incurred by the concession holder.[82] In the case of *Orthopadie Schutechnik*, the Court of Justice held, *inter alia*, that the concessionaire did not enjoy the degree of economic freedom which would distinguish a concession, nor that the concessionaire was exposed to 'a significant risk' connected with the services it provided. In the *Müller* case the Court stated that the concessionaire had to bear 'the main' or at least 'the substantial operating risk'.[83] The latter was somewhat refined in the case-law following that case.

Thus, the Court of Justice held in several cases that it must be noted that when the remuneration of the service provider exclusively originates from third parties, it suffices for the conclusion that there is a concession agreement for services that the contracting authority transfers a 'very limited' operating risk.[84] It is not unusual that certain sectors of activity, in particular sectors involving public service utilities are subject to rules which may have the effect of limiting the financial risks entailed. It must in particular remain open to the contracting authorities, acting in all good faith, to ensure the supply of services by way of a concession, if they consider that to be the best method of ensuring the public service in question, even if the risk linked to such an operation is

---

[80] Opinion of AG Mazak of 9 September 2010 (Case C-274/09 *Privater Rettungsdienst und Krankentransport Stadler v Zweckverband für Rettungsdienst und Feuerwehralarmierung Passau*), para 28.

[81] European Commission, Interpretative communication on Concessions under community law, [2000] OJ C121/2 footnote 13; S. Van Garsse, *De concessie in het raam van de publiek-private samenwerking. Een analyse van het openbaar en het privaat domein, van de domeinconcessies, de concessies van openbare werken, de concessies van diensten en hun aanbesteding* (Antwerp: die Keure 2007) 555–63.

[82] Case C 437/07, *Commission of the European Communities v Italian Republic*, paras 32–34.

[83] Case C-451/08, *Helmutt Müller v Bundesanstalt fur Immobilienaufgaben*, para 75.

[84] Case C-274/09, *Privater Rettungsdienst und Krankentransport Stadler v Zweckverband für Rettungsdienst und Feuerwehralarmierung Passau*, para 33.

very limited.[85] In such sectors, the contracting authority has no influence on the detailed rules of public law governing the service, and thus on the level of the risk to transfer, and it would not, moreover, be reasonable to expect a public authority granting a concession to create conditions which were more competitive and involved greater financial risk than those which, on account of the rules governing the sector in question, exist in that sector.[86]

However, while that risk may, at the outset, be very limited, it is necessary for classification as a service concession that the contracting authority transfers to the concession holder all or, at least, a significant share of the risk which it faces.[87] As an Advocate General pointed out, in order for there to be a concession contract the risk which is borne by the service provider must not necessarily 'be "considerable in absolute terms", only that it be at least a "significant share" of the risk which the contracting entity would anyway be assuming if it were to provide the service in question itself ... The decisive factor is that there should be a significant transfer of the risk inherent in the operation of the service, whatever that risk may be in absolute terms, that is, when considered alone'.[88]

It is also noteworthy that the recent case-law specifically deals with the nature and the specific risk to which the concession holder would have to be exposed in order for there to be mention of a concession. According to the Court of Justice the operating risk must be understood to be the risk of exposure to the vagaries of the market,[89] which may consist in the risk of competition from other operators, the risk that supply of the services will not match demand, the risk that those liable will be unable to pay for the services provided, the risk that the costs of operating the services will not fully be met by revenue or for example also the risk of liability for harm or damage resulting

---

[85] Case C-274/09, *Privater Rettungsdienst und Krankentransport Stadler v Zweckverband für Rettungsdienst und Feuerwehralarmierung Passau*, para 34; Case C206/08, *Wasser- und Abwasserzweckverband Gotha und Landkreisgemeinden (WAZV Gotha) v Eurawasser Aufbereitungs- und Entsorgungsgesellschaft mbH*, paras 72–74.

[86] Case C-274/09, *Privater Rettungsdienst und Krankentransport Stadler v Zweckverband für Rettungsdienst und Feuerwehralarmierung Passau*, para 35; Case C206/08, *Wasser- und Abwasserzweckverband Gotha und Landkreisgemeinden (WAZV Gotha) v Eurawasser Aufbereitungs- und Entsorgungsgesellschaft mbH*, paras 74–76.

[87] Case C206/08, *Wasser- und Abwasserzweckverband Gotha und Landkreisgemeinden (WAZV Gotha) v Eurawasser Aufbereitungs- und Entsorgungsgesellschaft mbH*, paras 77 and 80; Case C-274/09, *Privater Rettungsdienst und Krankentransport Stadler v Zweckverband für Rettungsdienst und Feuerwehralarmierung Passau*, para 29; Case C206/08, *Wasser- und Abwasserzweckverband Gotha und Landkreisgemeinden (WAZV Gotha) v Eurawasser Aufbereitungs- und Entsorgungsgesellschaft mbH*, para 77; Case C-348/10, *Norma-A SIA and Dekom SIA v Latgales plānošanas regions*, para 51.

[88] Opinion of AG Cruz Villalon of 7 July 2011 (Case C-348/10, *Norma-A SIA and Dekom SIA v Latgales plānošanas regions*) paras 51 and 52.

[89] Case C206/08, *Wasser- und Abwasserzweckverband Gotha und Landkreisgemeinden (WAZV Gotha) v Eurawasser Aufbereitungs- und Entsorgungsgesellschaft mbH*, para 67: 'If the contracting authority continues to bear all of the risk by not exposing the supplier to the vagaries of the market, the awarding of the right to operate the service requires that the formalities provided for in Directive 2004/17 be applied ...'.

from an inadequacy of the service.[90] By contrast, risks such as those linked to bad management or errors of judgement by the economic operator are not decisive for the purposes of classification as a public service contract or a service concession, since those risks are inherent in every contract, whether it be a public service contract or a service concession.[91] It is for the national courts, on the basis of the statutory and the contractual provisions, to determine to what extent the contracting party actually bears risk.[92]

3. The Legal Regime in Accordance with the Directive 2004/18

A. Public works concessions in the classical sector

Public works concessions in the classical sectors above a defined threshold are subjected to advertising, timing and subcontracting requirements under the Directive 2004/18. Awarding authorities must publish a public works notice in the Official Journal of the European Communities in order to put this contract up for competition at European level. This advertising rule applies irrespective of the nature of the potential concessionaire.[93]

Besides this obligation (sub)contracts of works awarded by the concession contract holder are also regulated.[94] If the concessionaire is itself an awarding authority, contracts of works which are over the Community threshold must be awarded in full compliance with all the detailed provisions of the Directive on public works contracts. If the concessionaire is not an awarding authority, the Directive stipulates that he/she must comply only with certain advertising rules.

It is interesting to see that there are no specific rules in the directive on the choice of procedure or criteria for award. However, the Treaty principles of (for example) transparency, equal treatment and non-discrimination do apply.

---

[90] Case C-234/03, *Contse SA, Vivisol Srl and Oxigen Salud SA v Instituto Nacional de Gestión Sanitaria (Ingesa), formerly Instituto Nacional de la Salud (Insalud)*, para 22: 'As a preliminary point, it should be observed that the case in the main proceedings, contrary to the Spanish Government's submissions, appears to concern a public service contract and not a management contract for a service categorised as a concession. As Insalud stated at the hearing, the Spanish administration remains liable for all harm suffered on account of a failure of the service. That factor, which implies that there is no transfer of risks connected to the provision of the service concerned, and the fact that the service is paid for by the Spanish health administration, support that conclusion. It is, however, for the national court to determine whether in fact that is the case.'

[91] Case C-274/09, *Privater Rettungsdienst und Krankentransport Stadler v Zweckverband für Rettungsdienst und Feuerwehralarmierung Passau*, para 38.

[92] Case C206/08, *Wasser- und Abwasserzweckverband Gotha und Landkreisgemeinden (WAZV Gotha) v Eurawasser Aufbereitungs- und Entsorgungsgesellschaft mbH*, para 78.

[93] Except if the relation is 'in-house' (cf. Case C-458/03, *Parking Brixen GmbH v Gemeinde Brixen and Stadtwerke Brixen AG*, para 62) or another exception applies (cf cases which meet the exceptional conditions laid down by the Directive where contracting authorities may resort to a negotiated procedure without prior publication of a notice in awarding a public works contract.

[94] The specific rules are furthermore also not applicable if the works contracts are awarded to grouped or affiliated undertakings.

B. Service concessions in the classical sector and concessions in the special sector

Service concessions in the classical sectors and utilities concessions are not formally regulated; the Treaty principles also apply to them. This was also pointed out in the Interpretative Communication on Concessions under Community Law.[95] Works concessions (even the ones that are regulated (*supra* A)) and service concessions are subject to the rules and principles of the Treaty. These principles where clarified by the European Commission and the case-law of the Court of Justice.

The *Telaustria* ruling was a particular milestone for concessions. In this ruling the Court of Justice confirmed that concessions for services did not fall under the scope of the Procurement Directive, but that the contracting authorities which conclude these contracts nevertheless had to observe the fundamental rules of the Treaty in general and the prohibition of discrimination on the basis of nationality. The Court of Justice also stated with reference to the *Unitron* ruling that this prohibition also included, *inter alia*, an obligation of transparency.[96] That obligation of transparency which is imposed on the contracting authority consists in ensuring, for the benefit of any potential tenderer, a degree of advertising sufficient to enable the services market to be opened up to competition and the impartiality of procurement procedures to be reviewed.[97]

The Court of Justice has refined this approach in later case-law. Without necessarily implying an obligation to call for tenders, that obligation of transparency, which applies when the service concession in question may be of interest to an undertaking located in a Member State other than that in which the concession is granted, requires the concession-granting authority to ensure, for the benefit of any potential tenderer, a degree of publicity sufficient to enable the service concession to be opened up to competition and the impartiality of the award procedures to be reviewed. The grant of a concession, in the absence of any transparency, to an operator located in the Member State of the awarding authority constitutes a difference in treatment to the detriment of operators located in other Member States, who have no real possibility of manifesting their interest in obtaining the concession in question. Such a difference in treatment is contrary to the principle of equal treatment and the prohibition of discrimination on grounds of nationality, and constitutes indirect discrimination on grounds of nationality prohibited by Articles 43 EC and 49 EC, unless it is justified by objective circumstances.[98]

Concessions awarding authorities must therefore in principle guarantee a sufficient degree of transparency and companies in another Member State must be given the opportunity to acquire access to all relevant information for the awarding so that they, if they wish to, can manifest their interest in the concession. The contents of the notification must therefore be sufficient in order to be able to consider on the basis thereof whether or not to make the interest apparent. Furthermore, potential parties

---

[95] European Commission, Interpretative communication on Concessions under community law, [2000] OJ C121/6.

[96] Case C-324/98, *Telaustria Verlags GmbH and Telefonadress GmbH v Post & Telekom Austria AG*, para 61.

[97] Ibid, 62.

[98] Case C-64/08 *Ernst Engelmann*, paras 50 and 51.

would be in a mutually equal position, *inter alia*, concerning the essence of the information in the notice.[99]

How the notification must specifically be organised is not entirely clear. A public notice in plenty of time in advance seems certainly to offer the necessary safeguards. However, in theory it cannot be excluded that instead of organising a public notice, potentially interested companies could be written to directly.[100] However, it cannot be clearly seen in practice how all interested parties can be identified in advance.[101]

Which medium may be chosen and which method of awarding is on the agenda if there are several interested parties is also not entirely clear. In an interpretive communication the European Commission established that the larger the importance of the assignment the more publicity it must be given.[102] In *Brixen* the Court stated that is for the concession-granting public authority to evaluate, subject to review by the competent courts, the appropriateness of the detailed arrangements of the call for competition to the particularities of the public service concession in question.[103]

Concerning the specific procedures the Court of Justice repeatedly held that the procurement procedures must be testable on impartiality.[104] What was referred to thereby was not specifically a procurement procedure as can be found in the Public Procurement Directives, but a procedure whereby a form of competition between various interested parties can be organised. Such a procedure must, in accordance with the case-law of the Court of Justice, safeguard objectivity and transparency as well as equal treatment.

Nevertheless a direct awarding of a concession, therefore without any notification and without a specific procedure, indeed remains possible in exceptional cases. Thus the Court of Justice earlier declared the in-house-doctrine applicable to concessions.[105] Other cases of application concern the exceptions in the Treaty itself, but also in the

---

[99] P. Heijnsbroeck, *Grond voor gelijkheid Gelijke kansen op werken bij gronduitgifte door de overheid* (The Hague: IBR 2013) 111.

[100] Ibid 109; Opinion of AG Fenelly conclusion of 19 May 2000 (Case C-324/98, *Telaustria Verlags GmbH and Telefonadress GmbH v Post & Telekom Austria AG*) para 43; C. Bovis, 'The Notion of Public Service Concession as a Component of Public-Private Partnerships' (2007) 1 EPPPL 16.

[101] P. Heijnsbroeck, *Grond voor gelijkheid Gelijke kansen op werken bij gronduitgifte door de overheid* (The Hague: IBR 2013) 109. Contra Opinion of AG Fenelly conclusion of 19 May 2000 (Case C-324/98, *Telaustria Verlags GmbH and Telefonadress GmbH v Post & Telekom Austria* AG) 43; C. Bovis, 'The Notion of Public Service Concession as a Component of Public-Private Partnerships' (2007) 1 EPPPL 16.

[102] Commission interpretative communication on the Community law applicable to contract awards not or not fully subject to the provisions of the Public Procurement Directives, [2006] OJ C 179/02.

[103] Case C-458/03, *Parking Brixen GmbH v Gemeinde Brixen and Stadtwerke Brixen AG*, para 50.

[104] C-410/04, *Associazione Nazionale Autotrasporto Viaggiatori (ANAV) v Comune di Bari and AMTAB Servizio SpA*, para 21; Case C-458/03, *Parking Brixen GmbH v Gemeinde Brixen and Stadtwerke Brixen AG*, para 49.

[105] Case C-458/03, *Parking Brixen GmbH v Gemeinde Brixen and Stadtwerke Brixen AG*, para 62.

case-law of the Court of Justice whereby the derogations find their justification in overriding reasons in the public interest.[106]

We note last but not least that the principles described above are not only relevant during the initial awarding of a concession, but also during the effecting of important changes to ongoing contracts. Reference can thus be made to the ruling in *Wall AG* where it is made clear that one cannot automatically make 'material changes'. In *Wall AG* the court argued that:

> where amendments to the provisions of a service concession contract are materially different in character from those on the basis on which the original concession contract was awarded, and therefore such is to demonstrate the intention of the parties to re-negotiate the essential terms of the contract, all necessary measures must be taken, in accordance with the national legal system of the Member State concerned, to restore the transparency of the procedure, which may extend to a new award procedure. If need be, a new award procedure should be organised in the manner appropriate to the specific features of the service concession involved, and should ensure that an undertaking located in another Member State has access to sufficient information on that concession before it is awarded.[107]

4. Interim Conclusion

Although services concessions for the time being are formally unregulated in many countries and some works concessions are regulated in a limited manner, important steps have been made in the past years to provide more clarity about the demarcation of the concept as the legal regime of concessions. However, the standard bearing flow of rulings also illustrates immediately that legal uncertainty has for the time being not been reduced. The case-law is very casuistic and it is not always clear what its exact scope is: how can a sufficient degree of transparency be organised? When and how must the procedure be specifically organised? Which specific exceptions are there? And so on.

Especially the demarcations of concessions and more specifically the risk element during the identification of concessions appears in practice to create an exceptional number of interpretation problems.[108]

---

[106] Cf recently Case C-221/12, *Belgacom NV v Interkommunale voor Teledistributie van het Gewest Antwerpen (INTEGAN) and Others*, para 38 (grounds of an economic nature, such as the wish to avoid the depreciation of an economic activity, are not overriding reasons in the public interest liable to justify the direct grant of a licence for services relating to that activity or of an exclusive right to engage in that activity of certain cross-border interest, by way of derogation from the principles of equal treatment and non-discrimination enshrined in those articles).

[107] Case C-91/08, *Wall AG v La ville de Francfort-sur-le-Main and Frankfurter Entsorgungs- und Service (FES) GmbH*, para 43.

[108] Cf the discussion in Actes de la Conférence-débat: La nouvelle définition légale de la délégation de service public, 5 March 2002, Institut de la Gestion Déléguée, 19, available 4 February 2016 at http://www.fondation-igd.org/files/pdf/La%20nouvelle%20definition%20legale%20de%20la%20delegation%20de%20service%20public,%20conference%20debat%2010.pdf; M. Burnett, 'A New EU Directive on Concessions – the Right Approach for PPP' (2008) EPPPL 186–8; Typical in that context is that the Commission for International Trade of the United Nations would, *inter alia*, not want to take over 'the European definition' of the concept of concession for its legislative model provisions because specified elements would create

If one accepts the central role of the risk element, then the question remains in any case of how this term must be exactly interpreted and from what time there is sufficient risk to be able to mention a concession.[109] The term risk is at least an unambiguous concept. For example, what does the fact that there must be a risk that the costs are not covered mean?[110] What is the position with regard to the captivity of the users?[111] Is an exclusive right and the absence of an alternative not a contraindication for an actual risk?[112] And what should be thought of the effect of specified, frequently occurring financial contractual clauses? Can they, or can they not, change the nature of the concession or public contract?[113] For example, financial penalty clauses or 'incentives,[114] or the so-called 'rendez-vous' clauses in case of concessions, intended to review the rates at a specified time on the basis of actual costs of the goods or services and of the use?[115] How should all this be calculated? Is one thereby replacing legal thinking with economic thinking as a result of which the debate becomes even more complicated?[116]

And, incidentally, the list of specific risks which are summed up by the Court of Justice as a determining factor? What about the availability risk? Reference can thus be made to a decision of Eurostat of 11 February 2004 on the accounting treatment of public-private cooperation agreements in the national accounts.[117] According to Eurostat the assets in case of public-private partnership are not considered to be government assets (and therefore recorded off balance sheet for government) if the private party bears the majority of the risks. The economic risk is thereby deemed to be on the part of the market participant if both of the following conditions are met: (1) the private partner bears the construction risk, and (2) the private partner bears at least one of either availability or demand risk.

---

uncertainty. A major issue was the uncertainty about the degree of the risk which must be borne by the concession holder before there could be mention of a concession. B. de Cazalet and J. Crothers, 'Présentation des dispositions législatives type sur les projets d'infrastructures à financement privé' (2004) RDAI 38.

[109] D. Moreau, 'Pour une relativisation du critère financier dans l'identification des délégations de service public' (2003) AJDA 1418.

[110] Cf C. Guettier, *Droits des contrats administratifs* (Paris: PUF 2004) 227 and 230.

[111] Cf CE (Fr), Commune de Guilhernad-Granges, 7 April 1999 (1999) AJDJA 517.

[112] D. Moreau, 'Pour une relativisation du critère financier dans l'identification des délégations de service public' (2003) AJDJA 1422.

[113] Cf O. Raymundie, *Gestion déléguée des services publics en France et en Europe* (Paris: Le Moniteur 2005) 95 at 223.

[114] D. Moreau, 'Pour une relativisation du critère financier dans l'identification des délégations de service public', (2003) AJDJA 1421.

[115] Ibid.

[116] Cf L. Vidal, 'Le juge administratif, l'économie et le contrat: réflexions à propos de deux arrêts du Conseil d'Etat' (1999) RFD Adm 1159; D. Moreau, 'Pour une relativisation du critère financier dans l'identification des délégations de service public' (2003) AJDJA 1422: 'Si l'on peut imaginer avec Lucien Rapp que le juge administratif se forme un jour 'à l'Ecole de Chicago et au théorème de Coase' pour faire face à ses nouvelles difficultés d'analyse, on ne peut en exiger autant des praticiens des contrats publics et de leurs partenaires, qui ont besoin d'un cadre simple et opérationnel pour conduire leurs relations contractuelles en toute sécurité juridique.'

[117] Cf P. Lignières in 'Débat sur les contrats de partenariat' (2004) Dr.Adm août-septembre 11.

Does the criterion 'risk' as central element ultimately not raise more questions than it resolves, one may wonder?[118] Elsewhere we defended therefore that the role of this criterion could best be put into perspective.[119] There are several reasons. First, the Community legislator, or at least until recently, did not mention the risk element, as the term right to exploit stands central. Secondly, it is ultimately difficult to justify that similar agreements whereby a contracting party demonstrates a higher degree of risk would be subjected to entirely different legal regimes.[120] Thirdly, attention can be focused on the fact that also in international sources the risk element does not constitute a demarcation criterion for concessions. This does not mean that the risks are not deemed to be important. On the contrary. The risk distribution seems to be a point for attention which is not to be ignored during the negotiation and the formulation of the concession.[121] Lastly, it must be established that the criterion currently especially fulfils a role in the elaboration of 'the right to exploit' and the accompanying transfer of responsibilities.[122] During this elaboration it is justified for one to have reservations. Is the bearing of 'economic risks' actually a requirement, in addition to other elements such as the duration, the global aspect of the activity (financing, conception, technical management), the autonomy in the taking of decisions or, as one author writes, the legal risks and responsibilities? In that respect, is the criticism of the Economic and Social Committee of this traditional approach not correct by now:[123] the specific characteristics of the concession cannot be summarised in one single criterion.[124]

What we consider should be central is ultimately that the concession holder 'operates', (this means 'can' operate) a 'company' (with some autonomy and personal, transferred, responsibilities) and can acquire revenue from the goods or services which the concession holder must and may execute in accordance with the concession. The operation must enable the concession holder to acquire revenue as a result of which its investments can in principle be depreciated and where applicable a certain profit can be made. Whether the revenue comes from a third party or the government makes little

---

[118] D. Moreau 'Pour une relativisation du critère financier dans l'identification des délégations de service public', (2003) AJDJA 1424.

[119] S. Van Garsse, *De concessie in het raam van de publiek-private samenwerking. Een analyse van het openbaar en het privaat domein, van de domeinconcessies, de concessies van openbare werken, de concessies van diensten en hun aanbesteding* (Antwerp: die Keure 2007) 552–72.

[120] Cf J.-B. Auby in *Actes de la Conférence-débat: La nouvelle définition légale de la délégation de service public, d 5 march 2002,* Institut de la Gestion Déléguée, 18 and 19. Compare A. Sevino and A. Gauthier, 'La notion de rémunération substantiellement assurée par les résultats de l'exploitation' (2003) AJDJA 832.

[121] M. Klein, M. Kerf et al, *Concessions for infrastructure. A guide to their design and award* (Washington D.C.:, The World Bank 1998), IX, 6: 'The allocation of risks between the involved parties is at the core of concession design: One key difference among various concession arrangements is the nature and extent of the risk they transfer from the government to the concessionaire and we can classify the accordingly: management contracts with incentive payments, leases and pure concessions-BOTs-ROTs.'

[122] Ibid.

[123] Opinion of the Economic and Social Committee on the 'Strengthening of the law governing concessions and public/private partnership (PPP) contracts, [2001] OJ C14/19.

[124] Ibid, 2.1.3.3 and 4.1.2.

difference. Whether the company runs risks as a result of the use or the purchase also makes little difference. Such an interpretation has the advantage that a better link can be made to the history of the concept of concession for works and services. The term concession would also obtain more connection to the (term) concession for infrastructure and services as is used by other international organisations (such as the World Bank,[125] UNIDO[126] and Uncitral.[127]

II. THE NEW CONCESSIONS DIRECTIVE

1. The Run-up to the New Directive

An important step was taken with the Green Paper on *Public-Private Partnerships and Community Law on Public Contracts and Concessions*.[128]

The formulation of a Green Paper was not unexpected. In 2003 the Commission had already in its Internal Market Strategy 2003–2006 announced that it wished to publish

[125] Thus in 'technical paper no. 399' with the title 'Concessions for infrastructure. A guide to their design and award' the term concession is used in a very broad sense. The term is used for every arrangement whereby a company is given the right from the government to deliver a specified service 'under conditions of significant market power'. More specifically this concerns inter alia 'BOT agreements', leasing, 'franchise agreements' and even management contracts with performance related remunerations. In a more narrow meaning the term concession is also used for an arrangement in which the concession holder has investment responsibilities.

[126] In the 'UNIDO BOT Guidelines', as the title indicates, mention is mainly made of BOT projects. The BOT project is described as a concession for constructing and operating infrastructure. However the operation also appears to comprise of the financing and the design. Furthermore, the term BOT is very broadly interpreted in the book. It thus comprises also of other acronyms such as BOO (build own operate), BOOT (build own operate transfer), BLT or BRT (build lease transfer or build rent transfer), BT (build transfer), DBFO (design build finance operate), etc. The tern 'concession' is lastly used to indicate the specific concession agreement. Guidelines for Infrastructure Development through Build-Operate-Transfer (BOT) Projects (UNIDO 1996).

[127] One can, *inter alia*, read in the Uncitral guide for privately financed infrastructure projects that the term concessions is not used there with a specific meaning such as usual in a specific legal system. However, at a certain time it is suggested that the national legislature could apply the following description of concession projects: '... the law could generally provide that concessions may be awarded for the purpose of entrusting an entity, private or public, with the obligation to carry out infrastructure works and deliver certain public services, in exchange for the right to charge a price for the use of the facility or premises, or for the service or goods it generates, or remuneration agreed to by the parties'. One author rightly points out that the area of application seems to extend to the French law of 'convention de délégation de service public' from the 'METP' to the PPP contracts. L. Folliot-Lalliot, 'Vers une approche unifiée de la convention de délégation de service public: état d'avancement des travaux de la Commission des Nations Unies pour le droit International sur les projects d'Infrastructure à Financement Privé' (2003) RFDA 895; cf http://www.uncitral.org/uncitral/en/uncitral_texts/procurement_infrastructure/2001Guide_PFIP.html (available 4 February 2016).

[128] Green Paper on public-private partnerships and Community law on public contracts and concessions COM(2004) 327, April 2004.

a Green Paper about PPP (public-private partnerships) and Community Law concerning public procurement and concession agreements. The same happened in its communication 'Developing the trans-European transport network: Innovative funding solutions – Interoperability of electronic toll collection systems' and in a white paper on services of general interest.[129] Lastly, the publication of the Green Paper was one of the action points of the European Growth Initiative.[130]

It is especially interesting that with the Green Paper a sounding was taken of the need for regulatory action concerning concessions. It appeared from the responses that a majority of the respondents were in favour of an initiative in this field. The Commission very carefully endorsed this position.[131] The necessary steps were therefore taken to conduct an impact analysis of a regulatory initiative for concessions.

The impact assessment carried out by the Commission showed that rules and practices of Member States concerning the award of concessions were very different and that the principles of the Treaty were not applied in the same way everywhere.[132] The absence or inadequacy of national rules for awarding concessions is believed to prevent the integration of national markets with regard to concessions, is believed to increase the risks of national favouritism, fraud and corruption and is also believed to be at the source of violations of the principles of the Treaty. Action was therefore justified and needed.

On 20 December 2011 the European Commission issued a draft Directive on concession contracts.[133] The proposal was part of an overall programme aimed at modernising public procurement in the European Union. The negotiations and the search for compromises ultimately took more time than had been anticipated beforehand. The fact that, as stated, also new proposals for Procurement Directives were

---

[129] Communication from the Commission to the European Parliament, the Council, the European economic and social Committee and the Committee of the regions. White paper on services of general interest, Brussels, xxx, COM (2004) 374, 16.

[130] Communication from the Commission 'A European initiative for growth: Investing in networks and knowledge for growth and jobs', COM (2003) 690 final, 11 November 2003. This report was approved by the Brussels European Council on 12 December 2003.

[131] Communication from the Commission to the European Parliament, the Council, the European Economic and Social Committee and the Committee of the regions on Public-Private Partnerships and Community law on Public Procurement and Concessions, Brussels, 15 November 2005, COM(2005) 569 final., 8 nr. 3.2: '… it would currently appear that a legislative initiative is the preferable option as regards concessions. However, as mentioned above, before formally proposing legislation further in-depth analysis will need to be undertaken in accordance with the principles of "Better Regulation", in order to determine whether indeed a Community initiative to regulate procedures for awarding concessions is necessary, if so, to shape such an initiative, and to better understand its possible impact.'

[132] Commission Staff Working Document Impact Assessment of an Initiative on Concessions. Accompanying the document Proposal for a directive of the European Parliament and of the Council on the award of concession contracts COM(2011) 897 final, SEC(2011) 1589 final, Brussels, 20 December 2011 SEC(2011) 1588 final.

[133] Proposal for a Directive of the European Parliament and of the Council on the award of concession contracts (Text with EEA relevance) SEC(2011) 1588 final, SEC(2011) 1589 final, available 4 February 2016 at http://www.europarl.europa.eu/RegData/docs_autres_institutions/commission_europeenne/sec/2011/1588/COM_SEC%282011%291588_EN.pdf.

being detailed at the same time and were on the agenda for discussion ensured that solutions (initially text proposals, but since then also compromise texts) which had been elaborated during first order and discussed for the Public Procurement Directives were also included in the Concessions Directive.

Following the suggestions from the legal literature and the public consultations the Commission has removed the most important legal uncertainties by including, *inter alia*, provisions about the following subjects: definition, exclusions, award procedures, duration and performance.[134] Hereinafter a number of points will be considered very briefly. First the concept of concessions for works and services will be considered. Thereupon some analysis will be made of the legal regime.

2. The Concept of Concessions for Works and Services in the Directive

A. The definition

The new Directive covers the award of works and services concessions both in the classic sector and in the special sector ('Utilities'). Building on the Court's case-law, the directive provides a clearer and more precise definition of a (works and services) concession. In line with the jurisprudence the most important factor remains the (definition of) operational risk. This risk is clarified in the directive itself and in many recitals in the preamble of the directive. The award of a concession shall imply the transfer to the concessionaire of an operating risk if the demand and/or supply risk is transferred.[135] Demand risk is to be understood as the risk on actual demand for the works or services which are the object of the contract (for example a toll road concession). Supply risk is to be understood as the risk on the provision of the works or services which are the object of the contract, in particular the risk that the provision of the services will not match the demand.[136]

Although the notion of supply risk was defined in the preamble it is not really clear what this means in practice. It was sufficiently remarkable that the first proposal of the European Commission also did not mention supply risk. That version mentioned (demand and) availability risk.[137] This approach originally raised the suspicion that the European Commission intended with the proposal to specifically regulate a broader category of PPP contract, something which some institutions had also earlier expressed being in favour of.[138] Therefore not only concessions on the basis of demand risk, but also contracts with remunerations on the basis of availability would be covered. This

---

134 http://ec.europa.eu/internal_market/consultations/2010/concessions/index_en.htm (available 4 February 2016).

135 Article 2, 1(1)b in fine of the proposal for a Directive of the European Parliament and of the Council on the award of concession contracts ('Concessions' Directive) (First reading) – Approval of the final compromise text, Brussels, 12 July 2013 (11748/13 MAP 61), hereinafter referred to as compromise text.

136 Cf. Preamble at 8a of the compromise text.

137 Article 2 in fine of the Proposal for a Directive of the European Parliament and of the Council on the award of concession contracts (Text with EEA relevance) SEC(2011) 1588 final. SEC(2011) 1589 final, hereinafter referred to as proposal.

138 For example, European Parliament resolution on public-private partnerships and Community law on public procurement and concessions (2006/2043(INI)), at 3.

was also in line with the impact assessment study which was conducted prior to the draft Directive, as it appeared from this research that 60 per cent of public-private partnership agreements took the form of concessions.[139] However, that result seems to have been influenced because design, build, finance, maintain and operate (DBFMO) contracts seem to have been included. In DBFMO contracts, the concessionaire designs, finances, builds and maintains and operates the infrastructure (for example, schools, prisons). The concessionaire is fully or to a large extent paid by the contracting authority (annual availability payments), and the payment is reduced, in some cases suspended, if the availability service is not rendered in conformity with the contractual requirements and performance and/or if risks occur that are allocated to the concessionaire.

Because of this the term concession would also have acquired immediate connection to the concept of PPP contract as applied in the context of the ESA rules. As was explained earlier, in case of PPP contracts a transfer of the economic risk takes place for Eurostat when the construction and the availability risk of the construction and the demand risk are transferred.

The fact that the term availability risk ultimately was left out of the entire Concessions Directive makes it clear that this was ultimately not the intention. This is evident from the fact that, to prevent confusion, different terminology was opted for, namely supply risk.

However, it is interesting that the new Directive also pays a lot of attention to the operating risk concept. The concessionaire shall be deemed to assume the operating risk where, 'under normal operating conditions', it is not guaranteed to recoup the investments made or the costs incurred in operating the works or services which are the subject matter of the concession, even if a part of the risk remains with the contracting entity.[140] When assessing the operating risk the net present value of all the investments, costs and revenue of the concessionaire can be taken into account.[141]

If the contracting authority relieves the concessionaire (under normal operating conditions) of any potential loss by guaranteeing a minimal revenue, equal or higher to the investments made and the costs the concessionaire incurs in relation to the performance of the contract, the contract will no longer qualify as a concession.[142]

As in the past to qualify as a concession, it is not necessary that third-party users are paying for the services or the infrastructure that is exploited. Arrangements which are exclusively remunerated by a contracting entity qualify as concessions if the payments relate to the actual demand for or the supply of the service of the asset (for example a shadow toll concession).[143] As was made clear in the court's case-law, the operating

---

[139] Commission Staff Working Document Impact Assessment of an Initiative on Concessions. Accompanying the document Proposal for a directive of the European Parliament and of the Council on the award of concession contracts COM(2011) 897 final, SEC(2011) 1589 final, Brussels, 20 December 2011 SEC(2011) 1588 final, 8.

[140] Article 2, 1(1)b in fine of the compromise text.

[141] Cf Preamble at 8a of the compromise text.

[142] Ibid at 7. For example this will be the case where specific regulation eliminates the risk by providing for a guarantee to the concessionaire on breaking even on investments and costs incurred when operating the contract.

[143] Ibid.

risk should stem from factors which are outside the control of the parties. The part of the risk transferred to the concessionaire shall therefore involve a real exposure to the vagaries of the market implying that any potential estimated loss incurred by the concessionaire shall not be merely nominal or negligible. Risk elements that are common to other contracts (for example, risks linked to bad management) are not decisive.[144]

From the above it appears that the fact that, as is usual in practice, specified risks can be shared or taken back by the government must be included. The latter is not unimportant seeing as otherwise interested market participants could not be found quickly to make a tender on the concession, or as the case may be very high risk premiums would be charged in the rates.[145] It is therefore in our view even appropriate that the government retains the risk of force majeure and act of state. Concerning the part of market and commercial risks it is clear that more care must be demonstrated. In our view it cannot be excluded that, for example, a 'floor' can be used in the concession subject to the condition that this does not result in the concessionaire 'under normal operating conditions', is not guaranteed to recoup the investments made or the costs incurred in operating the works or services which are subject matter of the concession. Lastly, it also appears not to be excluded that, for example in the context of financing, guarantees are provided to third parties (for example guarantees to the providers of external financing).

As in the past the concessions are considered to be 'contracts' by means of which the authority entrusts the execution of works or the provision and management of services to the concessionaire.[146] This implies mutually binding obligations where the executions of the works or services are subject to specific requirements which are legally enforceable. As a consequence other legal acts and agreements (authorisations, licences, public domain concessions, land lease contracts) should, like they did in the past, normally not qualify as concessions for works or services.[147]

B. Duration

In the *Müller* Case the Court of Justice pointed out that, with regard to the duration of concessions, there are serious grounds, including the need to guarantee competition, for holding the grant of concessions of unlimited duration to be contrary to the European Union legal order.[148] Also in the legal literature it is usually assumed that concessions can only be entered into for a fixed period and that this period must be in reasonable proportion to the investments and the achieving of a reasonable return.[149] The same thought was expressed by the European Parliament.[150]

---

144 Ibid at 8a.

145 Cf also A. Sanchez Graells, 'What Need and Logic for a New Directive on Concessions, Particularly Regarding the Issue of Their Economic Balance?' (2012) 2 EPPPL 94–104.

146 Cf Preamble at 6 of the compromise text.

147 Cf Preamble at 6a and 6b of the compromise text.

148 Case C-451/08, *Helmutt Müller v Bundesanstalt fur Immobilienaufgaben*, para 79.

149 P. Heijnsbroeck, *Grond voor gelijkheid Gelijke kansen op werken bij gronduitgifte door de overheid* (The Hague: IBR 2013) 250.

150 European Parliament resolution on public-private partnerships and Community law on public procurement and concessions (2006/2043(INI)), 29.

The original proposal of the European Commission confirmed this point of view by limiting the duration of concessions to the time necessary to the recoupment of investments and a reasonable return of invested capital.[151] Such a provision was somewhat problematic for (smaller) service concessions which do not require important upfront investments. In fact it is difficult in such a case to exclusively justify the duration by reference to the 'possibility to recover investment and to make reasonable return on investment'. As the purpose of the Directive was to prevent clear abuse and not to impose very short terms in case of concessions with insignificant investments, the proposal was modified. Article 16 on the duration of the concession now states that the duration of concessions shall be limited and the grantor of the concession shall estimate the duration on the basis of the works or services requested. For concessions lasting more than five years, the maximum duration of the concession shall not exceed the time that a concessionaire could reasonably be expected to take to recoup the investments made for operating the works or services together with a return on invested capital taking into account the investments required to achieve the specific contractual objectives. Article 16 in fine clarifies that the investments taken into account for the purposes of the calculation shall include both initial and investments during the life of the concession. The preamble of the directive stresses in its turn that contracting authorities can always award a concession for a period that is shorter (for example the concession contract could include a clause that in year X the authority will take over the concession), provided that the related compensation does not eliminate the operating risk.[152]

C. Exclusions

In the Concessions Directive, a relatively large amount of attention has been paid to exclusions. Exclusions were an important source of controversy during the negotiation and preparation of the Concessions Directive. In the final text the list of exclusions is rather long. It would be too much in this context to discuss all the exclusions. Some of the exclusions are easy to understand: for example, the exclusion of concessions currently governed by Regulations 1370/2007 on public transport services and 1008/2008 establishing common rules for the operation of air services.

Several exclusions seem to have been copy and pasted from the new Public Procurement Directives. It is doubtful if they are really relevant. Examples include: the acquisition or rental, by whatever financial means, of land, existing buildings or other immovable property or concerning rights thereon, political campaign services and specified legal services.

Other exclusions seem to be the result of effective lobbying and the search for a compromise. A striking example is the exclusion of the water sector.[153]

A somewhat specific category of exclusions which lastly is also still noteworthy concerns the public-public cooperation between public entities as well as vertical (in-house) cooperation. The issue of 'in-house' was also considered earlier in this chapter. The new in-house exclusion is in fact anchored to a certain extent in the

151 Article 16 of the proposal.
152 Preamble at 19a in fine of the compromise text.
153 Article 9a of the compromise text.

case-law of the European Court of Justice concerning concessions and public procurement although it at the same time attempted to clarify, refine and even adjust this case-law. The exclusion of public-public cooperation originates from the case-law in the field of public procurement. However, it is for the time being not entirely clear if this exclusion is relevant in the case of concessions.

3. The Legal Regime

From now on, the basis of the legal regime for the awarding of concessions is the fact that concessions from €5 million in principle must be obligatorily published in the Official Journal of the EU. Contracting authorities wishing to award a concession will be required to publish a concession notice (using a standard form and containing prescribed information). In this manner the contract is publicised to all potential interested contractors in the EU. Award of a concession without prior publication is only permitted in very exceptional circumstances, as is evident from the new Directive.

Although the threshold of €5 million at first instance does not seem very low, one must, however, take into consideration the fact that during the calculation of the value of the concession a very extensive series of elements (some of them very similar to those under the procurement directives) must be taken into consideration so that the threshold can be reached quickly, and apart from this many authorities will have a tendency to rather be safe than sorry and will publish the concession so as to be sure. This is due to the fact that a calculation in advance of the total value of a concession is in practice not very simple. Many of the elements will be very difficult to estimate at the commencement of the concession. How, for example, will the contracting authority be able to take into account the amount of the rates to be paid by the contracting authority and/or the users, as these amounts will be determined during the awarding procedure? The contracting authority may correctly apply a valuation method, yet still come to an amount that will not reflect the value of the concession at the end of the awarding procedure nor be in line with the actual revenues during the concession contract. It appears that the Community legislator was very aware of this problem. Thus in comparison with the initial draft Directive text a specific provision is currently included which permits a certain margin.[154]

Furthermore, the Directive contains for some services an extra light regime. Following the new Public Procurement Directive for the classis sector an ('extra') 'light' regime has been created for concessions in social and a number of specific sectors. Only specified publication obligations apply to those concessions pursuant to the Directive. One can read about this in the preamble:[155]

---

[154] Article 6(1) in fine: 'That estimate shall be valid at the moment at which the concession notice is sent or, in cases where such notice is not provided for, at the moment at which the contracting authority or the contracting entity commences the concession award procedure. For the purpose of paragraph -1, if the value of the concession at the moment of the award is more than 20% higher than its estimated value, the valid estimate shall be the value of the concession at the moment of the award'.

[155] Cf Preamble at 20 of the compromise text.

> It is appropriate to exclude from the full application of this Directive only those services which have a limited cross-border dimension, such as certain social, health, or educational services. These services are provided within a particular context that varies widely amongst Member States, due to different cultural traditions. A specific regime should therefore be established for concession for these services which takes into account the fact that they are newly regulated. An obligation to publish a prior information notice and a concession award notice of any concession with a value equal to or greater than the threshold established in this Directive is an adequate way to provide information on business opportunities to potential tenderers as well as on the number and type of contracts awarded to all interested parties.

However, this approach and justification is not very convincing when one takes into consideration that the argumentation also concerns many other concessions. That there is a need for those concessions for a flexible and adjusted regime is undoubtedly patently obvious, but that also applies to many other concessions and was also in fact the objective of the Concessions Directive. Furthermore, a 'basic regime' also continues to apply to those concessions which has in the meantime become more detailed in case-law, which the Concessions Directive ultimately, for reasons of legal uncertainty, intends to clarify.[156] Therefore, whilst the creation of a light regime for this type of service in the context of public procurement is fully understandable given the rigid and very comprehensive regulation thereof, the case of concessions is therefore an entirely different matter.

Under the regular regime the Directive contains various rules to promote the transparency and the objectivity of the procedure for the awarding of concessions. A lot of them are less rigid than similar provisions currently applicable to public contracts, others are quite similar. The Directive thus contains certain obligations with respect to the selection, exclusion and award criteria to be applied by the contracting authorities and contracting entities. The award criteria are thereby already more generally formulated than in the new classic Directive and the Utilities Directive.[157] Furthermore, it is interesting that a contracting authority or entity, in the event that it receives a very innovative proposal, which it could not have foreseen in advance, may, exceptionally, modify the ranking order of the award criteria to take into account this innovative solution. However, in such a case the contracting authority or entity must inform all tenderers about the modification and shall issue a new invitation to submit tenders.[158]

No further specific procedures were imposed for the awarding of concessions, but all sorts of general safeguards and principles were included. The contracting authority must in advance give, *inter alia*, a description of the concession and the technical

---

[156] See also preamble at 20: 'Furthermore, Member States should put in place appropriate measures with reference to the award of concession contracts for these services aimed at ensuring compliance with the principles of transparency and equal treatment of economic operators while allowing contracting authorities and contracting entities to take into account the specificities of the services in question'.

[157] Article 39 of the compromise text.

[158] Article 40 of the compromise text. It also states 'Where the award criteria have been published at the moment of the publication of the concession notice, the contracting authority or entity shall publish a new concession notice, in respect of the minimal time-limits referred to in Article 37 paragraph 2a'.

specifications. The contracting authority should also establish in advance and communicate to all participants the rules on the organisation of the concession award procedure. It has been expressly determined that negotiations are permitted. However, it can be read in the Directive that the subject-matter of the concession, the award criteria and the minimum requirements shall not be changed during the course of the negotiations.[159]

Thereupon the Directive also contains various information obligations concerning the awarding of concessions designed to guarantee effective means of challenging award decisions.[160]

We lastly report that the Concessions Directive has also, just like the new Public Procurement Directives, included provisions about the performance of the contracts. One of the most important provisions of the Directives concerns undoubtedly the provision concerning (future substantial) amendments.[161] Since the *Pressetext* ruling in the case of public procurement and *Wall AG* for concessions, as has already been seen, it appears that the amendment right of the government is seriously curtailed because in accordance with this case-law important amendments usually will result in the obligation to organise a new award procedure. This approach is certainly open to serious criticisms in the case of concessions for services and works. Seeing that concessions are 'incomplete' agreements whereby often for a very long period the implementation of works and services will be delegated and whereby the government traditionally has in the general interest an extensive – but certainly not unlimited[162] – *ius variandi*. Concession holders are very used to this in practice and accept this amendment right, which is not surprising seeing as the amendment right is accompanied by a duty of compensation by the government.

The Directives attempted to anchor and refine the *Pressetext* case-law. That this was in quite a few Member States a sensitive issue became clear on the agenda during the preparation of the new Directives. The ultimate text which is in fact very difficult to read, and contains various nuances, is clearly also the result of a compromise (which in fact at first instance seems to have been reached in the negotiations concerning the Public Procurement Directives). Although one could have expected that such a provision would be different in the case of concessions compared to in the case of public procurement (given their still different nature and the fact that renegotiations in case of concessions are more the rule than the exception)[163] this is not the case. We consider this to be a missed opportunity.

---

159 Article 35(6) of the compromise text.

160 Article 38 c of the compromise text. Cf also Articles 44 and 45 (remedy directive will apply).

161 Article 42 of the compromise text.

162 It may also not be used if this would result in an alteration of the nature of the overall concession.

163 S. Saussier, *An Economic Analysis of the Closure of Markets and other Dysfunctions in the Awarding of Concession Contracts* (2012), available 4 February 2016 at http://www.europarl.europa.eu/document/activities/cont/201206/20120626ATT47715/20120626ATT47715EN.pdf.

III. CONCLUSIONS

As forms of public-private partnership the concessions for works and services are not a new and unknown phenomena. Over the past decades the European institutions have repeatedly attempted to regulate concessions for works and (public) services. These attempts originally had limited success. The European Court of Justice and the European Commission did make it clear over the past years that various basic principles must be taken into consideration for all concessions. Through quite a few rulings it slowly became clear how concessions for works and services must be distinguished from public procurement contracts. The most important criterion hereby became the operating risk. This approach is open to criticism.

Very recently the European institutions succeeded in agreeing on a new Directive which contains a general scheme for concessions for works and services. In this chapter a number of aspects of this new Directive have been subjected to a first analysis. It appears, *inter alia*, from this that the European institutions have opted to link up as much as possible to the case-law of the Court of Justice. For example, for the distinction between concessions and public procurement the main criterion of the operating risk is upheld. However, important clarification has been provided on various points.[164] Therefore, some of the observations formulated elsewhere in this chapter have been met. However, certainly not all problems have been resolved. Thus a whole series of, sometimes hard to understand or justify, exceptions have been created, new concepts introduced (for example supply risk) and it will continue to be difficult in practice to assess whether the risk is sufficiently transferred to qualify a contract as a concession.

With regard to the legal regime it is clearly noticeable that the European institutions have made a serious effort to create a light regime for concessions with special attention to transparency and flexibility and – as stated first and foremost – with special attention to the specificic character of concessions.[165]

Nevertheless, in spite of everything, the Concessions Directive did still include quite a few elements from the parallel negotiated Public Procurement Directives. Their relevance or pertinence is not always as clear and in the author's view has also ensured that the text with the numerous recitals has ultimately become 'denser' and longer than was in fact necessary. The same can be said about some text amendments which took place in order to reach a compromise.[166]

Whether the new rules in the Directive are ultimately in fact 'clear and simple' and their application will not result in 'an excessive amount of bureaucracy' as was also stated first and foremost will become evident in the following years.[167] Since it also applies here that 'the proof of the pudding is in the eating'.

---

[164] For example, on the nature of the risks and on the threshold and on the duration.

[165] Cf Preamble at 1 and 1a of the compromise text.

[166] Although it must be admitted that other text amendments did indeed result in a simplification and contributed to a more suitable regime (for example the provisions on the award of concessions).

[167] Cf Preamble at 1a of the compromise text.

Conclusions

The vision and aspirations of European Institutions towards a Single Market Act[1] have identified public procurement reforms as essential components of competitiveness and growth[2] and as indispensable instruments of delivering public services.[3]

Public procurement in the European Union has been an integral part of the concept of the common market. Its regulation provides for economic and policy justifications for eliminating existing non-tariff barriers in inter-state trade. The identification of public procurement as a major non-tariff barrier has revealed the economic importance of its regulation. Savings and price convergence appear as the main arguments for liberalising the trade patterns of public procurement. The economic approach to the regulation of public procurement aims at the integration of public markets across the European Union. Through the principles of transparency, non-discrimination and objectivity in the award of public contracts, it is envisaged that the regulatory system will bring about competitiveness in the relevant product and geographical markets, will increase import penetration of products and services destined for the public sector, will enhance the tradability of public contracts across the common market, will result in significant price convergence and finally it will be the catalyst for the needed rationalisation and industrial restructuring of the European industrial base. Public procurement liberalisation reflects the wish of European institutions to eliminate preferential and discriminatory purchasing patterns by the public sector and create seamless intra-community trade patterns between the public and private sectors. Public procurement by Member States and their contracting authorities is often susceptible to a rationale and policy that favour indigenous undertakings at the expense of more efficient competitors. As the relevant markets have been sheltered from competition, distorted patterns emerge in the trade of goods, works and services destined for the pubic sector. These trade patterns represent a serious impediment in the functioning of the common market and inhibit the fulfilment of the principles enshrined in the Treaties. Alongside the economic arguments, legal arguments have emerged supporting the regulation of public procurement, as a necessary ingredient of the fundamental principles of the Treaties such as the free movement of goods and services, the right of establishment and the prohibition of discrimination on nationality grounds. The legal

[1] See European Commission, Communication to the European Parliament, the Council, the Economic and Social Committee and the Committee of the Regions, *Towards a Single Market Act,* COM(2010) 608 final.

[2] See European Commission, Communication, Europe 2020, A strategy for smart, sustainable and inclusive growth, 3 March 2010, COM (2010) 2020 final.

[3] See European Commission, Guide to the application of the European Union rules on state aid, public procurement and the internal market to services of general economic interest, and in particular to social services of general interest, 7 December 2010, SEC(2010) 1545 final. See European Commission, Buying Social: A Guide to Taking Account of Social Considerations in Public Procurement, SEC(2010) 1258, final.

significance of the regulation of public procurement in the common market has been well documented through the jurisprudence of the European Court of Justice.

Significant legal reasons have emerged by positioning the regulation of public procurement as a necessary ingredient of the fundamental principles of the EU Treaties, such as the free movement of goods and services, the right of establishment and the prohibition of discrimination on grounds of nationality. Finally, policy justifications of public procurement regulation have revealed a *sui generis* market place often referred to as *marchés publics* (public markets), where despite the inability of competition law to regulate it, an overwhelming need for transparency and accountability points towards the regime of public procurement as a safeguard to the above principles.

The regulation of public procurement reflects on two opposite dynamics: one of a community-wide orientation and one of national priorities. Litigation and jurisprudential inferences will be extremely important in understanding the thrust of the new regime. The role of the Court of Justice of the European Union has been instrumental in shaping many of the newly introduced concepts and in the future will be invaluable in interpreting the new public procurement regime and pronounce on the compatibility of implementing national provisions with the *acquis communautaire*.

The need for simplification of public procurement in the European Union is imperative. Simplification will result from procedural efficiencies and streamlining the application of the substantive rules. However, the challenge of the forthcoming reforms will be to demarcate the exhaustive harmonisation of the public procurement Directives in the light of market access of undertakings from third countries and sheltered markets for small and medium enterprises. Public procurement will be an essential part of the Single Market Act and its regulation will play a pivotal role for the Europe 2020 Growth Strategy. Its success will be constantly evaluated by Member States and the public markets.

Index